COMPUTERS

Tools for an Information Age

D0138963

A note about the Instructor's Edition with Annotations

Sixth Edition

The Instructor's Edition with Annotations provides you with a teaching tool that puts lecture and course organization at your fingertips. Thoroughly updated for the sixth edition of *Computers: Tools for an Information Age,* the Instructor's Edition offers the complete student text with a variety of annotations that give you flexibility and support in the classroom.

The Instructor's Edition provides chapter outlines and learning objectives at the beginning of each chapter, to make lecture preparation quicker and easier. In addition, the Instructor's Edition offers annotations to supplement your lecture. Notice the different types of annotations in the margin, in blue type:

- InfoBits
- Critical Thinking questions
- Learn By Doing notes
- Group Work notes
- Global Perspective notes

For further information about *Computers: Tools for an Information Age* and its instructional package, please contact your local sales representative. You can also visit our web site at **http://www.prenhall .com.** We look forward to hearing from you and to helping you meet your teaching needs.

COMPUTERS

Tools for an Information Age

Sixth Edition

H. L. CAPRON

Annotations by Jerry Reed with H. L. Capron

Prentice Hall
Upper Saddle River, New Jersey 07458

Sponsoring Editor	Anita Devine
Senior Production Supervisor	Juliet Silveri
Senior Project Manager	Patricia Mahtani
Senior Marketing Manager	Tom Ziolkowski
Art Director, Cover Design	Gina Hagen
Text Design	Mark Ong
Composition, Illustration, and Packaging Services	Lachina Publishing Services
Photo Researcher	Kathleen Cameron
Manufacturing Supervisor	Sheila Spinney/Tim McDonald
Cover Illustration	Joseph Maas

Many of the designations used by manufacturers and sellers to distinguish their products are claimed as trademards. Where those designations appear in this book, and Prentice Hall was aware of a trademark claim, the designations have been printed in initial caps or all caps.

Library of Congress Cataloging-in-Publication Data

Capron, H. L.
    Computers : tools for an information age: instructor's edition with annotations /
      H.L. Capron ; annotations by Jerry Reed with H.L. Capron. — 6th ed.
      p.   cm.
    ISBN 0-201-47659-2 — 0-201-61191-0 (instructor)
      1. Computers   I. Title
QA76.5.C363 2000
000—dc21   99-23915
                                      CIP

Prentice-Hall International (UK) Limited, London
Prentice-Hall of Australia Pty. Limited, Sydney
Prentice-Hall Canada, Inc., Toronto
Prentice-Hall Hispanoamericana, S.A., Mexico
Prentice-Hall of India Private Limited, New Delhi
Prentice-Hall of Japan, Inc., Tokyo
Pearson Education Asia Pte. Ltd., Singapore
Editora Prentice-Hall do Brasil, Ltda., Rio de Janeiro

Printed in the United States of America

10 9 8 7 6 5 4 3 2 1

COMPUTERS
Tools for an Information Age, Sixth Edition

Complete Instructional Support System

New Electronic Supplements

Interactive Edition Student CD-ROM. A discovery-based learning tool packaged with every new book that offers interactive multimedia explorations of key textbook topics, seamless integration to the Companion Web Site, and the complete text on CD-ROM.

- Navigation is easy and intuitive because it is done through an Internet browser
- Computer labs illustrating text concepts include sound and video
- Connect instantly to the Companion Web Site for the Interactive Study Guide and Planet Internet Exercises at the click of an icon

Companion Web Site. The Companion Web Site is an online learning environment for instructors and students. The range of activities available through the Companion Web Site include:

- *Online Study Guide*—different types of self-assessment exercises including multiple choice, true/false and fill-in-the-blank questions, with instant feedback available at the click of a button—all written by author H. L. Capron.

- *Planet Internet Exercises*—takes the text feature one step further by providing the links listed in the exercises.

- *Communication*—since learning is not conducted in a vacuum, we have integrated several ways for students and faculty to communicate from within the Companion Web Site.

- *Faculty Resources*—ancillary materials accessible for instant download, and syllabus creation and management tools are integrated into the Companion Web Site.

- *Syllabus Manager*—An online syllabus creation and management utility. Syllabus Manager™ provides instructors with an easy, step-by-step process to create and revise syllabi, with direct links into the Companion Web Site and other online content. Students access Syllabus Manager™ directly from within the Companion Web Site, providing quick access to course assignments.

Test Manager. Test Manager™ is a comprehensive suite of tools for testing and assessment. Test Manager™ allows educators to easily create and distribute tests for their courses, either by printing and distributing through traditional methods or by on-line delivery via a Local Area Network (LAN) server. Four question formats are available: multiple choice, true/false, matching, and completion exercises. Answer keys and page references for test questions are provided.

Lecture-Launcher Videotapes. Qualified adopters can receive our all-new videotapes. We have taken the best clips from many commercially available videotapes and put them together in 10-minute segments that relate to chapters in the text. These tapes are ideal for adding information and interest to your lectures. Your sales representative has details about this offer.

More Supplements

Capron's Pocket Internet: 4001 Sites. This pocket reference guide is available upon request when you place your order for new copies of the student text. The author personally selected 4001 Internet sites with interesting content, relevant to students' lives. Sites are grouped by topic. A sample of topics includes Animation, Architecture, Arts, Best-Hot-Cool, Finance and Investing, Career/Jobs, Computer Science, Cool Companies, Education, Entertainment, Entrepreneurs, Financial Aid, Fitness and Health, Free Stuff, and more.

Instructor's Edition with Annotations. This special edition contains over 50% new annotations (by Jerry Reed) for lecture preparation, and includes supplementary material not found in the Instructor's Resource Manual. The annotations include Group Work notes, Critical Thinking questions, InfoBits, Global Perspective notes, Learn By Doing notes, and alphabetized key terms.

Instructor's Resource CD. This CD-ROM provides the complete contents of the printed Instructor's Manual and Test Bank in Microsoft Word®, and Test Manager™ test generator, along with an Image Library and PowerPoint presentation slides.

Instructor's Manual and Test Bank, by H.L. Capron. Written by the author, this comprehensive manual provides the printed support you need for easier class preparation. Teaching notes from the author include learning objectives for each chapter, a chapter overview, a detailed lecture outline, and a list of key words for each chapter.

A printout of the complete electronic test bank is included. Question formats include multiple choice, true/false, matching, and completion exercises. Answer keys and page references for test questions are provided.

Additional Topics. We are offering two topics as a separate supplement: *The Programming Process: Planning the Solution Using Visual Basic* and *Number Systems.* Both supplements are available to be packaged with the text upon request.

Prentice-Hall Points Program. As a publisher, we are aware of the need to have the most current software application programs available to students in introductory computer courses. We are pleased to partner with colleges and universities to achieve this goal through our Prentice-Hall Points Program.

By adopting our text and lab books, your school may qualify for free software programs and site licenses to be used by your students in your school's computer lab.

BRIEF CONTENTS

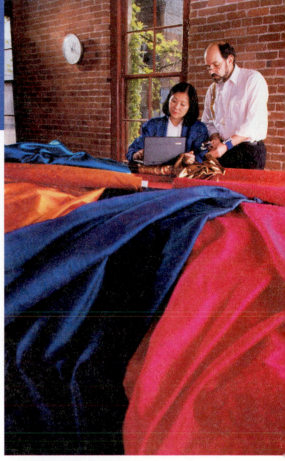

DETAILED CONTENTS

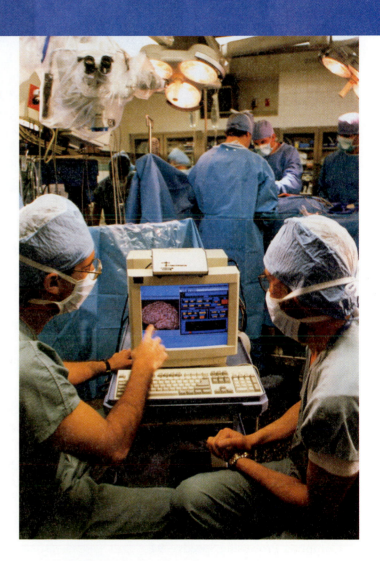

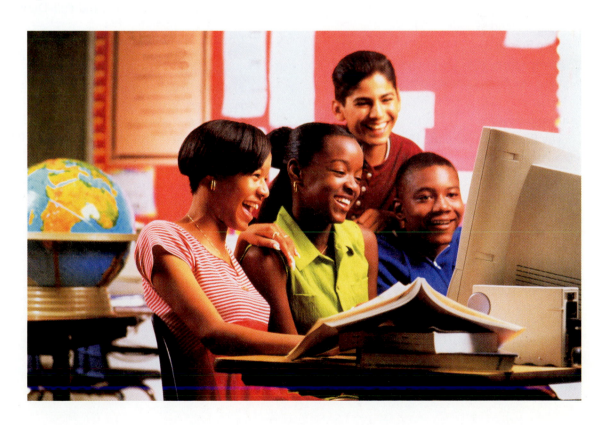

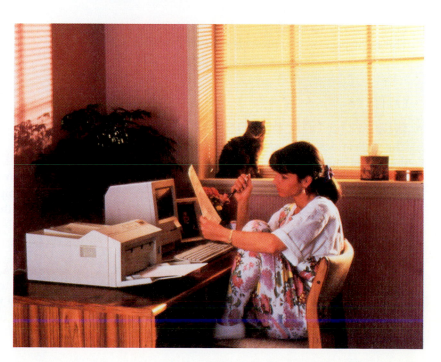

THE BUYER'S GUIDE AND GALLERIES

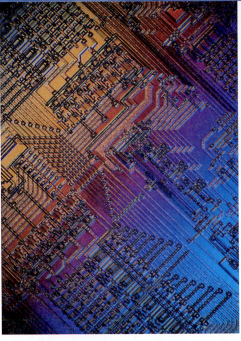

PREFACE

H. L. Capron, well-known and respected author of *Computers: Tools for an Information Age,* has once again given students the most comprehensive, up-to-date introduction to computers text in every respect. This Sixth Edition has new coverage from live banners to cupcakes to virtual private networks that ensures that students have the most current information at their fingertips as they learn about today's technology. Connectivity is paramount in today's society. In this edition, the connectivity theme is integrated into several aspects of the book. And exploring the Internet is made easy with the Quick Start in Chapter 1, Internet Chapters 8 and 9, Planet Internet, New Online Study Guide Companion Web Site, and Test Manager.

Focus on the Internet

Quick Start in Chapter 1. Jump start the text with an Introduction to the Internet in Chapter 1. Learn basic information about the Web, browsers, servers, and Internet protocol at the beginning and be able to use it throughout your course.

Internet chapters. The Internet is now covered in three independent chapters; so you can read the Internet material you need, when you need it.

> Chapter 7: "The Internet: A Resource for All of Us" explains the important aspects of Internet technology, from URLs to links to search engines.

> New Chapter 8: "The Internet in Business: Corporations, Small Businesses, and Entrepreneurs" focuses on various aspects of business use of the Internet, particularly electronic commerce.

> New Chapter 9: "Writing Your Own Web Page: Using HTML or FrontPage" offers students basic web-writing tools and detailed examples.

Planet Internet. The Planet Internet feature offers a non-technical look at various aspects of the World Wide Web in a two-page spread at the end of each chapter. Topics include places to start, global aspects of the Inter-

net, FAQs, business, shopping, careers, the great outdoors, multimedia, entertainment, resources, and Americana. Each Planet Internet suggests hands-on Internet exercises and is supported through the Planet Internet pages on the Capron Companion Web Site.

Web site. The Capron Companion Web Site provides links to all sites mentioned in the book chapters, galleries, and Planet Internet features. The site also features an interactive study guide to give students more self-quizzes, a chat room, and online testing.

Internet Gallery. The Visual Internet gallery features the visual impact of World Wide Web sites. The gallery focuses on attractive sites for designers and multimedia buffs, and also has a two-page spread on graphics-rich sites.

Internet security and history. Internet security issues, including cookies and government intervention, are examined in Chapter 10. The history of the Internet is described briefly in Chapter 7. Internet coverage is also integrated throughout several other chapters.

Pocket Internet. Students love the companion *Pocket Internet: 4001 Sites.* Now this popular pocket resource guide, has been updated and expanded to include 2000 more sites and even more disciplines.

Distinctive Learning Features

Multimedia. Whether on CD-ROMs or on the Internet, multimedia continues to be a major newsmaker in the computer industry. Underlying CD-ROM technology and multimedia applications are described in Chapter 5. Multimedia is also featured in the Visual Internet gallery and in its own Planet Internet following Chapter 8.

Ethics. In addition to a feature called Focus on Ethics that appears in each chapter, three major ethics categories are included in the chapters: Ethics and Software, Ethics and Data, and Ethics and Privacy. Further, one Planet Internet is devoted to ethics on the Internet.

Office 2000. All screens for hands-on applications have been produced using Microsoft Office 2000®.

Getting Practical. Various topics of practical interest to students, such as using your computer as a digital darkroom to produce semi-professional pictures, using software to keep your personal computer humming, and learning which computer skills are on the most-wanted list are covered in the Getting Practical box in each chapter.

2000 and Beyond. Examines computer-related trends as they may affect people today and into the 21st century. Examples include the E-Corporation, computerized space maps, and a computer in the form of a pen.

Making the Right Connections. Links people to computers. Topics include registering to vote online, the Microsoft TerraServer, online auctions, and Bluetooth communications.

Margin notes. To further engage the student, margin notes are placed throughout the text. The margin notes extend the text material by highlighting interesting applications of computers. Sample topics are virtual advertisements, web rings, online groceries, and the wired campus.

Buyer's Guide gallery. Students and their families are making important economic decisions about the purchase of a computer for their educational, personal, and business needs. This concise eight-page guide beginning on page forty offers students information to aid in hardware and software purchases.

Making Microchips gallery. The gallery text, supplemented by color photos, describes how microprocessors are made.

Appealing writing style. The author's writing style is known to be student-friendly. More importantly, the material is presented with real-life examples. Each chapter begins with a real-world vignette that leads the student into the material. Additional real-world examples are sprinkled throughout the chapter.

In-Text Learning Aids

Each chapter includes the following pedagogical support:

Learning Objectives at the beginning of each chapter provide key concepts for students.

Key terms are boldfaced throughout the text.

A *Chapter Review* offers a summary of core concepts and boldfaced key terms.

Discussion Questions encourage students to take what has been presented in the chapter and discuss it more thoroughly.

The *Student Study Guide* offers objective questions that students can answer to check their comprehension of essential concepts.

A *Glossary* and a comprehensive *Index* are included at the end of the text.

Student Learning Supplements

Interactive Edition Student CD-ROM

The Interactive Edition is a discovery-based learning tool packaged with every new book that offers interactive multimedia explorations of key textbook topics, seamless integration to the Companion Web Site, and the complete text on CD-ROM.

- Navigation is easy and intuitive because it is done through an Internet browser
- Computer labs illustrating text concepts include sound and video
- Connect instantly to the Companion Web Site for the Interactive Study Guide and Planet Internet Exercises at the click of an icon

Companion Web Site

The Companion Web Site is an online learning environment for instructors and students. The range of activities available through the Companion Web Site include:

- *Online Study Guide*—different types of self-assessment exercises including multiple choice, true/false, and fill-in-the-blank questions, with instant feedback available at the click of a button all written by author H. L. Capron.
- *Planet Internet Exercises*—takes the text feature one step further by providing the links in the exercises.
- *Communication*—since learning is not conducted in a vacuum, we have integrated several ways for students and faculty to communicate from within the Companion Web site.

Capron's Pocket Internet: 4001 Sites

This pocket reference guide is packaged upon your professor's request with new copies of the student text. The author personally selected 4001 Internet sites with interesting content, relevant to students' lives. Sites are grouped by topic and cover a number of disciplines. A sample of topics includes Animation, Architecture, Arts, Best-Hot-Cool, Finance and Investing, Career/Jobs, Computer Science, Cool Companies, Education, Entertainment, Entrepreneurs, Financial Aid, Fitness and Health, Free Stuff, and more.

CAPRON'S PROVEN PEDAGOGY

Internet Coverage. Jump start the text with an introduction to the Internet in Chapter 1. Learn basic information about the Web, browsers, servers, and Internet protocol at the beginning and be able to use it throughout your course. The Internet is now covered in three independent chapters: 7, 8, and 9 (Chapter 9 is not included in the Brief Edition); so you can read the Internet material you need, when you need it.

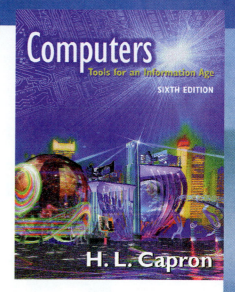

Complete Student Learning Package.
The sixth edition of Capron includes
an all-new student learning package of text,
CD-ROM and Web site. The Interactive Edition Student
CD-ROM is a discovery-based learning tool that offers
interactive multimedia explorations of key textbook topics, seamless integration to the Companion Web Site and
the complete text on CD-ROM. The Companion Web
Site provides links to all sites mentioned in the book
chapters, galleries, and Planet Internet features. The site
also features an interactive study guide to give students
more self-quizzes, a chat room, and online testing.

Each chapter of the text features a
two-page spread devoted to helping students
appreciate the variety of information available
on the Internet. Explanations are written in nontech-
nical terms. Hands-on **Planet Internet** exercises
include links to web pages where students can continue their exploration.

Focus on Ethics
boxes appear in
the margins to
raise ethical, thought-
provoking questions
and issues for you to
consider.

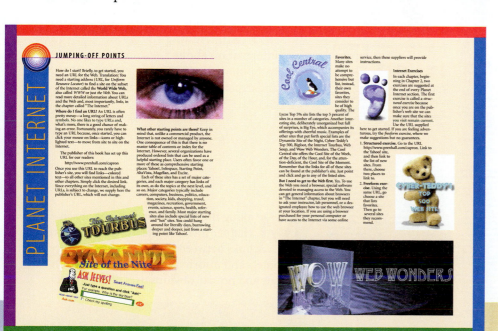

GETTING PRACTICAL
DIGITAL DARKROOM

Never mind the traditional dark room, where a photo buff squints under a tiny colored light while sloshing photos through smelly development chemicals. And, frankly, the results of all that sloshing, especially enlargements, probably would not be confused with professional work. But now that has changed. With the right computer equipment, you can be a professional—or close enough. You can make prints and enlargements that could not be differentiated from professional work without the aid of a magnifying glass.

First, let us consider the source of your pictures. How does one get the photos in the computer in the first place? There are several possibilities. A straightforward approach is to use a digital camera, storing the

pictures in some computer-sensible form—chip or card or disk—and transferring the images directly to the computer. If your photos were recorded on the camera's embedded chip, they can be transferred by means of a cable hooked up to your computer's serial port, a plug-like input in the back. Input from a digital camera is co...

load images from professional services on the Internet. Whatever method is chosen to input photos, then can edit and reproduce those photos.

Once you have the photos in digital form, you will probably want to use some photo imaging software to manipulate them. Such soft-

home. One such system, shown here, is produced by Hewlett Packard. The HP PhotoSmart PC photography system includes a photo printer, photo scanner, digital camera, and photographic papers for printing your pictures. Each component may be purchased separately.

The HP PhotoSmart scanner handles prints up to 5 by 7 inches, mounted slides, and even negatives. The printer can produce glossy pictures on heavy photo stock paper, in standard photo sizes, such as 5 by 7 inches, or 8 by 10 inches. The results are so crisp and vibrant that an average person could not distinguish them from a photo produced by a photo-processing chain. Keep in mind that this must be a second printer; the PhotoSmart printer is slow, and mediocre at printing traditional text.

Processing photographs at home is a trend is

I n each chapter, a **Getting Practical** box describes how students can enhance their experiences with computers inside or outside the classroom.

2000 and Beyond
THE E-CORPORATION

Every retail company must change to get in step with the Internet or else go out of business. Soon. There is no grace period for those that hesitate. E-commerce goes far beyond setting up an attractive web site.

If these statements seem too harsh, consider the reality of the numbers. In 1995 only 5 percent of Americans used the Internet every day. In 2000, that number has risen to 35 percent—a stunning change in a very short period of time. And are Internet users buying yet? Yes. It is only a trickle compared with the overall retail economy, but the advantages of e-commerce to the consumer are so outstanding that it is just a matter of time until many make the switch.

The new e-commerce reality is controlled by the consumer. The elements of consumer control that make e-commerce inevitable can be summarized as follows:

- **Smart customers.** Users can take advantage of the Internet to find information about products before buying.
- **Come to me.** Consumers no longer must take the car or a bus to the retail store. No, the merchandise is much handier than that—a click or two away.

can order a computer made up of exactly the components you want, no more, no less, by clicking off options on a screen. The customization of products has only begun.

- **Disappearing geographical lines.** Users need not be limited to regional boundaries. Internet retailers span the globe. For example, customers can order a book from Amazon.com whether they are in Pittsburgh or Zimbabwe.
- **No further obstacles.** People want to try before they buy? Tell that to the folks in the multibillion-dollar catalog business. Although Internet entrepreneurs easily convinced people to buy books and CDs, items they know, it is just a matter of time until they buy everything else online.

Comparison shopping. The phrase *hunting for a bargain* ha...

ware agent, a type of software that does

For all these consumer—

2 000 and Beyond. Examines computer-related trends as they may affect people today and into the 21st century. Examples include the E-Corporation, computerized space maps, and a computer in the form of a pen.

You're on File at Domino's

If you consider what items of personal information might be stored on disk files, you may think of your Social Security records or perhaps the information stored with your bank account. But small businesses also know about you. They store information you readily provide on their own disk files.

If, for example, you phone a Domino's, an outlet that delivers pizza, your name, address, phone number, and product ordered will be recorded in the company's disk files. When you call again in the future, this information can be retrieved quickly by keying in your phone number. This saves time and effort and speeds your pizza on its way.

MAKING THE RIGHT CONNECTIONS
ONLINE AUCTIONS

How would you like to have a business in which, each time a sale is made, both the seller and the buyer pay you money? An auction house is such a business. Sellers pay the auctioneer to set up a sale and the auctioneer takes a cut from the money the buyer pays. Of course, in a real live auction, the auctioneer must rent a warehouse or barn to hold the goods and the buyers, advertise the auction, hire people to move merchandise around, spend hours shouting and urging sales, and eventually collect money from the buyers.

Just like other retailers, auctioneers have moved online. Consider how this simplifies matters: no warehouse, no movers, no shouting, and precious little advertising. This streamlined operation does impose new tasks, however: photographing every item, maintaining a web site that can display the items, accepting bids, and collecting payments. Further, the ever-changing merchandise means greater-than-average site maintenance.

Many auction sites sell commercial items of little interest to the general public—scrap metal, salvaged vehicles, and excess inventory. The online auction sensations are the retail-like sites, such as eBay, whose site is shown here. Sellers pay between 25¢ and $2 per item just to have it made available for auction. eBay conducts an

electronic auction that runs for multiple days, with anyone who happens by the site submitting bids as they please. If the goods are sold, eBay collects a commission of 1.25 to 5 percent of the selling price.

Categories of merchandise on the eBay site include toys, antiques, books, movies, jewelry, collectibles, computers, dolls, photos, pottery, and more. On a typical day, merchandise might include an autographed picture of Joe DiMaggio, a 1937 Indian head nickel, a commercial balloon imprinter, a Chevy Blazer, a 1780 German bird engraving, a biography of Colin Powell, Super Bowl tickets, and a blue swirl glass paperweight. But this tiny list cannot even give the flavor of the vast amount of mer-

chandise available. There are, for example, over 8000 Barbie doll items. Buyers trade on eBay because of the large number of items available. If you want it, someone is probably selling it. Similarly, sellers are attracted to eBay because eBay has the most buyers. There are over a million auctions happening on eBay every day.

For any given item, a potential bidder can see the number of bids that have been made on an item, the current price, the date the bidding ends, and the e-mail address of the current high bidder. Most items are accompanied by detailed descriptions and photos. In order to bid on or sell an item, you will first need to register. You only need to register once. This way the buyer will know who the

seller is in order to pay him or her, and the seller will be able to answer any product questions potential buyers may have. Registration requires a real-world address and telephone number. eBay will not use this information for marketing, or disclose it to an outside party; the company will, however, supply your phone number, city, and state to another registered user upon request.

There are two appealing aspects for auction buyers—convenience and savings. The convenience is the usual convenience of buying online instead of moving from place to place, auction to auction. The savings are there if you know the merchandise and recognize a good price.

M argin notes provide interesting information about computers that motivates, entertains, and expands on chapter content.

M aking the Right Connections. Each chapter includes a feature that explores links between computers and people or computers and information. Students discover obvious and not-so-obvious uses of computers.

ACKNOWLEDGMENTS

Many people contributed to this project. I am struck by the geographic diversity of the team. The publishing anchors are in Massachusetts: editor Anita Devine, developmental editor Patricia Mahtani, production supervisor Juliet Silveri, art director Regina Hagen, and marketing manager Tom Ziolkowski. Other key players are scattered around the country: cover illustrator Joseph Maas in New Mexico, copy editor Ursula Smith in Vermont, production manager Lorne Franklin in Ohio, annotator Jerry Reed in Florida, ethics writer Jack Bresenham in South Carolina, designer Mark Ong and photo researcher Kathleen Cameron in California, and the author in Washington. Most of our communication was by e-mail. If anything, our communiqués were more efficient than if we had been office neighbors. In e-mail, one tends to get to the point. This book truly was a team effort. My sincere thanks to each and every one of you.

I would also like to thank the reviewers and survey respondents of the Sixth Edition. Your input is very much appreciated.

Beverly Amer, Northern Arizona University
Roger L. Anderson, College of Lake County
Madeline L. Baugher, Southwestern Oklahoma State University
Linda M. Beach, Potomac College
Jay Benson, Anne Arundel Community College
Kelly Black, California State University, Fresno
Jack E. Bresenham, Winthrop University
Peter Brown, Duquesne University
Debra L. Burgin, Kishwaukee College
Carl Scharpf, Seattle Community College
Art Dearing, Tarleton State University
Frank E. Green, University of Maryland Baltimore County
Nancy Hansen, Mankato State University
Ron Harkins, Miami University, Hamilton
Lee A. Hunt, Collin County Community College
Norman Jacobson, University of California, Irvine
Cherylee Kushida, Santa Ana College
William E. McTammany, Florida Community College, Jacksonville
Stephen L. Priest, Daniel Webster College
Tim Sylvester, Glendale Community College
Gerald L. Tatar, Duquesne University
William T. Verts, University of Massachusetts, Amherst

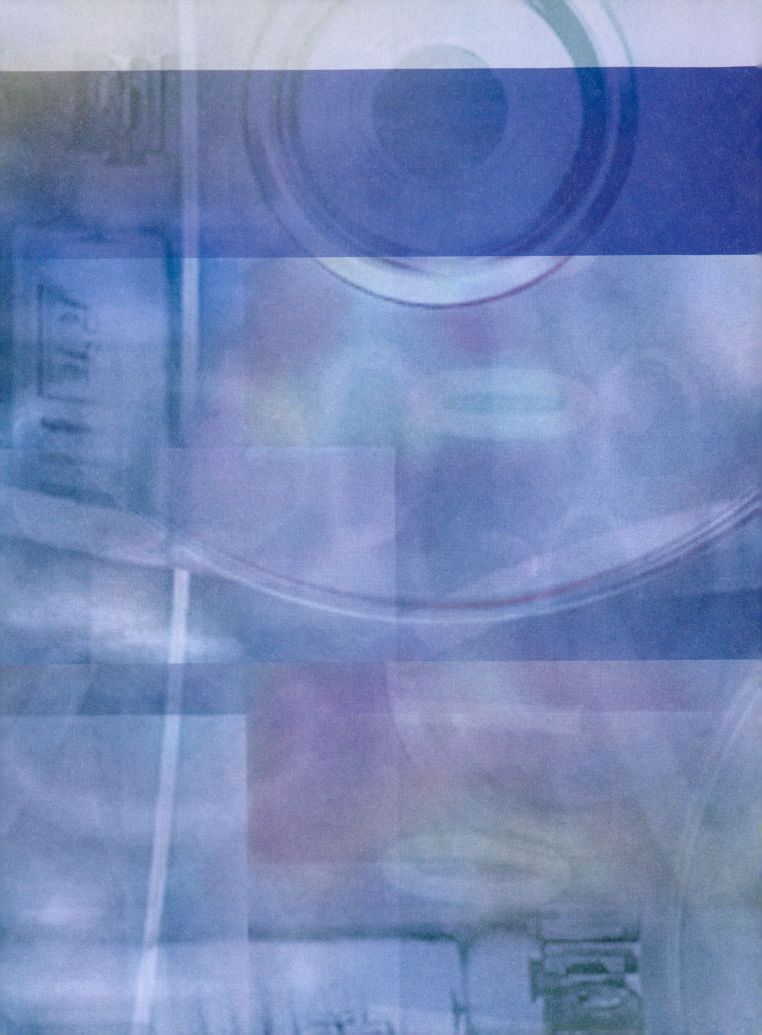

PHOTO ESSAY

The Age of Information

The dawn of a new age–the Information Age–glows before us with the promise of new ways of thinking, living, and working. The amount of information in the world is said to be doubling every six to seven years. Can we keep up? We can, but not without an understanding of how computers work and the ability to control them for our own purpose.

Stepping Out

Your first steps toward joining the Information Age include under-standing how we got to where we are today. Perhaps you recall from history books how the Industrial Age took its place in our world. In just a few years, society accepted the dizzying introduction of electricity, telephones, radio, automobiles, and airplanes. However, compared to the Industrial Age, the Information Age is evolving even more rapidly. It is likely to continue to evolve well into the twenty-first century.

Forging a Computer-Based Society

Traditional economics courses define the cornerstones of an economy as land, labor, and capital. Today we can add a fourth key economic element: information. As we evolve from an industrial to an information society, our jobs are changing from physical to mental labor. Just as people moved physically from farms to factories in the Industrial Age, so today people are shifting muscle power to brain power in a new, computer-based society.

You are making your move, too, taking your first steps by signing up for this computer class and reading this book. But should you go further and get your own computer? We look next at some of the reasons why you might.

A Computer in Your Future

Computers have moved into every nook and cranny of our daily lives. Whether or not you personally know anything about it, you invoke computers when you make a bank withdrawal, buy groceries at the supermarket, and even when you drive your car. But should you have a computer at your personal disposal? The answer today is "probably." Although only a third of Americans have personal computers in their homes, a much higher percentage use computers on the job. Almost any career in your future will involve a computer in some way.

In their homes people use various forms of computer technology for writing papers and memos, for keeping track of bank accounts, for communicating with friends and associates, for accessing knowledge, for purchasing goods, and so much more.

Computer Literacy for All

Why are you studying about computers? In addition to curiosity (and perhaps a course requirement), you probably recognize that it will not be easy to get through the rest of your life without knowing about computers. We offer a three-pronged definition of computer literacy:

- **Awareness.** As you study about computers, you will become aware of their importance, their versatility, and their pervasiveness in our society.
- **Knowledge.** You will learn what computers are and how they work. This requires learning some technical jargon, but do not worry—no one expects you to become a computer expert.
- **Interaction.** There is no better way to understand computers than through interacting with one. So being computer literate also means being able to use a computer for some simple applications.

Note that no part of this definition suggests that you must be able to create the instructions that tell a computer what to do. That would be akin to saying that anyone who plans to drive a car must first become an automotive engineer. Someone else can write the instructions for the computer; you simply use the instructions to get your work done. For example, an accountant might use a computer to prepare a report, a teenager to play a video game, a construction worker to record data from the field.

6

The Nature of Computers

Every computer has three fundamental characteristics. Each characteristic has by-products that are just as important. The three fundamental characteristics are:

- **Speed.** Computers provide the processing speed essential to our fast-paced society. The quick service we have come to expect—for bank withdrawals, stock quotes, telephone calls, and travel reservations, to name a few—is made possible by computers.

Businesses depend on the speedy processing provided by computers for everything from balancing ledgers to designing products, such as the camera and set of gears shown here.

- **Reliability.** Computers are extremely reliable. Of course, you

might not think this from some of the stories you may have seen in the press about "computer errors." However, most errors supposedly made by computers are really human errors.

■ **Storage Capability.** Computer systems can store tremendous amounts of data, which can be located and retrieved efficiently. The capability to store volumes of data is especially important in an information age.

These three characteristics—speed, reliability, and storage capability—have the following by-products:

■ **Productivity.** When computers move into business offices, managers expect increased productivity as workers learn to use computers to do their jobs better and faster. Furthermore, jobs like punching holes in metal or monitoring water levels can be more efficiently controlled by computers.

■ **Decision making.** To make decisions, managers need to take into account financial, geographical, and logistical factors. The computer helps decision makers sort things out and make better choices.

■ **Cost reduction.** Finally, because it improves productivity and aids decision making, the computer helps us hold down the costs of labor, energy, and paperwork. As a result, computers help reduce the costs of goods and services in our economy.

Next we look at some of the ways we use computers to make the workday more productive and our personal lives more rewarding.

Where Computers Are Used

Computers can do just about anything imaginable, but they really excel in certain areas. This section lists some of the principal areas of computer use.

- **Graphics.** Business people make bar graphs and pie charts from tedious figures to convey information with far more impact than numbers alone convey. Architects use computer-animated graphics to experiment with possible exteriors and to give clients a visual walk-through of proposed buildings. Finally, a new kind of artist has emerged, one who uses computers to express his or her creativity. The work shown here, called *Evolution,* was created by artist Darren Fisher.

- **Education.** Most schools in the United States have computers available for use in the classroom, and some colleges require entering freshmen to bring their own. Many educators prefer learning by doing—an approach uniquely suited to the computer.

- **Retailing.** Products from meats to magazines are packaged with zebra-striped bar codes that can be read by computer scanners at supermarket checkout stands to determine prices and help manage inventory. Computers operate behind the scenes too; for example, this book was tracked from printer to warehouse to bookstore with the help of computers and the bar code on the back cover.

- **Energy.** Energy companies use computers to locate oil, coal, natural gas, and uranium. Electric companies use computers to monitor vast power networks. In addition, meter readers use hand-held computers to record how much energy is used each month in homes and businesses.

- **Law enforcement.** Recent innovations in computerized law enforcement include national fingerprint files, a national file on the mode of operation of serial killers, and the computer modeling of DNA, which can be used

to match traces from an alleged criminal's body, such as blood at a crime scene.

■ **Transportation.** Computers are used in cars to monitor fluid levels, temperatures, and electrical systems. Computers also are used to help run rapid transit systems, load containerships, and track railroad cars across the country. The worker shown here in an airport tower rely on computers to help monitor air traffic.

■ **Money.** Computers speed up record keeping and allow banks to offer same-day services and even do-it-yourself banking over the phone. Computers have helped fuel the cashless economy, enabling the widespread use of credit cards and instantaneous credit checks by banks and retailers.

■ **Agriculture.** Farmers use small computers to help with billing, crop information, cost per acre, feed combinations, and market price checks. Cattle ranchers can also use computers for information about livestock breeding and performance.

■ **Government.** Among other tasks, the federal government uses computers to forecast weather, to manage parks, to process immigrants, to produce Social Security benefit checks, and—of course—to collect taxes. State and local governments also use computers routinely.

■ **The Home.** People have a computer in the home, often justifying it as an educational tool for their children. But that is only the beginning. Personal computers are being used at home to keep records, write letters, prepare budgets, draw pictures, publish newsletters, and connect with others.

■ **Health and medicine.** Computers help monitor the gravely ill in intensive care units and provide cross-sectional views of the body. Physicians can also use computers to assist in diagnoses; in fact, computers have been shown to correctly diagnose heart attacks more frequently than physicians do. If you are one of the thousands who suffer one miserable cold after another, you will be happy to know that computers have been able to map, in exquisite atomic detail, the structure of the human cold virus—the first

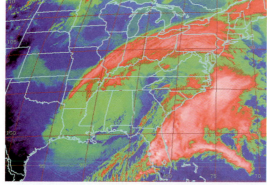

Hurricane Georges. First captured by a satellite, this photo of Hurricane Georges was computer-enhanced to provide color distinctions and a 3-D pop.

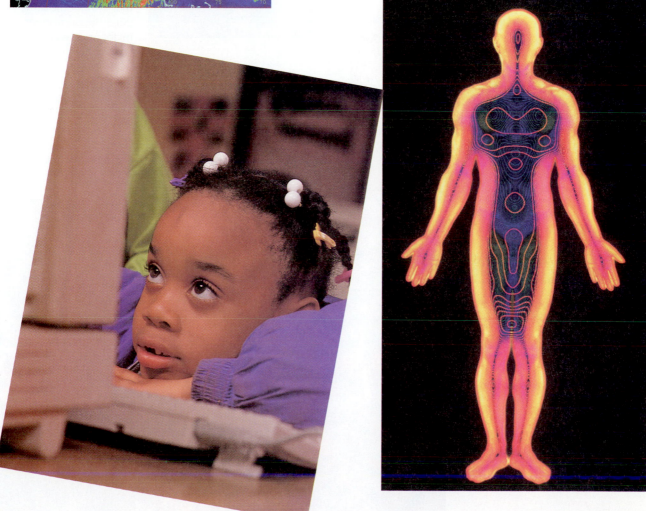

step toward a cure for the common cold.

- **Robotics.** Computers have paved the way for robots to take over many of the jobs that are too unpleasant or too dangerous for humans, such as opening packages believed to contain bombs. Robots are best known for their work in factories, but they can do many other things, not the least

of which is finding their way through the bloodstream.

- **The human connection.** Are computers cold and impersonal? The disabled do not think so; children, in particular, consider the computer their main education tool. Can the disabled walk again? Some can, with the help of computers. Can dancers and ath-

letes improve their performance? Maybe they can, by using computers to monitor their movements. Can we learn more about our ethnic backgrounds and our cultural history with the aid of computers? Indeed we can.

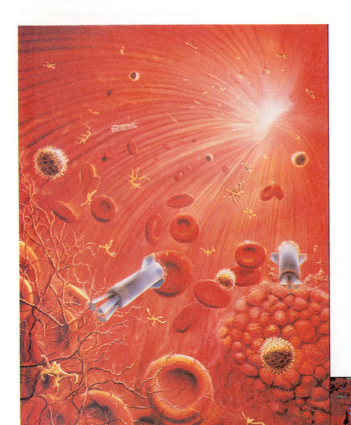

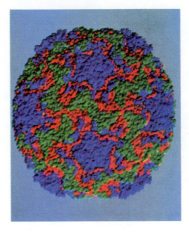

Cold virus. This computer-produced model of the cold virus named HRV 14 raises hopes that a cure for the common cold may be possible after all. With the aid of a computer, the final set of calculations for the model took one month to complete. Researchers estimate that without the computer the calculations might have required ten years of manual effort.

Robots. (below) This factory robot welds a new car under the direction of the computer. (at left) In the not-so-distant future, nanorobots, as shown here, will be able to destroy diseased tissues inside a human blood vessel.

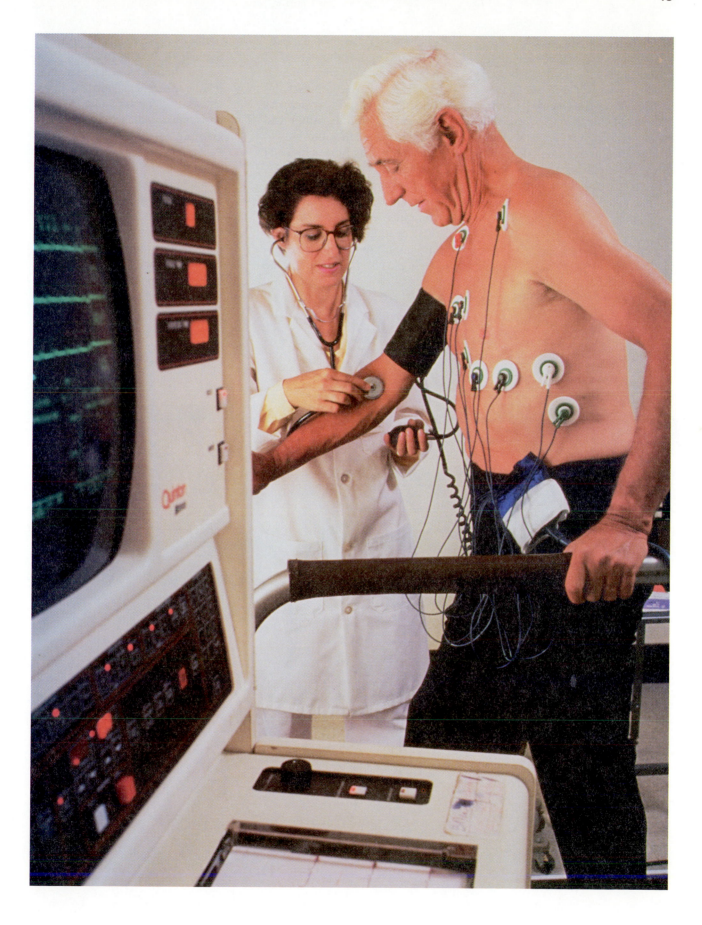

■ **The sciences.** Scientific researchers have long benefited from the high-speed capabilities of computers. Computers can simulate environments, emulate physical characteristics, and allow scientists to provide proofs in a cost-effective manner. Also, many mice—and other animals—have been spared since computers have taken over their roles in research.

■ **Connectivity.** One of the most popular uses of computers today is communicating with other people who have computers, whether for business or personal reasons. In addition, computers can give people the option of working at their homes instead of in city offices.

■ **Training.** It is much cheaper to teach aspiring pilots to fly in computerized training "cockpits," or simulators, than in real airplanes. Novice railroad engineers can also be given the expe-

rience of running a train with the help of a computerized device. Training simulations are relatively inexpensive and are always available on a one-to-one basis, making for very personal learning.

■ **Paperwork.** In some ways the computer contributes to paper use by adding to the amount of junk mail you find in your mailbox. However, in many ways it cuts down on paper handling. Using a computer, for example, you might type several drafts of a term paper before printing anything. Computerized record keeping and

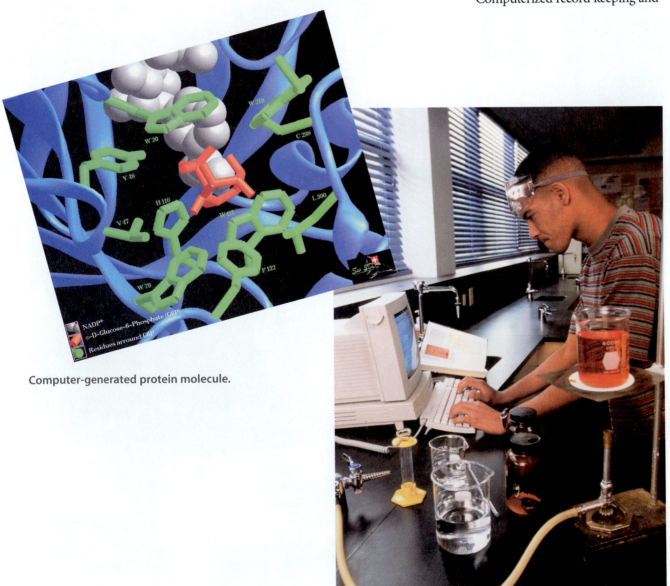

Computer-generated protein molecule.

ordering have also made paper-work more efficient.

▲

Computers are all around us. You have been exposed to computer hype, computer advertisements, and computer headlines. You have interacted with computers in your everyday life—at the grocery store, your school, the library, and more. You know more than you think you do. The beginnings of computer literacy are already apparent.

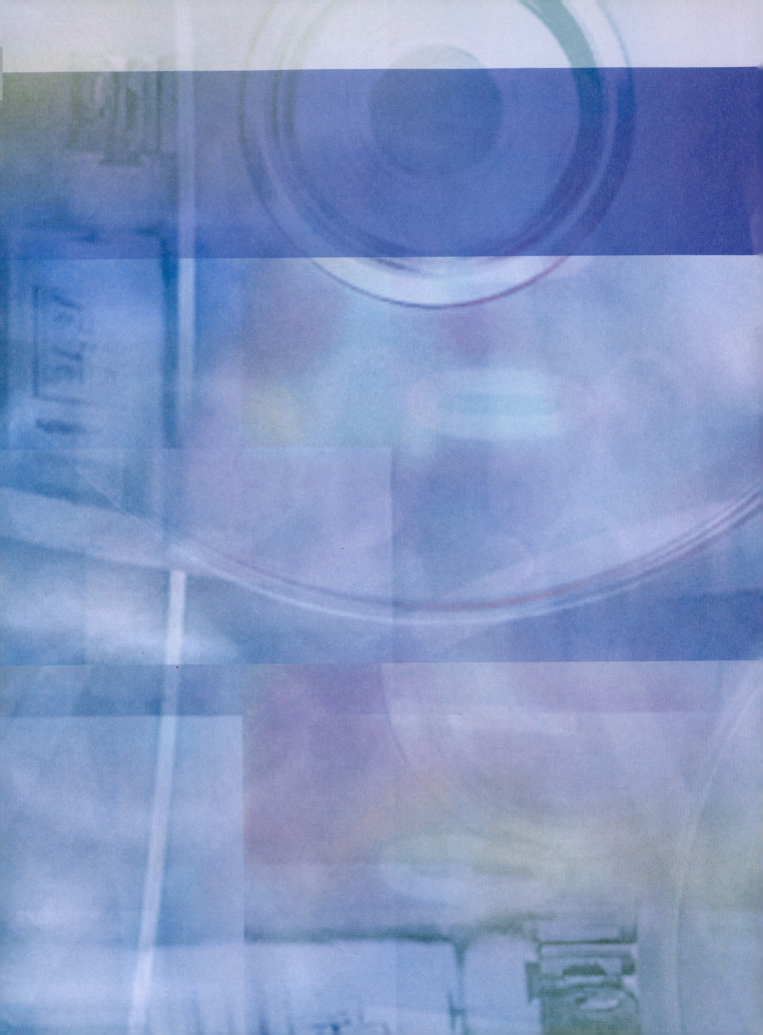

COMPUTER HARDWARE

Meeting the Machine

LEARNING OBJECTIVES

- Identify the basic components of a computer system: input, processing, output, and storage
- List some common input, output, and storage media
- Distinguish data from information
- Appreciate the significance of networking
- Understand the significance of the Internet
- Become familiar with the various classifications of computers

For years, Mike McDowell refused to buy a personal computer. The 38-year-old McDowell, owner of a 1200-acre farm in Wisconsin, told his disappointed children that they would just have to use the computers at school. The family simply could not justify the expense of a computer in the home. "If I buy a new tractor," he noted, "I can make the farm more profitable. But a computer? I just can't see it."

He can now. Mr. McDowell took a look at the new price tags. As personal computer prices ducked below $1000, they attracted a whole new audience of home users. The I-don't-need and I-can't-afford folks are taking the plunge. In fact, more than half of new computers are purchased by first-time buyers. In addition, computers are continuing their winning ways: Almost 80 percent of computer buyers are "satisfied" or "very satisfied" with their computers.

Mr. McDowell ticks off the uses his family has found for the computer. He took a class at his local community college and learned to use spreadsheets, a kind of rows-and-columns report, to plan his crop planting and rotations. When he can get it out of the hands of his Internet-surfing son, he uses the computer to send for weather and crop reports from agencies of the federal government. His wife favors e-mail, which lets her use the computer to send messages back and forth to her sisters in Duluth and Omaha. His teenage daughter, who wrote her high school reports using word processing, saved her summer job earnings to buy a laptop computer to take with her to college. Mr. McDowell now counts himself in the "very satisfied" category.

Global Perspective

Manufacturers of software and hardware must now take extra care to ensure that their software can be "localized"—that it can support translation into multiple languages, including some that do not use our conventional western alphabet. This involves supporting some different keyboard characters and different screen displays.

The Big Picture

A computer system has three main components: hardware, software, and people. The equipment associated with a computer system is called **hardware**. A set of instructions called **software** tells the hardware what to do. People, however, are the most important component of a computer system—people use the power of the computer for some purpose.

Software is also referred to as programs. To be more specific, a **program** is a set of step-by-step instructions that directs the computer to do the required tasks and produce the desired results. A **computer programmer** is a person who writes programs. **Users** are people who purchase and use computer software. In business, users are often called **end-users** because they are at the end of the "computer line," actually making use of the computer's capabilities.

2000 and Beyond

HAVE IT YOUR WAY

Your way exactly. The name of the new movement is *mass customization,* and the computer makes it possible.

Companies with millions of customers are starting to build products designed just for you. The woman shown in the photo is being measured for a pair of Levi jeans, which will be cut to fit her body. But clothes are just the beginning. You can buy a Dell computer made to your exact specifications. You can also buy eyeglasses molded to fit your face, CDs with music tracks you select, cosmetics mixed to match your skin tone, or a specially designed Barbie doll. Although these are mass-marketed goods, they can be uniquely tailored to the customers who buy them.

Computer-controlled factory equipment makes it possible to track every component of production and to readjust assembly lines quickly. Massive computer files can store information that includes the preferences of individual customers. Computer printers make it possible to change product packaging as necessary. The Internet is an important component too. For example, customers can go to the Mattel site and design a doll by choosing skin tone, eye color, hairdo, clothes, name, and even the doll's likes and dislikes. The new Barbie pal arrives in the mail with the doll's name on the package, along with a paragraph about her personality.

Mass customization is a novelty today. It will be common tomorrow.

This chapter examines hardware. The chapter looks at the "big picture"; thus many of the terms introduced in this chapter are discussed only briefly here. Subsequent chapters will define the various parts of a computer system in greater detail.

InfoBit

Some sources estimate that computer staff—the "peopleware"—are responsible for about half of every dollar spent on computing.

Hardware: The Basic Components of a Computer

InfoBit

One of the most startling aspects of the computer industry today is growth. During the past five years production of computers and computer-related equipment has quadrupled. This growth is over ten times as great as industry in general.

What is a computer? A 6-year-old called a computer "radio, movies, and television combined!" A 10-year-old described a computer as "a television set you can talk to." The 10-year-old's definition is closer but still does not recognize the computer as a machine that has the power to make changes.

Figure 1 Four primary components of a computer system. To function, a computer system requires input, processing, output, and storage.

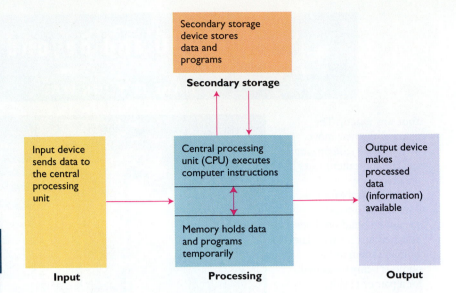

A **computer** is a machine that can be programmed to accept **data** *(input)*, process it into useful **information** *(output)*, and store it away (in a *secondary storage* device) for safekeeping or later reuse. The *processing* of input to output is directed by the software but performed by the hardware, the subject of this chapter.

To function, a computer system requires four main aspects of data handling: input, processing, output, and storage (Figure 1). The hardware responsible for these four areas is as follows:

- ■ *Input devices* accept data or commands in a form that the computer can use; they send the data or commands to the processing unit.
- ■ The *processor*, more formally known as the *central processing unit (CPU)*, has electronic circuitry that manipulates input data into the information people want. The central processing unit actually executes computer instructions.
- ■ *Output devices* show people the processed data—information—in understandable and usable form.
- ■ *Storage* usually means *secondary storage*, which consists of secondary storage devices such as disk—hard disk or diskettes or some other kind of disk—that can store data and programs outside the computer itself. These devices supplement *memory* or *primary storage*, which can hold data and programs only temporarily.

Before looking at each of these hardware aspects, consider them in terms of what you would find on a personal computer.

Your Personal Computer Hardware

Let us look at the hardware of a personal computer. Suppose you want to do word processing on a personal computer, using the hardware shown in Figure 2. Word processing software allows you to input data such as an essay, save it, revise and re-save it, and print it whenever you wish. The *input device*, in this case, is a keyboard, which you use to key—type—the original essay and any subsequent changes to it. You will also probably use the mouse as an input device. All computers, large and small, must have a *central pro-*

Curling Up with a Good Computer

It looks like a book, sort of, but it holds 50,000 pages. It weighs less than three pounds. It is, in fact, a computer book and it has a beautiful screen. It can hold reference books and several of your favorite novels.

In addition to the familiar comforts, this book knows a few tricks. You can still dog-ear a page by pressing a corner of the touch-sensitive screen, and you can use a stylus-type pen to write notes or underline. But you can also enlarge the typeface or touch a word to look it up in the dictionary.

Computer books are not cheap—yet. And, of course, you have to pay for the books too, but less than they would cost in their original form. New books can be charged and sent from the Internet directly to the computer book.

cessing unit, so yours does too—it is within the personal computer housing. The central processing unit uses the word processing software to accept the data you input through the keyboard. Processed data from your personal computer is usually *output* in two forms: on a screen and by a printer. As you key in the essay on the keyboard, it appears on the screen in front of you. After you have examined the essay on the screen, made changes, and determined that it is acceptable, you can print the essay on the printer. Your *secondary storage* device, as shown in Figure 2, which stores the essay until it is needed again, will probably be a hard disk or diskette. For reasons of convenience and speed, you are more likely to store your data—the essay—on a hard disk than on a diskette. (However, if you are using someone else's computer, such as a school computer, you will probably keep your own files on your own diskette.)

Next is a general tour of the hardware needed for input, processing, output, and storage. These same components make up all computer systems, whether small, medium, or large.

InfoBit

Input, processing, storage, and output can be found not only in general purpose computers, but also in smart appliances. Advanced sewing machines intended for small or home-based embroidery businesses feature the ability to scan in stitch designs, store them on diskettes, process them with a built-in microprocessor, and finally output the design as embroidery on fabric.

Figure 2 A personal computer system. In this personal computer system, the input device is a keyboard or a mouse. The input device feeds data to the central processing unit, which is inside the computer housing, the vertical box to the left of the screen. The output devices in this example are the screen, the printer, and the speakers. The secondary storage devices are a hard drive, a 3 1/2-inch disk drive, and a CD-ROM drive, all within the computer housing. This popular configuration, with the housing standing on end, is called a minitower.

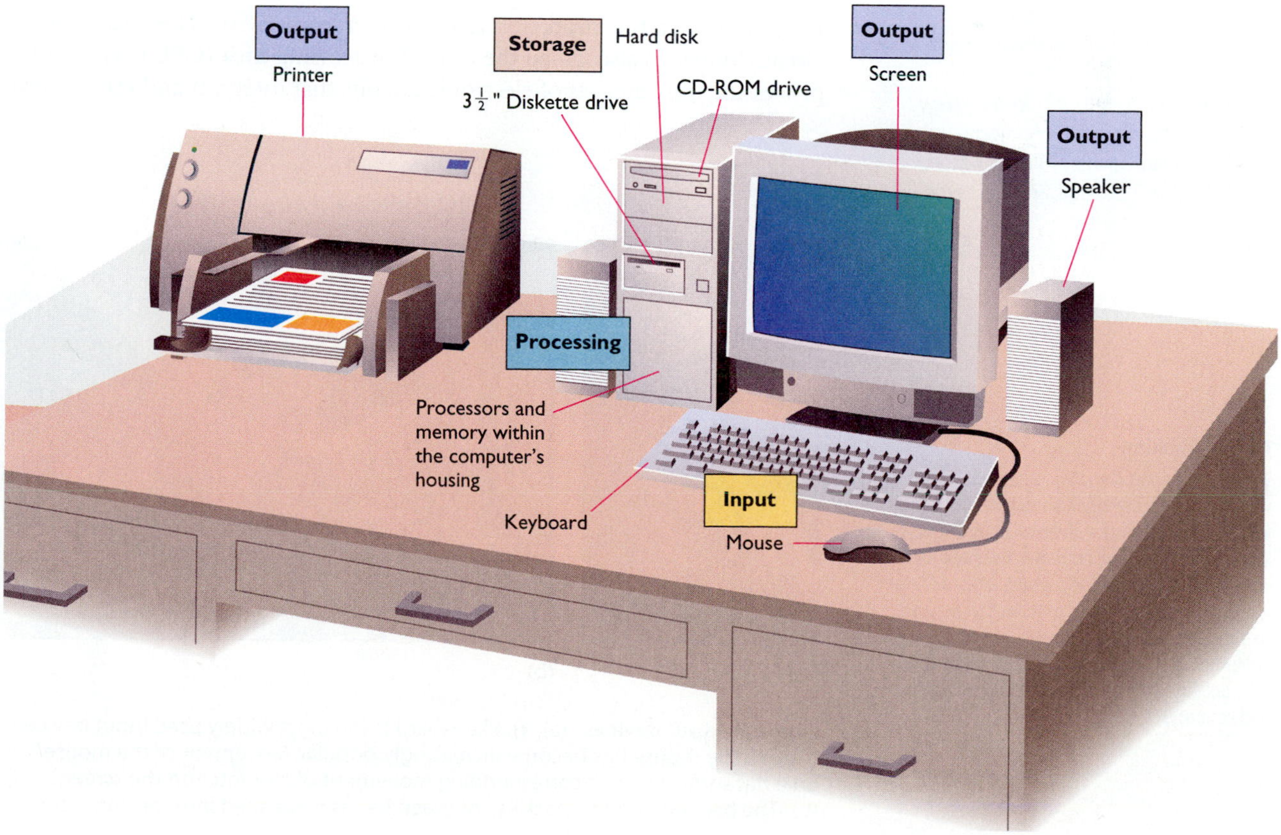

Critical Thinking
What social impact do you foresee occurring in the workplace if voice recognition software continues to increase in performance and popularity. (Possible societal effects include decreased need and jobs for clerical and administrative support, a lessened market for transcription equipment like that used in medical and legal offices, greater accessibility to computers by the some of the physically disabled, and reduction in the importance of typing speed and accuracy)

Input: What Goes In

Input is the data that you put into the computer system for processing. Here are some common ways of feeding input data into the system:

- *Typing* on a **keyboard** (Figure 3a). The keys on a computer keyboard are arranged in much the same way as those on a typewriter. The computer responds to what you enter; that is, it "echoes" what you type by displaying it on the screen in front of you.
- *Pointing* with a **mouse** (Figure 3a). A mouse is a device that is moved by hand over a flat surface. As the ball on its underside rotates, the mouse movement causes corresponding movement of a pointer on the computer screen. Pressing buttons on the mouse lets you select commands.
- *Scanning* with a **wand reader** or **bar-code reader** (Figure 3b). These devices, which you have seen used by clerks in retail stores, use laser beams to read special letters, numbers, or symbols such as the zebra-striped bar codes found on many products.

An input device may be part of a terminal. A **terminal** includes an input device, a television-like screen display, and some connection to a computer. For example, operators taking orders over the phone for a mail-order house would probably use terminals to input the order and send it to be processed by a large computer. You can input data to a computer in many other interesting ways, including by writing, speaking, pointing, or even just looking at the data.

The Processor and Memory: Data Manipulation

In a computer the processor is the center of activity. The **processor,** as already noted, is also called the **central processing unit (CPU)**. The central processing unit consists of electronic circuits that interpret and execute pro-

(a)   (b)

Figure 3 Input devices. (a) The keyboard is the most widely used input device, though the mouse has become increasingly popular. Movement of the mouse on a flat surface causes corresponding movement of a pointer on the screen. (b) The bar code on this package of green beans is scanned into the conputer.

gram instructions as well as communicating with the input, output, and storage devices.

It is the central processing unit that actually transforms data into information. **Data** is the raw material to be processed by a computer, such as grades in a class, touchdowns scored, or light and dark areas in a photograph. Processed data becomes **information**—data that is organized, meaningful, and useful. In school, for instance, an instructor could enter various student grades (data), which can be processed to produce final grades and perhaps a class average (information). Data that is perhaps uninteresting on its own may become very interesting once it is converted to information. The raw facts (data) about your finances, such as a paycheck or a donation to charity or a medical bill, may not be captivating individually, but together these and other items can be processed to produce the refund or amount you owe on your income tax return (information).

Computer **memory,** also known as **primary storage,** is closely related to the central processing unit but separate and distinct from it. Memory holds the data after it is input to the system and before it is processed; also, memory holds the data after it has been processed but before it has been released to the output device. In addition, memory holds the programs (computer instructions) needed by the central processing unit. Memory can hold data only temporarily because it requires a continuous flow of electric current; if the current is interrupted, the data is lost.

Output: What Comes Out

Output—the result produced by the central processing unit—is, of course, a computer's whole reason for being. Output is usable information—that is, raw input data that has been processed by the computer into information. Common forms of output are text, numbers, graphics, and even sounds. Text output, for example, may be the letters and memos prepared by office workers using word processing software. Other workers may be more interested in numbers, such as those found in formulas, schedules, and budgets. In many cases numbers can be understood more easily when output is in the form of graphics.

The most common output devices are computer screens and printers. A **screen,** the visible part of the **monitor,** can vary in its form of display, producing text, numbers, symbols, art, photographs, and even video, in full color (Figure 4a). **Printers** produce printed reports as instructed by a computer program (Figure 4b). Many printers, particularly those associated with personal computers, can print in color.

You can produce output from a computer in other ways, including film, voice, and music.

Secondary Storage

Secondary storage provides additional storage separate from memory. Recall that memory holds data and programs only temporarily; thus there is a need for secondary storage. The two most common secondary storage media are magnetic disks and magnetic tape. A **magnetic disk** can be a diskette or a hard disk. A **diskette** usually consists of a magnetic disk 3 1/2 inches in diameter, enclosed in a plastic case (Figure 5a). **Hard disks** usually have more storage capacity than diskettes and also offer faster access to the data they hold. With large computer systems, hard disks are often contained

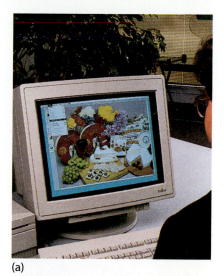
(a)

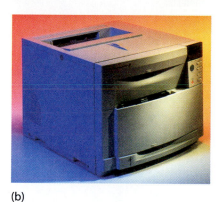
(b)

Figure 4 Output devices. Screens and printers are two types of output devices. (a) This screen can display text or the colorful graphics shown here. (b) This laser printer is used to produce high-quality output.

Critical Thinking

What cost and usability factors would you consider in purchasing an output device like a printer or a fax for an office installation? (Important factors include initial cost, cost per use, size, flexibility, reliability, warranty, manufacturer's reputation, compatibility with other equipment, and ease of use).

Learn by Doing

Consider asking students to interview someone who makes purchasing decisions about the types of computers they use in their workplace. What are the typical criteria used by these decision makers, and what types of computers do they buy now versus what types of hardware would they expect to buy three years from now?

InfoBit

A critical but often overlooked computer peripheral is an Uninterruptible Power Supply (UPS). Knowing that data on primary and secondary storage devices is likely to be lost or damaged in an unexpected power failure, many companies and home users purchase a UPS that will continue to supply power from a back-up battery during brief power outages.

in disk packs. Disk data is read by **disk drives.** Personal computer disk drives read diskettes; most personal computers have hard disk drives also. **Optical disks,** such as **CD-ROMs,** use a laser beam to read large volumes of data relatively inexpensively (Figure 5b).

Magnetic tape is used primarily with large computer systems. This tape usually comes on a cartridge and is similar to tape that is played on a tape recorder. Magnetic tape reels are mounted on **tape drives** when the data on them needs to be read by the computer system or when new data is to be written on the tape. Magnetic tape is usually used for backup purposes—for "data insurance"—because tape is inexpensive. The chapter on storage presents more detailed information about storage media, notably alternative disk storage.

The Complete Hardware System

The hardware devices attached to the computer are called peripheral equipment. **Peripheral equipment** includes all input, output, and secondary storage devices. In most personal computers, the CPU and disk drives are all contained in the same housing, a metal case; the keyboard, mouse, and screen are separate.

In larger computer systems, however, the input, processing, output, and storage functions may be in separate rooms, separate buildings, or even separate countries. For example, data may be input on terminals at a branch bank and then transmitted to the central processing unit at the bank's headquarters. The information produced by the central processing unit may then be transmitted to the international offices, where it is printed out. Meanwhile, disks with stored data may be kept at the bank headquarters, and duplicate data may be kept on disk or tape in a warehouse across town for safekeeping.

(a)   (b)

Figure 5 Secondary storage devices. (a) A 3 1/2-inch diskette is being inserted into a disk drive. (b) Optical disks can hold enormous amounts of data: text, music, graphics—even video and movies.

GETTING PRACTICAL

THOSE NECESSARY EXTRAS

Just like people who have boats or cameras, computer owners are tempted to buy the latest gadget. There are many from which to choose, some new, neat, and nifty—and some more useful than others.

For greater flexibility, check out a wireless keyboard or mouse, which works well as long as it is within direct line of sight of the computer. For everyday computer comfort, consider a gel-based mouse pad with a place to rest your wrist. To reduce

neck strain, get a document holder that attaches to the side of your monitor. While you are at it, you can reduce eyestrain by attaching a magnifier to the screen itself.

If you prefer to say what you think instead of writing it, you can purchase a

microphone and accompanying software to accept your voice input. Road warriors can buy practical laptop cases, with lots of pockets. If music and gaming are your computer life, you could invest in the very best: Bose speakers.

Although the equipment may vary widely from the simplest computer to the most powerful, by and large the four elements of a computer system remain the same: input, processing, output, and storage. These basic components are supplemented by hardware that can make computers much more useful, giving them the ability to connect to one another.

Networking

Many organizations find that their needs are best served by a **network,** a computer system that uses communications equipment to connect computers and their resources. Resources include printers and hard disks and even software and data. In one type of network, a **local area network (LAN),** personal computers in an office are connected together so that users can communicate with one another. Users can operate their personal computers independently or in cooperation with other computers to exchange data and share resources. The networking process can be much more complex; we will describe how large computers can be involved in networks in the chapter on networking.

Individual users in homes or offices have joined the trend to "connectivity" by hooking up their personal computers, usually via telephone lines, to other computers. Users who connect their computers to other computers via the phone lines must use a hardware device called a **modem** as a go-between to reconcile the inherent differences between computers and the phone system. From their own homes, users can connect to all sorts of computer-based services, performing such tasks as getting stock quotes, making airline reservations, and shopping for videotapes. An important service for individuals is **electronic mail,** or **e-mail,** which lets people send and receive messages via computer.

Whether the user is operating in a business capacity or simply exploring the options, a popular conduit for connectivity is the Internet.

InfoBit

While LANs are widely used in businesses today, an area that is just starting to take off is local area networking in the home. An industry study group predicts almost 6 million network nodes will ship into homes in 1999. The need for in-home connectivity comes from current PC owners who are buying additional PCs faster than non-PC owners are buying their first PC.

FOCUS ON thics

Can the Government Really Do That?

State governments have sold lists of driver license holder names and addresses for many years, with little citizen reaction. That changed in 1999 when citizens in South Carolina, Colorado, and Florida discovered that their driver license photos would be sold to a private company, which then would make them available via computer to other commercial parties, notably as an identification check for store cashiers. People were outraged at a perceived invasion of privacy. Ethical questions become more prominent when new technology makes a practice faster and more affordable.

The Internet

The **Internet,** sometimes called simply "the Net," is the largest and most far-flung network system of them all, connecting users worldwide. Surprisingly, the Internet is not really a single network but a loosely organized collection of thousands of networks. Many people are astonished to discover that no one owns the Internet. It has no central headquarters, no centrally offered services, and no comprehensive index to tell you what information is available.

Originally developed and still subsidized by the United States government, the Internet connects libraries, college campuses, research labs, businesses, and any other organization or individual who has the capacity to hook up.

Getting Connected

How are all kinds of different computers able to communicate with one another? To access the Internet, a user's computer must connect to a type of computer called a **server.** Each server uses the same special software called **TCP/IP** (for **Transmission Control Protocol/Internet Protocol**); it is this standard that allows different types of computers to communicate with each other (Figure 6). The supplier of the server computer, often called an **Internet service provider (ISP),** charges a fee, usually monthly, based on the amount of service provided. Once a user has chosen a service provider, he or she will be furnished with the information needed to connect to the server and, from there, to the Internet.

Figure 6 The Internet. (1) At his or her own computer, a user accesses the server computer, (2) probably over the phone line. (3) The server computer communicates with the Internet, perhaps passing on e-mail messages or requests for certain web sites, and picking up responses. (4) Incoming messages, e-mail, or requested Internet information are returned to the original requesting computer. This back-and-forth communication goes on as long as the user wishes to remain connected to the Internet.

Getting Around

Since the Internet did not begin as a commercial customer-pleasing package, it did not initially offer attractive options for finding information. The arcane commands were invoked only by a hardy and determined few. Furthermore, the vast sea of information, including news and trivia, can seem an overwhelming challenge to navigate. As both the Internet user population and the available information grew, new ways were developed to tour the Internet.

The most attractive method used to move around the Internet is called *browsing.* Using a program called a **browser,** you can use a mouse to point and click on screen text or pictures to explore the Internet, particularly the **World Wide Web (WWW or the Web),** an Internet subset of text, images, and sounds linked together to allow users to peruse related topics. Each different location on the Web is called a **web site** or, more commonly, just a **site.** You may have heard the term **home page;** this is just the first page of a web site.

The Internet is an important and complex topic. Although it is easy to use once you know how, there is much to learn about its use and its place in the world of computers. This opening chapter merely scratches the surface. More detailed information can be found in specific chapters devoted to the Internet. In addition, this book has a two-page spread, called "Planet Internet," at the end of each chapter, giving examples of some aspect of the Internet. Further, the more generic topic of connectivity is discussed in the feature "Making the Right Connections," offered in each chapter of the book.

Classification of Computers

Computers come in sizes from tiny to monstrous, in both appearance and power. The size of a computer that a person or an organization needs depends on the computing requirements. Clearly, the National Weather Service, keeping watch on the weather fronts of many continents, has requirements different from those of a car dealer's service department that is trying to keep track of its parts inventory. And the requirements of both of them are different from the needs of a sales person using a small notebook computer to record client orders or of a student writing a paper. Although we will describe categories of computers here, keep in mind that computers do not fall too readily into groups of distinct islands; the reality is blurry and overlapping—and changing all the time.

Supercomputers

The mightiest computers—and, of course, the most expensive—are known as **supercomputers**. Supercomputers are also the fastest: They can process trillions of instructions per second. Supercomputers can be found in mainstream activities as varied as stock analysis, automobile design, special effects for movies, and even sophisticated artwork (Figure 7). However, for many

Learn by Doing

If you have Internet access, a number of simple browser demonstrations are possible. One technique that is effective in demonstrating the breadth of content available on the Internet is to have students write down topics and then randomly select choices to search for on the Internet, using one of the available search engines.

Group Work

If you are planning to have students cooperate in teams, a number of "icebreaker" activities are possible, ranging from issuing students name cards to place at their seat, having them introduce themselves to the class, or even having them introduce the person who sits beside them (after a brief "interview" period).

InfoBit

National supercomputer laboratories already boast supercomputers that can deliver trillions of real numbered math operations per second. Within the next few decades we can expect supercomputers to achieve rates 1000 times faster than today's performance.

Figure 7 Supercomputer graphics. Thes graphic images, called fractals, are formed by using the computer to repeat geometric shapes with color, size, and angle variations. (a) Note the basic triangle and circle elements on which the fractals are built. (b) Here, the artist makes slight adjustments to make the fractals appear to be in motion.

(a)

(b)

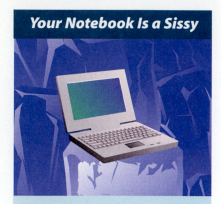

Your Notebook Is a Sissy

Where does your notebook computer travel? From home to school, snuggled in your backpack? From home to office or hotel, cradled in its own cushioned case? Your notebook has probably never had to defend itself from life's knocks.

Compare your notebooks to notebooks that have been, to use a term of art, *ruggedized*. That is, they have been made sufficiently rugged to pass any number of torture tests—-shock, falls, vibration, dust, and water. Typically, the machine's innards are housed in a magnesium alloy case, about 20 times as strong as the plastic generally used in conventional notebooks. The keyboard is sealed to prevent liquid from seeping into the internal circuitry, and all external connections are dust-resistant. The disk drives are mounted in a shock-absorbing gel compound.

So, who needs all this hardiness? The military, for openers. Also, construction engineers, oil-rig managers, and anyone else whose center of operations is based on sand, water, or ice.

Critical Thinking

What advantages could a company get from leasing computers rather than buying them? (While there may be purely financial reasons like lessened capital expenditures, another reason is that PC's become obsolete so quickly that leasing a new one every two to three years is much more attractive than owning a personal computer outright).

years supercomputer customers were an exclusive group: agencies of the federal government. The federal government uses supercomputers for tasks that require mammoth data manipulation, such as worldwide weather forecasting and weapons research (Figure 8a).

Mainframes

In the jargon of the computer trade, large computers are called **mainframes** (Figure 8b). Mainframes are capable of processing data at very high speeds—millions of instructions per second—and have access to billions of characters of data. The price of these large systems can vary from several hundred thousand to many millions of dollars. With that kind of price tag, you will not buy a mainframe for just any purpose. Their principal use is for processing vast amounts of data quickly, so some of the obvious customers are banks, insurance companies, and manufacturers. But this list is not all-inclusive; other types of customers are large mail-order houses, airlines with sophisticated reservation systems, government accounting services, aerospace companies doing complex aircraft design, and the like. As you can tell from these examples of mainframe applications, a key characteristic of large computers is that they are designed for multiple users. For example, many reservations clerks could be accessing the same computer at the same time to make reservations for waiting customers.

As computer users have marched inexorably toward personal computers and networking, pundits erroneously have predicted the demise of mainframes. But "big iron," the affectionate nickname for these computers, is proving to be hardy and versatile. More recent uses include helping large businesses carry out critical applications such as running automated teller machines and delivering e-mail. Thus the mainframe has taken on the coloration of a server and is often referred to as a *server*. On the Internet, where computers of all stripes can coexist and even work in concert, vast data stores are being kept on the "large servers." The large server—the mainframe—is still the most reliable way to manage vast amounts of data. As an example, national retailer L. L. Bean is using an IBM mainframe system to offer its entire catalog on the Internet.

Personal Computers

Most often called **personal computers,** or just **PCs,** these desktop computers are occasionally known as **microcomputers** or, sometimes, **home computers** (Figure 8c). Personal computers now fall into categories; most are low-end functional computers (sometimes ungallantly referred to as "cheap PCs") or else fully powered personal computers. A third category of upper-end PCs, called **workstations,** is used by specialized workers such as engineers, financial traders, and graphic designers. Workstations are small enough to fit on a desktop but approach the power of a mainframe.

Most users choose between personal computers in the first two categories: less expensive or more expensive. For many years PCs were offered only in the fully powered state-of-the-art category and bore price tags over $2000, enough to make some home buyers hesitate. But now, for a few hundred dollars, anyone can own a personal computer. At the low end, a cheap PC has less of everything: a slower and less powerful microprocessor, less memory, a smaller and less crisp screen, less hard drive space, and fewer software choices. Nevertheless, cheap PCs perform primary functions more than adequately. Customers who want a computer mainly for basic applications such as word processing, personal finance, record-

Figure 8 Computer classifications. Here are some examples of computers by their informal classifications. (a) This Cray supercomputer has been nicknamed Bubbles because of its bubbling, shimmering coolant liquids. Cray computers have 75 percent of the supercomputer market. (b) Mainframe computers are usually shown in multiple units, looking like a group of sterile refrigerators. IBM has chosen to add a little flair to its presentation of the IBM 9672. (c) Individuals use personal computers in both the home and the office. (d) People who work in various locations favor portable notebook computers.

Critical Thinking

Notebook computers are not without operational (and even social) problems. What problems do you imagine arise for notebook owners? (Travel is risky for notebooks, airport security is problematic, theft is a real possibility, inclement weather requires packing, persons nearby may be annoyed by noise of keystrokes, batteries run down, work may increasingly invade the home, and the computer must be kept dry at all times).

keeping, games, and access to the Internet are usually happy with computers at the low end.

There are, of course, people who should buy the more expensive, cutting-edge computers. You will want all the computer you can get if you plan to spend a lot of time on graphic images, heavy-duty calculations, programming, and—above all—action-oriented arcade games.

A variation on the personal computer is the **network computer** (NC), or simply a **net computer** or **net box,** a limited piece of hardware with a central processing unit and minimal memory, offered with Internet access in mind. The net computer hooks up to the Internet via a telephone line. In the home, people can use a net computer with the television set as the computer screen. (Commercially, televisions sold with this setup are marketed as "Web TVs.") In the office, keyboards and monitors are provided. Most net computers have no disk storage at all. The original idea behind this un-PC was simplicity and low price. However, net computers have faltered in the marketplace, mainly because cheap PCs have cut into their territory.

Notebook Computers

A computer that fits in a briefcase? A computer that weighs less than a newborn baby? A computer you do not have to plug in? A computer to use on your lap on an airplane? Yes to all these questions. **Notebook computers** are wonderfully portable and functional, and they are popular with travelers who need a computer that can go with them (Figure 7d). Somewhat larger, heavier versions of these computers are known as **laptop computers.**

The memory and storage capacity of notebook computers today can compete with those of desktop computers. Notebooks have a hard disk drive and most accept diskettes, so it is easy to move data from one computer to another. Many offer a CD-ROM drive. Furthermore, notebooks can run most software available. Notebooks are not as inexpensive as their size might suggest; most carry a price tag greater than that of a full-size personal computer. However, like other technology, notebook computers are getting faster, lighter, and more feature-rich (Figure 9).

Smaller Still: Personal Digital Assistants

A handheld computer called a **personal digital assistant** (PDA) can be used to keep track of appointments and other business information, such as customer names and orders. PDAs are also called **pen-based computers** because, through a pen-like stylus, they can accept handwritten input directly on a touch-sensitive screen. Many PDAs offer multiple functions, including wireless e-mail and fax capabilities (Figure 10).

Users of PDAs are often clipboard-carrying workers, such as parcel delivery drivers and meter readers. Other potential users are workers who cannot easily use a notebook computer because they are on their feet all day: nurses, sales representatives, real estate agents, and insurance adjusters. But the biggest group of users is found right in the office; these users like the fact that this convenient device can keep their lives organized.

▲

This chapter has taken a rather expansive look at computer hardware. However, hardware by itself is just an empty shell. Software is the ingredient that gives value to the computer.

Figure 9 Notebook computers. All these users, whether working in the office or in the field, find it convenient to use notebook computers.

MAKING THE RIGHT CONNECTIONS

ROCK THE VOTE

The anthem of several Internet sites, "rock the vote," refers to getting out the vote and, especially, making sure that people are registered to vote. In fact, people can—almost—register to vote entirely via the Internet. Talk about the "right connections. . . ."

The phenomenon goes back to 1993 when Congress passed the law commonly known as the "motor voter" law, referring to the possibility of registering at the same time you get your driver's license. The same law also required the Federal Election Commission to create one single uniform voter registration application that can be used to register voters in nearly all 50 states.

Enter the Internet. Several Internet sites—notably, the Net Vote site—provide a form containing name, address, and other blanks for you to fill out right on the computer's screen. The completed form is then submitted, again via the Internet, to the sponsoring organization. In a week or two you will receive your voter registration card in the mail. Once you sign and return it, you are registered to vote.

Figure 10 Pen-based computers. The popular Palm V, which weighs just over four ounces, has some rivals but no real competition. (a) The Palm V lets you manage your calendar and contact list, keep a to-do list, send e-mail with a wireless modem, and even jot short memos with the accompanying stylus. (b) Placed in its cradle, which is attached to a desktop computer, the Palm V can send data back and forth.

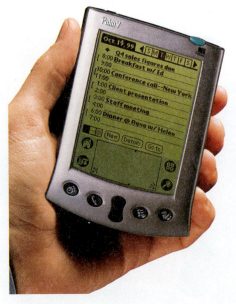

(a)

(b)

CHAPTER REVIEW

Summary and Key Terms

- The equipment associated with a computer system is called hardware. The **programs,** or step-by-step instructions that run the machines, are called **software. Computer programmers** write programs for **users,** or **end-users**—people who purchase and use computer software.

- A **computer** is a machine that can be programmed to process **data** (input) into useful **information** (output). A computer system comprises four main aspects of data handling—input, processing, output, and storage.

- **Input** is data to be accepted into the computer. Common input devices are the **keyboard;** a **mouse,** which translates movements of a ball on a flat surface to actions on the screen; and a **wand reader** or **bar-code reader,** which uses laser beams to read special letters, numbers, or symbols such as the zebra-striped bar-codes on products.

- A **terminal** includes an input device, such as a keyboard or wand reader; an output device, usually a television-like screen; and a connection to the main computer.

- The **processor,** or **central processing unit (CPU),** processes raw data into meaningful, useful information. The CPU interprets and executes program instructions and communicates with the input, output, and storage devices. **Memory,** or **primary storage,** is related to the central processing unit but is separate and distinct from it. Memory holds the input data before processing and also holds the processed data after processing, until the data is released to the output device.

- **Output,** which is raw data processed into usable information, is usually in the form of words, numbers, and graphics. Users can see output displayed on a **screen,** part of the **monitor,** and use **printers** to display output on paper.

- **Secondary storage** provides additional storage space separate from memory. The most common secondary storage devices are **magnetic disks,** but **magnetic tape** also provides secondary storage. Magnetic disks are **diskettes,** usually 3 1/2 inches in diameter, or **hard disks.** Hard disks on large systems are contained in a disk pack. Hard disks hold more data and offer faster access than diskettes do. Some hard disks come in removable cartridge form. Disk data is read by **disk drives. Optical disks,** such as **CD-ROMs,** use a laser beam to read large volumes of data. Magnetic tape comes on reels or in cassettes and is mainly used for backup purposes. Magnetic tape reels are mounted on **tape drives.**

- **Peripheral equipment** includes all the input, output, and secondary storage devices attached to a computer. Some peripheral equipment may be built into one physical unit, as in many personal computers, or contained in separate units, as in many large computer systems.

- Often organizations use a **network** of personal computers, which allows users to operate independently or in cooperation with other computers, exchanging data and sharing resources. Such a setup is called a **local area network (LAN).**

- Users who connect their computers via the phone lines must use a hardware device called a **modem** to reconcile the inherent differences between computers and the phone system.

- Individuals use networking for a variety of purposes, especially **electronic mail,** or **e-mail.**

- The **Internet,** sometimes called simply "the Net," connects users worldwide. To access the Internet, a user's computer must connect to a type of computer called a **server,** which has special software called **TCP/IP** (for **Transmission Control Protocol/Internet Protocol**) that allows different types of computers to communicate with one another. The supplier of the server computer, often called an **Internet service provider (ISP),** charges a fee based on the amount of service provided.

■ With software called a **browser,** a user can manipulate a mouse to point and click on screen text or pictures to explore the Internet, particularly the **World Wide Web** (**WWW** or **the Web**), an Internet subset of text, images, and sounds linked together to allow users to view related topics. Each different location on the Web is called a **web site** or, more commonly, just a **site**. A **home page** is the first page of a web site.

■ The most powerful and expensive computers are called **supercomputers.** Large computers called **mainframes** are used by businesses such as banks, airlines, and manufacturers to process very large amounts of data quickly.

■ Desktop computers are called **personal computers (PCs), microcomputers,** or sometimes **home computers. Workstations** combine the compactness of a desktop computer with power that almost equals that of a mainframe. Lower-priced PCs are sometimes called "cheap PCs." A **network computer (NC)**, sometimes called simply a **net computer** or **net box,** is a limited machine that has had difficulty competing with cheap PCs. **Notebook computers** are small portable computers; somewhat larger, heavier versions are called **laptop computers.**

■ **Personal digital assistants (PDAs),** also called **pen-based computers,** are handheld computers that accept handwritten input directly on a screen.

Discussion Questions

1. Consider the hardware used for input, processing, output, and storage for personal computers. Most personal computer systems come configured in a standard way, but you may find differences in how you would use that equipment.

   a. Input. You would probably use a keyboard to input data. For what purposes would you use a mouse?

   b. Output: You would, of course, have a screen. After the computer itself, the biggest expense is the printer. Can you imagine getting along without a printer?

   c. Is a 3 1/2-inch diskette drive sufficient? Why would a hard disk be of value to you? Why might you want a CD-ROM drive?

2. Discuss this statement: "I see myself using word processing to prepare term papers and the Internet to do research. Other than that, I doubt if I would have any use for computers during my college years."

3. Are you considering a particular career? Discuss how computers are used, or could be used, in that field.

Student Study Guide

Multiple Choice

1. The central processing unit is an example of

   a. software   c. a program

   b. hardware   d. an output unit

2. Additional data and programs not being used by the processor are stored in

   a. secondary storage   c. input units

   b. output units   d. the CPU

3. Step-by-step instructions that run the computer are
   a. hardware   c. documents
   b. CPUs   d. software

4. A computer whose primary input mode is hand-written input on a screen is a
   a. supercomputer   c. desktop computer
   b. mainframe   d. pen-based computer

5. Desktop and personal computers are also known as
   a. microcomputers c. supercomputers
   b. mainframes   d. peripheral equipment

6. The raw material to be processed by a computer is called
   a. a program   c. data
   b. software   d. information

7. A home page is part of a(n)
   a. terminal   c. NC
   b. web site   d. LAN

8. A bar-code reader is an example of a(n)
   a. processing device   c. storage device
   b. input device   d. output device

9. The computer to which a user's computer connects in order to access the Internet is called a
   a. server   c. notebook
   b. supercomputer   d. PDA

10. Printers and screens are common forms of
    a. input units   c. output units
    b. storage units   d. processing units

11. The unit that transforms data into information is the
    a. CPU   c. bar-code reader
    b. disk drive   d. wand reader

12. The device that reconciles the differences between computers and phones is the
    a. TCP/IP   c. wand reader
    b. LAN   d. modem

13. PDA stands for
    a. protocol disk administrator
    b. processor digital add-on
    c. primary digital assistant
    d. personal digital assistant

14. An example of peripheral equipment is the
    a. CPU   c. spreadsheet
    b. printer   d. microcomputer

15. A computer that interacts with a television set is the
    a. desktop computer   c. supercomputer
    b. net computer   d. PDA

16. Software used to access the World Wide Web is called
    a. a browser   c. a server
    b. web   d. e-mail

17. A device that inputs data by scanning letters and numbers is the
    a. keyboard   c. wand reader
    b. mouse   d. diskette

18. Another name for memory is
    a. secondary storage   c. disk storage
    b. primary storage   d. tape storage

19. Which is not a computer classification?
    a. maxicomputer   c. pen-based computer
    b. microcomputer   d. mainframe

20. A web site may be found on the
    a. PDA   c. TCP/IP
    b. WWW   d. CPU

21. An input device that translates the motions of a ball rolled on a flat surface to the screen is a
    a. wand reader   c. keyboard
    b. bar-code reader d. mouse

22. Computer users who are not computer professionals are sometimes called
    a. librarians   c. peripheral users
    b. information officers d. end-users

23. The most powerful computers are
    a. super PCs   c. workstations
    b. supermainframes d. supercomputers

24. Raw data is processed by the computer into
    a. number sheets   c. updates
    b. paragraphs   d. information

25. Laser beam technology is used for
    a. terminals   c. optical disks
    b. keyboards   d. magnetic tape

True/False

T F 1. The processor is also called the central processing unit, or CPU.

T F 2. Secondary storage units contain the instructions and data to be used immediately by the processor.

T F 3. A home page is the first page of a web site.

T F 4. Two secondary storage media are magnetic disks and magnetic tape.

T F 5. A diskette holds more data than a hard disk.

T F 6. PDAs accept handwritten data on a screen.

T F 7. The most powerful personal computers are known as supercomputers.

T F 8. A supplier of access to a server is called an Internet service provider.

T F 9. Processed data is called information.

T F 10. The Internet is a subset of the World Wide Web.

T F 11. A modem is the hardware device that is the go-between for computers and telephones.

T F 12. Secondary storage is another name for memory.

T F 13. The most powerful personal computer is the workstation.

T F 14. TCP/IP is hardware that connects to the Internet.

T F 15. These computers are arranged from least powerful to most powerful: microcomputer, mainframe, supercomputer.

T F 16. The Internet is an example of a peripheral device.

T F 17. The best-selling personal computer is the network computer.

T F 18. A LAN is usually set up between two cities.

T F 19. Magnetic tape is most often used for backup purposes.

T F 20. Another name for memory is secondary storage.

T F 21. Most users use supercomputers to access the Internet.

T F 22. A modem is used to accept handwritten input on a pen-based computer.

T F 23. A notebook computer is a small, portable computer.

T F 24. A location on the World Wide Web is called a site.

T F 25. Another name for workstation is personal digital assistant.

Fill-In

1. The four general components of a computer are

   a. _____

   b. _____

   c. _____

   d. _____

2. The part of the Internet noted for images and sound is the _____.

3. After data is input to the system but before it is processed, it is held in _____.

4. What are magnetic tape reels mounted on when their data is to be read by the computer system? _____.

5. The input, output, and secondary storage devices attached to a computer are known as _____.

6. Large computers in the computer industry are called _____.

7. Lower-priced PCs are sometimes called _____.

8. The term used for raw material given to a computer for processing is _____.

9. People who purchase and use software are called _____.

10. A hardware device that is the intermediary between a computer and the phone system is the _____.

11. The computer that must be accessed to reach the Internet is called the _____.

12. The software used to access the Internet is called a _____.

13. CPU stands for _____.

14. Three types of input methods mentioned in the chapter are

    a. _____

    b. _____

    c. _____

15. Another name for a microcomputer is

    _____.

16. TCP/IP stands for _____.

17. Messages sent via computer are called

    _____.

18. The supplier of the server is the

    _____.

19. The opening screen on a web site is called the

    _____.

20. LAN stands for _____.

21. PDA stands for _____.

22. Limited computers offered mainly to access the Internet are called _____.

23. A computer that is as compact as a desktop but has power almost equal to that of a mainframe is the _____.

24. The software that makes it possible for different kinds of computers to communicate on the Internet is called _____.

25. The most powerful computers are called

    _____.

26. A computer and its associated equipment are called _____.

27. The CPU processes data into

    _____.

Answers

Multiple Choice

1. b	6. c	11. a	16. a	21. d
2. a	7. b	12. d	17. c	22. d
3. d	8. b	13. d	18. b	23. d
4. d	9. a	14. b	19. a	24. d
5. a	10. c	15. b	20. b	25. c

True/False

1. T	6. T	11. T	16. F	21. F
2. F	7. F	12. F	17. F	22. F
3. T	8. T	13. T	18. F	23. T
4. T	9. T	14. F	19. T	24. T
5. F	10. F	15. T	20. F	25. F

Fill-In

1. a. input unit
   b. processor
   c. output unit
   d. storage unit
2. World Wide Web (or just the Web)
3. memory (or primary storage)
4. tape drives
5. peripheral equipment
6. mainframes
7. cheap PCs
8. data
9. users, or end-users
10. modem
11. server
12. browser
13. central processing unit
14. keyboard, mouse, wand reader, or bar-code reader
15. personal computer
16. Transmission Control Protocol/Internet Protocol
17. electronic mail (or e-mail)
18. Internet service provider
19. home page
20. local area network
21. personal digital assistant
22. network computers, or net computers, or net boxes
23. workstation
24. TCP/IP (Transmission Control Protocol/Internet Protocol
25. supercomputers
26. hardware
27. information

WHAT IS IT ALL ABOUT?

First, just what is the Internet? The Internet is a loosely organized global collection of thousands of networks. It can be accessed by anyone who has a computer, appropriate software, and a connection to a computer called a server.

Why has it become so popular? The main reason is that the Internet offers so much information in a convenient way. The information is both high in volume and extremely varied in content. The Internet is also quite easy to use, at least compared with other technologies. A person with relatively minimal knowledge can access the Internet from the nearest connected computer, even from home.

OK, let's assume that it's easy enough even for me. Why should I jump in? The one answer that fits everyone is that you dare not risk being left behind. Futurists predict that networking of some kind will be as necessary to work and to living as technologies such as the telephone or computers.

After that, the answer to this question depends a lot on the individual. Are you curious? Would you like to connect with people around the world? Would you like an amazing library at your fingertips? Would you like the convenience of finding out about almost anything current—the weather in London, the score of your team's ball game, the verdict of a court case—by typing at the keyboard? Would it amuse you just to see what other folks are up to?

Give me some more for-instances. OK. Do you plan to look for a car in the near future? The Internet offers information-loaded sites describing cars, such a the Jeep site shown here. Need some information on what your U.S. Senators are up to? The Senate site shown here is a good place to begin. Consider some other sites that could show up during your Internet travels. One of the most fascinating is the AfriCam site, which relays a new image every 30 seconds from cameras stashed high in the trees; you can watch as wild animals pass in and out of view. You can also find out what it is like to be a roadie, learn about the history of roller coasters, and see an astronomer's view of the Virgo cluster.

Is this going to cost money? Maybe. Free Internet access is common in schools and libraries and other government organizations. Your employer may offer free access. If you want to hook up from your own personal computer, the required software is probably free, but you will have to pay some sort of

PLANET INTERNET

monthly charge to the company providing the physical connection.

Speaking of usage, I have heard that people spend hours and hours on the Internet. This is not uncommon. The Internet has so much

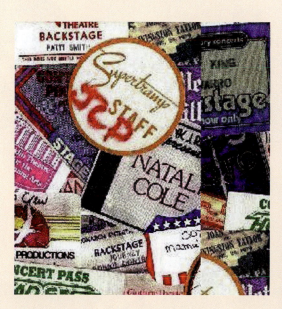

to offer that a user can easily drift from one thing to another without realizing how time is passing. But a specific task can often be done in a reasonable amount of time.

What's coming up later in the Internet discussions? For the most part, we'll examine various offerings on the Internet, some serious, some less so. Information about using the Internet will be tucked in here and there, so your knowledge will grow. In the next Planet Internet we'll start traveling on the most popular part of the Internet, the World Wide Web.

BUYER'S GUIDE

HOW TO BUY YOUR OWN PERSONAL COMPUTER

Where Do You Start?

We cannot choose your new computer system for you any more than we can select a new car for you. But we can tell you to look for or avoid various features. We will not be able to lead you to a particular brand and model—so many new products are introduced every month that doing so would be impossible. If you are just starting out, however, we can help you define your needs and ask the right questions.

Maybe you have already done some thinking and have decided that owning your own personal computer offers advantages. Now what? You can start by talking to other personal computer owners about how they got started and how to avoid pitfalls. Or you can read some computer magazines, especially ones with evaluations and ratings, to get a feel for what is available. Next find several dealers. Most dealers are listed in the Yellow Pages of the phone book, and many advertise in your local newspaper. Visit several. Don't be afraid to ask questions. You are considering a major purchase, so plan to shop around.

Finally, you may consider buying a computer system over the Internet or by direct mail. You can find advertisements in any computer magazine. Access the site (presumably, using someone else's computer) or call the listed toll-free number and ask them to send you a free brochure.

THE MAJOR CHOICES

The PC Standard?

Although computers are sold under many brand names, most offer the "PC standard," also referred to as the business standard. The PC standard usually is a computer that uses the Microsoft Windows operating system and an Intel microprocessor, a combination sometimes called "Wintel." If you will be using your computer for business applications and, in particular, if you need to exchange files with others in a business environment, consider sticking with the standard. However, the Apple iMac, noted for its ease of use, is an attractive alternative, especially for beginners.

Family Computer or Business Computer?

Although the basic machine is probably the same, many dealers offer a computer labeled a "family computer." The package typically comes with a good modem and sound system, a joystick, and plenty of educational, financial, and entertainment software. A "business computer" will have a modest sound system and, most likely, one good suite of business software for such tasks as word processing and spreadsheets.

Desktop or Notebook?

Do you plan to use your computer in one place, or will you be moving it around? Notebook computers—also called laptop computers—have found a significant niche in the market, mainly because they are packaged to travel easily. A notebook computer is lightweight (most about 7 pounds and some as little as 2-1/2 pounds) and small enough to fit in a briefcase or backpack. Today's notebook computers offer power and functionality that are equivalent to that of a desktop computer. They also carry a similar price tag and are sometimes even more expensive.

Internet or In-Store?

Several reputable manufacturers sell reliable hardware via their Internet sites at good prices. However, they tend to be patronized by experienced users, businesses that order in bulk or individuals who are on their second or third computer and who know what they want. These buyers peruse the site and pick and choose the computer and options they want. They place an order via the site (or possibly over the phone), and have the new machine(s) delivered to the door. Since there is no retail middleman, they save money and also get the latest technology fast.

A first-time buyer, however, usually wants to kick the tires. You will probably be more comfortable looking over the machines, tapping the keyboard, and clicking the mouse. An in-store visit also gives you the opportunity to ask questions.

What to Look For in Hardware

The basic personal computer system consists of a central processing unit (CPU) and memory, a monitor (screen), a keyboard and a mouse, a modem, and assorted storage devices—probably a 3 1/2-inch diskette drive, a CD-ROM drive, a hard disk drive. Most people also want a printer, and many merchants offer package deals that include a printer. Unless you know someone who can help you out with technical expertise, the best advice is to look for a packaged system—that is, one in which the above components (with the exception of the printer) are assembled and packaged by the same manufacturer. This gives you some assurance that the various components will work together. Perhaps even more important, if something should go wrong, you will not have to deal with multiple manufacturers pointing fingers at one another.

Computer Housing

Sometimes called the computer case or simply "the box," the housing holds the electronic circuitry and has external receptors called ports to which the monitor, printer, and other devices are connected. It also has the bays that hold the various disk drives. The monitor traditionally was placed on top of the computer case; there are still systems offered in that configuration. More common, however, is the minitower, in which the case stands on end and the monitor sits directly on the desk. The minitower was orig-

inally designed to be placed on the floor, conveniently out of the way. But the floor location turned out to be somewhat inconvenient, so many users keep their minitowers on the desk next to the monitor. The Apple iMac encloses all its internal equipment in a combination monitor-housing box; the see-through teal version is shown here.

Central Processing Unit

If you plan to purchase a PC-standard machine, you will find that most software packages run most efficiently on computers using a Pentium Pro microprocessor. Any lesser version of the Pentium should carry a bargain-

basement price. A microprocessor's speed is expressed in megahertz (MHz), and it is usually 100 MHz and up. The higher the number, the faster—and more expensive—the microprocessor.

Memory

Memory, or RAM, is measured in bytes, with each byte representing a character of data. The minimum memory threshold keeps rising, as software makers produce sophisticated products that run efficiently only with ever-larger amounts of memory. What is more, some users want or need to have several software programs open at the same time, to be able to switch conveniently among them. Lots of memory will help keep everything running smoothly and speedily. We suggest a minimum of 64 megabytes of memory for serious users, and 96 or 128 megabytes if possible. It will make all the difference in the speediness of your computer.

Monitor

The monitor is a very important part of your computer system—you will spend all your computer time looking at it. Except in the case of the very cheapest personal com-

CHEAP OR NOT-SO-CHEAP?

A personal computer for under $1000? How about under $500? These bargain systems can handle what most home users want from a computer: word processing, games, e-mail, and Web surfing. The minimal system, however, has limitations: The hard disk is smallish, there is marginal memory for games and other graphics-heavy programs, there is minimal expandability, and sound quality from built-in speakers is only adequate. Worse, given its razor-thin margins, the vendor's customer service may be minimal too.

Sophisticated users know they cannot get by with such a system; for example, they are likely to need several programs open at the same time, a strain on memory. But an inexpensive computer may be ideal for first-time buyers, especially those who are watching their budgets.

puters, you can expect a monitor—in color—as standard equipment.

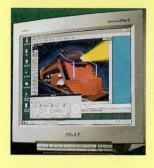  

Screen Size

Monitors usually have a screen display of between 12 and 17 inches, measured diagonally. Generally, a larger screen provides a display that is easier to read, so most monitors sold today have at least 15-inch screens. However, the 17-inch screen reduces eyestrain and it is well suited for displaying Internet web pages, graphics, and large photos and illustrations.

Screen Readability

You may wish to compare the readability of different monitors. First, make certain that the screen is bright and has minimum flicker. Glare is another major consideration. Harsh lighting nearby can cause glare to bounce off the screen, and some screens seem more susceptible to glare than others. A key factor affecting screen quality is resolution, a measure of the number of dots, or pixels, that can appear on the screen. The higher the resolution—that is, the more dots there are—the more solid the text characters appear. For graphics, more pixels means sharper images. Color monitors most commonly available are Super VGA (SVGA) and Extended Graphics Array (XGA), with XGA best for graphic animations.

Ergonomic Considerations

Can the monitor swivel and tilt? If so, this will eliminate your need to sit in one position for a long period. The ability to adjust the position of the monitor becomes an important consideration when several users share the same computer, particularly people of different sizes, such as parents and children. Furthermore, if you expect to type for long periods of time, you would be wise to buy a wrist pad to support your hands and wrists.

Input Devices

There are many input devices. We will mention only the two critical ones here: a keyboard and a mouse.

Keyboard

Keyboards vary in quality. To find what suits you best, sit down in the store and type. You may be surprised by the real differences in the feel of keyboards. Make sure the keys are not cramped together; you will find that your typing is error prone if your fingers are constantly overlapping more than one key. Assess the color and layout of the keyboard. Ideally, keys should be gray with a matte finish. The dull finish reduces glare.

Should you consider a wireless keyboard? A wireless keyboard uses infrared technology rather than wires to communicate with the computer. Thus, you could use the keyboard at the far end of a conference table or on the kitchen table—any place within 50 feet of the computer. Furthermore, a touchpad—a mouse substitute—that can be used to drag the cursor or click on screen objects is built into the keyboard.

Mouse

A mouse is a device that you roll on a tabletop to move the pointer on the screen. Since most software is designed to be used with a mouse, it is a necessary purchase and will likely come with any new desktop computer. Microsoft has introduced the IntelliMouse Explorer, shown here, whose IntelliEye operates by optical tracking technology rather than the traditional mouse ball on the bottom, making a smooth pointer movement.

Secondary Storage

You will need disk drives to read software into your computer and to store software and data that you wish to keep.

Diskette and Zip Drives

Some personal computer software today comes on diskettes, so you need a diskette drive to accept the software. Diskettes are also the common medium for exchange of data among computer users.

Most computer systems today come with a 31/2-inch diskette drive. A zip drive is also an option for users who be transporting large or numerous files.

CD-ROM and DVD Drives

Most personal computer software comes on CD-ROM disks, far handier than multiple diskettes. But the main attraction is the use of high-capacity CD-ROMs for holding byte-rich images, sounds, and videos—the stuff of multimedia. The smoothness of a CD-ROM video presentation is indicated by the "X factor"—16X, 24X, 40X—the higher the better. However, it is just a matter of time before CD-ROM is supplanted by even higher-capacity DVD-ROMs.

Hard Disk Drive

A hard disk drive is a standard requirement. A hard disk is fast and reliable and holds large amounts of data. Software comes on a set of several diskettes or on optical disk; it would be unwieldy to load these each time the software is used. Instead, the software is stored on the hard drive, where it is conveniently accessed from that point forward.

All computer systems offer a built-in hard disk drive, with variable storage capacity—the more storage, the higher the price. Storage capacity is measured in terms of bytes—characters—of data. Keep in mind that software, as

well as your data files, will be stored on the hard disk; just one program can take many millions of bytes. Hard disk capacity may be offered in megabytes—millions of bytes—but it is more likely to be offered with gigabytes—billions of bytes. The more the better.

Printers

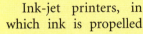

A printer is probably the most expensive peripheral equipment you will buy. Some inexpensive models are available, but those who have a great concern for quality output may pay a hefty price. When choosing a printer, consider speed, quality, and cost—not necessarily in that order.

Ink-jet printers, in which ink is propelled

SYSTEM REQUIREMENTS

Make sure your hardware is compatible with the requirements of the software you are buying. You can find the requirements by reading the fine print on the software package. Here is a typical requirements blurb from a software package: Requires a personal computer with a Pentium or higher processor (Pentium Pro or higher recommended) running Microsoft Windows 98 or later operating system, 16MB of memory (RAM) minimum, 32MB recommended. Hard disk minimum installation 70 MB, typical installation 120MB.

costs for staples such as special coated paper and color ink cartridges. Still, color printers, once prohibitively expensive, are both attractive and affordable. The images shown here, as well as the opening image Audio Archives, were all produced by Hewlett Packard color laser printers.

All-in-Ones

An All-in-One machine combines the capabilities of a full range of office equipment into one device: Printing, faxing, scanning and copying abilities are all available on the same machine. There are certain advantages, such as installing and learning just one software package. Further, the all-in-one reduces the number of cables cluttering the floor and, perhaps most importantly, takes up less space than that required by multiple machines. You may purchase an adequate but somewhat limited all-in-one for a few hundred dollars. Businesses that want color capabilities, speedy printing, and all-day fax capabilities will pay a steeper price.

Portability: What to Look For in a Notebook Computer

Generally, you should look for the same hardware components in a notebook computer as you would in a desktop computer: a fast microprocessor, plenty of memory, a clear screen, and diskette and hard drives. A CD-ROM drive is an option in some models.

Most models include an internal modem. Another option is a PC card modem that fits in a slot on the notebook. In either case, you merely run a cord from the modem jack to the phone jack in the wall. Thus, from your hotel room or from any place else that has a phone jack, you can be connected to online services, e-mail, and the Internet.

You will have to make some compromises on input devices. The keyboard will be attached and the keys may be more cramped than those on a standard keyboard. Also, traveling users often do not have a handy surface for rolling a mouse, so the notebook will probably come with a built-in trackball or a touchpad. If you prefer a mouse, you can purchase it separately.

onto the paper by a battery of tiny nozzles, can produce excellent text and graphics. In fact, the quality of ink-jet printers approaches that of laser printers. The further attractions of low cost and quiet operation have made the ink-jet printer a current favorite among buyers, especially those who want color output.

Laser printers, which use technology similar to copying machines, are the top-of-the-line printers for quality and speed. The price of a low-end laser printer is within the budget of most users. Laser printers are particularly favored by desktop publishers to produce text and graphics on the same page. Affordable laser printers can produce output at 600 dots per inch (dpi), giving graphic images a sharpness that rivals that of photographs. At the high end, more expensive laser printers offer 1200 dpi. However, this rich resolution may be of little value to a buyer who plans to produce mostly text.

Affordable color printers are available for a few hundred dollars, although some are priced much higher. Even at a high price, color printers are not perfect. The rich color seen on the computer screen is not necessarily the color that will appear on the printed output. Furthermore, note that color printers often have fairly high operating

Other Hardware Options

There are a great many hardware variations; we will mention a few here. Note that, although we are describing the hardware, these devices may come with accompanying software, which must be installed according to directions before the hardware can be used.

Communications Connections

If you want to connect your computer via telephone lines to the office computer, or to an online service such as America Online, or to the Internet, or if you want to send and receive electronic mail, you need a communications device. Although the choices are many, the most common device, by far, is the modem. This device converts outgoing computer data into signals that can be transmitted over telephone lines, and does the reverse for incoming data.

Most computers come with an internal modem, out of sight inside the computer housing. Furthermore, most people choose a fax modem, which serves the dual purpose of modem and fax. Using a fax modem, you can receive a fax and then print it out, or send a fax if it originated in your computer (using, for example, word processing software) or was scanned into your computer. Most new computers come equipped with a fax modem.

Other Input Devices

If you are interested in action games, you may wish to acquire a joystick, which looks similar to the stick shift on a car. A joystick allows you to manipulate a cursor on the screen. A scanner is useful if you need to store pictures and typed documents in your computer. Scanners are often  purchased by people who want to put their photographs on the computer or to use their computers for desktop publishing. Finally, you can purchase voice input hardware, which is basically a microphone.

Surge Protectors

These devices protect against the electrical ups and downs that can affect the operation of your computer. In addition,

a surge protector provides a receptacle for all power plugs and a handy switch to turn everything on or off at once. Some of the more expensive models, really uninterruptible power supply systems, provide up to ten minutes of full power to your computer if the electric power in your home or office is knocked out. This gives you time to save your work on disk (so that the work will not be lost if the power fails) or to print out a report you need immediately.

What to Look For in Software

The first software decision is made by the choice of the PC-standard or Macintosh computer: You will use software that was written for the operating system software of that machine. Almost all new PC-standard computers come with Microsoft Windows preinstalled; Windows users will want applications software written for the Windows environment.

Hardware Requirements for Software

Identify the type of hardware required before you buy software. Under the heading System Requirements (sometimes called specifications) right on the software package, a list will typically include a particular kind of computer and operating system and a certain amount of memory and hard disk space.

Brand Names

In general, publishers of well-known software offer better customer support than lesser-known companies. Support may be in the form of tutorials, classes by the vendor or others, and the all-important hotline assistance. In addition, makers of brand-name software usually offer superior documentation and upgrades to new and better versions of the product.

Where to Buy Software

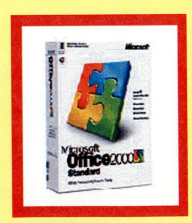

Not very long ago, computer users bought their software at small specialty stores, where they hoped they could understand the esoteric language of the sales staff. In contrast, in enormous stores, buyers now pile software packages into their shopping carts like so many cans of soup. The choice of software vendors has expanded considerably.

Computer Superstores

The superstores, such as CompUSA, sell a broad variety of computer hardware and software. Although their primary advantage is a vast inventory, they also offer on-site technical support.

Warehouse Stores Often billed as clubs, such as Wal-Mart's SAM's, these giant stores sell all manner of merchandise, including computer software.

Mass Merchandisers Stores such as Sears sell software along with their other various merchandise.

Computer Dealers

Some small retail stores sell hardware systems and the software that runs on them. Such a store usually has a well-informed staff and may be your best bet for in-depth consulting.

Mail Order

Users who know what they want can get it conveniently and reasonably through the mail. Once an initial contact is made, probably from a magazine advertisement, the mail-order house will send catalogs of software regularly.

Over the Internet

Users who connect to the Internet often find it convenient to purchase software online. Each major software vendor has its own web site and, among other things, offers its wares for sale. A buyer usually is given the choice of receiving typical packaging—disks and documentation—through the mail or of downloading the software directly from the vendor's site to the buyer's computer.

Now That You Have It, Can You Use It?

Once the proud moment has come and your computer system is at home or in the office with you, what do you do with it?

Documentation

Computer systems today come with extensive documentation, the written manuals and disk files that accompany the hardware. Usually, a simple brochure with detailed drawings will help you plug everything together. The installation procedure, however, is often largely (and conveniently) on disk. The same brochure that helps you 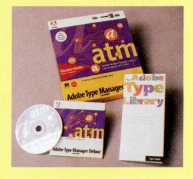 assemble the hardware will guide you to the software on the diskette or CD-ROM. Using the software, the computer configures itself, mostly without any assistance from you.

Software documentation usually includes a user's guide, a reference manual for the various commands available with the software. Software tutorials are also common and are useful for the novice and experienced user alike. Software tutorials usually come on a separate diskette or CD-ROM, and they guide you as you work through sample problems using the software.

Training

Can you teach yourself? In addition to the documentation supplied with your computer, numerous books and magazines offer help and answer readers' questions. Other sources are classes offered by computer stores and local colleges. These hands-on sessions may be the most effective learning method of all.

Maintenance Contract

Finally, when purchasing a computer, you may wish to consider a maintenance contract, which should cover labor and parts and possibly advice on a telephone hotline. Such contracts vary in comprehensiveness. Some cover on-site repairs; others require you to pack up the computer and mail it in. Another option is that the replacement part, say a new monitor, is sent to you and you then return the old monitor in the same packaging.

WHY ARE COMPUTERS BEIGE?

When personal computers debuted in the late 1970s, they were colored beige, partly to fit into the '70s office earth tone motif, but also because the warm color reduced eye strain and did not show dust. It has been a beige world ever since until Apple heavily marketed its color choices for the iMac.

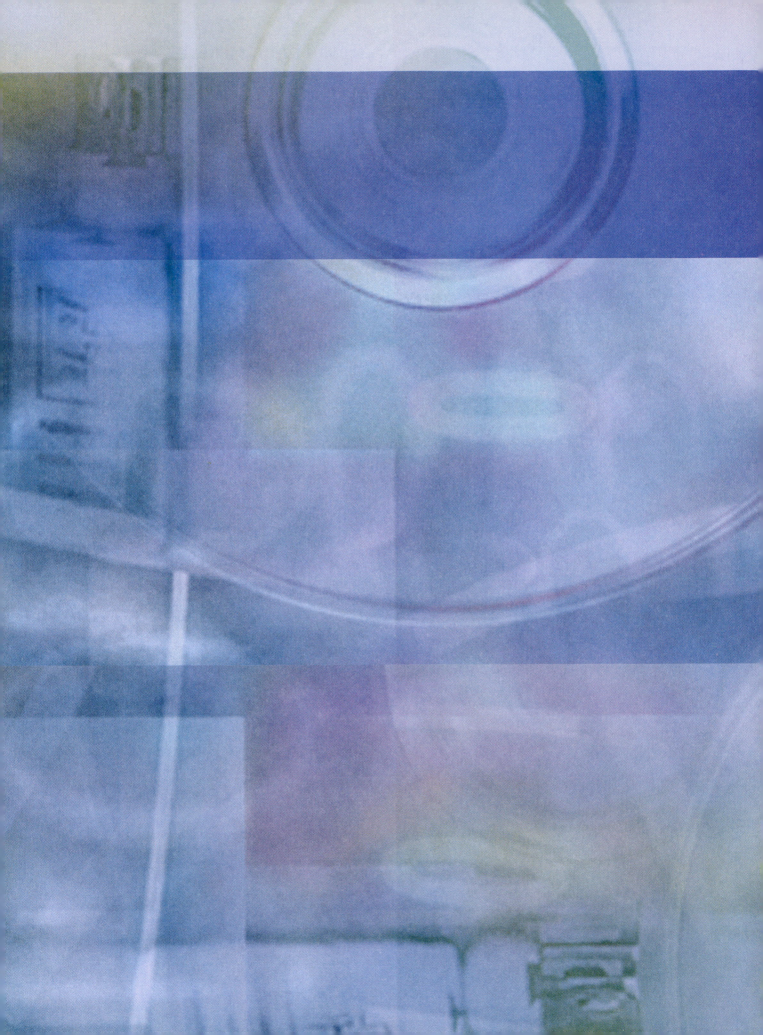

CHAPTER TWO

COMPUTER SOFTWARE

Applications Software and Operating Systems

LEARNING OBJECTIVES

- Understand the difference between operating systems and applications software
- List various types of task-oriented software
- Understand, in a general way, the kinds of software available for both large and small businesses
- Know the functions of an operating system
- Understand the basics of a personal computer operating system
- Understand the need for resource allocation on large computers
- Appreciate ethical issues associated with software
- Learn the functions of various computer people

After her first year in college, Anita Jefferson got a summer job in the resort town of Friday Harbor. She waited tables for both the noon and evening shifts. Her wages were supplemented nicely by generous tips from tourists. An accounting major, Anita would have preferred a job in a business office, but at least her summer income would make a significant dent in her upcoming tuition.

As it turned out, Anita's summer was more valuable than she expected. On her second day on the job, she learned that a colleague had signed up for a morning computer class at the local branch of a community college. Since it was a beginning class and did not interfere with her work schedule, Anita signed up too.

Anita's previous computer experiences were limited to math drills in elementary school and playing games on her mother's home computer. She knew that, as an accountant, she would certainly use a computer. In fact, according to the schedule, two of her fall classes would require computer lab time. Although somewhat apprehensive, Anita was hoping to get a head start on computers.

The course included both lectures on the fundamentals of computer hardware and software and hands-on computer experience. By the end of the summer, Anita had a good grasp of computer basics and could perform such tasks as preparing memos on the computer. But her greatest reward was learning how to use spreadsheets, which let her enter, revise, and print numerical data in rows and columns. She recognized that budgets, ledgers, inventories, and other keystones of accounting would all be maintained using spreadsheets on a computer. She definitely got a head start.

InfoBit

While the cost to develop packaged software is mostly in research and development, and in the labor of programmers, most of the cost of manufacturing it is in making an attractive package. In fact, the box may cost more to produce than the CD-ROM or diskette it contains. Some manufacturers of software deliberately make the package larger than necessary, filling it with padding or packing material in an effort to make the package more visible on the shelf and to—literally—displace the competition from retail shelves.

Software: Telling the Machine What to Do

When people think about computers, they usually think about machines. The tapping on the keyboard, the rumble of whirling disk drives, the changing flashes of color on a computer screen—these are the attention getters. However, it is really the **software**—the planned, step-by-step set of instructions required to turn data into information—that makes a computer useful.

Generally speaking, software can be categorized as *systems software* or *applications software*. However, people rarely speak of systems software; it is more common to discuss a subset of systems software known as the **operat-**

ing system, the underlying software found on all computers. **Applications software** is *applied* to a real-world task. It can be used to solve a particular problem or to perform a particular task—to keep track of store inventory or design a car engine or draft the minutes of the PTA meeting or play a game of solitaire. We will begin with the kinds of applications software that you might use, then move on to a discussion of the underlying operating system.

Applications Software

Applications software may be either custom or packaged. Many large organizations pay **computer programmers**—people who design, write, test, and implement software—to write **custom software,** software that is specifically tailored to their needs. Custom software for the tasks of a large organization may be extremely complex and take a lot of time—possibly years—to write.

The average person is most likely to deal with software for personal computers, called **packaged software** or **commercial software.** This software is literally packaged in a container of some sort, usually a box or folder, and is sold in stores or catalogs. Packaged software for personal computers often comes in a box that is as colorful as that of a board game. Inside the box you will find one or more disks holding the software and, usually, an instruction manual, also referred to as **documentation** (Figure 1). Note, however, that some packaged software has little written documentation; the information about the software is mostly stored on disk with the software for handy future reference.

Although it is not possible to tell you how to use a specific software package, we can say, in general, that you begin by inserting the disk in the disk drive. Software usually comes on a CD-ROM and requires a setup—installation—process before use. Furthermore, for future convenience, the setup process copies some or all of the new software to the hard disk drive. Some software may require the CD-ROM to be in the drive whenever the software

Figure 1 Packaged software. Each of the colorful software packages shown here includes one or more disks containing the software and at least a minimal instruction manual, or documentation, describing how to use the software.

Robot Redux

Most of us have heard of robots. Many of us have played with Legos. Now Lego offers a kit, called the Lego Mindstorms Robotic Invention System, for building a robot whose actions will be based on software. The kit includes the robot's programmable controller, two motors, touch and light sensors, and, of course, hundreds of Lego pieces.

You start by constructing a robot. Once your robot is built, you can use the accompanying software to write instructions that let the robot respond to something, such as contact with its touch sensors or a change in light level. You could, for example, program the robot to navigate an obstacle course. No serious knowledge of programming is needed, nor do you even need to type. A tutorial shows you how to build a simple robot. There are several sample programs. Although adults may enjoy the kit, a child can understand it.

Lego maintains its own web site, which offers more tips and challenges.

Critical Thinking

Why does custom software take so much time and effort to write? (Software is abstract, and is therefore difficult to plan, manage, and create. Also, software is more easily changed than hardware so there is immense pressure to revise it even as it is being written. Further, much of the complexity that used to go into hardware has "migrated" into software now.)

InfoBit

Just because software is available for downloading via the Internet doesn't mean it is either free or legal. The organized, electronic distribution of pirated commercial software or "warez" has become a significant problem on the Internet. Warez (pronounced as though spelled "wares" or possibly by some pronounced like the city of "Juarez") is a term used by software pirates to describe software that has been stripped of its copy-protection and made available on the Internet for downloading.

Critical Thinking

What are the positives and negatives of distributing documentation for programs exclusively on disk or CD-ROM? (Positives include the ability to search the documentation online, lower cost, and little danger of losing or misplacing a manual. Negatives include having to read on a screen that is markedly smaller than a page, the need to use a program to learn about a program, and the lack of paper's "portability.")

Figure 2 Happy and Max. This software lets children follow the adventures of the dog Happy and his friend Max.

is used. Once the software is installed, you can click its **icon,** its picture image on the screen, or type an instruction—command—to get the program started.

A great assortment of software is available to help you with a variety of tasks—writing papers, preparing budgets, storing and retrieving information, drawing graphs, playing games, and much more. This wonderful array of software is what makes computers so useful.

Most personal computer software is designed to be user-friendly. The term **user-friendly** has become a cliché, but it still conveys meaning: It usually means that the software is supposed to be easy—perhaps even intuitive—for a beginner to use or that the software can be used with a minimum of training and documentation.

But What Would I Use It For?

New computer owners soon discover a little secret: The box is only the beginning. Although they may have agonized for months over their hardware choice, they are often uncertain as to how to proceed when purchasing software. The most common pattern for a new user is to start out with some standard software packages, such as word processing and other basic applications, that are preinstalled by the computer manufacturer. Later, this base may be expanded as the user becomes aware of what software is available. The needs of different people will be met with different software. Here are two real-life scenarios.

Kristin Bjornson is a private detective who, using a computer, runs her business from her home. Her computer came with word processing software, plus some CD-ROMs holding an encyclopedia, a "family doctor" reference program, and several games. Kristin's primary interest in the software focused on business information and certain public files on the Internet. She selected an Internet service provider and used software supplied by the provider. She also prepared her income taxes using a question-and-answer tax preparation program. Over the next year, Kristin purchased other software unrelated to business applications: software to draw maps of highways for planned trips, a program to help her son study for the Scholastic Assessment Test, and a combination game/book called Happy and Max for her six-year-old (Figure 2).

As a second example, consider Max Prentiss, whose first job as an apprentice carpenter did not involve computers. But Max made a computer one of his first acquisitions. He subsequently purchased various software: software containing an atlas and quotations; an on-screen version of *The Far Side* calendar; and an all-in-one package that included software for a personal phone book, home budget planning, and home repair. But he eventually

focused on the large *National Geographic* map images available on CD-ROM (Figure 3).

The point of these stories is that different people want different software applications. You have only to stroll through a few aisles of software racks to appreciate the variety of software available. Whether you want to learn to type or tour a museum or build a deck, or perhaps try such crazy-but-real titles as Internet for Cats or the sci-fi thriller called I Have No Mouth and I Must Scream, someone offers the software.

Acquiring Software

Sometimes software is free. Software is called **freeware** if its author chooses to provide it free to all. However, freeware may or may not be copyrighted—that is, have restrictions of use placed upon it. Uncopyrighted software is considered to be in the **public domain** and may be used, or even altered, without restriction. Sometimes freeware, perhaps written by a student or educator, is offered without fee and without copyright. Other freeware may be offered to the public as a marketing tool by a major manufacturer, who will most certainly copyright it and maintain all ownership rights. Software called **shareware** is also given away free, but the maker hopes for voluntary payment—that is, he or she hopes that you like it well enough to send a contribution.

The software that people use most often, packaged software such as word processing or spreadsheet software, sometimes called *commercial software,* is probably both copyrighted and at least somewhat costly. This kind of software must not be copied without permission from the manufacturer. In fact, software manufacturers call making illegal copies of commercial software **software piracy** and pursue miscreants to the full extent of the law.

What is the best way to purchase commercial software? The legendary small retail software store is disappearing fast because the price of software has declined too much to provide an acceptable profit margin. So software has moved to the warehouse stores and to mail-order houses, each with thousands of software titles. The high sales volume takes up the slack for slim per-unit profits. From the individual consumer's point of view, the lower prices and convenient one-stop shopping are significant advantages.

An organization, as opposed to individual users, must take a different approach in acquiring software. Most organizations—businesses, government, nonprofit agencies—have computers, and their users, of course, need

Critical Thinking

What problems or concerns would you have about electronic software distribution? (Possible problems—what to do about incomplete or corrupt downloads, no master CD or diskettes in the event of accidental deletion, no printed manuals, need to use credit card or transmit other banking information on the Internet.)

InfoBit

One of the hottest terms applied to freeware and public domain software is "open-source." This means that the author distributes the programming language source code, as well as the freeware application program. This allows other programmers to modify and improve the product, and then freely redistribute their work.

InfoBit

One of the largest sources of public domain software is the federal government. Many programs developed with government grant money are available free on the Internet. Examples include software for displaying maps, processing medical images, tracking the space shuttle, and many other applications.

Figure 3 Images from CD-ROM software. These images are from a *National Geographic* CD-ROM of maps that have been featured in the magazine.

2000 and Beyond

THIS OLD HOUSE

The future is in sight. "This old house" will become the intelligent networked home. This artist's depiction shows household computers and most appliances hooked to and under the control of an in-home central computer.

That central computer is linked to the outside world, providing access to information networks and to community services such as the fire department.

Satellite input

Lights

Smoke detector

Desktop PC

Security

Central server

Electric utilities

Cable input

Portable PC

Telephone

Lawn sprinklers

TV and VCR

software. The most widespread solution is obtaining vendor permission to copy software legally, an approach called site licensing. Typically, a **site license** permits an organization, for a fee, to make a limited number of copies of a software product. The customer agrees to keep track of who uses it and takes responsibility for copying and distributing manuals to its own personnel. Incidentally, if you work for a large corporation, check with your employer before you buy a copy of the expensive software you use at the office. Under some license agreements, employees are allowed to use the same software at home.

Organizations with local area networks usually install widely used software such as word processing on the network's server computer. Thus the software is available to users connected to the network without the necessity of installing the software on each user's computer.

Another software movement is afoot: **electronic software distribution.** Never mind the trip to the store. A user can simply pay to **download** the software—move it from another computer to the user's computer over data communications links. In fact, in the not-so-distant future, users will not need to purchase software but will be able merely to download it temporarily from a vendor via the Internet for a per-use rental fee. Downloading software from the Internet is already a reality; many users get freeware, shareware, and even copyrighted software from the Internet. One common scenario is to download copyrighted software free for a trial period. Anytime you use the software you will be encouraged to go back online and "register" (pay with a credit card); unregistered software automatically disables itself after a given time period, such as 21 days.

Some Task-Oriented Software

Most users, whether at home or in business, are drawn to task-oriented software, sometimes called *productivity software,* that can make their work faster and their lives easier. The major categories of task-oriented software are word processing (including desktop publishing), spreadsheets, database management, graphics, and communications. Further, software designated as office suites offers some combination of these categories in a single package. A brief description of each category follows.

Word Processing/Desktop Publishing

The most widely used personal computer software is **word processing** software. Business people use word processing for memos, reports, correspondence, minutes of meetings, and anything else that someone can think of to type. Users in a home environment type term papers, letters, journals, movie logs, and much more. Word processing software lets you create, edit, format, store, and print text and graphics in one document. Since you can store on disk the memo or document you typed, you can retrieve it another time, change it, reprint it, or do whatever you like with it. Unchanged parts of the stored document do not need to be retyped; the whole revised document can be reprinted as if new.

As the number of features in word processing packages has grown, word processing has crossed the border into desktop publishing territory. **Desktop**

Disney Magic

© Disney Enterprises, Inc.

New users sometimes worry that a computer will be used mostly for games. Surveys show that about 70 percent of personal computer users happily admit that they play games—at least a little—almost daily. In fact, entertainment is a perfectly valid use of a personal computer in the home. But the entertainment need not be limited to games. There are many types of entertainment packages.

Here is an example: Disney's Magic Artist software lets young children have fun coloring Disney images—and learn a bit at the same time. For instance, children can use a mouse to select images and apply different tools—such as pen, paintbrush, chalk, and spray paint—to color the image. They can also resize, flip, and rotate images. They can combine images with backgrounds and even, if they wish, add music.

Global Perspective

Among the many factors driving growth in computer-related careers in Europe is the requirement that nations convert banking, trading, and electronic commerce systems to use the Euro currency.

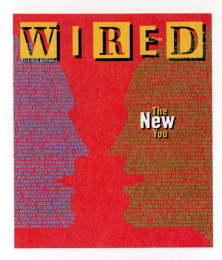

Figure 4 Desktop publishing. Many novice computer users produce attractive newsletters and brochures with desktop publishing, but professional publications, such as this cover for *Wired Magazine,* are also produced with desktop publishing. This magazine cover was generated by computer software. The art was created with graphics software. The photo was digitized with imaging software. The type and layout were produced with desktop publishing software, which was also used to combine the text and art. The completed cover was then printed to film, which a printer used to produce the finished product.

Critical Thinking

Compare and contrast electronic spreadsheets and conventional electronic calculators. (Some advantages of spreadsheets are clear –the ability to automatically recalculate as data values change, the ability to save and print copies, and large capacity. Handheld calculators still hold a few advantages, however. Among them are extreme portability, low-cost, ease of use and almost instant availability—no need to "boot" a calculator or "launch" its applications.)

publishing packages are usually better than word processing packages at meeting high-level publishing needs, especially when it comes to typesetting and color reproduction. Many magazines and newspapers today rely heavily on desktop publishing software (Figure 4). Businesses use it to produce professional-looking newsletters, reports, and brochures—both to improve internal communication and to make a better impression on the outside world.

Electronic Spreadsheets

Spreadsheets, made up of columns and rows of numbers, have been used as business tools for centuries (Figure 5). A manual spreadsheet can be tedious to prepare, and when there are changes, a considerable amount of calculation may need to be redone. An **electronic spreadsheet** is still a spreadsheet, but the computer does the work. In particular, spreadsheet software automatically recalculates the results when a number is changed. If, for example, one chore of a spreadsheet is to calculate distance based on rate and time, a change in the rate would automatically cause a new calculation so that the distance would change too. This capability lets business people try different combinations of numbers and obtain the results quickly. The ability to ask, "**What if . . . ?**" and then see the results on the computer before actually committing resources helps business people make better, faster decisions.

What about spreadsheet software for the user at home? The ability to enter combinations of numbers in a meaningful way—such as different combinations of down payments and interest rates for the purchase of a home—gives users financial vision that they could not readily produce on their own. Users at home employ spreadsheets for everything from preparing budgets to figuring out whether to take a new job to tracking their progress at the gym.

Database Management

Software used for **database management**—the management of a collection of interrelated facts—handles data in several ways. The software can store data, update it, manipulate it, retrieve it, report it in a variety of views, and print it in as many forms. By the time the data is in the reporting stage—given to a user in a useful form—it has become information. A concert promoter, for example, can store and change data about upcoming concert dates, seating, ticket prices, and sales. After this is done, the promoter can use the software to retrieve information, such as the number of tickets sold in each price range or the percentage of tickets sold the day before the concert.

Database software can be useful for anyone who must keep track of a large number of related facts. Consider crime detection, which involves a process of elimination—a tedious task. Tedious work, however, is often the kind the computer does best. Once data is entered into a database, searching by computer is possible. Consider these examples: Which criminals use a particular mode of operation? Which criminals are associates of this suspect? Does license number AXB221 refer to a stolen car? And so on. One particularly successful crime-detection database application is a fingerprint-matching system, which can match crime-scene fingerprints with computer-stored fingerprints.

Home users apply database software to any situation in which they want to retrieve stored data in a variety of ways. For example, one hobbyist stores data about her coin collection. She can retrieve information from the coin database by country, date, value, or size. Another user, a volunteer who helps

EXPENSES	JANUARY	FEBRUARY	MARCH	APRIL	TOTAL
RENT	425.00	425.00	425.00	425.00	1700.00
PHONE	22.50	31.25	17.00	35.75	106.50
CLOTHES	110.00	135.00	156.00	91.00	492.00
FOOD	280.00	250.00	250.00	300.00	1080.00
HEAT	80.00	50.00	24.00	95.00	249.00
ELECTRICITY	35.75	40.50	45.00	36.50	157.75
WATER	10.00	11.00	11.00	10.50	42.50
CAR INSURANCE	75.00	75.00	75.00	75.00	300.00
ENTERTAINMENT	150.00	125.00	140.00	175.00	590.00
TOTAL	1188.25	1142.75	1143.00	1243.75	4717.75

(a)

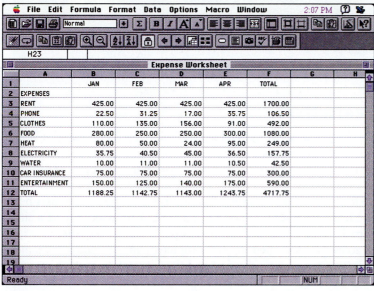

(b)

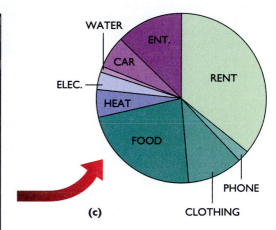

(c)

find blood donors for the American Red Cross, maintains a file of all donors in his area so that he can retrieve names and phone numbers by asking questions based on blood type, zip code, or the last date blood was donated.

Graphics

It might seem wasteful to show **graphics** to business people when standard computer printouts of numbers are readily available. However, graphs, maps, and charts can help people compare data, spot trends more easily, and make decisions more quickly. In addition, visual information is usually more compelling than a page of numbers. Besides dressing up facts and figures, graphics are often used by business people, or anyone with a message to deliver, as part of a presentation (Figure 6a).

The most pleasing use of graphics software is the work produced by **graphic artists,** people who have both artistic ability and the skills to use sophisticated graphics software to express their ideas. Artists use software as a tool of their craft to produce stunning computer art (Figure 6b).

Figure 5 A simple expense spreadsheet. (a) This paper-and-pencil expense sheet is a typical spreadsheet of rows and columns. You have to do the calculations to fill in the totals. (b) This screen shows the same information on a computer spreadsheet program, which does the calculations for you. (c) The spreadsheet program can also present the expenses graphically in the form of a pie chart.

InfoBit

Graphics are older than computers, but not nearly as old as numbers and tables. Abstract graphs and charts only became popular as recently as the 19th century.

(a)

Figure 6 Graphics. (a) Colorful computer-generated graphics can help people compare data and spot trends. (b) This artwork was generated on the computer with graphics software. Artist Karl Manning titled this piece *A Fine Day.*

(b)

Communications

From the viewpoint of an individual with a personal computer at home, **communications** means—in simple terms—that he or she can hook a phone up to the computer and communicate with the computer at the office or access data stored in another computer in another location. The most likely way for such a user to connect to others is via the Internet. A user needs software called a **browser** to access the Internet. A browser may be a single software package or it may be included as part of other software offerings. Internet access is described more completely in subsequent chapters. Meanwhile, you can pick up the flavor of the Internet from the home page screens shown in Figure 7.

Although the Internet is heavily used by both individuals and businesses, organizations—mostly business and government—were major users of communications software long before the Internet was in the mainstream. Consider weather forecasting. Some businesses, such as agriculture, amusement parks, and ski areas, are so dependent on the weather that they need constantly updated information. Various services offer analysis of live weather data, including air pressure, fog, rain, and wind direction and speed.

For a totally different type of communications application, consider the stock exchange. Stock portfolios can be managed by software that takes quotations over communication lines directly from established market monitors such as Dow Jones. The software keeps records and offers quick and accurate investment advice. And, of course, the stock exchange itself is a veritable beehive of computers, all communicating with one another and with remote computers that can provide current information.

Office Suites

Since most people need to use the kinds of task-oriented software just described, some choose to buy a **suite**—a group of basic software designed to work together. The phrase *work together* is the key. If you buy word pro-

(a)

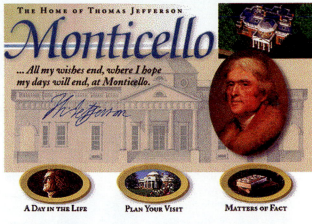

(b)

(c)

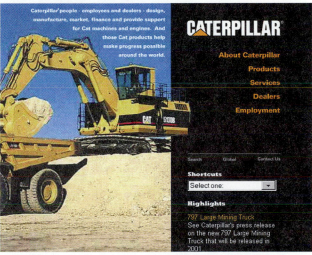

(d)

Figure 7 A sample of home pages from the Internet. These screens give some indication of the variety of sites that can be found on the Internet: (a) Esprit, selling fine sports clothes, (b) a historical view of Thomas Jefferson's Monticello home, (c) *Zark* comics, and (d) Caterpillar's products and services.

cessing software from one manufacturer and a spreadsheet package from another, they may be incompatible. Using suite software, however, means that you could easily build a spreadsheet and then move it into a report you are preparing using word processing. Another advantage of suites is that the various packages have the same "look and feel"—the same buttons and menus and overall appearance.

Most personal computers come with simple suites that feature word processing, spreadsheet, and graphics programs. But even moderately sophisticated users may quickly outgrow such programs. The next step up, whether you are a professional working from home, a small business owner, or just a hobbyist, includes more sophisticated versions of these applications and additional software types, such as database management. In fact, one of the most common office applications of suites is **mail merge,** in which certain names and addresses from a database are used on letters prepared using word processing. Two or three software makers have dominated the suite market for years and continue to offer software upgrades—newer and better versions.

Critical Thinking

Clearly office software suites have advantages for users. What advantages do they have for software vendors? (Ability to charge more and sell more software, ability to supplant competition by closely coupling programs from same vendor, reduced packaging costs, wider appeal to consumers.)

GETTING PRACTICAL

FIX-IT SOFTWARE

There are several programs on the market that profess to keep your personal computer running smoothly. The First Aid program is easy for novice users to navigate and powerful enough to provide more advanced users with some serious tools.

Easy? Just look at the screen shown here. All you need to do is click the peripheral with which you are having trouble—printer, monitor, whatever—and First Aid will get to work to find a solution, asking questions and checking your internal set-

tings. The program also can examine your computer's Internet setup, including modem, browser, and Internet service provider.

First Aid offers a Check-Up button that, when clicked, will scan your system and alert you to any difficulties. Further, the program categorizes a

problem as either critical, meaning it needs fixing immediately, or as a problem likely to cause trouble some time in the future. First Aid also provides tips and suggestions on ways you can improve your computer's performance in the areas checked.

If you want to educate yourself on how to tweak your computer's settings, click the How Do I button. This brings up informative videos that demonstrate how to use these functions.

Software makers have long tried to outdo one another by offering software with myriad seldom-used features. However, they have recently begun to take a different approach. Vendors now focus on ease of use and on throwing in nifty programs such as personal time organizers, to-do list makers, e-mail programs, and—best of all—access to the Internet.

The do-everything programs, of course, need significant amounts of memory and also require a lot of disk space, so be sure that the requirements listed on the software box fit your hardware. The good news, however, is that competition continues to heat up the price wars, causing the prices of these packages to fall.

Learn by Doing

Consider asking students to visit local software retailers and measure the following: number of feet of shelf space devoted to each major category of software (office suites, games, databases, communications, educational). Another thing students may note is how the software is organized—which applications get the highly visible locations on the end of the aisles, in the window, at the checkout, and so forth.

Business Software

We have already mentioned that many large organizations often hire their own programmers to write custom software. The Boeing Company, for example, will not find software to plan the electrical wiring of an airplane among off-the-rack packages. However, not all of a company's software need be custom-made. Many companies use standard packages for standard tasks such as payroll and accounts receivable. Furthermore, some software vendors specialize in a certain "vertical" slice of the business community, serving similar customers such as plumbers or accountants.

Vertical Market Software

Software written especially for a particular group of like businesses, such as dentists or plumbers, is called **vertical market software.** This user-oriented software usually presents options with a series of easy-to-follow screens that minimize the training needed.

An auto repair shop is a good example of a business that can make use of vertical market software. Designed in conjunction with people who understand the auto repair business, the comprehensive software for an auto shop can prepare work orders, process sales transactions, produce invoices, evaluate sales and profits, track parts inventory, print reorder reports, and update the customer mailing list.

Software for Workgroups

If you work on a project with a group of people, it is likely that you will use software especially made for that scenario. **Groupware,** also called **collaborative software,** can be defined generally as any kind of software that lets a group of people share information or track information together. Using that general definition, some people might say that electronic mail is a form of groupware. But simply sending data back and forth by e-mail has inherent limitations for collaboration, the most obvious being confusion if there are more than two group members. To work together effectively on a project, the data being used must be in a central place that can be accessed and changed by anyone working on the project. That central place is a database, or databases, on disk. Having the data in just one place eliminates the old problem of separate and possibly different versions of the same project.

A popular groupware package called Notes combines electronic mail, networking, scheduling, and database technology (Figure 8). Using such groupware, business people can work with one another and share knowledge or expertise unbounded by factors such as distance or time zone differences. Notes can be installed on all computers on the network.

Groupware is most often used by a team for a specific project. A classic example is a bid prepared by Price Waterhouse, an accounting firm, for a consulting contract. They had just a few days to put together a complex proposal, and the four people who needed to write it were in three different states. They were able to work together using their computers and Notes, which permitted a four-way dialogue on-screen. They also extracted key components of the proposal from existing company databases, including the résumés of company experts, and borrowed passages from similar successful proposals.

Getting Software Help at Work: The Information Center

More often than not, a worker in an office has a computer on his or her desk. It is just a matter of time until that user needs help. If personal computer users compared notes, they would probably find that their experiences are similar. The experience of budget analyst Manuela Lopez is typical. She was given her own personal computer so that she could analyze financial data. She learned to use a popular spreadsheet program. She soon thought about branching out with other software products. She wanted a statistics software

Figure 8 Notes. These three screens are from a groupware package called Notes. Groupware lets workers use the computer to collaborate on a project.

package but was not sure which one was appropriate or how to get it. She saw that a colleague was using a database management program but had no idea how to use it herself. Most of all, Manuela felt her productivity would increase significantly if she knew how to use the software to access certain data in the corporate data files.

The company **information center,** often called simply the *help desk,* is one solution to these kinds of needs. Although no two centers are alike, all information centers are devoted exclusively to giving users service. Information centers usually offer help with software selection, software training, and, if appropriate, access to corporate computer systems.

Software for a Small Business

Suppose that, as a fledgling entrepreneur with some computer savvy, your ambition is to be as competitive as one personal computer will let you be. You are not alone. Two interesting statistics are that more than half of American workers would like to own their own businesses and that the number of home-office workers is increasing by 5 percent a year. Savvy entrepreneurs realize that a computer is a major asset in running the business, even at the very start. The software industry has responded to this need with various packages that come under the generic heading of **small office, home office,** or **SOHO** for short.

You know you cannot afford expensive software, but you also know that there is an abundance of moderately priced software that can enhance all aspects of your business. A look through any store display of software packages will reveal several aimed at small businesses, from marketing strategy software to software for handling mailing lists.

The following basic list is presented according to business functions— things you will want to be able to do. The computer can help.

■ **Accounting.** Totaling the bottom line must be the number one priority for any business. If you are truly on your own, or have just one or two employees, you may be able to get by with simple spreadsheet software to work up a ledger and balance sheet and generate basic invoices and payroll worksheets. Larger operations can consider a complete accounting package, which produces profit-and-loss statements, balance sheets, cash flow reports, and tax summaries. Most packages will also write and print checks, and some have payroll capability.

■ **Writing and advertising.** Word processing is an obvious choice because you will need to write memos and the like. Desktop publishing can be a real boon to a small business, letting you design and produce advertisements, flyers, and even your own letterhead stationery, business forms, and business cards. A big advantage of publishing your own advertisements or flyers is that you can print small quantities and start anew as your business evolves. Finally, you may think it is worthwhile to publish your own newsletter for customers.

■ **Customer service.** Customer service is a byword throughout the business world, but the personal touch is especially important in a small business. Database software can be useful here. Suppose, for example, that you run a pet grooming service. You surely want to keep track of each customer by address and so forth for billing and advertising purposes. But this is just the beginning. Why not store data about each pet too? Think how impressed the customer on the phone will be when you recall that Sadie is a standard poodle, seven years old, and that it is time for her to have her booster shots.

- **Keeping up and making contacts.** Even if you have only one computer, you can still be networked to the outside world. Business connections are available in many forms from dozens of sites on the Internet.
- **Making sales pitches.** If your business depends on pitching your product or service in some formal way, presentation software can help you create colorful demonstrations that are the equivalent of an electronic slide show. Presentation software is designed for regular people, not artists, so putting together a slick sequence of text and graphics is remarkably simple (Figure 9).

Finally, consider an all-in-one software package specifically designed to help you get your home office organized. This is a variation on the suites described earlier but is geared specifically to the small business. If you are on your own, you need the organizational skills of a secretary, the research skills of a librarian, the accounting skills of a bookkeeper, and the experience of someone who has done it before. Comprehensive SOHO packages address all these needs, providing a searchable library of resources, a legal guide, and a tax guide. The packages also include collections of business documents for every situation, from asset depreciation to press release announcements. Such packages also typically offer links to useful business and government sites on the Internet.

Ethics and Applications Software

The most sizzling ethics issue related to software is the acquisition and use of illegal software copies, the software piracy we mentioned earlier. Lamentations by both business and the computer industry are so persistent and so loud that we are devoting a separate section to this issue.

Have you ever copied a friend's music CD or tape onto your own blank tape? Many people do so without much thought. It is also possible to photocopy a book. Both acts are clearly illegal, but there is much more fuss over

Figure 9 A computer-produced presentation. Shown here are just two of the screens that Jean Lake uses when making a presentation about her business. She was able to prepare them quickly using graphics software (Microsoft PowerPoint). She can show the screens directly with a projector connected to a computer or have them converted to conventional slides.

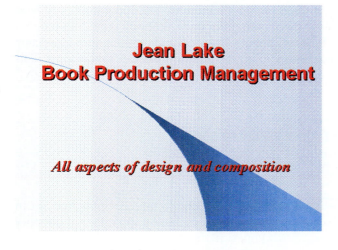

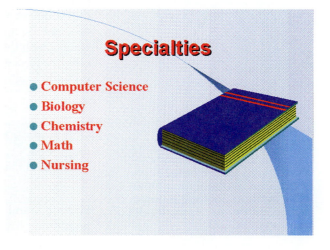

illegal software copying than over copying music or books. Why is this? Well, to begin with, few of us are likely to undertake the laborious task of reproducing *War and Peace* on a copy machine. Another difference is that a copied tape or book is never quite as good as the original; copied software, on the other hand, is identical to the original and works just as well. The other part of the issue is money. A pirated copy of a top-20 CD will set the recording company—and the artist—back just a few dollars. But pirated software may be valued at hundreds of dollars. The problem of stolen software has grown right along with the personal computer industry.

OK If I Copy That Software?

Consider this incident. Bill Huston got his computer education at a local community college. One of his courses taught him how to use software on personal computers. He had access to a great variety of copyrighted software in the college computer lab. After graduating, he got a job at a local museum, where he used database software on a personal computer to catalog museum wares. He also had his own computer at home.

One day Bill stopped back at the college and ran into a former instructor. After greetings were exchanged, she asked him why he happened to drop by. "Oh," he said, "I just came by to make some copies of software." He wasn't kidding. Neither was the instructor, who, after she caught her breath, replied, "You can't do that. It's illegal." Bill was miffed, saying, "But I can't afford it!" The instructor immediately alerted the computer lab. As a result of this encounter, the staff strengthened policies on software use and increased the vigilance of lab personnel. In effect, schools must protect themselves from people who lack ethics or are unaware of the law.

There are many people like Bill. He did not think in terms of stealing anything; he just wanted to make copies for himself. But, as the software industry is quick to point out, unauthorized copying *is* stealing because the software makers do not get the revenues to which they are entitled. If Bill had used illegally copied software at his place of work, his employer could be at risk for litigation.

Why Those Extra Copies?

Copying software is not always a dirty trick—there are lots of legitimate reasons for copying. To begin with, after paying several hundred dollars for a piece of software, you will definitely want to make a backup copy in case of disk failure or accident. You probably want to copy the program onto a hard disk and use it, more conveniently, from there. Software publishers have no trouble with these types of copying. But thousands of computer users copy software for another reason: to get the program without paying for it. This is clearly unethical and illegal.

InfoBit

How complex are operating systems? Programmers often measure complexity by the number of lines of programming language "code" required. A simple operating system, like Linux, is made up of about 750 thousand lines of code. A complex operating system, Microsoft Windows, is made up of over 15 million lines of code.

Operating Systems: Hidden Software

When a brand-new computer comes off the factory assembly line, it can do nothing. The hardware needs software to make it work. Part of the story

User
Applications programs
Operating system
Hardware

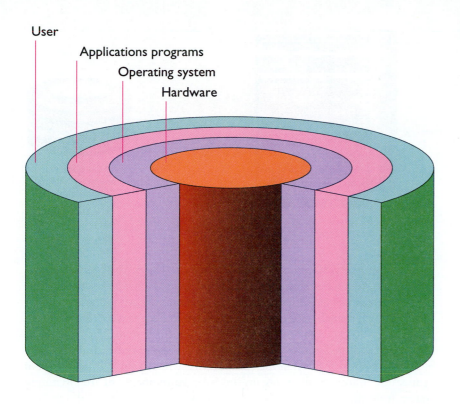

Figure 10 A conceptual diagram of an operating system. Closest to the user are applications programs—software that helps a user compute a payroll or play a game or calculate the trajectory of a rocket. The operating system is the set of programs between the applications programs and the hardware.

is the applications software, such as word processing or spreadsheet software, that we discussed earlier in the chapter. But applications software cannot communicate directly with the hardware, so the operating system serves as intermediary software between the applications software and the hardware. An **operating system** is a set of programs that lies between applications software and the computer hardware; it is the fundamental software that controls access to all other software and hardware resources. Figure 10 gives a conceptual picture of operating system software as an intermediary between the hardware and the applications software. Incidentally, the term **systems software** is sometimes used interchangeably with *operating system,* but systems software means all programs related to coordinating computer operations. Systems software includes the operating system, but it also includes programming language translators and a variety of service programs.

Operating systems for mainframe and other large computers are complex indeed, since they must keep track of several programs from several users all running in the same time frame. Although some personal computer operating systems—most often found in business or learning environments—can support multiple users, most are concerned only with a single user at a time.

Note that we said that an operating system is a set of programs. The most important program in the operating system, the program that manages the operating system, is the **supervisor program,** most of which remains in memory and is thus referred to as *resident.* The supervisor controls the entire operating system and loads into memory other operating system programs (called *nonresident*) from disk storage only as needed (Figure 11).

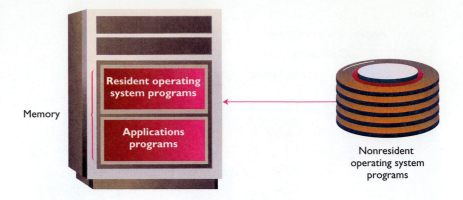

Figure 11 Retrieving operating system programs from disk. The supervisor program of the operating system is resident in memory and calls in nonresident operating system programs from the disk as needed.

Memory

Resident operating system programs

Applications programs

Nonresident operating system programs

Most users today have a computer with a hard disk drive. No matter what operating system is being used, when the computer is turned on, the operating system will be loaded from the hard drive into the computer's memory, thus making it available for use. The process of loading the operating system into memory is called *bootstrapping,* or **booting** the system. The word *booting* is used because, figuratively speaking, the operating system pulls itself up by its own bootstraps. When the computer is switched on, a small program in memory automatically pulls up the basic components of the operating system from the hard disk.

An operating system has three main functions: (1) to manage the computer's resources, such as the central processing unit, memory, disk drives, and printers; (2) to establish a user interface; and (3) to execute and provide services for applications software. Keep in mind, however, that much of the work of an operating system is hidden from the user; many necessary tasks are performed behind the scenes. In particular, the first listed function, managing the computer's resources, is taken care of without the user being aware of the details. Furthermore, all input and output operations, although invoked by an applications program, are actually carried out by the operating system.

Although much of the operating system functions are hidden from view, you will know when you are using an applications software package, and this requires that you invoke—call into action—the operating system. Thus you establish a user interface and also execute software.

We now focus on the interaction between a single user and a personal computer operating system.

Operating Systems for Personal Computers

If you peruse software offerings at a retail store, you will generally find the software grouped according to the operating system on which the software can run. Generally, applications software—word processing, spreadsheets, games, whatever—can run on just one operating system. Just as you cannot place a Nissan engine in a Ford truck, you cannot take a version of WordPerfect—a word processing program—designed to run on a computer

MAKING THE RIGHT CONNECTIONS

CLASSIC PHOTO COLLECTIONS

You may have seen this photo before. People are so fond of it that it has appeared in various museum photo exhibitions and in many magazine and book collections. Photographer Alfred Eisenstaedt snapped this picture in 1963 at a Paris puppet show, capturing the children's reactions just as the evil dragon was slain.

Now, of course, the computer improves access to such photos. Famous photos—thousands of them—have been digitized and assembled into collections that are available on the Internet. Thus the interested and the curious can conveniently browse through some of the world's most compelling photo exhibitions. And most such images are for sale.

using the Microsoft Windows operating system and run it on an Apple iMac, which uses its own operating system, OS 8.5. The operating systems must certainly be different if the computers' processors are different. Software makers must decide for which operating system to write an applications software package, although some make versions of their software for more than one operating system.

Users, though, do not set out to buy an operating system; they want computers and the applications software to make them useful. However, since the operating system determines what software is available for a given computer, they must at the least be aware of their own computer's operating system.

Although operating systems differ, many of their basic functions are similar. Let us examine some of the basic functions of operating systems by examining the software that is used on most personal computers—Microsoft Windows.

Microsoft Windows

The operating system called **Microsoft Windows**—Windows for short—uses a colorful graphics interface that, among other things, eases access to the operating system. Microsoft Windows defines the operating environment standard for computers with Intel processors. Most new personal computers come with Windows already installed (Figure 12).

A Windows Overview

The feature that makes Windows so easy to use is a **graphical user interface** (**GUI,** pronounced "Goo ee"), in which users work with on-screen pictures called **icons** and with **menus** rather than with keyed-in commands (Figure 13). Clicking icons or menu items activates a command or function. The menus in Figure 13 are called **pull-down menus** because they appear to pull down like a window shade from the original selection. Some menus, in contrast, called **pop-up menus,** originate from a selection on the bottom of the screen. Furthermore, icons and menus encourage pointing and clicking with a mouse, an approach that can make computer use fast, easy, and intuitive.

As millions of users can attest, Windows is an unqualified success. But even a popular software product can be improved, hence the subsequent versions called Windows 95 and Windows 98. Windows 95 was offered as a new and distinct operating system. Windows 98 is a variation on Windows 95 and has much the same screen look.

Windows features a Start button in the lower-left corner just waiting to be clicked (Figure 12). From this beginning you can conveniently find a program or a file. Programs can also be invoked—started—by a double-click on an icon on the desktop, the Windows opening screen. Figure 12 shows several program icons; you could double-click the icon labelled *Hearts* to launch that program—a game. Perhaps the greatest convenience, as you can see in Figure 12, is the task bar along the bottom of the screen, an array of buttons for each active program, that is, a program in current use. You can click from one active program to another as easily as changing channels on your TV. As another example of convenience, long file names, up to 255 characters, are permitted.

Anyone who has added a new component, perhaps a modem or a sound card, to an existing computer knows that it must be configured to the system, a process that may involve some software and even hardware manipulations. Windows supports **plug and play,** a concept that lets the computer

Figure 12 Windows screen. The screen on this user's computer shows an icon for each of several software packages available on the computer. A double-click of the mouse on the icon invokes—runs—the desired program. Note the task bar at the bottom of the screen: It shows a button for each program currently in use. Note that the names of the programs on the buttons are abbreviated; the names become shorter and shorter as added buttons crowd the early arrivals.

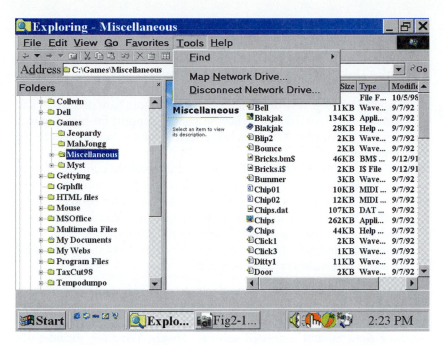

Figure 13　Windows menus. This is a Windows Explorer screen. Explorer helps you keep track of your files. Explorer shows file folders on the left. The folder currently open is the subfolder Miscellaneous within the folder Games. The files that are contained in subfolder Miscellaneous are shown on the right. This screen also illustrates menus; note the pull-down menu for Tools near the top. Also, when the Start button on the lower left is clicked, it issues a pop-up menu (not shown here) with various options, including shutting down. The Start button is part of the task bar, which shows tiny clickable icons for (left to right) Internet Explorer, Outlook Express, Dell options, return to desktop, and "channels," an option for retrieving data from certain Internet sites. To the right of these icons, there is a button for each program currently open, from left to right, Windows Explorer and PhotoSuite (manipulating images). Proceeding right, the next set of icons, mostly added by the user, are sound volume, the Microsoft Network, Zing (images while awaiting web sites), and Personal Web Server. Finally, rightmost is the time; if you rest your mouse on it, the day and date appear.

configure itself when a new component is added. However, for plug and play to become a reality, hardware components must also feature the plug-and-play standard. Once a peripheral is built to the plug-and-play standard, a user can install it simply by plugging it in and turning on the computer. Windows recognizes that a new device has been added and proceeds to configure it.

A Windows technology called **object linking and embedding** (OLE—wonderfully pronounced "oh LAY") lets you embed or link one document with another. For instance, you could embed a graphic within a document created in a desktop publishing program that supports OLE. When you click the graphic to edit it, you are taken to the graphics program in which you created the graphic.

Some notable features of the latest version of Windows are

■　**Internet/intranet browsing capabilities.** Microsoft's browser, Internet Explorer, is included with Windows. In fact, Windows itself has been made to look more like a browser. Note, for example, in Figure 13, the

Figure 14 Windows CE. This handheld computer, showing a Windows CE screen, rests in a desktop cradle when not on the road.

Address slot at the top of the Exploring window; this is reminiscent of a browser screen.

- **Support for state-of-the-art hardware.** This includes support for Digital Video Disk (DVD) and the latest multimedia components. DVD and multimedia are described in the chapter on storage.
- **Support for huge disk drives.** Everyone wants more hard disk space, and today's enormous drives provide the answer. Support for high-capacity drives is provided in Windows in the form of tables that can handle the larger numbers.
- **TV viewer and broadcast ability.** A broadcast-enabled computer blends television with new forms of information and entertainment. It blurs the line between television, web pages, and computer content. It also enables the reception of broadcast web pages and other live data feeds, such as across-the-screen news headlines and stock quotes.
- **Wizards.** Windows lets users accomplish various tasks using "wizards," software that makes tasks user-friendly.

Further, Windows includes technologies to help reduce the cost of owning and maintaining a personal computer. Other features include improved backup, improved interfaces with other software, new and improved networking features, and increased security. Finally, Windows includes Dr. Watson, which provides technical information about the state of the computer when it suffers a general protection fault, commonly called a "crash."

The stripped-down version called Windows CE (for *consumer electronics*) is meant for handheld organizers and other new digital appliances (Figure 14). It is a subset of Windows, scaled back to work with less memory on smaller screens and without much, if any, file storage. It looks roughly like Windows and has rudimentary word processing, spreadsheet, e-mail, and web browsing software. It also allows contact and calendar information and documents to be swapped between a desktop personal computer and a handheld computer.

Windows NT

The operating system called **Windows NT** (for *new technology*) is meant mostly for corporate, networked environments. Beginning with version 4.0, NT looks exactly like Windows 98 and runs most of the software that runs under Windows 98. But beneath the surface, Windows NT is far more robust and heavy-duty. It has been engineered for stability and, as befits a networked environment, has much stronger security features.

For home users, the features that make Windows NT attractive to businesses may be overkill. Furthermore, Windows NT requires much more memory and hard disk space—probably triple for each—than does Windows 98. Technical support costs more too, closer to what a business would expect to pay.

Windows 2000

Windows NT becomes Windows 2000, which merges Windows NT 4.0's stability with Windows 98's setup and hardware awareness. Windows 2000 is designed for both work and home use.

The most noticeable feature is that Windows 2000 software knows who you are. One computer can serve many people. Once you tell it who you are, it will immediately reconfigure to your preferences. It personalizes the Start menu so programs used most frequently are visible and others are hidden. Windows 2000 also knows what you are using. Dynamic layout features will consider what kind of screen you are on (handheld, TV, PC), what size it is, and so on, and then adjust its size and format accordingly. A particularly attractive feature is the self-healing applications software—if you accidentally delete a necessary component, Windows will restore it. Gone are the traditional user-interface elements such as menus. Windows 2000 lets you ask for something in ordinary language and get an answer. You can, for example, type, "Start a new document," without telling it to launch your word processing program.

Computers and People

These first two chapters have described hardware, software, and data, but the most important element in a computer system is people. Anyone nervous about a takeover by computers will be relieved to know that computers will never amount to much without people—the people who help make the system work and the people for whom the work is done.

Computers and You, the User

As noted earlier, computer users have come to be called just *users,* a nickname that has persisted for years. Whereas once computer users were an elite breed—highly educated scientists, research-and-development engineers, government planners—today the population of users has broadened considerably. This expansion is due partly to user-friendly software for both work and personal use and partly to the availability of small, low-cost personal computers. There is every likelihood that all of us will be computer users, even if our levels of sophistication vary.

Computer People

Many organizations have a department called **Management Information Systems (MIS)** or **Computer Information Systems (CIS), Computing Services, Information Services,** or **Information Technology.** Whatever it is called, this department is made up of people responsible for the computer resources of an organization. Large organizations, such as universities, government agencies, and corporations, keep much of the institution's data in computer files: research data, engineering drawings, marketing strategy, accounts receivable, accounts payable, sales facts, manufacturing specifications, transportation plans, and so forth. The people who maintain the data are the same people who provide service to the users: the computer professionals. Let us touch on the essential personnel required to run large computer systems.

Data entry operators prepare data for processing, usually by keying it in a machine-readable format. **Computer operators** monitor the computer, review procedures, keep peripheral equipment running, and make backup copies of data. **Librarians** catalog the processed disks and tapes and keep them secure.

Global Perspective

The demand for programming talent is so strong in the United States that employers have repeatedly petitioned the government to increase the quotas for foreign programmers allowed to immigrate and work on American soil.

OPERATING SYSTEMS FOR LARGE COMPUTERS

Large computers—mainframes—are usually owned by businesses, universities, and the government, which make them available to many people for use, all at the same time. This presents special problems, which must be addressed by the operating system.

Computer users often have questions when they first realize that their program is "in there" with all those other programs. At any given moment, which program gets the CPU? If several programs are in memory at the same time, what keeps the programs from getting mixed up with one another? How is storage handled when several programs may want to get data from or send processed data to disk at the same time? Why doesn't printer output from several programs get all jumbled up? The operating system anticipates these problems and takes care of them "behind the scene" so that users can share the computer's

resources without worrying about how it is done.

Notice that the questions above all address sharing problems, that is, multiple users sharing the central processing unit, memory, storage, and the printer. Shared resources are said to be allocated. **Resource allocation** is the process of assigning computer resources to programs for their use.

Sharing the Central Processing Unit

If a computer has a single central processing unit, all programs running on the computer must share it. Two approaches to sharing are multiprogramming and time-sharing. But first, let us distinguish multiprogramming from multiprocessing. **Multiprocessing** refers to the use of a powerful computer with more than one central processing unit, so that multiple programs can run simultaneously, each using its own processor.

If there is only one central processing unit, it is not physically possible for more than one program to use it at the same time. **Multiprogramming** means two or more programs are being executed in the same time frame, that is, **concurrently,** on a computer. What this really means is that the programs are taking turns; one program runs for a while and then another one runs. The key word here is *concurrently,* as opposed to *simultaneously.* In concurrent use, for example, one program could be using the CPU while another does something else, such as send output to the printer, which gives the illusion of simultaneous processing. Typical examples of programs that run in a multiprogramming environment are payroll, accounts receivable, and stock reporting.

A special case of multiprogramming, **time-sharing,** gives each user a **time slice**—a fraction of a

second—during which the computer works on a single user's tasks. At the end of the time slice—that is, when time is up—the resources are taken away from that user and given to someone else. **Response time** is the time between your typed computer request and the computer's reply. Even if you are working on a calculation and the operating system interrupts it, sending you to the end of the line until the other users have had their turns, you may not notice that you have been deprived temporarily of service. Typical time-sharing applications are those with many users, each of whom is allowed to run a series of brief, randomly occurring actions; examples include credit checking, retail sales transactions, and airline reservation systems.

Sharing Memory
The process of allocating memory to programs and

Global Perspective

Recently there has been increased interest in moving some traditional programming tasks offshore to the developing nations. Advantages here include the availability of skilled, inexpensive labor, with many foreign programmers actually having been educated in American universities.

Computer programmers, as noted earlier, design, write, test, implement, and maintain the programs that process data on the computer system; they also maintain and update the programs. **Systems analysts** are knowledgeable in the programming area but have broader responsibilities. They plan and design not just individual programs but entire computer systems. Systems analysts maintain a working relationship with both programmers and the users in the organization. The analysts work closely with the users to plan new systems that will meet the users' needs. A professional called a **network manager** implements and maintains the organization's network(s). The department manager, often called the **chief information officer (CIO),** must understand more than just computer technology. This person must under-

of keeping programs in memory separate from one another is called **memory management.** There are many methods of memory management. Some systems simply divide memory into separate areas, each of which can hold a program. The problem is how to know how big the areas, sometimes called **partitions or regions,** should be; at least one of them should be large enough to hold the largest anticipated program.

Many computer systems manage memory by using a technique called **virtual storage** (also called **virtual memory**). The virtual storage concept means that part of the program is stored on disk and is brought into memory for execution only as needed. (Since only one part of a program can be executing at any given time, the parts not currently needed are left on the disk.) Virtual storage causes the program to appear to be using more memory space than is

actually the case. Since only part of the program is in memory at any given time, the amount of memory needed for a program is minimized. Memory, in this case, is considered *real storage,* while the secondary storage (hard disk, most likely) holding the rest of the program is considered *virtual storage.*

Virtual storage is often implemented using the paging method. Suppose you have a very large program, which means there will be difficulty finding space for it on the computer's shared memory. If your program is divided into small pieces, it will be easier to find places to put those pieces. This is essentially what paging does. **Paging** is the process of dividing a program into equal-size pieces called **pages** and storing them in equal-size memory spaces called **page frames.** The pages are stored in memory in noncontiguous locations, that is, locations not necessarily next to each other.

Even though the pages are not right next to each other in memory, the operating system is able to keep track of them. It does this by using a **page table,** which, like an index, lists each page that is part of the program and the corresponding beginning memory address where it has been placed.

In a multiprogramming environment it is theoretically possible for one program to accidentally hop into the middle of another, causing destruction of data and general chaos. To avoid this problem, the operating system confines each program to certain defined limits in memory; this process is called **memory protection.**

Sharing Storage Resources

The operating system keeps track of which file is where and responds to commands to manipulate files. But the situation is complicated by the possibility that more

than one user may want to read or write a record from the same disk pack at the same time. Again, it is the operating system that keeps track of the input and output requests and processes them, usually in the order received. Any program instruction to read or write a record is routed to the operating system, which processes the request and then returns control to the program.

Sharing Printing Resources

Suppose the computer has only one printer. If programs took turns printing their output a line or two at a time, interspersed with the output of other programs, the resulting printed report would be worthless. To get around this problem, a process called **spooling** is used: Each program first sends to disk any output to be printed. When the entire output is on the disk, it is sent to the printer.

stand the goals and operations of the entire organization and be able to make strategic decisions.

These are some standard jobs and standard titles. There are many others, most notably those associated with creation and maintenance of Internet sites; these will be discussed in detail in the Internet chapters.

▲

These opening chapters have painted a picture with a broad brush. Now it is time to get down to details. The next chapters describe hardware in more detail.

CHAPTER REVIEW

Summary and Key Terms

- **Software** is the planned, step-by-step set of instructions required to turn data into information. **Applications software** can be used to solve a particular problem or to perform a particular task. Applications software may be either custom or packaged.

- **Computer programmers** are people who design, write, test, and implement software. Organizations may pay computer programmers to write **custom software,** software that is specifically tailored to their needs.

- **Packaged software,** also called **commercial software,** is packaged in a container of some sort, usually a box or folder, and is sold in stores or catalogs. Inside the box are one or more disks holding the software and perhaps an instruction manual, also referred to as **documentation.**

- The term **user-friendly** means that the software is supposed to be easy for a beginner to use or that the software can be used with a minimum of training.

- **Freeware** is software for which there is no fee. Software is considered to be in the **public domain** if it is uncopyrighted, and thus may be altered. Software called **shareware** is also given away free; the maker hopes for voluntary payment.

- *Commercial software* is copyrighted, costs money, and must not be copied without permission from the manufacturer. Making illegal copies of commercial software is called **software piracy** and is punishable under the law.

- A **site license** permits an organization, for a fee, to make a limited number of copies of a software product. **Electronic software distribution** means a user can pay to **download** the software—move it from another computer to the user's computer.

- **Word processing** software lets you create, edit, format, store, and print text and graphics in one document. It is those three words in the middle—*edit, format,* and *store*—that reveal the difference between word processing and plain typing. **Desktop publishing** packages meet high-level publishing needs to produce professional-looking newsletters, reports, and brochures.

- An **electronic spreadsheet,** made up of columns and rows of numbers, automatically recalculates the results when a number is changed. This capability lets business people try different combinations of "**what if . . .**" numbers and obtain the results quickly.

- **Database management** software manages a collection of interrelated facts. The software can store data, update it, manipulate it, retrieve it, report it in a variety of views, and print it in as many forms.

- **Graphics** software can produce graphs, maps, and charts and can help people compare data, spot trends more easily, and make decisions more quickly. **Graphic artists** use graphics software to express their ideas visually.

- A **browser** is software used to access the Internet.

- A **suite** is a group of basic software designed to work together. A typical suite application is **mail merge,** in which certain names and addresses from a database are applied to letters prepared using word processing.

- Software written especially for a group of like businesses is called **vertical market software.**

- **Groupware,** also called **collaborative software,** is any kind of software that lets a group of people share information or track information together.

- The company **information center,** or help desk, is devoted to giving users help with software selection, software training, and, if appropriate, access to corporate computer systems.

- Software designed for small businesses is termed **SOHO,** for **small office, home office.**

- An **operating system** is a set of programs that lies between applications software and the computer hardware. **Systems software** refers to all programs related to coordinating computer operations, including the operating system, programming language translators, and service programs.

- The **supervisor program,** most of which remains in memory, is called *resident.* The supervisor controls the entire operating system and loads into memory *nonresident* operating system programs from disk storage as needed.

- An operating system has three main functions: (1) to manage the computer's resources, such as the central processing unit, memory, disk drives, and printers; (2) to establish a user interface; and (3) to execute and provide services for applications software.

- Loading the operating system into memory is called **booting** the system.

- A key product is **Microsoft Windows,** software with a colorful **graphical user interface (GUI).** Windows offers on-screen pictures, which are called **icons,** and both **pull-down** and **pop-up menus.** These features encourage pointing and clicking with a mouse, an approach that can make computer use faster and easier.

- A key feature of Microsoft Windows is **plug and play,** a concept that lets the computer configure itself when a new component is added. A Windows technology called **object linking and embedding (OLE)** lets you embed or link one document with another.

- **Windows NT** (for *new technology*) is meant mostly for corporate, networked environments. Windows 2000 merges Windows NT 4.0's stability with Windows 98's setup and hardware awareness and can be used in either a work or home environment. Windows CE (for *consumer electronics*) is a scaled-back version of Windows, meant for handheld organizers and other new digital appliances.

- **Resource allocation** is the process of assigning computer resources to certain programs for their use. **Multiprocessing** means that a computer with more than one central processing unit can run multiple programs simultaneously, each using its own processor.

- **Multiprogramming** is running two or more programs in the same time frame, **concurrently,** on the same computer. **Time-sharing** is a special case of multiprogramming in which several people use one computer at the same time. Each user is given a **time slice** in which the computer works on that user's tasks before moving on to another user's tasks. **Response time** is the time between the user's typed computer request and the computer's reply.

- **Memory management** is the process of allocating memory to programs and of keeping the programs in memory separate from each other. Some systems divide memory into separate areas, sometimes called **partitions** or **regions,** each of which can hold a program.

- In the **virtual storage** (or **virtual memory**) technique of memory management, part of the application program is stored on disk and is brought into memory only when needed for execution. Memory is considered real storage; the secondary storage holding the rest of the program is considered virtual storage. **Paging** divides a program into equal-size pieces (**pages**) that fit exactly into corresponding noncontiguous memory spaces (**page frames**). The operating system keeps track of page locations using an index-like **page table.**

- **Memory protection** defines the limits of each program in memory, thus preventing programs from accidentally destroying or modifying one another.

- **Spooling** writes each file to be printed temporarily onto a disk instead of printing it immediately.

- Many organizations have a department called **Management Information Systems (MIS)** or **Computer Information Systems (CIS), Computing Services, Information Services,** or **Information Technology.** This department is made up of people responsible for the computer resources of an organization.

- **Data entry operators** prepare data for processing, usually by keying it in a machine-readable format. **Computer operators** monitor the computer, review procedures, and keep peripheral equipment running. **Librarians** catalog the processed disks and tapes and keep them secure. **Computer programmers** design, write, test, and implement the programs that process data on the computer system; they also maintain and update the programs. **Systems analysts** are knowledgeable in the programming area but have broader responsibilities; they plan and design not just individual programs but entire computer systems. A professional called a **network manager** implements and maintains the organization's network(s). The department manager, often called the **chief information officer (CIO)**, must understand computer technology as well as the goals and operations of the entire organization.

Discussion Questions

1. Consider these firms. What uses would each have for computer software? Mention as many possibilities as you can.

   a. Security Southwestern Bank, a major regional bank with several branches

   b. Azure Design, a small graphic design company that produces posters, covers, and other artwork

   c. Checkerboard Taxi Service, whose central office manages a fleet of 160 cabs that operate in an urban area

   d. Gillick College, a private college that has automated all student services, including registration, financial aid, and testing

2. If you have, or will have, a computer of your own, how will you get software for it?

Student Study Guide

Multiple Choice

1. An operating system is a(n)

   a. set of users   c. application

   b. set of programs   d. supervisor program

2. A computer professional who writes and tests software is called a(n)

   a. programmer   c. librarian

   b. systems analyst   d. operator

3. Step-by-step instructions that run the computer are called

   a. hardware   c. documents

   b. CPUs   d. programs

4. CIS stands for

   a. Computer Internet System

   b. Commercial Internet System

   c. Collaborative Information Systems

   d. Computer Information Systems

5. The actions that separate word processing from typing are

   a. format, store, print   c. create, edit, format

   b. edit, format, store   d. create, store, print

6. Paging divides a program into pages that fit in

   a. the page table   c. page frames

   b. the page index   d. virtual pages

7. The underlying software is called

   a. applications   c. groupware

   b. the operating system   d. shareware

8. Which of the following terms is *not* a description of certain software?

   a. custom   c. download

   b. freeware   d. collaborative

9. The department within an organization that is designed to help users with software is the

   a. browser   c. information center

   b. SOHO   d. network

10. Software written especially for a group of like businesses is called

    a. freeware   c. shareware

    b. word processing   d. vertical market software

11. Making illegal copies of copyrighted software is called

    a. software piracy   c. collaboration

    b. browsing   d. electronic distribution

12. Loading the operating system into the memory of a personal computer is called

    a. booting   c. supervising

    b. applying   d. graphing

13. Software that allows the production of professional newsletters and reports is called

    a. database management   c. spreadsheets

    b. groupware   d. desktop publishing

14. The type of software that can store, update, manipulate, and retrieve data is called

    a. desktop publishing   c. database management

    b. spreadsheet   d. graphics

15. Another name for available-for-purchase software is

    a. secondary software   c. systems software

    b. packaged software   d. peripheral software

True/False

T F 1. A browser is software used to access the Internet.

T F 2. The most important program in an operating system is the supervisor program.

T F 3. Making illegal copies of copyrighted software is called software piracy.

T F 4. Vertical market software is designed for a group of like businesses.

T F 5. Workers using groupware must be physically in the same office.

T F 6. Software documentation may be written or may be included as part of the software.

T F 7. The operating system is an example of applications software.

T F 8. Under multiprogramming, programs can run concurrently.

T F 9. Windows uses a graphical interface.

T F 10. User-friendly refers to a special kind of computer.

T F 11. Custom software is specially tailored to user needs.

T F 12. Complex software usually requires a setup process before use.

T F 13. Word processing is a type of task-oriented software.

T F 14. Desktop publishing software is used to manage numbers in columns and rows.

T F 15. Spooling means that virtual pages are written directly to the printer.

T F 16. The person who plans new systems is the network manager.

T F 17. Another name for groupware is SOHO.

T F 18. Copyrighted software is in the public domain.

T F 19. An advantage of groupware is collaboration.

T F 20. A site license entitles an individual to freeware.

Fill-In

1. A group of basic software designed to work together is called a(n) _____.

2. What kind of software presents numbers in columns and rows? _____.

3. SOHO stands for _____.

4. The name for collaborative software is _____.

5. The general name for software that can be used to solve a problem or perform a task is _____.

6. Software written for a group of like businesses is called _____.

7. Software that is given away free is called _____.

8. The underlying software found on all computers is the _____.

9. The department within an organization that is dedicated to giving software help is the _____.

Answers

Multiple Choice

1. b	6. c	11. a
2. a	7. b	12. a
3. d	8. c	13. d
4. d	9. c	14. c
5. b	10. d	15. b

True/False

1. T	6. T	11. T	16. F
2. T	7. F	12. T	17. F
3. T	8. T	13. T	18. F
4. T	9. T	14. F	19. T
5. F	10. F	15. F	20. F

Fill-In

1. suite
2. spreadsheet
3. small office, home office
4. groupware
5. applications software
6. vertical market software
7. freeware
8. operating system
9. information center

JUMPING-OFF POINTS

How do I start? Briefly, to get started, you need an URL for the Web. Translation: You need a starting address (*URL,* for *Uniform Resource Locator*) to find a site on the subset of the Internet called the **World Wide Web,** also called *WWW* or just *the Web.* You can read more detailed information about URLs and the Web and, most importantly, *links,* in the chapter called "The Internet."

Where do I find an URL? An URL is often pretty messy—a long string of letters and symbols. No one likes to type URLs and, what's more, there is a good chance of making an error. Fortunately, you rarely have to type an URL because, once started, you can click your mouse on links—icons or highlighted text—to move from site to site on the Internet.

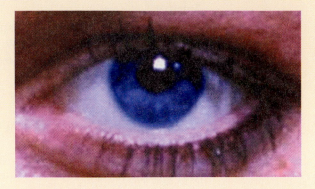

The publisher of this book has set up this URL for our readers:

http://www.prenhall.com/capron

Once you use this URL to reach the publisher's site, you will find links—colored text—to all other sites mentioned in this and other chapters. Simply click the desired link. Since everything on the Internet, including URLs, is subject to change, we supply here the publisher's URL, which will not change.

What other starting points are there? Keep in mind that, unlike a commercial product, the Internet is not owned or managed by anyone. One consequence of this is that there is no master table of contents or index for the Internet. However, several organizations have produced ordered lists that can be used as a helpful starting place. Users often favor one or more of these as comprehensive starting places: Yahoo!, Infospace, Starting Point, AltaVista, Magellan, and Excite.

Each of these sites has a set of major categories, and each major category has links of its own, as do the topics at the next level, and so on. Major categories typically include careers, computers, business, politics, education, society, kids, shopping, travel, magazines, recreation, government, events, science, sports, health, reference, and family. Most major starting sites also include special lists of new and "hot" sites. You could hang around for literally days, burrowing deeper and deeper, just from a starting point like Yahoo!.

PLANET INTERNET

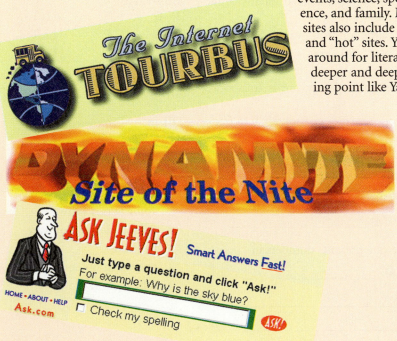

Favorites. Many sites make no attempt to be comprehensive but list, instead, their own favorites, sites they consider to be of high quality. The Lycos Top 5% site lists the top 5 percent of sites in a number of categories. Another interesting site, deliberately unorganized but full of surprises, is Big Eye, which accompanies its offerings with cheerful music. Examples of other sites that put forth special lists are the Dynamite Site of the Night, Cyber-Teddy's Top 500, Bigfoot, the Internet Tourbus, Web Soup, and Wow Web Wonders. The Cool Central site offers the Cool Site of the Week, of the Day, of the Hour, and, for the attention-deficient, the Cool Site of the Moment. Remember that the links for all of these sites can be found at the publisher's site. Just point and click and go to any of the listed sites.

But I need to get to the Web first. Yes. To use the Web you need a browser, special software devoted to managing access to the Web. You can get general information about browsers in "The Internet" chapter, but you will need to ask your instructor, lab personnel, or a designated employee how to use the web browser at your location. If you are using a browser purchased for your personal computer or have access to the Internet via some online

service, then these suppliers will provide instructions.

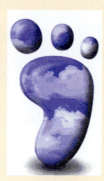

Internet Exercises

In each chapter, beginning in Chapter 2, two exercises are suggested at the end of every Planet Internet section. The first exercise is called a *structured exercise* because once you are on the publisher's web site we can make sure that the sites you visit remain current. Use the URL supplied here to get started. If you are feeling adventurous, try the *freeform exercise,* where we make suggestions but no guarantees.

1. **Structured exercise.** Go to the URL http://www.prenhall.com/capron. Link to the Yahoo! site, and then link to the list of new sites. From there, choose two places to link to.

2. **Freeform exercise.** Using the same URL, go choose a site that lists favorites. Then go to several sites they recommend.

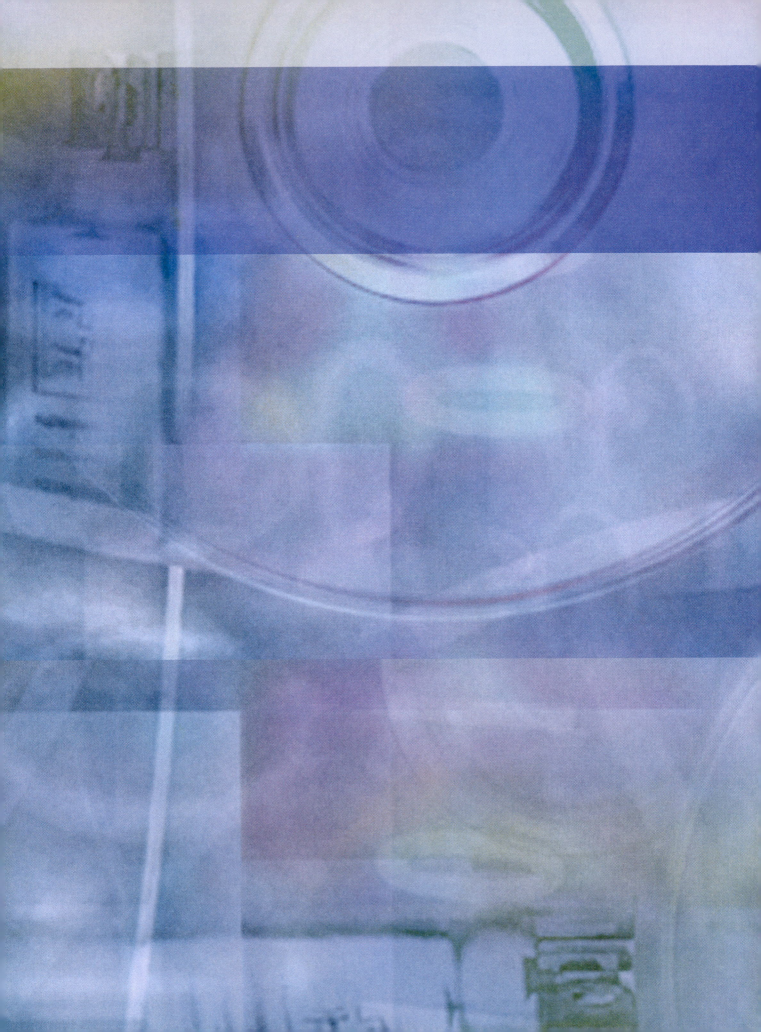

CHAPTER THREE

THE CENTRAL PROCESSING UNIT

What Goes On inside the Computer

LEARNING OBJECTIVES

- Identify the components of the central processing unit and how they work together and interact with memory
- Describe how program instructions are executed by the computer
- Understand how data is represented in the computer
- Describe how the computer finds instructions and data
- Become acquainted with personal computer chips
- Understand the measures of computer processing speed and approaches that increase speed

Mark Ong, who hoped to be a scriptwriter, planned a double major in creative writing and drama. In the summer before he entered college, he took a summer job as an intern editorial assistant, where he first used word processing. He decided that it would be helpful to have a personal computer of his own when he went to college in the fall. But he felt unsure of how to make a purchase. In fact, he felt that he did not even know what questions to ask. He discussed this with an office colleague, who casually noted that any computer setup comes with the "standard stuff"—processor, keyboard, mouse, screen, disk drives—and that all he had to do was go to a computer store and pick one that fit his price range. Mark was not satisfied with this approach, especially in light of the advertisements he had seen in the local

newspaper and in computer magazines.

Most advertisements displayed photos of personal computers, accompanied by cryptic descriptions of the total hardware package. A typical ad was worded this way: Pentium II, 500MHz, 64MB RAM, 512KB cache, 1.44MB diskette drive, 40X CD-ROM, 17.2GB hard drive. The price for this particular machine was pretty hefty—over $2000. Mark noticed that the ads for machines with lower numbers, for example, only 400MHz, also had lower price tags. Similarly, higher numbers meant higher price tags. Although he did recognize the disk drives, he had no idea what the other items were or why the numbers mattered. Clearly, there was more to a purchasing decision than selecting a system with the "standard stuff."

Mark tore out some of the ads and marched to a nearby computer store. After asking a lot of questions, he learned that Pentium II is a microprocessor type, that MHz stands for megahertz and is a measurement of the microprocessor's speed, that RAM

is the computer's memory, that cache is a kind of handy storage place for frequently used data and software instructions, and that GB is an abbreviation for gigabytes, a measurement of storage size for the hard disk. Most importantly, Mark learned that the number variations mattered because they were factors in determining the computer's capacity and speed.

Many buyers do select their personal computer system merely on the basis of a sales pitch and price range. Those people could argue, with some success, that they do not need to know all the computer buzzwords any more than they need to know the technical details of their television sets or sound systems. They know that they do not have to understand a computer's innards to put it to work.

But there are rewards for those who want to dig a little deeper, learn a little more. Although this chapter is not designed to help you purchase a computer, it does provide some background information and gives you the foundation on which future computer knowledge can be built.

The Central Processing Unit

The computer does its primary work in a part of the machine we cannot see, a control center that converts data input to information output. This control center, called the **central processing unit** (CPU), is a highly complex, extensive set of electronic circuitry that executes stored program instructions. All computers, large and small, must have at least one central processing unit. As Figure 1 shows, the central processing unit consists of two parts: the *control unit* and the *arithmetic/logic unit.* Each part has a specific function.

Before examining the control unit and the arithmetic/logic unit in detail, consider data storage and its relationship to the central processing unit. Computers use two types of storage: primary storage and secondary storage. The CPU interacts closely with primary storage, or memory, referring to it for both instructions and data. For this reason this chapter will discuss memory in the context of the central processing unit. Technically, however, memory is not part of the CPU.

Memory holds data only temporarily, at the time the computer is executing a program. Secondary storage holds permanent or semipermanent data on some external medium, such as a disk, until it is needed for processing by the computer. Since the physical attributes of secondary storage devices determine the way data is organized on them, secondary storage and data organization will be discussed together in the chapter on storage.

Now let us consider the components of the central processing unit.

Figure 1 The central processing unit. The two parts of the central processing unit are the control unit and the arithmetic/logic unit. Memory holds data and instructions temporarily while the program they are part of is being executed. The CPU interacts closely with memory, referring to it for both instructions and data.

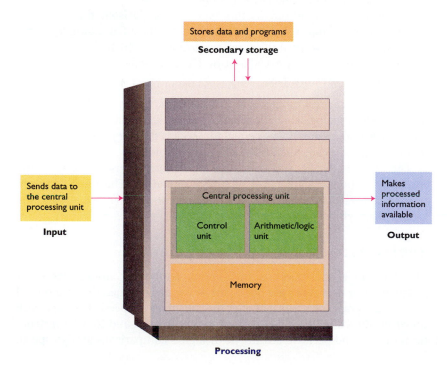

Secondary storage — Stores data and programs

Input — Sends data to the central processing unit

Central processing unit — Control unit / Arithmetic/logic unit

Memory

Output — Makes processed information available

Processing

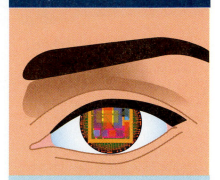

Chips That See

No, we won't be inserting chips into your eyes anytime soon. It's the other way around: The power to "see" is being given to chips. They are called *imaging chips* because they can see, and respond to, images put in front of them. An example on the market today is a machine at the checkout stand that is like the one that scans your groceries, but this one is for your fingertips. In just seconds, a computer with an imaging chip can compare your fingerprint with thousands on file and send a yes or no decision. When used, this technology has eliminated check fraud.

What might an imaging chip watch over? Technical futurists see several possibilities. Chips on airplanes could watch to see that the landing gear descends properly. Imaging chips in cars could detect the size of a passenger and adjust the force of the air bag accordingly. surgeons could plant tiny chips in the chest of a patient to watch over their handiwork in the critical hours following an operation.

InfoBit

Ever wonder why the very highest performing computers seem to cost substantially more than those with more middling performance? One reason is that computer chip manufacturers make a lot more money on high speed processors than on lower speed chips. The Pentium III chip costs Intel about $70 to manufacture and will sell for up to $700. The less powerful Celeron chip still costs about $65 to make but sells for as little as $70.

Are You Being Watched?

The disconcerting answer is—maybe. MHz and GB and the like are obvious measures to judge speed and capacity of a computer you consider purchasing. Less obvious is what else may be lurking in the computer or in the software. Is the CPU a model that has its own unique identifier so that documents or e-mail can be traced back to the owner of that computer? This was the case with Intel's Pentium III. Will your software create a unique identifier hidden in documents created with word processing software? This was once the case with Microsoft Word. Public outcry over the ethics of these privacy invasions appears to have motivated Intel and Microsoft to rethink their covert identification. For now at least, the hidden ID can be made inoperative.

InfoBit

An instruction containing a logical operation is almost always followed by an instruction that branches, or jumps to another part of the program, depending on the result of the comparison performed. This "conditional branching" allows parts of the program to be skipped or repeated, to carry out the logic of its designers.

InfoBit

In the never-ending search for higher performance, manufacturers are placing special high-speed memory on the same silicon chip as the microprocessor itself. Besides increasing speed, such "embedded memory" designs reduce power consumption, increase reliability, and make circuitry more compact.

Learn by Doing

Gather some microprocessor hardware manuals, either in printed form or from the Internet, and ask students to examine the very different ways in which processors may describe a single operation, such as "ADD."

The Control Unit

The **control unit** contains circuitry that uses electrical signals to direct the entire computer system to carry out, or execute, stored program instructions. Like an orchestra leader, the control unit does not execute program instructions; rather, it directs other parts of the system to do so. The control unit must communicate with both the arithmetic/logic unit and memory.

The Arithmetic/Logic Unit

The **arithmetic/logic unit** (ALU) contains the electronic circuitry that executes all arithmetic and logical operations.

The arithmetic/logic unit can perform four kinds of **arithmetic operations,** or mathematical calculations: addition, subtraction, multiplication, and division. As its name implies, the arithmetic/logic unit also performs logical operations. A **logical operation** is usually a comparison. The unit can compare numbers, letters, or special characters. The computer can then take action based on the result of the comparison. This is a very important capability. It is by comparing that a computer is able to tell, for instance, whether there are unfilled seats on airplanes, whether charge-card customers have exceeded their credit limits, and whether one candidate for Congress has more votes than another.

Logical operations can test for three conditions:

- **Equal-to condition.** In a test for this condition, the arithmetic/logic unit compares two values to determine if they are equal. For example, if the number of tickets sold *equals* the number of seats in the auditorium, then the concert is declared sold out.
- **Less-than condition.** To test for this condition, the computer compares values to determine if one is less than another. For example, if the number of speeding tickets on a driver's record is *less than* three, then insurance rates are $425; otherwise, the rates are $500.
- **Greater-than condition.** In this type of comparison, the computer determines if one value is greater than another. For example, if the hours a person worked this week are *greater than* 40, then the program should multiply every extra hour by 1 1/2 times the usual hourly wage to compute overtime pay.

A computer can test for more than one condition. In fact, a logic unit can usually discern six logical relationships: equal to, less than, greater than, less than or equal to, greater than or equal to, and less than or greater than. Note that less than or greater than is the same as *not equal to.*

The symbols that let you define the type of comparison you want the computer to perform are called **relational operators.** The most common relational operators are the equal sign ($=$), the less-than symbol ($<$), and the greater-than symbol ($>$).

Registers: Temporary Storage Areas

Registers are special-purpose, high-speed, temporary storage areas for instructions or data. They are not a part of memory; rather, they are special additional storage locations that offer the advantage of speed. Registers work under the direction of the control unit to accept, hold, and transfer instructions or data and perform arithmetic or logical comparisons at high speed.

The control unit uses a register the way a store owner uses a cash register—as a temporary, convenient place to store what is used in transactions.

Computers usually assign special tasks to registers, including collecting the results of computations, keeping track of where a given instruction or piece of data is stored in memory (each storage location in memory is identified by an address, just as each house on a street has an address), and temporarily holding data taken from or about to be sent to memory.

Consider registers in the context of all the means of storage discussed so far. Registers hold data *immediately* related to the operation being executed. Memory is used to store data that will be used in the *near future*. Secondary storage holds data that may be needed *later* in the same program execution or perhaps at some more remote time in the future.

Now let us look at how a payroll program, for example, uses all three types of storage. Suppose the program calculates the salary of one employee. The data representing the hours worked and the data for the rate of pay are ready in their respective registers. Other data related to the salary calculation—overtime hours, bonuses, deductions, and so forth—is waiting nearby in memory. The data for other employees is available in secondary storage. As the computer finishes calculations for one employee, the data for the next employee is brought from secondary storage into memory and eventually into the registers.

Memory

Memory is also known as **primary storage, primary memory, main storage, internal storage,** and **main memory;** all these terms are used interchangeably by people in computer circles. Manufacturers often use the term **RAM,** which stands for *random-access memory.* Memory is the part of the computer that holds data and instructions for processing. Although closely associated with the central processing unit, memory is separate from it. Memory stores program instructions or data only as long as the program they pertain to is in operation. Keeping these items in memory when the program is not running is not feasible for these reasons:

- Most types of memory store items only while the computer is turned on; data is lost when the machine is turned off.
- If more than one program is running at once (usually the case on large computers and sometimes on small computers), a single program cannot lay exclusive claim to memory.
- There may not be room in memory to hold all the processed data.
- Secondary storage is more cost-effective than memory for storing large amounts of data.

The CPU cannot process data from an input device or disk directly; the data must first be available in memory. How do data and instructions get from an input or storage device into memory? The control unit sends them. Likewise, when the time is right, the control unit sends these items from memory to the arithmetic/logic unit, where an arithmetic operation or logical operation is performed. After being processed, the result is sent to memory, where it is held until it is ready to be released—sent—to an output or storage device.

Learn by Doing

Have students come up with everyday situations that require decisions applying the logical operators and connectives. For example, "If my grade point average IS GREATER THAN 2.99 then I will receive a B," and "if the weather IS NOT EQUAL TO rain, OR brought umbrella IS EQUAL TO true, then I can go out."

InfoBit

One trend in the design of microprocessors to create more and more registers. While early CPUs might have only a single "accumulator" register, a recent chip may have 30 or more general purpose registers.

Critical Thinking

What does the "Random" mean in "Random Access Memory"—RAM? (It does not mean that the memory responds or is accessed "at random." In some ways "random" is a misnomer—"direct" would be a better synonym. The term is meant to imply that—unlike sequential storage media—the CPU can access any location directly without having to read through any preceding or succeeding locations.)

The chief characteristic of memory is that it allows very fast access to instructions and data, no matter where the items are within it. A discussion of the physical components of memory—memory chips—appears later in this chapter.

How the CPU Executes Program Instructions

Let us examine the way the central processing unit, in association with memory, executes a computer program. We will be looking at how just one instruction in the program is executed. In fact, most computers today can execute only one instruction at a time, though they execute it very quickly. Many personal computers can execute instructions in less than one-millionth of a second, whereas those speed demons known as supercomputers can execute instructions in less than one-trillionth of a second.

Before an instruction can be executed, program instructions and data must be placed into memory from an input device or a secondary storage device. (The process is further complicated by the fact that, as noted earlier, the data will probably make a temporary stop in a register.) As Figure 2 shows, once the necessary data and instruction are in memory, the central processing unit performs the following four steps for each instruction:

1. The control unit *fetches* (gets) the instruction from memory.
2. The control unit *decodes* the instruction (decides what it means) and directs that the necessary data be moved from memory to the arithmetic/

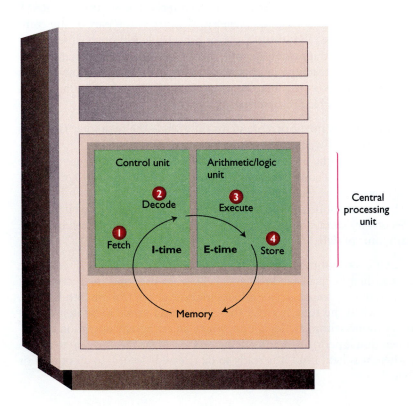

Figure 2 The machine cycle. Program instructions and data are brought into memory from an external source, either an input device or a secondary storage medium. The machine cycle executes instructions one at a time, as described in the text.

MAKING THE RIGHT CONNECTIONS
A TECHIE'S DREAM SUPERPHONE

A phone is just a phone. It may be a cordless phone, a cellular phone, or a phone hooked up to a computer, but it is still just a phone. Right? Don't bet on it. That handy portable device is about to become—*super-phone.*

Giving brains—microchips—to mobile phones lets them receive e-mail, surf the Internet, and even pay the bills. Now give that little phone a different look, say, a small vertical screen, and you are ready for video phone, the

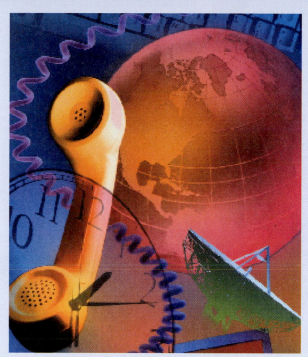

ability to see the person to whom you are speaking. Another type of phone lives a double life: phone on one side and, flipped over, handheld computer on the other side.

The mobile phone is becoming an everyday appliance. In fact, to some it is even a fashion statement, available in a rainbow of colors. But some parents see a more serious purpose; they give each child a portable phone that can call only one number—home.

logic unit. These first two steps together are called instruction time, or **I-time.**

3. The arithmetic/logic unit *executes* the arithmetic or logical instruction. That is, the ALU is given control and performs the actual operation on the data.

4. The arithmetic/logic unit *stores* the result of this operation in memory or in a register. Steps 3 and 4 together are called execution time, or **E-time.**

The control unit eventually directs memory to send the result to an output device or a secondary storage device. The combination of I-time and E-time is called the **machine cycle.** Figure 3 shows an instruction going through the machine cycle.

Each central processing unit has an internal **clock** that produces pulses at a fixed rate to synchronize all computer operations. A single machine-cycle instruction may be made up of a substantial number of subinstructions, each of which must take at least one clock cycle. Each type of central processing unit is designed to understand a specific group of instructions—such as ADD or MOVE—called the **instruction set.** Just as there are many different languages that people understand, so too are there many different instruction sets that different types of CPUs understand.

Figure 3 The machine cycle in action.
Suppose a program must find the average of five test scores. To do this, it must total the five scores and then divide the result by 5. The program would begin by setting the total to 0; it then would add each of the five numbers, one at a time, to the total. Suppose the scores are 88, 76, 91, 83, and 87. In this figure the total has been set to 0, and then 88, the first test score, has been added to it. Now examine the machine cycle as it adds the next number, 76, to the total. Follow the four steps in the machine cycle. (1) *Fetch:* The control unit fetches the instruction from memory. (2) *Decode:* The control unit decodes the instruction. It determines that addition must take place and gives instructions for the next number (76) to be placed in a register for this purpose. The total so far (88) is already in a register. (3) *Execute:* The ALU does the addition, increasing the total to 164. (4) *Store:* In this case the ALU stores the new total in the register instead of in memory, since more numbers still need to be added to it. When the new total (164) is placed in the register, it displaces the old total (88).

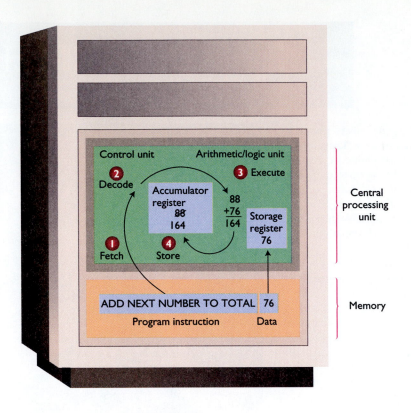

Storage Locations and Addresses: How the Control Unit Finds Instructions and Data

It is one thing to have instructions and data somewhere in memory and quite another for the control unit to be able to find them. How does it do this?

The location in memory for each instruction and each piece of data is identified by an **address.** That is, each location has an address number, like the mailboxes in front of an apartment house. And, like the mailboxes, the address numbers of the locations remain the same, but the contents (instructions and data) of the locations may change. That is, new instructions or new data may be placed in the locations when the old contents no longer need to be stored in memory. Unlike a mailbox, however, a memory location can hold only a fixed amount of data; it can hold only one number or one word.

Figure 4 shows how a program manipulates data in memory. A payroll program, for example, may give instructions to put the rate of pay in location 3 and the number of hours worked in location 6. To compute the employee's salary, then, instructions tell the computer to multiply the data in location 3 by the data in location 6 and move the result to location 8. The choice of locations is arbitrary—any locations that are not already spoken

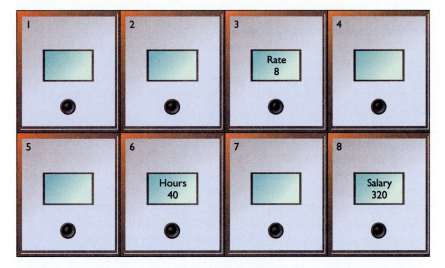

Figure 4 Addresses are like mailboxes. The addresses of memory locations are like the identifying numbers on apartment-house mailboxes. Suppose you want to compute someone's salary as the number of hours multiplied by the rate of pay. Rate ($8) goes in memory location 3, hours (40) in location 6, and the computed salary ($8 x 40 hours, or $320) in location 8. Thus, the addresses are 3, 6, and 8, but the contents are $8, 40, and $320, respectively. Note that the program instructions are to multiply the contents of location 3 by the contents of location 6 and move the result to location 8. (A computer language used by a programmer would use some kind of symbolic name for each location, such as Rate or Pay-Rate instead of the number 3.) The data items are the actual contents—what is stored in each location.

Critical Thinking

Why does base 10—the decimal system—seem so natural for humans? (One reason suggested by anthropologists is that we learned to count using our ten fingers. The ancient Mayans had a base 20 system, and it is believed that they counted on their fingers and on their toes).

InfoBit

In most computer systems, electricity turned on to a level between 2 1/2 and 5 volts represents a binary 1, while electricity turned off to a level less than about 1/2 volt stands for a binary 0. For comparison, a typical two-cell flashlight produces about 3 volts—just enough voltage to stand for a digital 1.

for can be used. Programmers using programming languages, however, do not have to worry about the actual address numbers, because each data address is referred to by a name. The name is called a **symbolic address**. In this example, the symbolic address names are Rate, Hours, and Salary.

Data Representation: On/Off

We are accustomed to thinking of computers as complex mechanisms, but the fact is that these machines basically know only two things: on and off. This two-state on/off system is called a **binary system**. Using the two states—which can be represented by electricity turned on or off—the computer can construct sophisticated ways of representing data.

Let us look at one way the two states can be used to represent data. Whereas the decimal number system has a base of 10 (with the ten digits 0, 1, 2, 3, 4, 5, 6, 7, 8, and 9), the binary system has a base of 2. This means it contains only two digits, 0 and 1, which correspond to the two states off and on. Combinations of 0s and 1s represent larger numbers (Figure 5).

Bits, Bytes, and Words

Each 0 or 1 in the binary system is called a **bit** (for *bi*nary digi*t*). The bit is the basic unit for storing data in computer memory—0 means off, 1 means

BINARY EQUIVALENT OF DECIMAL NUMBERS 0–15	
Decimal	**Binary**
0	0000
1	0001
2	0010
3	0011
4	0100
5	0101
6	0110
7	0111
8	1000
9	1001
10	1010
11	1011
12	1100
13	1101
14	1110
15	1111

Figure 5 Decimal and binary equivalents. Seeing numbers from different systems side by side clarifies the patterns of progression. The two numbers in each row have the same value; they are simply expressed differently in different number systems.

Character	ASCII–8
A	0100 0001
B	0100 0010
C	0100 0011
D	0100 0100
E	0100 0101
F	0100 0110
G	0100 0111
H	0100 1000
I	0100 1001
J	0100 1010
K	0100 1011
L	0100 1100
M	0100 1101
N	0100 1110
O	0100 1111
P	0101 0000
Q	0101 0001
R	0101 0010
S	0101 0011
T	0101 0100
U	0101 0101
V	0101 0110
W	0101 0111
X	0101 1000
Y	0101 1001
Z	0101 1010
0	0011 0000
1	0011 0001
2	0011 0010
3	0011 0011
4	0011 0100
5	0011 0101
6	0011 0110
7	0011 0111
8	0011 1000
9	0011 1001

(a)

Letter	ASCII–8
K	0100 1011
I	0100 1001
L	0100 1100
O	0100 1111
B	0100 0010
Y	0101 1001
T	0101 0100
E	0100 0101

(b)

Figure 6 The ASCII-8 code. (a) Shown are the ASCII-8 binary representations for letters and digits. This is not the complete code; there are many characters missing, such as lowercase letters and punctuation marks. The binary representation is in two columns to improve readability. (b) The ASCII-8 representation for the word KILOBYTE.

on. Notice that since a bit is always either on or off, a bit in computer memory is always storing some kind of data.

Since single bits by themselves cannot store all the numbers, letters, and special characters (such as $ and ?) that a computer must process, the bits are put together in a group called a **byte** (pronounced "bite"). There are usually 8 bits in a byte. Each byte usually represents one **character** of data—a letter, digit, or special character.

Computer manufacturers express the capacity of memory and storage in terms of the number of bytes they can hold. The number of bytes can be expressed as **kilobytes.** *Kilo* represents 2 to the tenth power (2^{10}), or 1024. *Kilobyte* is abbreviated **KB,** or simply **K.** A kilobyte is 1024 bytes. In an older computer, a memory of 640K means the computer can store 640×1024, or 655,360 bytes. Memory capacity is usually expressed in terms of **megabytes** (1024×1024 bytes). One megabyte, abbreviated **MB,** means roughly one million bytes. Personal computer memory may have 64MB and more. With secondary storage devices, manufacturers sometimes express capacity in terms of **gigabytes** (abbreviated **GB**)—billions of bytes. Also, mainframe memories can hold gigabytes.

A computer **word,** typically the size of a register, is defined as the number of bits that constitute a common unit of data, as defined by the computer system. The length of a word varies by computer. Generally, the larger the word, the more powerful the computer. There was a time when word size alone could classify a computer. Word lengths have varied from 8 bits for very early personal computers to 32 or 64 bits for most personal computers today.

Coding Schemes

As noted, a byte—a collection of bits—can represent a character of data. But just what particular set of bits is equivalent to which character? In theory we could each make up our own definitions, declaring certain bit patterns to represent certain characters. Needless to say, this would be about as practical as each person speaking his or her own special language. Since we need to communicate with the computer and with each other, it is appropriate that we use a common scheme for data representation. That is, there must be agreement on which groups of bits represent which characters.

The code called **ASCII** (pronounced "AS key"), which stands for American Standard Code for Information Interchange, uses 7 bits for each character. Since there are exactly 128 unique combinations of 7 bits, this 7-bit code can represent only 128 characters. A more common version is ASCII-8, also called extended ASCII, which uses 8 bits per character and can represent 256 different characters. For example, the letter A is represented by 01000001. The ASCII representation has been adopted as a standard by the U.S. government and is found in a variety of computers, particularly personal computers. Figure 6 shows part of the ASCII-8 code.

Personal Computer Chips

The chips discussed here would be attached to the **motherboard,** the flat board within the personal computer housing that holds the computer circuitry (Figure 7). The motherboard, also called the main circuit board, is a

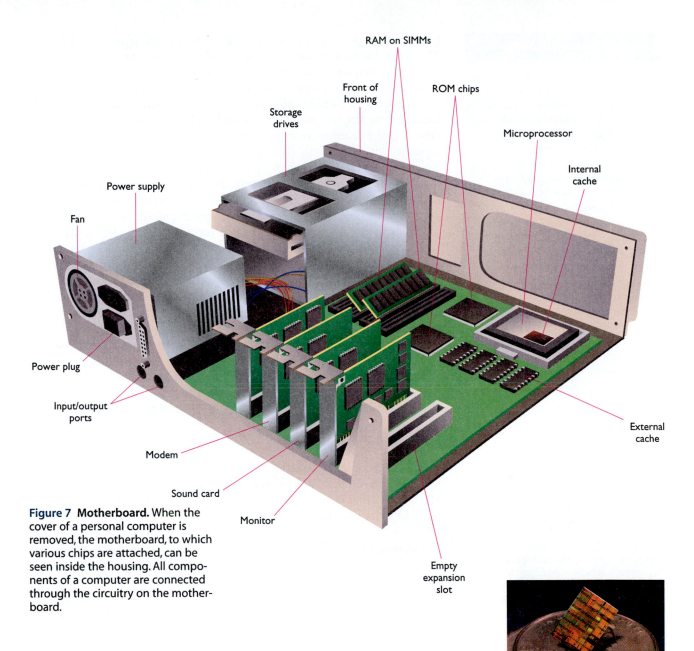

RAM on SIMMs

Front of
housing

ROM chips

Storage
drives

Microprocessor

Internal
cache

Power supply

Fan

Power plug

Input/output
ports

Modem

Sound card

Monitor

Empty
expansion
slot

External
cache

Figure 7 Motherboard. When the cover of a personal computer is removed, the motherboard, to which various chips are attached, can be seen inside the housing. All components of a computer are connected through the circuitry on the motherboard.

mass of chips and connections that organize the computer's activities. The motherboard also holds **expansion slots** into which other circuit boards can be inserted to link peripheral devices to the processor. It is the central processing unit, the microprocessor, that is the most important component of the motherboard.

Microprocessors

A miniaturized central processing unit can be etched on a chip, a tiny square of silicon, hence the term *computer on a chip.* A central processing unit, or processor, on a chip is a **microprocessor** (Figure 8), or **microchip** for short. A microprocessor may be called a **logic chip** when it is used to control specialized devices (such as the fuel system of a car). Microprocessors contain tiny **transistors,** electronic switches that may or may not allow current to pass through. If current passes through, the switch is on, representing the 1

Figure 8 A microprocessor chip. This Pentium chip is shown on a stack of pennies to give perspective to its small size.

InfoBit

What hazards do RAM chips face? A surprising one is naturally occurring radiation. Because the 1's and 0's that make up the stored data are actually represented as tiny electrical charges, passing radioactive particles from sources such as cosmic rays can disturb the stored information, turning a 1 into a 0, or vice versa, and wreaking havoc with the stored data. On earth this is an unlikely occurrence, but in space—where radiation levels are much higher—special RAM chips called "radiation-hardened" must be used to prevent memory errors from causing CPU "crashes."

InfoBit

The key to making microprocessors faster is to make their transistors smaller. As an example, the very earliest microprocessors used a geometry of 10 microns. Each transistor was then about 10 millionths of a meter across. Even though 10 microns is small, the recent Pentium Pro chip was produced in a geometry under one quarter of a micron—some 40 times smaller.

bit. If current does not pass through, the switch is off, representing a 0 bit. Thus combinations of transistors can stand for combinations of bits, which, as noted earlier, represent digits, letters, and special characters.

The transistor is the basic building block of the microprocessor. Today's microprocessors contain millions of transistors. Microprocessors usually include these key components: a control unit and an arithmetic/logic unit (the central processing unit), registers, and a clock. (Clocks are often on a separate chip in personal computers.) Notably missing is memory, which usually comes on its own chips.

How much smaller? How much cheaper? How much faster? Three decades of extraordinary advances in technology have packed increasingly greater power onto increasingly smaller chips. Engineers can now imprint as much circuitry on a single chip as filled room-size computers in the early days of computing. But are engineers approaching the limits of smallness? Current development efforts focus on a three-dimensional chip built in layers. Chip capacities in the future do seem almost limitless.

In addition to factors such as increased speed, microprocessors have historically increased their power by swallowing up functions previously accomplished by other hardware. For example, in the 1980s, chipmaker Intel incorporated a math coprocessor, a separate chip favored by engineers, into its microprocessor. Currently, Intel's Pentium chip includes multimedia instructions that boost a computer's ability to produce graphics, video, and sound. The more functions that are combined on a microprocessor, the faster the computer runs, the cheaper it is to make, and the more reliable it is.

Memory Components

The first part of this chapter described the central processing unit and how it works with memory. Next is an examination of the memory components. Historically, memory components have evolved from primitive vacuum tubes to today's modern semiconductors.

Semiconductor Memory   Most modern computers use semiconductor memory because it has several advantages: reliability, compactness, low cost, and lower power usage. Since semiconductor memory can be mass-produced economically, the cost of memory has been considerably reduced. Chip prices have fallen and risen and fallen again—all on the basis of a variety of economic and political factors—but they remain a bargain. Semiconductor memory is **volatile,** that is, it requires continuous electric current to represent data. If the current is interrupted, the data is lost.

Semiconductor memory is made up of thousands of very small circuits—pathways for electric currents—on a silicon chip. A chip is described as **monolithic** because all the circuits on a single chip together constitute an inseparable unit of storage. Each circuit etched on a chip can be in one of two states: either conducting an electric current or not—on or off. The two states can be used to represent the binary digits 1 and 0. As noted earlier, these digits can be combined to represent characters, thus making the memory chip a storage bin for data and instructions.

One important type of semiconductor design is called **complementary metal oxide semiconductor (CMOS).** This design is noted for using relatively little electricity. This makes it especially useful for computers requiring low power consumption, such as portable computers. In personal computers, one use for CMOS is CMOS RAM; this is a tiny 64-bit region that, thanks to battery power, retains data when the computer is shut off. Thus CMOS RAM can be used to store information your computer needs when it boots up, such as time and date.

RAM and ROM   Memory keeps the instructions and data for whatever programs you happen to be using at the moment. Memory is referred to as **RAM—random-access memory**—in this discussion, both to emphasize its random function and to distinguish it from ROM. Data in memory can be accessed randomly, no matter where it is, in an easy and speedy manner. RAM is usually volatile; as noted above, this means that its contents are lost once the power is shut off. RAM can be erased or written over at will by the computer software.

In recent years the amount of RAM storage in a personal computer has increased dramatically. An early personal computer, for example, was advertised with "a full 4K RAM." Now 64MB RAM or even more is common. More memory has become a necessity because sophisticated personal computer software requires significant amounts of memory. You can augment your personal computer's RAM by buying extra memory chips to install in your memory board or by purchasing a **single in-line memory module** (**SIMM**), a board that contains memory chips. The SIMM board plugs into sockets on the computer's motherboard, which is more convenient than attaching individual chips. In general, the more memory your computer has, the more (and bigger) tasks the computer can do.

RAM can be of two types: static RAM (**SRAM**)—pronounced "s-ram"—and dynamic RAM (**DRAM**), pronounced "d-ram." DRAM must be constantly refreshed (recharged) by the central processing unit or it will lose its contents, hence the name dynamic. Static RAM will retain its contents without intervention from the CPU. Although SRAM is faster, DRAM is used in most personal computer memory because of its size and cost advantages (Figure 9).

Read-only memory (ROM) contains programs and data that are permanently recorded into this type of memory at the factory; they can be read and used, but they cannot be changed by the user. For example, a personal computer probably has a program for calculating square roots in ROM. ROM is nonvolatile—its contents do not disappear when the power is turned off.

Using specialized tools called **ROM burners**, the instructions within some ROM chips can be changed. These chips are known as **PROM** chips, or **programmable read-only memory chips**. There are other variations on ROM chips, depending on the methods used to alter them. Programming and altering ROM chips is the province of the computer engineer.

Figure 9   DRAM chip. This DRAM chip is smaller than a button.

InfoBit

RAM memory chips are produced using the same technology of etched silicon as microprocessors, and contain a comparable number of transistors. Why then are RAM chips so much cheaper than processor chips? One reason is that RAM is made up of a series of simple, repeated structures, while processors have the additional complexity of individually-located and irregularly interconnected transistors.

InfoBit

Anyone who has played a cartridge-based video game has used software that was stored in a ROM chip.

Speed and Power

The characteristic of speed is universally associated with computers. Power is a derivative of speed as well as of other factors such as memory size. What makes a computer fast? Or, more to the point, what makes one computer faster than another? Several factors are involved, including microprocessor speed, bus line size, and the availability of cache. A user who is concerned about speed will want to address all of these. More sophisticated approaches to speed include flash memory, RISC computers, and parallel processing. A discussion of each of these factors follows.

Critical Thinking

What software on a personal computer must reside in ROM? (Software for "booting," that is, software that starts the computer running when it is turned on. Since the contents of RAM are volatile it cannot contain boot programs, and some software must be loaded initially to tell the CPU how to access secondary storage. All personal computers contain some ROM for this purpose.)

GETTING PRACTICAL

SHOULD YOU BUILD YOUR OWN COMPUTER?

Building your own computer may seem like a fanciful idea indeed, especially if you have not even decided whether to buy a computer that comes prepackaged. However, the option of building a computer, once the territory of hard-core techies, is now a possibility for mainstream consumers. Some people like the idea of the adventure, and they also like the cost savings.

What skills do you need? And what equipment? Surprisingly, very little of either. You will not need to do anything as dramatic as welding. In truth, your task is really to acquire and then assemble the various components, screwing and snapping them into place, rather like an electronic Lego set.

Let us begin with the shopping list. You will need a motherboard, microprocessor, RAM, case with power supply, diskette drive, hard drive, video card, monitor, keyboard, and mouse. You will likely also want a modem, CD-ROM drive, sound card, and speakers. Now the question becomes which ones. A visit to your local electronics store can be a high-tech reconnaissance mission, in which you can gather information from both sales people and fellow customers. Be sure to check the store's return policy; you should be able to return any component unconditionally within a certain time frame. If reduced personal service is an acceptable trade-off for lower costs, you may prefer to buy from a mail-order house or an Internet site; check the advertising section of any major computer magazine. But do buy the major components from the same company to cut down on compatibility problems.

We do not have the space here to describe the components in detail, much less the assembly process. Detailed instructions, which you should read carefully, accompany each software item. You can get further advice from magazines, perhaps a local computer club, and the Internet.

We mentioned cost savings, but most of the savings are not up front. The total component cost will not be significantly less than what you would pay for a fully assembled computer. The real savings come in the future when you are able to upgrade your computer on your own, adding more memory, a new microprocessor, a new hard drive, or whatever, rather than buying a new computer.

Building a computer can be a satisfying experience, but it is not for everyone. Generally speaking, if you have any doubts, don't do it.

Computer Processing Speeds

Although all computers are fast, there is a wide diversity of computer speeds. The execution of an instruction on a very slow (old) computer may be measured in less than a **millisecond,** which is one-thousandth of a second, or perhaps in **microseconds,** each of which is one-millionth of a second. Modern computers have reached the **nanosecond** range—one-billionth of a second. Still to be broken is the **picosecond** barrier—one-trillionth of a second.

Microprocessor speeds are usually expressed in **megahertz (MHz),** millions of machine cycles per second. Thus, a personal computer listed at 500MHz has a processor capable of handling 500 million machine cycles per second. A top-speed personal computer can be much faster, with some even approaching GHz (gigahertz—billions of machine cycles per second) speeds.

Another measure of computer speed is **MIPS,** which stands for *one million instructions per second.* For example, a computer with speed of 0.5 MIPS can execute 500,000 instructions per second. High-speed personal computers can perform at 100 MIPS and higher. MIPS is often a more accurate measure than clock speed, because some computers can use each tick of the clock more efficiently than others. A third measure of speed is the **megaflop,** which stands for *one million floating-point operations per second.* It measures the ability of the computer to perform complex mathematical operations.

Bus Lines

As is so often the case, the computer term *bus* is borrowed from its common meaning—a mode of transportation. A **bus line** is a set of parallel electrical paths, usually copper tracing on the surface of the motherboard, that internally transports data from one place to another within the computer system. The amount of data that can be carried at one time is called the *bus width,* which indicates the number of electrical paths. The greater the width, the more data can be carried at a time. A larger bus size means:

- The computer can transfer more data at a time, making the computer faster.
- The computer can reference larger memory address numbers, allowing more memory.
- The computer can support a greater number and variety of instructions.

In general, the larger the word size or bus width, the more powerful the computer.

Cache

A **cache** (pronounced "cash") is a relatively small block of very fast memory designed for the specific purpose of speeding up the internal transfer of data and software instructions. Think of cache as a selective memory: The data and instructions stored in cache are those that are most recently or most frequently used. When the processor first requests data or instructions, these must be retrieved from main memory, which delivers at a pace that is relatively slow compared with the speed of the microprocessor. As they are retrieved, those same data or instructions are stored in cache. The next time the microprocessor needs data or instructions, it looks first in cache; if the needed items can be found there, they can be transferred at a rate that far exceeds a trip from main memory. Of course, cache is not big enough to hold everything, so the wanted data or instructions may not be there. But there is a good chance that frequently used items will be in cache. Thus, since the most frequently used data and instructions are kept in a handy place, the net result is an improvement in processing speed.

Caching has become such a vital technique that some newer microprocessors offer **internal cache** built right into the processor's design. This is the fastest sort, since it is right there for the microprocessor to access. However, cache memory takes up precious space on the microprocessor, so a processor would probably have only about 8KB of on-board cache. Most

Critical Thinking

What difficulties do you think manufacturers face in attempting to test microprocessor chips? (One problem is speed—to test a 500 MHz chip requires a test machine capable of running considerably faster than 500 MHz, and the immense number of possible combinations. A processor adding together two 32 bit numbers can get any of 2^{64} results. Obviously, exhaustive testing is impractical).

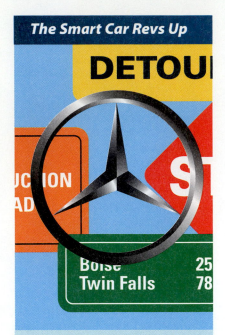

The Smart Car Revs Up

You may have heard of microprocessors controlling fuel injection and all kinds of other things under the hood, but that is old news. Starting with luxury models, new cars have on-board computers that can supply driving directions and warn of upcoming traffic conditions and road problems. It is even possible for the car's computer to respond to voice commands to change the radio channel or send a fax, all without fumbling with dials or the car phone.

But what is being done about that worst of problems, a breakdown on the freeway? In the very near future, experts in a remote monitoring center may be able to transmit corrective software to fix the problem on the spot.

computers include **external cache** on separate chips, probably 512KB. Obviously, the more cache a computer has, the more likely it is to have the instructions or data the processor needs in the cache.

Flash Memory

We have stated that memory is volatile—that it disappears when the power is turned off—hence the need for secondary storage to keep data on a more permanent basis. A long-standing speed problem has been the slow rate at which data is accessed from a secondary storage device such as a disk, a rate significantly slower than internal computer speeds. It seemed unimaginable that data might someday be stored on nonvolatile memory chips—nonvolatile RAM—close at hand. A breakthrough has emerged in the form of nonvolatile **flash memory.** Flash chips are currently being used in cellular phones and cockpit flight recorders, and they are replacing disks in some handheld computers.

Flash memory chips are being produced in credit card–like packages, which are smaller than a disk drive and require only half the power; that is why they are being used in notebook computers and the handheld personal digital assistants.

RISC Technology: Less Is More

It flies in the face of computer tradition: Instead of reaching for more variety, more power, more everything-for-everyone, proponents of **RISCs—reduced instruction set computers**—suggest that we could get by with a little less. In fact, reduced instruction set computers offer only a small subset of instructions; the absence of bells and whistles increases speed. So there is a back-to-basics movement in computer design.

RISC supporters say that on conventional computers (called **CISCs,** or **complex instruction set computers**), a hefty chunk of the instruction set is rarely used. Those underused instructions, they note, are an impediment to speedy performance. RISC computers, with their stripped-down instruction sets, zip through programs like racing cars—at speeds 4 to 10 times those of CISC computers. This is heady stuff for the merchants of speed who want to attract customers by offering more speed for the money.

Parallel Processing

The ultimate speed solution is **parallel processing,** a method of using several processors at the same time. Consider the description of computer processing you have seen so far in this chapter: The processor gets an instruction from memory, acts on it, returns processed data to memory, and then repeats the process. This is conventional **serial processing,** the execution of one instruction at a time. A variation on this approach is **pipelining,** in which an instruction's actions—fetch, decode, execute, store—need not be complete before the next instruction is begun. For example, once fetch is complete for an instruction and it moves to decode, fetch is begun for the next instruction.

The problem with the conventional computer is that the single electronic pathway, the bus line, acts like a bottleneck. The computer has a one-track mind because it is restricted to handling one piece of data at a time. For many applications, such as simulating the airflow around an entire airplane in flight, this is an exceedingly inefficient procedure. A better solution? Many

2000 and Beyond

SICK COWS AND TALKING TOASTERS

The ubiquitous microchip, already in our cars and refrigerators, is moving into new territory. No need, for example, for a farmer to worry if Bossie, out there alone in the field, might take sick. A chip, packaged with a tiny battery and sensor, sits in one of her four stomachs, and alerts the farmer within half an hour if there is a problem. What could possibly be next? What indeed. How about a toaster that talks to you? "Toast is done." But talking appliances are child's play

compared with what is coming next.

Sunglasses will answer when you call out to find them. Grocery packages will open themselves when you tell them and also update your shopping list.

The ultimate in hidden chips might be the one in

the heel of your shoe, bearing your personal information. If you should happen to meet a person similarly equipped, a simple handshake will cause a swap of phone numbers and other information via a low-level current that races along your skin's surface, then into your partner's; data is thus transferred from one wired heel into another. If romance is in the air, consider the chip-powered diamond brooch from jeweler Henry Winston: Light flashes from the brooch with each beat of the wearer's heart.

processors, each with its own memory unit, working at the same time: parallel processing. Some parallel processors are capable of operating in terms of **teraflops**—that is, trillions of floating-point instructions per second. Recall, for comparison, that a megaflop is a mere one million floating-point operations per second.

A number of parallel processors are being built and sold commercially. Parallel processing has, until recently, been strictly the territory of large computers. However, some high-end personal computer chips now use parallel processing.

▲

The future holds some exciting possibilities for computer chips. One day we may see computers that operate using light (photonics) rather than electricity (electronics) to control their operation. Light travels faster and is less likely to be disrupted by electrical interference. And would you believe that someday computers might actually be grown as biological cultures? So-called biochips may replace today's silicon chip. As research continues, so will the surprises.

Whatever the design and processing strategy of a computer, its goal is the same: to turn raw input into useful output. Input and output are the topics of the next chapter.

Critical Thinking

RISC computers were designed by removing instructions from the CPU that were little used or unnecessary. Why would computer engineers persist in putting in instructions that are unnecessary? (There are several possible reasons: hardware is often designed long before any software for it is written, so computer engineers cannot know for certain what instructions programmers and applications will really use. Also, once a chip is produced containing some set of instructions, designers will be very reluctant to remove any instructions from future versions, because that has the potential to make lots of programs obsolete and would ruin "backward compatibility.")

Summary and Key Terms

- The **central processing unit** (**CPU**) is a complex set of electronic circuitry that executes program instructions; it consists of a control unit and an arithmetic/logic unit.

- The central processing unit interacts closely with primary storage, or memory. Memory provides temporary storage of data while the computer is executing the program. Secondary storage holds the data that is permanent or semipermanent.

- The **control unit** of the central processing unit coordinates execution of the program instructions by communicating with the arithmetic/logic unit and memory—the parts of the system that actually execute the program.

- The **arithmetic/logic unit** (**ALU**) contains circuitry that executes the arithmetic and logical operations. The unit can perform four **arithmetic operations**: addition, subtraction, multiplication, and division. Its **logical operations** usually involve making comparisons that test for three conditions: the **equal-to condition,** the **less-than condition,** and the **greater-than condition.** The computer can test for more than one condition at once, so it can discern three other conditions as well: less than or equal to, greater than or equal to, and less than or greater than.

- Symbols called **relational operators** ($=$, $<$, $>$) can define the comparison to perform.

- **Registers** are special-purpose, high-speed areas for temporary data storage.

- **Memory** is the part of the computer that temporarily holds data and instructions before and after they are processed by the arithmetic/logic unit. Memory is also known as **primary storage, primary memory, main storage, internal storage,** and **main memory.** Manufacturers often use the term **RAM,** which stands for *random-access memory.*

- The central processing unit follows four main steps when executing an instruction: It (1) fetches—gets—the instruction from memory, (2) decodes the instruction and gives instructions for the transfer of appropriate data from memory to the ALU, (3) directs the ALU to perform the actual operation on the data, and (4) directs the ALU to store the result of the operation in memory or a register. The first two steps are called **I-time** (instruction time), and the last two steps are called **E-time** (execution time).

- A **machine cycle** is the combination of I-time and E-time. The internal **clock** of the central processing unit produces pulses at a fixed rate to synchronize computer operations. Each central processing unit has a set of commands it can understand called the **instruction set.**

- The location in memory for each instruction and each piece of data is identified by an **address.** Address numbers remain the same, but the contents of the locations change. A meaningful name given to a memory address is called a **symbolic address.**

- Since a computer can recognize only whether electricity is on or off, data is represented by an on/off **binary system,** represented by the digits 1 and 0.

- Each 0 or 1 in the binary system is called a **bit** (binary digit). A group of bits (usually 8 bits) is called a **byte,** which usually represents one **character** of data, such as a letter, digit, or special character. Memory capacity was once expressed in **kilobytes** (**KB** or **K**). One kilobyte equals 1024 bytes. A **megabyte** (**MB**), about one million bytes, is used today to express memory size. A **gigabyte** (**GB**) equals about one billion bytes.

- A computer **word** is the number of bits that make up a unit of data, as defined by the computer system.

- A common coding scheme for representing characters is **ASCII** (American Standard Code for Information Interchange), which uses 7-bit characters. A variation of the code, called ASCII-8, uses 8 bits per character.

■ The **motherboard,** the flat board within the personal computer housing, holds the chips and circuitry that organize the computer's activities. The motherboard also holds **expansion slots** into which other circuit boards can be inserted to link peripheral devices to the processor.

■ A central processing unit, or processor, on a chip is a **microprocessor,** or **microchip** for short. A microprocessor may be called a **logic chip** when it is used to control specialized devices. Microprocessors contain tiny **transistors,** electronic switches that may or may not allow current to pass through, representing a 1 or 0 bit, respectively.

■ The more functions that are combined on a microprocessor, the faster the computer runs, the cheaper it is to make, and the more reliable it is.

■ **Semiconductor memory,** thousands of very small circuits on a silicon chip, is **volatile.** A chip is described as **monolithic** because the circuits on a single chip constitute an inseparable unit of storage.

■ An important type of semiconductor design is called **complementary metal oxide semiconductor (CMOS);** it is noted for using little electricity, making it especially useful for computers requiring low power consumption, such as portable computers.

■ **Random-access memory (RAM)** keeps the instructions and data for whatever programs you happen to be using at the moment.

■ A **single in-line memory module (SIMM)** is a plug-in board that contains memory chips.

■ RAM is often divided into two types: static RAM **(SRAM),** which is faster, and dynamic RAM **(DRAM),** which is smaller and less expensive.

■ **Read-only memory (ROM)** contains programs and data that are permanently recorded into this type of memory at the factory; they can be read and used, but they cannot be changed by the user. ROM is nonvolatile. The instructions within some ROM chips can be changed using **ROM burners;** these chips are known as **PROM** chips, or **programmable read-only memory chips.**

■ Computer instruction speeds fall into various ranges, from a **millisecond,** which is one-thousandth of a second; to a **microsecond,** one-millionth of a second (for old computers); to a **nanosecond,** one-billionth of a second. Still to be achieved is the **picosecond** range—one-trillionth of a second.

■ Microprocessor speeds are usually expressed in **megahertz (MHz),** millions of machine cycles per second. Another measure of computer speed is **MIPS,** which stands for one million instructions per second. A third measure is the **megaflop,** which stands for one million floating-point operations per second.

■ A **bus line** is a set of parallel data paths that transports data from one place to another internally within the computer system. The amount of data that can be carried at one time is called the *bus width.*

■ A **cache** is a relatively small amount of very fast memory that stores data and instructions that are used frequently, resulting in an improved processing speed. **Internal cache,** the fastest kind, refers to cache built right into the processor's design. Most computers include **external cache** on separate chips.

■ The emerging technology of **flash memory** will provide memory chips that are nonvolatile.

■ RISCs—**reduced instruction set computers**—are fast because they use only a small subset of instructions. Conventional computers, called **CISCs,** or **complex instruction set computers,** include many instructions that are rarely used.

■ Conventional **serial processing** uses a single processor and can handle just one instruction at a time. **Pipelining** means that an instruction's actions—fetch, decode, execute, store—need not be complete before the next instruction is begun. **Parallel processing** uses several processors in the same computer at the same time. Some parallel processors are capable of operating in terms of **teraflops**—that is, trillions of floating-point instructions per second.

Discussion Questions

1. Why is writing instructions for a computer more difficult than writing instructions for a person?

2. Do you think there is a continuing need to increase computer speed? Can you think of examples in which more speed would be desirable?

3. It will soon be possible to have microchips implanted in our bodies to monitor or improve our physical conditions. Do you think this is a good or bad idea?

Student Study Guide

Multiple Choice

1. The electrical circuitry that executes program instructions is the
   a. register
   b. operator
   c. central processing unit
   d. bus line

2. The entire computer system is coordinated by
   a. the ALU
   b. the control unit
   c. registers
   d. arithmetic operators

3. A bus line consists of
   a. registers
   b. parallel data paths
   c. megabytes
   d. machine cycles

4. Equal to, less than, and greater than are examples of
   a. logical operations
   b. subtraction operations
   c. locations
   d. arithmetic

5. The primary storage unit is also known as
   a. a register
   b. mass storage
   c. secondary storage
   d. memory

6. Data and instructions are put into primary storage by
   a. memory
   b. secondary storage
   c. the control unit
   d. the ALU

7. Tools to change PROM chips are called
   a. chip kits
   b. PROM burners
   c. RAM burners
   d. none of these

8. During E-time the ALU
   a. examines the instruction
   b. executes the instruction
   c. enters the instruction
   d. elicits the instruction

9. When the control unit gets an instruction it is called
   a. E-time
   b. I-time
   c. machine time
   d. ALU time

10. When the control unit directs the ALU to perform an operation on the data, the machine cycle is involved in its
    a. first step
    b. second step
    c. third step
    d. fourth step

11. Computer operations are synchronized by
    a. the CPU clock
    b. the binary system
    c. megabytes
    d. E-time

12. Another name for primary storage is
    a. secondary storage
    b. binary system
    c. ROM
    d. main storage

13. Which is not another name for memory?
    a. primary storage
    b. internal storage
    c. main storage
    d. secondary storage

14. Another name for a logic chip is
    a. PROM
    b. microprocessor
    c. memory
    d. ROM

15. Data is represented on a computer by a two-state on/off system called
    a. a word
    b. a byte
    c. the binary system
    d. RAM

16. A letter, digit, or special character is represented by a
    a. bit
    b. byte
    c. kilobyte
    d. megabyte

17. Memory capacity may be expressed in
    a. microseconds
    b. bits
    c. megabytes
    d. cycles

True/False

T F 1. The control unit consists of the CPU and the ALU.

T F 2. Secondary storage holds data only temporarily.

T F 3. The control unit directs the entire computer system.

T F 4. MIPS is an abbreviation for megaflop.

T F 5. The electronic circuitry that controls all arithmetic and logical operations is contained in the ALU.

T F 6. The three basic logical operations may be combined to form a total of nine commonly used operations.

T F   7. Memory allows fast access to instructions in secondary storage.

T F   8. Registers are temporary storage areas located in memory.

T F   9. Memory is usually volatile.

T F   10. RISC computers use fewer instructions than traditional computers.

T F   11. All computers except personal computers can execute more than one instruction at a time.

T F   12. The machine cycle consists of four steps, from the first step of fetching the instruction to the last step of storing the result in memory.

T F   13. The internal clock of the CPU produces pulses at a fixed rate to synchronize all computer operations.

T F   14. A cache is a small amount of secondary storage.

T F   15. Computers represent data using the two-state binary system.

T F   16. A bit is commonly made up of 8 bytes.

T F   17. A kilobyte (KB) is 1024 bytes.

Fill-In

1. A millionth of a second is called a(n)

2. The unit that consists of both the control unit and the arithmetic/logic unit is the

3. Processing instructions one at a time is called

4. When the control unit decodes an instruction, is the machine cycle in I-time or E-time?

5. MHz is an abbreviation for

6. The abbreviation used for memory chips that can be altered is

7. The combination of I-time and E-time is called a

8. The name for the symbols = , <, and > is

9. Each memory location is identified by a(n)

10. A 0 or 1 in the binary system is called a(n)

11. MIPS stands for

12. A disadvantage of semiconductor memory is that

Answers

Multiple Choice
1. c	6. c	11. a	16. b
2. b	7. d	12. d	17. c
3. b	8. b	13. d	
4. a	9. b	14. b	
5. d	10. c	15. c	

True/False
1. F	6. F	11. F	16. F
2. F	7. F	12. T	17. T
3. T	8. F	13. T	
4. F	9. T	14. F	
5. T	10. T	15. T	

Fill-In
1. microsecond
2. central processing unit
3. serial processing
4. I-time
5. megahertz
6. PROM
7. machine cycle
8. relational operators
9. address
10. bit
11. one million instructions per second
12. it is volatile

PLANET INTERNET

The Internet is big, really big. Some say that working on the Internet gives new meaning to the word *infinity.* One way to grasp the vastness of the Internet is to link to sites in other countries.

So far away. As intriguing as these faraway sites may be, it can take some time to access a complex and popular site. An option that may be available is a *mirror site,* a nearby site that has the identical offering. The WebMuseum site in Paris, for example, which offers paintings from the Louvre on your screen, urges you right away to switch (link) to one of the mirror sites on its list. Using a mirror site dramatically improves the speed of data access.

The CERN site. It is entirely appropriate that we mention the CERN site, a laboratory for particle physics in Geneva, Switzerland. CERN is the birthplace of the World Wide Web. This site includes a link to the history of CERN's relationship with the Web.

English or not English. Many foreign sites offer an English version of their site to visitors whose language is English; comprehension-wise, you could just as easily be connected to a site in Kansas. These sites usually offer a choice: Would you prefer English or Swedish? Others simply launch into their native tongue. You either speak it or you just go along for the pictures. More sophisticated sites note your location and immediately present their site in English, with an option to switch to the native tongue.

Worth the trip? You decide. A good place to begin is the World Communities site, where you can hop from country to country. Be prepared for the fact that some developing countries have relatively primitive offerings at this point; in fact, despite being on the list, some cannot be reached at all. But many sites are fascinating. The sites may offer detailed information about the country. Others officially represent the commercial and tourist

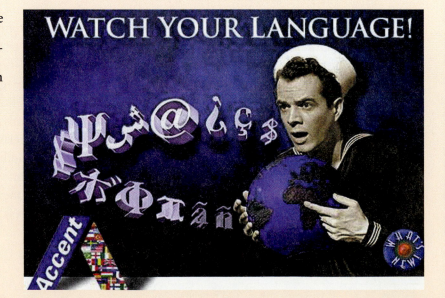

interests of the country or community.

Global information at home.
Businesses with a global presence need to maintain a global awareness. There are many sites devoted to information about international customs and trade, represented by the Internationalist logo shown here. The tourist industry has a significant presence on the Internet; you can learn about all kinds of package tours and about places to visit. The Tutankhamen image shown here often appears on Egyptian tourism sites and the picture of the Cliffs of Moher may show up on an Irish tourism site.

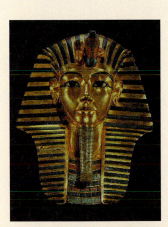

Many "global" sites have no particular commercial viability are enjoyable for the same reasons a local site would be enjoyable. Good examples are the English Spywatch game, and the Chateau de Versailles sites shown here.

What if you want to learn the language of a country that you may visit or in which you may decide to live? Not to worry. The Internet has many offerings in that department, as indicated by the Watch Your Language! image shown here.

Internet Exercises

1. **Structured exercise.** Begin with the URL http://www.prenhall.com/capron and use the link supplied to go to the CERN site.

2. **Freeform exercise.** Beginning with the World Communities site, compare the home pages you find for countries in Europe, Asia, the Pacific, and South America.

Microchips form the lightning-quick "brain" of a computer. These devices, though complex, work on a very simple principle: They "know" when electric current is on and when it is off. They can process information because it is coded as a series of on-off electric signals. Before the invention of microchips, these signals were controlled by thousands of separate devices laboriously wired together to form a single circuit. However, thousands of circuits can be embedded on a single microchip; a microchip is often called an integrated circuit.

Silicon is a semiconductor—it conducts electricity only "semi" well. This does not sound like such an admirable trait, but the beauty of silicon is that it can be doped, or treated, with different materials to make it conduct electricity well or not at all. By doping various areas of a silicon chip differently, designers can set up pathways for electricity to follow. The pathways consist of grooves etched into layers placed over a silicon substrate. The silicon is doped so that the pathways conduct electricity. The surrounding areas do not conduct electricity at all.

1. This simplified illustration shows the layers and grooves within a transistor, one of thousands of circuit components on a single chip. Pathway C controls the flow of electricity through the circuit. (a) When no electric charge is added to pathway C, electricity cannot flow along the circuit pathway from area A to area B. Thus the transistor is "off." (b) A charge added to pathway C temporarily allows electricity to travel from area A to area B. Now the transistor is "on," and electricity can continue to other components in the circuit. The control of electricity here and elsewhere in the chip makes it possible for the computer to process information coded as "on-off" electric signals.

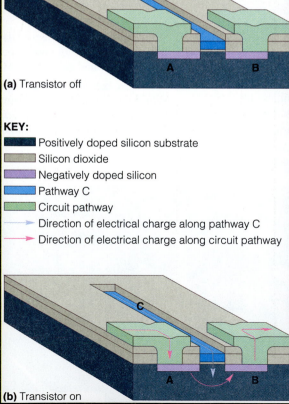

(a) Transistor off

KEY:

- Positively doped silicon substrate
- Silicon dioxide
- Negatively doped silicon
- Pathway C
- Circuit pathway
- → Direction of electrical charge along pathway C
- → Direction of electrical charge along circuit pathway

(b) Transistor on

MAKING MICROCHIPS

Computer power in the hands of the people—we take it for granted now, but not so long ago computers existed only in enormous rooms behind locked doors. The revolution that changed all that was ignited by chips of silicon smaller than your fingernail: microchips.

Silicon is one of the most common elements on Earth, but there is nothing commonplace about designing, manufacturing, testing, and packaging the microprocessors that are made from silicon. In this gallery we will explore the key elements in the process by which those marvels of miniaturization—microchips—are made.

Preparing the Design

Each microprocessor is constructed like a multistory building, with multiple layers of material combining to create a single complex unit. Try to imagine figuring out a way to place thousands of circuit components next to one another so that electricity flows through the whole integrated circuit the way it is supposed to. That is the job of chip designers. Essentially, they are trying to put together a gigantic multilayered jigsaw puzzle. The circuit design of a typical chip requires over a year's work by a team of designers. Computers assist in the complex task of mapping out the most efficient pathways for each circuit layer.

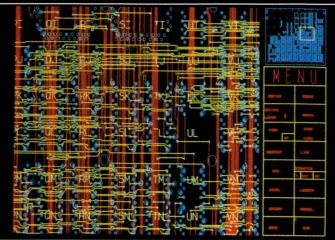

3. Close-up of what a chip designer sees on the screen.

2. A designer can arrange and modify circuit patterns and display them on a screen. Superimposing the color-coded circuit layers allows the designer to evaluate the relationships between them. The computer allows the designer to electronically store and retrieve previously designed circuit patterns.

3. Here the designer has used computer graphics software to display a screen image of the circuit design.

4. The computer system can also provide a printed version of any or all parts of the design. This large-scale printout allows the design team to discuss and modify the entire chip design.

2. Microchip designers execute their plans using the computer.

4. A chip designer team works with an enlarged printout of the design.

Manufacturing the Chip

The silicon used to make computer chips is extracted from common rocks and sand. It is melted down into a form that is 99.9 percent pure silicon and then doped with chemicals to make it either electrically positive or electrically negative.

6. A silicon wafer.

5. A cylinder of silicon that will be sliced into wafers.

5. The molten silicon is then "grown" into cylindrical ingots in a process similar to candle dipping.
6. A diamond saw slices each ingot into circular wafers four or six or eight inches in diameter and four-thousandths of an inch thick. The wafers are sterilized and polished to a perfectly smooth, mirror-like finish. Each wafer will eventually contain hundreds of identical chips. One silicon wafer can produce more than 100 microprocessors.

Since a single speck of dust can ruin a chip, chips are manufactured in special laboratories called clean rooms. The air in clean rooms is filtered, and workers dress in "bunny suits" to lessen the chance of chip contamination. A chip-manufacturing lab is 100 times cleaner than a hospital operating room.
7. Chip-manufacturing processes vary, but one step is common: Electrically positive silicon wafers are placed in an open glass tube and inserted in a 1200° Celsius oxidation furnace. Oxygen reacts with the silicon, covering each wafer with a thin layer of silicon dioxide, which does not conduct electricity well. Each wafer is then coated with a gelatin-like substance called photoresist, which hardens. The final design of each circuit

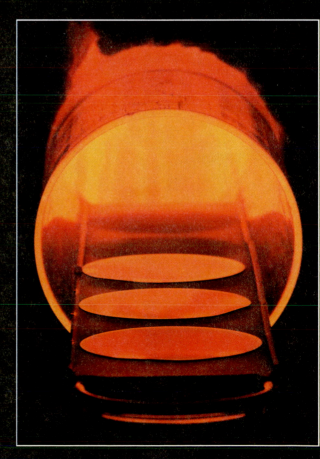

7. Analogy of silicon being cooked.

layer must be reduced to the size of the chip. A stencil called a mask, representing the schematic design of the circuit, is placed over the wafer. Ultraviolet light is shined through the mask, softening the exposed—nonmasked—photoresist on the wafer.

8. The wafer is then taken to a washing station in a specially lit "yellow room," where the wafer is washed in solvent to remove the soft photoresist. This leaves ridges of material—hardened photoresist in the pattern of the mask—on the wafer. Next the silicon dioxide revealed by the washing is etched away by hot gases. The silicon underneath, which forms the circuit pathway,

is then doped to make it electrically negative. In this way, the circuit pathway is distinguished electrically from the rest of the silicon. In the final step, aluminum is deposited to connect the circuit components and form the bonding pads to which wires will later be connected.

9. The result: one wafer with many chips.

10. Computerized coloration enhances this close-up view of a wafer with chips.

11. This image shows circuit paths on a microprocessor chip magnified 3000 times.

8. Wafer washing room.

9. Close-up of chips on a wafer.

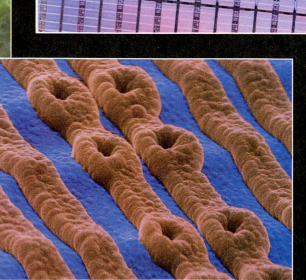

10. Chips still on the wafer.

11. A chip magnified 3000 times.

Testing the Chip

Microprocessor manufacturers devote extraordinary efforts to testing their chips. The chips are tested all along the way, from design to manufacturing to packaging. A microprocessor is so complex that it is impossible to literally check every possible state it could be in; the number of elements—millions of transistors—and the number of different combinations is simply too great. However, months of continuous, specialized, and extremely expensive testing will yield a working, reliable product. Even after a chip reaches production, testing continues. Each new chip is tested while still on the wafer and after it is packaged.

Although chips on a particular wafer may look identical, they do not perform identically.

12. A probe machine must perform millions of tests on each chip, to determine whether it conducts electricity in the precise way it was designed to. The needle-like probes contact the bonding pads, apply electricity, measure the results, and mark ink spots on defective chips.

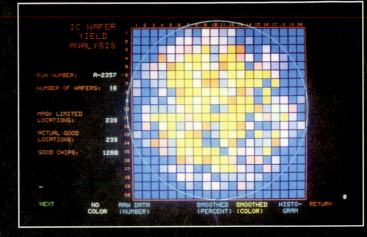

13. Classifying defects and eliminating bad chips.

13. A defect review performed by a computer finds and classifies defects in order to eliminate them from the wafer.
14. After the initial testing, a diamond saw cuts each chip from the wafer, and defective chips are discarded.

12. Needle-like probes test each chip.

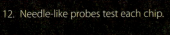

14. Cutting chips from the wafer.

Packaging the Chip

Each acceptable chip is mounted on a protective package.

15. An automated wire-bonding device wires the bonding pads of the chip to the electrical leads on the package, using aluminum or gold wire thinner than a human hair. A variety of packages are in use today.

16. Dual in-line packages have two rows of legs that are inserted into holes in a circuit board.

17. Square pin-grid array packages, which are used for chips requiring many electrical leads, look like a bed of nails. The pins are inserted into holes in a circuit board. In this photo the protective cap has been cut away, revealing the ultrafine wires connecting the chip to the package.

16. Chip mounted on surface so that legs can be inserted into holes on the circuit board.

15. Wiring the chip.

17. Square pin-grid chip package..

From Chip to Computer

At a factory that manufactures circuit boards, 18. a robot makes a circuit board and 19. another robot inserts a pin-grid package into holes in a circuit board. Several surface mount packages have already been placed on the board.

20. Dual in-line packages of various sizes have been attached to this circuit board.
21. This circuit board is being installed in a Compaq computer.

18. A factory robot makes a circuit board.

19. A factory robot lines up the pins on the chip package with holes on the receiving circuit board.

20. A finished circuit board.

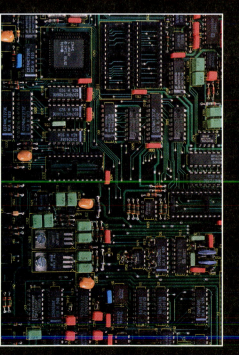

21. Installing the circuit board.

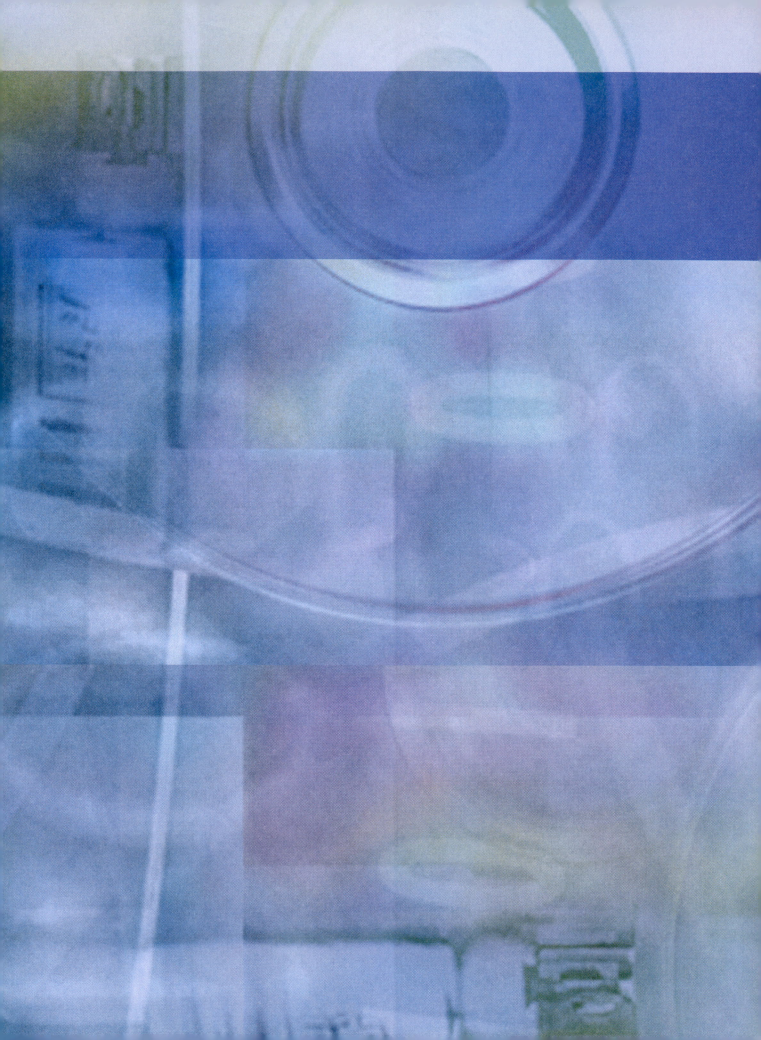

INPUT AND OUTPUT

The User Connection

LEARNING OBJECTIVES

- Appreciate the user relationship with computer input and
  output
- Understand how data is input
  to a computer system and differentiate among various
  input equipment
- Describe how a monitor
  works and know the characteristics that determine
  quality
- List the different methods of
  computer output
- Differentiate among different
  kinds of printers

McKenna University long ago abandoned the practice of standing in line to register for classes. Now almost everything is handled by phoning a computer. Since these procedures save time and trouble, they suit Rose Sierra just fine. Rose did begin with a manual procedure when she first applied to the university. Her application, the source document, was prepared by her and, after she was accepted, scanned into the university's computer. From that point forward, Rose has communicated directly with the computer.

Rose can phone the computer and supply it with her data, using her touch-tone phone as a sort of miniature keyboard. Once the computer responds to the number she dials, she enters her Social Security number, followed by the unique personal identification number (PIN) assigned to her by the university. She can then follow the procedure to register for classes, entering class item numbers from the college's class schedule. Various options are available, such as taking a class for credit or audit, by entering a number from her phoneset. The computer delivers voice output, telling her she has—or has not—been accepted in a class. Once she has entered all classes, Rose can push other buttons for other options, such as hearing her class schedule, dropping a class, hearing the tuition amount owed, and paying by credit card.

Once Rose is registered, the computer will print her student identification card, complete with bar code, which she can pick up in the library. The ID card is used for checking books out of the library and for making use of computer and science labs. The computer produces a lot of other output, such as class rosters for instructors and registration summaries, that are only indirectly related to Rose.

Rose is not particularly familiar with computer-related input/output terms such as *source document, scan, keyboard, voice output, bar code,* and so forth, nor does she need to be to register. But understanding these terms, and other terms related to input and output, will help users navigate all sorts of computer systems.

How Users See Input and Output

The central processing unit is the unseen part of a computer system; users are only dimly aware of it. But users are very much aware of the input and output associated with the computer. They submit input data to the computer to get processed information, the output.

MAKING THE RIGHT CONNECTIONS

FACE TO FACE

Perhaps you can send e-mail, and you may even have learned how to send along a photograph. But can you talk face-to-face with someone using a computer connection? You can if you buy one of the video kits that have made the process easy and affordable. A typical kit includes a camera and software, both easy to install. Shown here is Intel's Create & Share Camera Pack; note the camera atop the monitor. Of course, this only works if the party at the other end of your communication has a video setup too.

The technology for video telephones has been around for a long time, but it never caught on with the general public. Perhaps people didn't want to be seen with their hair in curlers or in their bathrobes. But computer video telephony is attractive, partly because it is inexpensive even over long distances, and partly because it is still sufficiently novel that it is planned in advance— no curlers.

Sometimes the output is an instant reaction to the input. Consider these examples:

- Zebra-striped bar codes on supermarket items provide input that permits instant retrieval of outputs—price and item name—right at the checkout counter.
- A forklift operator speaks directly to a computer through a microphone. Words like *left, right,* and *lift* are the actual input data. The output is the computer's instant response, which causes the forklift to operate as requested.
- A sales representative uses an instrument that looks like a pen to enter an order on a special pad. The handwritten characters are displayed as "typed" text and are stored in the pad, which is actually a small computer.
- Factory workers input data by punching in on a time clock as they go from task to task. The time clock is connected to a computer. The outputs are their weekly paychecks and reports for management that summarize hours per project on a quarterly basis.

Input and output may be separated by time or distance or both. Here are some examples:

- Data on checks is used as input to the bank computer, which eventually processes the data to prepare a bank statement once a month.
- Charge-card transactions in a retail store provide input data that is processed monthly to produce customer bills.

(a)

(b)

Figure 1 Keyboards. (a) A traditional computer keyboard. (b) Chinese characters are significantly more complicated than the letters and digits found on a standard keyboard. To enter Chinese characters into the computer system, a person uses a special keyboard. Each letter key shows the characters that a user can type by holding down other keys while pressing that letter (as you would hold down a Shift key to make capital letters).

Group Work

Some corporations have found it cheaper to ship their source documents to foreign countries for data entry. Labor costs are lower and non-English speakers may make fewer errors in data entry because they read letter by letter, rather than word by word.

InfoBit

The computer mouse has a long history. A prototype—made partly of wood—was first demonstrated by Douglas Englebart in 1968. Trackballs are at least as old as the computer mouse, and allowed operators to move a tracking cursor over targets in an air-traffic control system of the mid-1960s.

■ Water-sample data is collected at lake and river sites, keyed in at the environmental agency office, and used to produce reports that show patterns of water quality.

The examples in this section show the diversity of computer applications, but in all cases the process is the same: input–processing–output. This chapter examines input and output methods in detail.

Input: Getting Data from the User to the Computer

Some input data can go directly to the computer for processing. Input in this category includes bar codes, speech that enters the computer through a microphone, and data entered by means of a device that converts motions to on-screen action. Some input data, however, goes through a good deal of intermediate handling, such as when it is copied from a **source document** (jargon for the original written data) and translated to a medium that a machine can read, such as a magnetic disk. In either case the task is to gather data to be processed by the computer—sometimes called *raw data*—and convert it into an electronic form the computer can understand. Conventional input devices include the keyboard, mouse, and trackball, explained in the following sections.

Keyboard

A **keyboard,** which usually is similar to a typewriter keyboard, may be part of a personal computer or part of a terminal that is connected to a computer somewhere else (Figure 1a). Not all keyboards are traditional, however. A fast-food franchise like McDonald's, for example, uses keyboards whose keys represent items such as large fries or a Big Mac. Even less traditional is the keyboard shown in Figure 1b, which is used to enter Chinese characters. Figure 2 shows the complete layout of a traditional keyboard.

Mouse

A **mouse,** which has a ball on its underside, is rolled on a flat surface, usually the desk on which the computer sits or perhaps a separate flat item called a *mouse pad* (Figure 3a). The rolling movement causes a corresponding movement of a **pointer** on the screen. The pointer can be a number of shapes but is most often an arrow. A mouse usually has two buttons, the left for common actions and the right for operating system or application-defined actions. Actions with the mouse consist of positioning the pointer and then clicking (sometimes double-clicking) a button. Move the mouse pointer to the desired place in the screen text, then click the button to set the **insertion point,** or **cursor.** (The insertion point can also be moved by pressing various keyboard keys.) The next text typed will begin at the insertion point.

You can also use the mouse to communicate commands to the computer by clicking a button on top of the mouse. In particular, a mouse button is often used to click on an icon (Figure 3b), a pictorial symbol on a screen; the **icon** represents a computer activity—a command to the computer—so clicking the icon invokes the command. The command may be to launch an application, such as word processing or a game. The environment permitting communication with the computer by clicking on icons is referred to as a **graphical user interface (GUI).**

As mice have evolved, new features and new buttons have been added. Some mice are even cordless. Microsoft's IntelliMouse offers an extra wheel, positioned between the two mouse buttons, that can be clicked like a button or rolled to affect the cursor (Figure 3c). With software designed to be used with this mouse, it can move through a document line by line or page by page or zoom in on a special spreadsheet cell or flip backwards through web pages already seen.

Trackball

A variation on the mouse is the **trackball.** You may have used a trackball to play a video game. The trackball is like an upside-down mouse—you roll the ball directly with your hand. The popularity of the trackball surged with the advent of laptop computers, when traveling users found themselves without a flat surface on which to roll the traditional mouse. Trackballs are often built in on portable computers, but they can also be used as separate input devices with standard desktop computers (Figure 4).

A variation on this theme is the **track pad,** with your finger as the pointer (Figure 5). Just wiggle your finger across the pad of the tiny surface and corresponding movements will be made on the screen. Tabs at the bottom of the unit serve the same functions as mouse buttons.

Source Data Automation: Collecting Data Where It Starts

Efficient data input means reducing the number of intermediate steps required between the origination of data and its processing. This is best accomplished by **source data automation**—the use of special equipment to collect data at the source, as a by-product of the activity that generates the data, and send it directly to the computer. Recall, for example, the supermarket bar code, which can be used to send data about the product directly to the computer. Source data automation eliminates keying, thereby reducing costs and opportunities for human-introduced mistakes. Since data about a transaction is collected when and where the transaction takes place, source data automation also improves the speed of the input operation and is much less expensive than other methods.

For convenience, this discussion is divided into the primary areas related to source data automation: magnetic-ink character recognition, scanners and other optical recognition devices, and even your own voice, finger, or eye.

Magnetic-Ink Character Recognition

Abbreviated **MICR, magnetic-ink character recognition** involves using a machine to read characters made of magnetized particles. The most common example of magnetic characters is the array of numbers across the bottom of your personal check. Figure 6 shows what some of these numbers and symbols represent.

Most magnetic-ink characters are preprinted on your check. If you compare a check that you wrote that has been cashed and cleared by the bank with one that is still unused in your checkbook, you will note that the

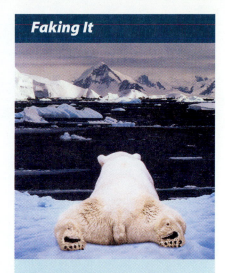

Faking It

This polar bear seems right at home but, in fact, he is not. Photographer Art Wolfe used computer photo imaging software to doctor the photo, placing the nonnative bear in Antarctica.

Photo imaging software is quite sophisticated. In addition to adding and subtracting items, any novice can tinker with an image. Some possibilities are rotating, resizing, cropping, brightening, and removing "red eye." For further amusement, the same software will let you warp an image, elongating Uncle Harry's ears or giving yourself a gracious pompadour.

InfoBit

Trackballs must be cleaned frequently if they are to operate smoothly. The problem of erratic operation is aggravated on trackballs because they have openings on top, surrounding the ball, into which fine dust and dirt particles eventually descend. The problem is particularly acute with trackballs on laptop computers, since laptops are exposed to a wide variety of "dirty" environments.

InfoBit

Properly operated Magnetic Ink Character Recognition machines can scan checks at rates in excess of 2,000 per minute with error rates under 0.5 percent.

FINDING YOUR WAY AROUND A KEYBOARD

Most personal computer keyboards have three main parts: function keys, the main keyboard in the center, the numeric keys to the right. Extended keyboards, such as the keyboard shown here, have additional keys between the main keyboard and the and the numeric keys and status lights in the upper-right corner.

Function Keys

The function keys (highlighted in tan on the diagram) are an easy way to give certain commands to the computer. What each function key does is defined by the particular software you are using. Some keyboards have function keys to the left instead of across the top.

Main Keyboard

The main keyboard includes the familiar keys found on a typewriter keyboard (dark blue), as well as some special command keys (light blue). The command keys have different uses that depend on the software being used. Some of the most common uses are listed here.

 The Escape key, Esc, is used in different ways by different programs; often it allows you to "escape" the program.

 The Tab key allows you to tab across the screen and set tab stops as you would on a typewriter.

 When the Caps Lock key is pressed, uppercase letters are produced.

 The Shift key allows you to produce uppercase letters and the upper symbols shown on the keys.

 The Control key, Ctrl, is pressed in combination with other keys to initiate commands as specified by the software.

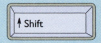 The Alternate key, Alt, is also used in combination with other keys to initiate commands.

Three keys—Ctrl/Alt/Del—depending on the system, can be used in combination to stop a program or to reboot. Hold down Ctrl and Alt while pressing Del.

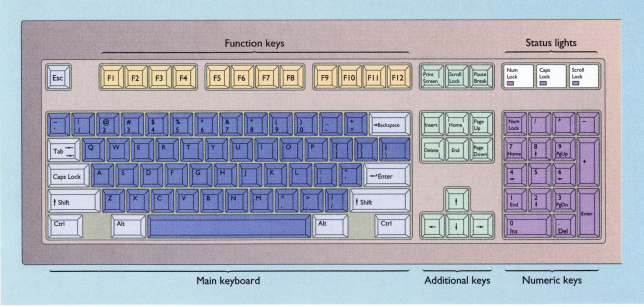

Figure 2 **Finding your way around a keyboard.**

amount of the cashed check has been reproduced in magnetic characters in the lower-right corner. These characters were added by a person at the bank by using a **MICR** ("MIKE er") **inscriber.**

Scanner

There was a time when the only way to transfer an existing document into the computer was to retype it. Now, however, a **scanner** can convert text or even a drawing or picture into computer-recognizable data by using a form

The Backspace key is most often used to delete a character to the left of the cursor, moving the cursor back one position. (The cursor is the flashing indicator on the screen that shows where the next character will be inserted.)

The Enter key moves the cursor to the beginning of the next line. It is used at the end of the paragraph, for instance.

Numeric Keys

The numeric keys (purple) serve one of two purposes, depending on the status of the Num Lock key. When the computer is in the Num Lock mode, these keys can be used to enter numeric data and mathematic symbols (/ for "divided by," * for "multiplied by," -, and +). In the Num Lock mode, the status light under "Num Lock" lights up. When the computer is not in the Num Lock mode, the numeric keys can be used to move the cursor and perform other functions. For example:

In some programs the End key moves the cursor to the bottom-right corner of the screen or to the right end of the current line.

This key moves the cursor down.

The Page Down key, PgDn, advances one full screen while the cursor stays in the same place.

This key moves the cursor to the left.

This key moves the cursor to the right.

In some programs the Home key moves the cursor to the top-left corner of the screen or to the left end of the current line.

This key moves the cursor up.

The Page Up key, PgUp, backs up to the previous screen while the cursor stays in the same place.

The Insert key, Ins, when toggled off, causes keyed characters to override existing characters.

The Delete key, Del, deletes a character or space to the right of the cursor or deletes selected text.

Additional Keys

Extended keyboards include additional keys (green) that duplicate the cursor movement functions of the numeric keys. Users who enter a lot of numeric data can leave their computers in the Num Lock mode and use these additional keys to control the cursor.

The Arrow keys, to the left of the numeric keys, move the cursor position, just as the numeric keys 2, 4, 6, and 8 do when they are not in the Num Lock mode.

Just above the arrow keys are six keys—Insert, Delete, Home, End, Page Up, and Page Down—which duplicate functions of the numeric keys 0, decimal point (Del), 7, 1, 9, and 3.

At the top of the keyboard, to the right of the function keys, are keys that perform additional tasks. For example:

The Print Screen key causes the current screen display to be placed on the computer's clipboard, a memory place from which it can be saved or moved elsewhere.

The Scroll Lock key controls the way the cursor control keys work for some programs. Many applications ignore the Scroll Lock setting.

The Pause/Break key can temporarily freeze data that is being scrolled to the screen. Used together with the Ctrl key, Ctrl/Break may stop a program.

of optical recognition. **Optical recognition** systems use a light beam to scan input data and convert it into electrical signals, which are sent to the computer for processing. Optical recognition is by far the most common type of source input; just think of all those supermarket scanners.

Now consider all those drawers filled with receipts, warranties, and old checks. If you would let the computer take care of them, you could save space and, even better, be able to find an item when you want it. In a process called **imaging,** a scanner converts those papers to an electronic version, which can then be stored on disk and retrieved when needed. But most consumers use

Learn by Doing

Have students develop and collect data for a short survey addressing the features of scanners used by businesses (e.g., type of scanner used, reliability, ease of use, data collected). Students should be encouraged to include a variety of types of scanners and businesses in their sample.

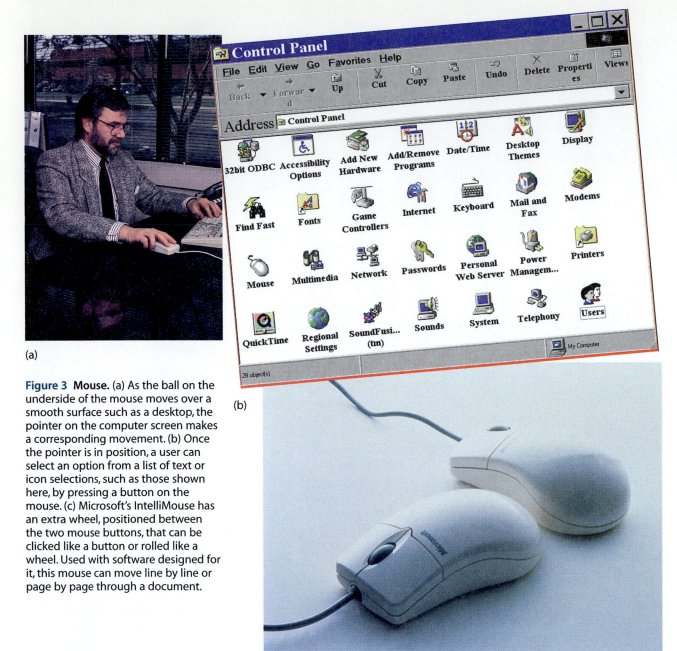

(a)

(b)

(c)

Figure 3 Mouse. (a) As the ball on the underside of the mouse moves over a smooth surface such as a desktop, the pointer on the computer screen makes a corresponding movement. (b) Once the pointer is in position, a user can select an option from a list of text or icon selections, such as those shown here, by pressing a button on the mouse. (c) Microsoft's IntelliMouse has an extra wheel, positioned between the two mouse buttons, that can be clicked like a button or rolled like a wheel. Used with software designed for it, this mouse can move line by line or page by page through a document.

InfoBit

A problem with handheld scanners occurs when the picture being scanned is wider than the scanner's field of view. Then the user of a handheld scanner must scan the picture as two separate images, and attempt to use computer software to join the pieces. This is a tedious and demanding task, at best.

a scanner to turn snapshots into images that can be printed, incorporated into a craft project, e-mailed, or posted on their web site. Another popular use is converting printed documents, perhaps a letter or magazine article, into text that can be edited—changed or revised—by word processing software.

Business people also find imaging useful, since they can view an exact computer-produced replica of the original document at any time. Processed by related software, the words and numbers of the document can be manipulated by word processing and other software. The Internal Revenue Service uses imaging to process 17,000 tax returns per hour, a significant improvement over hand processing.

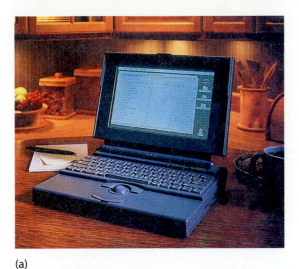

(a)

(b)

Figure 4 Trackball. The rotation of the ball causes a corresponding movement of the pointer on the screen. (a) Trackballs are often used with laptop computers because, especially on an airplane, there may be no handy surface on which to roll a mouse. Notice that the ball is placed in the center, both for compactness and to accommodate both right- and left-handed users. (b) This trackball, looking rather like an oversized egg, is called EasyBall because it can be grasped and manipulated by a child's small hand.

Scanners fall into three categories. A **flatbed scanner** typically scans one sheet at a time, although some offer an attachment for scanning multiple sheets. Flatbed scanners are space hogs, taking up about as much room as a tabletop copy machine (Figure 7c). The advantage of a flatbed scanner is that it can be used to scan bound documents, such as pages from books and other bulky items. In a **sheetfeed scanner,** motorized rollers feed the sheet across the scanning head. A key attraction of sheetfeed scanners is that they are usually designed to fit neatly between the keyboard and the monitor (Figure 7a). However, sheetfeed scanners are less versatile than flatbed scanners and are more prone to errors. A **handheld scanner,** the least expensive and least reliable of the three, is a handy portable option (Figure 7b). It is often difficult to get a good scan with a handheld scanner, because the user must move the scanner in a straight line at a fixed rate.

Figure 5 Track pad. Use your finger on this pad to move the pointer on the screen. The tabs at the bottom serve the same functions as mouse buttons.

Many users like scanners because they can use them to feed photographs directly into the computer. If, however, you want to scan text and then be able to edit it using word processing, you need special software—usually called OCR software, for *optical character recognition*—that can identify the individual letters as opposed to treating the entire text document as one big picture. Most scanners come accompanied by OCR software.

More Optical Recognition Methods

In addition to text and images, optical recognition can process data appearing in a variety of forms: optical marks, optical characters, bar codes, and even handwritten characters.

Optical Mark Recognition   Abbreviated **OMR, optical mark recognition** is sometimes called *mark sensing*, because a machine senses marks on a piece

Critical Thinking

What uses can you imagine for a computer scanner? (Scanning and retouching old photographs, scanning fabric patterns for crafts, and acting as a home Xerox machine are easy possibilities. In fact, many scanners will scan originals that are not completely flat and creating images of dolls, small toys, or even carefully scanning pets is also possible.)

Group Work

Have students mark their responses to a practice quiz on machine scored answer sheets. Do not instruct them to be careful about erasures or stray marks. Generate two or three demonstration answer sheets, where you do not carefully erase "changed" responses, and mark two responses for at least one question. Show students the results of the computer grading program (e.g., items marked incorrect due to "multiple responses" from insufficiently erased answer changes, duplicate responses, stray marks).

InfoBit

One of the more novel applications of Optical Character Recognition is the avoidance of legal restrictions on the publication of cryptographic information. Barred by law from publishing the software source code for their DES code-breaking program on the web, the Electronic Frontier Foundation published the source code as a book. The book is designed to be scanned using OCR, and uses special font and layouts to facilitate the correct electronic entry of the controversial computer program.

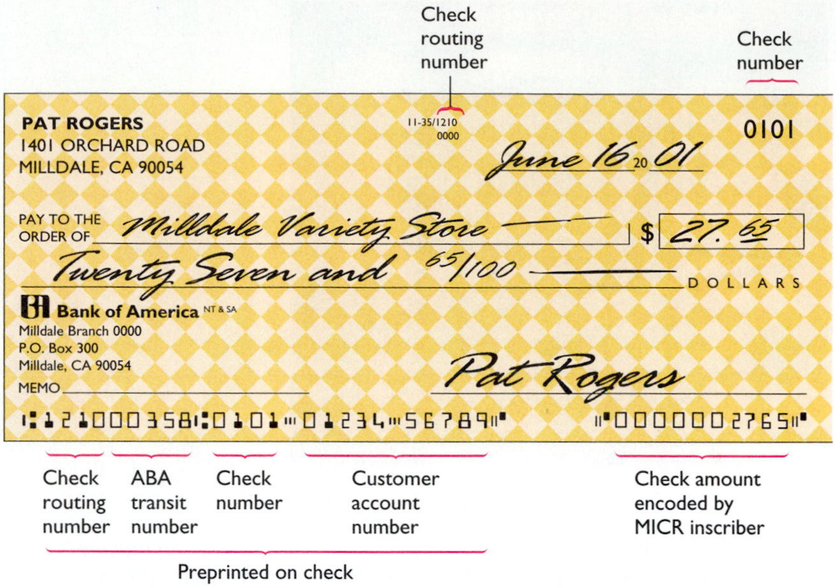

Figure 6 The symbols on your check. Magnetic-ink numbers and symbols run along the bottom of a check. The symbols on the left are preprinted. The MICR characters in the lower-right corner of a cashed check are entered by the bank that receives it; these numbers should correspond to the amount of the check.

Translate as You Scan

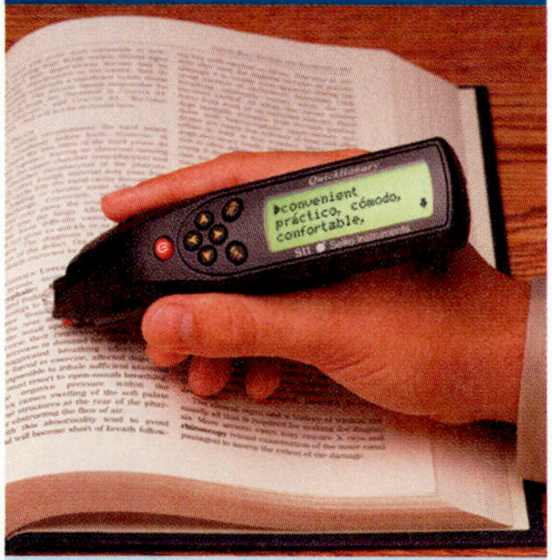

This hand-held scanner, called Quicktionary by Seiko, can translate text from one language to another. Just slide the tip of the pen across the text and the translation appears in the pen's window. The pen holds a vocabulary of approximately 400,000 words. Popular combinations (one set per pen) are French/English and Spanish/English.

of paper. As a student, you may immediately recognize this approach as the technique used to score certain tests. Using a pencil, you make a mark in a specified box or space that corresponds to what you think is the answer. The answer sheet is then graded by an optical device that recognizes the patterns and converts them to computer-recognizable electrical signals.

Optical Character Recognition Abbreviated **OCR, optical character recognition** devices also use a light source to read special characters and convert them into electrical signals to be sent to the central processing unit. The characters—letters, numbers, and special symbols—can be read by both humans and machines. They are often found on sales tags on store merchandise. A standard typeface for optical characters, called **OCR-A,** has been established by the American National Standards Institute (Figure 8).

The handheld **wand reader** is a popular input device for reading OCR-A. There is an increasing use of wands in libraries, hospitals, and factories, as well as in retail stores. In retail stores the wand reader is connected to a **point-of-sale (POS) terminal.** This terminal is somewhat like a cash register, but it performs many more functions. When a clerk passes the wand reader over the price tag, the computer uses the input merchandise number to retrieve a description (and possibly the price, if it is not on the tag) of the item. A small printer produces a customer receipt that shows the item description and price. The computer calculates the subtotal, the sales tax (if any), and the total. This information is displayed on the screen and printed on the receipt.

The raw purchase data becomes valuable information when it is summarized by the computer system. This information can be used by the accounting department to keep track of how much money is taken in each day, by

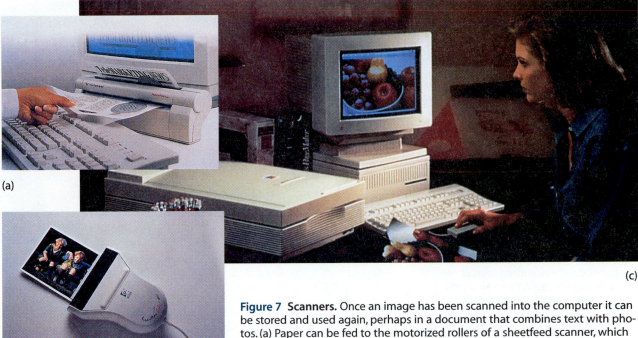

(a)

(b)

(c)

Figure 7 Scanners. Once an image has been scanned into the computer it can be stored and used again, perhaps in a document that combines text with photos. (a) Paper can be fed to the motorized rollers of a sheetfeed scanner, which has the added advantage of fitting nicely between keyboard and monitor. (b) A handheld scanner is manually passed over the image to be scanned. (c) With a flatbed scanner, the image to be scanned is laid face down on the scanner, which looks something like a small copy machine.

buyers to determine what merchandise should be reordered, and by the marketing department to analyze the effectiveness of their ad campaigns.

Bar Codes　Each product on the store shelf has its own unique number, which is part of the **Universal Product Code** (UPC). This code number is represented on the product label by a pattern of vertical marks, or bars, called **bar codes.** (UPC, by the way, is an agreed-upon standard within the supermarket industry; other kinds of bar codes exist. You need only look as far as the back cover of this book to see an example of another kind of bar code.) These zebra stripes can be sensed and read by a **bar-code reader,** a photoelectric device that reads the code by means of reflected light. Like the wand reader in a retail store, the bar-code reader in a bookstore or grocery store is part of a point-of-sale terminal. When you buy, say, a can of corn at the supermarket, the checker moves it past the bar-code reader (Figure 9a). The bar code merely identifies the product to the store's computer; the code does not contain the price, which may vary. The price is stored in a file that can be accessed by the computer. (Obviously, it is easier to change the price in the computer than it is to restamp the price on each can of corn.) The computer automatically tells the point-of-sale terminal what the price is; a printer prints the item description and price on a paper tape for the customer. Some supermarkets are moving to do-it-yourself scanning, putting the bar-code reader—as well as the bagging—in the customer's hands.

Although bar codes were once found primarily in supermarkets, there are a variety of other interesting applications. Bar coding has been described as an inexpensive and remarkably reliable way to get data into a computer. It is

Learn by Doing

Have students collect as many different examples of bar codes as possible. Possible sources beyond the UPC code found on almost every product include junk mail, envelopes, express packages, books, mailing labels, railroad cars, library cards, and prerecorded videos.

Figure 8 Reading the OCR-A typeface. This is a common typeface for optical character recognition.

(a)

(b)

Figure 9 Bar codes. (a) This photoelectric bar-code scanner, often seen at supermarket checkout counters, reads the product's zebra-stripe bar code. The bar code identifies the product for the store's computer, which retrieves price and description information. The price is then automatically rung up on the point-of-sale terminal. (b) FedEx uses a bar code system to identify and track packages in transit.

InfoBit

Handwriting recognition is much more difficult than optical character recognition. In contrast to the neatly printed characters produced by a computer printer or a fax, handwriting varies widely in shape, style and legibility. To aid those developing handwriting recognition systems in benchmarking their systems, the National Institute of Standards and Technology (NIST) maintains a special database of words, each penned by 500 different humans.

no wonder that virtually every industry has found a niche for bar codes. Federal Express, for example, attributes a large part of the corporation's success to the bar-coding system it uses to track packages (Figure 9b). Each package is uniquely identified by a 10-digit bar code, which is input to the computer at each point as the package travels through the system. An employee can use a computer terminal to query the location of a given shipment at any time; the sender can request a status report on a package or track the package on the FedEx website.

Handwritten Characters Machines that can read handwritten characters are yet another means of reducing the number of intermediate steps between capturing data and processing it. In many instances it is preferable to write the data and immediately have it usable for processing rather than having data entry operators key it in later. However, not just any scrawl will do; the rules as to the size, completeness, and legibility of the handwriting are fairly rigid (Figure 10).

		Good	Bad
1.	Make your letters big	EWING	EWING
2.	Use simple shapes	57320	57320
3.	Use block printing	KENT	Kent
4.	Connect lines	5BE4	5BE4
5.	Close loops	9068	9068
6.	Do not link characters	LOOP	LOOP

Figure 10 Handwritten characters. Legibility is important in making handwritten characters readable by optical recognition.

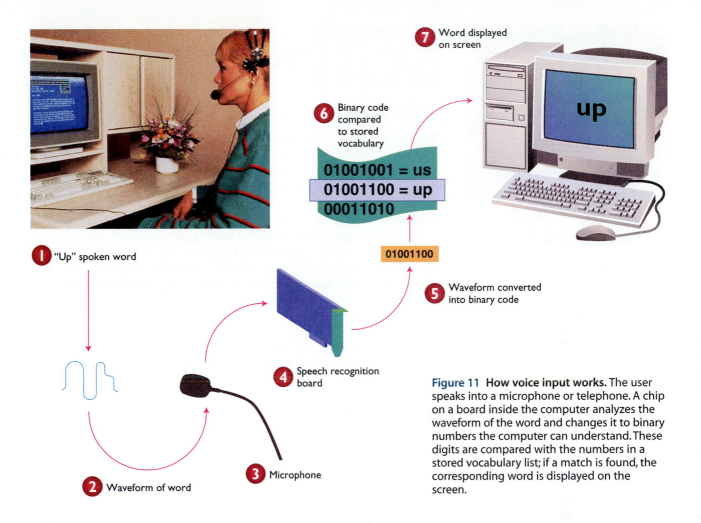

1 "Up" spoken word

2 Waveform of word

3 Microphone

4 Speech recognition board

5 Waveform converted into binary code

6 Binary code compared to stored vocabulary

01001001 = us
01001100 = up
00011010

01001100

7 Word displayed on screen

up

Figure 11 How voice input works. The user speaks into a microphone or telephone. A chip on a board inside the computer analyzes the waveform of the word and changes it to binary numbers the computer can understand. These digits are compared with the numbers in a stored vocabulary list; if a match is found, the corresponding word is displayed on the screen.

Voice Input

Speaking to a computer, known as **voice input** or **speech recognition,** is another form of source input. **Speech recognition devices** accept the spoken word through a microphone and convert it into binary code (0s and 1s) that can be understood by the computer (Figure 11). Typical users are the disabled, those with "busy hands" or hands too dirty for the keyboard, and those with no access to a keyboard. Uses for speech recognition include changing radio frequencies in airplane cockpits, controlling inventory in an auto junkyard, asking for stock-market quotations over the phone, inspecting items moving along an assembly line, and allowing physically disabled users to issue commands (Figure 12).

Most speech recognition systems are speaker-dependent—that is, they must be separately trained for each individual user. The speech recognition system "learns" the voice of the user, who speaks isolated words repeatedly. The voiced words the system "knows" are then recognizable in the future.

Speech recognition systems that are limited to isolated words are called **discrete word systems,** and users must pause between words. Experts have tagged speech recognition as one of the most difficult things for a computer to do. However, the technology for **continuous word systems,** which can interpret sustained speech, so that users can speak almost normally, has

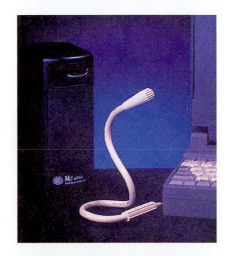

Figure 12 Microphone. This twistable—and inexpensive—microphone is an input device for speech recognition.

Figure 13 Touch-screen kiosk. This kiosk is in a grocery store in Avon, Connecticut. Customers can touch the screen to make a series of choices, and a suitable recipe is then printed out.

improved dramatically in the last few years. A key advantage of delivering input to a computer in a normal speaking pattern is ease of use. It is faster and easier to dictate a letter than to key it. Soon, most new personal computers will be equipped with speech recognition.

Touch Screens

One way of getting input directly from the source is to have a human simply point to a selection. The edges of a **touch screen** emit horizontal and vertical beams of light that crisscross the screen. When a finger touches the screen, the interrupted light beams can pinpoint the location selected on the screen.

Kiosks—self-contained self-help boxes often found in public places such as malls and supermarkets—offer a variety of services. A kiosk's touch screen is so easy to use that it attracts patrons (Figure 13). Wal-Mart, for example, uses kiosks to let customers find needed auto parts. Many delicatessens use kiosks to let you point to salami on rye, among the other selections. But the most widespread use of kiosks is in government offices. They are becoming sufficiently commonplace that people are no longer startled when the voice of an attractive woman on the kiosk screen says "If you want to file for divorce, touch here." In fact, kiosks in California, Arizona, and Utah handle uncontested divorces, probates, evictions, small claims, and other legal matters.

Looking

Delivering input simply by looking at the computer would seem to be the ultimate in capturing data at the source. The principles involved are similar to those used in making a screen selection by touching the screen with a finger. Electrodes attached to the skin around the eyes respond to movement of the eye muscles, which produce tiny electric signals when they contract. The signals are read by the computer system, which determines the location on the screen where the user is looking.

Such a system is not yet in the mainstream. The first people to benefit will likely be those who, because of disabilities or busyness, cannot use their hands or voices for input.

Output: Information for the User

As noted earlier, computer output usually takes the form of screen or printer output. Other forms of output include voice, sound, and various forms of graphics output.

A computer system often is designed to produce several kinds of output. An example is a travel agency that uses a computer system. If a customer asks about airline connections to, say, Toronto, Calgary, and Vancouver, the travel agent will probably make a few queries to the system and receive on-screen output indicating availability on the various flights. After the reservations have been confirmed, the agent can ask for printed output that includes the tickets, the traveler's itinerary, and the invoice. In addition, agency management may periodically receive printed reports and charts, such as monthly summaries of sales figures or pie charts of regional costs.

2000 and Beyond

PEN AND INK

Computers of the future will get smaller and smaller and will be found in everyday objects. In fact, your new computer is . . . a pen. Christened Digital Ink, the pen, shown here, is close to a fully functioning computer. It can accept input; you simply write—in ink—on any surface and the pen will record your motions, inscribing your message in digital code. It processes with an embedded chip. Later, output can be loaded to your desktop computer by placing the pen in the computer-connected "inkwell," a peripheral device that doubles as a charger for the pen's battery. If speed is of the essence, the pen can transmit the data immediately. In short, you can use the pen to do many tasks that you may or may not use a computer to do now—take notes, organize your life, send e-mail, and calculate your bank balance.

You have not seen this pen in stores yet; it is still on the drawing board at Carnegie Mellon University. But, backed by Intel, Digital Ink has raised high expectations for use in the not-too-distant future.

Computer Screen Technology

A user's first interaction with a computer screen may be to view the screen response to that user's input. When data is entered, it appears on the screen. Furthermore, the computer response to that data—the output—also appears on the screen. The screen is part of the computer's **monitor,** which also includes the housing for its electrical components. Monitors usually include a stand that can be tilted or swiveled to allow the monitor to be easily adjusted to suit the user.

Screen output is known in the computer industry as **soft copy** because it is intangible and temporary, unlike **hard copy,** produced by a printer on paper, which is tangible and can be permanent.

Computer screens come in many varieties (Figure 14), but the most common kind is the **cathode ray tube (CRT).** Cathode ray tube monitors that display text and graphics are in common use today. Although most CRTs are color some are **monochrome,** meaning that only one color, usually green or amber, appears on a dark background. Monochrome screens, which are less expensive than those with color, are used in business applications such as customer inquiry or order entry, which have no need for color.

Most CRT screens use a technology called **raster scanning,** a process of sweeping electron beams across the back of the screen. The backing of the screen display has a phosphorous coating that glows whenever it is hit by a

Global Perspective

Homonyms—words of differing meaning that are pronounced the same—are confusing to speech recognition software. While this is a problem in English, with some 10,000 syllables to choose from, the problem is much more acute in Japanese, which has only 120 distinct syllables. With so few syllables, many more Japanese words are homonyms.

InfoBit

Computer users can add optically coated, tempered glass filters and monitor lenses to their screens. These are designed to reduce glare, enhance contrast, improve viewability, and help relieve the eyestrain, blurred vision, and fatigue caused from working long hours on a computer.

(a)

(b)

Figure 14 A variety of screens.
(a) Laptop computers, once limited to monochrome screens, now usually have color screens. (b) This high-resolution brilliance is available only on a color graphics display.

beam of electrons. But the phosphorus does not glow for very long, so the image must be **refreshed** often. If the screen is not refreshed often enough, the fading screen image appears to flicker. A **scan rate**—the number of times the screen is refreshed—of 80 to 100 times per second is usually adequate to retain a clear screen image. As the user, you tell the computer what image you want on the screen, by typing, say, the letter M, and the computer sends the appropriate image to be beamed on the screen. This is essentially the same process used to produce television images.

A CRT display has several hundred horizontal lines, which are scanned from left to right, and from top to bottom. The screen is sometimes scanned in **interlaced** fashion: first the odd-numbered lines, and then the even-numbered lines. This allows for a lower refresh rate without producing flicker. With text and fixed graphics displays, this scheme can work well. However, with animated graphics—especially images that move or change form rapidly—interlacing can produce an irritating flutter effect. Thus most screens today are advertised as **non-interlaced (NI),** that is, all lines are scanned in order.

A computer display screen that can be used for graphics is divided into dots that are called **addressable** because they can be *addressed* individually by the graphics software. Each dot can be illuminated individually on the screen. Each dot is potentially a *pic*ture *el*ement, or **pixel.** The **resolution** of the screen—its clarity—is directly related to the number of pixels on the screen: The more pixels, the higher the resolution. Another factor of importance is **dot pitch,** the amount of space between the dots. The smaller the dot pitch, the better the quality of the screen image. Most computers come with built-in graphics capability. Others need a device, called a **graphics card** or **graphics adapter board,** which has to be added.

Graphic standards were established in the early years of the personal computer. The intention of standards is to agree upon resolutions, colors, and so forth, to make it easier for the manufacturers of personal computers, monitors, and software to ensure that their products work together.

The standards in most common use today are SVGA and XGA. There are several varieties of **SVGA (Super VGA),** each providing a different resolution: 800 by 600 (pixels), 1024 by 768, 1280 by 1024, and 1600 by 1200. All SVGA standards support a palette of 16 million colors, but the number of colors that can be displayed simultaneously is limited by the amount of video memory installed in a system. One SVGA system might display only 256 simultaneous colors while another displays the entire palette of 16 million colors.

XGA (extended graphics array) is a high-resolution graphics standard designed to replace older standards. It provides the same resolutions but supports more simultaneous colors. In addition, XGA allows monitors to be noninterlaced.

Is bigger really better? Screen sizes are measured diagonally. However, unlike television screens, computer screen size is not regulated. Manufacturers sometimes fudge a bit. When making comparisons, a user would do well to bring a ruler. A typical office worker who handles light word processing and spreadsheet duties will probably find a 15- or 17-inch screen adequate. A user involved with high-powered graphics will probably want a 19-inch screen. At the high end, screens can be purchased that are as large as television sets, 21 inches and up.

To answer the question, yes, bigger is usually better, but it is also more expensive and takes up more space on your desk. For your own personal computer, once you try a larger screen you will not want to go back. In addition to the reduced strain on the eyes, it is particularly useful for web pages, page layout, graphics, and large photos and illustrations.

Flat Screens

Another type of screen technology is the **liquid crystal display (LCD),** a flat display often seen on watches and calculators. LCD screens are commonly used on laptop computers. But flat screens are getting bigger and are making their way to desktop computers (Figure 15). Although traditional CRT monitors get deeper as they get wider, flat panel monitors maintain their depth—a superskinny few inches—regardless of screen size. Flat panel screens are wonderful to look at, with crisp, brilliant images. Further, they are easy on the eyes; they do not flicker but, instead, just brightly shine on. Flat screen monitors are more expensive than CRTs.

Terminals

A **screen** may be part of the monitor of a self-contained personal computer, or it may be part of a terminal attached to a large computer. A **terminal** consists of an input device, an output device, and a communications link to the main computer. Most commonly, a terminal has a keyboard for an input device and a screen for an output device, although there are many variations on this theme. Most terminals these days have some processing ability of their own—a CPU—and are thus called **smart terminals.** Bank tellers use terminals to communicate directly with a central computer to determine bank balances and other information.

Printers

A **printer** is a device that produces information on paper output. Some older printers produce only letters and numbers, but most printers used with personal computers today can also produce information in graphic form. Most printers have two **orientation** settings, portrait and landscape mode. The default setting is **portrait mode,** in which output, such as a memo, is printed in a vertical alignment, that is, with the longest end north and south. **Landscape mode** prints output "sideways," or horizontally, on the paper; this is especially useful for spreadsheets that have a lot of data across the sheet. Graphics images may be more suitable to one mode over another (Figure 16).

There are two ways of printing an image on paper: the impact method and the nonimpact method. An **impact printer** uses some sort of physical contact with the paper to produce an image, physically striking paper, ribbon, and print hammer together. Mainframe users who are more concerned about high volume than high quality usually use line printers—impact printers that print an entire line at a time. These users are likely to print hearty reports, perhaps relating to payroll or costs, for internal use. Impact printers are needed when multiple copies of a report are printed; the impact carries the output through to the lower copies.

A **nonimpact printer** places an image on a page without physically touching the page. The major technologies competing in the nonimpact market are laser and ink-jet, the two kinds of printers you will find in your local computer store. **Laser printers** use a light beam to help transfer images to

Figure 15 Flat panel desktop monitor. Flat panel screens are slim and present bright images.

Disappearing Act

It looks just like a copy machine. But, unlike a copier, it does not add to the glut of paper in the office. In fact, it *subtracts*. The Decopier removes text and other detritus from the sheets of used paper fed to it.

The machine applies a nontoxic chemical at low heat to a sheet of printed paper in order to loosen up the toner and ink, then sweeps away the flakes. The paper emerges at the other end spanking new—or, at least, recycled.

Figure 16 Printer output orientation. Printers offer the option of printing output (a) taller than wide in *portrait* mode or (b) "sideways" in *landscape* mode. In this example, the rectangular image has more pleasing proportions in landscape mode. However, landscape mode is most often used for printing spreadsheets. Artist Kelly Thibodeau calls this work *Lantern*.

(a)

(b)

paper (Figure 17). Today's laser printers print 600 or 1200 **dpi (dots per inch)**, producing extremely high quality results. Laser printers print a page at a time at impressive speeds, using technology similar to that of a photocopier. Organizations use laser printers to produce high-volume, customer-oriented reports. Low-end black-and-white laser printers for use with personal computers can now be purchased for a few hundred dollars. Color laser printers are more expensive.

Figure 17 Laser printers. (a) The high-quality print and durability of the Hewlett-Packard laser printers make them bestsellers. (b) A laser printer works like a photocopy machine. Using patterns of small dots, a laser beam conveys information from the computer to a positively charged drum inside the laser printer. Wherever an image is to be printed, the laser beam is turned on, causing the drum to become neutralized. As the drum passes by a toner cartridge, toner sticks to the neutral spots on the drum. The toner is then transferred from the drum to a piece of paper. In the final printing step, heat and pressure fuse the toner to the paper. The drum is then cleaned for the next pass.

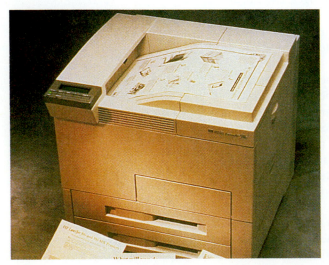
(a)

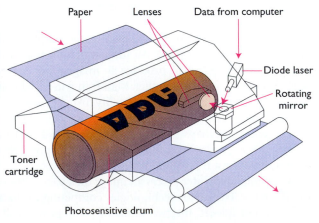
(b)

Ink-jet printers, which spray ink from multiple jet nozzles, can print in both black and white and several different colors of ink to produce excellent graphics (Figure 18). However, the print quality of an ink-jet printer, although more than adequate, usually will not match that of a laser printer. Nor will the printing be as speedy. Furthermore, ink-jet printers need a fairly high quality of paper so that the ink does not smear. Nevertheless, low-end ink-jet printers, which cost just a few hundred dollars, are a bargain for users who want color output capability. Unfortunately, they have also become vehicles for counterfeiters (Figure 19).

If you choose a color printer, whether ink-jet or laser, you will find that its colors are not perfect. The color you see on your computer screen is not necessarily the exact color you will see on the printed output. Nor is it likely to be the color you would see on a professional four-color offset printing press.

Choosing between a laser printer and an ink-jet printer comes down to a few factors. If printing speed is important to you, or if the quality of the printed text is a top priority, you probably want a black-and-white laser printer. If you cannot resist the prospect of color and are not overly concerned about text quality or speed, an ink-jet may be your best choice. If you want it all, color laser printers are available, but in a higher price range.

Figure 18 Ink-jet printers. A color ink-jet printer is an affordable and popular addition to many computer systems.

Voice Output

We have already examined voice input in some detail. As you will see in this section, however, computers are frequently like people in the sense that they find it easier to talk than to listen. **Speech synthesis**—the process of enabling machines to talk to people—is much easier than speech recognition. "The key is in the ignition," your car says to you as you open the car door to get out. Machine voices are the product of **voice synthesizers** (also called **voice-output devices** or **audio-response units**), which convert data in main storage to vocalized sounds understandable to humans.

There are two basic approaches to getting a computer to talk. The first is **synthesis by analysis,** in which the device analyzes the input of an actual human voice speaking words, stores and processes the spoken sounds, and reproduces them as needed. The second approach to synthesizing speech is **synthesis by rule,** in which the device applies a complex set of linguistic rules to create artificial speech. Synthesis based on the human voice has the advantage of sounding more natural, but it is limited to the number of words stored in the computer.

Voice output has become common in such places as airline and bus terminals, banks, brokerage houses, and even some automobiles. It is typically used when an inquiry is followed by a short reply, such as a bank balance or flight time. Many businesses have found other creative uses for voice output over the telephone. Automatic telephone voices take surveys, inform customers that catalog orders are ready to be picked up, and, perhaps, remind consumers that they have not paid their bills.

Figure 19 Computer counterfeiting. It is, unfortunately, pretty easy for an amateur to print money: All that is needed is an investment of a few hundred dollars in a scanner, an ink-jet printer, and some high-quality paper. However, it is also fairly easy to get caught, especially in view of the unprintable watermark on each new bill. The U.S. Secret Service, responsible for the integrity of the country's money, does not view counterfeiting as a lark and prosecutes to the fullest extent of the law.

Music Output and Other Sounds

In the past, personal computer users occasionally sent primitive musical messages, feeble tones that wheezed from the tiny internal speaker. Today's personal computers can be equipped with speakers placed on either side of the computer or, in some cases, mounted on the sides of the monitor or buried in the computer housing. Users want good-quality sound from certain kinds of software, especially the sophisticated offerings called *multimedia,* which includes multiple sight and sound effects. Even the zap-and-crash sounds of action games deserve to be heard. To enhance the listening experience further, manufacturers are now producing audio chips that, by varying the frequencies and timing of the sound waves as they reach the human ear, can fool the brain into thinking that it is hearing three-dimensional sound from two speakers.

MIDI (Musical Instrument Digital Interface), pronounced "MID dee," is a set of rules designed for recording and playing back music on digital synthesizers. Much in the same way that two computers communicate via modems, two synthesizers communicate via MIDI. The information exchanged between two MIDI devices is musical in nature. MIDI information tells a synthesizer, in its most basic mode, when to start and stop playing a specific note. Other information shared may include the volume and modulation of the note. A number of software programs are available for composing and editing music that conforms to the MIDI standard. They offer a variety of functions: For instance, when you play a tune on a keyboard connected to a computer, a music program can translate what you play into a written score. MIDI is supported by many makes of personal computer sound cards.

Computer Graphics

Now for everyone's favorite, computer graphics. You have probably seen the lines and charts of business (Figure 20). Just about everyone has seen TV commercials or movies that use computer-produced animated graphics. Computer graphics can also be useful in education, science, sports, computer art, and more (Figure 21). But their most prevalent use today is still in business.

Business Graphics

Graphics can be a powerful way to impart information. Colorful graphics, maps, and charts can help managers compare data more easily, spot trends, and make decisions more quickly. Also, the use of color helps people get the picture—literally. Although color graphs and charts have been used in business for years—usually to make presentations to upper management or outside clients—the computer allows them to be rendered quickly, before information becomes outdated. One user refers to business graphics as "computer-assisted insight."

Video Graphics

Video graphics can be as creative as an animated cartoon (Figure 22). Although they operate on the same principle as a moving picture or cartoon—one frame at a time in quick succession—**video graphics** are produced by computers. Video graphics have made their biggest splash on television, but many people do not realize they are watching a computer at

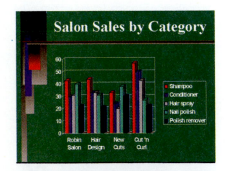

Figure 20 Business graphics. These charts were made with powerful but easy-to-use graphics software.

(a)

(b)

(c)

(d)

Figure 21 Computer graphics. These works are done completely on the computer by computer graphic artists. (a) Artists Jean-Marie Haerens and Fabien Mosen title this work *Roger, Gary and Bob* as a spoof on the colors red, green, and blue. (b) Artist Nathan O'Brien did not name this image but describes it as what you might see on a summer day if you looked down instead of around. (c) Artist Gena Obukhov calls this image *Gomusic*. (d) Artists Ian and Ethel MacKay named this work *Toco Toucan*.

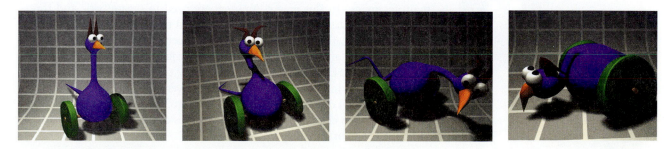

Figure 22 Video graphics. These images, featuring a character named Rolly, are part of a multiframe animated set developed by students Bret Battery, Mark Manca, and Angela Woods at the University of Washington. Student groups work on a series of projects introducing them to modeling, shading, lighting, and animation.

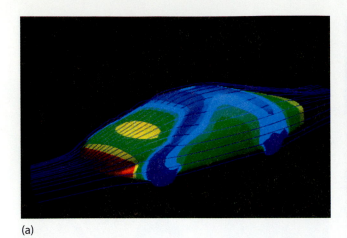

(a)

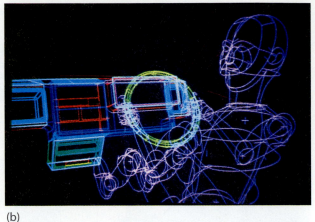

(b)

Figure 23 CAD/CAM. With computer-aided design and computer-aided manufacturing (CAD/CAM), the computer can keep track of all details, maintain designs of parts in storage, and combine parts electronically as required. (a) A computer-aided design wireframe of a car used to study design possibilities. (b) Engineers also use graphics to test designs relative to the consumer.

FOCUS ON *Ethics*

Saving Your Face

What responsibility does a computer user have when using a picture of a person? Can an employer ethically include photos of employees on a web site page without express permission from each individual? Can a university create web sites that include faculty faces without potentially compromising the person's privacy and safety?

work. The next time you watch television, skip the trip to the kitchen and pay special attention to the commercials. If there is no live human in the advertisement (and perhaps even if there is), the moving objects you see, such as floating cars and bobbing electric razors, are doubtlessly computer output. Another fertile ground for video graphics is a television network's logo and theme. Accompanied by music and swooshing sounds, the network symbol spins and cavorts and turns itself inside out, all with the finesse that only a computer could supply.

Video graphics are well known to people who like to play arcade games; their input device is a **joystick,** a sort of quickly reacting mouse with a handle that allows fingertip control of figures on the screen.

Computer-Aided Design/ Computer-Aided Manufacturing

Computer graphics have become part and parcel of a field known by the abbreviation **CAD/CAM,** short for **computer-aided design/computer-aided manufacturing.** In this area computers are used to create two- and three-dimensional pictures of everything from hand tools to tractors to highway designs. CAD/CAM provides a bridge between design (planning what a product will be) and manufacturing (actually making the planned product). As a manager at DaimlerChrysler said, "Many companies have design data and manufacturing data, and the two are never the same. At Chrysler, we have only one set of data that everyone dips into." Keeping data in one place, of course, makes changes easier and encourages consistency. For an example of Chrysler's efforts, see Figure 23.

Figure 24 Digital cameras. Digital cameras do not use film. They store images internally then send them via cable or disk to your computer.

Digital Cameras

Point, shoot, edit, print; the steps noticeably missing are loading film and, later, the trips to the photo-processing lab. A **digital camera** takes photos that it stores internally on a chip; there is no film (Figure 24). The photos can then be sent by cable directly to your computer; some cameras place the image on a removable card that can be added to an adapter and inserted in the computer's disk drive. Some cameras record images directly on a diskette. Once in the computer, the photos can be edited with the software that accompanied the camera. When you are satisfied with a photo, you can print it. Photos printed on your everyday printer will not rival film-based images, but you may buy a special printer designed for photos that uses heavyweight paper and produces good results.

A particular advantage of digital cameras is their little LCD windows that let you see the photo you just took. If you do not like it, simply delete it and try again.

Ethics and Data

Few people pause to ponder the relationship between ethics and data, but it is an important one. Once the data is in the computer, there are many ways it can be used, sold, or even altered. Data can also be input and be stored in a great variety of ways. Consider these data ethics issues, all of which are at least debatable and most of which could be defensible in some situations:

- Is it ethically acceptable to use a computer to alter photographs? Is it ethical to substitute one person for another in a photograph? Should we be able to change pictures of ourselves? of group photos from school or work? Is it ethical to use a computer to add a celebrity to a photo? Does it matter if the celebrity is alive or dead?
- Suppose you perceive that the contents of certain e-mail messages may be of interest to a plaintiff suing your company. Is it ethical to just erase them?
- A friend who has worked on a political campaign has a disk file of donors. Is it ethical to use that same list to solicit for your candidate?

Note that not all of these scenarios inherently require a computer. But the computer makes it that much easier.

▲

New forms of computer input and output are announced regularly, often with promises of multiple benefits and new ease of use. Part of the excitement of the computer world is that these promises are usually kept, and users reap the benefits directly. Input and output just keep getting better.

Virtual Ads

Are you in the stands, watching the game? Then you see the scene in the top image shown here. But if you are watching the game on television, you may see an altered version, as shown in the bottom image. The computer is at work again, this time producing a virtual ad—one that does not exist in the ballpark.

Prior to the event, an operator selects which advertisements to insert and chooses where in the stadium they will appear. During the broadcast, the system then automatically inserts the advertisement into position, correctly adjusted for the position of the television camera. The inserted images appear as if they actually exist in the stadium, even to the extent that players pass in front of—obscure—the inserted image.

Unlike the usual 30-second television commercial, this ad may loom in front of a viewer for much of the game. Furthermore, advertisers can target local audiences, showing an ad for hot soup in Juneau while, in the same spot, showing an ad for cold soda in San Diego.

GETTING PRACTICAL

DIGITAL DARKROOM

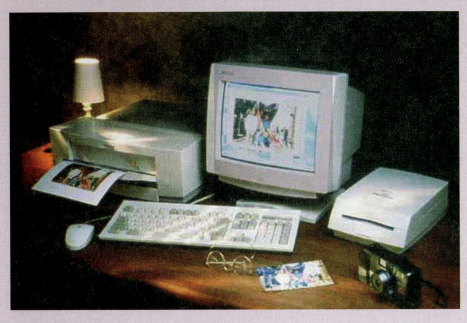

Never mind the traditional dark room, where a photo buff squints under a tiny colored light while sloshing photos through smelly development chemicals. And, frankly, the results of all that sloshing, especially enlargements, probably would not be confused with professional work. But now that has changed. With the right computer equipment, you can be a professional—or close enough. You can make prints and enlargements that could not be differentiated from professional work without the aid of a magnifying glass.

First, let us consider the source of your pictures. How does one get the photos in the computer in the first place? There are several possibilities. A straightforward approach is to use a digital camera, storing the pictures in some computer-sensible form—chip or card or disk—and transferring the images directly to the computer. If your photos were recorded on the camera's embedded chip, they can be transferred by means of a cable hooked up to your computer's serial port, a plug-like input in the back. Input from a digital camera is convenient but is limited in quality. Another choice is to scan photos into the computer; a good quality scanner will maintain the quality of the photos.

Another possible photo source is the Internet, which offers free images, some as part of clip-art collections. Keep in mind, however, that professional photos on Internet sites are probably fee-based. Thus, if your photo interest goes beyond casual snapshots, you can pay for and download images from professional services on the Internet. Whatever method is chosen to input photos, the net result is that you then can edit and reproduce those photos.

Once you have the photos in digital form, you will probably want to use some photo imaging software to manipulate them. Such software is an option rather than a necessity, but many people find that they like to improve or change their pictures in some way. However, despite a bit of photo manipulation by software, the printed photo image you hope for can only be as good as the image the program is given to work with.

Several vendors offer equipment specifically geared to the photography market, that is, systems designed to help real people produce real photos at home. One such system, shown here, is produced by Hewlett Packard. The HP PhotoSmart PC photography system includes a photo printer, photo scanner, digital camera, and photographic papers for printing your pictures. Each component may be purchased separately.

The HP PhotoSmart scanner handles prints up to 5 by 7 inches, mounted slides, and even negatives. The printer can produce glossy pictures on heavy photo stock paper, in standard photo sizes, such as 5 by 7 inches, or 8 by 10 inches. The results are so crisp and vibrant that an average person could not distinguish them from a photo produced by a photo-processing chain. Keep in mind that this must be a second printer; the PhotoSmart printer is slow, and mediocre at printing traditional text.

Processing photographs at home is a trend is progress. People love to take pictures. People also love enlargements. Yet, mostly due to the high cost, only a tiny per cent of photos are enlarged. Home computer photography systems offer a new level of flexibility and creativity, enabling users to make professional-looking prints, reprints, and enlargements of photos that can be incorporated into personalized greeting cards, calendars, and postcards.

Summary and Key Terms

- A **keyboard** is a common input device that may be part of a personal computer or a terminal connected to a remote computer. A **source document** is the original written data to be keyed into the computer.

- A **mouse** is an input device with a ball on its underside, whose movement on a flat surface causes a corresponding movement of the **pointer** on the screen. Moving the mouse (or pressing keyboard keys) allows you to reposition the pointer, then click the mouse button to set the **insertion point,** or **cursor.** An **icon,** a pictorial symbol on a screen, can be clicked to invoke a command to the computer, a process called a **graphical user interface (GUI).**

- A **trackball** is like an upside-down mouse—the ball is rolled with the hand. A **track pad** invokes a command with finger movement.

- **Source data automation** involves the use of special equipment to collect data at its origin and send it directly to the computer.

- **Magnetic-ink character recognition (MICR)** allows a machine to read characters made of magnetized particles, such as the preprinted characters on a personal check. Some characters are preprinted, but others, such as the amount of a check, are added by a person using a **MICR inscriber.**

- A **scanner** can convert text or even a drawing or picture into computer-recognizable form by using **optical recognition,** a system that uses a light beam to scan input data and convert it into electrical signals that are sent to the computer for processing. In a process called **imaging,** a scanner converts those papers to an electronic version, which can then be stored on disk and retrieved when needed.

- A **flatbed scanner,** a tabletop machine, typically scans a sheet at a time, although some offer an attachment for scanning multiple sheets. A **sheetfeed scanner,** usually designed to fit neatly between the keyboard and the monitor, uses motorized rollers to feed the sheet across the scanning head. A **handheld scanner,** the least expensive and least reliable of the three, is handy for portability.

- **Optical mark recognition (OMR)** devices recognize marks on paper. **Optical character recognition (OCR)** devices read special characters, such as those on price tags. These characters are often in a standard typeface called **OCR-A.** A commonly used OCR device is the handheld **wand reader,** which is often connected to a **point-of-sale (POS) terminal** in a retail store. A **bar-code reader** is a photoelectric scanner used to input a **bar code,** a pattern of vertical marks; one standard represents the **Universal Product Code (UPC)** that identifies a product. Some optical scanners can read precise handwritten characters.

- **Voice input,** or **speech recognition,** is the process of presenting input data to the computer through the spoken word. **Speech recognition devices** convert spoken words into a digital code that a computer can understand. The two main types of devices are **discrete word systems,** which require speakers to pause between words, and **continuous word systems,** which allow a normal rate of speaking.

- Input can be given directly to a computer via a **touch screen;** a finger touching the screen interrupts the light beams on the monitor edge, pinpointing the selected screen location.

- The **monitor** features the computer's screen, includes the housing for its electrical components, and probably sits on a stand that tilts and swivels. Screen output is known in the computer industry as **soft copy** because it is intangible and temporary, unlike **hard copy,** produced by a printer on paper, which is tangible and can be permanent.

■ The most common kind of computer screen is the **cathode ray tube (CRT).** Some computer screens are **monochrome**—the characters appear in one color, usually green or amber, on a dark background. Most CRT screens use a technology called **raster scanning,** in which the backing of the screen display has a phosphorous coating, which will glow whenever it is hit by a beam of electrons. The screen image must be **refreshed** often to avoid flicker. The **scan rate** is the number of times the screen is refreshed per second. **Interlaced** screens are scanned every other line, but **non-interlaced (NI)** screens are preferred for animated graphics.

■ A computer display screen that can be used for graphics is divided into dots that are called **addressable** because they can be *addressed* individually by the graphics software. Each screen dot is called a **pixel.** The more pixels, the higher the **screen resolution,** or clarity. **Dot pitch** is the amount of space between the dots on a screen. If a computer does not come with built-in graphics capability, you will have to add a **graphics card** or **graphics adapter board.**

■ Common graphics standards are **SVGA (Super VGA),** providing various high resolutions and potentially supporting a palette of 16 million colors, and **XGA (extended graphics array),** a high-resolution graphics standard that provides the same resolutions but supports more simultaneous colors and can be non-interlaced.

■ A **liquid crystal display (LCD)** is a type of flat screen found on laptop computers and on some desktop computers. These screens are noted for their slimness and bright, flicker-free images, but they are more expensive than CRTs.

■ A **screen** may be part of the monitor of a self-contained personal computer, or it may be part of a **terminal,** an input/output device linked to a main computer. Most terminals these days have some processing ability of their own—a CPU—and are thus called **smart terminals.**

■ **Printers** produce printed paper output. The default printer **orientation** setting is **portrait mode,** in which output is printed with the longest end north and south; **landscape mode** prints output "sideways" on the paper. Printers can be classified as either **impact printers,** which form characters by physically striking the paper, or **nonimpact printers, laser** and **ink-jet printers,** which use a noncontact printing method. Today's laser printers print 600 or 1200 **dpi (dots per inch),** producing extremely high-quality results.

■ Computer **speech synthesis** has been accomplished through **voice synthesizers** (also called **voice-output devices** or **audio-response units**). One approach to speech synthesis is **synthesis by analysis,** in which the computer analyzes stored tapes of spoken words. In the other approach, called **synthesis by rule,** the computer applies linguistic rules to create artificial speech.

■ **MIDI (Musical Instrument Digital Interface),** pronounced "MID dee," is a set of rules designed for recording and playing back music on digital synthesizers.

■ **Video graphics** are a series of computer-produced pictures. Video-graphic arcade games are played with a **joystick,** which allows fingertip control of figures on the screen.

■ In **computer-aided design/computer-aided manufacturing (CAD/CAM),** computers are used to design and manufacture products.

■ A **digital camera** takes photos that are stored internally on a chip or card, then sent directly to your computer, where they can be edited and printed.

Discussion Questions

1. For this question, use your knowledge from either reading or experience, or imagine the possibilities. What kind of input device might be convenient for these types of jobs or situations?

   a. A supermarket stock clerk who takes inventory by surveying items currently on the shelf

   b. A medical assistant who must input existing printed documents to the computer

   c. An airport automated luggage-tracking system

d. A telephone worker who takes orders over the phone

e. A restaurant in which customers place their own orders from the table

f. An inspector at the U.S. Bureau of Engraving who monitors and gives a go/no go response on printed money passing by on an assembly line

g. A retailer who wants to move customers quickly through checkout lines

h. A psychologist who wants to give a new client a standard test

i. An environmental engineer who hikes through woods and streams to inspect and report on the effects of pollutants

j. A small-business owner who wants to keep track of employee work hours

2. Do you think that voice input is practical for your own use?

3. If price were not a consideration, what kind of printers would you buy for your home or business personal computers?

Student Study Guide

Multiple Choice

1. The amount of space between the dots on a screen is called
   a. OCR   c. dot pitch
   b. LCD   d. OMR

2. A pictorial screen symbol that represents a computer activity is called a(n)
   a. pointer   c. touch screen
   b. icon   d. MICR

3. Using computers to design and manufacture products is called
   a. inscribing   c. detailing
   b. CAD/CAM   d. imaging

4. Soft copy refers to
   a. OCR-A   c. screen output
   b. music sounds   d. digitizing

5. The type of scanner that fits between the keyboard and the monitor is the
   a. sheetfeed scanner c. flatbed scanner
   b. handheld scanner   d. video scanner

6. An ink-jet printer is an example of a(n)
   a. laser printer   c. LCD printer
   b. impact printer   d. nonimpact printer

7. Entering data as a by-product of the activity that generates the data is known as
   a. source data automation   c. CAD/CAM
   b. a discrete word system   d. MICR entry

8. The rate of screen refreshment is called
   a. pixel speed   c. raster rate
   b. bit-map speed   d. scan rate

9. Magnetic characters are produced on your bank checks by
   a. bar-code readers c. MICR inscribers
   b. mice   d. OCR

10. "Mark sensing" is another term for
    a. MICR   c. OMR
    b. POS   d. XGA

11. A device used for optical character recognition is a
    a. wand reader   c. pen
    b. cursor   d. MICR reader

12. OCR-A is a
    a. portrait   c. wand reader
    b. standard typeface d. bar code

13. POS terminals are similar to
    a. calculators   c. UPCs
    b. touch-tone telephones   d. cash registers

14. A one-color screen on a black background is called
    a. monochrome   c. addressable
    b. blank   d. liquid crystal display

15. Voice input devices convert voice input to
    a. digital codes   c. OCR-A
    b. bar codes   d. optical marks

16. Imaging uses what device to input data?
    a. scanner   c. icon
    b. bar-code reader d. tablet

17. The pointer can be moved by rolling this device on a flat surface:
    a. mouse   c. wand reader
    b. UPC   d. interactive tablet

18. Which input device is often attached to laptop computers?
    a. trackball   c. inscriber
    b. graphic display   d. wand reader

19. A screen that is lighter and slimmer than a CRT is a(n)
    a. OCR   c. flat panel
    b. graphics card   d. terminal

20. Computer animation is a form of
    a. LCD   c. video graphics
    b. CAD/CAM   d. color printer output

True/False

T F   1. The greater the number of pixels, the poorer the screen clarity.

T F   2. Printers produce hard copy.

T F   3. Video graphics are computer-produced pictures.

T F   4. Discrete word systems allow a normal rate of speaking.

T F   5. Data is scanned into the computer using a mouse.

T F   6. In a discrete word system, the user must pause between words.

T F   7. CRT stands for computer remote terminal.

T F   8. Optical recognition technology is based on magnetized data.

T F   9. OMR senses marks on paper.

T F 10. A wand reader can read OCR characters.

T F 11. A "sideways" printer orientation is called portrait mode.

T F 12. LCD is a type of flat screen found on laptop computers.

T F 13. LCD stands for liquid crystal display.

T F 14. The personal computer screen standard with the highest resolution is CGA.

T F 15. A mouse can be clicked to invoke a command.

T F 16. The MICR process is used mainly by retail stores.

T F 17. A cursor indicates the location of the next interaction on the screen.

T F 18. Dot pitch refers to the number of pixels on a screen.

T F 19. The best way to scan a page from a book is with a flatbed scanner.

T F 20. One color screen standard today is XGA.

T F 21. Non-interlaced screens are best for animated graphics.

T F 22. A track pad is used by moving it across a hard surface.

T F 23. MIDI is the accepted standard for LCD screens.

T F 24. To avoid flicker a screen needs to be refreshed often.

T F 25. The most common use for a joystick is CAD/CAM applications.

T F 26. A terminal that has the capability of doing some processing is called a smart terminal.

T F 27. Flat screens can be found on desktop computers as well as laptop computers.

T F 28. A laser printer is an impact printer.

T F 29. A digital camera uses an embedded chip to focus the picture but records the picture on regular film.

T F 30. The type of scanner that produces the highest quality image is the handheld scanner.

Fill-In

1. The original written data to be keyed into the computer is called the _____.

2. LCD stands for _____.

3. The standard optical typeface is known as
   _____.

4. POS stands for _____
   _____.

5. Another name for a pictorial screen symbol that represents a command is
   _____.

6. MICR stands for
   _____.

7. Using a scanner to input documents to the computer is called
   _____.

8. The phrase used to describe collecting computer data at the source is
   _____
   _____.

9. UPC stands for

_____.

10. The input method used mainly by banks for processing checks is known as

_____.

11. The CRT technology in which the phosphorus-coated screen glows when it is hit by a beam of electrons is called _____.

12. The method that uses a light beam to sense marks on machine-readable test forms is called

_____.

13. The tabletop scanner that can handle a book page is the _____.

14. Which technology is more challenging, voice input or voice output? _____.

15. The kind of terminal that reads bar codes but is like a cash register is the

_____.

16. Screen output is called

_____.

17. Printed computer output is called

_____.

18. The type of scanner that accepts a sheet of paper and moves it with motorized rollers is the

_____.

19. An input device that reads OCR tags is the

_____.

20. A screen that accepts input from a pointing finger is called a _____.

Answers

Multiple Choice

1. c	6. d	11. a	16. a
2. b	7. a	12. b	17. a
3. b	8. d	13. d	18. a
4. c	9. c	14. a	19. c
5. a	10. c	15. a	20. c

True/False

1. F	7. F	13. T	19. T	25. F
2. T	8. F	14. F	20. T	26. T
3. T	9. T	15. T	21. T	27. T
4. F	10. T	16. F	22. F	28. F
5. F	11. F	17. T	23. F	29. F
6. T	12. T	18. F	24. T	30. F

Fill-In

1. source document
2. liquid crystal display
3. OCR-A
4. point of sale
5. icon
6. magnetic-ink character recognition
7. imaging
8. source data automation
9. Universal Product Code
10. MICR
11. raster scanning
12. OMR
13. flatbed
14. voice input
15. POS terminal
16. soft copy
17. hard copy
18. sheetfeed
19. wand reader
20. touch screen

When people begin to learn something new, they usually have many questions. In fact, people being introduced to the same new subject often have exactly the same questions. Rather than answer each question individually, it makes sense to keep the most frequently asked questions—FAQs—in a handy place that anyone can access. FAQs are a long-standing tradition on the Internet.

Where are FAQs on the Internet? The use of FAQs is so widespread that you are likely to come across them on many sites. However, some sites specialize in comprehensive Internet-related FAQs—and answers—for beginners, notably the long-standing Web Browser Open FAQs. Another good place to start is Beginner's Central. Several sites, such as the Net Lingo site, offer lists of Internet-related definitions. You can also pose questions to the Surf Guru.

Can I get some general information about the Internet? Some sites include a history of the Internet as one of many offerings. Others, like the History of the Internet, Net History, Hobbes Internet Timeline, and World Wide Web: Origins and Beyond sites, offer a long and detailed history, with names, organizations, and timelines. You can get demographic information about the Internet—official and unofficial statistics—from sites such as Internet Statistics.

What is Doonesbury doing over there? Look closely and you will see that one of the circles contains the cartoon's artist, Garry Trudeau, with "FAQs" printed nearby. This icon links to a portion of the site where the artist answers questions about the comic strip. Similarly, the Car Talk image represents a page that offers, among other things, a list of FAQs on car repair. These two sites typify the use of FAQs related to the material

on individual sites, as opposed to topics related to the Internet as a whole.

What about going beyond the basic facts to get help on making a home page? Advice abounds, usually with titles such as the Getting Started site. Most users with an interest in making a web page start with information about HTML. A good place to start would be the Beginner's Guide to HTML; actually, there are several sites with that exact name. Another is the HTML Guide, whose clickable reference-book logo is shown here. There are dozens of HTML sites. If you find one HTML site, it probably will have a list of links to others.

Anything else for making a page? There are many sites that offer design advice and free clip-art images. Getting Started is a popular home page advice site. David Seigel's Casbah site, shown here, is highly regarded for its excellent page design advice.

Are there other places to get help? There are several possibilities besides teaching yourself. Many colleges include home page creation as part of an Internet course. This may be via HTML or in one of several authoring languages, such as FrontPage. Private firms advertise courses to teach you the basics in a

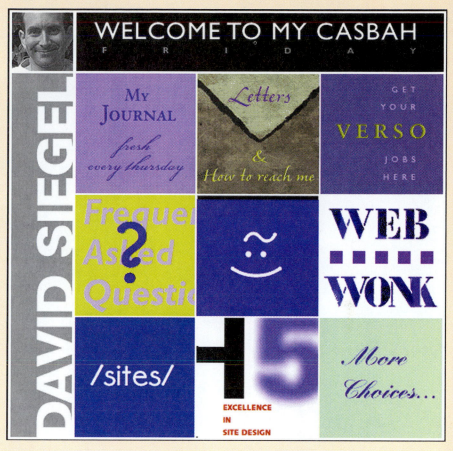

few hours. Serious users, usually businesses that want a "Web presence," may engage the services of consultants who can create a sophisticated home page.

Internet Exercises

1. **Structured exercise.** Begin with the URL http://www.prenhall.com/capron and link to the Web Browser Open FAQs.
2. **Freeform exercise.** Go to the Beginner's Guide to HTML and click on some of the links listed there.

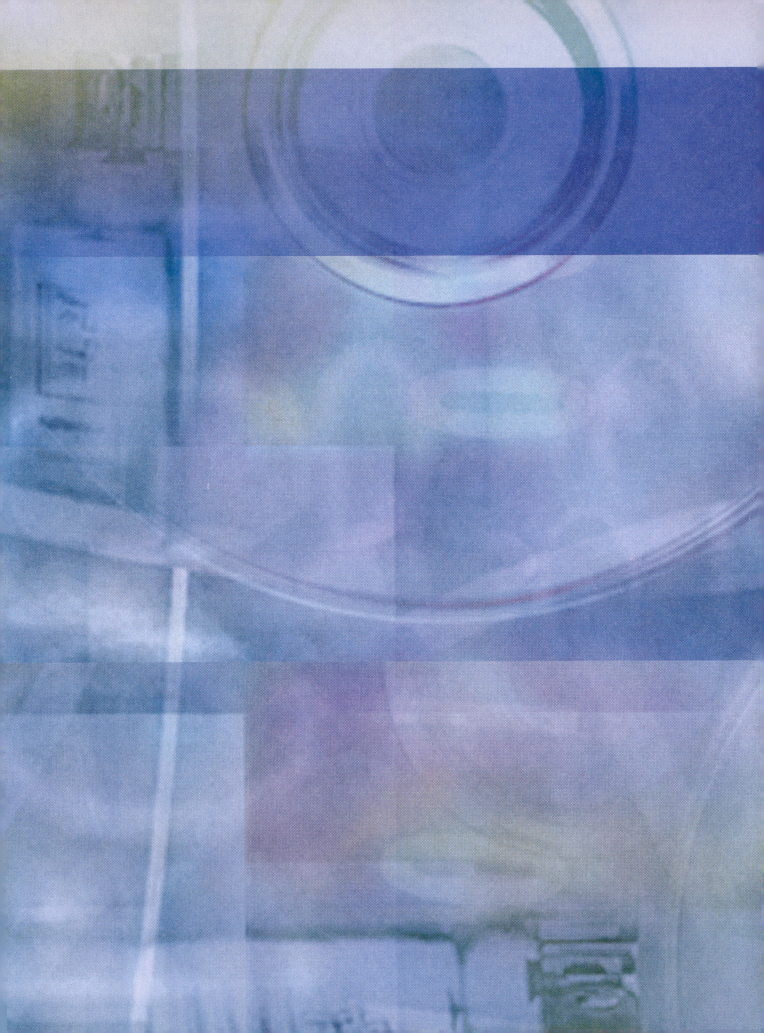

CHAPTER FIVE

STORAGE AND MULTIMEDIA

The Facts and More

LEARNING OBJECTIVES

- List the benefits of secondary storage
- Identify storage media available for personal computers
- Differentiate the principal types of secondary storage
- Describe how data is stored on a disk
- Understand and appreciate the benefits of multimedia
- Understand how data is organized, accessed, and processed

Cheri Urquhart, Tate Kirschner, and Taylor Russell met in college, where they were studying to become architects. They did both undergraduate and graduate work together and then went their separate ways into the workforce. But they remained in the same city and kept in touch.

Seven years later, at a professional conference, their casual conversation over dinner turned serious and they began to consider forming their own architectural firm. The details of accomplishing this were complex and involved many months of planning. Our concern here is what they decided to do about computers and, particularly, computer storage.

Architectural drawings are made with special software; the software alone takes up many millions of bytes of storage. In addition, the architectural drawings themselves are storage hogs. The three architects did not hesitate to include hard disk with many gigabytes of storage.

Another problem was the need to be able to produce computer-generated "walk-through" movies, a simulated tour to show their clients the planned structure. For this, they chose DVD-ROM, a type of high-capacity storage disk that can hold a full-length movie with room to spare.

Further, the architects each had computers at home. They thought they should upgrade the storage capacity of their individual computers so that they could bring work home. They also wanted some sort of transfer storage device, so they could bring drawings on disk between home and office; they settled on the Zip drive, which holds a high-capacity diskette.

The issues just described are more complicated than most people face. However, it is true that disk storage is an ongoing issue for most users—we can never seem to get enough. A rule of thumb among computer professionals is to estimate disk needs generously and then double that amount. But estimating future needs is rarely easy.

The Benefits of Secondary Storage

Picture, if you can, how many filing-cabinet drawers would be required to hold the millions of files of, say, tax records kept by the Internal Revenue Service or historical employee records kept by General Motors. The record storage rooms would have to be enormous. Computers, in contrast, permit storage on tape or disk in extremely compressed form. Storage capacity is unquestionably one of the most valuable assets of the computer.

Secondary storage, sometimes called **auxiliary storage,** is storage separate from the computer itself, where you can store software and data on a semi-

MAKING THE RIGHT CONNECTIONS

REBANET

Do you want to know more about Brad Pitt? Kobe Bryant? Reba? You will have no trouble finding a connection on the Internet to almost any celebrity. In addition to casual fan sites, most famous folks maintain their own official sites, such as the Reba McIntire page shown here. The sites of show business and sports celebrities offer lists of accomplishments, such as recordings, movies, and statistics. The sites may also offer photos to download and memorabilia for sale. But, most important, almost all official sites let visitors pose questions that will be answered via e-mail.

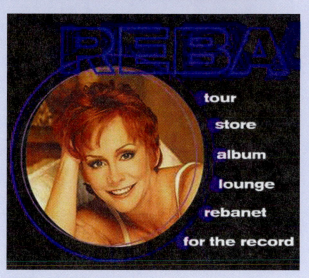

permanent basis. Secondary storage is necessary because memory, or primary storage, can be used only temporarily. However, you probably want to reuse information you have derived from processing; that is why secondary storage is needed.

The benefits of secondary storage can be summarized as follows:

- **Space.** Organizations may store the equivalent of a roomful of data on sets of disks that take up less space than a breadbox. A simple diskette for a personal computer can hold the equivalent of 500 printed pages, or one book. An optical disk can hold the equivalent of approximately 500 books.
- **Reliability.** Data in secondary storage is basically safe, since secondary storage is physically reliable. (We should note, however, that disks sometimes fail.) Also, it is more difficult for untrained people to tamper with data on disk than with data stored on paper in a file cabinet.
- **Convenience.** With the help of a computer, authorized users can locate and access data quickly.
- **Economy.** Together the three previous benefits indicate significant savings in storage costs. It is less expensive to store data on tape or disk (the principal means of secondary storage) than to buy and house filing cabinets. Data that is reliable and safe is less expensive to maintain than data subject to errors. But the greatest savings can be found in the speed and convenience of filing and retrieving data.

These benefits apply to all the various secondary storage devices, but, as you will see, some devices are better than others. The discussion begins with a look at the various storage media, including those used for personal computers, and then moves to what it takes to get data organized and processed.

Group Work

The pace of change in computing is amazing, and students may be able to share in this perspective if they work in teams to interview a computer professional about some concrete area of change. Possibilities for questions include changes in cost, reliability, capacity and functionality the interviewee has witnessed in secondary storage devices, or in computer networking speeds and connections.

Figure 1 **Surface of a disk.**

Magnetic Disk Storage

Diskettes and hard disks are magnetic media; that is, they are based on a technology of representing data as magnetized spots on the disk—with a magnetized spot representing a 1 bit and the absence of such a spot representing a 0 bit. Reading data from the disk means converting the magnetized data to electrical impulses that can be sent to the processor. Writing data to disk is the opposite; it involves sending electrical impulses from the processor to be converted to magnetized spots on the disk. As Figure 1 shows, the surface of each disk has concentric tracks on it. The number of tracks per surface varies with the particular type of disk.

Diskettes

A **diskette** is made of flexible mylar and coated with iron oxide, a substance that can be magnetized. A diskette can record data as magnetized spots on tracks on its surface. Diskettes became popular along with the personal computer. Most computers use the 3 1/2-inch diskette, whose capacity is 1.44 megabytes of data (Figure 2). The diskette has the protection of a hard plastic jacket and fits conveniently in a shirt pocket or purse. The key advantage of diskettes is portability. Diskettes easily transport data from one computer to another. Workers, for example, carry their files from office computer to home computer and back on a diskette instead of carrying a stack of papers in a briefcase. Students use the campus computers but keep their files on their own diskettes. Diskettes are also a convenient vehicle for backup: It is convenient to place an extra copy of a hard disk file on a diskette.

However, the venerable 3 1/2-inch diskette, a standard for a decade, is being challenged. A new standard could be a higher-capacity disk whose drive can handle both the new disk type and the traditional 3 1/2-inch disk. However, the technology with a head start is Iomega's Zip drive, already installed by 20 million users. The Zip drive holds 100-megabyte disks, 70 times the capacity of traditional diskettes (Figure 3). The disadvantage of the Zip drive is that it is not compatible with 3 1/2-inch diskettes.

Even a high-capacity diskette can be problematic if, for example, you want to take a large file back and forth between your office and home computers. One possibility is **data compression,** the process of squeezing a big file into a small place. Compression can be as simple as removing all extra space characters, inserting a single repeat character to indicate a string of repeated characters, and substituting smaller data strings for frequently

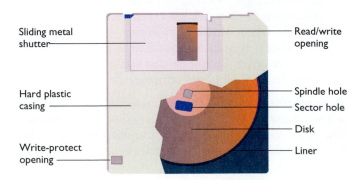

Sliding metal shutter

Hard plastic casing

Write-protect opening

Read/write opening

Spindle hole

Sector hole

Disk

Liner

Figure 2 **Diskette.** A cutaway view of a 3 1/2-inch diskette.

occurring characters. This kind of compression can reduce a text file to 50 percent of its original size. Compression is performed by a program that uses a formula to determine how to compress or decompress data. To be used again, the file must, of course, be uncompressed. Incidentally, to speed up the transfer, many users choose to compress files that will be sent from one computer to another via data communications.

Hard Disks

A **hard disk** is a metal platter coated with magnetic oxide that can be magnetized to represent data. Hard disks come in a variety of sizes (Figure 4a). Several disks can be assembled into a **disk pack.** There are different types of disk packs, with the number of platters varying by model. Each disk in the pack has top and bottom surfaces on which to record data. Many disk devices, however, do not record data on the top of the top platter or on the bottom of the bottom platter.

A **disk drive** is a device that allows data to be read from a disk or written on a disk. A disk pack is mounted on a disk drive that is a separate unit connected to the computer. Large computers have dozens or even hundreds of external disk drives; in contrast, the hard disk for a personal computer is within the computer housing. In a disk pack all disks rotate at the same time, although only one disk is being read from or written on at any one time. The mechanism for reading or writing data on a disk is an **access arm;** it moves a read/write head into position over a particular track (Figure 5a). The **read/write head** on the end of the access arm hovers just above the track but does not actually touch the surface. When a read/write head does accidentally touch the disk surface, it is called a **head crash** and data can be destroyed. Data can also be destroyed if a read/write head encounters even minuscule foreign matter on the disk surface (Figure 5b). A disk pack has a series of access arms that slip in between the disks in the pack (Figure 5c). Two read/write heads are on each arm, one facing up to access the surface above it and one facing down to access the surface below it. However, only one read/write head can operate at any one time.

Most disk packs combine the disks, access arms, and read/write heads in an airtight, sealed module. These disk assemblies are put together in clean rooms so that even microscopic dust particles do not get on the disk surface.

Hard disks for personal computers are 3 1/2-inch disks in sealed modules (Figure 6). Hard disk capacity for personal computers has soared in recent years; older hard disks have capacities of tens of megabytes, but new ones offer multiple gigabytes of storage. Terabyte capacity is on the horizon. Although an individual probably cannot imagine generating enough output—letters, budgets, reports, pictures, and so forth—to fill a hard disk, software packages take up a lot of space and can make a dent rather quickly. Furthermore, graphics images and audio and video files require large amounts of disk space. Perhaps more important than capacity, however, is the convenience of speed. Personal computer users find that accessing files on a hard disk is significantly faster and more convenient than accessing files on a diskette.

Hard Disks in Groups

No storage system is completely safe, but a **redundant array of independent disks,** or simply **RAID,** comes close. RAID storage uses several small hard disks that work together as a unit. The most basic RAID system—RAID level 1—simply duplicates data on separate disk drives, a concept called **disk mirroring** (Figure 7b). Thus no data is lost if one drive fails. This process is reli-

Figure 3 The Iomega Zip disk drive. Shown here is a separate drive unit, but many users have their Zip drive installed in a bay in the computer's housing.

InfoBit

One reason a "head crash" does so much damage to a disk has to do with the speed of the disk surface relative to the stationary head. The disk surface is actually moving under the head at 60 miles per hour or more and so even a brief collision between the two can be fatal to the stored data and damaging to the head.

(a)

(b)

Figure 4 Magnetic disks. (a) Hard magnetic disks come in a variety of sizes. Shown here is a 3 1/2-inch hard drive for a personal computer. (b) These 3 1/2-inch diskettes are protected by a firm plastic exterior cover.

(a)

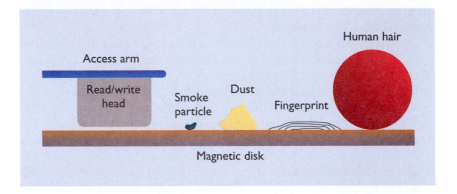

(b)

Learn by Doing

Provide students with a recent issue of any major personal computer or computer "trade" magazine, and an issue—preferably of the same periodical—from about a year ago. Have students scan the advertisements and compute the following: average advertised hard disk capacity, average hard disk price, average price per megabyte. Compare the capacities, prices and ratios from one year ago with recent prices. What trend do you see?

InfoBit

How reliable are hard disks? Mathematical calculations performed by drive manufacturers now predict Mean Times Between Failures (MTBF) of up to a million hours. However, studies of actual disk drive failure rates suggest that the real MTBF is only about 200,000 hours—still an impressive number.

Critical Thinking

Much data on diskette and CD-ROM is not compressed, even though this would often save space. What tradeoffs do you see in compressing data? (Compression slows down access to files because the CPU has to do many calculations to compress and decompress, decompression software must be available on every machine in which the diskette is to be used, and some files cannot be compressed very much, perhaps because they have already been compressed by some other program.)

(c)

Figure 5   Read/write heads and access arms. (a) This photo shows a read/write head on the end of an access arm poised over a hard disk. (b) When in operation, the read/write head comes very close to the surface of the disk. On a disk, particles as small as smoke, dust, a fingerprint, and a hair loom large. If the read/write head encounters one of these, data is destroyed and the disk damaged. (c) Note that there are two read/write heads on each access arm. Each arm slips between two disks in the disk pack. The access arms move simultaneously, but only one read/write head operates at any one time.

Figure 6 Hard disk for a personal computer. The innards of a 3 1/2-inch hard disk with the access arm visible.

able but expensive. Expense, however, may not be an issue when the value of the data is considered.

Higher levels of RAID take a different approach called **data striping** (Figure 7c), which involves spreading the data across several disks in the array, with one disk used solely as a check disk, to keep track of what data is where. If a disk fails, the check disk can reconstitute the data. Higher levels of RAID process data more quickly than simple data mirroring does. RAID is now the dominant form of storage for mainframe computer systems.

How Data Is Organized on a Disk

There is more than one way of physically organizing data on a disk. The methods considered here are the sector method and the cylinder method.

The Sector Method   In the **sector method** each track on a disk is divided into sectors that hold a specific number of characters (Figure 8a). Data on the track is accessed by referring to the surface number, track number, and sector number where the data is stored. The sector method is used for diskettes.

The fact that a disk is circular presents a problem: The distance around the tracks on the outside of the disk is greater than that around the tracks on the inside. A given amount of data that takes up one inch of a track on the inside of a disk might be spread over several inches on a track near the outside of a disk. This means that the tracks on the outside are not storing data as efficiently.

Zone recording takes maximum advantage of the storage available by dividing a disk into zones and assigning more sectors to tracks in outer zones than to those in inner zones (Figure 8b). Since each sector on the disk holds the same amount of data, more sectors mean more data storage than if all tracks had the same number of sectors.

The Cylinder Method   A way to organize data on a disk pack is the **cylinder method,** shown in Figure 9. The organization in this case is vertical. The

Critical Thinking

RAID systems do increase disk system reliability, but they are not a panacea. What reasons can you think of why data can still be lost even with RAID? (RAID may actually inspire false confidence and reduce the diligence with which backups are performed. RAID protects against disk failures, not against power failures, software bugs, programmer carelessness, or user mistakes. Very destructive events, like building fires, storms and floods can still damage disks protected by RAID by damaging or destroying the entire array.)

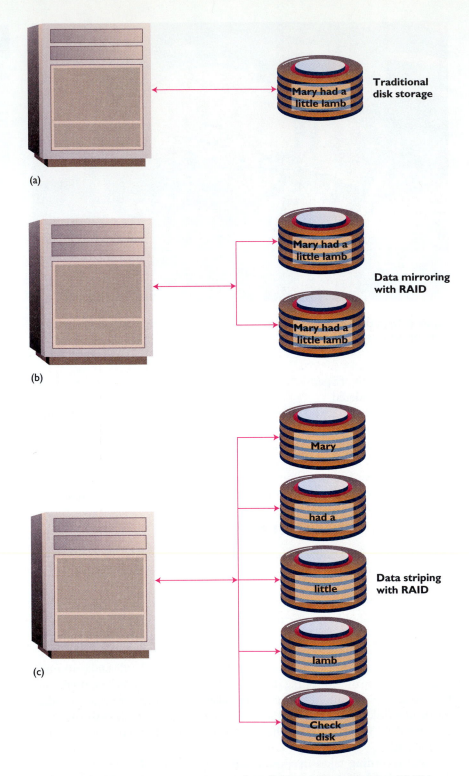

(a)

(b)

(c)

Traditional
disk storage

Data mirroring
with RAID

Data striping
with RAID

Figure 7 RAID storage. (a) Data is stored on disk in traditional fashion. (b) Disk mirroring with RAID stores a duplicate copy of the data on a second disk. (c) In a system called data striping with RAID, data is scattered among several disks, with a check disk that keeps track of what data is where so that data lost on a bad disk can be re-created.

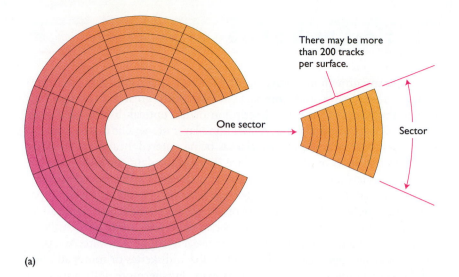

There may be more than 200 tracks per surface.

One sector

Sector

(a)

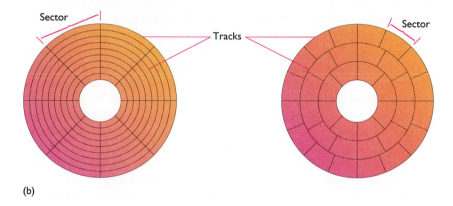

Sector

Tracks

Sector

(b)

Figure 8 Sectors and zone recording. (a) When data is organized by sector, the address is the surface, track, and sector where the data is stored. (b) If a disk is divided into traditional sectors, as shown here on the left, each track has the same number of sectors. Sectors near the outside of the disk are wider, but they hold the same amount of data as sectors near the inside. If the disk is divided into recording zones, as shown on the right, the tracks near the outside have more sectors than the tracks near the inside. Each sector holds the same amount of data, but since the outer zones have more sectors, the disk as a whole holds more data than the disk on the left.

purpose is to reduce the time it takes to move the access arms of a disk pack into position. Once the access arms are in position, they are in the same vertical position on all disk surfaces.

To appreciate this, suppose you had an empty disk pack on which you wished to record data. You might be tempted to record the data horizontally—to start with the first surface and fill track 000, track 001, track 002, and so on and then move to the second surface and again fill tracks 000, 001, 002, and so forth. Each new track and new surface, however, would require movement of the access arms, a relatively slow mechanical process.

Recording the data vertically, on the other hand, substantially reduces access arm movement. The data is recorded on the tracks that can be accessed by one positioning of the access arms—that is, on one **cylinder.** To visualize cylinder organization, pretend that a cylindrically shaped item, such as a tin can, is dropped straight down through all the disks in the disk pack. All the tracks thus encountered, in the same position on each disk surface, make up a cylinder. The cylinder method, then, means that all tracks of a certain cylinder on a disk pack are lined up one beneath the other, and all the vertical tracks of one cylinder are accessible by the read/write heads with one positioning of the access arm mechanism. Tracks within a cylinder are numbered according to this vertical perspective, from 0 on the top down to the last surface on the bottom.

Track 150 on each surface

Figure 9 Cylinder data organization. To visualize the cylinder form of organization, imagine dropping a cylinder such as a tin can straight down through all the disks in the disk pack. Within cylinder 150, the track surfaces are vertically aligned and are numbered vertically from top to bottom.

Optical Disk Storage

The explosive growth in storage needs has driven the computer industry to provide inexpensive and compact storage with greater capacity. This demanding shopping list is a description of the **optical disk** (Figure 10a). The technology works like this: A laser hits a layer of metallic material spread over the surface of a disk. When data is being entered, heat from the laser produces tiny spots on the disk surface. To read the data, the laser scans the disk, and a lens picks up different light reflections from the various spots. Optical storage technology is categorized according to its read/write capability. **Read-only media** are disks recorded by the manufacturer and can be read from but not written to by the user. Such a disk cannot, obviously, be used for your files, but manufacturers can use it to supply software. An applications software package could include a dozen diskettes or more; all these can fit on one optical disk with room to spare. Furthermore, software can be more easily installed from a single optical disk than from a pile of diskettes.

Write-once, read-many media, also called **WORM media,** may be written to once. Once filled, a WORM disk becomes a read-only medium. A WORM disk is nonerasable. For applications demanding secure storage of original versions of valuable documents or data, such as legal records, the primary advantage of nonerasability is clear: Once they are recorded, no one can erase or modify them.

A hybrid type of disk, called **magneto-optical (MO),** combines the best features of magnetic and optical disk technologies. A magneto-optical disk has the high-volume capacity of an optical disk but can be written over like a magnetic disk. The disk surface is coated with plastic and embedded with magnetically sensitive metallic crystals. To write data, a laser beam melts a tiny spot on the plastic surface and a magnet aligns the crystals before the

(a)

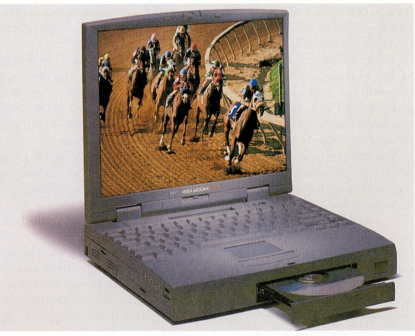

(b)

Figure 10 Optical disks. (a) Optical disks store data using laser beam technology. (b) Many laptop computers include a CD-ROM drive. Laptop users can use CD-ROM applications to make on-the-road presentations or can pop in a CD-ROM encyclopedia to find some needed information.

GETTING PRACTICAL

STAMPS FROM YOUR COMPUTER

That's right: No more trips to the post office, no standing in line. Several sites on the Internet, including PostagePlus, shown here, let you pay for postage and store it right on your hard disk. When you need a stamp, you just print it on the envelope. Well, it does not look much like a real stamp, but the post office accepts it just the same.

Here is how it works. From your personal computer, you access a site that sells postage. This can be done at any time, day or night. You pay for postage, usually with a credit card. The money goes to the U.S. Postal Service, but the company with which you are dealing takes care of the accounting. The postage company grants you permission to print a certain amount of postage, sending that amount and the stamp image to your "vault"—a file—on your hard disk.

(Alternatively, some companies keep your account on their own files.) Then, just print and mail. Another advantage, of interest to a small business, is software that lets you manage multiple address lists and track your mailing costs.

The convenience is remarkable, but there are downsides: signup and monthly fees in addition to the postage—and fewer colorful stamps in circulation.

plastic cools. The crystals are aligned so that some reflect light and others do not. When the data is later read by a laser beam, only the crystals that reflect light are picked up.

CD-ROM

A variation on optical storage technology is the **CD-ROM,** for **compact disk read-only memory.** CD-ROM has a major advantage over other optical disk designs: The disk format is identical to that of *audio* compact disks, so the same dust-free manufacturing plants that are now stamping out digital versions of Kenny G or Jewel can easily convert to producing anything from software to a digitized encyclopedia. Furthermore, CD-ROM storage is substantial—up to 660 megabytes per disk, the equivalent of more than 400 standard 3 1/2-inch diskettes.

Keep in mind that a CD-ROM cannot be used in your personal computer's diskette drive; you must have a CD-ROM drive on your computer (or, as we will discuss shortly, a DVD drive). Today, even laptop computers have CD-ROM drives (Figure 10b). Although CD-ROMs are read-only, a different technology called **CD-R** permits writing on optical disks—but just once; mistakes cannot be undone. CD-R technology requires a CD-R drive, CD-R disks, and the accompanying software. Once a CD-R disk is written on, it can be read not only by the CD-R drive but by any CD-ROM drive. Another variation, **CD-RW,** is more flexible, permitting reading, writing, and rewriting.

InfoBit

An example of the benefits of CD-ROM is the release of important legal documents, like the U.S. Code (the text of current public laws enacted by Congress), on CD rather than paper. When the U.S. Code was published on paper, it was so expensive and so large that it was only updated every six years. The entire U.S. Code now fits on a single CD, is updated every year, and saves about one million dollars a year in printing costs.

DVD-ROM

The new storage technology that outpaces all others is called **DVD-ROM,** for **digital versatile disk** (originally *digital video disk*). Think of a DVD, as it is called for short, as an overachieving CD-ROM. Although the two look the same, a DVD has an astonishing 4.7-gigabyte capacity, seven times more

Global Perspective

The compact disk was not an American invention. The technology was originally developed by Phillips Corporation of the Netherlands and Sony Corporation of Japan.

Single-sided DVDs   **Double-sided DVDs**

Single-layer (4.76GB)   Dual-layer (8.56GB)   Single-layer (9.46GB)   Dual-layer (17GB)

Figure 11 DVD-ROM. A DVD-ROM can use one or two sides, with each side having one or two layers. Since a single layer holds 4.7 gigabytes, and the second almost as much, a DVD-ROM with two sides and two layers per side can hold almost four times that much, or 17 gigabytes.

InfoBit

The possible space—and weight—savings from using CD-ROM instead of paper are truly astounding. For instance, the Navy studied the impact of using CD-ROM to contain a ship's manuals and documentation instead of paper copies. They found that a cruiser carried almost 36 tons of documentation, enough that the stability of the ship could be adversely affected if the papers were stored above the main deck. In theory an equivalent amount of information—5 million pages—could be stored on 20 CD-ROMs, weighing about 10 pounds.

InfoBit

DVD capacity is well-suited to movie viewing. A single sided, single layer DVD can contain 133 minutes of video—sufficient to hold 95% of all movies. Longer movies require "flipping" over a double-sided DVD.

FOCUS ON **Ethics**

Not So Fast . . .

When preparing a multimedia presentation, take a moment to reflect before adding music, images, or video clips. Have you obtained copyright clearance from the copyright owner? Even featuring statuary you have photographed in front of a civic structure may not be a simple matter. The artist who created the work of art may still own the copyright even if the statues themselves have been sold. In general, unless a work of art was created by you, you must consider ownership issues.

than that of the CD-ROM. And that is just the plain variety. DVDs have two layers of information, one clear and one opaque, on a single side; this so-called double-layered DVD surface can hold about 8.5GB. Furthermore, DVDs can be written on both sides, bumping capacity to 17GB (Figure 11). And a DVD-ROM drive can also read CD-ROMs. It is not surprising that DVD-ROM technology is seen as a replacement for CD-ROMs over the next few years.

Operating very much like CD-ROM technology, DVD uses a laser beam to read microscopic spots that represent data. But DVD uses a laser with a shorter wavelength, permitting it to read more densely packed spots, thus increasing the disk capacity. The benefits of this storage capacity are many—full-length movies and exquisite sound. Audio quality on DVD is comparable to that of current audio compact disks. DVDs will eventually hold high-volume business data. It is just a matter of time until all new personal computers will come with a DVD drive as standard equipment. The writable version of DVD is *DVD-RAM*, whose standards are being hammered out.

If you have a CD-ROM or a DVD-ROM drive, you are on your way to one of the computer industry's great adventures: multimedia.

Multimedia

Multimedia stirs the imagination. For example, have you ever thought that you could see a film clip from *Gone with the Wind* on your computer screen? One could argue that such treats are already available on videocassette, but the computer version provides an added dimension for this and other movies: reviews by critics, photographs of movie stars, lists of Academy Awards, the possibility of user input, and much more. Software described as **multimedia** typically presents information with text, illustrations, photos, narration, music, animation, and film clips (Figure 12). Until the optical disk, placing this much data on a disk was impractical. However, the large capacity of optical disks means that the kinds of data that take up huge amounts of storage space—photographs, music, and film clips—can now be readily accommodated.

Multimedia Requirements

To use multimedia software, you must have the proper hardware. In addition to the aforementioned CD-ROM or DVD-ROM drive, you also need a sound card or sound chip (installed internally) and speakers, which may rest externally on either side of the computer or be built into the computer housing. Special software accompanies the drive and sound card. In particular, if full-motion video is important to you, be sure your computer includes **MPEG (Motion Picture Experts Group)**, a set of widely accepted video standards. Another video-related issue is the speed of the drive: the faster the better. The higher the drive speed, the faster the transfer of data and the smoother the video showing on the screen.

Critical Thinking

Will multimedia make text—and reading—obsolete? What are the advantages and disadvantages of each? (It seems unlikely that audio and visual information via computer will ever completely supplant text. Multimedia advantages include realism, high interest level and the idea that "a picture is worth a thousand words." Advantages of text are that it remains compact, is easily compressible, lends itself to hard copy printing, and conveys information at a high rate, since most people can read much faster than anyone can speak or listen.)

(a)

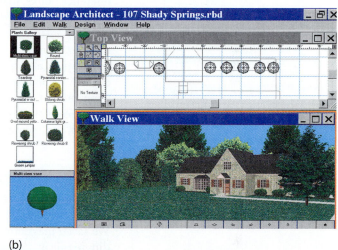

(b)

(c)

(d)

Figure 12 **Multimedia applications.** Multimedia applications offer everything from games to business advice. These four samples include (a) a look at Dangerous Creatures, complete with movie clips, fierce animal sounds, and not-so-fierce baby animals; (b) selections of plants and scenes to help plan landscaping; (c) everything you need to learn Russian, including the clicked/spoken alphabet and phrases; and (d) the popular interactive game Riven, which uses movement and music to enhance the adventure.

Should your next computer be a multimedia personal computer? Absolutely. There is no doubt that multimedia is the medium of choice for all kinds of software.

Multimedia Applications

If you take a moment to peruse the racks of multimedia software in your local store, you can see that most of the current offerings come under the categories of entertainment or education—or possibly both. You can study *and hear* works by Stravinsky or Schubert. You can explore the planets or the ocean bottom through film clips and narrations by experts. You can be "elected" to Congress, after which you tour the Capitol, decorate your office, hire staff, and vote on issues. You can study the battle of Gettysburg—and even change the outcome. You can study the Japanese language, seeing the symbols and hearing the intonation. You can buy multimedia versions of reference books, magazines, children's books, and entire novels.

But this is just the beginning. Businesses are already moving to this high-capacity environment for street atlases, national phone directories, and sales catalogs. Coming offerings will include every kind of standard business application, all tricked out with fancy animation, photos, and sound. Educators will be able to draw upon the new sight and sound for everything from human anatomy to time travel. And just imagine the library of the future, consisting not only of the printed word but also of photos, film, animation, and sound recordings—all flowing from the computer.

Magnetic Tape Storage

We saved magnetic tape storage for last because it now has taken a subordinate role in storage technology. **Magnetic tape** looks like the tape used in music cassettes—plastic tape with a magnetic coating. As in other magnetic media, data is stored as extremely small magnetic spots. Tapes come in a number of forms, including 1/2-inch-wide tape wound on a reel, 1/4-inch-wide tape in data cartridges and cassettes, and tapes that look like ordinary music cassettes but are designed to store data instead of music. The amount of data on a tape is expressed in terms of **density**, which is the number of **characters per inch** (cpi) or **bytes per inch** (bpi) that can be stored on the tape.

The highest-capacity tape is the **digital audio tape,** or DAT, which uses a different method of recording data. Using a method called **helical scan recording,** DAT wraps around a rotating read/write head that spins vertically as it moves. This places the data in diagonal bands that run across the tape rather than down its length. This method produces high density and faster access to data.

Figure 13 shows a **magnetic tape unit** that might be used with a mainframe. The tape unit reads and writes data using a **read/write head.** When the computer is writing on the tape, the **erase head** first erases any data previously recorded.

Two reels are used, a **supply reel** and a **take-up reel.** The supply reel, which has the tape with data on it or on which data will be recorded, is the reel that is changed. The take-up reel always stays with the magnetic tape unit. Many cartridges and cassettes have the supply and take-up reels built into the same case.

Figure 13 Magnetic tape units. Tapes are always protected by glass from outside dust and dirt. These modern tape drives, called "stackers," accept several cassette tapes, each with its own supply and take-up reel.

Tape now has a limited role because disks have proved to be the superior storage medium. Disk data is quite reliable, especially within a sealed module. Furthermore, as will be shown, disk data can be accessed directly, as opposed to sequential data on tape, which can be accessed only by passing by all the data ahead of it on the tape. Consequently, the primary role of tape today is as an inexpensive backup medium.

Backup Systems

Although a hard disk is an extremely reliable device, it is subject to electro-mechanical failures that cause loss of data, as well as physical damage from fire and natural disasters. Furthermore, data files, particularly those accessed by several users, are subject to errors introduced by users. There is also the possibility of errors introduced by software. With any method of data storage, a **backup system**—a way of storing data in more than one place to protect it from damage and errors—is vital. As already noted, magnetic tape is used primarily for backup purposes. For personal computer users, an easy and inexpensive way to back up a hard disk file is simply to copy it to a diskette or Zip disk whenever it is updated. But this is not practical for a system with many files or many users.

Personal computer users have the option of purchasing their own tape backup system, to be used on a regular basis for copying all data from hard disk to a high-capacity tape. Data thus saved can be restored to the hard disk later if needed. A key advantage of a tape backup system is that it can copy the entire hard disk in minutes; also, with the availability of gigabytes of hard disk space, it is not really feasible to swap diskettes in and out of the machine. Further, tape backup can be scheduled to take place when you are not going to be using the computer.

Organizing and Accessing Stored Data

As users of computer systems, we offer data as we are instructed to do, such as punching in our identification code at an automated teller machine or perhaps filling out a form with our name and address. But data cannot be dumped helter-skelter into a computer. Some computer professional—probably a programmer or systems analyst—has to have planned how data from users will be received, organized, and stored and also in what manner data will be processed by the computer.

This kind of storage goes beyond what you may have done to store a memo created in word processing. Organizations that store data usually need a lot of data on many subjects. For example, a charitable organization would probably need detailed information about donors, names and schedules of volunteers, perhaps a schedule of fund-raising events. A factory would need to keep track of inventory (name, identification number, location, quantity, and so forth), the scheduled path of the product through the assembly line, records of quality-control checkpoints, and much more. All this data must be organized and stored according to a plan. First consider how data is organized.

Digital Dog Tags

Traditional dog tags carry a soldier's name and other bits of information that can be seen in a small space. But now, in practically the same amount of space, a multimedia tag called a Personal Information Carrier (PIC) can store a soldier's full medical history, including X-ray images and cardiograms.

InfoBit

Since backing up every file on your hard disk drive—whether it has changed or not—can be very time consuming, many users of tape backup combine periodic "full" backups with more frequent "incremental" backups. The full backups make a copy of every file on disk. The incremental backups copy only those files that have changed since the last full backup.

Critical Thinking

Backups should always be made onto removable media. Besides the unlimited capacity afforded by replaceable media, what other reasons can you see for using removable media in backups? (A major reason is the ability to take the backups to a safe, off-site storage area. Building fires, employee sabotage and water damage can destroy both the original data and the backup copies if the copies are physically close to the originals).

Dupeless
Dupeless

Is it possible that you have more than one copy of the same file on your hard disk? That second copy, of course, would take up extra space. To make the scenario even worse, suppose that you had a dozen copies of the same file. Is this even possible? Alas, yes.

This may seem surprising because people first think of files in terms of their own creations, and they know they did not make multiple copies of the same file. But the duplicate files—and there likely are some—appear as part of software you have added. Each software package comes complete with needed files, as if it were the only software you have. Thus, as you install new software, you will probably include files that you already have installed with other software.

A program called Dupeless, which can be downloaded from the Internet, ferrets out the extra files, notifies the user, and deletes them on command.

Critical Thinking

What fields would make good keys and which fields would make poor keys for databases with the following records: people, cars, books, dogs, and telephones? (Workable keys include the following: Social Security Number for people, Vehicle Identification Number—VIN—for cars, ISBN for books, rabies vaccination tag number or AKC registered name for dogs, area code and telephone number—and possibly country code—for telephones. Poor keys include: name for people, model number for cars, title for books, "Rover" for dogs, local phone number for telephones.)

Data: Getting Organized

To be processed by the computer, raw data is organized into characters, fields, records, files, and databases. First is the smallest element, the character.

- A **character** is a letter, digit, or special character (such as $, ?, or *).
- A **field** contains a set of related characters. For example, suppose that a health club is making address labels for a mailing. For each person it might have a member number field, a name field, a street address field, a city field, a state field, a zip code field, and a phone number field.
- A **record** is a collection of related fields. Thus, on the health club mailing list, one person's member number, name, address, city, state, zip code, and phone number constitute a record.
- A **file** is a collection of related records. All the member records for the health club compose a file. Figure 14 shows how data for a health club member might look.
- A **database** is a collection of interrelated files stored together with minimum redundancy. Specific data items can be retrieved for various applications. For instance, if the health club is opening a new outlet, it can pull out the names of people with zip codes near the new club and send them an announcement.

A field of particular interest is the **key,** a unique identifier for a record. It might seem at first that a name—of a person, say, or a product—would be a good key; however, since some names may be the same, a name field is not a good choice for a key. When a file is first computerized, existing description fields are seldom used as keys. Although a file describing people might use a Social Security number as the key, it is more likely that a new field will be developed that can be assigned unique values, such as customer number or product number.

In addition to organizing the expected data, a plan must be made to access the data on files.

The File Plan: An Overview

Now that you have a general idea of how data is organized, you are ready to look at the process used to decide how to place data on a storage medium. Consider this chain: (1) It is the application—payroll, airline reservations, inventory control, whatever—that determines how the data must be accessed by users. (2) Once an access method has been determined, it follows that there are certain ways the data must be organized so that the needed access is workable. (3) The organization method, in turn, limits the choice of storage medium. The discussion begins with an appreciation of application demands, then moves to a detailed look at organization and access.

The following application examples illustrate how an access decision might be made.

1. A department store offers its customers charge accounts. When a customer makes a purchase, a sales clerk needs to be able to check the validity of the customer's account while the customer is waiting. The clerk needs immediate access to the individual customer record in the account file.
2. A major oil company supplies its charge customers with credit cards, which it considers sufficient proof for purchase. The charge slips collected by gas stations are forwarded to the oil company, which processes

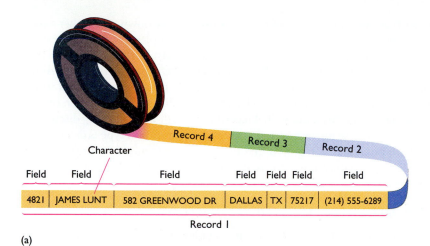

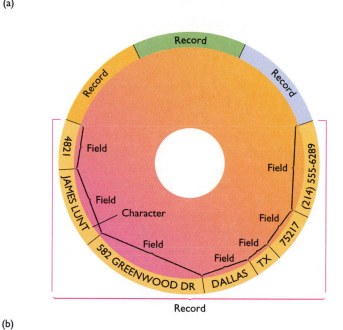

Figure 14 How data is organized.
Whether stored on tape or on disk, data is organized into characters, fields, records, and files. A file is a collection of related records. These drawings represent (a) magnetic tape and (b) magnetic disk.

them in order of account number. Unlike the retail example just given, the company does not need access to any one record at a specific time but merely needs access to all customer charge records when it is time to prepare bills.

3. A city power and light company employee accepts reports of burned-out streetlights from residents over the phone. Using a key made up of unique address components, the clerk immediately finds the record for the offending streetlight and prints out a one-page report that is routed to repair units within 24 hours. To produce such quick service for an individual streetlight, the employee needs to be able to access the individual streetlight record.

4. Next-month schedules for airline flight attendants are computer-produced monthly and delivered to the attendants' home-base mailboxes. The schedules are put together from information based on flight records, and the entire file can be accessed monthly at the convenience of the airline and the computer-use plan.

You're on File at Domino's

If you consider what items of personal information might be stored on disk files, you may think of your Social Security records or perhaps the information stored with your bank account. But small businesses also know about you. They store information you readily provide on their own disk files.

If, for example, you phone a Domino's, an outlet that delivers pizza, your name, address, phone number, and product ordered will be recorded in the company's disk files. When you call again in the future, this information can be retrieved quickly by keying in your phone number. This saves time and effort and speeds your pizza on its way.

As you can see, the question of access seems to come down to whether a particular record is needed right away, as it was in examples 1 and 3. This immediate need for a particular record means access must be *direct*. It follows that the organization must also be direct, or at least *indexed,* and that the storage medium must be disk. Furthermore, the type of processing, a related topic, must be *transaction processing.* The critical distinction is whether or not immediate access to an individual record is needed. The following discussion examines all these topics in detail. Although organization type is determined by the type of access required, the file must be organized before it can be accessed, so organization is the first topic.

File Organization: Three Methods

There are three major methods of storing files of data in secondary storage:

- Sequential file organization, in which records are organized in a particular order
- Direct file organization, in which records are not organized in any special order
- Indexed file organization, in which records are organized sequentially but indexes are built into the file to allow a record to be accessed either sequentially or directly

Sequential File Organization **Sequential file processing** means that records are in order according to a key field. As noted earlier, a file containing information on people will be in order by a **key** that uniquely identifies each person, such as Social Security number or customer number. If a particular record in a sequential file is wanted, all the prior records in the file must be read before the desired record is reached. Tape storage is limited to sequential file organization. Disk storage may be sequential, but records on disk can also be accessed directly.

Direct File Organization **Direct file processing,** or **direct access,** allows the computer to go directly to the desired record by using a record key; the computer does not have to read all preceding records in the file as it does if the records are arranged sequentially. Direct processing requires disk storage; in fact, a disk device is called a **direct-access storage device (DASD)** because the computer can go directly to the desired record on the disk. It is this ability to access any given record instantly that has made computer systems so convenient for people in service industries—for catalog order-takers determining whether a particular sweater is in stock, for example, or bank tellers checking individual bank balances. An added benefit of direct-access organization is the ability to read, change, and return a record to its same place on the disk; this is called **updating in place.**

Obviously, if we have a completely blank area on the disk and can put records anywhere, there must be some predictable system for placing a record at a disk address and then retrieving the record at a subsequent time. In other words, once the record has been placed on a disk, it must be possible to find it again. This is done by choosing a certain formula to apply to the record key, thereby deriving a number to use as the disk address. **Hashing,** or **randomizing,** is the name given to the process of applying a mathematical operation to a key to yield a number that represents the address. Even though the record keys are unique, it is possible for a hashing scheme to produce the same disk address, called a **synonym**, for two different records; such an occurrence is called a **collision**. There are various ways to recover from a collision; one way is simply to use the next available record slot on the disk.

There are many different hashing schemes; although the example in Figure 15 is too simple to be realistic, it can give you a general idea of how the process works. An example of how direct processing works is provided in Figure 16.

Indexed File Organization   Indexed file processing, or **indexed processing,** is a third method of file organization, and it represents a compromise between the sequential and direct methods. It is useful in applications where a file needs to be in sequential order, but, in addition, access to individual records is needed.

An indexed file works as follows: Records are stored in the file in sequential order, but the file also contains an index. The index contains entries consisting of the key to each record stored on the file and the corresponding disk address for that record. The index is like a directory, with the keys to all

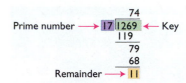

Figure 15 A hashing scheme. Dividing the key number 1269 by the prime number 17 yields a remainder of 11, which can be used to indicate the address on a disk.

Figure 16 An example of direct access. Assume there are 13 addresses (0 through 12) available in the file. Dividing the key number 661, which is C. Kear's employee number, by the prime number 13 yields a remainder of 11. Thus, 11 is the address for key 661. However, for the key 618, dividing by 13 yields a remainder of 7, a synonym, since this address has already been used by the key 137, which also has a remainder of 7. Hence the address becomes the next location—that is, 8. Note, incidentally, that keys (and therefore records) need not appear in any particular order. (The 13 record locations available are, of course, too few to hold a normal file; a small number was used to keep the example simple.)

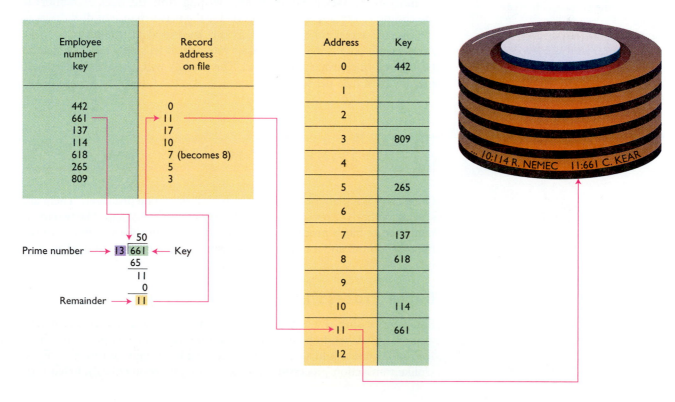

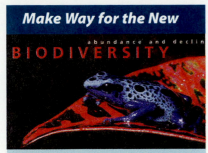

There was a time when sales representatives worked a neighborhood door to door, eager to convince parents that their child needed a 20-volume encyclopedia set of his or her own. Anxious to give their youngsters every educational advantage, parents signed up for extended payment plans to take care of the purchase, often costing hundreds of dollars.

No more. Now a parent can purchase a CD-ROM for a few dollars. Digital encyclopedias such as Encarta, whose sample images are shown here, go beyond what books can offer, with features such as a timeline of clickable objects, inter- activities, collages, and links to the Internet.

records listed in order. For a record to be accessed directly, the record key must be located in the index; the address associated with the key is then used to locate the record on the disk. Accessing the entire file of records sequen- tially is simply a matter of beginning with the first record and proceeding one at a time through the rest of the records.

Before proceeding with the actual processing of data, consider the physi- cal activity of the disk as it accesses records directly.

Disk Access to Data

Three primary factors determine **access time,** the time needed to access data directly on disk:

- **Seek time.** This is the time it takes the access arm to get into position over a particular track. Keep in mind that all the access arms move as a unit, so they are simultaneously in position over a set of tracks that make up a cylinder.
- **Head switching.** The access arms on the access mechanism do not move separately; they move together, all at the same time. However, only one read/write head can operate at any one time. Head switching is the acti- vation of a particular read/write head over a particular track on a par- ticular surface. Since head switching takes place at the speed of electric- ity, the time it takes is negligible.
- **Rotational delay.** Once the access arm and read/write head are in posi- tion and ready to read or write data, the read/write head waits for a short period until the desired data on the track moves under it.

Once the data has been found, the next step is **data transfer,** the process of transferring data between memory and the place on the disk track—from memory to the track if the computer is writing, from the track to memory if the computer is reading. One measure for the performance of disk drives is the average access time, which is usually measured in milliseconds (ms). Another measure is the **data transfer rate,** which tells how fast data can be transferred once it has been found. This usually will be stated in terms of megabytes of data per second.

Processing Stored Data

Once there is a plan for accessing the files, they can be processed. There are several methods of processing data files in a computer system. The two main methods are batch processing (processing data in groups at a more conve- nient later time) and transaction processing (processing data immediately, as it is received).

Batch Processing

Batch processing is a technique in which transactions are collected into groups, or batches, to be processed at a time when the computer may have few online users and thus be more accessible, usually during the night. Unlike transaction processing, a topic coming up momentarily, batch pro-

2000 and Beyond

THE BLACK BOX UNDER YOUR HOOD

In the last month, you and your family have taken your truck on 113 trips, long and short, for a total of 667 miles. You have moved the gearshift lever 402 times, sped down the highway at 83 miles per hour, and let the truck idle each morning for approximately 16 seconds.

Is this Big Brother watching the way you drive? No. Not yet, anyway. It is the Ford Motor Company, which records everything from the engine temperature to how often you hit the brakes. In new cars there are tiny sensors and computers that track a car's every gurgle; it is a relatively simple matter to store the results and then download the data to the Ford research center.

Engineers have long designed cars by hunch, assuming, for example, that drivers often gun the engine and that they rarely let the car warm up properly. Wrong on both counts, as it turns out. The actions of the Ford drivers (paid for their participation) supply useful, and sometimes surprising,

information. Data has shown, for example, that sometimes elderly drivers tool along just as fast as young whippersnappers.

The ultimate goals in gathering this data are more durable vehicles, safer roads, and cleaner air.

cessing involves no direct user interaction. Let us consider updating the health club address-label file. The **master file,** a semipermanent set of records, is, in this case, the list of all members of the health club and their addresses. The **transaction file** contains all changes to be made to the master file: additions (transactions to create new master records for new members), deletions (transactions with instructions to delete master records of members who have resigned from the health club), and revisions (transactions to change items such as street addresses or phone numbers in fields in the master records). Periodically, perhaps monthly or weekly, the master file is **updated** with the changes called for in the transaction file. The result is a new, up-to-date master file (Figure 17).

In batch processing, before a transaction file is matched against a master file, the transaction file must be sorted (usually by computer) so that all the transactions are in sequential order according to a key field. In updating the health club address-label file, the key is the member number assigned by the health club. The records on the master file are already in order by key. Once the changes in the transaction file are sorted by key, the two files can be matched and the master file updated.

During processing, the computer matches the keys from the master and transaction files, carrying out the appropriate action to add, revise, or delete. At the end of processing, a newly updated master file is created; in addition, an error report is usually printed. The error report shows actions such as an attempt to delete a nonexistent record or an attempt to add a record that already exists.

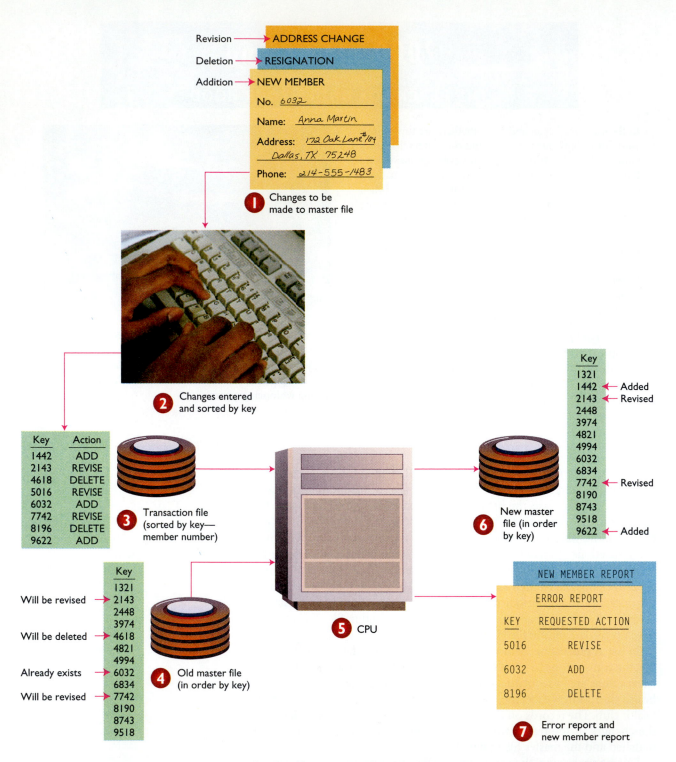

Figure 17 How batch processing works. The purpose of this system is to update the health club's master address-label file. The updating will be done sequentially. (1) Changes to be made (additions, deletions, and revisions) are input with (2) a keyboard, sorted, and sent to a disk, where they are stored in (3) the transaction file. The transaction file contains records in sequential order, according to member number, from lowest to highest. The field used to identify the record is called the key; in this instance the key is the member number. (4) The master file is also organized by member number. (5) The computer matches transaction file data and master file data by member number to produce (6) a new master file and (7) an error report and a new member report. Note that since this was a sequential update, the new master file is a completely new file, not just the old file updated in place. The error report lists member numbers in the transaction file that were not in the master file and member numbers that were included in the transaction file as additions that were already in the master file.

Transaction Processing

Transaction processing is a technique of processing transactions—a bank withdrawal, an address change, a credit charge—in random order, that is, in any order they occur. Note that although batch processing also uses transactions, in that case they are grouped together for processing; the phrase *transaction processing* means that each transaction is handled immediately. Transaction processing is real-time processing. **Real-time processing** means that a transaction is processed fast enough for the result to come back and be acted upon right away. For example, a teller at a bank can find out immediately what your bank balance is. For processing to be real-time, it must also be **online**—that is, the terminals must be connected directly to the computer. Transaction processing systems use disk storage because the disk drive can move directly to the desired record.

Advantages of transaction processing are immediate access to stored data (and thus immediate customer service) and immediate updating of the stored data. A sales clerk, for example, could access the computer via a terminal to verify the customer's credit and also record the sale via the computer (Figure 18). Later, by the way, those updated records can be batch-processed to bill all customers.

Global Perspective

The rise of the standard European currency—the Euro—poses problems for transaction processing systems at banks and commercial institutions. Transaction processing systems worldwide risk increased errors as they are reprogrammed to convert between two or more different national currency units. Business systems programmers may have to create additional internal checks and controls to ensure accurate processing and rule out fraud when the Euro is involved.

Group Work

Students can glean a better understanding of the speed and reliability required for transaction processing when they interview local businesses about the number and kind of transactions their computers process. Examples of businesses that may cooperate in providing some numbers of transactions for students include cellular phone providers, banks, electric and gas utilities, and college admissions and records systems.

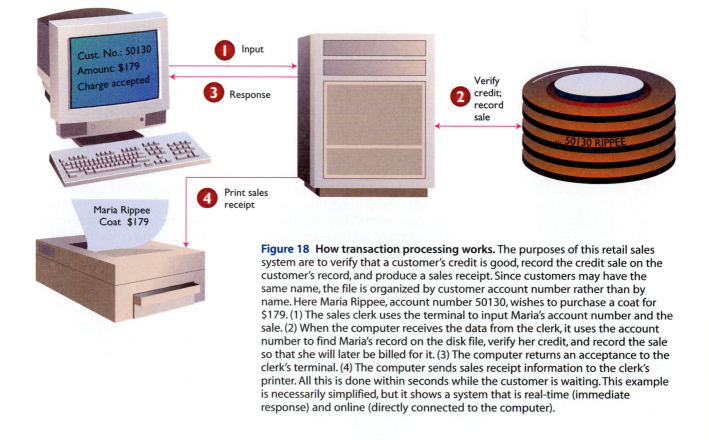

Figure 18 How transaction processing works. The purposes of this retail sales system are to verify that a customer's credit is good, record the credit sale on the customer's record, and produce a sales receipt. Since customers may have the same name, the file is organized by customer account number rather than by name. Here Maria Rippee, account number 50130, wishes to purchase a coat for $179. (1) The sales clerk uses the terminal to input Maria's account number and the sale. (2) When the computer receives the data from the clerk, it uses the account number to find Maria's record on the disk file, verify her credit, and record the sale so that she will later be billed for it. (3) The computer returns an acceptance to the clerk's terminal. (4) The computer sends sales receipt information to the clerk's printer. All this is done within seconds while the customer is waiting. This example is necessarily simplified, but it shows a system that is real-time (immediate response) and online (directly connected to the computer).

Batch and Transaction Processing: The Best of Both Worlds

Numerous computer systems combine the best features of both methods of processing. Generally speaking, transaction processing is used for activities related to the current needs of people—especially workers and customers—as they go about their daily lives. Batch processing, by comparison, can be done at any time, even in the middle of the night, without worrying about the convenience of the people ultimately affected by the processing.

A bank, for instance, may use transaction processing to check your balance and individually record your cash withdrawal transaction during the day at the teller window. However, the deposit that you leave in an envelope in an "instant" deposit drop may be recorded during the night by means of batch processing. Printing your bank statement is also a batch process. Most store systems also combine both methods: A point-of-sale terminal finds the individual item price as a sale is made, but that same process captures inventory data, which may be batched and totaled to produce inventory reports.

Police license-plate checks for stolen cars work the same way. As cars are sold throughout the state, the license numbers, owners' names, and so on, are updated in the motor vehicle department's master file, usually via batch processing on a nightly basis. But when police officers see a car they suspect may be stolen, they can radio headquarters, where an operator with a terminal uses transaction processing to check the master file immediately to see if the car has been reported missing. Some officers have a laptop computer right in the car and can check the information themselves.

Auto junkyards, which often are computerized big businesses, can make an individual inquiry for a record of a specific part needed by a customer waiting on the phone or in person. As parts are sold, sales records are kept to update the files nightly using batch processing.

As you can see from these examples, both workers and customers eventually see the results of transaction processing in the reports output by batch processing. Managers will see further batch processing output in the form of information gathered and summarized about the processed transactions. And, finally, new transaction processing is possible based on the results of previous batch processing.

▲

What is the future of storage? Perhaps holographic storage, which would be able to store thousands of pages on a device the size of a quarter and would be much faster than even the fastest hard drives. Whatever the technology, it seems likely that there will be greater storage capabilities in the future to hold the huge data files for law, medicine, science, education, business, and, of course, the government.

To have access to all that data from any location, we need data communications, the subject of the next chapter.

CHAPTER REVIEW

Summary and Key Terms

- Secondary storage, sometimes called **auxiliary storage,** is storage separate from the computer itself, where software and data can be stored on a semipermanent basis. Secondary storage is necessary because memory, or primary storage, can be used only temporarily.

- The benefits of secondary storage are space, reliability, convenience, and economy.

- Diskettes and hard disks are magnetic media, based on a technology of representing data as magnetized spots on the disk. The surface of each disk has concentric tracks on it.

- **Diskettes** are made of flexible mylar. Advantages of diskettes, as compared with hard disks, are portability and backup. The 3 1/2-inch diskette standard may be challenged by a new, higher-capacity disk whose drive can handle both the new disk and the traditional 3 1/2-inch disk, or perhaps by Iomega's Zip drive, whose disk has a high capacity but is not compatible with 3 1/2-inch diskettes.

- **Data compression** makes a large file smaller by temporarily removing nonessential items.

- A **hard disk** is a metal platter coated with magnetic oxide that can be magnetized to represent data. Several disks can be assembled into a **disk pack.**

- A **disk drive** is a machine that allows data to be read from a disk or written on a disk. A disk pack is mounted on a disk drive that is a separate unit connected to the computer. The disk **access arm** moves a **read/write head** into position over a particular track, where the read/write head hovers above the track. A **head crash** occurs when a read/write head touches the disk surface and causes all data to be destroyed.

- A **redundant array of independent disks,** or simply **RAID,** uses several small hard disks that work together as a unit. RAID level 1 duplicates data on separate disk drives, **disk mirroring.** Higher levels of RAID use **data striping,** spreading the data across several disks in the array, with one disk used solely as a check disk to keep track of what data is where.

- The **sector method** of recording data on a disk divides each track into sectors that hold a specific number of characters. Data on the track is accessed by referring to the surface number, track number, and sector number where the data is stored. **Zone recording** involves dividing a disk into zones to take maximum advantage of the storage available by assigning more sectors to tracks in outer zones than to those in inner zones.

- The **cylinder method** is a vertical organization of data on a disk pack. The set of tracks that can be accessed by one positioning of the access arms is called a **cylinder.**

- **Optical disk** technology uses a laser beam to enter data as spots on the disk surface. To read the data, the laser scans the disk, and a lens picks up different light reflections from the various spots. **Read-only media** are recorded on by the manufacturer and can be read from but not written to by the user. **Write-once, read-many media,** also called **WORM media,** may be written to once. A hybrid type of disk, called **magneto-optical (MO),** has the large capacity of an optical disk but can be written over like a magnetic disk. **CD-ROM,** for **compact disk read-only memory,** which has a disk format identical to that of audio compact disks, can hold up to 660 megabytes per disk. CD-R technology permits writing on optical disks. CD-RW technology is more flexible, permitting reading, writing, and rewriting.

- **DVD-ROM,** for **digital versatile disk,** has astonishing storage capacity, up to 17GB if both layers and both sides are used.

- **Multimedia** software typically presents information with text, illustrations, photos, narration, music, animation, and film clips—possible because of the large capacity of optical disks. **MPEG (Motion Picture Experts Group)** is a set of widely accepted video standards.

■ **Magnetic tape** stores data as extremely small magnetic spots. The amount of data on a tape is expressed in terms of **density,** which is the number of **characters per inch (cpi)** or **bytes per inch (bpi)** that can be stored on the tape. The highest-capacity tape is **digital audio tape,** or **DAT,** which uses a different method of recording data. Through a method called **helical scan recording,** the data is placed in diagonal bands that run across the tape rather than down its length.

■ A **magnetic tape unit** reads and writes data using a **read/write head;** when the computer is writing on the tape, the **erase head** first erases any data previously recorded. Two reels are used: a **supply reel** that has the data tape and a **take-up reel** that stays with the magnetic tape unit.

■ A **backup system** is a way of storing data in more than one place to protect it from damage and loss. Most backup systems use tape.

■ A **character** is a letter, digit, or special character (such as $, ?, or *). A **field** contains a set of related characters. A **record** is a collection of related fields. A **file** is a collection of related records. A **database** is a collection of interrelated files stored together with minimum redundancy; specific data items can be retrieved for various applications.

■ **Sequential file processing** means that records are in a certain order according to a unique identifier field called a **key.** If a particular record in a sequential file is wanted, then all the prior records in the file must be read before the desired record is reached.

■ **Direct file processing,** or **direct access,** allows the computer to go directly to the desired record by using a record key. Direct processing requires disk storage; a disk device is called a **direct-access storage device (DASD).** In addition to instant access to any record, an added benefit of direct-access organization is the ability to read, change, and return a record to its same place on the disk; this is called **updating in place. Hashing,** or **randomizing,** is the name given to the process of applying a formula to a key to yield a number that represents the address for the record that has that key. A hashing scheme may produce the same disk address, called a **synonym,** for two different records; such an occurrence is called a **collision.**

■ **Indexed file processing,** or **indexed processing,** stores records in the file in sequential order, but the file also contains an index of keys; the address associated with the key is then used to locate the record on the disk.

■ Three factors determine **access time,** the time needed to access data directly on disk: **seek time,** the time it takes to get the access arm into position over a particular track; **head switching,** the activation of a particular read/write head over a particular track on a particular surface; and **rotational delay,** the brief wait until the desired data on the track moves under the read/write head. Once data has been found, **data transfer,** the transfer of data between memory and the place on the disk track, occurs.

■ Access time is usually measured in milliseconds (ms). The **data transfer rate,** which tells how fast data can be transferred once it has been found, is usually stated in terms of megabytes of data per second.

■ **Batch processing** is a technique in which transactions are collected into groups, or batches, to be processed at a time when the computer has few online users and thus is more accessible. A **master file** is a semipermanent set of records. A **transaction file,** sorted by key, contains all changes to be made to the master file: additions, deletions, and revisions.

■ Transaction processing is a technique of processing transactions in any order they occur. **Real-time processing** means that a transaction is processed fast enough for the result to come back and be acted upon right away. **Online processing** means that the terminals must be connected directly to the computer.

Discussion Questions

1. If you were buying a personal computer today, what would you expect to find as standard secondary storage? What storage might you choose as an option?

2. Can you imagine new multimedia applications that take advantage of sound, photos, art, and perhaps video?

3. Provide your own example to illustrate how characters of data are organized into fields, records, files, and (perhaps) databases. If you wish, you may choose one of the following examples: department store, airline reservations, or Internal Revenue Service data.

Student Study Guide

Multiple Choice

1. The density of data stored on magnetic tape is expressed as
   - a. units per inch
   - b. tracks per inch
   - c. packs per inch
   - d. bytes per inch

2. Another name for secondary storage is
   - a. cylinder storage
   - b. density
   - c. auxiliary storage
   - d. memory

3. A magnetized spot represents
   - a. cpi
   - b. a zone
   - c. MB
   - d. 1 bit

4. A field contains one or more
   - a. characters
   - b. databases
   - c. records
   - d. files

5. Processing transactions in groups is called
   - a. data transfer
   - b. transaction processing
   - c. head switching
   - d. batch processing

6. A hard disk can be backed up efficiently using
   - a. zoning
   - b. a tape backup system
   - c. a transaction file
   - d. WORM

7. Relatively permanent data is contained in
   - a. a field
   - b. memory
   - c. a transaction
   - d. a master file

8. A limitation of magnetic tape as a method of storing data is that it is
   - a. not reusable
   - b. organized sequentially
   - c. expensive
   - d. not portable

9. DASD refers to
   - a. disk storage
   - b. tape storage
   - c. fields
   - d. sorting

10. Optical disk technology uses
    - a. helical scanning
    - b. DAT
    - c. a laser beam
    - d. RAID

11. The mechanism for reading or writing data on a disk is called a(n)
    - a. track
    - b. WORM
    - c. key
    - d. access arm

12. Higher levels of RAID spread data across several disks, a method called
    - a. helical scanning
    - b. hashing
    - c. data striping
    - d. duplication

13. The time required to position the access arm over a particular track is known as
    - a. rotational delay
    - b. seek time
    - c. data transfer
    - d. head switching

14. A way of organizing data on a disk pack to minimize seek time is through use of
    - a. sequential files
    - b. the cylinder method
    - c. sequential order
    - d. hashing

15. The speed with which a disk can find data being sought is called
    - a. access time
    - b. direct time
    - c. data transfer time
    - d. cylinder time

16. The disk storage that uses both a magnet and a laser beam:
    - a. hashing
    - b. CD-ROM
    - c. magneto-optical
    - d. WORM

17. The RAID method of duplicating data:
    - a. zoning
    - b. the sector method
    - c. data mirroring
    - d. data striping

18. Before a sequential file can be updated, the transactions must first be
    - a. numbered
    - b. sorted
    - c. labeled
    - d. updated

19. Hashing, to get an address, is the process of applying a formula to a
    - a. key
    - b. file
    - c. record
    - d. character

20. The maximum number of recordable layers on a DVD-ROM disk is
    - a. 1
    - b. 8
    - c. 2
    - d. 4

21. A CD-ROM has the same format as a(n)
    a. backup tape   c. RAID
    b. diskette   d. audio compact disk

22. Several small disk packs that work together as a unit:
    a. CD-ROM   c. RAID
    b. WORM   d. MO

23. Assigning more sectors to outer disk tracks:
    a. zone recording   c. randomizing
    b. data transfer   d. sectoring

24. The ability to return a changed disk record to its original location is called
    a. magneto-optical   c. rotational delay
    b. multimedia   d. updating in place

True/False

T F   1. Real-time processing means that a transaction is processed fast enough for the result to come back and be acted upon right away.
T F   2. CD-R technology permits writing on CD-ROMs.
T F   3. A field is a set of related records.
T F   4. A magnetic tape unit records data on tape but cannot retrieve it.
T F   5. A transaction file contains records to update the master file.
T F   6. WORM can be written once; then it becomes read-only.
T F   7. Rotational delay comes before seek time.
T F   8. Density is the number of characters per inch.
T F   9. The most common backup medium is CD-ROM.
T F   10. Another name for randomizing is zoning.
T F   11. Transaction processing systems are real-time systems.
T F   12. Multimedia software can include film clips.
T F   13. Hard disks have disks, access arms, and read/write heads in a sealed module.
T F   14. Magneto-optical refers to a special type of tape that records data diagonally.
T F   15. A magnetic disk has concentric tracks.

Fill-In

1. Adding more sectors to the outer tracks of a disk is called _____ _____.

2. Processing transactions in a group is called _____.

3. The primary advantage of optical disk technology lies in its _____ _____.

4. The type of software that can offer photos, narration, music, and more is called _____.

5. DASD stands for _____ _____.

6. The type of access required by a file is determined by _____ _____.

7. Two types of RAID are
   a. _____.
   b. _____.

8. If a read/write head touches a hard disk surface, this is called a _____.

9. What does CD-ROM stand for?
   _____
   _____.

10. A disk that has magnetically sensitive metallic crystals embedded in the plastic coating is called _____.

11. The concept of using several disks together as a unit is known as _____ _____.

12. A unique identifier for a record is called a _____.

13. The smallest unit of raw data is the

    _____.

14. The method of organizing data vertically on a disk
    pack is the _____

    _____.

15. Another name for hashing is:

    _____.

16. Four benefits of secondary storage:

    a. _____

    b. _____

    c. _____

    d. _____

17. The three kinds of components in a sealed data
    module:

    a. _____

    b. _____

    c. _____

18. The three primary factors that determine access
    time for disk data?

    a. _____

    b. _____

    c. _____

19. Three major methods of file organization:

    a. _____

    b. _____

    c. _____

20. A required process before transactions can be used
    to update a sequential file is

    _____.

Answers

Multiple Choice

1. d	6. b	11. d	16. c	21. d
2. c	7. d	12. c	17. c	22. c
3. d	8. b	13. b	18. b	23. a
4. a	9. a	14. b	19. a	24. d
5. d	10. c	15. a	20. d	

True/False

1. T	6. T	11. T
2. T	7. F	12. T
3. F	8. T	13. T
4. F	9. F	14. F
5. T	10. F	15. T

Fill-In

1. zone recording
2. batch processing
3. capacity
4. multimedia
5. direct-access storage device
6. the application
7. a. disk mirroring
   b. data striping
8. head crash
9. compact disk read-only memory
10. magneto-optical
11. redundant array of independent disks (RAID)
12. key
13. character
14. cylinder method
15. randomizing
16. a. space
    b. reliability
    c. convenience
    d. economy
17. a. disks
    b. access arms
    c. read/write heads
18. a. seek time
    b. head switching
    c. rotational delay
19. a. sequential
    b. direct
    c. indexed sequential
20. sorting

FREE OR NOT FREE

Many people, especially those associated with schools and government organizations, have free access to the Internet. But is the information available on Internet sites also free? Often, the answer is yes.

What information is free and what isn't? There are no uniform rules to guide you. Although some information providers make a blanket "help yourself" statement, much information is unaccompanied by a proprietary statement. You could collect freebies safely on sites that are clearly designated, such as the Free and Neat Stuff site and the Free Site, shown here. However, business people

and others who do not want their works copied post clear notices on their pages, using phrases such as *Copyrighted* and *All rights reserved*.

Freebies. Several types of information tend to be free. Categories of free information include health care, the environment, government agencies, consumer information, humor, lists of events, family issues, the weather, hobby information, clip art, web design and home page advice, academic offerings, and most topics found on individual home pages. Images on the Storm Photos site, for example, are provided by a government agency. Note the cartoon, shown here, of a woman leaning against a door. The room behind the door is bursting with files of clip art, which are always free. Clip art is handy for building home pages.

As a category, software is not generally free. However, many sites do offer free software, which can usually be downloaded directly to a user's computer. The PC

Computing site includes a comprehensive list of free software. The 3M company offers free downloadable software to place the yellow "sticky" Post-it Notes on your screen. However, the free part is only for a trial period, a sales device used effectively by many companies. The Neoplanet site goes further, offering to dowload a product that will overlay your browser and provide categories of the best (read: advertisers') sites and permit customizing. Neoplanet also includes free e-mail.

Other companies offer free services right on the Internet. Blue Mountain is one of several greeting card companies that offer a variety of cards that you

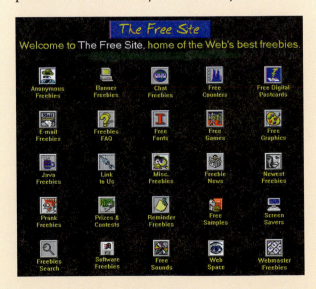

can fill in with your name and the name and e-mail address of the recipient and then send free. The Maps on Us site will draw a map of any location for which you provide an address.

Some companies on the Web offer free samples of their products. For example, the Jelly Belly site offers free samples that they send through the mail. Of course, this means providing your mailing address. The form you fill out probably will ask for other information too, especially your e-mail address, all of which the company can use for promotional purposes.

Internet to be shared freely by all. Most browsers allow you to capture such items by clicking the right mouse button and then Save (back to the left button) to save the image to a file. Another possibility is screen-capture software.

However, many artist and photographers, usually professionals, state that their works are copyrighted and may be used only with permission. An example is the Stock

Solution, whose logo is shown here. The Stock Solution is an agency that represents professional photographers whose works can be seen right on your screen. But you must agree to a lease fee before you can make any further use of the photos.

Not free. Business products and services are likely to have a fee. Even information on sites related to sports and entertainment may not be freely available. Such sites often require at least that you "register," that is, provide your name and address and e-mail address, all of which—again—are used for marketing purposes.

Art and photography. Many artists and photographers put their works on the

Internet Exercises

1. **Structured exercise.** Begin with URL http://www.prenhall.com/capron and examine the free (save frog lives!) Virtual Frog Dissection Kit.

2. **Freeform exercise.** Beginning with Yahoo! or your own favorite online directory, find the maps to track the weather in your home state.

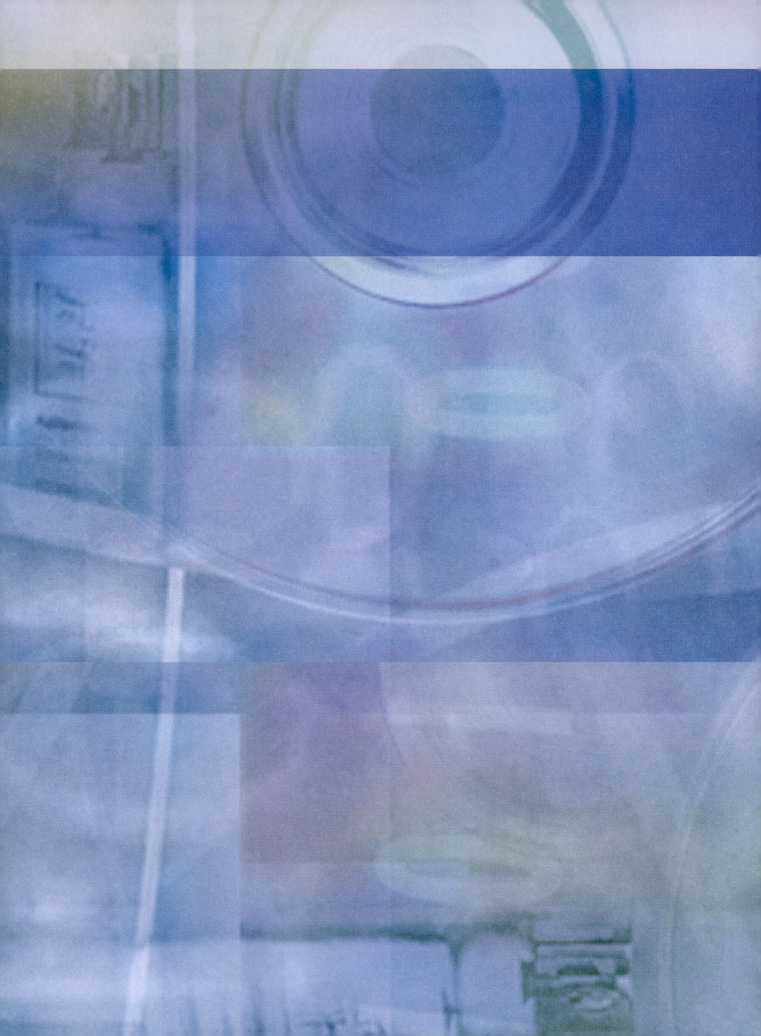

CHAPTER SIX

NETWORKING
Computer Connections

LEARNING OBJECTIVES

- Know the basic components of a network
- Know data transmission methods, including types of signals, modulation, and choices among transmission modes
- Differentiate the various kinds of communications links and appreciate the need for protocols
- Understand network configurations
- Know the components, types, and protocols of a local area network
- Appreciate the complexity of networking
- Become acquainted with examples of networking

Bob Emerson is retired. He lives half the year in Seattle and the other half in Florida, and he has a personal computer in each location. Bob was heard to remark that most people use their computers for just one thing—word processing. This comment was greeted with hoots from his daughter, who teaches computer courses at a community college, and by his three grandchildren, who use computers at school and at home. Although they did not dispute the importance of word processing, they noted that he was overlooking a key activity—connectivity. That is, most people also use their computers to send and receive e-mail and to connect to the Internet. In particular, they thought it would be fine to be able to communicate with him by e-mail when he was away in Florida.

Bob knew all this, more or less, but was not anxious to sign up. He worried about "one more monthly bill" and also about the difficulty of discontinuing the service if he chose to do so. He was persuaded to sign up for a free trial period, with the promise of family help if he needed an escape clause.

The end of this true story is predictable. Bob now e-mails the family regularly. He surfs the Internet on many topics, particularly genealogy, and has connected with other Emersons worldwide. He hardly notices the extra monthly bill.

Data Communications

Mail, telephone, TV and radio, books, newspapers, and periodicals—these are the traditional ways users send and receive information. However, **data communications systems**—computer systems that transmit data over communications lines such as telephone lines or cables—have been evolving since the mid-1960s. Let us take a look at how they came about.

In the early days of computing, **centralized data processing** placed everything—all processing, hardware, and software—in one central location. But centralization proved inconvenient and inefficient. All input data had to be physically transported to the computer, and all processed material had to be picked up and delivered to the users. Insisting on centralized data processing was like insisting that all conversations between people occur face-to-face in one designated room.

In the late 1960s businesses began to use computers that were often at a distance from the central computer. These systems were clearly decentralized because the smaller computers could do some processing on their own, yet some also had access to the central computer. This new setup was labeled **distributed data processing**, which accommodates both remote *access* and

Figure 1 Local area network. Although allocated to individual workers, the computers shown here are wired together so that their users can communicate with one another.

remote *processing*. A typical application of a distributed data processing system is a business or organization with many locations—perhaps branch offices or retail outlets.

The whole picture of distributed data processing has changed dramatically with the advent of networks of personal computers. A **network** is a computer system that uses communications equipment to connect two or more computers and their resources. Distributed data processing systems are networks. Of particular interest in today's business world are *local area networks (LANs)*, which are designed to share data and resources among several individual computer users in an office or building (Figure 1). Networking will be examined in more detail in later sections of this chapter.

The next section previews the components of a communications system, to give you an overview of how these components work together.

Putting Together a Network: A First Look

Even though the components needed to transmit data from one computer to another seem quite basic, the business of putting together a network can be extremely complex. This discussion begins with the initial components and then moves to the list of factors that a network designer needs to consider.

① Sending device

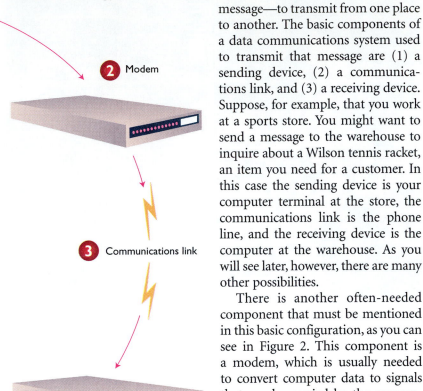
② Modem

③ Communications link

⑤ Central processing unit or terminal

④ Modem

Figure 2 Communications system components. Data originating from (1) a sending device is (2) converted by a modem to data that can be carried over (3) a communications link and (4) reconverted by a modem at the receiving end before (5) being received by the destination computer.

Getting Started

The basic configuration—how the components are put together—is rather straightforward, but there is a great variety of components to choose from, and the technology is ever changing. Assume that you have some data—a message—to transmit from one place to another. The basic components of a data communications system used to transmit that message are (1) a sending device, (2) a communications link, and (3) a receiving device. Suppose, for example, that you work at a sports store. You might want to send a message to the warehouse to inquire about a Wilson tennis racket, an item you need for a customer. In this case the sending device is your computer terminal at the store, the communications link is the phone line, and the receiving device is the computer at the warehouse. As you will see later, however, there are many other possibilities.

There is another often-needed component that must be mentioned in this basic configuration, as you can see in Figure 2. This component is a modem, which is usually needed to convert computer data to signals that can be carried by the communications channel and vice versa. Modems will be discussed in detail shortly. (And, by the way, most modems now are internal, that is, out of sight within the computer's housing. We use the external variety in the illustration just to make a point.)

Large computer systems may have additional components. At the computer end, data may travel through a communications control unit called a **front-end processor,** which is actually a computer in itself. Its purpose is to relieve the central computer of some of the communications tasks and thus free it for processing applications programs. In addition, a front-end processor usually performs error detection and recovery functions.

Network Design Considerations

The task of network design is a complex one, usually requiring the services of a professional specifically trained in that capacity. Although you cannot learn how to design a network in this brief chapter, you can ask some questions that can help you appreciate what the designer must contemplate. Here, in the vernacular, is a list of questions that might occur to a customer who was considering installing a network; these questions also provide hints of what is to come in the chapter.

Question: I've heard that different kinds of modems and cables send data at different speeds. Does that matter?

Answer: Yes. The faster the better. Generally, faster means lower transmission costs too.

Question: Am I limited to communicating via the telephone system?

Answer: Not at all. There are all kinds of communications media, with varying degrees of speed, reliability, and cost. There are trade-offs. A lot depends on distance too—you wouldn't choose a satellite, for example, to send a message to the office next door.

Question: So the geographical area of the network is a factor?

Answer: Definitely. In fact, network types are described by how far-flung they are: A *wide area network* might span the nation or even the globe, but a *local area network* would probably be campuswide or cover an office.

Question: Can I just cable the computers together and start sending data?

Answer: Not quite. You must decide on some sort of plan. There are various standard ways, called *topologies,* to physically lay out the computers and other elements of a network. Also available are standard software packages, which provide a set of rules, called a *protocol,* that defines how computers communicate.

Question: I know one of the advantages of networking is sharing disk files. Where are the files kept? And can any user get any file?

Answer: The files are usually kept with a particular computer, one that is more powerful than the other computers on the network. Access depends on the network setup. In some arrangements, for example, a user might be sent a whole file, but in others the user would be sent only the particular records needed to fulfill a request. The latter is called *client/server,* a popular alternative.

Question: This is getting complicated.

Answer: Yes.

These and other related considerations will be presented first, followed by an example of a complex network or, rather, a set of networks. You need not understand all the details, but you will have an appreciation for the effort required to put together a network. Let us see how the components of a communications system work together, beginning with how data is transmitted.

Data Transmission

A terminal or computer produces digital signals, which are simply the presence or absence of an electric pulse. The state of being on or off represents the binary number 1 or 0, respectively. Some communications lines accept digital transmission directly, and the trend in the communications industry is toward digital signals. However, most telephone lines through which these digital signals are sent were originally built for voice transmission, and voice transmission requires analog signals. The next section describes these two types of transmission, and then modems, which translate between them.

High-Tech Souvenir

So, where did you ski today? If you visit Vail, Colorado, and sign up for MapTrek, you can wear a fanny pack loaded with global-positioning devices that will interact with a satellite to track your every turn and bump on the slopes. At day's end you will be presented with a map showing your precise path and approximate speed.

Critical Thinking

Even if you have a good plan for what kind of network to put into place, problems often occur. What problems can you predict may arise when attempting to install and operate a network in a small office for the first time? (Although physical installation of the network wiring is expensive in old buildings, the really daunting problems may have to do more with people than hardware. Someone must be responsible as the Network Administrator, and no existing employee may qualify—or want—this job. Users will require training in how to use the network or they may be unsuccessful in actually operating it. Some older programs may need to be modified or at least reinstalled to work with the network.)

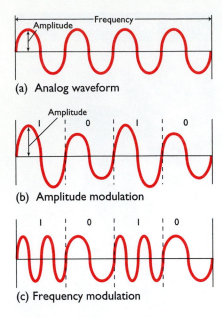

(a) Analog waveform

(b) Amplitude modulation

(c) Frequency modulation

Figure 3 **Analog signals.** (a) An analog carrier wave moves up and down in a continuous cycle. (b) The analog waveform can be converted to digital form through amplitude modulation. As shown, the wave height is increased to represent a 1 or left the same to represent a 0. (c) In frequency modulation the amplitude of the wave stays the same but the frequency increases to indicate a 1 or stays the same to indicate a 0.

Digital and Analog Transmission

Digital transmission sends data as distinct pulses, either on or off, in much the same way that data travels through the computer. However, some communications media are not digital. Communications devices such as telephone lines, coaxial cables, and microwave circuits are already in place for voice (analog) transmission. The easiest choice for most users is to piggyback on one of these. Thus the most common communications devices all use **analog transmission,** a continuous electrical signal in the form of a wave.

To be sent over analog lines, a digital signal must first be converted to an analog form. It is converted by altering an analog signal, called a **carrier wave,** which has alterable characteristics (Figure 3a). One such characteristic is the **amplitude,** or height of the wave, which can be increased to represent the binary number 1 (Figure 3b). Another characteristic that can be altered is the **frequency,** or number of times a wave repeats during a specific time interval; frequency can be increased to represent a 1 (Figure 3c).

Conversion from digital to analog signals is called **modulation,** and the reverse process—reconstructing the original digital message at the other end of the transmission—is called **demodulation.** An extra device is needed to make the conversions: a modem.

Modems

A **modem** is a device that converts a digital signal to an analog signal and vice versa (Figure 4). Modem is short for *mo*dulate/*dem*odulate.

Types of Modems   Modems vary in the way they connect to the telephone line. Most modems today are directly connected to the phone system by a cable that runs from the modem to the wall jack. A **direct-connect modem** is directly connected to the telephone line by means of a telephone jack. An **external modem** is separate from the computer (Figure 5). Its main advantage is that it can be used with a variety of computers. For a modem that is out of sight—literally—an **internal modem** board can be inserted into the computer by the user; in fact, most personal computers today come with an internal modem as standard equipment.

Notebook and laptop computers often use modems that come in the form of **PC cards,** originally known as PCMCIA cards, named for the

Figure 4 **Modems.** Modems convert—modulate—digital data signals to analog signals for sending over communications links, then reverse the process—demodulate—at the other end.

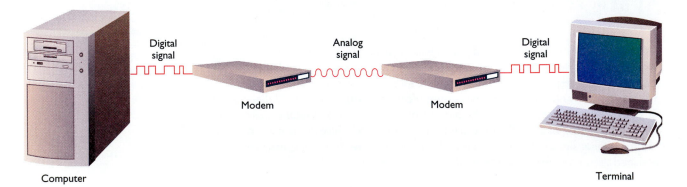

Personal Computer Memory Card International Association. The credit card–sized PC card slides into a slot in the computer (Figure 6). A cable runs from the PC card to the phone jack in the wall. PC cards have given portable computers full connectivity capability outside the constraints of an office.

Modem Data Speeds   The World Wide Web has given users an insatiable appetite for fast communications. This, and costs based on time use of services, provides strong incentives to transmit as quickly as possible. The old— some very old—standard modem speeds of 9600, 14,400, 28,800, and 33,600 **bits per second (bps)** have now been superseded by modems that transmit 56,000 bps. Note, however, that the 56K speed is only for receiving data, and often not even that is up to full speed.

ISDN

As noted earlier, communication via phone lines requires a modem to convert between the computer's digital signals and the analog signals used by phone lines. But what if another type of line could be used directly for digital transmission? One technology is called **Integrated Services Digital Network,** usually known by its acronym, **ISDN.** The attraction is that an **ISDN adapter** can move data at 128,000 bps, a vast speed improvement over any modem. Another advantage is that an ISDN circuit includes two phone lines, so a user can use one line to connect to the Internet and the other to talk on the phone at the same time. Still, ISDN is not a panacea. Although prices are coming down, initial costs are not inexpensive. You need both the adapter and phone service and possibly even a new line, depending on your current service. Also, ongoing monthly fees may be significant. Furthermore, ISDN is unavailable in some geographic areas.

Emerging communication technologies are overtaking even the speeds of ISDN, and these are described in an Internet chapter. They are more appropriately included in the discussion of the need-for-speed by the folks who can afford it, commercial users of the Internet.

Asynchronous and Synchronous Transmission

Sending data off to a far destination works only if the receiving device is ready to accept it. But *ready* means more than just available; the receiving device must be able to keep in step with the sending device. Two techniques commonly used to keep the sending and receiving units dancing to the same tune are asynchronous and synchronous transmission.

When **asynchronous transmission** (also called **start/stop transmission**) is used, a special start signal is transmitted at the beginning of each group of message bits—a group is usually just a single character. Likewise, a stop signal is sent at the end of the group of message bits (Figure 7a). When the receiving device gets the start signal, it sets up a timing mechanism to accept the group of message bits.

Synchronous transmission is a little trickier because characters are transmitted together in a continuous stream (Figure 7b). There are no call-to-action signals for each character. Instead, the sending and receiving devices are synchronized by having their internal clocks put in time with each other via a bit pattern transmitted at the beginning of the message. Furthermore, error-check bits are transmitted at the end of each message to make sure all characters were received properly. Synchronous transmission equipment is more complex and more expensive but, without all the start/stop bits, transmission is much faster.

Figure 5 An external modem.

Figure 6 A PC card modem. This PC card modem, although only the size of a credit card, packs a lot of power: data reception at 56,000 bytes per second. The card, shown here resting against a laptop keyboard, is slipped into a slot on the side of the keyboard. Look closely at the right end of the modem and you can see the pop-out jack. So, it goes in this order: Slide in the card, pop out the jack, and snap in the phone cord.

InfoBit

Synchronous transmission is widely used in digital telephone networks. It is still startling to realize, however, just how accurate that synchronization must be at high speeds. Telephone switches connected by loops of optical fiber are kept synchronized by atomic clocks to within nanoseconds— billionths of a second. This lowers error rates caused by "dropping" a bit almost to zero.

Learn by Doing

Have students obtain data from local telephone companies and providers on the cost of installing and operating an ISDN connection to a private residence. This would include an installation charge, a monthly charge and the cost for an ISDN "terminal adapter"—rather like an ISDN modem. Compare these costs to the cost of a high speed analog modem and an ordinary telephone line in your area.

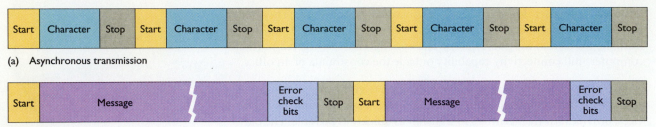

| Start | Character | Stop | Start | Character | Stop | Start | Character | Stop | Start | Character | Stop | Start | Character | Stop |

(a) Asynchronous transmission

| Start | Message | Error check bits | Stop | Start | Message | Error check bits | Stop |

(b) Synchronous transmission

Figure 7 Asynchronous and synchronous transmission. (a) Asynchronous transmission uses start/stop signals surrounding each character. (b) Page-width constraints preclude showing the true amount of continuous data that can be transmitted synchronously between start and stop characters. Unlike asynchronous transmission, which has one start/stop set per character, synchronous transmission can send many characters, even many messages, between one start/stop set. Note that synchronous transmission requires a set of error-check bits to make sure all characters were received properly.

Simplex, Half-Duplex, and Full-Duplex Transmission

Data transmission can be characterized as simplex, half duplex, or full duplex, depending on permissible directions of traffic flow. **Simplex transmission** sends data in one direction only; everyday examples are television broadcasting and arrival/departure screens at airports. **Half-duplex transmission** allows transmission in either direction, but only one way at a time. An analogy is talk on a CB radio. In a bank a teller using half-duplex transmission can send the data about a deposit and, after it is received, the computer can send a confirmation reply. **Full-duplex transmission** allows transmission in both directions at once. An analogy is a telephone conversation in which, good manners aside, both parties can talk at the same time.

Communications Links

The cost for linking widely scattered computers is substantial, so it is worthwhile to examine the communications options. Telephone lines are the most convenient communications channel because an extensive system is already in place, but there are many other options. A communications **link** is the physical medium used for transmission.

Types of Communications Links

There are several kinds of communications links. Some may be familiar to you already.

Wire Pairs One of the most common communications media is the **wire pair**, also known as the **twisted pair**. Wire pairs are wires twisted together to form a cable, which is then insulated (Figure 8a). Wire pairs are inexpensive. Further, they are often used because they have already been installed in a building for other purposes or because they are already in use in telephone systems. However, they are susceptible to electrical interference, or noise. **Noise** is anything that causes distortion in the signal when it is received. High-voltage equipment and even the sun can be sources of noise.

Coaxial Cables Known for sending a strong signal, a **coaxial cable** is a single conductor wire within a shielded enclosure (Figure 8b). Bundles of cables can be laid underground or undersea. These cables can transmit data much faster than wire pairs and are less prone to noise.

Focus on Ethics

Too Perfect?

Most electronic transmission today is digital. Satellites, television, computers—all are or soon will be digital. Even your watch is probably digital. But not all is fair to see. An evolving social and legal matter is protecting intellectual property such as music and movies, which can be recorded and transmitted digitally. In contrast to a slightly degraded analog copy, a digital copy is almost perfect.

Fiber Optics   Traditionally, most phone lines transmitted data electrically over wires made of metal, usually copper. These metal wires had to be protected from water and other corrosive substances. **Fiber optics** technology eliminates this requirement (Figure 8c and d). Instead of using electricity to send data, fiber optics uses light. The cables are made of glass fibers, each thinner than a human hair, that can guide light beams for miles. Fiber optics transmits data faster than some technologies, yet the materials are substantially lighter and less expensive than wire cables. It can also send and receive a wider assortment of data frequencies at one time. The range of frequencies that a device can handle is known as its bandwidth; **bandwidth** is a measure of the capacity of the link. Fiber optics offer very high bandwidth and very low noise susceptibility.

Microwave Transmission   Another popular medium is **microwave transmission,** which uses what is called line-of-sight transmission of data signals through the atmosphere (Figure 9a). Since these signals cannot bend to follow the curvature of the earth, relay stations—often antennas in high places such as the tops of mountains and buildings—are positioned at points approximately 30 miles apart to continue the transmission. Microwave transmission offers speed, cost-effectiveness, and ease of implementation.

Satellite Transmission   The basic components of **satellite transmission** are **earth stations,** which send and receive signals, and a satellite component called a transponder. The **transponder** receives the transmission from an

Figure 8 Communications links. (a) Wire pairs are pairs of wires twisted together to form a cable, which is then insulated. (b) A coaxial cable is a single conductor wire surrounded by insulation. (c) Fiber optics consists of hairlike glass fibers that carry voice, television, and data signals. (d) This photo shows light emitted from a handful of fiber optic cables.

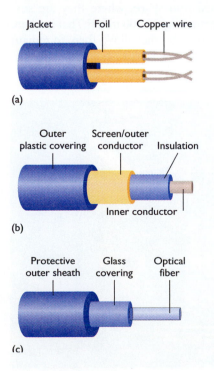

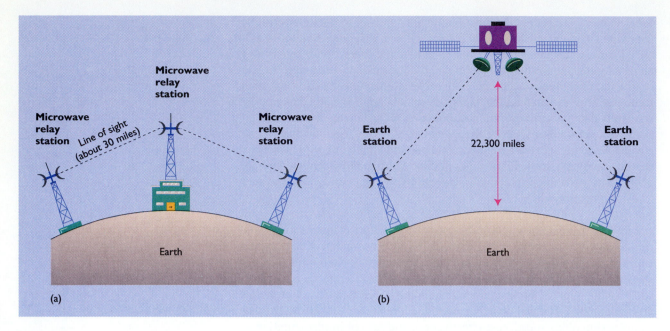

Microwave
relay
station

Microwave
relay
station

Microwave
relay
station

Line of sight
(about 30 miles)

Earth
station

22,300 miles

Earth
station

Earth

Earth

(a)

(b)

Figure 9 Microwave and satellite transmission. (a) To relay microwave signals, dish-shaped antennas such as these are often located atop buildings, towers, and mountains. Microwave signals can follow a line-of-sight path only, so stations must relay this signal at regular intervals to avoid interference from the curvature of the earth. (b) In satellite transmission, a satellite acts as a relay station and can transmit data signals from one earth station to another. A signal is sent from an earth station to the relay satellite, which changes the signal frequency before transmitting it to the next earth station.

earth station, amplifies the signal, changes the frequency, and retransmits the data to a receiving earth station (Figure 9b). (The frequency is changed so that the weaker incoming signals will not be impaired by the stronger outgoing signals.) This entire process takes only a few seconds.

If a signal must travel thousands of miles, satellites are usually part of the link. A message being sent around the world probably travels by cable or some other physical link only as far as the nearest earth-satellite transmission station (Figure 10). From there it is beamed to a satellite, which sends it back to earth to another transmission station near the data destination. Communications satellites are launched into space, where they are suspended about 22,300 miles above the earth. Why 22,300 miles? That is where satellites reach geosynchronous orbit—the orbit that allows them to remain

Figure 10 A satellite dish. A satellite dish is not usually the prettiest sight on the horizon, but a photographer has taken this shot of a dish with an exaggerating "fish-eye" lens, emphasizing the relationship of the dish to the signals that come from the satellite in space.

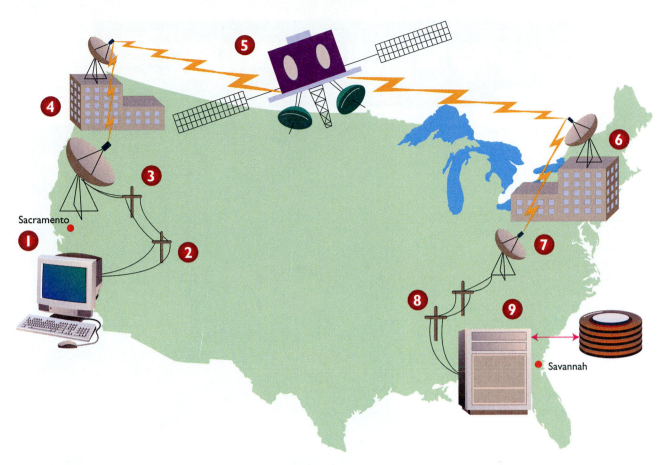

positioned over the same spot on the earth. However, not all satellites are in geosynchronous orbit; some are much closer to earth.

Mixing and Matching   A network system is not limited to one kind of link and, in fact, often works in various combinations, especially over long distances. An office worker who needs data from a company computer on the opposite coast will most likely use wire pairs in the phone lines, followed by microwave and satellite transmission (Figure 11). Astonishingly, the trip across the country and back, with a brief stop to pick up the data, may take only seconds.

Protocols

A **protocol** is a set of rules for the exchange of data between a terminal and a computer or between two computers. Think of protocol as a sort of precommunication agreement about the form in which messages or data is to be sent and receipt acknowledged. Protocols are handled by hardware and software related to the network, so that users need only worry about their own data.

Protocol Communications   Two devices must be able to ask each other questions (Are you ready to receive a message? Did you get my last message? Is there trouble at your end?) and to keep each other informed (I am sending data now). (Of course, we are referring here to coded signals, not words in the vernacular.) In addition, the two devices must agree on how data is to be transferred, including data transmission speed and duplex setting. But this must be done in a formal way. When communication is desired among

Figure 11 A variety of communications links. Say an accountant working in the Sacramento office needs certain tax records from the headquarters computer files in Savannah. One possibility for the route of the user request and the response is as follows. (1) The accountant makes the request for the records, which (2) goes out over the local phone system to (3) a nearby microwave station, which transmits the request to (4) the nearest earth-satellite transmission station, where (5) it is relayed to a satellite in space, which relays it back to earth (6) to an earth-satellite station near Savannah, where it is sent to (7) a microwave station and then (8) via the phone lines to (9) the headquarters computer. Once the tax records are retrieved from the Savannah computer files, the whole process is reversed as the requested records are sent back to Sacramento.

MAKING THE RIGHT CONNECTIONS
LIFE BY SATELLITE

The satellite boom is the practical way to wire the world. Furthermore, it is an entirely egalitarian method, providing a communication structure for Africa and Argentina just as surely as for American cities, no matter what commercial sponsors may have intended. In fact, the hundreds of satellites in the sky hold the potential for changing the way we live and work.

A person with a cell phone can dial, literally, from anywhere on earth to anywhere else. The call can zip from one satellite to another and finally to the receiving party. Although, in theory, this can benefit people in developing countries who have no installed phone base, it is likely to first benefit people in economically developed countries, letting them communicate from home to office to car. Hikers and bikers can use the same technology to call for help from a distant place. The communication will pinpoint the exact location of the transmission, determined by a global positioning satellite receiver.

computers from different vendors (or even different models from the same vendor), the software development can be a nightmare because different vendors use different protocols. Standards help.

Setting Standards   Standards are important in the computer industry; it saves money if users can all coordinate effectively. Communications standards exist and are constantly evolving and being updated for new communications forms. Perhaps the most important protocol is the one that makes Internet universality possible. Called **Transmission Control Protocol/ Internet Protocol (TCP/IP)**, this protocol permits any computer at all to communicate with the Internet. This is rather like everyone in the world speaking one language.

Network Topologies

The physical layout of a network is called a **topology**. There are three common topologies: star, ring, and bus networks. In a network topology, a com-

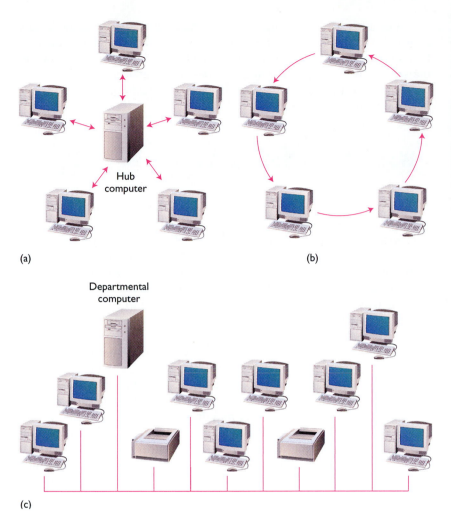

(a)

(b)

Departmental computer

(c)

Figure 12 Topologies. (a) The star network topology has a central computer that runs the network. (b) The ring network topology connects computers in a circular fashion. (c) The bus network topology connects all nodes in a line and can preserve the network if one computer fails.

ponent is called a **node,** which is usually a computer on a network. (The term *node* is also used to refer to any device connected to a network, including the server, computers, and peripheral devices such as printers.)

A **star network** has a hub computer that is responsible for managing the network (Figure 12a). All messages are routed through the central computer, which acts as a traffic cop to prevent collisions. Any connection failure between a node and the hub will not affect the overall system. However, if the hub computer fails, the network fails.

A **ring network** links all nodes together in a circular chain (Figure 12b). Data messages travel in only one direction around the ring. Any data that passes by is examined by the node to see if it is the addressee; if not, the data is passed on to the next node in the ring. Since data travels in only one direction, there is no danger of data collision. However, if one node fails, the entire network fails.

Really Big Plans

A private company called Teledesic is building a global "Internet in the Sky," scheduled to be operational in 2003. On its very first day of service, Teledesic (pronounced "tel eh DEH sic") expects to enable broadband telecommunications access for businesses, schools, and individuals everywhere on the planet. Big plans, indeed, especially when you consider that the company was founded only in 1990.

The Teledesic system's low orbit eliminates the long signal delay normally experienced with faraway geosynchronous satellite communications and enables the use of small, low-power terminals and antennas. The system will have 288 satellites, plus spares. Laptop-size terminals, mounted flat on rooftops, will receive and send signals, and connect to a computer network or a personal computer indoors.

The Teledesic system is designed to support millions of simultaneous users. Teledesic will offer a family of user equipment to access the network. Most users will have two-way connections that can receive data at 64MB per second and 2MB per second in the other direction (this is appropriate, since most users of high-volume data are receiving, not sending). The receiving speed is more than 2000 times faster than today's standard modems.

End-user rates will be set by service providers, but Teledesic expects rates to be comparable to those of future urban services for broadband access, which will be lower than rates for those services today.

In summary: very fast, very convenient, very high capacity—all for a lower price.

A **bus network** has a single line to which all the network nodes are attached (Figure 12c). Computers on the network transmit data in the hope that it will not collide with data transmitted by other nodes; if this happens, the sending node simply tries again. Nodes can be attached to or detached from the network without affecting the network. Furthermore, if one node fails, it does not affect the rest of the network.

Wide Area Networks

There are different kinds of networks. It is appropriate to begin with the geographically largest, a wide area network.

A **wide area network** (WAN) is a network of geographically distant computers and terminals. A network that spans a large city is sometimes called a **metropolitan area network,** or **MAN.** In business, a personal computer sending data any significant distance is probably sending it to a mainframe computer. Since these larger computers are designed to be accessed by terminals, a personal computer can communicate with a mainframe only if the personal computer emulates, or imitates, a terminal. This is accomplished by using **terminal emulation software** on the personal computer. The larger computer then considers the personal computer or workstation as just another user input/output communications device—a terminal.

When smaller computers are connected to larger computers, the result is sometimes referred to as a **micro-to-mainframe** link. The larger computer to which the terminal or personal computer is attached is called the **host computer.** If a personal computer is being used as a terminal, **file transfer software** permits users to download data files from the host or upload data files to the host. To **download** a file means to retrieve it from another computer. To **upload,** a user sends a file to another computer.

Local Area Networks

A local area network (LAN) is a collection of computers, usually personal computers, that share hardware, software, and data. In simple terms, LANs hook personal computers together through communications media so that each personal computer can share the resources of the others. As the name implies, LANs cover short distances, a campus or office or building.

Local Area Network Components

LANs do not use the telephone network. Networks that are LANs are made up of a standard set of components.

- All networks need some system for interconnection. In some LANs the nodes are connected by a shared **network cable.** Low-cost LANs are connected with twisted wire pairs, but many LANs use coaxial cable or fiber optic cable, which may be more expensive but faster. Some local area networks, however, are **wireless,** using infrared or radio wave transmissions instead of cables. Wireless networks are easy to set up and reconfigure, since there are no cables to connect or disconnect, but they have slower transmission rates and limit the distance between nodes.

- A **network interface card,** sometimes called a **NIC,** connects each computer to the wiring in the network. A NIC is a circuit board that fits in one of the computer's internal expansion slots. The card contains circuitry that handles sending, receiving, and error checking of transmitted data.

- Similar networks can be connected by a **bridge,** a hardware/software combination that recognizes the messages on a network and passes on those addressed to nodes in other networks. For example, a fabric designer whose computer is part of a department LAN for a textile manufacturer could send cost data, via a bridge, to someone in the accounting department whose computer is part of another company LAN, one used for financial matters. It makes sense for each department, design and finance, to maintain separate networks because their interdepartmental communication is only occasional. A **router** is a special computer that directs communications traffic when several networks are connected together. If traffic is clogged on one path, the router can determine an alternative path. More recently, now that many networks have adopted the Internet protocol (IP), routers are being replaced with **IP switches,** which are less expensive and, since no translation is needed, faster than routers.

- A **gateway** is a collection of hardware and software resources that lets a node communicate with a computer on another dissimilar network. One of the main tasks of a gateway is protocol conversion. A gateway, for example, could connect an attorney on a local area network to a legal service offered through a wide area network.

Now let us move on to the types of local area networks. Two ways to organize the resources of a LAN are client/server and peer-to-peer.

Client/Server Networks

A **client/server** arrangement involves a **server,** the computer that controls the network. In particular, a server has hard disks holding shared files and often has the highest-quality printer, another resource to be shared (Figure 13). The clients are all the other computers on the network. Under the client/server arrangement, processing is usually done by the server, and only the results are sent to the client. A computer that has no disk storage ability and is used basically to send input to the server for processing and then receive the output is called a **thin client.** Sometimes the server and the client computer share processing. For example, a server, upon request from the

Figure 13 Server and peripheral hardware. In this network for a clinic with seven doctors, the daily appointment records for patients are kept on the hard disk associated with the server. Workers who, using their own computers, deal with accounting, insurance, and patient records can access the daily appointment file to update their own files.

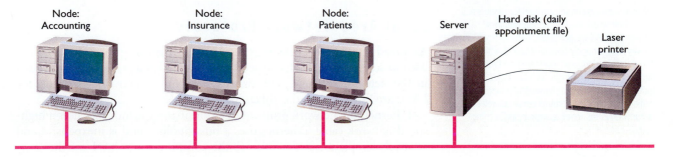

Node: Accounting   Node: Insurance   Node: Patients   Server   Hard disk (daily appointment file)   Laser printer

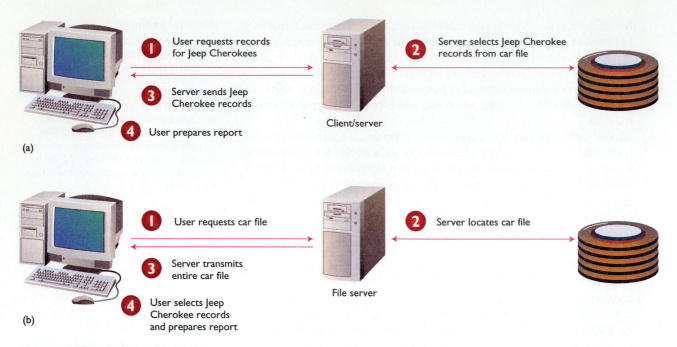

(a)

1 User requests records for Jeep Cherokees

2 Server selects Jeep Cherokee records from car file

3 Server sends Jeep Cherokee records

4 User prepares report

Client/server

(b)

1 User requests car file

2 Server locates car file

3 Server transmits entire car file

4 User selects Jeep Cherokee records and prepares report

File server

Figure 14 Client/server contrasted with file server. (a) In a client/server relationship, (1) a user makes a request to the server to select only Jeep Cherokee records from a state car file; (2) the server does so and (3) sends the records back to the user, who (4) uses those specific records to prepare a report. (b) In a file server relationship, (1) a user asks for the entire state car file, which (2) the server locates and then (3) transmits to the user, who then (4) selects the Jeep Cherokee records and prepares a report. The client/server setup places most of the processing burden on the more powerful server and also significantly reduces the amount of data being transferred between server and user.

client, could search a database of cars in the state of Maryland and come up with a list of all Jeep Cherokees. This data could be passed on to the client computer, which could process the data further, perhaps looking for certain equipment or license-plate letters. This method can be contrasted with a **file server** relationship, in which the server transmits the entire file to the client, which does all its own processing. Using the Jeep example, the entire car file would be sent to the client, instead of just the extracted Jeep Cherokee records (Figure 14).

Client/server has attracted a lot of attention because a well-designed system reduces the volume of data traffic on the network and allows faster response for each client computer. Also, since the server does most of the heavy work, less-expensive computers can be used as nodes.

Peer-to-Peer Networks

All computers in a **peer-to-peer** arrangement have equal status; no one computer is in control. With all files and peripheral devices distributed across several computers, users share one another's data and devices as needed. Peer-to-peer networks are common in small offices with perhaps a dozen personal computers. The main disadvantage is lack of speed—peer-to-peer networks slow down under heavy use. Many networks are hybrids, containing elements of both client/server and peer-to-peer arrangements.

Local Area Network Protocols

As already noted, networks must have a set of rules—protocols—that are used to access the network and send data. Recall that a protocol is embedded in the network software. The two most common network protocols for LANs are Ethernet and the Token Ring network.

Ethernet, the network protocol that dominates the industry, uses a high-speed network cable. Ethernet uses a bus topology and is inexpensive and relatively simple to set up. Since all the computers in a LAN use the same

2000 and Beyond

MAPPING SPACE

A skyscraper? Look again. This structure is an oversized telescope, with a task no less daunting than making an atlas of the universe. That's right—maps. The telescope, the main component of a project called the Sloan Digital Sky Survey, records data with the aid of light-sensitive silicon semiconductors. Hundreds to thousands of stars can be viewed every few minutes. That data is stored and analyzed by computer.

The Sky Survey will systematically map one-quarter of the entire sky, producing a detailed image of it and determining the positions and absolute brightnesses of more than 100 million celestial objects. It will also measure the distance to a million of the nearest galaxies, giving us a three-dimensional picture of the universe through a volume one hundred times larger than that explored to date. The Sky Survey will also record the distances to 100,000 quasars, the most distant objects known, giving us an unprecedented hint at the distribution of matter to the edge of the visible universe.

The Sky Survey is the latest in an ancient and honorable tradition of surveying the sky. Many of humanity's earliest permanent records describe the attempts to frame the universe. The Sky Survey will advance this tradition in a number of ways. As the first large-area survey to use electronic light detectors, the image it produces will be substantially more sensitive and accurate than earlier surveys, which relied on photographic techniques. The Sky Survey also represents a significant increase in scale. The total quantity of information produced, about 15 terabytes (trillion bytes), rivals the information content of the Library of Congress.

A sample map a yard wide and 33 feet long displays only six minutes of observations. It will take years into the twenty-first century to complete the project. We will not be able to pick up space maps anytime soon.

---

cable to transmit and receive data, they must follow a set of rules about when to communicate; otherwise, two or more computers could transmit at the same time, causing garbled or lost messages. Operating much like a party line, a computer "listens" to find out if the cable is in use before transmitting data. If the cable is in use, the computer must wait. When the cable is free from other transmissions, the computer can begin transmitting immediately. This transmission method is called by the fancy name of **carrier sense multiple access with collision detection**, or **CSMA/CD.**

If by chance two computers transmit data at the same time, the messages collide. When a **collision** occurs, a special message, lasting a fraction of a second, is sent out over the network to indicate that it is jammed. Each computer stops transmitting, waits a random period of time, and then transmits again. Since the wait period for each computer is random, it is unlikely that they will begin transmitting again at the same time. This all happens without the user being aware of it.

A **Token Ring network,** which is closely associated with IBM, works on the concept of a ring network topology, using a token—a kind of electronic signal. The method of controlling access to the shared network cable is called **token passing.** The idea is similar to the New York City subway: If you want to ride—transmit data—you must have a token. However, unlike the subway, there is only one token available. The token circulates from computer to computer along the ring-shaped LAN.

When a computer on the network wishes to transmit, it first captures the token; only then can it transmit data. When the computer has sent its message, it releases the token back to the network. Since only one token is circulating around the network, only one device is able to access the network at a time.

The Work of Networking

The use of automation in the office is as varied as the offices themselves. As a general definition, however, **office automation** is the use of technology to help people do their jobs better and faster. Much automated office innovation is based on communications technology. This section begins with several important office technology topics—electronic mail, facsimile technology, groupware, teleconferencing, and electronic data interchange.

Electronic Mail

Electronic mail, or **e-mail,** is the process of sending messages directly from one computer to another, where it is stored until the recipient chooses to receive it. A user can send data to a colleague downstairs, a message across town to that person who is never available for phone calls, a query to the headquarters office in Switzerland, and even memos simultaneously to regional sales managers in Chicago, Raleigh, and San Antonio. Electronic mail users shower it with praise. It can reach many people with the same message, it reduces the paper flood, and it does not interrupt meetings the way a ringing phone does. Since e-mail does not require both participants to be present at the time of transmission, it is a boon to people who work on the same project but live in different time zones.

Facsimile Technology

Operating something like a copy machine connected to a telephone, **facsimile technology** uses computer technology and communications links to send graphics, charts, text, and even signatures almost anywhere in the world. The drawing—or whatever—is placed in the facsimile machine at one end, where it is digitized (Figure 15). Those digits are transmitted across the miles and then reassembled at the other end to form a nearly identical version of the original picture. All this takes only minutes—or less. Facsimile is not

Figure 15 Faxing it. This facsimile machine can send and receive text, drawings, and graphs long-distance.

only faster than overnight delivery services, it is less expensive. Facsimile is abbreviated **fax,** as in "I sent a fax to the Chicago office."

Personal computer users can send and receive faxes directly by means of a **fax modem,** which also performs the usual modem functions. A user can send computer-generated text and graphics as a fax. When a fax comes in, it can be reviewed on the computer screen and printed out. The only missing ingredient in this scheme is paper; if the document to be sent is available only on paper, it must be scanned into the computer first or else be sent using a separate fax machine.

Groupware

Groupware is any kind of software that lets a group of people share things or track things together. The data the workers share is in a database on disk. But the key to their being able to share that data is their access to it via communications lines. We mention groupware to emphasize the role of communications systems in letting people, who may be in far-flung locations, work together.

Teleconferencing

An office automation development with cost-saving potential is **teleconferencing,** a method of using technology to bring people and ideas together despite geographic barriers. There are several varieties of teleconferencing, but most common today is **videoconferencing,** whose components usually include a large screen, video cameras that can send live pictures, and an online computer system to record communication among participants (Figure 16). Although this setup is expensive to rent and even more expensive to own, the costs seem trivial when compared with travel expenses—airfare, lodging, meals—for in-person meetings.

Figure 16 A videoconferencing system. Geographically distant groups can hold a meeting with the help of videoconferencing. A camera transmits images of local participants for the benefit of distant viewers.

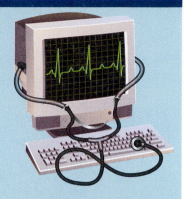

E-mail Your Doctor

Though your doctor is not looking for electronic penpals, she or he may want to hear from patients by e-mail. Many doctors have added regular stints in front of their computers to their schedules. The most obvious advantage is avoiding telephone tag, with no one sitting by the phone and both sides leaving messages.

Doctors in universities lead the way, but now the practice is spreading to managed care organizations and will probably become standard service in the health care industry.

Patients who want to take advantage of this service should keep a few things in mind. By law, all e-mail communications must be filed in a patient's medical record. To avoid mix-ups, be sure to include your proper name and patient identification number. Keep your message short and stick to one issue per e-mail. Do not expect a speedy response; most doctors try to reply within 48 hours. If it is an emergency, pick up the phone.

Global Perspective

The availability of worldwide e-mail makes new simplifications in business processes possible. Complex business decisions that would originally have required expensive, real-time, teleconferences or face-to-face meetings can often be resolved by using an e-mail "Delphi" technique. Participants circulate draft proposals via e-mail, and reach a consensus decision with the help of a moderator, avoiding the problems with jet-lag, time-zones, passports, and off-hours meeting times.

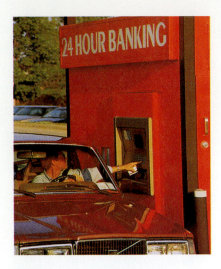

Figure 17 An automated teller machine. Users can obtain bank services 24 hours a day through ATMs.

Videoconferencing has some drawbacks. Some people are uncomfortable about their appearance on camera. A more serious fear is that the loss of personal contact will detract from some business functions, especially those related to sales or negotiations.

Electronic Data Interchange

Businesses use a great deal of paper in transmitting orders. One method devised to cut down on paperwork is **electronic data interchange** (EDI). EDI is a series of standard formats that allow businesses to transmit invoices, purchase orders, and the like electronically. In addition to eliminating paper-based ordering forms, EDI can help to eliminate errors in transmitting orders that result from transcription mistakes made by people. Since EDI orders go directly from one computer to another, the tedious process of filling out a form at one end and then keying it into the computer at the other end is eliminated. Many firms use EDI to reduce paperwork and personnel costs. Some large firms, especially discounters such as Wal-Mart, require their suppliers to adopt EDI and, in fact, have direct computer hookups with their suppliers.

Electronic Fund Transfers: Instant Banking

Using **electronic fund transfers** (EFTs), people can pay for goods and services by having funds transferred from various accounts electronically, using computer technology. One of the most visible manifestations of EFT is the **ATM**—the **automated teller machine** that people use to obtain cash quickly (Figure 17). A high-volume EFT application is the disbursement of millions of Social Security payments by the government directly into the recipients' checking accounts.

Computer Commuting

A logical outcome of computer networks is **telecommuting,** the substitution of communications and computers for the commute to work (Figure 18). That is, a telecommuter works at home on a personal computer and proba-

Figure 18 Telecommuting. Using CAD/CAM software, this architect works at home four days a week. He goes into the office one day a week for meetings and conferences.

GETTING PRACTICAL

EVERYTHING YOU ALWAYS WANTED TO KNOW ABOUT E-MAIL

I know generally what hardware and software need to be in place for e-mail, but how do I get in on the action? You must first sign up for some service, probably giving a credit card number for monthly payments and then being prompted to make up your own e-mail address and password. Thus established, you will probably click a screen icon to invoke your e-mail service whenever you want it.

I don't know how I actually send e-mail. Your e-mail service will provide menus of choices, one of which is to write e-mail. The look of the screen may vary, but, generally, all e-mail write systems have the same elements—a place for the e-mail address of the recipient, a place to put the message title, and a place for you to type your message. You can see these three elements on the America Online (AOL) screen shown here.

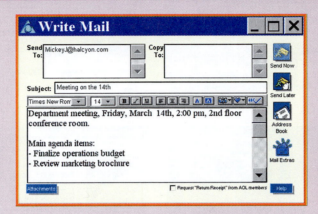

That's it? Well, many services will let you get a bit fancier if you wish. For example, as you can see here, AOL offers buttons for changing fonts, checking spelling, adding a photo, and so on.

How does my message get to the recipient? First, you click a Send button, Send Now if you are online—connected to AOL—or Send Later if you are offline. AOL, or whatever service you are using, will take care of delivery.

How do I know someone's e-mail address? Just ask.

You will have a collection of your friends' and colleagues' addresses in no time. And, since you are not expected to memorize them, just keep them in the clickable address book.

How do I get my own e-mail? It varies by the service, of course, but, generally, when you go online you will be informed that you have mail; AOL intones the famous "You've got mail!" In offices, where users are online to their company servers all day, a quiet chiming sound may indicate that new mail has arrived. Other systems sim-

ply display a small window on the screen, with a message that mail has arrived. You click the list of mail and click each item to read it. You may also, of course, choose to ignore it.

Can I just stay online for hours writing e-mail? Theoretically, yes, but it is not a good idea. You would be tying up a connection unnecessarily. You can write your e-mail offline and then, once the mail is ready, go online and send it. Most people write—and read—their e-mail offline.

Can I get free e-mail? Probably. You may be able to hook up to your college system. You will likely have e-mail at your place of work, although your employer may limit personal messages. You can get free e-mail on your personal computer from several sources, notably Juno, which will set you up on its own server in return for supplying some personal information used for marketing.

---

bly uses the computer to communicate with office colleagues or customers. In fact, some telecommuters are able to link directly to the company's network. Many telecommuters stay home two or three days a week and come into the office the other days. Time in the office permits the needed face-to-face communication with fellow workers and also provides a sense of participation and continuity. Approximately 20 million people are classified as telecommuters.

Online Services

Users can connect their personal computers to consumer-oriented communications services. These services, formally called **information utilities,** or,

InfoBit

According to a recent survey, of those companies that support telecommuting, approximately 56% reimburse home workers for desktop personal computers.

(a)

(b)

(c)

(d)

Figure 19 Online services. Computer users can use their personal computers to get information on a variety of topics through online services such as America Online. Shown here are (a) a clickable weather map, (b) a screen showing flowers, cards, and candy offerings for online shoppers, (c) a colorful screen to encourage kid creativity, and (d) a screen with activities associated with business research.

Global Perspective

While the networks which make up the Internet in the United States are operated by many independent governmental agencies and commercial businesses, data networking in many European countries is under more centralized control. Data communication networks are often run by organizations known as PTTs—Postal, Telephone and Telegraph administrations—the same organizations which operate the post offices in these countries.

more popularly, **online services,** are widely used by both home and business customers. Popular online services include America Online and the Microsoft Network. You need only set up the software, provided free by the service, and answer questions about how you will arrange to pay (probably a credit card).

These online services each offer myriad choices, including news, weather, shopping, games, educational materials, electronic mail, forums, financial information, and software product support (Figure 19). Online services typically offer an easy-to-use graphical environment, with mouse-controlled icons and overlaid screen windows.

Charges for online services vary. Often package deals are available. One possibility is a monthly fee that includes all basic services, including e-mail and access to the Internet, and a certain amount of connection time, with extra charges for extra time. For a higher monthly fee, a user can purchase unlimited access. People who live in densely populated areas can connect to the service through a local phone number, avoiding extra phone charges. However, people in remote areas may have to access the service through a long-distance phone number, a disadvantage that can generate a shocking phone bill for the uninitiated.

The Internet

The Internet, as indicated earlier in this book, is not just another online activity. The other topics discussed in this section pale in comparison. The

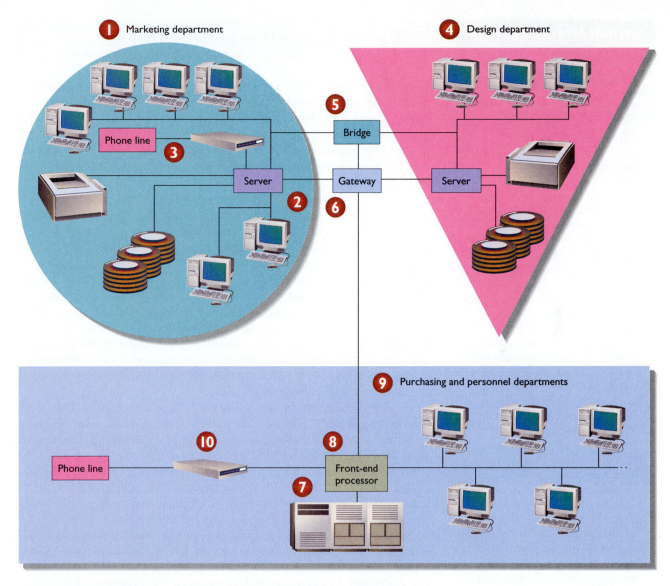

Figure 20 Example of a network. In this set of networks for a toy manufacturer, (1) the marketing department has a bus local area network whose six personal computers use a shared printer. Both program and data files are stored with the (2) server. Note (3) the modem that accepts outside inquiries from field representatives. (4) The design department, with just three personal computers, has a similar LAN. The two LANs can communicate via (5) a bridge. Either LAN, via (6) a gateway, can access (7) the mainframe computer, which uses (8) a front-end processor to handle communications. Users in (9) the purchasing and personnel departments have terminals attached directly to the mainframe computer. The mainframe computer also has (10) a modem that connects to the telephone lines and then, via satellite, to the mainframe at the headquarters office in another state.

Internet is considered by many to be the defining technology of the beginning of the 21st century, and it may well hold that status for several years. Since we are devoting separate chapters and features exclusively to the Internet, we mention it here only to make the list complete.

Instant Messaging

It is fast. In fact it is nearly instant: A message sent from a colleague arrives in a separate smaller window on your screen. (The instant message shown here appears on top of the Motley Fool site, which the recipient was viewing when the instant message arrived.) In that same window you can type a reply and send it off; it too will be received instantly. The dialogue can continue, back and forth. For instant messaging to work, both parties must be online at the same time. Contrast this with e-mail, which does not depend on your being at the computer; your e-mail will be there whenever you happen to get to your computer and ask for it.

Businesses use instant messaging to send time-sensitive messages, to exchange drafting files, or to keep people in touch on the road. However, businesses usually run instant messaging on their own servers so they can control security.

The Complexity of Networks

Networks can be designed in an amazing variety of ways, from a simple in-office group of three personal computers connected to a shared printer to a global spread including thousands of personal computers, servers, and mainframes. The latter, of course, would not be a single network but, instead, a collection of connected networks. You have already glimpsed the complexity of networks. Now let us consider a set of networks for a toy manufacturer (Figure 20).

The toy company has a bus local area network for the marketing department, consisting of six personal computers, a modem used by outside field representatives to call in for price data, and a server with a shared laser printer and shared marketing program and data files. The LAN for the design department, also a bus network, consists of three personal computers and a server with shared printer and shared files. Both LANs use the Ethernet protocol and have client/server relationships. The design department sometimes sends its in-progress work to the marketing representatives for their evaluation; similarly, the marketing department sends new ideas from the field to the design department. The two departments communicate, one LAN to another, via a bridge. It makes sense to have two separate LANs, rather than one big LAN, because the two departments need to communicate with each other only occasionally.

In addition to communicating with each other, users on each LAN, both marketing and design, occasionally need to communicate with the mainframe computer, which can be accessed through a gateway. All communications for the mainframe are handled by the front-end processor. Users in the purchasing, administrative, and personnel departments have terminals connected directly to the mainframe computer. The mainframe also has a modem that connects to telephone lines and then, via satellite, to the mainframe computer at corporate headquarters in another state.

Network factors that add to complexity but are not specifically addressed in Figure 20 include the electronic data interchange setups between the toy manufacturer's purchasing department and seven of its major customers, the availability of electronic mail throughout the networks, and the fact that—via a modem to an outside line—individual employees can access the Internet.

The near future in data communications is not difficult to see. The demand for services is just beginning to swell. Electronic mail already pervades the office and the campus and is growing rapidly in the home. Expect instant access to all manner of information from a variety of convenient locations. Prepare to become blasé about communications services available in your own home and everywhere you go.

CHAPTER REVIEW

Summary and Key Terms

- **Data communications systems** are computer systems that transmit data over communications lines, such as telephone lines or cables.

- **Centralized data processing** places all processing, hardware, and software in one central location.

- Businesses with many locations or offices often use **distributed data processing,** which allows both remote access and remote processing. Processing can be done by the central computer and the other computers that are hooked up to it.

- A **network** is a computer system that uses communications equipment to connect two or more computers and their resources.

- The basic components of a data communications system are a sending device, a communications link, and a receiving device.

- Data may travel to a large computer through a communications control unit called a **front-end processor,** which is actually a computer in itself. Its purpose is to relieve the central computer of some communications tasks.

- **Digital transmission** sends data as distinct on or off pulses. **Analog transmission** uses a continuous electric signal in a **carrier wave** having a particular **amplitude** and **frequency.**

- Digital signals are converted to analog signals by **modulation** (change) of a characteristic, such as the amplitude of the carrier wave. **Demodulation** is the reverse process; both processes are performed by a device called a **modem.**

- A **direct-connect modem** is connected directly to the telephone line by means of a telephone jack. An **external modem** is not built into the computer and can therefore be used with a variety of computers. An **internal modem** is on a board that fits inside a personal computer. Notebook and laptop computers often use a **PC card** modem that slides into a slot in the computer.

- Modem speeds are usually measured in **bits per second (bps).**

- An **ISDN adapter,** based on **Integrated Services Digital Network (ISDN),** can move data at 128,000 bps, a vast improvement over any modem.

- Two common methods of coordinating the sending and receiving units are **asynchronous transmission** and **synchronous transmission.** The asynchronous, or **start/stop,** method keeps the units in step by including special signals at the beginning and end of each group of message bits—a group is usually a character. In synchronous transmission the internal clocks of the units are put in time with each other at the beginning of the transmission, and the characters are transmitted in a continuous stream.

- **Simplex transmission** allows data to move in only one direction (either sending or receiving). **Half-duplex transmission** allows data to move in either direction but only one way at a time. With **full-duplex transmission,** data can be sent and received at the same time.

- A communications **link** is the physical medium used for data transmission. Common communications links include **wire pairs** (or **twisted pairs**), **coaxial cables, fiber optics, microwave transmission,** and **satellite transmission.** In satellite transmission, which uses **earth stations** to send and receive signals, a **transponder** ensures that the stronger outgoing signals do not interfere with the weaker incoming ones. **Noise** is anything that causes distortion in the received signal. **Bandwidth** refers to the number of frequencies that can fit on one link at the same time, or the capacity of the link.

- A **protocol** is a set of rules for exchanging data between a terminal and a computer or between two computers. The protocol that makes Internet universality possible is **Transmission Control Protocol/Internet Protocol (TCP/IP),** which permits any computer at all to communicate with the Internet.

- The physical layout of a local area network is called a **topology.** A **node** usually refers to a computer on a network. (The term *node* is also used to refer to any device connected to a network, including the server, computers, and peripheral devices such as printers.) A **star network** has a central computer, the hub, that is responsible for managing the network. A **ring network** links all nodes together in a circular manner. A **bus network** has a single line, to which all the network nodes and peripheral devices are attached.

- Computers that are connected so that they can communicate among themselves are said to form a network. A **wide area network (WAN)** is a network of geographically distant computers and terminals. A network that spans a large city is sometimes called a **metropolitan area network,** or **MAN.** To communicate with a mainframe, a personal computer must employ **terminal emulation software.** When smaller computers are connected to larger computers, the result is sometimes referred to as a **micro-to-mainframe link.** The large computer to which a terminal or personal computer is attached is called the **host computer.** In a situation in which a personal computer or workstation is being used as a network terminal, **file transfer software** enables a user to **download** files (retrieve them from another computer and store them) and **upload** files (send files to another computer).

- A **local area network (LAN)** is usually a network of personal computers that share hardware, software, and data. The nodes on some LANs are connected by a shared **network cable** or by **wireless** transmission. A **network interface card (NIC)** may be inserted into a slot inside the computer to handle sending, receiving, and error checking of transmitted data.

- If two LANs are similar, they may send messages among their nodes by using a **bridge.** A **router** is a special computer that directs communications traffic when several networks are connected together. Since many networks have adopted the Internet protocol (IP), some use **IP switches,** which are less expensive and faster than routers. A **gateway** is a collection of hardware and software resources that connects two dissimilar networks, including protocol conversion.

- A **client/server** arrangement involves a **server,** a computer that controls the network. The server has hard disks holding shared files and often has the highest-quality printer. Processing is usually done by the server, and only the results are sent to the node. A computer that has no disk storage capability and is used basically for input/output is called a **thin client.** A **file server** transmits the entire file to the node, which does all its own processing.

- All computers in a **peer-to-peer** arrangement have equal status; no one computer is in control. With all files and peripheral devices distributed across several computers, users share each other's data and devices as needed.

- **Ethernet** is a type of network protocol that accesses the network by first "listening" to see if the cable is free; this method is called **carrier sense multiple access with collision detection,** or **CSMA/CD.** If two nodes transmit data at the same time, it is called a **collision.** A **Token Ring network** controls access to the shared network cable by **token passing.**

- **Office automation** is the use of technology to help people do their jobs better and faster. **Electronic mail (e-mail)** allows workers to transmit messages to other people's computers. **Facsimile technology (fax)** can transmit text, graphics, charts, and signatures. **Fax modems** for personal computers can send or receive faxes, as well as handle the usual modem functions.

- **Groupware** is any kind of software that lets a group of people share things or track things together, often using data communications to access the data.

- **Teleconferencing** is usually **videoconferencing,** in which computers are combined with cameras and large screens. **Electronic data interchange (EDI)** allows businesses to send common business forms electronically.

- In **electronic fund transfers (EFTs),** people pay for goods and services by having funds transferred from various checking and savings accounts electronically, using computer technology. The **ATM**—the **automated teller machine**—is a type of EFT.

- **Telecommuting** means a worker works at home on a personal computer and probably uses the computer to communicate with office colleagues or customers.

- America Online and the Microsoft Network are examples of major commercial communications services called **information utilities** or **online services.**

Discussion Questions

1. Suppose you ran a business out of your home. Pick your own business or choose one of the following: catering, motorcycle repair, financial services, a law practice, roofing, or photo research. Now, assuming that your personal computer is suitably equipped, determine for what purposes you might use one or more—or all—of the following: e-mail, fax modem, online services such as America Online, the Internet, electronic fund transfers, and electronic data interchange.

2. Discuss the advantages and disadvantages of telecommuting versus working in the office.

3. Do you expect to have a computer on your desk on your first full-time job? Do you expect it to be connected to a network?

Student Study Guide

Multiple Choice

1. Internet protocol is governed by
   a. EFT   c. MAN
   b. TCP/IP   d. EDI

2. A computer that has no hard disk storage but sends input to a server and receives output from it is called a
   a. thin client c. MAN
   b. host   d. transponder

3. Devices that send and receive satellite signals are called
   a. modems   c. tokens
   b. earth stations d. servers

4. Housing all hardware, software, storage, and processing in one site location is called
   a. time-sharing processing c. centralized
   b. a distributed system   d. a host computer

5. Transmission permitting data to move only one way at a time is called
   a. half duplex c. simplex
   b. full duplex d. start/stop

6. The process of converting from analog to digital is called
   a. modulation   c. line switching
   b. telecommuting   d. demodulation

7. The device used with satellite transmission that ensures that strong outgoing signals do not interfere with weak incoming signals is the
   a. microwave   c. transponder
   b. cable   d. modem

8. A network that spans a large city is known as a(n)
   a. ISDN   c. LAN
   b. MAN   d. NIC

9. The Token Ring network controls access to the network using
   a. facsimile technology c. a bus
   b. ISDN   d. token passing

10. The arrangement in which most of the processing is done by the server is known as
    a. simplex transmission c. electronic data interchange
    b. a file server relationship d. a client/server

11. Distortion in a signal is called
    a. phase   c. noise
    b. IP switch   d. amplitude

12. One or more computers connected to a hub computer is a
    a. ring network c. node
    b. CSMA   d. star network

13. A connection for similar networks is a
    a. router   c. gateway
    b. bridge   d. fax

14. The physical layout of a LAN is called the
    a. topology   c. contention
    b. link   d. switch

15. The network type in which all computers have equal status is called
    a. a communications link c. peer-to-peer
    b. WAN   d. a gateway

16. The type of modulation that changes the height of the signal:
    a. frequency   c. phase
    b. amplitude   d. prephase

17. A network that places all nodes on a single cable:
    a. star   c. ring
    b. switched   d. bus

18. Signals produced by a computer to be sent over phone lines must be converted to
    a. modems   c. analog signals
    b. digital signals   d. microwaves

19. The device used between LANs that use the Internet protocol:
    a. bus   c. IP switch
    b. gateway   d. token

20. Microwave transmission, coaxial cables, and fiber optics are examples of
    a. modems   c. routers
    b. communication   d. ring networks
       links

21. A network of geographically distant computers and terminals is called a(n)
    a. bus   c. WAN
    b. ATM   d. LAN

22. Two dissimilar networks can be connected by a
    a. gateway   c. node
    b. bus   d. server

23. Graphics and other paperwork can be transmitted directly using
    a. CSMA/CD   c. token passing
    b. facsimile   d. transponder

24. The number of frequencies that can fit on a link:
    a. WAN   c. EFT
    b. bandwidth   d. EDI

25. Software used to make a personal computer act like a terminal:
    a. fax   c. videoconferencing
    b. bridge   d. emulation

True/False

T F   1. Frequency modulation varies the position in time of a complete wave cycle.

T F   2. Local area networks are designed to share data and resources among several computers in the same geographical location.

T F   3. A WAN is usually limited to one office building.

T F   4. A front-end processor is a computer.

T F   5. A thin client has no disk storage.

T F   6. An internal modem is normally used with a variety of computers.

T F   7. A modem can be used for either modulation or demodulation.

T F   8. Start/stop transmission sends characters in a stream.

T F   9. A transponder ensures that the stronger incoming signals do not interfere with the weaker outgoing ones.

T F   10. Full-duplex transmission allows transmission in both directions at once.

T F   11. Fiber optics are a cheaper form of communication than wire cables.

T F   12. A standard modem can transmit data faster than ISDN can.

T F   13. Another name for file server is peer-to-peer.

T F   14. A digital signal can be altered by frequency modulation.

T F   15. Synchronous transmission is also called start/stop transmission.

T F   16. Interactions among networked computers must use a protocol.

T F   17. The term node may refer to any device connected to a network.

T F   18. Ethernet and Token Ring are identical protocols.

T F   19. A ring network has no central host computer.

T F   20. A file server usually transmits the entire requested file to the user.

T F   21. A gateway connects two similar computers.

T F   22. A bus network uses a central computer as the server

T F   23. Fax boards can be inserted inside computers.

T F   24. Ethernet systems "listen" to see if the network is free before transmitting data.

T F   25. Telecommuting is a type of information utility.

Fill-In

1. The term for computer systems that transmit data over telephone lines is _____ _____.

2. TCP/IP stands for _____.

3. The kind of signal most telephone lines require is

   _____.

4. What device converts a digital signal to an analog

   signal and vice versa? _____

   _____

5. What is America Online an example of?

   _____

6. Distortion in the received signal is called

   _____.

7. The number of frequencies that can fit on a link at

   one time is determined by the

   _____.

8. What is the general term for the use of technology

   in the office? _____

9. The name of the extra computer often used by

   large computers to perform communications func-

   tions is _____.

10. What kind of network links distant computers and

    terminals? _____

11. The physical layout of a network is called the

    _____.

12. The type of server that delivers the entire file to a

    user node is the _____.

13. How does a Token Ring network control access to

    the cable? _____

14. Another name for an information utility is a(n)

    _____.

15. NIC stands for _____.

Answers

Multiple Choice

1. b	6. d	11. c	16. b	21. c
2. a	7. c	12. d	17. d	22. a
3. b	8. b	13. b	18. c	23. b
4. c	9. d	14. a	19. c	24. b
5. a	10. d	15. c	20. b	25. d

True/False

1. T	6. F	11. T	16. T	21. F
2. T	7. T	12. F	17. T	22. F
3. F	8. F	13. F	18. F	23. T
4. T	9. F	14. F	19. T	24. T
5. T	10. T	15. F	20. T	25. F

Fill-In

1. data communications systems
2. Transmission Control Protocol/Internet Protocol
3. analog
4. a modem
5. information utility, or online service
6. noise
7. bandwidth
8. office automation
9. front-end processor
10. wide area network
11. topology
12. file server
13. token passing
14. online service
15. network interface card

PLANET INTERNET

Shopping conveniences have existed since catalogs were invented. Convenience is at a high point today because computer shopping offers goods and services handily bundled together. The variety of available goods is stunning. What would you like to buy? A watch? A book? A knife? Bicycle shocks? Coffee? Pet gifts? Sports clothing? Clown shoes?(!) A gift of boxed fruit? All of these products, and thousands more, are available from companies that sell their wares on the Internet. As for the service, with a few clicks of a mouse and taps on the keyboard, an order can be on its way to you. The products just mentioned tend to be at individual specialty sites. But hundreds more shops have banded together to form electronic malls.

So many stores. The term *electronic mall* refers to a group of Internet stores that rivals physical malls in size and variety. A good place to start is the Mall of Cyberspace. There are many similar malls. You can even buy an inch of Maui at the Aloha Mall site. Many shoppers find that, in a rather short time, they have stumbled on favorite stores. We offer these from our list: Patagonia, Cybershop, Amazon, Bagel Oasis, Mexican Pottery, Southpaw Enterprises, 1-800-Flowers, College Depot, and the Chocolate Lovers' Page. You will soon have your own list.

Finding what you want. It is all well and good to know the names and the URLs of several shopping sites. But, although shopping on the Internet is more convenient than traipsing around by car and foot, you are still faced with the prospect of searching for what you want, store by Internet store. What if there was a better way? There is such a way, of course: a search engine, a site that allows you to type in a request of one or more words. The search engine then returns lists of sites matching your search words. You merely click on the name of a desired site and you're to be transported there. Search engines, of course, are not just for shopping; they can come in handy any time you need to find something specific on the Internet. Perhaps you need something more expensive, like a car. Go the Volkswagen Beetle site to check out features.

Welcome to

Mall of Cyberspace

Your Storefront on the Information Superhighway

A Better Way to Travel.

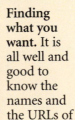

Use a search engine to find other car sites and compare features. **What if I don't want to buy anything?** No problem. It's just like old-fashioned window shopping, where you are welcome to look to your heart's content. Of course, as do retailers in real stores, Internet businesses hope you will see something you want to buy.

Internet Exercises

1. **Structured exercise.** Begin with the URL http://www.prenhall.com/capron and go to the Amazon site. Check the price of a certain title and then call your local bookstore for a comparison price.
2. **Freeform exercise.** Check first, if you wish, at the mall of Cyberspace. Then put the words *shop* and *mall* to a search engine and explore several other malls.

Charge it? Standards for secure transmission of transactions have evolved to the point where many people feel comfortable using the "secure server" to place orders, including sending credit-card numbers. Others prefer to do their shopping on the Internet but to place the actual order by telephone or some other secure means.

Such a bargain! If you are a comparison shopper, you will be delighted to discover that merchandise offered via the Internet is often a bargain. This is because overhead is low when compared with that of physical retail stores and even when compared with shopping by mail. No attractive displays, no sales people, no security devices clipped to merchandise, no printed catalogs, and possibly even no advertising. And, of course, a successful business has a potentially worldwide audience and can thus purchase in high volume and pass the savings on to consumers.

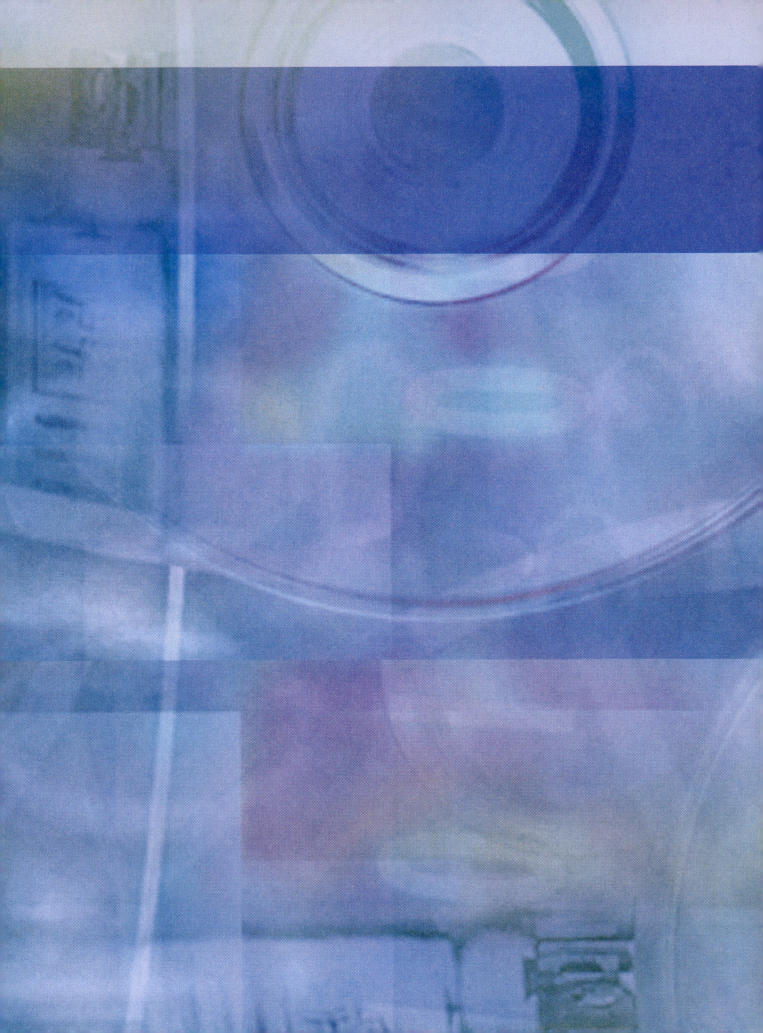

THE INTERNET

A Resource for All of Us

LEARNING OBJECTIVES

- Appreciate the history of the Internet
- Learn what is needed to get on the Internet
- Understand generally what an Internet service provider does
- Know the rudimentary functions of a browser
- Understand how to search the Internet
- Appreciate the non-Web parts of the Internet
- Appreciate the ongoing problems associated with the Internet

Whitney Bonilla had heard about the Internet, although she did not know quite what it was. She thought it had something to do with connecting to other people in other places. She also thought that it somehow contained a lot of information, information that might be handy for research for her college papers. She was right on both counts.

During her first week on campus, Whitney set out to hunt down the Internet. She discovered that there were several computer labs on campus and that one specialized in helping students get started on the Internet. But Whitney needed a lab pass to gain entry. A lab pass, for a fee, entitled a student to a certain number of hours on the Internet. The lab passes went first to students enrolled in computer classes and then to other students on a first-come, first-served basis. Unfortunately, Whitney was not among the first and was not able to get a pass at all.

All was not lost, however. Whitney found Internet access at the main library on campus. A librarian (who liked to call herself a "cybrarian") offered an hour-long beginners' class, repeated every day at noon and available to any student. Although subsequent computer access was limited to 30 minutes per session and no more than twice a week, Whitney found this sufficient to get her feet wet. She learned to get on the Internet, to move from site to site, and to find what she wanted.

She registered at the earliest possible date for the following quarter and included a beginning Internet course in her class schedule. She also got a lab pass.

InfoBit

One major survey concluded that there are significant gender differences in just what aspects of the Internet males and females choose to use. While men were reportedly more likely to use specialized applications like FTP and Usenet, women were more likely to use e-mail and associated mailing lists.

The Internet as a Phenomenon

The Internet is a loosely configured, rapidly growing labyrinth of networks of computers from around the world, from corporations, organizations, and individuals. Since the numbers change daily, the growth rate of Internet sites and Internet users can only be described as unprecedented. Ironically, the original idea behind the personal computer was to provide individual—and separate—computing. But, instead of remaining solo acts, users now find the greatest utility in connecting to every resource they can find. Although the growth of personal computers over the last few decades has been noteworthy, the increase has been steady rather than spectacular. The rise of connectivity, especially the use of the Internet, has been much faster. Millions of users hook up to the Internet every day.

Some people have tried to figure out who all those users are. Some have guessed that it is mostly teenage boys who hang out on the Internet and that they are there for hours and hours at a time. This is partly right. There are certainly lots of teenage boys on the Internet, and they probably have more time than most of us to surf the Internet. But they are by no means the majority. Although statistics are fleeting, Internet demographic trends indicate that the vast majority of users are adults and that almost half are female.

To many people who are recent users, it seems as if the Internet sprang up overnight. That, of course, is not true, but its popularity caught a lot of people by surprise. A look at its history explains why.

Don't Know Much about History

The history of the Internet bears telling. It is mercifully short. The reason that there is little to say is that it slumbered and stuttered for approximately 30 years before the general public even knew it existed. The Internet was started by obscure military and university people as a vehicle for their own purposes. They never in their wildest dreams thought it would become the international giant it is today. Let us look back briefly, to understand their point of view.

First Stirrings at the Department of Defense

Ever heard of a fallout shelter? In the cold war of the 1950s, people worried about "the bomb," about a nuclear attack whose radiation aftereffects—fallout—would be devastating. Some people built underground shelters, usually under their own houses, to protect themselves. It was in this climate of fear that the U.S. Department of Defense became concerned that a single bomb could wipe out its computing capabilities. Working with the Rand Corporation, they decided to rely on not one but several computers, geographically dispersed, and networked together. No one computer would be in charge.

A message to be sent to another computer would be divided up into **packets,** each labeled with its destination address. Each packet would wind its way individually through the network, probably taking different routes, but each heading in the direction of its destination and eventually being reconstituted into the original message at the end of the journey. The idea was that even if one computer was knocked out, the others could still carry on by using alternative routes. A packet can travel a variety of paths; the chosen path does not matter as long as the packet reaches its destination. The software that took care of the packets was Transmission Control Protocol/Internet Protocol (TCP/IP). TCP does the packeting and reassembling of the message. The IP part of the protocol handles the addressing, seeing to it that packets are routed across multiple computers.

They called the new set of connections **ARPANet,** an acronym that stands for Advanced Research Projects Agency Network. The year was 1969. Before long, computers from research universities and defense contractors joined the network. But the network was limited to people who had some technical expertise—a major reason why it was not yet of particular interest to the general public.

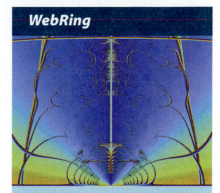

WebRing

WebRing is a free Internet service that offers groups of similar sites—the "ring"—on a given topic. Most of the sites are noncommercial. WebRing subjects vary greatly and include topics such as aviation, cartoons, science fiction, international news, water sports, real estate, and theatre.

At the main WebRing site, you can click on a category, such as the Eye Candy ring, featuring attractive graphics—"eye candy." The Eye Candy ring site opens with an index of the sites in the ring. You may accept the optional random site or click on one of your own choice. If, in the Eye Candy ring, you choose the Erd Ogivae site, you can see a couple dozen fractals, two of which are shown here. Fractal art is formed by using the computer to repeat geometric shapes with color, size, and angle variations. Once you get on the ring, you have the option of going to the next site on the ring, round and round until you come back to the original ring site.

Any web site owner can apply to join an existing ring or create a new ring. Rings are listed in the WebRing directory once they contain at least five sites.

Tim and Marc

Tim Berners-Lee is arguably the pivotal figure in the surging popularity of the Internet: He made it easy. In 1990, Dr. Berners-Lee, a physicist at a laboratory for particle physics in Geneva, Switzerland, perceived that his work would be easier if he and his far-flung colleagues could easily link to one another's computers (Figure 1). He saw the set of links from computer to computer to computer as a spider's web; hence the name **Web.** The **CERN site,** the particle physics laboratory where Dr. Berners-Lee worked, is considered the birthplace of the **World Wide Web.**

A **link** on a web site is easy to see: It is either colored text called **hypertext** or an icon or image called a **hyperregion** (Figure 2). A mouse click on the link appears to transport the user to the site represented by the link, and in common parlance one speaks of moving or transferring to the new site; actually, data from the new site is transferred to the user's computer.

Marc Andreessen was a student when, in 1993, he led a team that invented the *browser,* software used to explore the Internet (Figure 3). The browser featured a graphical interface, so that users could see and click on pictures as well as text. That first browser was named **Mosaic,** and it made web page multimedia possible. For the viewing public, the Internet now offered both easy movement with Dr. Berners-Lee's links and attractive images and a graphical interface provided by the browser. Today there are several competitive browsers, one of which is Netscape Communicator, produced by a company founded by Marc Andreessen and others. Netscape, Inc. was later purchased by America Online.

The Internet Surges Ahead

TCP/IP is software in the public domain. Since no one was really in charge of the network, there was no one to stop others from just barging in and linking up wherever they could. The network became steadily more valuable as it embraced more and more networks. Meanwhile, corporate networks, especially LANs of personal computers, were growing apace. Companies and organizations, noting an opportunity for greater communication and access to information, hooked their entire networks to the burgeoning network. A new name, taken from the name of the TCP/IP protocol, evolved: the Internet. The original ARPANet eventually disappeared altogether. Its users hardly noticed. Its functions continued and improved under the broader Internet.

In summary, the emergence of the Internet is due to four factors: (1) the universal TCP/IP standard, (2) the web-like ability to link from site to site, (3) the ease of use provided by the browser's graphical interface, and (4) the growth of personal computers and their local area networks that could be connected to the Internet.

Although statistics and projections vary, the growth of the Internet has been swift and unprecedented. No one thinks it is a fad. Almost everyone agrees that it is a true technological revolution. It continues to evolve.

Figure 1 **Dr. Tim Berners-Lee.** Working at a physics lab in Geneva, Switzerland, Dr. Berners-Lee invented a method of linking from site to site so that he could easily communicate with his colleagues worldwide. Thus was born the World Wide Web or, simply, the Web.

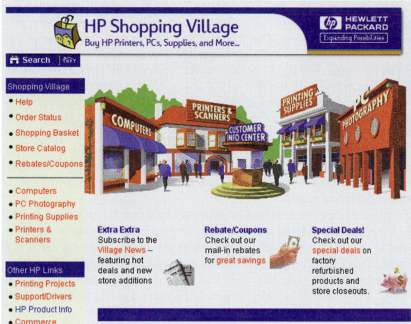

Figure 2 Links. This HP Shopping Village site, one of several associated with Hewlett-Packard, is typical in that it permits linking via icons—the village "buildings" that say Computers, Printers & Scanners, and so forth—or just text, as seen to the left. Many sites have icons in the form of clickable cartoons or artwork. Note that most of the text links are in red, indicating that they have not yet been clicked. The blue text, for HP Product Info, lower left, indicates that the link has been visited previously. However, there is nothing standard about which text color means what.

Figure 3 Marc Andreessen. As a student, Mr. Andreessen led a college team that developed the first browser, called Mosaic. He later developed a commercial product, the Netscape Navigator browser (later Netscape Communicator), which was an instant success and is widely used on the Internet.

Getting Started

History is interesting, but most people want to know how to use the Internet, or at least how to get started. We cannot be specific here because many factors—computers, servers, browsers, and more—vary from place to place and time to time. But we can talk about overall strategy and what the various services and software applications have to offer.

The Internet Service Provider and the Browser

An Internet user needs a computer with a modem (or possibly cable) and its related software, an Internet service provider, and a browser. An **Internet service provider (ISP)** provides the server computer and the software to connect to the Internet. A **browser** is the software on the user's computer that allows the user to access the Internet via the service provider, using a graphical interface. If you are accessing the Internet from a school, an organization, or a workplace, it is likely that these elements are already in place. The only task would be to activate the browser and know how to use it.

InfoBit

Although your browser won't require a supercomputer to handle your web surfing, there is a connection between supercomputers and Internet history. Marc Andreessen was working at NCSA—the National Center for Supercomputer Applications, at the University of Illinois, where he was a student—when he invented the graphical browser.

Things Aren't What They Used To Be

The original ARPANet environment was set among professionals with sound ethical standards. An unfortunate collateral effect of Internet growth has been the infiltration of hackers and other charlatans. No longer can the network be viewed as a safe, self-policed environment. Like social mores that evolved among users of old party line telephones, one needs to be aware that others can "listen in" and even do malicious damage.

InfoBit

You can use your browser's menu to change text size. You will probably find it on the default setting Medium; change it to largest.

InfoBit

Want to know what others folks are doing on the Web? The Magellan search engine site will let you click *voyeur* to see what other people are searching for. Of course, you don't know who they are.

InfoBit

Big changes are occurring in the area of retail ISPs, the kind that sell access to individuals and small businesses. The larger ISPs are gradually assimilating the smaller ones. Although there will always be Mom& Pop ISPs that specialize in personal service, they will probably need another income stream beyond Internet service because prices will be lowered and profits squeezed.

InfoBit

Don't be surprised if your friends don't recommend their Internet service provider. Almost half of the respondents in one major survey were dissatisfied enough with their ISP that they were thinking about switching.

If you wish to access the Internet from your own personal computer, one possibility is to sign up for an **online service,** such as America Online, that includes Internet access. The Internet service provider and browser are included in the package, and thus Internet access is available to you as soon as you have signed up for the online service. The main difference between an ISP and an online service is that an ISP is a vehicle to access the Internet, but an online service offers, in addition, members-only information. Online services provide content on every conceivable topic, all in a colorful, clickable environment that even a child can use. You will probably prefer an online service over an ISP if you are new to the online experience, if most of your friends and colleagues use the same online service, if people of different skill levels will use your computer to go online, or if you want to control what your children see online.

Approximately two-thirds of Internet users connect via an online service; the other one-third use an ISP. People who prefer an ISP are usually less interested in the managed resources of an online service and more interested in a freewheeling Internet experience that they can control themselves. You probably want an ISP if you prefer a different browser, plan to use a special communications link such as ISDN, or want to publish a complex web home page.

If you elect to go directly to an Internet service provider, you will first need to select one. Some people seek advice from friends; others begin with advertisements in their phone books or the business section of the newspaper. Note the Getting Practical feature called "Choosing an Internet Service Provider." Once you have arranged to pay the fees (probably an installation fee and certainly a monthly fee), you will set up your ISP interaction according to your provider's directions. The ISP may provide a disk that, once inserted into your computer's disk drive, will automatically set up the software, dial up the ISP, and set up your account, all with minimal input from you.

The next step is to install browser software on your computer. You can purchase a browser in your local software retail outlet or, if you have some other online access vehicle, possibly download it free from the browser vendor's web site. As you are installing the browser, you will be asked for information about your ISP, for which your ISP will have prepared you. (An ISP typically furnishes several pages of detailed instructions.) Once you are set up, you invoke the browser as you would any software on your computer, and it will begin by dialing the Internet service provider for you. You are on your way to the Internet experience.

The Browser in Action

As mentioned earlier, a browser is software used to explore the Internet. When they first came on the scene, browsers were a great leap forward in Internet friendliness. A number of browsers are available, some better organized and more useful than others. Two popular browsers are Netscape Communicator and Microsoft's Internet Explorer.

When you invoke your browser software, it will dial up the Internet service provider and, once successfully connected, display either the **home page**—initial page—of the web site that created your particular browser or some other site designated by your ISP. The browser shows three parts on the screen: two very obvious chunks and a third that is just a line at the bottom (Figure 4). The top part is the *browser control panel,* consisting of lines of menus and buttons, to be described momentarily. The lower part, by far the largest part of the screen, is the *browser display window.* At the very bottom of the screen is a *sta-*

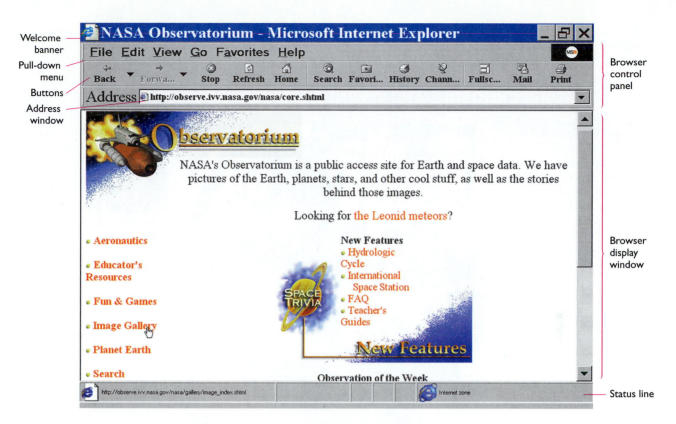

Figure 4 Browser control panel. Most browsers offer pretty much the same functions; the example here is a popular browser called Internet Explorer. Just below the browser's welcome banner, showing the name of the web site and browser display, is a set of pull-down menus; each such menu has several submenus. Just below the menus is a line of buttons. The buttons grouped to the left refer to the current web site in the browser display window: Back (go to the previous site), Forward (go forward to the next site, assuming you already went back), Stop (stop an incoming site that is taking too long to load or that, after just a brief look, you wish to see no further), Refresh (redo the current site), and Home (return to browser's home page). The middle buttons are Search (find sites on the Web), Favorites (keep a list of sites to which one might return), History (lists of sites you visited, by week and by day), and Channels (a list of web sites chosen to deliver content from the Internet to your computer). The buttons on the right are Fullscreen (let the browser display window take up the entire screen), Mail (get e-mail if you are set up on an account) and Print (print the content of the current site). Below the button line is the Address window, which contains the URL of the site in the browser display window.

tus line, which indicates the progress of data being transferred as you move from site to site. The status line may also show other messages, depending on the browser. The browser control panel at the top stays the same—except for the changing address of the visited site—as you travel from site to site through the Web; the browser display window changes, showing, in turn, each new Internet site you visit. Note, by the way, that it is common to refer to traveling "from site to site," but in actual fact you are traveling nowhere; the information from the site is coming to you. The data from the "visited" site is sent from its source computer across the Internet to your computer.

When you first invoke the browser, the web site window generally shows material according to the browser vendor's wishes, usually useful informa-

GETTING PRACTICAL

CHOOSING AN INTERNET SERVICE PROVIDER

If you have decided that you want to connect your computer to the Internet directly via an Internet service provider, you have to choose among many offerings. Many ISPs are national in scope; others are regional or local services. The best rates generally come from local ISPs. Local ISPs are usually what are called *retail ISPs;* that is, they deal primarily with individuals and small businesses.

You can begin by checking the Yellow Pages of your local phone directory, which probably has listings under "Internet." Also check out ISP advertisements in monthly computer magazines and, in urban areas, in your local newspaper. Many advertisements include a toll-free number that you can call for free software and a free trial subscription of a month or of a certain number of online hours.

An online resource called The List is by far the most comprehensive and useful list of ISPs (http://www.thelist.com). It is, of course, available only to people who are already able to get online. How-

ever, you may be able to persuade a friend or colleague to access the site for you. It features thousands of ISPs and is searchable by state, province (in Canada), and telephone area code.

Here are some further tips:

- Look for an ISP whose access is only a local phone call away. Otherwise, long distance charges will figure prominently in your monthly

phone bill. Even if a seemingly toll-free number is offered, the provider will recoup the cost in charges to you.
- Seek a provider with speedy access. *Speedy access* is a relative and changeable term, so we will not fixate on it now. But do not assume that all ISPs have the same access speed. Ask and compare.
- Ideally, find a provider with software that will

automate the registration process. Configuring the right connections on your own is not a trivial task.
- Figure out how likely you are to get help. At the very least, ask for the phone numbers and hours of the help line. If help is available only via e-mail, take your business elsewhere.
- ISPs are volatile. Make sure your contract includes terms that let you opt out if your ISP wants to transfer your account to a different ISP or if your ISP is bought out. For that matter, make sure you can opt out for your own reasons.

Finally, don't fall for an unrealistic bargain. Like anything else, if it sounds too good to be true, it probably is. You will probably find that a "bargain" service is oversubscribed, underpowered, and full of busy signals. Even worse, your call for technical help may garner only a "this number has been disconnected" message. Stability is worth something.

tion and possibly advertisements for their products (most browsers, however allow you to change the first page you see when you sign on to one of your own preference). Note that the site display is not limited to the size of your screen; your screen merely limits how much of the site you can see at one time (Figure 5). The page can be **scrolled**—moved up and down—by using

(a)

Figure 5 Web page view. A web page has an indeterminate length. (a) Your first look at the Campbell Soup web site will match the size and shape of your screen. (b) The Campbell Soup site is, of course, much longer than can be seen in one screenful.

(b)

the **scroll bar** on the right; simply press your mouse button over a scroll bar arrow to see the page move. As you move the page, note that the browser control panel stays in place; it is always available no matter what the browser display window shows.

Browser Functions and Features

Next, let us examine the functions of the browser control panel. You can follow along on Figure 4 as you read these descriptions. Again, this discussion is necessarily generic and may vary from browser to browser. First, note the browser's welcome banner, touting its own name and logo, across the top of the screen. Next, usually off to the right, is the browser logo, such as the circled *msn* shown in Figure 4. The logo is active—shimmering, changing colors, rotating, *something*—when it wants to let you know that it is in the process of moving you to a new site. Since this sometimes takes a while, it would be disconcerting to stare at a static screen and think nothing is happening. Note also that the status line at the bottom of the page provides information about the progress in contacting and receiving data from the desired site. If the transfer to the new site takes too long, you can cancel the move by clicking the browser's Stop button.

Menus and Buttons   Using a mouse lets you issue commands through a set of **menus,** a series of choices normally laid out across the top of the screen. The menus are called **pull-down menus** because each initial choice, when clicked with a mouse, reveals lower-level choices that pull down like a window shade from the initial selection at the top of the screen. You can also invoke commands using **buttons** for functions such as Print to print the current page, Home to return to the browser home page, and—perhaps the

URL:

http://www.intel.com/pressroom/index.htm

Protocol   ISP address   Path, directory,
                  (domain)   file name

Figure 6 A dissected URL. The Uniform Resource Locator represents a unique address of an Internet site or file. Whenever you are looking at a web site, you can see its URL near the top of the screen in the browser's control panel, in the location (address) slot. The example here shows a web address for the Intel host, using a file called index.htm in the pressroom directory.

ones you will use the most—Back and Forward, to help you retrace sites you have recently traversed. If you rest the cursor over a button for just a few seconds, a small text message will reveal its function. Note that all functions are listed in the pull-down menus; the buttons are just convenient repetitions of the most commonly used functions.

URL The location slot, sometimes called the address window, will usually contain a **Uniform Resource Locator (URL)**, a rather messy-looking string of letters and symbols, which is the unique address of a web page or file on the Internet. An URL (pronounced "earl" or, alternatively, "U-R-L") has a particular format (Figure 6). A web page URL begins with the protocol *http*, which stands for **HyperText Transfer Protocol.** This protocol is the means of communicating by using links, the clickable text or image that transports a user to the desired site. Next comes the **domain name,** which is the address of the Internet service provider (ISPs, by the way, must register each domain name and pay an ongoing fee). The last part of the domain name, *com* in Figure 6, is called a **top-level domain** and represents the purpose of the organization or entity—in this case, *com* for "commercial." In some cases, the end of the domain name stands for the country of origin. Note the usage of top-level domain names in Figure 7. The last part of the URL, usually the most

Figure 7 Distribution of top-level domain names. A glance at the chart shows that the majority of web sites, worldwide, have the top-level domain *com;* that is, they are business sites. Sites using *net* are often business sites too. The other domains shown here are *edu* for education; *mil* for military; *jp* for Japan; *us* for United States, for those wishing to distinguish it from sites in other countries; *org* for nonprofit organizations; and *gov* for government. Country domains use two letters; typical examples are *fi* (Finland), *uk* (United Kingdom), *de* (Germany), *ca* (Canada), *au* (Australia), *nl* (Netherlands), and *se* (Sweden). Seven new top-level domain names have been added: *firm* for business sites, *store* for sites offering goods to purchase, *web* for sites emphasizing activities related to the WWW, *arts* for sites emphasizing cultural and entertainment activities, *rec* for sites emphasizing recreation/entertainment activities, *info* for sites providing information services, and *nom* for those wishing individual or personal nomenclature.

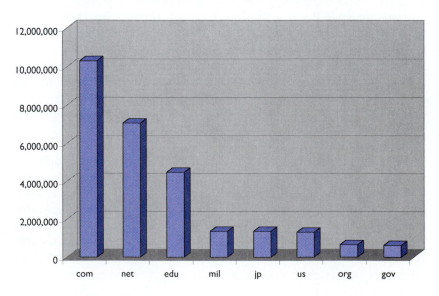

Figure 8 Frames. This unusual site, WhatIs, has a total of five separate rectangular sections, called frames. The site is designed to offer computer-related definitions. The narrow frame across the top contains clickable alphabet letters, which cause the frame just below to change; in this example, the letter T has been clicked in the top frame, calling up the list of terms beginning with T. The list of terms is movable, up and down, as are the frame along the left side and also the center section. Note that each of these three frames has its own scroll bar. Once a term has been highlighted, its definition will appear in the large frame below; in this case, the word *telephony* is defined. A fifth frame, across the bottom, holds a banner advertisement.

complex, contains directories and file names to help zero in on a very specific part of a site. Parts of the URL to the right of the domain, that is, the directory and file names, are case-sensitive; that is, you must type uppercase or lowercase characters exactly as indicated.

Many URLs end right after the domain. Although there may be many pages that are part of the site and thus have longer URLs, it is simplest to start at the top with the short URL. In fact, many advertised URLs neglect to even mention the *http://* part of their address, partly because newer browser versions supply the *http://* for you.

No one likes to type URLs. There are several ways to avoid it. The easy way, of course, is simply to click links to move from one site to another. Another way is to click a pre-stored link on your browser's **hot list**—called Bookmarks or Favorites or something similar—where you can store your favorite sites and their URLs.

Frames   Most browsers support a concept called **frames,** which allow a given page to be divided into rectangular sections, each of which can operate independently of the others (Figure 8). It is like having several small pages on the same screen; some may be static and others may be scrolled up and down. The advantage is that a site can offer several different functions or areas of focus. A disadvantage of frames is that a small screen, notably a laptop screen, may look cluttered. A classic approach to frames is the three-frame look: a static title frame and a left-side navigation frame that target the main content frame to the right (Figure 9).

Competition   Not just functional buttons, but buttons that illuminate when the cursor passes over them. Not just English, but French, German, and Italian. Not just frames, but borderless frames. You begin to get the idea. As browsers compete to be the best, they get fancier. And we, the users, get more browser functionality. In fact, some browsers are considered a whole suite of programs, including rich software tools for communicating and sharing information and offering support for mail, security, collaboration, and web page authoring.

Plug-ins   In addition to the browsers themselves, various vendors offer **plug-ins,** software that enhances the value of a browser by increasing its functionality or features. Typical plug-ins can enhance a site's audio-video experience or improve image viewing. Most plug-ins can be downloaded from their own web sites. Once the plug-in is downloaded and installed, usually a sim-

Exact Time

How accurate is the clock on your personal computer? Not very. The quartz crystals that are used to regulate the clock logic are accurate only to 0.005 percent, allowing a drift of about two minutes per month. You can, of course, use your telephone to call a time-of-day service and reset your computer clock manually. Or you can do it the easy way: Use the Internet.

A program called ExactTime will get the correct time from a web site dedicated to that purpose. In fact, it picks up the date too and uses the collected information to reset your computer's date and time. You can set up the program to do this automatically at regular intervals. Your computer will then have the most accurate clock in your house or office.

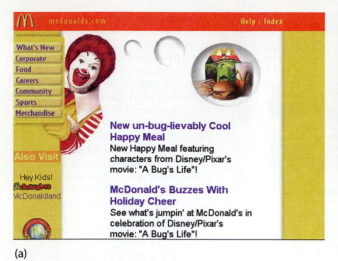

(a)

(b)

Figure 9 Classic frames structure. McDonald's and IBM have adopted the popular three-frame configuration—top, left, right. (a) The McDonald's title frame, across the top, stays the same. The left-hand side is a navigation frame whose items can be clicked to bring up new content to the right. (b) IBM also has a title frame across the top and a navigation frame left but has varied the configuration by adding a list of clickable options just below the title frame.

ple procedure, the browser can automatically handle the newly enabled features. An example of a plug-in is Adobe Acrobat, which is used to put documents in Portable Document Format (PDF). Since everything from product descriptions to IRS forms is on the Web in PDF, it is important that a browser be equipped to handle the format. Perhaps the most popular plug-in is Shockwave, from a company named Macromedia. Shockwave permits viewing sites that have quality animation and other effects (Figure 10).

Java

In the early days of the Web, everything presented on a web page was static, composed of material that had already been prepared. A user was basically accessing the electronic version of a printed page. Even though that access was certainly a convenience, the content of the web page offered nothing innovative. Until Java. It is Java that permits the dancing icons, sound clips, flashing messages, banners that scroll across the page—and much more. **Java** is a programming language, developed by Sun Microsystems, that is used to write software that can run on any machine, hence its appeal to the multifaceted Internet.

The programs that provide multimedia effects, the moving images and sound clips on a web page, are called **applets,** a sort of abbreviation for "little applications" (Figure 11). Applets can make web pages perform virtually any task—display animations, receive input, perform calculations, and so forth. Java also provides the possibility of dynamic interaction, where the user can receive immediate feedback and the programs actually do things on their own.

To benefit from applets, a user must have a browser that is capable of running Java, as, indeed, the most popular browsers are. If you are thus equipped, you will doubtless see many applets in action as you cruise the Web.

Moving from Site to Site

There are several ways to leave your browser's home page and start moving to other sites. Most browsers provide a list of clickable categories, such as sports, weather, news, technology, and even comic strips. Also a button click away are lists of new sites, "cool" sites, and various comprehensive directories. All of these come under the category of—yes—browsing.

But suppose you have something more specific in mind. If you know the URL for a desired site, delete the current URL in the location box, then type in the new one—carefully—and press Enter on the keyboard. You will be moved to the site just as if you had clicked a link. Sometimes—too often—an URL does not work. That is, a message is returned saying Unable to Locate Server or, simply, Not Found. The former may mean that you typed the URL incorrectly. The latter probably means that the specific site you want is no longer on that ISP. People do move around, from ISP to ISP, and they do not always provide a forwarding address.

Keep in mind that moving from site to site, whether by link or URL, is not magic. Although the movement from site to site is relatively effortless for the user, all the concepts described here are in play. That is, link requests move from your computer to your server and across networks of computers, all using TCP/IP, until the destination site is reached. Then, carrying the desired information back to your computer, the process is reversed.

Searching the Internet

Although a browser, true to its name, lets a user browse by listing clickable categories of information—sports, business, kids, whatever—most users soon want to find something specific. A **search engine** is software, usually located at its own web site, that lets a user specify search terms; the search engine then finds sites that fit those terms. A browser usually offers links to one or more search engines, or a user can simply link to the site of a favorite search engine.

Now, a search engine does not actually go out to the Web and "look around" each time a search is requested. Instead, the search engine, over time, builds a database of searchable terms that can be matched to certain

Figure 10 Shockwave plug-in. The site for Rod Stewart includes eye-catching Shockwave animation, as various elements move around and banners slide into place. Incidentally, this site also includes album sound tracks, which you can appreciate with an audio plug-in from RealNetworks.

Figure 11 Applets. Applets are extremely common on web sites; you probably will see a great variety. In these simple applets, the flag waves, the WOW bounces, and the cow's propeller spins.

MAKING THE RIGHT CONNECTIONS

SITE SNAGGER

Sometimes making the "right connections" means staying online far too long. Some sites are lengthy and complex, so it can take some time to peruse them carefully. Worse, they may take forever, or so it seems, to load. What if you could, so to speak, pack up the site and take it with you? That is the notion behind Site Snagger software, which lets you download—"snag"—an entire site to your hard disk, to be examined offline at your leisure. While it is downloading, you can do other work or go out for a sandwich.

PC Magazine Online, shown here, is a complex site with much to offer—a perfect application of a site to examine offline at your leisure. It also is appropriate to use this site as an example, since it is the source of the free Site Snagger software.

Site Snagger lets you set up each new "project" with a name. You supply the URL and the Site Snagger software goes after the site, even dialing the connection for you. Once Site Snagger has downloaded the desired site to your hard disk, you can examine the list of pages and click on those that interest you. When you are done with the site, you delete the project file as you would any other file.

web sites. To build this database, a search engine uses software to follow links across the Web, calling up pages and automatically indexing to a database some or all the words on the page. In addition, sites are submitted by their owners to the search engine, which indexes them.

As the result of a search request, the search engine will present a list of sites in some format, which varies by search engine. In fact, the nature of the search varies according to the search engine. Initially, users are astonished at the number of sites found by the search engine, often hundreds and perhaps thousands.

Hot Search Engines

The title of this section is somewhat facetious, since a new "hot" search engine can show up overnight. Further, some early search engines, less than half-a-dozen years old, are considered hackneyed and dull. Nevertheless, of the dozens of search engines in existence, a list of a few useful search engines is appropriate. Note that the use of these search engines is free, although you will, of course, encounter some advertising. See the comparison chart in Table 1.

Although it may seem that the same search query ought to produce the same list of sites no matter what the search engine, this is hardly the case. Search engines vary widely in size, content, and search methodology. Keeping this in mind, serious researchers sometimes put the same query to each of several search engines and expect to be given a somewhat different list of sites from each. The ultimate search device is software that searches the search engines. That is, it runs your query on several different search engines, probably the top seven or eight, simultaneously.

Table 1   Top search engines

	Search Engine	Features
AltaVista logo	AltaVista	Very fast; indexes every word on every page of every site; searches Usenet too; excellent for custom searches.
HotBot logo	HotBot	Fast; unique search options let you restrict searches; very comprehensive; excels at finding current news.
Northern Light logo	Northern Light	Powerful and well organized; groups results by subject, type, source, and language.
Lycos logo	Lycos	Numerous search options, a comprehensive directory, and good returns on simple searches.
Infoseek logo	Infoseek	Searches not only the Web but also newsgroups, FAQs, and e-mail addresses; extras such as foreign language searching and searching by geographical region.
Excite logo	Excite	Good returns for simple searches; provides related hints and an array of extra content.
WebCrawler logo	WebCrawler	Good for simple searches; also returns clickable links related to the search topic.
Yahoo! logo	Yahoo!	Well-organized categories let the user switch from browsing to searching in a certain area; but finds only keywords, not any word on a site.

Narrowing the Search

A simple one-word search will yield many sites, most of which will be irrelevant to your purposes. Suppose, for example, you are considering a driving trip through Utah. If you submit the word *Utah* as your search criterion, you will retrieve everything from Utah Lake to the Utah Jazz basketball team. The trick is to customize your search criteria. In this case, adding the word *vacation* to the search criteria will produce a list that begins with various hotels and parks in Utah. You can refine and narrow your search repeatedly.

There are more sophisticated methods for narrowing your search and for getting it right the first time. Different search engines offer different methods. Take a look at the search site's page, and you will probably see a clickable phrase such as Custom Search or Advanced Search or Options. Click the phrase to see how your request can be made to order. For example, the AltaVista search engine permits quotation marks. If you type *"World Trade*

Learn By Doing

The Alta Vista search engine offers the ability to count the number of links to a particular URL by using a search such as "link:jpl.nasa.gov." This feature is fully explained on the help pages. Have students find out how many links point to their favorite web page.

Table 2 Boolean Search Terms

Operator	Use
AND	Include both terms; example: life AND insurance
OR	Include either or both terms; example: university OR college
NOT	Exclude any site with terms preceded by NOT; example: browsers AND NOT Microsoft

Learn By Doing

Demonstrate or have students try the action of the Boolean operators AND and OR by comparing the number of search engine "hits" from searches like "dog OR dancing" versus "dog AND dancing." Show how NOT can be used with AND to exclude particular matches from your search, as in "(horse AND talking) AND NOT 'Mr. Ed.'"

Learn By Doing

If you have classroom Internet access, have students jot down possible keywords for searches and then use an Internet search engine to find pages that reference some of the keywords. Try combining suggestions from different students into one search with AND or OR. For instance, combining a suggestion like "Chicago Bulls" with "weather" often turns up some surprising connections.

InfoBit

Many web pages offer their own miniature search engines that allow searching only the pages on that site by keyword. If you know that the information you are seeking is on a particular site, but you don't know exactly where, these site-based search engines may prove more useful than a full Internet search, with its thousands of irrelevant matches.

Center" as your search criterion, you will get results that focus on that institution. If, instead, you type *World, Trade,* and *Center* as just three words in a row, the search engine will find every instance of each of the three words, alone and in combination—possibly several thousand sites. Alas, even the quote method is imperfect. For example, a site on a completely different topic will show up if the words *World Trade Center* appear anywhere in the site.

Most search engines offer operators with special functions based on a mathematical system called **Boolean logic.** The operators most commonly used are AND, OR, and NOT. The words can be further qualified with parentheses. AND means both; OR means either or both. Used correctly, these simple words can reduce search output to a dozen relevant sites instead of thousands of unrelated ones (Table 2). Consider these examples: You want information on the companies called Cirrus and Intel. Key *Cirrus* OR *Intel* for output that gives any site that mentions either or both companies. Suppose you need the population of the country of Jordan. If you key *Jordan,* you will see many sites for Michael Jordan, among others. Instead, key *Jordan* AND NOT *Michael.* Most requests combine several terms and operators. For example, suppose you want to go to college in Illinois but want to live in a town smaller than Chicago, and you want to inquire about tuition. Try *Illinois* AND NOT *Chicago* AND (*college* OR *university*) AND *tuition* AND *admission.* This query is quite specific and it will produce mostly desired sites.

Other ways of refining search results are to specify the language (English, Russian, and so forth) of the site, its most recent update, and whether the page includes an image or audio or video.

Search Engine Limitations

Search engines are known for turning up too *much* information, hence the need for Boolean terms and other methods to fine-tune the results. It is perhaps counterintuitive, then, to realize that search engines examine only a fraction of the Web. The Web's vastness simply foils even the best search engines. The two search engines that have the broadest coverage, HotBot and AltaVista, search only about a third of all the pages on the Web. Some search engines cover less than 20 percent of available web pages. That leaves page after page, floating out there somewhere, unreachable by anyone lacking the specific web address.

Furthermore, the problem is going to get worse. The Web has approximately 400 million pages, with millions of pages being added every year. It is probably impossible to index the entire Web. Thus the futility of trying to build giant databases will probably lead to a trend toward smaller, specialized search sites. For instance, HotBot now runs a special search engine called NewsBot that constantly patrols a special set of news-related sites. With a concentrated effort, such a site can be made smarter and more thorough in its own field. Some services avoid the issue entirely by providing only highlights of the Web. Yahoo!, one of the most widely used sites, is really not a search engine in the literal sense. Yahoo! employs human researchers to sift through sites and list them under appropriate categories instead of indexing every page in the electronic universe.

For now, the best bet for users hunting down some elusive piece of information is to use multiple search engines. Using a half-dozen search engines approximately doubles the results obtained with the most prolific individual search engine.

2000 and Beyond

INTERNET 2, 3, 4, 5

Making predictions about the future is a notoriously foolish business, but that has rarely stopped people from trying. The Internet, growing by leaps and bounds, will be very different, even in the near future, not to mention in a quarter-century.

We can see some new directions already. Universities that were major players in the development of the Internet saw their pioneering efforts appropriated by the rest of the world. So they have gone off on their own. A superfast network, called Internet 2, has been developed by a consortium of 120 universities for research and education purposes. However,

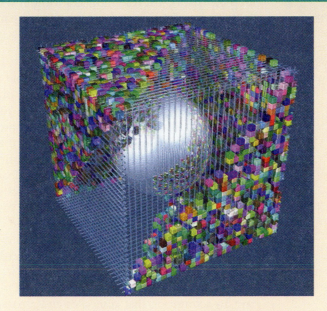

Internet 2 is not open to the general public.

It is not just universities that want a new and better Internet. The Next

Generation Internet Initiative is a federally funded effort to develop a high-speed Internet that is 1000 times faster than

today's model and available to everyone. This may be dubbed Internet 3.

We can imagine, eventually, an Internet 4 and 5 and beyond, offering features that are exotic by today's standards: systems that let you see and hear and touch computer-generated images, chip-embedded appliances that can let you know when they need repair, even remote surgery. If these seem too far-fetched, keep in mind that only a few years ago you would have had difficulty imagining sending instant mail across the globe or carrying a phone in your pocket or owning Internet-related stocks.

Branching Out

Although the World Wide Web is usually the focus of any Internet discussion, there are other parts of the Internet that deserve attention. All of them, in fact, predate the Web. One way to identify such sites is to observe the protocol. Instead of *http*, which you may be accustomed to seeing used for web sites, you may see *news* or *ftp*.

Newsgroups

Usenet is an informal network of computers that allows the posting and reading of messages in newsgroups that focus on specific topics. A more informal name is simply **newsgroups.** Topics of newsgroup discussions cover almost any subject you could imagine. If you have a passion for herbal remedies or for Macintosh computers or for Chinese politics, you can find not just one person but an entire group of people who share your interest and have something to say about it. Today there are more than 10,000 newsgroups. All of them offer conversation, and many offer files to download.

Group Work

Internet Scavenger Hunt. If you have Internet access, you can try the following experiments with searching and navigating the Web. Pick a fairly narrow topic, and have teams of no more than three students each search for entries on this topic. Encourage students not to rely exclusively on the search engines themselves; they should follow the links on pages they initially find to reach subsequent, more detailed pages. This is often described as an "expanding" search.

Global Perspective

Some of the topics that arise in newsgroups have international repercussions. Because there is no central authority for the Internet, and because laws differ widely from country to country, postings that may be perfectly legal in one country may constitute a violation of the law in others. Usenet postings of information about the making of explosives, however ethically repugnant, appear to be legal in the United States but are prohibited in many other countries.

InfoBit

One particularly effective technique for "lurking" is to download and read the FAQ—Frequently Asked Questions—for the particular newsgroup in which you are interested. These documents are usually informative and entertaining, and it is considered poor etiquette to post questions to the newsgroup if they have already been answered in the FAQ.

Critical Thinking

Usenet groups offer an incredibly wide range of topics, some of which are very controversial. Examples include groups that exchange recipes for explosives or that distribute pornographic images. Do you think these groups should be censored or eliminated? Why or why not? (This is clearly not a question with objective answers. Arguments in favor of restricting these groups usually turn on security, anti-crime, and antiterrorism concerns; fears of access by minors; and religious beliefs. Arguments against restriction are based on First Amendment and freedom of expression issues, as well as the argument that the "cure" might be worse than the problem.)

Think of a newsgroup as one large bulletin board marked off by category. If you happen along, you can read other people's postings. If you wish to respond to a message or just contribute your own original thought, you leave a message. The process is just about that simple. A suggested rule is that you observe the newsgroup for a while, an activity called **lurking,** before you jump in. That is, just read messages without writing any. That way you will get the flavor of the group before you participate.

FTP: Downloading Files

You already know that you can access files that reside on remote computers through the Internet and view them on your own computer screen. That is, you are allowed to look at them. But what if you wanted to *keep* a file; that is, what if you wanted your own copy of a file on your own computer? It may be possible to download—get—the file from the distant computer and place it on the hard disk of the computer you are using.

Whether or not a file is available for downloading depends on two things: (1) whether you are allowed to download files to the hard disk of the computer you are using and (2) whether the file you want is available for copying. Whether or not you are permitted to download files to the computer you are using may depend upon the availability of disk space, which is at a premium in some locations. Of course, if you are using your own personal computer, you may do whatever you like.

Many computer files are proprietary, and a user who wants them must have an account on that computer and a password. However, all kinds of files—programs, text, graphics images, even sounds—are available to be copied without restriction. The free files are public archives, often associated with an educational institution or the government.

There are many reasons you might want someone else's file. Perhaps, for example, a colleague in another city has just written a 150-page grant proposal and wants to send it to you; it is not convenient to send large files via e-mail. Perhaps you want some NASA space photos or some game software. Perhaps you have nothing particular in mind but, knowing that free stuff is out there, you simply go to a popular FTP site and look around. You can also upload—send your own files to another computer—but most people do a lot more downloading than uploading.

Computers on the Internet have a standard way to transfer copies of files, a program called **FTP,** for **file transfer protocol.** The term has become so common that FTP is often used as a verb, as in "Jack FTP-ed that file this morning." Most downloading is done by a method called **anonymous FTP.** This means that instead of having to identify yourself with a proper account on the remote computer, you can simply call yourself Anonymous. Also, instead of a password, you just use your e-mail address. This is merely background information; your browser will do all this work for you when you indicate that you want to transfer to an ftp site to select a file and download it.

Not Quite Perfect Yet

The Internet has been heaped with well-deserved praise. But still there are concerns. To begin with, no one really knows exactly who is out there on the Internet and what they are doing online. It's a little worrisome. On the other hand, many users find the freewheeling, no-controls aspect of the Internet appealing. Many fear government attempts, such as the Communications Decency Act of 1996, which proposed fines and jail time for offenders, to tame the Internet. Although this bill was struck down by the courts, the issues remain.

Behavior Problems

There really are some behavior problems on the Internet. But there are behavior problems in any aspect of society, from the playground to the boardroom. Those who abuse the Internet are, relatively speaking, small in number. Even so, solutions to the problems posed by abusers include a proposed ratings system and software for parental control of the types of sites or newsgroups accessed.

Meanwhile, the community of Internet users has made serious efforts to monitor behavior on the Internet. One consistent effort is **netiquette,** which refers to appropriate behavior in network communications. For example, users are admonished not to type in caps (IT'S LIKE SHOUTING). Netiquette rules are published on several sites and in every book about the Internet.

Useless, Overburdened, and Misinformed

Some people consider some home pages useless. In fact, there is a site called Useless Pages that maintains a listing of pages the site manager deems useless. However, many people are willing to pay for the connection to a web server in order to promote a home page they fancy, whatever anyone else may think. Others put out birth or wedding announcements, complete with photos. One useless page does nothing except count the number of times that page is accessed. At the other end of the spectrum are sites that apparently have so much value that their popularity renders them mostly inaccessible. Any list of "cool" sites, a favorite web word, is likely to be crowded.

There are no guarantees. The Internet is full of misinformation. Just because something is on the Internet does not mean it is true. If someone steps up to announce that the government uses black helicopters to spy on us or that tapes sound better if you soak them in water first, you need not accept such information as fact. It's not that people intend to be wrong, it's just that they sometimes are. If you are doing serious research on the Internet, be sure to back it up with other sources, especially non-Internet sources.

▲

The Internet is interesting and even fun. Perhaps the best aspect of the Internet is that even a novice computer user can learn how to move from site to site on the Internet with relative ease.

No time to brush up on your French? How about when you are staring at the screen, waiting for a web site to load? An engaging little program called Zing can give you a tiny blast of entertainment: a French flashcard, a music clip, a joke, or a pretty picture. As soon as you click on a site, a random Zing screen pops up on the screen. The Zing screen diminishes to a very small corner (and can be deleted) once the site you have clicked begins loading or, at your option, when the site is completely loaded.

Zing, which can be downloaded from its own web site, offers a variety of messages, images, and sounds. You can select as many as you wish from several channels, which update automatically to stay fresh. Channels include car culture, comix, digital art, entertainment, French, jokes, an on-this-day feature, photography, quotes, and Spanish. Of course, you must have room on your own disk to store all these images so they can be summoned quickly.

In a sense, you can say goodbye to the World Wide Wait.

Critical Thinking

Some people get so wrapped up in the Internet that they may even battle what has come to be called Internet addiction. What signs might signal such a problem? (Some possibilities are productivity loss at work and at home, skipping meals, abandoning former interests and activities, excessive fatigue, and, at work, guilty looks when someone enters the area.)

CHAPTER REVIEW

Summary and Key Terms

- A message to be sent to another computer is divided up into **packets,** each labeled with its destination address; the packets are reassembled at the destination address. The software that takes care of the packets is Transmission Control Protocol/Internet Protocol (TCP/IP). TCP does the packeting and reassembling of the message. The IP part of the protocol handles the addressing, seeing to it that packets are routed across multiple computers.

- The new set of connections, officially established in 1969, was called **ARPANet,** for Advanced Research Projects Agency Network.

- In 1990, **Dr. Tim Berners-Lee** made getting around the Internet easier by designing a set of links for one computer to connect to another. He saw the set of links as a spider's web; hence the name **Web.** The **CERN site** at Berners-Lee's laboratory is considered the birthplace of the **World Wide Web.** A **link** on a web site is easy to see: It is colored text called **hypertext** or an icon or image called a **hyperregion.** A mouse click on the link transports the user to the site represented by the link.

- As a student in 1993, **Marc Andreessen** led a team that invented the *browser,* graphical interface software used to explore the Internet. That first browser was named **Mosaic.**

- An Internet user needs a computer with a modem and its related software, an Internet service provider, and a browser. An **Internet service provider (ISP)** provides the server computer and the software to connect to the Internet. A **browser** is the software on the user's computer that allows the user to access the Internet via the service provider, using a graphical interface.

- When you invoke your browser software, it will dial up the Internet service provider and, once successfully connected, display the **home page** of the browser's web site. The browser shows three parts on the screen, the *browser control panel,* consisting of lines of menus and buttons; the *browser display window* to show the current site; and a *status line* at the bottom. The page can be **scrolled**—moved up and down—by using the **scroll bar** on the right.

- Using a mouse permits commands to be issued through a series of **menus,** a series of choices normally laid out across the top of the screen. The menus are called **pull-down menus** because each initial choice, when clicked with a mouse, reveals lower-level choices. **Buttons** can also invoke commands.

- The **Uniform Resource Locator (URL)** is a string of letters and symbols that is the unique address of a web page or file on the Internet. A web page URL begins with the protocol *http,* which stands for **HyperText Transfer Protocol,** the means of communicating using links. Next comes the **domain name,** which is the address of the Internet service provider. The last part of the domain name is called a **top-level domain** and represents the purpose of the organization or entity.

- A **hot list**—called Bookmarks or Favorites or something similar—stores favorite sites and their URLs.

- In browsers, **frames** allow a given page to be divided into rectangular sections, each of which can operate independently of the other.

- A **plug-in** is software that enhances the functionality of a browser.

- **Java,** a programming language developed by Sun Microsystems, can be used to write software that can be used on any machine. Java **applets** are small programs that provide multimedia effects on web pages.

- A **search engine** is software that lets a user specify search terms; the search engine then finds sites that fit those terms. A way to narrow a search is to use a mathematical system called **Boolean logic,** which uses the operators AND, OR, and NOT.

- **Usenet,** or **newsgroups,** is an informal network of computers that allow the posting and reading of messages in newsgroups that focus on specific topics. Reading messages without writing any is called **lurking.**

■ Computers on the Internet have a standard way to transfer copies of files, a set of rules called **FTP,** for **file transfer protocol.** Most downloading is done by a method called **anonymous FTP,** meaning that a user can be named Anonymous and the password can be simply the user's e-mail address.

■ **Netiquette** refers to appropriate behavior in network communications.

Discussion Questions

1. After he left school, Marc Andreessen, in his own words, wanted to make a "Mosaic killer." He felt he had not been given sufficient credit for his college efforts and set out to make his fortune commercially with Netscape Navigator, the forerunner of Netscape Communicator. He did. Dr. Tim Berners-Lee, however, rejected numerous commercial offerings. He felt that if he cashed in on his invention it would compromise the Web, which he wanted to be available to everyone. Are both these positions defensible? Comment.

2. How reliable are search engines? Why might one give a different set of results than another?

Student Study Guide

Multiple Choice

1. The author of the Web was
   a. Rand Corporation   c. Tim Berners-Lee
   b. ARPANet   d. Marc Andreessen

2. Which is not a Boolean operator?
   a. OR   c. AND
   b. IN   d. NOT

3. The protocol for downloading files carries the abbreviation
   a. HTTP   c. ISP
   b. FTP   d. URL

4. The action of moving a page up or down on the screen is called
   a. scrolling   c. lurking
   b. linking   d. framing

5. The software on a user's computer that employs a graphical interface to access the Internet is called
   a. URL   c. ISP
   b. FTP   d. a browser

6. Which factor was not a major contributor to the emergence of the Internet?
   a. links   c. frames
   b. browsers   d. TCP/IP

7. The first browser was called
   a. Internet Explorer   c. ARPANet
   b. FTP   d. Mosaic

8. The birth of the World Wide Web took place at
   a. Rand Corporation   c. ARPA
   b. CERN   d. Microsoft

9. Giving this factor would *not* help narrow a search:
   a. language   c. Boolean operator
   b. applet   d. date

10. A message to be sent to another computer is divided into
   a. URLs   c. packets
   b. hyperregions d. frames

True/False

T F   1. Browser software is kept on the server computer.

T F   2. In an URL, the domain name is the address of the ISP.

T F   3. The inventor of the browser is Marc Andreessen.

T F   4. TCP/IP is the standard Internet protocol.

T F   5. Dr. Tim Berners-Lee started ARPANet.

T F   6. A web page using frames must use exactly three frames: top, left, and right.

T F   7. The first ISP was Mosaic.

T F   8. Plug-ins increase the functionality of browsers.

T F   9. Com is an example of a top-level domain.

T F   10. A link on a web site is usually colored text or an image or icon.

Answers

Multiple Choice
1. c	3. b	5. d	7. d	9. b
2. b	4. a	6. c	8. b	10. c

True/False
1. F	3. T	5. F	7. F	9. T
2. T	4. T	6. F	8. T	10. T

Many people, whether college students or experienced employees, dread the prospect of facing the world and begging for a job. Resources for this onerous task are often limited to the classified ads and perhaps a placement center. You need have no such limitation if you have access to the Internet. A number of services specialize in matching employers with job seekers.

However, although assistance is available for first-time job seekers, and some sites even specialize in helping college students, it would be fair to say that many jobs posted on the Internet lean toward experienced people in the computer field.

Online help for students. You could start with Ask the Headhunter, which provides interesting job-search tips. The Online Career Center, whose monster symbol is shown here, offers career support services such as a list of keywords to use to search for jobs from thou-

sands of companies. JobWeb offers employment information, job listings, and tips; it also permits a job seeker to fill out a form online to create a listing on its pages. JobTrak is the largest online job listing service in the United States and, as you can see from its home page image, shown here, offers a large variety of services. Other good possibilities are the Career Central, CareerWeb, and Employease sites.

These sites, and others like them, have one thing in common: They all promote their list

The Job Resource

- Student Resources
- Recruiter Resources
- Student Groups

of job seekers to employers. This is their profit center. For a fee, an employer can search the site's database of job candidates. The database search can be narrowed by using keywords that represent job titles or particular skills required. This connection between employer and job seeker is much more efficient and speedy than the traditional shuffling of piles of resumés.

Your home page resumé. Some job seekers have taken advantage of Web exposure by developing their own home page resumés. This goes so far beyond the traditional resume that a new name should be invented for it. Typically, the candidate includes a nice photo and then offers perhaps a 10- to 15-line resumé. Why so short? Each resumé line has links! For example, one line may refer to classes taken, with classes being a link.

A potential employer merely clicks on the word *Classes* to pop up a list of classes the job seeker has taken. Similarly, links can be made to intern work, laboratory assignments, extracurricular activities, work experience, special skills, and so forth. A person developing such a home page from scratch can make the resumé as varied as desired. Some schools permit students to post resumés on their site for a certain time period.

There are a few dozen sites devoted exclusively to resumés. They usually offer, among other things, tips on resumé writing. Other sites feature a resumé service as one of many options; the Virtual Job Fair site, whose opening image is shown here, offers resumé services. As so many sites do, this one will let you post your resumé on its site. Resumé service is sometimes free, but more often a fee is required. Other resumé sites of note are Tripod's Resume Builder and Resumail Network.

Internet Exercises

1. **Structured exercise.** Hook up through the URL http://www.prenhall.com/capron and take a look at the Virtual Job Fair site. Find out what you have to do to submit a resumé for posting on this site.

2. **Freeform exercise.** To expand your set of resources, begin with the Yahoo! site. Find and click on Business and Economy and then click Employment.

in with some Internet "eye candy" — sites deliberately created to have visual appeal. Although definitely in business, neither Rollerblade nor Pepsi, shown on this page, presents a "plain vanilla" business site. Both offer plenty of content of interest to cons

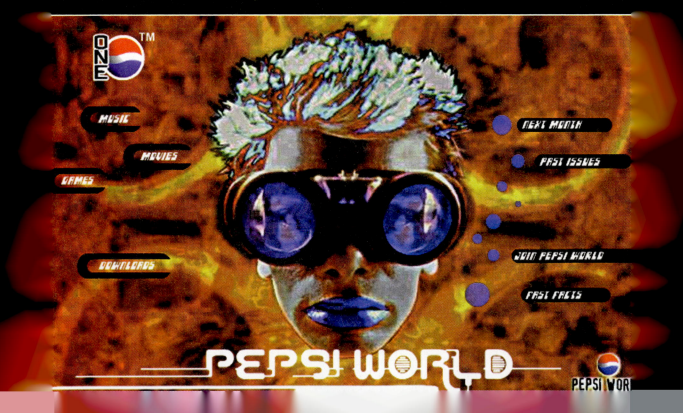

THE VISUAL INTERNET

Internet Site Designers

Compared to plain text, graphics images take far more bytes. A single image may take a half-million bytes. The more bytes of data in a web site, the longer it takes the site to load. Since site owners do not want visitors to be discouraged by a long wait, most limit their graphics to a few small images. Thus it is not common to find graphics-rich sites.

However, people who specialize in designing web sites want to show their wares, so they usually display more graphics than the average site. The title page of this gallery shows the brilliant-red Jiong designer site, bright but still subtle; each of the small objects can be revealed with mouse-over action and all are clickable.

Many people specialize in some phase of web site design and offer their services on their own web sites. Here are some of the best. On this page are Dahlin Smith White (to the right) and Eclectica (below). On the facing page are (across the top) Egomedia and John Hersey; in the middle are P2 Output and Juxt Interactive. At the bottom on the facing page is the site for the Cooper-Hewitt National Design Museum.

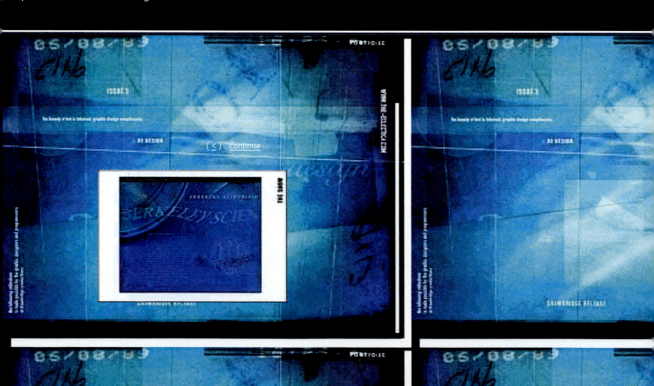

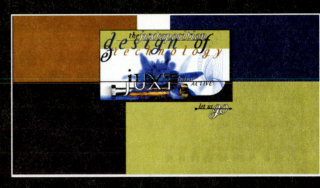

Design

[100 years of collecting]
[birthday gift]

for Daily Life

for Shaping Space

for Communicating

Multimedia

The sites shown here are all have animation and sound powered by the popular software plug-in called Shockwave. The Shockwave player software is included with many popular browsers and is also available free from the Macromedia site. You can download Shockwave, and it will be "plugged in" to your browser. It is in Macromedia's interest to have many users able to appreciate "shocked" sites because it helps sell the software that generates the animation and sound.

The Pooh page shown here is just one of hundreds of pages at Disney, an accomplished mass media site. The Dreamworks site has animation and—especially—music. On the opposite page, top to bottom: Gillette takes advantage of multimedia to demonstrate its product, the Mach 3 razor, in an attractive way; Leo's Great Day is an animated feature on the Pepworks online entertainment site; the highly pixilated image is one of many smooth sights and sounds on the impressive site for the Balthasar online advertising agency.

At bottom right is the Colony Wars site, offering impressive animation. On-screen games are key applications for animation and sound. People who want to play a game may be more patient than, say, a potential business customer when it comes to waiting for the site to download. This is just as well because a multimedia-rich site can take an inordinate amount of time to download, depending, of course, on the speed of the data transmission vehicle.

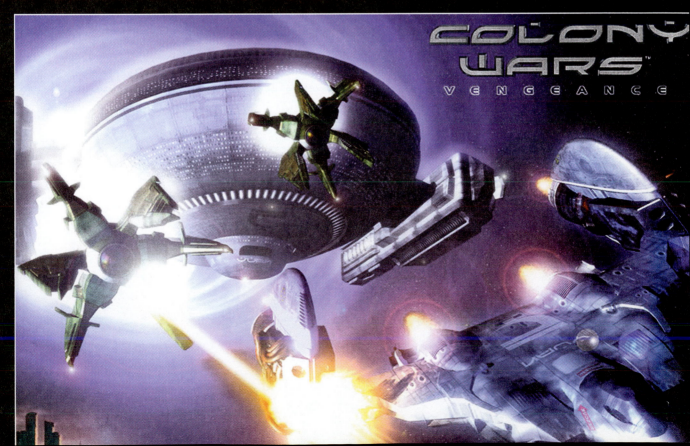

Graphics-rich Sites

As we have noted, site owners, especially owners of business sites, want their sites to load quickly, and so they avoid time-consuming graphics. So, what kinds of sites are likely to be attractive, graphics-rich sites? We have already considered the sites of the designers themselves.

Another good bet for attractive graphics are sites aimed at children; web designers know that they must make a colorful splash to get and keep their attention. Other candidates for especially attractive sites are artists, photographers, and online magazines. We offer a representative sample here. Below is a series of works by master glass artist Dale Chihuly.

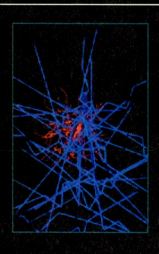

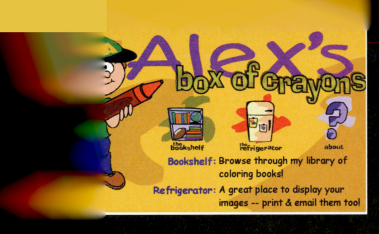

Bookshelf: Browse through my library of coloring books!

Refrigerator: A great place to display your images -- print & email them too!

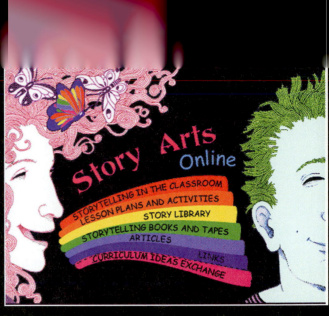

Story Arts Online

STORYTELLING IN THE CLASSROOM
LESSON PLANS AND ACTIVITIES
STORY LIBRARY
STORYTELLING BOOKS AND TAPES
ARTICLES
CURRICULUM IDEAS EXCHANGE
LINKS

...rnation is back with good
... New exciting stuff is
...ening every day, and it's going
...ange the world as we know it.
... And pop. It's all a revolution
01Remix or Archive

SUPERMODEL: LAETITIA CASTA · PHOTO: UNKNOWN

A LIFETIME EDUCATION *FREE*
FOR HIGH SCHOOL GRADUATES WHO QUALIFY
U.S. CADET NURSE CORPS

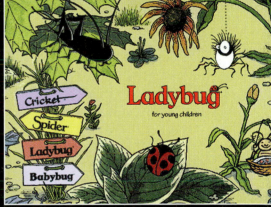

Cricket
Spider
Ladybug
Babybug

Ladybug
for young children

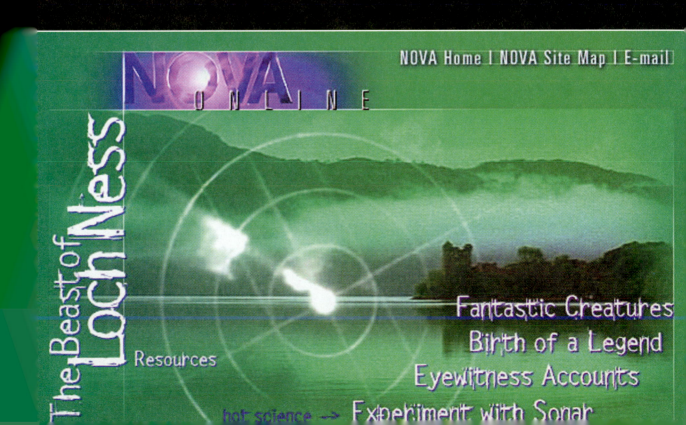

NOVA Home I NOVA Site Map I E-mail

NOVA ONLINE

The Beast of Loch Ness

Resources

hot science →

Fantastic Creatures
Birth of a Legend
Eyewitness Accounts
Experiment with Sonar

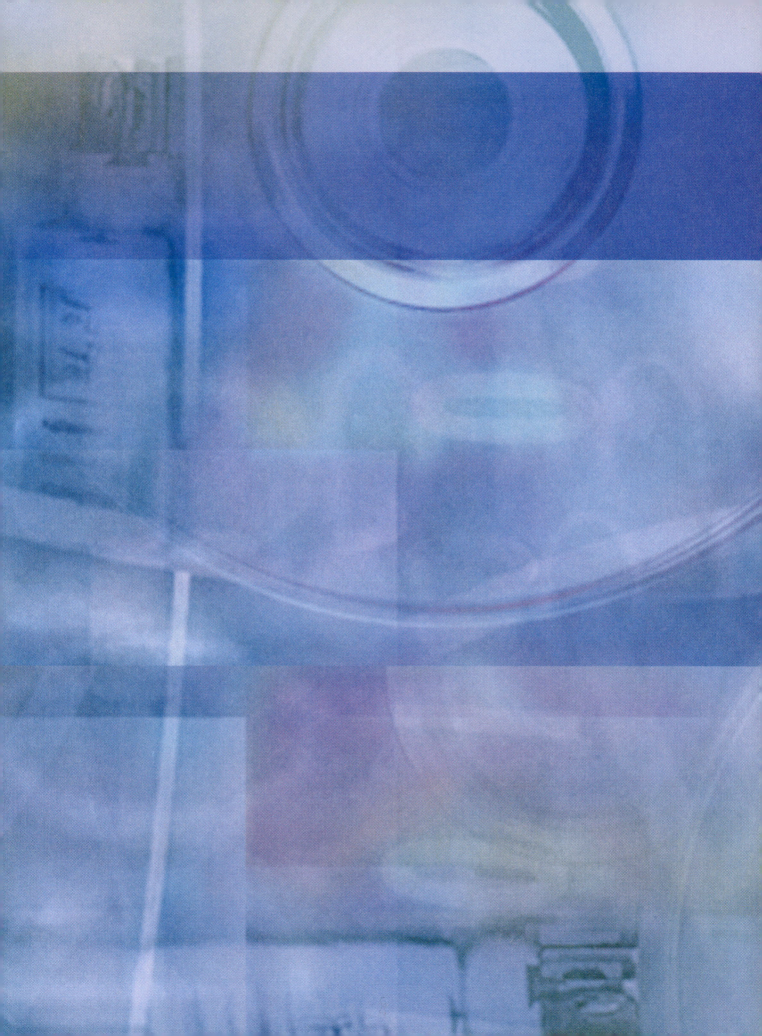

CHAPTER EIGHT

THE INTERNET IN BUSINESS

Corporations, Small Businesses, and Entrepreneurs

LEARNING OBJECTIVES

- Understand the pervasiveness and inevitability of business on the Internet
- Comprehend how money factors, especially advertising, affect the Web
- Understand the likely success factors for Web entrepreneurs
- Appreciate the need for ever-greater Internet transmission speed
- Differentiate intranets, extranets, and virtual private networks

Her friends, only half-teasing, tell everyone that Kathleen Cameron is "browsing for housing." Although Kathleen and her husband, John, are mildly amused, they actually see their approach as practical. They are buying a house on the Internet.

The adventure began in San Francisco, where Kathleen and John were living when he took a new job with a venture capital firm in Atlanta. Kathleen, a photo researcher, had plenty of experience searching the Internet and figured that was a good place to get a head start on house hunting.

When real estate professionals dream of the ideal customer, they may have someone like the tech-savvy Kathleen in mind. She is, in fact, the harbinger of the future, a user of the houses-on-computers system that has taken many dollars to put in place. Both national and local real estate web sites are racing to attract customers.

The National Real Estate Association estimates that there are approximately 100,000 real estate and related web sites. Many sites offer an amazing amount of information, including maps of cities and neighborhoods, listings showing the outside of the house, and even a virtual tour through the inside of the house. Kathleen is particularly interested in the search feature that allows her to narrow her focus by zip code, price, number of bedrooms, view, schools, and more. Most sites also offer help with planning home financing.

Before Kathleen and John made the cross-country trip to go house hunting in person, they already knew what neighborhood they wanted to live in and had preselected seven possible houses. They enlisted the aid of a local real estate agent, chose one of the preselected houses, and closed the deal—all within three days.

Real estate sales are, in fact, a local activity requiring in-person encounters, so perhaps to say that you can "buy a house on the Internet" is a bit of an exaggeration. But this is about as close as one can get. Home buying is just one of many business activities on the Internet.

Business Sites

The very word *business* seems boring to some people. Those same folks may be disinclined to visit a "business site" on the Internet. They would be missing out.

There are business sites for any kind of business you can imagine, from the most venerable bank to the latest gotta-have-it fad. They include sites that represent conglomerates who just want to have a "presence" on the Internet and the entrepreneurs who want you to buy something—now. Their appearance may be staid or may be exotic. As a group, they are far from boring.

However, business sites have, for the most part, evolved to the point of looking a bit the same (Figure 1). There are reasons. One reason is that they

(a)

(b)

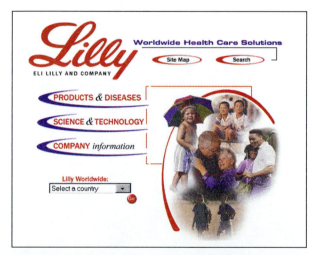

(c)

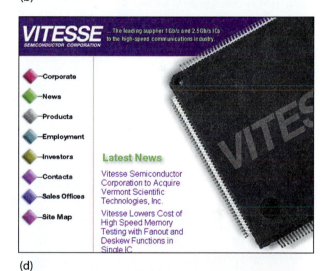

(d)

(e)

(f)

Figure 1 Various business sites. The companies represented are (a) BabyCenter, an online retail company; (b) UPS (United Parcel Service), a delivery service; (c) Eli Lilly, a pharmaceutical manufacturer; (d) Vitesse, a semiconductor manufacturer; (e) Merrill Lynch, a stock broker; and (f) GE (General Electric), a manufacturer of various electrical products.

Who's Over Your Shoulder?

As you move from site to site, give some thought to nearby folks who may or may not appreciate the content of your travels across the Internet. What you find funny or interesting may be offensive to others. Paying attention to others is a considerate move in a college environment but a critical one in a work environment. Your employer will take a dim view of your Internet activities if they are perceived to create a hostile workplace—and possibly even support legal action.

InfoBit

One of the more novel applications of electronic commerce is the "Cyber-Bail" kiosk. Working like an Automated Teller Machine, the accused can insert a credit card, and for 10% surcharge, post bail for minor offenses in California.

are mostly all the same width and anchored to the left side of the screen. *Ice, jello,* and *liquid* are related terms describing three approaches to controlling content placement on a web page. Because the browser user can control and change both screen resolution and window size, the web page designer is challenged to design a page that will achieve its intended effect in spite of user resizing. An **ice page** is one in which the primary content has a fixed width and is "frozen" to the left margin. A **jello page** has a fixed width but "wiggles and jiggles" to center itself on the screen. A **liquid page** is a web page that will re-flow to fit no matter what size window you "pour" it into. Unlike the ice and jello approaches, a liquid page leaves no blank margin on the right or the left. A liquid page is considered good page design (Figure 2).

The second reason a lot of business sites look the same is that they want to jam as much information as possible—at the very least several clickable links—on the small space available for the opening screen of their site. Thus that first screen may be crowded. But the most important reason they have a sameness is that they avoid large graphics. They do not want you to become discouraged by waiting for slow-loading graphics to appear, so they use a flurry of little graphics, each of which can be loaded quickly.

(a)

(b)

Figure 2 Sites adjusted for screen width. A user with a large screen often sees the screen only partially filled because it gets the same page width as that of a small screen. But some web sites adjust their content to fit the screen. The images shown here are wide because they look this way on a wide screen. Shown here are (a) The Nature Conservancy, a land conservation organization, and (b) Fox Kids, a television channel.

Whether a site is promoting an image or is providing product information or is offering online transactions, in the end it is all about trying to sell the public a product or service. But the sites that overtly seek online retail sales form the concept called e-commerce.

E-Commerce: Retail Sites

The world of **electronic commerce,** or, more commonly, **e-commerce,** buying and selling over the Internet, represents nothing less than a new economic order. Even the word *retail* is evolving to *etail,* for electronic retail. With a few clicks of your mouse, you can buy a suit in Thailand, an out-of-print biography, a particular used car, or a bargain airline ticket. Or, considering more mundane items, you can buy music CDs, videos, clothes, computers, baby equipment, jewelry, sporting goods, office supplies, cosmetics, flowers, gifts, and your weekly groceries—still with just a few clicks (Figure 3). You can make those clicks from the comfort of your home, in the middle of the night, and with your hair in curlers, if you wish.

Figure 3 Retail web sites. All these businesses have physical "bricks and mortar" stores, but they also sell their goods directly from their web sites. Just click an item into your "shopping cart" and, when done, "check out" by supplying your credit card and a shipping address. Shown here are (a) Exploria, (b) J. Crew, (c) The Nature Company, and (d) OfficeMax.

(a)

(b)

(c)

(d)

Figure 4 Site content. Retail sites may offer extra site content, something beyond a list of products, to attract visitors. Lands' End, a retail clothier specializing in sportswear, adds content to its site by including first-person adventure stories. Shown here is the story of one man's life in the wilderness.

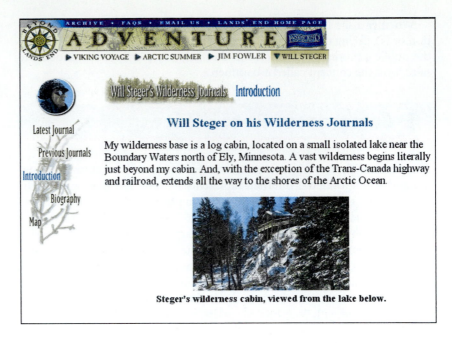

Retail businesses understand the attractions of online shopping to consumers and are scrambling to capture their share of sales. They also understand that Internet sales mean cost savings, including the costs of a physical store building and sales people. And, finally, they understand that consumers are in a unique position to comparison-shop; in fact, there are sites devoted exclusively to helping consumers compare prices. So the bottom line is that cost savings will probably translate to more competitive prices. But first they must attract potential customers to their sites.

Adding Content

Retail web sites have begun adding **content** to attract visitors and boost sales. That is, rather than just the usual lists and views of products and prices, the site includes something of more general interest to attract visitors. Lands' End, for example, a retail clothier specializing in sportswear, has added true-life adventure tales, with text and photos, to its site (Figure 4). Notice that the outdoor adventures are related to the products sold by the company. As markets get more crowded, strong content can be a differentiator.

Interestingly, content-rich sites that were not originally retail sites are adding products and pitching sales. Thus the difference between content and commerce sites is becoming more narrow.

Only Flirting with the Internet

Some companies would love to embrace the Internet but must settle for half measures. Although manufacturers know that the Internet could be an effective sales tool, they fear that selling a product from their own site will alienate the sales representatives and stores with whom they have established relationships. In fact, online commerce is seen as a menace to the men and women who do in-person selling or distribution and who still control a high percentage of most companies' order flow. As a result, jittery corporate strategists are trying to capitalize on the Internet's potential without sabotaging traditional sales channels.

There are a variety of solutions, none completely satisfactory. Some companies keep prices on their web sites high, so the flesh-and-blood sales person can offer an obvious discount. Others placate dealers and sales people with a cut of each transaction, regardless of whether they played a part in generating it. For the moment, the most popular approach may be site marketing up to the point of actual sale, then recommending a local store to complete the transaction.

Looking at it from a different point of view, sometimes a successful web site can alienate others who are only indirect business associates. Take Dave Smith Motors, in Kellogg, Idaho, seller of Chrysler cars and trucks. Dave put up his own web site and it attracted so much attention that customers came to Dave's from miles around. Other dealers boycotted Chrysler because it allocated more cars to Dave's successful lot. The Federal Trade Commission declared the boycott anticompetitive and illegal, but Chrysler came to the rescue by making a generic web site that can be used by all its dealers (Figure 5). Chrysler's site lets customers configure a vehicle, pick a dealer, and request a price quote.

Once a retail site exists, it must make its presence known. There are various ways to promote a site, but one of the most effective ways is to advertise on a portal.

Portals and Advertising

You know how network television earns money: Although it is free to viewers, the networks collect revenues from advertisers. Further, the amount of money the networks charge advertisers is directly related to how popular the show is, that is, how many viewers are on hand to see the advertising. Now apply this technique to web sites. Web sites that carry advertisements can charge for them at rates that are directly related to the number of visitors to the site, that is, the more visitors, the higher the advertising rates.

Thus it is that a web site wants to be your **portal** to the Internet, your everyday first stop, your neighborhood, your hangout. The site owners want you to come early and often. But, most of all, they want to persuade you to use them as your guide.

Online Groceries

It is not yet a major activity on the Internet. But, why not? Internet users already pay their bills, trade stocks, send gifts, and even buy cars on the Internet. Can groceries be far behind? Peapod, whose site is shown here, was a pioneer. Although not yet available in all areas of the country, it is a hit with Internet shoppers in the Midwest.

Here is how Peapod works. You place your order at the Peapod site by strolling the "aisles," lists of just about any available product, organized by brand name. All categories are covered, including produce, seafood, meat and poultry, deli, dairy, household, frozen, bakeshop, snacks, baby, pets, and general grocery. As you click items, they are added to your grocery cart, whose contents—and the mounting bill—can be seen along the side of the screen. Your order is filled by Peapod employees who shop at regular supermarkets and then deliver the groceries to your home.

You must supply a credit-card number and there must be someone at the house to receive the groceries when they arrive. Arrival time is at your convenience, provided you order a day in advance.

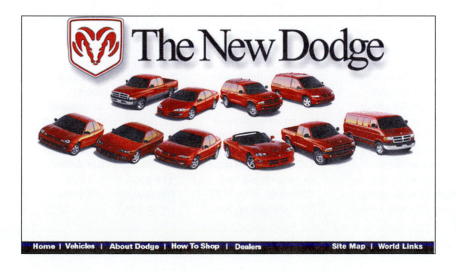

Figure 5 Dealers and manufacturers. Chrysler established a site that could be used by all Chrysler dealers, letting customers configure cars and find a dealer.

2000 and Beyond

THE E-CORPORATION

Every retail company must change to get in step with the Internet or else go out of business. Soon. There is no grace period for those that hesitate. E-commerce goes far beyond setting up an attractive web site.

If these statements seem too harsh, consider the reality of the numbers. In 1995 only 5 percent of Americans used the Internet every day. In 2000, that number has risen to 35 percent—a stunning change in a very short period of time. And are Internet users buying yet? Yes. It is only a trickle compared with the overall retail economy, but the advantages of e-commerce to the consumer are so outstanding that it is just a matter of time until many make the switch.

The new e-commerce reality is controlled by the consumer. The elements of consumer control that make e-commerce inevitable can be summarized as follows:

■ **Smart customers.** Users can take advantage of the Internet to find information about products before buying.
■ **Come to me.** Consumers no longer must take the car or a bus to the retail store. No, the merchandise is much handier than that—a click or two away.

■ **Comparison shopping.** The phrase *hunting for a bargain* has little true meaning in a traditional retail society. Who has time? But it takes only a jiffy on the Internet. Consumers can check the price of new lawnmowers by jumping from site to site, or by using one of the sites especially set up for comparison shopping, or even by using a soft-

ware agent, a type of software that does the hunting and comparing.
■ **My way.** For some products, there is no reason to settle for a mass-produced variety found in traditional stores. Over the Internet, you can order a CD made up of tracks of your choice and download the CD to your computer. You

can order a computer made up of exactly the components you want, no more, no less, by clicking off options on a screen. The customization of products has only begun.
■ **Disappearing geographical lines.** Users need not be limited to regional boundaries. Internet retailers span the globe. For example, customers can order a book from Amazon.com whether they are in Pittsburgh or Zimbabwe.
■ **No further obstacles.** People want to try before they buy? Tell that to the folks in the multibillion-dollar catalog business. Although Internet entrepreneurs easily convinced people to buy books and CDs, items they know, it is just a matter of time until they buy everything else online.

For all these consumer-centric reasons, users flock to the Internet to buy. The final happy reason to do so is that prices usually are lower on the Internet. Retailers who understand the seismic change of their industry also understand that e-commerce competition brings prices down. The good news is that the retailers' costs come down too.

Getting Personal

To be a good guide, the portal site begins by presenting content and links on a wide variety of topics, from health to movies to shopping. But to be a good guide to you personally, the portal site needs some information from you that it can use to personalize your use of the site. You will see a link on the portal site saying something like My _____ (fill in the site name), or perhaps Personalize or Customize. On the basis of the personal data you supply, the site can present local weather conditions, local news and sports scores, and even a portfolio of stocks you own. The more the portal offers you, the greater the likelihood that you will drop by often. Some portals go further, offering instructions on how to make the portal site the "home page" you encounter first each time you access the Internet.

Another Source of Money

Portal web sites have an even more significant revenue stream, basically a referral fee. The portal web site offers the news, sports, shops, and so forth from sources called **affiliates,** which the portal chooses. The affiliates—based on deals made with the portal—pay for the privilege. They may pay only for being listed on the portal site or—more likely—pay a percentage of a sale to any visitor who has clicked there from the portal site. If, for example, a visitor at the Yahoo! site clicks on Clifford's Flowers, and then sends balloons from Clifford's to her sister across the country, Yahoo! will get a percent of the profit from that sale, simply because it made the referral.

Just who are these portal sites? Most are familiar names to Web surfers. Many started out as search engines and then expanded their content and retail connections. A well-known portal is Yahoo!, begun as a search site by two college students (Figure 6). (They named it Yahoo!, by the way, as an acronym for Yet Another Hierarchical Officious Oracle, although no one bothers with that windy title anymore.) Yahoo!'s advertising campaign is so

Figure 6 A portal. Portal sites hope to be your main site, the place where you jump off to the rest of the Web. Yahoo!, shown here, is a popular portal site.

Clicking for Coupons

Discount coupons have been around for a long time, but it took the Internet to make them inexpensive to produce and convenient to use. Manufacturers now can bypass the mass printing and distribution of coupons in circulars and newspapers. Users can skip the hunting and clipping processes. So, at both ends, time and money are saved.

In Internet fashion, users can find the coupons they want with a search engine and then print them on their own printers. The search can be minimized by using sites that specialize in coupons, such as ValuPage, whose site is shown here.

There have been some concerns about fraud, say, printing unauthorized coupons. But manufacturers note that the same thing is possible using regular newspaper coupons, which could be scanned into a computer, then altered and printed. Interestingly, neither fear has materialized. Perhaps thieves are looking for bigger game.

InfoBit

One radical business model being tried on the Internet involves companies selling products at or below their cost. The idea is that they will attract enough users to their sites so that advertising revenue from banner ads will more than offset any losses on the sales of product.

successful that it is familiar even to people who have never used the Internet. Other content-rich portals are Lycos, Snap!, Excite, Infoseek, Microsoft Start, Go Network, and America Online. The America Online site, by the way, is indeed the first site seen by AOL customers jumping from AOL-specific content to the Internet, but it is also a portal site in its own right that often is accessed by non–AOL members.

Portals continue to grow in number and in content. The ultimate goal of each portal is to make its site your one-stop site on the Internet. Surfers, of course, would never settle for one site, but it seems likely that they will settle on one site as their personalized—and oft-visited—home page. Home sweet home page.

More Advertising

We have lived with advertising all our lives. It can be intrusive and annoying, but often it is informative, interesting, or even funny. For the most part, however, it is just in the background. For the user, the main advantage of advertising is that it pays all or most of the costs of the message on radio and television, in magazines and newspapers—and on the Internet.

Most advertisements on web sites are in the form of **banner ads,** which were originally in the shape of a long rectangle (Figure 7). Advertisers pay the host site for the privilege of showing their ad on the site; it is their hope, of course, that users will be sufficiently attracted to the ad that they will click the banner and thus be transported to the site of the advertiser. Many small ads are, in fact, in a variety of shapes. Some of them are little applets, showing some sort of motion to get our attention.

Banners do not work as well as advertisers would like because users are often reluctant to **click through,** that is, leave the current site, in which they are presumably interested, and go the advertised site. One solution to this problem is the **live banner,** which lets a user get more information about a product—a pitch—without leaving the current site. This approach has proved popular but is not without drawbacks: The live banners work slowly, especially with slower modems, and are expensive to develop.

The most effective Web advertisements are **context-sensitive;** that is, the ad is related to the subject matter on the screen. As the advertisers put it, there is greater "click through and conversion," meaning the ad is more likely to be clicked and, once at the advertised site, the user is more likely to buy something. Notice, for example, in Figure 7, that choosing the topic Computers elicits ads about software, whereas the topic Travel summons ads for cars and planes. Since the user is in control of the path through the Web, it is reasonable to assume that he or she is receptive to ads on his or her chosen topic.

There are disadvantages of web site ads for users. One is that they often have graphics and perhaps even applets, both of which take time to load. Another disadvantage is that as the page is loading on the screen, the ads load first, or at least early, so that you will not see the entire page until the ads are in place. That is, the site manager wants to make sure that you see the advertisements before you go clicking off somewhere else.

Payments and Taxes

You have seen the ads and perused the site and now you want to make a purchase. How will you pay for it? And must you pay taxes on your purchase?

(a)

(b)

Figure 7 Banner ads. Major traffic sites carry banner advertisements strategically placed to match the subject matter. (a) The Lycos site, which is a search engine as well as a portal, opens with an extensive list of categories. If you click Computers, you will see the screen shown here, which includes three computer-related ads (only one of them in the actual shape of a banner). (b) Starting with the HotBot search engine/portal, click Travel to see the screen shown here, which has three travel-related ads.

These simple questions have rather complex answers that have kept the industry's attention since the beginning of online sales.

E-Commerce Payments

Some retail sites give you the option of phoning or faxing your order. They do this because they know that some people are leery of submitting their credit-card numbers over the network to an online retail site. They fear that the card number may be intercepted in transit and then used illicitly to run up charges on the card. Although this is theoretically possible, it is highly unlikely. To begin with, the messages between the buyer and the online retailer are encrypted—encoded—so that they are not readable to the casual observer. It would take a skilled programmer to undo the encryption; frankly, there are more fruitful places to attack. The de facto standard for online transaction payments is the *Secure Sockets Layer (SSL)* protocol. However, most sites simply refer to it as "our secure server," and many customers have become comfortable using it.

E-Commerce Taxes

One of the little thrills of catalog shopping is that you may not have to pay local sales taxes on articles purchased. Under American federal law, if a company from which you order is out of state, you need pay sales taxes to your own state only if the catalog company has some sort of *presence* (sometimes called a *nexus*) in your state, such as a branch store or a warehouse. Now try to apply that to Internet commerce, whose sellers are likely to be far away and whose "presence" anyplace is debatable. But that is just the beginning of the long-running debate on taxing the Internet. Some folks want to tax even using the Internet.

There are approximately 30,000 taxing entities—states, counties, cities—in the United States. If all of them were to be turned loose to get their slice of the pie, the Internet would be seriously burdened and perhaps irreparably harmed. The compromise, passed into law in October 1998, is called the **Internet Tax Freedom Act.**

The act has four basic components:

1. It prohibits state and local governments from imposing taxes on Internet access charges, such as those billed by America Online or an Internet service provider.
2. It prohibits taxes from being imposed on out-of-state businesses through strained interpretations of "presence."
3. It creates a temporary commission to study taxation of Internet commerce and report back to Congress on whether the Internet ought to be taxed.
4. It calls on the executive branch to demand that foreign governments keep the Internet free of taxes and tariffs.

In summary, the act provides that the Internet be free of new taxes for three years while a committee determines if taxes should be imposed and, if so, how to do so in a uniform way. Further, notice that nothing has changed in regard to imposing sales taxes. The act refers only to *new* taxes or to trying to cook up "presence" in some new way. State and local governments are allowed to impose sales taxes on Internet sales, provided that the tax is the same as that which would be imposed on the transactions if they were conducted in a more traditional manner, such as over the phone or through mail order.

Entrepreneurs

Starting your own business on the Internet is a game anyone can play. And we do mean anyone, from those involved in agriculture to real estate to finance. Even the smallest entrepreneur can get in on the act. Individuals can gain access to people and markets—including global markets—not readily affordable or even available elsewhere. For a minimum investment, far less than that needed for a physical store or office, you can have a server link and a smashing home page that exactly expresses the nature of your business. You can even alter the page as your business grows and changes.

The statements just made are true, if a bit rosy in color. Even though "anyone can play," the Internet is not a level playing field. Firms with multimillion-dollar marketing budgets and customer bases in the hundreds of thousands are more likely to be able to draw large numbers of people to their web sites than the most creative garage-based entrepreneur. Does this mean that the little guys do not have a chance? They have a chance, but not a level playing field.

Success Factors

Nothing guarantees success, defined as making a profit from your Internet business. It can be done, and most certainly is being done, but business on the Internet is not a panacea. Just as in a regular store, the key success factor for any commercial web site is repeat business. How do you keep customers coming back? Some primary success factors are content, uniqueness, self-help, and community.

The body of your site, what you have to say and offer, is the *content*. The site must offer something—preferably several somethings—to keep interest up. What will it be? News about the product, scores, contests, searches, and much more. Observe the variety of content as you examine business sites. The site cannot be static. If it is exactly the same as on a previous visit, most users will not bother returning.

One site loaded with daily-changing content is The Motley Fool (Figure 8). The name is inspired by Shakespeare's *As You Like It*: "I met a fool i' the forest, a motley fool." Despite their trademark jester costumes, no one would take brothers David and Tom Gardner for fools. The Motley Fool is the name of their online forum, which lets investors ask questions and share knowledge. Hundreds of thousands of visitors, frustrated by lack of investing knowledge from traditional sources, visit the site each month.

Can you be *unique?* One recommendation for success is to have a specialty, something not offered elsewhere. Twins Jason and Matthew Olim, jazz fans who had trouble finding a good selection of recordings in their local stores, decided to set up a web site that they called CDnow, offering every jazz album made in the United States and thousands of imports. The beauty of the scheme was that there was no initial outlay for a store or even for inventory. A shopper places an order with CDnow, which in turn contacts distributors. The disk is usually delivered within 24 hours. CDnow eventually added other kinds of music and also movies. Another successful specialty site is Hot Hot Hot, whose logo is shown here, offering an enormous variety of hot sauces from around the world (Figure 9). Note that in each of these two examples, the site not only offers something unique but also appeals to an audience that will be repeat customers.

Customers like to take care of themselves as much as possible, so some *self-help* features are both useful and a winning strategy. If your site is, or becomes, large, you should include a search component so that users can find what they want easily. Again, depending on the complexity of the site, customers want to be able to do research, configure and order products, troubleshoot problems, check on the status of an order, or track a delivery.

Figure 8 A successful entrepreneur site. One of the hallmarks of the Motley Fool web site is that it has ever-changing content, which brings investors to the site again and again, many of them daily or even hourly.

A key to the success of a commercial site is a sense of *community*. An outstanding example of this is the Amazon Books site. Amazon features notes from authors about their own books and lets any customer write a review about a book. Customers perusing book offerings can just click an icon to read the reviews for a certain book. People who love books return again and again to this site. Customers who agree to register by filling out an on-screen form are eligible for book prizes. The prizes are attractive, and the registration data—name, e-mail address, and possibly book interests—provides Amazon with future marketing information.

My Mother, the Conglomerate

Mom-and-pop businesses have learned that, on the Web, anybody can look like a conglomerate. The same is true for teenagers, college students, stay-at-homes, and anyone else who is operating a business from a den or garage. Visitors at the College Depot site, which sells college-type merchandise, may be surprised to learn that the business is based in the Gleeson family home in Trumbull, Connecticut. The site offers 50,000 different products, has secure online ordering, and gives the impression of a large retail operation. The Gleesons want to convey the image that they are a substantial company because they think it helps to build trust.

As we noted, anyone can do this—in theory. We do not want to convey the impression that success is automatic. Many small businesses, even those on the Internet, do not succeed. But, still, success is a possibility—and the initial investment need not be daunting.

Traffic Jams

The Internet was not planned for its current users. The original Internet was a low-speed, text-based network designed to send messages among a few government sites and the research and defense contracting community. No one then envisioned today's millions of users, some surfing for hours at a time and sending high-volume multimedia data. The Internet is a victim of its own success, its arteries so clogged that a user often crawls and stutters through cyberspace.

Figure 9 A specialty entrepreneur site. The site HotHotHot, whose logo is shown here, specializes in hot sauces.

GETTING PRACTICAL

SETTING UP A RETAIL SITE

If you were setting up a physical store (commonly referred to as "bricks and mortar" to distinguish it from a retail web site) you would need merchandise and sales people. But that is just the beginning. You must have some mechanism for customers to gather merchandise to purchase; they may simply hold the goods in hand, but a shopping cart is common. You must supply some way of charging customers—cash, check, credit card. You

"storefront" software can handle all aspects of a web site retail operation.

A good example is iCAT Commerce Online, whose Chef's Catalog, Mountain Zone, and Ethel M Chocolates customers are shown here. These are some of the functions that iCAT will handle:

- Create a storefront web site that looks professional. This may not include fancy graphics or fonts, but it does

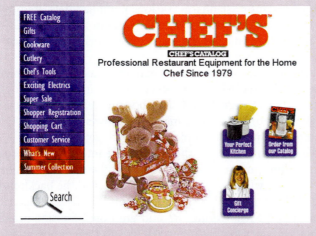

probably want to be able to deliver goods to customers if they phone in an order.

A retail web site has similar activities, but they are handled in a different way, a way suitable to the physical gap between store and customer. You may have the expertise to set up a simple web page, but including the software to handle sales transactions is much more complex. Fortunately, user-friendly

mean that your site will be free of typos, easy to navigate, and clearly laid out.

- Set up an order and payment processing system. This includes letting customers add merchandise to their "shopping cart" and accepting payment by credit card in a secure environment.
- Market your site. To make sales, you need

traffic. iCAT will see that you are listed with the major search engines.

Storefront software helps get you started by offering easy-to-use templates, basically fill-in-the-blank screens that the software converts to a site. You visit the company's web site, fill in the options you want, and enter your product information. With iCAT there is no risk because there is a free trial period.

You may be interested in what iCAT considers the "hot" categories of online best sellers in the immediate future. They include personal care products; sports paraphernalia; music-related theme merchandise; health and nutrition-related products; home furnishing products; auto repair and home repair products; and patterned sets of china, glass, and silverware.

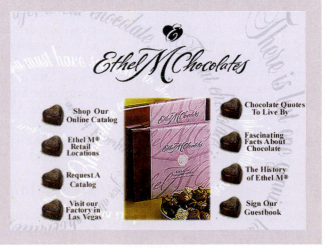

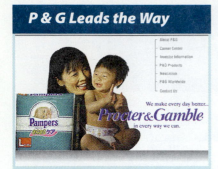
The "speed problem," as it is succinctly known, hangs like a cloud over all Internet transactions. A casual user may be merely annoyed by a delay as a site downloads. For serious users sending high volume data, the problem can be crippling. The speed problem impacts every aspect of business on the Internet.

Numerous solutions to the speed problem have been proposed. Still more are on the drawing table. Most solutions are aimed at increasing **bandwidth,** the measure of the capacity of a communications link. The idea is to expand "the pipes" so that more data can flow through. Some speedy alternatives to a 56Kbps modem are satellite, ISDN, DSL and its variations, and cable modem (Table 1).

Satellite transmission is wireless and widely available. But this method is expensive and may be clogged in peak hours. **Integrated Services Digital Network,** usually known by its acronym, **ISDN,** transmits data at up to 128,000 bps. ISDN requires special equipment and is somewhat complicated to set up and somewhat expensive, but it is very speedy and widely available.

Digital subscriber line (DSL) service uses advanced electronics to send data over conventional copper telephone wires. Like traditional analog modems, DSL modems translate digital computer messages to analog signals to send over the lines and then convert the message back to digital signals at the destination. However, DSL spreads the analog signals over a large range of frequencies, acting as if dozens of modems were sending signals at the same time. xDSL is a catchall for the varieties of DSL: ADSL, RDSL, and others. Since DSL lacks industry standards, various manufacturers are proposing their own variations. The majority of xDSL systems are sold to businesses. xDSL is available only on a limited basis; a user must be near a central office and have copper wiring in place.

Another approach, now available in limited markets, is a **cable modem,** a speedster that uses the coaxial television cables already in place without interrupting normal cable TV reception. Cable modems can be stunningly fast: 10 *million* bps. Furthermore, a cable modem is always "on," like a TV channel, and does not require dialing or placing a call to get started.

The speed problem is complicated by the fact that the Internet comprises many communication links, and no one "fix" can affect them all. The major links that tie servers across wide geographical areas are called the **backbone** of the Internet. Links that form the backbone bear well-known commercial names such as Sprint and MCI WorldCom, and are noted for significant bandwidth. Suppose, however, that many users increase their home-access bandwidth. Widespread use of high-speed home-access systems will place even more demands on the backbone, and that will, in turn, slow everyone's access to the system.

Part of the reason for Internet congestion, and thus slower speeds, is that people have not been charged on the basis of their usage of the Internet. In forum after forum, experts predict that users are going to have to pay for Internet use. A heavy user, it is thought, should pay more than an occasional browser. Economists assert that, as in other segments of society, if people do not pay for what they consume, there will be no economic incentive to keep building the Internet.

Streaming

Perhaps the most notable bandwidth user is **streaming,** the downloading of live audio, video, and animation content. Users can hear and see the digitized

Table 1   Comparison of Internet Connections

Connection	Download Time, 10MB file	Pros	Cons
56K modem	23 min.	In place now	Slow Must dial up
ISDN	10 min.	Easy to get Instant connection	Requires new equipment
DSL	50 sec.	Standard phone lines Simultaneous phone calls Always on	Limited availability Requires copper wiring Expensive hardware/service
Cable modem	26 sec.	Doesn't use phone line Simple, inexpensive setup Always on	Limited availability Expensive for business
Satellite	3 min.	No wires Doubles as TV dish	Must buy dish Expensive Slow at peak hours

content even as it is still being downloaded. Streamed sound and images usually appear via a browser plug-in, letting streaming begin within seconds of a user's click. But the price of that convenience is quality. The voluminous content of sight and sound over the network is a serious challenge to the bandwidth. Thus the results are less than satisfactory. Still, it really is something to get even a limited version of radio and television capability on your computer. As with all aspects of data traveling over a network, performance will improve as bandwidth problems are alleviated.

A popular plug-in is RealPlayer, which can be downloaded free from the RealNetworks site (Figure 10a). Once you have downloaded and installed an audio-video plug-in with your browser, you can start streaming from sites that offer such data. Start with the free samples from your plug-in's web site. Then move to other sites that specialize in video and sound.

One well-known site is broadcast.com, which presents live radio and some canned television shows (Figure 10b). When you indicate by a click that you want to receive some sort of streaming data, the site that has the data will immediately check your browser for an audio-video plug-in. If you have none, it will tell you so and, most likely, give you an icon for you to click so you can head to the appropriate site and download the needed plug-in. If you already have the plug-in, it will immediately spring into action in a separate window on your screen. In short order, you will hear or see, or perhaps both, the data you ordered. The quality you receive depends greatly on the speed of your connection. Audio usually is quite clear and could be mistaken for an actual radio broadcast. Video can be herky-jerky for users other than those with very speedy connections. However, even these limited offerings can give a sense of the future of streaming media.

Multicasting

Suppose you work for a company that develops documentary packages. You have written a report that should be seen not by everyone in the company—only by a few dozen selected individuals. Suppose, further, that your computer-produced report is not just some simple text but, instead, includes

InfoBit

Some users are concerned enough about the performance of the Internet backbone that they have set up web sites to give "Internet weather forecasts," a euphemism that refers not the weather but to Internet data traffic reports. These sites determine the network delay time and error rate from one major node to another along the backbone. Web graphics display the timings of the link, hour by hour, superimposed on a geographic map of the region.

InfoBit

One low-tech trick for reducing amount of bandwidth and online time consumed by advertisements is to select "text-only" on web sites that support this feature. Although the graphical elements of the page will disappear (being replaced with[Image]), most of the ads will no longer download either. This approach works best on some search engine pages, where the content in which you are interested is text and graphics are unnecessary anyway.

InfoBit

Some cable modem suppliers are limiting the duration of streaming video downloads to a ten minute maximum. While this is certainly influenced by the huge amount of bandwidth occupied by video streams, there may be some fear on the part of cable companies that web-based entertainment videos will infringe on the broadcast television market.

(a)

(b)

Figure 10 RealNetwork.
(a) RealNetwork is a popular browser plug-in (add-on software) that can be downloaded free and then used to accept streaming—live—audio and video on your computer. (b) The site called broadcast.com presents live radio and some canned television shows.

bandwidth-hogging items such as graphics, sounds, and video clips. How would you proceed to send the report to the designated recipients over the company's computer network?

You could send a separate copy from your computer to the computer of each recipient on your list, one at a time; this is called **unicasting** (Figure 11). This approach would waste bandwidth because the same files would be sent over and over, first to your company's server and then back out to the recipient. You could, instead, opt for **broadcast** mode, in which the server sends only one copy of the file, but it is sent to every computer on the network, whether or not the computer's user should receive it. This too is wasteful—and possibly compromises security by placing the report in the hands of inappropriate people.

There is a third, and better, solution. **Multicasting** sends just one copy of each file and drops it off only with appropriate recipients. Now expand the picture and imagine the impact of multicasting over the entire Internet. Multicasting network technology can reduce data traffic by delivering a single stream of data to thousands of recipients over whatever bandwidth is available. NASA space shuttle launchings and Rolling Stones concerts were some early multicasting events.

Push Technology

Businesses large and small have embraced the Internet. But businesses can find the Internet frustrating because they must sit idly by, so to speak, and hope that users will visit their sites. That is, in the jargon of the trade, they await users to *pull* data from their sites. The answer to this problem is the opposite approach: push technology.

Think of it this way: *Pull* is like going to the newsstand to pick up a paper, but *push* is like having it delivered to your door. More precisely, **push technology** refers to software that automatically sends—pushes—information from the Internet to a user's personal computer. From the sender's point of view, this process is akin to TV broadcasting, so push technology is some-

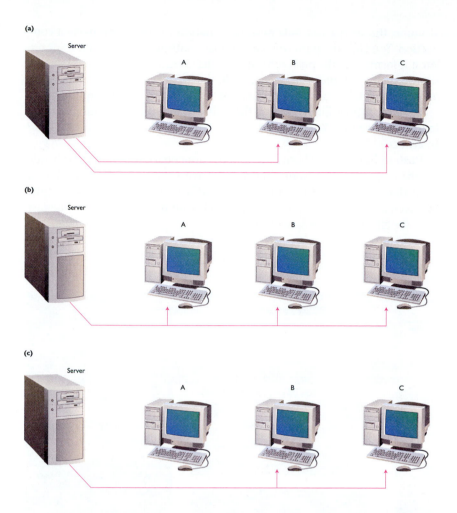

(a)

Server

A   B   C

(b)

Server

A   B   C

(c)

Server

A   B   C

Figure 11 Freeing up bandwidth. (a) Wasteful: In the unicast model, the server sends multiple copies of the same multimedia stream, one to each designated user—in this case, users B and C. (b) Perhaps better, depending on the total number of users: In the broadcast model, the server sends one copy of the multimedia stream, dropping it off to every user on the network, whether or not they should receive it, in this case users A, B, and C. (c) Best: In the multicast model, the server sends one copy of the multimedia stream, dropping it off only to designated users B and C.

times called **webcasting.** Proponents laud push technology as a time-saver for users: Instead of browsing and searching the Internet for what you want, customized information is gathered up for you from various sites and sent to you automatically. Detractors view it in less flattering terms, seeing it as marketing hype that will clog the Internet with frivolous graphics and unwanted advertising.

The pushing, however, begins only with the consent of the recipient. The concept was pioneered by PointCast Inc., which delivers information in the form of a screen-saver (Figure 12). It works like this: You download the free push software from the company's web site and install it. Then, using the software, you select "channels" you want to receive. The list of channels includes generic titles such as sports and business and also brand names such as CNN and the *New York Times.* You can narrow selections further within the channels. Then the push software goes out to the Internet and retrieves, from various sites, information—and ads—related to your declared interests. These are presented on your screen, complete with stock quotes and sports scores flowing across the bottom of the screen.

This concept works best for users who have a persistent connection via the office computer network. The information is downloaded to a corporate server and then relayed to employees. News and information is updated throughout the day. For people using the software on a personal computer

InfoBit

As an example of "push" technology, Internet bookseller Amazon.com automatically sends e-mail to you about new books published in the categories similar to those books you have bought from them previously. However, you can opt out of such mailings.

at home, the service can only push information to you if you make a connection. You click the push software's update button whenever you want the latest information; the push software will dial a connection, gather information from the Internet, disconnect itself, then display the new information on your screen. Further, the software can be set to connect and update automatically at regular intervals. Both the software and the information-gathering service are free. You must, of course, have the ability to connect to the Internet.

Push technology has been criticized in some quarters as being too bandwidth-hungry. In fact, some businesses have prohibited their employees from signing up for push technology. PointCast has made inroads recently, however, by switching to a multicast model, sending files down the line just once for all users on the same server.

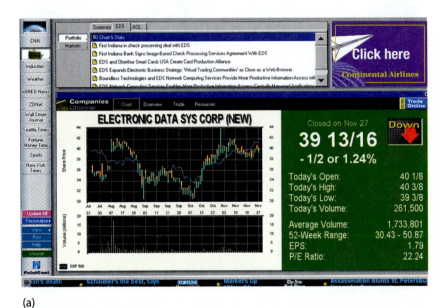

(a)

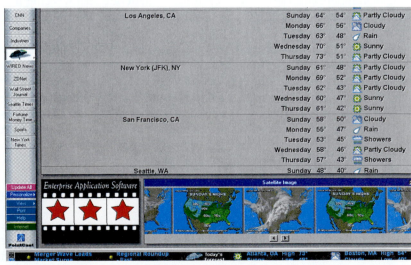

(b)

Figure 12 Push technology. PointCast downloads information in various categories from the Internet to the user's personal computer. Categories range from headline news to sports to lifestyles to business. Stock quotes, sports scores, and weather predictions stream across the bottom of the screen. (a) Note the briefcase image in the upper-left corner, indicating that the category Companies has been clicked. Users can keep a list of their own stocks. Shown here is a graph with statistics with Electronic Data Systems. Screens also show commercials; note the Continental Airlines ad in the upper-right corner. (b) The umbrella image in the upper-left corner indicates that the category Weather has been clicked. Predictions for major cities drift up the top half of the screen; below are enlargeable maps. The stars in the lower-left corner are part of an advertisement.

Intranets

Although many businesses use the Internet to promote their products and services to the public, they are finding that an even more useful application is for their internal—company-only—purposes, hence the intranet.

Vendors promoting their intranet software products in magazine advertisements often make a play on the word, perhaps InTRAnet or even Intranet. They do not want you to think that they are simply misspelling Internet. In fact, an **intranet** is a private Internet-like network internal to a certain company. The number of intranets has been growing rapidly. Every Fortune 500 company either has an intranet or is planning one. Part of the reason for the phenomenal growth is the relative ease of setting up an intranet.

Setting Up an Intranet

It's fast, it's easy, it's inexpensive. Relatively speaking, of course. The components of an intranet are familiar ones: the same ones used for the Internet. Hardware requirements include a server and computers used for access. These probably exist because most companies already have local area networks; this is why the intranet setup is fast, easy, and inexpensive. The Internet TCP/IP protocols must be in place. The server, which will act as a clearinghouse for all data regardless of source, needs its own software. The server will process requests and also perhaps pull data from traditional sources such as a mainframe computer. As on the Internet, each access computer needs a browser.

The intranet developers will doubtless devote the most time and attention to writing the web pages that employees will see and use. The pages must be well designed and easy to follow, opting for function over glitz. A typical opening page, for example, would probably have an attractive company logo and several clickable generic icons to represent functions. One click leads to a more detailed page and so on. By presenting information the same way to every computer, the developers can pull all the computers, software, and data files that dot the corporate landscape into a single system that helps employees find information wherever it resides.

Intranets at Work

A well-designed intranet can be used by most employees from day one. They can point and click and link to sites that contain information previously locked away behind functionaries and forms. Suppose, for example, that an employee needs to check up on the status of her benefits. Traditionally, she would probably have to find the right form, fill it out correctly, submit it, and wait a few days for a response. Now, it is point and click, give some identifying information such as Social Security number, and the information shows up on the screen and can be printed.

Employee information is just the beginning. Typical applications are internal job openings, marketing, vacation requests, corporate policy information, and perhaps company training courses. Some even include the local weather report and the daily cafeteria menu. Intranets even cut down on the flow of e-mail. A manager can, instead of sending out mass e-mail to employees, post notices on his or her own web site and leave it to employees to check it regularly.

The Internet Too

An intranet can remain private and isolated, but most companies choose to link their intranets to the Internet. This gives employees access to Internet resources and to other employees with their own intranets in geographically dispersed places. The employee access to the public Internet should not be confused with public access to the company intranet; the intranet is private.

However, companies may choose to link some parts of their intranets together. Such a hookup, intranet-to-intranet, is called an **extranet.** Some companies are finding that their long-standing relationships with customers and suppliers can often be handled more easily and more inexpensively with an extranet than with more traditional electronic data interchange—EDI—systems.

Virtual Private Networks

A **virtual private network** (VPN) provides technology that uses the public Internet backbone as a channel for private data communication. A VPN essentially carves out a private passageway through the Internet. Thus a VPN allows remote offices, company road warriors, and even business partners or customers to use the Internet, rather than pricey private lines, to reach company networks. The idea of the VPN is to give the company the same capabilities at much lower cost by sharing the public infrastructure.

Virtual private networks may be new, but the tunneling technology they are based on is well established. **Tunneling,** also called **encapsulation,** is a way to transfer data between two similar networks over an intermediate network. Tunneling software encloses one type of data-packet protocol into the packet of another protocol. Although as yet there is no standard protocol for the packet that is doing the tunneling, Microsoft, 3Com, and several other companies have proposed a standard protocol called *Point-to-Point Tunneling Protocol (PPTP)*. The original protocol, the one holding the tunnel, is the standard Internet TCP/IP protocol. Thus organizations can use the Internet to transmit data "privately" by embedding their own network protocol—PPTP technology—within the TCP/IP packets carried by the Internet.

VPN tunneling adds another dimension to the tunneling procedure. Before encapsulation takes place, the packets are encrypted—encoded—so the data is unreadable to outsiders. The encapsulated packets travel through the Internet until they reach their destination; the packets then are separated and returned to their original format. Authentication technology is used to make sure the client has authorization to contact the server.

By replacing expensive private network bandwidth with relatively low-cost bandwidth, a company can slash operating costs and simplify communications. No longer needed are the 800 lines and long-distance charges; employees simply place local or toll-free calls to Internet service providers

InfoBit

A vital term for e-commerce users selecting VPNs will be quality of service. Using advanced networking protocols, many carriers offering VPNs will be willing to make Service Level Agreements (SLAs). In these agreements, the VPN provider promises to meet specified availability and throughput standards, with financial penalties for non-compliance. Given the increasing importance of electronic messaging in business, customers should demand SLAs from their providers.

MAKING THE RIGHT CONNECTIONS
ONLINE AUCTIONS

How would you like to have a business in which, each time a sale is made, both the seller and the buyer pay you money? An auction house is such a business. Sellers pay the auctioneer to set up a sale and the auctioneer takes a cut from the money the buyer pays. Of course, in a real live auction, the auctioneer must rent a warehouse or barn to hold the goods and the buyers, advertise the auction, hire people to move merchandise around, spend hours shouting and urging sales, and eventually collect money from the buyers.

Just like other retailers, auctioneers have moved online. Consider how this simplifies matters: no warehouse, no movers, no shouting, and precious little advertising. This streamlined operation does impose new tasks, however: photographing every item, maintaining a web site that can display the items, accepting bids, and collecting payments. Further, the ever-changing merchandise means greater-than-average site maintenance.

Many auction sites sell commercial items of little interest to the general public—scrap metal, salvaged vehicles, and excess inventory. The online auction sensations are the retail-like sites, such as eBay, whose site is shown here. Sellers pay between 25¢ and $2 per item just to have it made available for auction. eBay conducts an electronic auction that runs for multiple days, with anyone who happens by the site submitting bids as they please. If the goods are sold, eBay collects a commission of 1.25 to 5 percent of the selling price.

Categories of merchandise on the eBay site include toys, antiques, books, movies, jewelry, collectibles, computers, dolls, photos, pottery, and more. On a typical day, merchandise might include an autographed picture of Joe DiMaggio, a 1937 Indian head nickel, a commercial balloon imprinter, a Chevy Blazer, a 1780 German bird engraving, a biography of Colin Powell, Super Bowl tickets, and a blue swirl glass paperweight. But this tiny list cannot even give the flavor of the vast amount of merchandise available. There are, for example, over 8000 Barbie doll items. Buyers trade on eBay because of the large number of items available. If you want it, someone is probably selling it. Similarly, sellers are attracted to eBay because eBay has the most buyers. There are over a million auctions happening on eBay every day.

For any given item, a potential bidder can see the number of bids that have been made on an item, the current price, the date the bidding ends, and the e-mail address of the current high bidder. Most items are accompanied by detailed descriptions and photos. In order to bid on or sell an item, you will first need to register. You only need to register once. This way the buyer will know who the seller is in order to pay him or her, and the seller will be able to answer any product questions potential buyers may have. Registration requires a real-world address and telephone number. eBay will not use this information for marketing, or disclose it to an outside party; the company will, however, supply your phone number, city, and state to another registered user upon request.

There are two appealing aspects for auction buyers—convenience and savings. The convenience is the usual convenience of buying online instead of moving from place to place, auction to auction. The savings are there if you know the merchandise and recognize a good price.

(ISPs) to make the connection. VPNs also reduce in-house network management responsibilities because much of the remote communications burden is turned over to ISPs.

Consolidation of the Web

The World Wide Web started out as—and still is—a freewheeling place where anyone who could publish a web page could participate. This participation meant that the Internet became the preferred medium for all kinds of ideological, political, cultural, and entertainment persuasions. A related notion is that the Internet is not owned by anyone; it is uncontrolled and uncontrollable.

But changes—business-related changes—have been in the wind for some time. The Internet, as it turns out, is not immune to the normal forces of consolidation, which bring efficiency and uniformity to new media and new industries. Indeed, the only thing different about the Web—a new trillion-dollar industry—is that the opportunities for consolidation are of such a large scale that it is occurring at warp speed, the Web's typical pace.

Ordinary Internet users first took notice of the consolidation process in 1999, when America Online bought Netscape. But less noticeable dealings have been proceeding apace. Although, for the great mass of consumers, the restructured Web will not look that different from prior communications media, a handful of well-known brands will determine the nature and content of the majority of what is seen and heard on a daily basis. The high-traffic, commercially viable sites will increasingly come into the hands of a few major conglomerates.

This process is not so different from what has happened in other industries in America. Mom-and-pop stores give way to regional and national chains. Then someone emerges to set a pace that everyone else must match—Wal-Mart Stores, Inc., in discount retailing or Blockbuster Entertainment in the video rental business. There always will be new players and lots of players. But there will also be defining players, players who consolidate. We cannot predict the players; we just know that they *are* there and they *will be* there—consolidating the Web.

We have said that the Internet is interesting and fun, and it is. But it is much more than that. The Internet represents a new and important buisness model and, indeed, an entire new way of looking at industry and commerce.

CHAPTER REVIEW

Summary and Key Terms

- An **ice page** has a fixed width and is on the left margin. A **jello page** has a fixed width but centers itself on the screen. A **liquid page** fits any screen.

- The world of **electronic commerce,** or, more commonly, **e-commerce,** buying and selling over the Internet, represents a new economic order. Customers can buy just about anything on the Internet.

- Retail web sites have begun adding **content** to attract visitors and boost sales.

- Some companies must settle for half measures because they fear that selling a product from their own web site will alienate the sales representatives and stores with whom they have established relationships.

- A web site that is used as a gateway or guide to the Internet is called a **portal.** Portals and other sites collect money from **banner ads** and referrals to **affiliate** sites.

- Users who leave the current site for an advertised site are said to **click through;** to get business from users who will not click through, a **live banner,** which lets a user get more information about a product without leaving the current site, may be used.

- The most effective Web advertisements are **context-sensitive;** that is, the ad is related to the subject matter on the screen.

- E-commerce payments by credit card are probably safe over a secure server.

- The **Internet Tax Freedom Act** imposes a three-year moratorium (which began in October 1998) on taxes imposed on the Internet and calls for a committee to study the matter.

- Some primary entrepreneurial success factors are content, uniqueness, self-help, and community.

- Numerous solutions to the speed problem have been proposed. Most solutions are aimed at increasing **bandwidth,** the measure of the capacity of a communications link. Satellite transmission is wireless and widely available, but it is also expensive and perhaps clogged in peak hours. **Integrated Services Digital Network,** usually known by its acronym, **ISDN,** transmits data at 128,000 bps. ISDN requires special equipment and is somewhat complicated to set up and somewhat expensive, but it is very speedy and widely available. **Digital subscriber line (DSL)** service uses advanced electronics to send data over conventional copper telephone wires. A **cable modem** uses coaxial television cables already in place for data transmission without interrupting normal cable TV reception.

- The major links that tie servers across wide geographical areas are called the **backbone** of the Internet.

- **Streaming** is the downloading of live audio, video, and animation content.

- **Unicasting** sends data from a computer to the computer of each designated recipient. In **broadcast** mode, the server sends only one copy of the files, but it is sent to every computer on the network. **Multicasting** sends just one copy of each file and drops it off only with appropriate recipients.

- **Push technology,** also called **webcasting,** refers to software that automatically sends—pushes—information from the Internet to a user's personal computer.

- An **intranet** is a private Internet-like network internal to a certain company.

- An **extranet** is a network of two or more intranets.

- A **virtual private network (VPN)** provides technology that uses the public Internet backbone as a channel for private data communication. **Tunneling,** also called **encapsulation,** is a way to transfer data between two similar networks over an intermediate network by enclosing one type of data packet protocol into the packet of another protocol.

Discussion Questions

1. Some established companies fret over whether or not to actually offer their goods and services over the Internet, in competition with their traditional outlets. If the decision were up to you, at what point might you go forward with a complete retail site?

2. Consider an Internet business site that could be started by an entrepreneur. Some possibilities are for a series of children's books, an invention that instantly melts snow on sidewalks, or the rental of a small getaway cabin—or consider a business of your own choice. How would you introduce the success factors of content, uniqueness, self-help, and community into your web site?

3. If you were on the committee decreed by the Internet Tax Freedom Act, what recommendations might you make about imposing taxes on Internet use? Do you see any comparisons with taxes already imposed on telephone use?

4. How much does the appearance of the opening page of a site matter? Is it worth the extra effort to make a page liquid instead of ice, for the sake of those viewers with larger screens? Would your answers be different for a commercial site as opposed to a personal site?

5. Sites that are heavy with graphics take longer to load than graphics-light sites. That is, a visitor must wait longer to view a graphics-rich site. Multimedia sites that include movement and sound take even longer to load. Which of these types of sites may be able to justify making visitors wait a bit longer to see the site: corporate presence, major retail, small entrepreneur, charitable organization, product demonstration, web site designers, entertainment, personal home page, and games. Finally, how long should a visitor be expected to wait? How long are you personally willing to wait for a site to show up on your screen? Should the length of a reasonable wait time vary with the type of site?

Student Study Guide

Multiple Choice

1. Another name for tunneling is
   a. portal
   b. cabling
   c. encapsulation
   d. bandwidth

2. A web site ad that does not require click-through is called
   a. context sensitive
   b. a live banner
   c. a portal
   d. streaming

3. Sending a file repeatedly, once for each recipient, is called
   a. webcasting
   b. unicasting
   c. broadcasting
   d. multicasting

4. The fastest communications link is via
   a. a cable modem
   b. a satellite
   c. a 56K modem
   d. ISDN

5. Downloading live audio, video, and animation is called
   a. tunneling
   b. unicasting
   c. cabling
   d. streaming

6. Software that automatically sends information from the Internet to the user employs
   a. an affiliate
   b. a banner
   c. push technology
   d. an extranet

7. Which is not a key success factor for an entrepreneurial web site?
   a. content
   b. uniqueness
   c. community
   d. streaming

8. A web site that is used as a gateway or guide to the Internet is a(n)
   a. portal
   b. backbone
   c. ISDN
   d. extranet

9. The name used to describe the major links that tie servers across wide geographical areas is
   a. encapsulation
   b. backbone
   c. tunneling
   d. e-commerce

10. A technology that uses the public Internet backbone as a channel for private data communications is known as
    a. e-commerce
    b. DSL
    c. VPN
    d. ISDN

11. DSL stands for
    a. Digital subscriber line
    b. Digital stream line
    c. Digital self-help line
    d. Digital service line

12. The Internet Tax Freedom Act
    a. allows taxes on streaming
    b. must be approved by individual states
    c. imposes a three-year Internet tax moratorium
    d. all of these

13. Users who leave the current site by clicking on a banner ad are said to
    - a. push
    - b. tunnel
    - c. stream
    - d. click through

14. When a single file is sent and dropped off only to designated recipients, this is called
    - a. broadcasting
    - b. multicasting
    - c. unicasting
    - d. web casting

15. An advertisement that is related to what is currently showing on the web page is called
    - a. encapsulation
    - b. context-sensitive
    - c. a portal
    - d. the backbone

16. A web page that fits any size screen is said to be
    - a. live
    - b. liquid
    - c. encapsulated
    - d. jello

17. To attract visitors and increase sales, many retail sites have added
    - a. VPN
    - b. backbone
    - c. content
    - d. context

18. The measure of the capacity of a communication link is called its
    - a. content
    - b. transmission
    - c. DSL
    - d. bandwidth

19. When a computer sends just one copy of a file but drops it off at every computer, whether or not the latter is a designated recipient, the sending computer is said to be
    - a. unicasting
    - b. multicasting
    - c. web casting
    - d. broadcasting

20. A private Internet-like network within a company is called a(n)
    - a. intranet
    - b. extranet
    - c. virtual private network
    - d. ISDN

21. The general term for buying and selling on the Internet is
    - a. click through
    - b. e-commerce
    - c. jello and ice
    - d. streaming

22. A web site may have ads that can be clicked to send a user to another site; the latter may be referred to as this kind of site:
    - a. live
    - b. ice
    - c. affiliate
    - d. portal

23. A network of two or more intranets is called a(n)
    - a. extranet
    - b. VPN
    - c. portal
    - d. DSL

24. A web page that occupies the center of the screen is said to be
    - a. live
    - b. cabled
    - c. ice
    - d. jello

25. A web page that is anchored to the left margin of the screen is said to be
    - a. live
    - b. encapsulated
    - c. ice
    - d. liquid

True/False

T F 1. Bandwidth is the measure of the capacity of a communications link.

T F 2. A major goal of Internet users is decreasing bandwidth.

T F 3. Retail web sites, by law, cannot include content other than products and services.

T F 4. The principal companies associated with the Internet backbone are DSL and ISDN.

T F 5. An intranet is a public network and an extranet is a private network.

T F 6. Multicasting sends one copy of each file to every user on the network.

T F 7. A cable modem is slower than a traditional modem.

T F 8. There are various versions of DSL.

T F 9. A live banner ad lets a user see advertised information without leaving the current site.

T F 10. Encapsulation is related to virtual private network technology.

T F 11. ISDN must be context-sensitive.

T F 12. Push technology is also called multicasting.

T F 13. E-commerce means downloading government-related web sites.

T F 14. An ad that is related to the subject matter on the screen is said to be context-sensitive.

T F 15. Streaming is downloading live audio, video, and animation.

T F 16. One reason that business sites have a similar look is that most limit their sites to small graphic images.

T F 17. One cost of establishing a web site is the physical requirement for "bricks and mortar."

T F 18. E-commerce sites display their wares but do not permit actual purchases of goods via the Internet.

T F 19. The advertising medium most often used for attracting visitors to a web site is outdoor billboards.

T F 20. The Internet Tax Freedom Act prohibits government entities from imposing any new taxes for a three year period.

T F 21. Retail web sites usually offer extra material, called content, that is totally unrelated to the product or service they sell.

T F 22. Some companies are nervous about actually selling a product or service on a web site for fear of alienating their established contacts with stores and sales representatives.

T F 23. Items that are offered for sale via web sites are limited to non-perishable goods, such as CDs, books, and cameras.

T F 24. An affiliate site shares the profit from a sale with the site that made the referral.

T F 25. A portal site does not permit the use of live banners ads.

T F 26. All retail businesses that have a web site offer to sell their product or service via the web site.

T F 27. One problem with banner ads is that users are often reluctant to leave the current site to go to the advertised site.

T F 28. A live banner must be context-sensitive.

T F 29. If a user invokes a search engine with the words "vacation" and "Maui" and the next screen includes a banner ad for a hotel in Maui, the ad is said to be context-sensitive.

T F 30. The most important success factor for an entrepreneurial web site is the use of sophisticated graphics.

T F 31. Portals use affiliates to generate revenue.

T F 32. The Internet Tax Freedom Act prohibits governing entities from collecting sales taxes across state lines.

T F 33. Users who purchase items via the Internet need not pay sales taxes.

T F 34. When a web site is visited, the advertisements are usually among the first elements to appear on the screen.

T F 35. A portal site has many offerings, mostly to encourage visitors to use that portal site as their guide to the Internet.

Fill-In

1. The major links that tie Internet servers across wide geographical areas are called collectively the _____.

2. Another name for webcasting is _____.

3. Downloading live audio, video, and animation is called _____.

4. The capacity of a communications link is measured as its _____.

5. Sending the same file to everyone on the network is known as _____.

6. The communications link that uses coaxial television cables is the _____.

7. VPN stands for _____.

8. A private Internet-like network internal to a certain company is called a(n) _____ _____.

9. An ad that matches the subject matter on the screen is said to be _____ _____.

10. DSN stands for _____.

11. A network of two or more intranets is called _____.

12. In the context of a virtual private network, another word for encapsulation is _____ _____.

13. Sending just one copy of a file and dropping it off only at designated recipients is called _____.

14. A web page that is of fixed width and anchored to the left side of the screen is said to be _____.

15. Portal sites collect money from sites to which they refer visitors; these sites are called _____.

16. Users who leave the current site to go to an advertised site are said to _____.

17. The type of page that fills a screen, no matter what the width, is called _____ .

18. The short name for electronic commerce is

    _____ .

19. When a computer sends a separate file to each designated recipient, this is known as

    _____ .

20. The federal law that imposes a three-year moratorium on taxes imposed on the internet is called

    _____ .

21. To attract visitors, retail web sites have added extra interesting information, called

    _____ .

22. A web site that is used as a gateway or guide to the Internet is called _____ .

23. A type of web site advertisement that lets a user get information about an advertised product without leaving the current site is _____ .

24. The primary entrepreneurial web site success factors are

    a. _____ .

    b. _____ .

    c. _____ .

    d. _____ .

25. A web site page that appears in the center of the screen is said to be _____ .

Answers

Multiple Choice

1. c	6. c	11. a	16. b	21. b
2. b	7. d	12. c	17. c	22. c
3. b	8. a	13. d	18. d	23. a
4. a	9. b	14. b	19. d	24. d
5. d	10. c	15. b	20. a	25. c

True/False

1. T	11. F	21. F	31. F
2. F	12. F	22. T	32. T
3. F	13. F	23. F	33. F
4. F	14. T	24. T	34. T
5. F	15. T	25. F	35. T
6. F	16. T	26. F	
7. F	17. F	27. T	
8. T	18. F	28. F	
9. T	19. F	29. T	
10. T	20. T	30. F	

Fill-In

1. backbone
2. push technology
3. streaming
4. bandwidth
5. broadcasting
6. cable modem
7. virtual private network
8. intranet
9. context-sensitive
10. digital subscriber line
11. extranet
12. tunneling
13. multicasting
14. ice
15. affiliates
16. click through
17. liquid
18. e-commerce
19. unicasting
20. Internet Tax Freedom Act
21. content
22. portal
23. live banner
24. a. content
    b. uniqueness
    c. self-help
    d. community
25. jello

PLANET INTERNET

For users who are Internet-savvy, a key buzzword is *multimedia*. The concept covers a lot of ground and, more specifically, much exciting software.

I think I understand the term *multimedia* in a general sense—text, images, photographs, sound effects, and even motion—but what does it mean on the Internet? Pretty much the same thing. Text, of course, has always been a component of the Internet. Images and photographs became easily available with the advent of browser software. Now users can hear narrations and music and other sounds. The advent of Java and other software has also made motion—video!—a possibility.

So I can hear music and see movement just by showing up at a site that has them? Not quite. You must have a browser that is up to the task. The newer versions of modern browsers can do many of these things. Some special effects require special software additions to your browser, called plug-ins. If your browser cannot take advantage of the full "experience," you will probably see a message on the site that tells you so and urges you get some specific software that will enhance site enjoyment. If so, the message will probably include a link to the site that offers the software, usually for free downloading to your computer.

How do I get this plug-in software and then get it to work with my browser? Go to the site

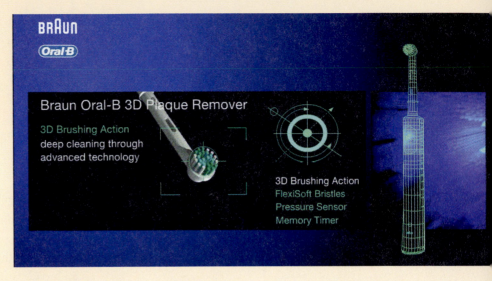

Braun Oral-B 3D Plaque Remover

3D Brushing Action
deep cleaning through
advanced technology

3D Brushing Action
FlexiSoft Bristles
Pressure Sensor
Memory Timer

of the software developer that makes the plug-in. You won't have to look far for a clickable download icon. Read the instructions carefully to make sure that you select the software that works with your browser and your operating system. You may also be asked to choose the directory—folder—in which you want the software placed; the default location is usually in the same place as your browser. You may be offered instructions, and it is usually suggested that you print them for later reference. These include installation instructions, that is, how to plug the new software into your browser once it is downloaded. This usually involves running one of the programs downloaded.

With sight as a single sensory input we judge...

Are there some standard software plug-ins that I should be sure to check out? Tough question. Standards are evolving. Once the standards battles are settled, it is likely that plug-in functions will be subsumed eventually into ever more sophisticated browsers. Meanwhile, there are definitely some software products that are widely used.

Can I see some sites that use these popular plug-ins? Yes, but first you need to have the plug-in software in order to appreciate its value to the site. (By the way, you can usually still see the multimedia site even if you don't have a suitable browser or the required plug-in software to appreciate its multimedia aspects; you just see a "plain vanilla" version of the site.) Before you do any downloading, the best approach is probably to go to the site of the software developer and see all the action with the plug-in software supplied on the site.

Let us consider two popular plug-ins. *Shockwave*, which can be seen and downloaded from the Macromedia site, can provide amazing animation. Text and images swoop and swirl and stream across the screen as the site loads, usually with audio accompaniment. Shockwave makes the site come alive. Shockwave is the main attraction on tens of thousands of sites, including the well-known Disney and Nike sites as well as less-well-known sites.

As an example, the Braun site opens with its toothbrush swirling and moving about in interesting ways, complemented by tooth-brushing sounds. Another interesting example is the site for Saatchi and Saatchi. As you would expect from an advertising agency, their site is clever. The cat shown here is part of a series of images in which the fish moves and the cat changes position accordingly, with various promotional subtitles included.

Another popular add-on is *RealNetworks*, whose sounds are sufficiently sophisticated to provide entire broadcasts, such as baseball games. RealNetworks audio supports sophisticated sites such as that of singer Alanis Morissette. To listen to RealAudio content, Internet users must have a RealPlayer installed on their computers. Once the player is installed on a user's computer, it works automatically whenever the user clicks on a RealAudio file on a web site. Buttons on the player's control panel enable users to control volume and other functions. The basic RealPlayer software is free and can be downloaded from the RealNetworks site.

Your browser, by the way, can probably support some sound without a plug-in; try The Soundry, The Answering Machine, and Historical Speeches sites. Perhaps the most popular music site is MP3, which uses a compression technique to shrink audio files. Aspiring musicians use it to submit their tunes to the Internet for anyone to download.

Internet Exercises

1. **Structured exercise.** Begin with the URL http://www.prenhall.com/capron and link to the Macromedia (Shockwave) site.

2. **Freeform exercise.** Put the word *multimedia* through a search engine and see what you find.

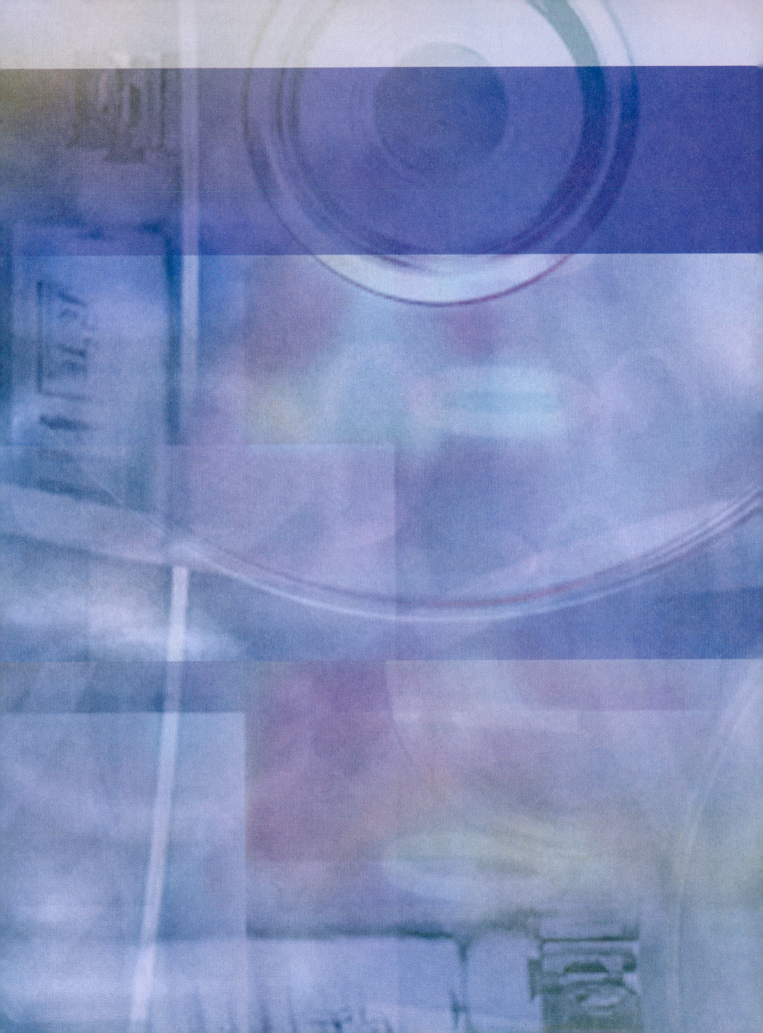

CHAPTER NINE

WRITING YOUR OWN WEB PAGE

Using HTML or FrontPage

Juliet Silveri is a marketing major in her junior year at Ohio State University. She is well acquainted with the Internet; she has used it for her own convenience, especially for ordering books and for student research. She has three friends who have written web pages but, until recently, has had no interest in writing her own web page. It seemed pointless to go through the learning process and the effort when she had nothing particular to say.

Juliet changed her mind when she took a marketing group project course that focused on promotional strategy—consumer behavior, setting goals and objectives, creative strategy, media strategy, and social and economic issues. Juliet's group decided that their project would be a web page that included a form for users to fill out regarding their concerns about making purchases online. They felt this would meet most of the course objectives and, in particular, be a creative challenge to convince users to participate.

Two of the group members knew how to write a web page and two members, including Juliet, did not. The group decided it would be a fair division of team labor for the nonweb folks to contribute to the content and help evaluate the results. But by the end of the first week Juliet was not satisfied with that approach; she wanted to work on the web page too.

She started saturation learning on her own, first studying HTML, the language used to write web pages, at some web sites set up for HTML beginners. This gave her some foundation. But, in talking to others, she decided she could accomplish her web page goals more quickly by learning a software package called FrontPage, which offered an easier and more powerful approach to page writing. She took a four-evening introductory course to FrontPage and managed to get by with this information, together with a couple of reference books and assistance from her more knowledgeable teammates.

Although she concedes that her learning approach was less than ideal, Juliet did manage to learn about writing web pages, and she made a significant contribution to the team project.

Before You Start

This chapter offers beginning instruction in the language called **HTML,** which stands for **HyperText Markup Language,** and also in Microsoft FrontPage 2000. It presents just enough information so that you can write a simple page for the Web in either HTML or FrontPage. Although we suggest at least skimming the HTML sections, it is possible to go directly from this section to the FrontPage sections of the chapter, beginning with the heading "Authoring Software."

We begin with some assumptions. The first is that you have studied the Internet, at least a little, and understand the meanings of the terms *World Wide Web,* browser, server, Internet service provider, site, home page, hypertext, URL, and link. Other assumptions are that you have already seen several web sites and have linked from site to site.

Before you plunge into coding, you need to understand the requirements for writing, testing, and publishing a page on the Web. Further, it will be helpful for you to see where this chapter is headed.

Requirements

You need to have access to appropriate hardware and software, including the following:

Writing Vehicle   You will need some software vehicle with which to write the HTML code for your web page. This can be a text editor such as Notepad that comes with Microsoft Windows, or perhaps a word processing program. Alternatively, there are HTML editors available for downloading from the Web. The software you use is not important as long as you can save the HTML file on disk as a text file. As we shall see later, files for FrontPage can be written using applications software such as Word or Excel.

Browser   You will need a browser to test the code and, later, to access the server. To use the browser to test your HTML file, you open the browser, but you need not actually make a connection to a server. That is, for testing purposes, at least at first, you can just use the browser, which understands HTML, on a personal computer or terminal not connected to the Internet. FrontPage offers a button that you can invoke to see your page in the browser.

Server   You will need to be connected to a server to test links to other sites. Once you have tested your page you will want to publish it, that is, make it accessible to others on the Internet. You will need to send your files—the coded files and any files it may use, such as an image—to a server, where they will be stored on the server's disk. The page file will be given its own unique URL. There are several server possibilities, such as your college's computer, a web site such as GeoCities that offers free web pages, or a local Internet service provider.

Where We Are Headed

We will begin by using HTML to create a simple page. Next we will expand a bit to create a resumé using HTML. Next we will incorporate more tags as we write HTML code for a web page that is a resumé. When we move on to FrontPage, we will remake the first HTML example using FrontPage and then go on to a more complex example.

The Basic Tags

HTML consists of a set of commands called **tags**; the tags tell the browser how to display the information provided. Many of them are quite simple. We will begin with just a few tags and then use them in a simple web page example. This way you can see right away how the HTML code and the resultant web page are related. We will expand that page a bit and incorporate other tags.

The Palace

When you are taking your first steps toward making a web page, it is useful, and perhaps entertaining, to see what others before you have done. The Palace fits in the "entertaining" category. It is also extremely complex.

Visitors to The Palace web site are encouraged to download free Palace-related software. The software can then be used to access various pages, which are all different in theme but have the same function: chat.

Conventional "chat rooms" are nothing more than screens of scrolling text produced by anywhere from two to a couple dozen users typing comments at one another. Palace chat rooms, in contrast, are lushly decorated spaces peopled by plumaged creatures, each of whom represents a chatter. When a chatter speaks a balloon containing the text appears over the bird's—speaker's—head.

It is the same chat gig, but a lot more colorful.

Table 1 Some HTML Tags

Tag	Description
\<HTML> . . . \</HTML>	Mark start and end of an HTML file
\<HEAD> . . . \</HEAD>	Mark start and end of the HEAD section
\<TITLE> . . . \</TITLE>	Title for the page
\<BODY> . . . \</BODY>	Mark the start and end of the content of the page
\<Hx> . . . \</Hx>	Heading, where *x* is 1 through 6
\<P> . . . \</P>	Paragraph
\ 	Break to a new line
\<EM> . . . \</EM>	Emphasis
\<STRONG> . . . \</STRONG>	Strong emphasis
\<I> . . . \</I>	Italic
\<B> . . . \</B>	Boldface
\<CENTER> . . . \</CENTER>	Center text horizontally
\<UL> . . . \</UL>	Unordered list
\<OL> . . . \</OL>	Ordered list
\<LI>	List item
\<HR>	Horizontal rule
\<IMG>	Image
\<A> . . . \</A>	Anchor; with attribute HREF provides a link

We begin with the basic tags that define the overall form of an HTML document—file—and then move to tags that give basic structure to the way the page will appear. Finally, we will submit the first, if limited, HTML code to the browser to see how the resulting page looks (Table 1).

Document Tags

Tags most often come in pairs, a beginning tag and an ending tag. The tag has a certain format: The command is enclosed in angle brackets—an opening angle bracket (\<) and a closing angle bracket (>). The very first tag of an HTML file, for example, must be \<HTML>. Paired tags have another tag that looks almost like the first but has a forward slash (/) just before the command. The paired tags for the HTML command, which go at the beginning and end of an HTML file, are \<HTML> and \</HTML> (Figure 1).

Tags, by the way, are not case-sensitive; they can be written in uppercase or lowercase or any combination of the two. Many people prefer uppercase because the tags are then easier to spot when looking at an HTML file.

Immediately following the HTML command is the **head tag** pair, \<HEAD> and \</HEAD>, which enclose the HEAD section. The HEAD command encloses the TITLE command, which is written with the **title tag** pair, \<TITLE> and \</TITLE>. This command will cause a page title to be displayed at the very top of the browser window in the title bar. After the HEAD section is the BODY section, enclosed by the **body tag** pair, \<BODY> and \</BODY>. All of the content of the page—headings, paragraphs, lists, images, and so forth—goes between the BODY tags.

Figure 1 has a complete set of the tags just described, with lines drawn to show how the matching tag pairs are related. Notice that it is permissible for one set of tags to be completely enclosed within another set of tags; the two HEAD tags, for example, are enclosed between the two HTML tags. The enclosed tags are called **nested tags.** It is not permissible, however, for sets of tags to overlap.

The code you see in Figure 1 is correct as it is. However, if you submitted it to a browser, the browser would produce only a blank page with the words *Test Title* in the title bar. A blank page shows because there is not yet any content between the \<BODY> and \</BODY> tags. In the next section, we will add some content to the basic document structure in Figure 1.

Text Structure Tags

All tags discussed from this point forward belong between the two BODY tags described in the previous section.

Heading tags (not to be confused with the HEAD tag) come in pairs and produce six text sizes, largest to smallest, as follows: \<H1> and \</H1>, \<H2> and \</H2>, and so forth, through \<H6> and \</H6>. The text to be printed is placed between a pair of tags. Text to be printed very large would use a number 1 heading, for example, \<H1>Theater Schedule\</H1>. The text generated by a number 6 heading, on the other hand, would be very small.

A paragraph of text is marked by the pair of **paragraph tags,** \<P> and \</P>. The browser inserts a blank line before the start of a paragraph. The text words within paragraph tags will be displayed by the browser with one space between any two adjacent words. You can, of course, use any kind of spacing when preparing an HTML file in order to make it easy to read. Extra white space—blank spaces or lines—is simply ignored by the browser.

If you want a line break, that is, to end a line and begin a new one but not start a new paragraph, use the **line break tag,**
. This is a single tag; it is not part of a pair. One more thing: A blank line follows a heading, so the only time you need to use the paragraph tag is when the paragraph follows another paragraph and you thus need to force a blank line.

A First Example

Examine Figure 2a, which shows the HTML code to describe a theater and mention its current plays. Note the file name at the top: Hayes. The first heading, a number 1 heading, will be the largest. The subheading will be of medium size, a number 3 heading. The first paragraph does not need paragraph tags because a blank line automatically follows the heading just above the paragraph. The second paragraph is marked with paragraph tags, so it will be set off with a blank line above it. The plays are listed within a paragraph, but they are forced by line breaks to appear on individual lines.

To test the HTML file, use the browser's Open command, and type in the exact path and name of the HTML file, as it is stored on disk. When the file is opened, the file name appears in the browser's Address window at the top of the browser, and the browser's interpretation of the HTML—the web page—appears in the browser display window.

Figure 2b shows the resulting page when the HTML text file Hayes.html is opened by the browser. Notice the title *The Hayes Theater* at the top of the browser window.

By the way, you may find on occasion that a displayed page is not what you thought the HTML code would produce. Whether this is due to an error or because you prefer a different outcome, you can simply return to the HTML file, make revisions, *remember to save the file,* and then reload—rerun—it through the browser using the browser's refresh button. If the browser still has the same file path/name in its Address window, you need only click the Address window and press Enter to make the page display again to see the changes you made to the HTML code.

Lists

A **list** is really a basic text structure, but it needs enough explanation to require its own section. The two kinds of lists used most often are unordered lists and ordered lists. An unordered list, also called a bulleted list, uses the **unordered list tag** pair, <UL> and </UL>, and produces an indented list, usually with a browser-supplied character in front of it, probably a small circle or square. An ordered list uses the **ordered list tag** pair, <OL> and </OL>, and causes the browser to number the indented list items in order, usually 1., 2., and so forth. Whether unordered or ordered, each item in a list is preceded by a single **list item tag,** <LI> (Figure 3).

Improving the Appearance of the Page

There are several things we can do to make a page more functional and more attractive. Although space prohibits listing all of them, we will mention some of the more common tags.

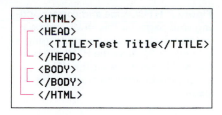

Figure 1 Basic HTML document structures. Lines have been drawn to mark pairs of tags. The <HTML> tag is used to define the document as containing HTML code. The <HEAD> tag defines the HEAD section, which contains the pair of <TITLE> tags that provide the title for the page. The entire content of the web page will be enclosed within the two <BODY> tags.

InfoBit

Font sizes on many browsers are approximate, so web authors cannot depend on the exact text sizes appearing for all users when designing the page. The tag <FONT SIZE=+3>, for example, is relative to the default font sizes selected by a particular browser. Cautious web page authors stay away from very large or very small fonts, knowing that browser variations can make extreme text sizes unreadable.

InfoBit

Some designers save special text, especially large fonts, as images rather than as text. This works especially well for large titles, and avoids a lot of problems with non-standard font and browser combinations. If you need a greeting page with a headline spelled out in 72 point "Wingdings," consider making the text into an image using special software (or even a high-end word processor like Word or WordPerfect). Display this image at the top of the page instead of text that would require special fonts. Observe that this is exactly what most professional sites do.

Figure 2 HTML code and corresponding web page. (a) This HTML code was entered and saved as a text file using a text editor. (b) After the HTML file is opened by the browser, the HTML causes the browser to produce this page.

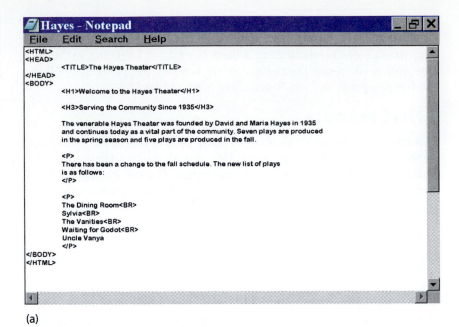

(a)

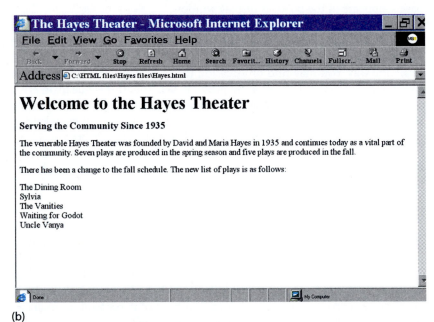

(b)

Figure 3 Lists. HTML code for an unordered list. A retail music site might list, in no particular order, albums on special that day. The browser will produce an indented, bulleted list of the albums.

```
<UL>
<LI>Music Box, Maria Carey
<LI>Miracles, Kenny G
<LI>Superunknown, Soundgarden
<LI>Q's Jook Joint, Quincy Jones
<LI>Blue, LeAnn Rimes
</UL>
```

Style Tags

A popular option is style tags, logical and physical. Logical tags are related to the fact that different browsers are written by different people who have different ideas about how things should be done. In fact, you can submit the same HTML code to different browsers and see slightly different browser displays of the page. (This becomes more obvious with more complex pages.) **Logical style tags** leave it up to a browser to display text in its own way. The **emphasis tags,** <EM> and </EM>, with the text to be highlighted between them, will usually display italics. The **strong emphasis tag** pair, <STRONG> and </STRONG>, will likely display the text between the tags as boldface.

However, most people prefer to use **physical style tags,** which tell a browser exactly how to display the text. Physical style tags are easy to use, and

GETTING PRACTICAL

SO YOU WANT TO BE A WEBMASTER

Generally speaking, a webmaster, as the name indicates, is a person who makes and takes care of web sites. Some students enjoy making web pages and wonder if they could do so for a living. Here is some information about what it takes. Many webmasters are freelancers, offering their services to all comers. Many more are in the employ of corporations or organizations that need an ongoing presence to maintain their web sites.

Jack of All Trades

Historically, webmasters have been multitalented and have performed a variety of tasks, being responsible for graphics design, site content, and site maintenance. But this is changing, as the sheer complexity of Web-related tasks overwhelms organizations. As job assignments become more specific, new job titles are emerging: web site developer, web content author, media integrator, web sales manager, director of electronic commerce,

extranet database specialist, and so on.

Many webmasters are self-taught or have learned much of what they know on the job. But that is changing too, as webmasters seek more formal training and even certification.

Certification

How does a company distinguish webmaster wannabes from the independent contractors who

can really do the job? Unfortunately, some businesses have used hired guns who can talk the talk but cannot perform adequately. Webmasters too have to face the problem of unqualified folks in their ranks. The solution is certification.

Certification is offered by the Association of Web Professionals. The association offers study programs and also prepares and administers tests that lead to the *Certified Web Technician* designation. Candidates must agree to abide by a code of ethics. Supported by Microsoft, IBM, and other industry heavyweights, the certificate sets the standards for competence and professionalism

for Web professionals. Individuals who gain the certificate increase their skill levels, achieve a recognized set of competencies, and increase their credibility with employers.

Among other skills, a certified web technician can connect a local area network to the Internet, troubleshoot client HTML pages, analyze network traffic to the client site, implement security features, and set up and maintain server hardware and software.

Webmasters are not legally bound to be certified. But they do need to join the Association of Web Professionals in order to earn the certificate. Candidates are not required to take the AWP's program of courses before testing; other programs and even self-study courses are available. Finally, the association offers a maintenance program, with continued education as deemed appropriate.

---

they work with most browsers. Some commonly used physical tag pairs are the **italic tag** pair, <I> and </I>, and the **boldface tag** pair, <B> and </B>. Another popular style tag pair is the **center tag** pair, <CENTER> and </CENTER>, for horizontal centering.

Enhancing the First Example

Returning to our first example, you can see some changes in the HTML code in Figure 4a. From top to bottom, the first heading has been centered, the second heading has been centered and made italic, and the plays have been put in an unordered list and also made boldface. Notice that both the paragraph tags and the break tags were removed from the group of plays when it

Automatic Copyright

Viewers sometimes assume that material on Internet sites is not copyrighted if they do not see a specific notice of copyright. They may conclude that, ethically, it is permissible to help themselves. Not so. Copyrighted material no longer needs to include notice of copyright by use of © or even the word "copyright." Copyright protection exists from the time the work is created in fixed form. That is, no one needs to include copyright warnings in order to be protected from predators; the notices you see on Internet sites are just reminders.

was made into a list. The new code has been saved (don't forget to save) before being submitted to the browser, which now shows the altered page shown in Figure 4b.

Adding Images

Few web sites offer only text. In fact, most are loaded with graphic images. But notice that sophisticated sites use graphics judiciously: They may be appropriate and attractive, but they are probably not enormous. This is

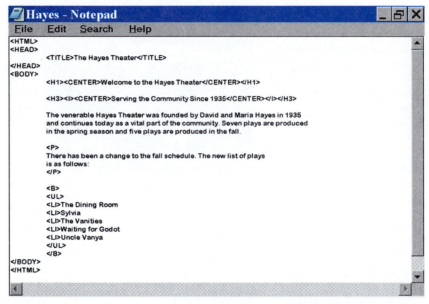

(a)

Figure 4 Altered HTML code and changed page. (a) The original code from Figure 2 has been changed to center the headings, make the second heading italic, and put the plays in a boldface unordered list. (b) The changed page.

(b)

because large graphics take too long to download, and visitors to the site get tired of waiting. But you certainly want images of some kind on your page, so we will cover the basics here.

The Resumé Example

The next HTML example will produce a resumé for a student majoring in computer science. He has written some web pages and is looking for a student internship at an Internet-related company. The HTML to create that page includes tags you already know and also image and link tags, the next two topics. You can preview the HTML for the resumé in Figure 5a and see the resumé page in Figure 5b.

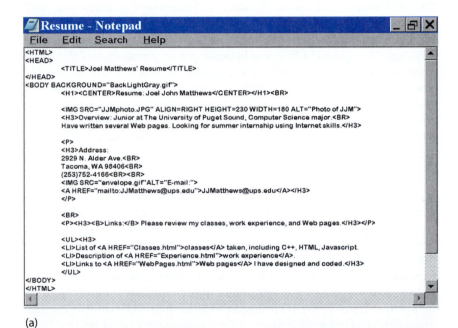

(a)

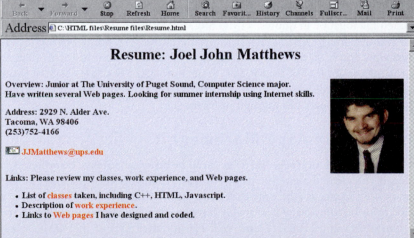

Figure 5 HTML code and the resulting resumé page. (a) The HTML code includes image and link tags. (b) This first page of the resumé is deliberately short because it includes links to more detailed information, such as classes and work experience.

(b)

Figure 6 Images and icons.
Thousands of images are available on the Web. The images shown here were downloaded from various web pages that offer them for free.

InfoBit

A GIF file can be small and loads more quickly, but allows a relatively small range of colors. The millions of colors used by JPEGs are needed for accurate color rendition.

InfoBit

If you depend on a clickable image map for navigating your site, consider including a series of textual links across the bottom of the page too. This lets users who may have difficulty loading the images navigate your page successfully, and adds very little time and effort to your page authoring.

Obtaining Images

There are several ways to obtain images to use on a web page. An easy way is to download them from a site that offers free images (Figure 6). You could even pay for the use of images offered on various professional photography sites on the Web; however, you cannot help yourself to copyrighted images. You can scan photographs or anything else (assuming that you own the item or have obtained permission) on paper to a disk file or ask a copy center to perform this service for you. If you wish to create original graphics, several software packages are available for this purpose.

Image File Formats

The file formats most commonly used for images on the Internet are **GIF** (pronounced "jif"), for **Graphic Interchange Format,** and **JPG** ("J peg"), for **Joint Photographic Experts Group.** These two formats are accepted by most browsers. The specific differences between the two formats and the situations that favor one over another are beyond the scope of this discussion; however, as a general rule of thumb, GIFs are for graphics and JPGs are for photographs. It is likely, however, that, because of patent problems, GIF files will be replaced by **PNG** ("ping"), for **Portable Network Graphics,** files. The photograph shown in Figure 5b was scanned to JPG format.

The Image Tag

An image that is referenced right in the HTML code and whose file is loaded with the HTML code is called an **inline image.** An image can be included in a page by using the single **image tag,** <IMG>. But there is something new here: **attributes** associated with the tag. Within the image tag you must use the attribute SRC, which stands for *source,* that is, the location of the image to be used. The most efficient location for the graphic is in a nearby file; for testing purposes, it is easiest if the file is in the same directory—folder—as the file that contains the HTML code. Professionals who handle sites with multiple images often place all images in a subdirectory called Images. Thus, unlike the text we used for pages in earlier examples, images are not embedded in the HTML code; only the reference to an image is in the code—the tag and the name of the file that holds the image.

The SRC attribute must be completely inside the image tag, and its associated file must be in quotes: <IMG SRC="JJMphoto.JPG">.

Another image attribute is ALT, for alternative text. Some browsers cannot view graphics, and some users (to save time) choose to turn off their browser's graphics capability. For these users, ALT includes text of your choosing that will be seen instead of the image. Note the alternative text for Joel John Matthews' photograph in Figure 5a.

Image Sizing and Placement

How big should an image be? This could be an exact science, but often it is not. If you created a graphic using software, then you know its exact height and width in pixels (the dots that make up the image). If you do not have this information, you will probably have to do a little experimenting to see what looks right. HEIGHT and WIDTH are attributes of the <IMG> tag; you can see them used in Figure 5a for JJMphoto.JPG. Most browsers will stretch the image to make it fit the height and width specified.

Placing an image may be easy or may take some experimenting. The <IMG> tag has an attribute called ALIGN, which lets you align the text with an adjacent image at the top (TOP), middle (MIDDLE), bottom (BOTTOM), or places in between. The default is that the text will be aligned with the bottom of the image. If you wanted to place an image so that the adjacent text runs next to the top of the image, you would use

    <IMG SRC="JJMphoto.JPG" ALIGN=TOP>

You can also set ALIGN to RIGHT (placing the image next to the right margin) or LEFT. Other <IMG> attributes that can help place an image are HSPACE and VSPACE, which force horizontal and vertical spacing, respectively.

Adding Links

The power of the Internet is in links: You can link to any other site, and anyone else can link to yours. Further, links can be used to divide a page into more manageable pieces, with the first page linking to lower levels of information; those pages, in turn, can also link to lower levels. In the resumé example, for instance, instead of having one long page, we use an initial page, short and to the point, with links to other topics of interest: classes, work experience, and links to web pages (Figure 5b).

The Anchor Tag

Links are accomplished by using the **anchor tag** pair, <A> and </A>. The key attribute of the anchor tag is HREF, which indicates a link destination. The anchor tag also includes the name of the word or words—the **hypertext**—that will be clicked to initiate the move to the new site. The format to link to another web page looks like this:

    <A HREF="URL">Name</A>

Here, URL is replaced by the address of the page destination. *Name* refers to the highlighted word that you want the user to click on. For example, the anchor

    <A HREF="http://www.kodak.com">Kodak</A>

links to the Kodak site, as indicated by its URL. On the page, a user would click the word *Kodak,* as indicated by the name after the URL.

In Figure 5b, note that, in the bulleted list at the bottom, the words *classes, work experience,* and *Web pages* are highlighted in red, indicating that they are links that can be clicked. Referring to the corresponding code in Figure 5a, note that the anchor tags use those words as the names in the anchors. The URLs shown in those same code lines refer to files that are in the same directory as the HTML file for the original page. It is beyond our scope to show those files or their corresponding pages.

Final Touches to the Resumé

Two additions will be made to make Joel's resumé a more polished product. The first is essential: If a potential employer found Joel's resumé on the Internet, the employer should be able to contact him via the Internet by

---

Home Page Snoops

Notice that this little item is not accompanied by a real family photo; we do not want to make things worse than they already are. "Click my picture to find out more about me." The plain fact is that people are abandoning privacy on their own web pages. Pictures of children, for example, provided by proud parents, can give valuable information, starting with appearance and names, that might be used to harm a child.

Identity thieves, who would like to pose as you and run up a mountain of debt in your name, can often find name, birth date, occupation, degrees, and maybe even your address. Think about it. A name, birth date, and birthplace will get a birth certificate. A driver's license, the de facto identifier, is not far behind, and it unlocks the keys to credit cards.

Suppose you are interested in genealogy and include part of the family tree on your site. So there is *mother's maiden name,* right? Bingo! That is a major identifier used by banks and other security-conscious organizations. You just compromised your bank account. Enough said.

InfoBit

Set up your page to allow text-only browsing, too. Although the majority of Internet surfers are equipped with graphical browsers such as Internet Explorer and Netscape, there are still millions of users who have only textual browsers such as Lynx, which is still quite popular in older public libraries. As one advocate of increased text and decreased graphics puts it: "Dare to be dull."

Color	Hexadecimal
Red	FF0000
Green	00FF00
Blue	0000FF
Black	000000
Dusty Rose	856363
Brass	B5A642
Cyan	00FFFF
Bronze	8C7723
Orange	FF7F00
Midnight Blue	2F2F4F
Neon Blue	4D4DFF
Violet	4F2F4F
Forest Green	238E23
Salmon	6F4242
Scarlet	8C1717
Khaki	9F9F5F
Pink	BC8F8F
Goldenrod	DBDB70
Yellow	FFFF00
Magenta	FF00FF
White	FFFFFF
Firebrick	8E2323
Cadet Blue	5F9F9F
Silver	E6E8FA

Figure 7 Background color digits. Full color charts, showing a swatch of color that matches a hexadecimal combination, can be found on several web sites.

Figure 8 Background graphics. These samples are graphics that can be tiled—moved across and down the screen—to fill in the complete background on a web page. The background on the bottom is used in the resumé example, Figure 5.

using e-mail. The anchor tag and the HREF attribute can be used to reference the e-mail protocol as follows:

<A HREF="mailto:e-mail address">name</A>

As you can see in Figure 5a, the e-mail address for Joel has been filled in as *JJMatthews@ups.edu;* he also uses the e-mail address as the name that will be printed on the page. We also used the <IMG> tag to sneak in a tiny letter icon just before the e-mail address.

One more thing. **Background** refers to the screen appearance behind the text and images. Rather than accepting a plain background, default white or gray in most browsers, we can take control and give a page a background with color or perhaps even texture. Backgrounds are added using an attribute of the <BODY> tag. One possibility is to use the attribute BGCOLOR with a six-digit hexadecimal code that signifies the desired background color, two digits each for red, green, and blue. For example, BGCOLOR= #FF0000 gives a red background. See Figure 7 for other possibilities.

We chose instead to use the attribute BACKGROUND, which uses a graphic that is a small square that is **tiled** by the browser—spread down and across the screen to make a complete background (Figure 8). In the resumé code, we told the browser to use a textured graphic file, BackLightGray.gif, to create the tiled background. Note the <BODY> tag in Figure 5a.

Authoring Software

A category of software, generally referred to as **authoring software,** lets you make a web page without having any knowledge of HTML; the software converts your specifications to HTML for you. Authoring software offers sufficient ease of use that the greenest user can make a simple web page with only minimum assistance. You could think of authoring software as an extra layer that takes care of the details for you.

One group that welcomes authoring software is office workers, who traditionally have written text for the company web site and handed it off to a worker who maintains the web site; that person then has typically coded it in HTML and included it on the web site. Authoring software lets users write their content themselves, using familiar software such as word processing or spreadsheet programs, and then add that content themselves to the appropriate company web site.

Although lauded for its access for beginners, authoring software is, at the same time, powerful enough for professional web designers. A notable feature is that the HTML to perform some obscure function can be inserted in the middle of the HTML generated by the authoring software. However, professionals may depend more heavily on HTML and use authoring software in a lesser role.

We will use the authoring software called FrontPage 2000 to show what you can do with this type of software. FrontPage 2000 was designed to interface smoothly with the Office 2000 suite; it is included with the premium version of Office 2000 but can be purchased separately. Although it is beyond the scope of this book to give complete hands-on detail, we can demonstrate the power of FrontPage with a few examples you can reproduce on a computer, and perhaps vary to your own taste, as we proceed.

Getting Started in FrontPage

When you launch the FrontPage program, an almost empty screen appears (Figure 9a). The menus and toolbars across the top of the FrontPage screen are similar to those of Microsoft Office 2000 programs such as Word and Excel. This is deliberate, to give users the same "look and feel" with which they already may be comfortable.

Initially, the only other item on the screen is a set of buttons along the left side under Views. These buttons provide different ways of looking at your web site so you can manage it conveniently. We will describe the effects of these buttons shortly, as soon as we have added some data to make them meaningful.

FrontPage calls a web site a web; a **web** is a set of related web pages. Although you can override it if you wish, webs and their pages are stored by default in the folder called My Webs. You need to start the process by creating a web. This is done by clicking New under the File menu, and then Web.

Figure 9 Getting started with a new web and new page. (a) Initial screen for FrontPage software. (b) There are many sophisticated offerings here to create a new web. We will choose Empty Web. The image shown here, by the way, is merely a window on a small part of the FrontPage screen; we have enlarged it to make it readable. (c) The list of files for the new web shows in the center frame. Notice that the name of the web—HayesWeb—now shows at the top of the screen. The still-blank space to the right will be where the new page goes. (d) A new page has been invoked. FrontPage gives it a temporary name (new_page_1.htm); we will name it as soon as we save the data in the page.

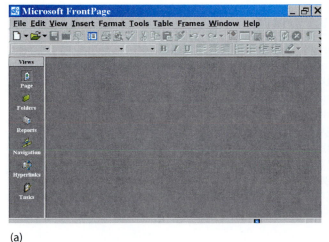

(a)

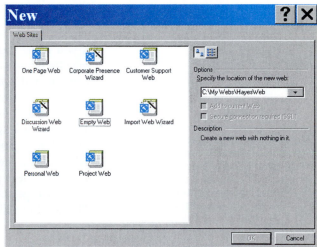

(b)

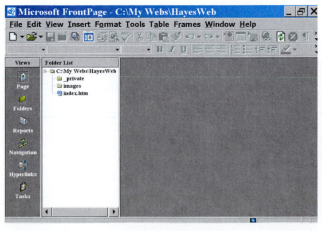

(c)

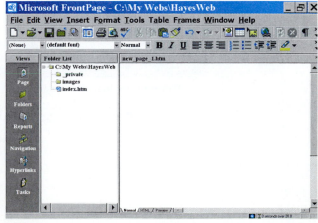

(d)

Figure 10 Hayes page and results in browser. (a) This is the Hayes Theater page, typed as you see it in FrontPage. (b) This is the preview of the Hayes page results as shown in the browser, that is, how it will look as a web page. Notice that it looks pretty much the same as the page prepared in FrontPage, that is, WYSIWYG: What You See Is What You Get.

(*Note:* Using the submenu New under the File menu often is preferable to using the New button  on the standard toolbar because the submenu New offers many options.)

A new window temporarily overlays the FrontPage screen; it shows different types of webs (Figure 9b). Now, recall that authoring software serves many audiences. Most of the webs here, such as Discussion Web Wizard, are for users with relatively complex needs and, presumably, more expertise than we have yet developed. Yet we do not want to be limited to something as simple as a one-page web, so we will select Empty Web. But first we need to give the new web a name. Since we will start with the Hayes Theater example, we will name it HayesWeb. Now double-click Empty Web and see the change on the FrontPage screen (Figure 9c). The center of the screen holds folders; you can see the new HayesWeb and some files under it. We will be adding pages to HayesWeb and they will show up under Folders too.

The still-blank part of the screen, to the right, is where a new page will be built. On this occasion, a plain page will do, so we merely click the New button on the standard toolbar (Figure 9d). Now we are ready to write a web page. Notice, as we begin, that the activated button under Views, on the left, indicates that we are in **Page view**; that is, a page in progress is the topic of the rightmost part of the screen.

FrontPage WYSIWYG

If you made your way through the HTML tags earlier in the chapter, you may be pleased to see that there are no such devices in FrontPage; instead you proceed with **WYSIWYG** (pronounced "Wizzy wig"), an acronym meaning *what you see is what you get*. Consider the Hayes Theater example, whose desired results, produced directly by HTML code, are shown in Figure 4b. No knowledge of HTML is needed to produce the same results using FrontPage; simply take the WYSIWYG approach: Key the Hayes title and other lines in the sizes you want, and use bullets for the list of plays (Figure 10a). Save the page as Hayes_main. You need to give the page a title, so right-click the page, then left-click Page Properties and fill in the title as The Hayes Theater. Now click the Preview button on the toolbar to see the web

(a)

(b)

page results in the browser, that is, the way it will look as a web page (Figure 10b). Notice that the title, The Hayes Theater, is across the top of the screen.

Navigation and Other Views

We will use the Hayes Theater example to add some links, clickable references to other web pages. We will add three subpages, each of which will be linked to from the Hayes_main page. The subpages are the Calendar, First-Nighters, and Support. The order of business is this: Create the subpages, set up the navigation structure showing how the subpages relate to the main page, and then add the links from the main page to the subpages.

The three subpages can be made as just skeleton pages for our purposes; once saved they show up as new pages under the HayesWeb folder. We will be sure to give them titles. Now that we have developed a set of related pages, we need to set up the **Navigation view** of the web site, the structure showing the relationships among the pages. Click the Navigation button under Views, then use your mouse under Folders to drag to the right frame first the Hayes_main page, and then (under it) the pages to which it links; as you drag the subpages into place, the connecting lines will form automatically (Figure 11). The names of the boxes in the Navigation view are the ones that were used as titles for the pages. The Navigation view is useful both for seeing the structure of a web site and as a prerequisite for using certain other features.

While we are at it, note the other views, as applied to this web (Figure 12). **Folders view** lists the files in more detail. **Reports view** gives detailed information about the site, which would be of interest to someone managing a site, especially a complex one. The **Hyperlinks view** gives a graphic picture of link relationships. In the HayesWeb the Hyperlinks view is identical to the Navigation view, but this is not always true; sometimes links go to other places on the same page or to pages that are totally separate from this web. The **Tasks view** shows a list of items that should be completed on the web and who is responsible. We have added a couple of items just so you can see what it might look like. But the value of the Tasks view is for collaboration: When several people are working together on a complex site, the Tasks view is one of their communication vehicles.

The Deadly Sins

In *Creating Killer Web Sites,* a book aimed at the design aspects of a web site, author David Siegel sets forth a list of "deadly sins," the most egregious offenses to be found on Web pages. The list of sins:

- **Blank line paragraph separators.** Indicate a new paragraph with an indentation, just as in written prose. Save the white space for separating sections.
- **Horizontal rules.** Horizontal line dividers, even if clever, are barriers that take up space and interrupt the natural flow of the page. You will not see them on well-designed sites.
- **Cluttered backgrounds.** Backgrounds composed of images interfere with the readability of the text superimposed on it. Keep it simple; a solid color background is best.
- **Slow loading.** Sites that take seemingly forever to load deter repeat visits. Keep most pages on the site under 30K bytes.

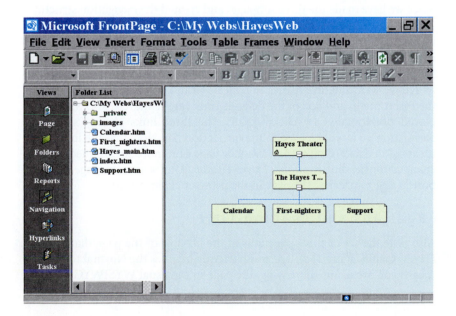

Figure 11 Navigation view. Note the activated Navigation button under Views. This causes the view of the relationship between the pages in HayesWeb.

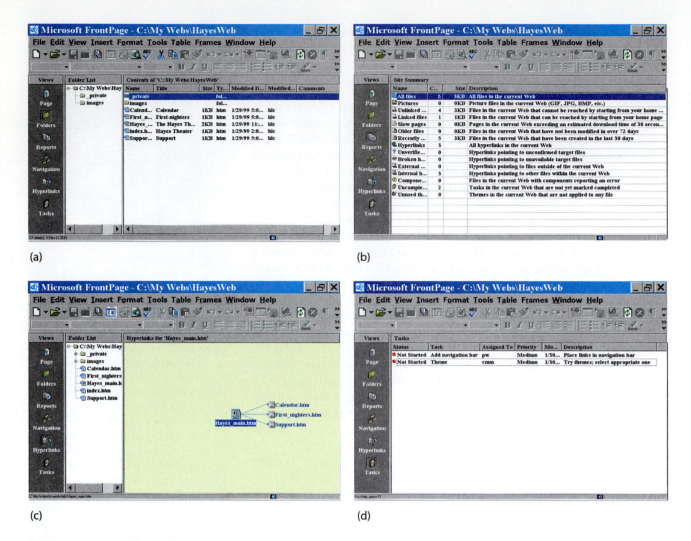

(a)

(b)

(c)

(d)

Figure 12 Other views. Each view reveals a different aspect of a web. Shown here, for HayesWeb, are (a) Folders view, (b) Reports view, (c) Hyperlinks view, and (d) Tasks view.

Adding Links in FrontPage

Since we have made the three subpages and created the navigation structure, we now are ready to add the links. Re-open Hayes_main. We could make individual links using the Hyperlink button 🔘 on the standard toolbar, but it is preferable to use a **Navigation bar** because this allows other options, such as displaying attractive buttons for links. Click on the Hayes_main page where we want the link names to appear. Next, click Navigation Bar under the Insert menu and accept the defaults (links are "children" and will be displayed horizontally) by clicking OK. The three links already set up in Navigation view will be used in the navigation bar. Note that the links show up as colored text (Figure 13a). To make page a bit more streamlined we have changed the heading to simply *Hayes Theater*. After saving the page, click the button 🔘 to preview the page in the browser (Figure 13b).

Page Tabs and Loading Time

Also note the set of three **page tabs** at the bottom of the page that displays Hayes_main (Figure 13a). The one currently in use is the **Normal tab,** which means you are using, or viewing, the page in the usual WYSIWYG mode. If

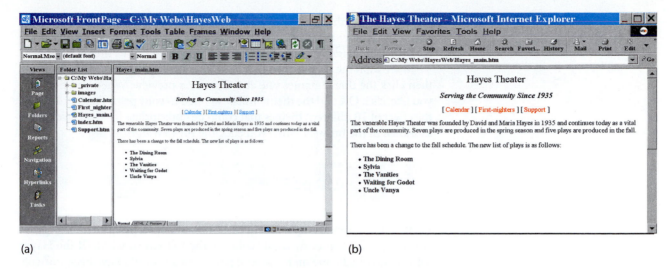

(a)   (b)

Figure 13 Hayes page with links. (a) The colored text indicates that Calendar, First-Nighters, and Support are hyperlinks to subpages. (b) The resulting page as shown in the browser.

you clicked the **HTML tab** you would see the HTML version of Hayes_main, which is generated automatically from the WYSIWYG version by the FrontPage software. This is convenient for knowledgeable users who want to add some lines in HTML to an existing page. The **Preview tab** lets you see how the page will look when it is displayed in the browser. When you are working on a page, it is handy to be able to switch back and forth to see the effects on the displayed page as you make changes.

There is one more important item at the bottom of the page. Look to the lower right to **estimated loading time.** Since it is desirable to keep loading time low so users do not get tired of waiting for the page to show up on their screens, this figure is very important, especially in professional web sites. The time in Figure 13a says (not surprisingly) that this simple page loads in 0 seconds using a 56K modem; the slot can be changed to show different modem speeds.

Themes

You can enhance the appearance of a page in a number of ways. As you can in just about any software, you can vary the font, size, and color of text. Another do-it-yourself option is to right-click the page, left-click Page Properties, and select a background color and margins. You can invoke Bullets under the Format menu and introduce your own pictures to be used as bullets. There are many other possibilities. Or . . . you can do it the easy way and select a preformatted theme for the entire page from the 60 or so offered by FrontPage.

A **theme** is a unified set of design elements and color schemes that you can apply to a page to give it a consistent and attractive appearance. Design elements include background, fonts, banners, bullets, and link buttons. Some theme names are targeted to certain audiences; examples are Construction Zone (barbed-wire fence), Blueprint (graph paper), Automotive (odometers), and Nature (leaves).

To take advantage of a theme, we will add a **banner,** a sort of pictorial heading. To add a banner to the Hayes page, click on the page near the top line (to indicate the location where we want the banner to be inserted), then click Page Banner under the Insert menu and insert the banner text. There is no noticeable evidence that a banner has been added until a theme is applied.

To see what the themes look like, click Theme under the Format menu and then click the theme names one at a time for a preview. When you find one you like, click OK and the theme will be applied to your page. Figure 14 shows the effect of 10 different themes that could be appropriate for the Hayes page, as shown in the browser when you click the preview button   .

Page Templates

We used the Hayes example first because it was simple. But it has one big disadvantage: The text body is one column, the full screen width. If the Hayes information had gone on for several paragraphs it would have been difficult to read. The eyes cannot easily scan across a wide area. Newspaper people know this, which is why they print everything in narrow columns. Even books have generous margins so that the body of the text is not too wide for comfortable reading. It is desirable to offer similar comforts for the readers of your web page.

Page Template Selections

It is certainly possible to write a web page placing text in columns. But FrontPage makes the exercise easier by offering **page templates,** predesigned pages that can contain page settings, formatting, and page elements. Templates can handle many features in addition to columns. There are templates for table of contents, searches, guest book, bibliography, frequently asked questions, forms for visitors and customers to fill out, and, of course, two-column and three-column pages. But the most attractive are those that include images. As with other features, there are procedures to add images to a page. But it is much easier to have an image already in place and just replace it with your own.

By selecting New under the File menu, then Page, you will see a window offering several choices of templates for your web page (Figure 15). Click

Figure 14 Themes. Compare the plain version of the Hayes main page with possible themes, named by FrontPage as (a) Network Blitz, and (b) Postmodern.

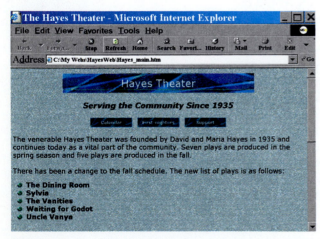

(a)

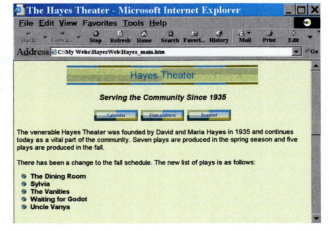

(b)

once on a selection to get a general idea, shown in the lower right corner of the screen, what the page template will look like; the example here shows a one-column body with contents on the left and an image at the top. If you double-click a selection it will then appear in Page view and you can begin to modify it for your own purposes. Figure 16 shows several page templates.

Page Template Example

We will use a page template, the one shown in Figure 16d, to quickly create a site about the orca, a type of sea mammal. We chose this particular template because it has elements that fit our needs: a commanding title; a narrow, readable text body in the center; a place on the right for an orca image and related text; and preset link text locations on the left that we can use to go to subpages about orcas.

Set Up Web, Page Template, Subpages   We need to start by making a new web, which we will call OrcaWeb, then plan the subpages and make at least skeletons of them on plain pages so that they can be linkable. The subpages will be for orca facts, orca location maps, photo gallery, and orca links. These tasks, making the new web and subpages, are done using methods similar to those described earlier in the chapter for the Hayes FrontPage example. Now we use the page template shown in Figure 16d for the main orca page. Click New under the File menu, then Page, and then double-click the template called "one-column body with two sidebars." This page will be saved as Orca_main. Once we have done this much, our page will look like Figure 17a. We also set up the navigation structure for OrcaWeb, with Orca_main at the top and all others as subpages.

Replace Text   On the Orca_main page, as shown in Figure 17a, think of the heading, sunflower photo, crazy text, and links text as placeholders. They are nicely aligned but the content is meaningless and temporary. We will write our own text over the placeholder text and insert a picture right over the

Critical Thinking

What criteria are appropriate for evaluating a web page? Would this vary by kind of page, say business or e-commerce versus personal? (This is really open-ended, but some possible criteria are aesthetic and artistic, content, and technical. Examples of artistic criteria include use of color, fonts, original artwork, and overall "impact." Criteria for content might be amount of factual content, accuracy and references, writing style, and frequency of updating. Technical criteria include load time, ease of navigation, good use of frames, and appropriate "add-ons" such as Java applets and e-mail forms.)

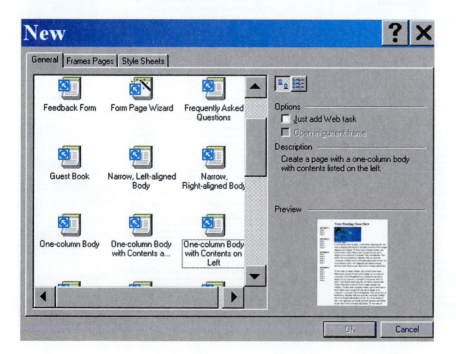

Figure 15 Page template selections. FrontPage offers several templates for a web page. Click once on a selection to get a general idea, shown in the lower-right corner of the screen, of what the page template will look like; the example here shows a one-column body with contents on the left. If you double-click a selection, it will then appear in your page.

placeholder photo. You can look ahead to Figure 17b to see the direction we are heading. To type new text, position the cursor appropriately on the page and type the new text in overtype mode, or else delete the unwanted text and replace it as you go along. Another option is to copy text from some other source to the Orca_main page. In this manner, replace the text in the header, the main body, the photo caption, and the paragraph under the photo.

Add Links   Next, each link will be set up individually. Click on one of the link-text locations, then click the Hyperlink button [icon] on the standard toolbar. When offered a list of files, click the matching saved-page file, and then click OK. For example, the first link is to be *Orca facts*. We click the location for that link, the top one, and then the Hyperlink button [icon] , and, given a list of file names, click on *Orca facts.htm*. The page title, Orca facts, shows up as the link, in underlined, colored text. (After each link is created, simply delete any remaining placeholder link text).

Replace Image   Now we are ready to replace the sunflower picture with an orca photo. Any images used with a web page need to be stored with other files that belong to the web. We will move the photo called *orca closeup.jpg* to

Figure 16 Sample page templates. FrontPage offers over two dozen page templates, formats already set up so that you can plug in your own data. The templates shown here are called (a) narrow left-aligned body, (b) one-column body with contents and sidebar, (c) narrow right-aligned body, and (d) one-column body with two sidebars. And, by the way, just what is that language? Latin? Not really.

(a)

(b)

(c)

(d)

MAKING THE RIGHT CONNECTIONS

GOT APPLETS?

Applets are tiny programs, written in the Java language from Sun Microsystems. Well, they are not so tiny any more. Applets were originally quite simple, perhaps an opening and closing mailbox to draw attention to e-mail. But, as these samples show, applets have moved uptown. Applets can wiggle, bounce, sing, dance, reverse direction, shimmer, fade, explode, or do anything else a Java programmer can dream up. Both visual and audio effects are possible. In the examples shown here, clockwise from top left, the Rubik's cube can be rotated and altered by dragging a mouse over it, the leopard runs, the shapes with Feedback quickly change positions to draw attention, the states and capitals can be rotated and matched, the colorful design can be manipulated with the buttons in the lower left, the goldfish moves around the bowl to wherever the mouse moves the pointer, and, most amazing of all, balloons float and move as the train passes by below.

Most browsers today are Java-compatible. When a browser accesses a Java-powered page, applets are copied to the browser's computer and executed there. This local execution makes possible a high level of Web interaction and multimedia effects, unhampered by HTML restrictions or network bandwidth.

If you would like to add applets to your web site, plenty are available free; just use a search engine to find them on the Web and follow instructions to download the code. If you would like to learn to write your own Java applets, introductions and tutorials are available on several web sites.

the Images folder under OrcaWeb, being sure to click Refresh under the View menu so that the addition of the photo will be reflected under Folders. We open the Images folder under Folders to be sure it is there. Now we click the sunflower image on Orca_main, click the button on the standard toolbar to Insert Picture from File ![icon], and then, when offered a list of photo file names, double-click on *orca-closeup.jpg*. We save the page. The changes to the page can be seen in Figure 17b.

The results are a bit unbalanced, so we enlarge both the main text body and the links text, and also boldface the links text. The result, as shown in the browser, is seen in Figure 18. This is the page a user would see first on the web site, the home page. A click on any of the links would cause the appropriate subpage to show up on the screen, replacing the home page. The subpages would have links letting a user return to the home page.

Frames

Rather than having all information sort of loosely assembled across a web page, you can divide the page up into a series of **frames**, rectangular areas that hold separate pages. A collection of frames displayed in a single page is

Critical Thinking

How would you divide up labor of creating web page. (Content, design, text, graphics, testing, publicity, and so forth. But first, you need to know what client or intended audience wants.)

Group Work

One way of presenting the vast content of the Web in terms understandable to students is to focus small teams on evaluating examples of different kinds of web sites. If you like, one team can compare personal web sites, another online news and magazines, a third e-commerce, entertainment and so forth. Each team is to evaluate at least three sites, compare notes, look for features, strengths, weaknesses by category. You may wish to emphasize to students that they should agree within the team and document the criteria used.

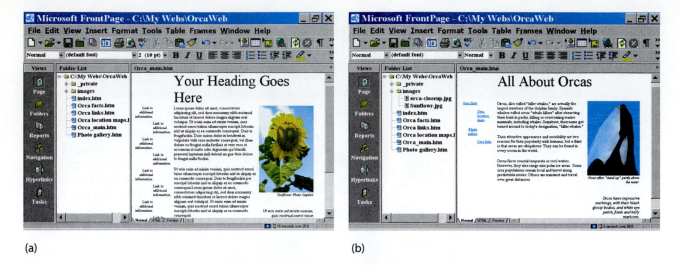

(a)   (b)

Figure 17 Template and orca page. (a) The template shown here has "placehold-ers" for text, an image, and text for links. (b) The Orca_main page after the tem-plate text, image, and text for links have been replaced with orca data.

Group Work

Even if you don't have classroom Internet access, students may find it useful to build model web pages on lab or stand-alone personal computers. If you elect to try this activity, you can form teams and assign roles. (Depending on team composition and interests, possible roles include graphic designer, technician, writer, producer, and so forth.) Target web pages include ones for your school, or your department, or a local charity or community organization.

called a **frameset.** Before creating a frameset, we will make the pages that will go into the frames. But first let us consider the possibilities.

Frame Templates

When you select New under the File menu, then Page, then choose the tab Frames, you will see a window with several frame templates (Figure 19). You can click a template to see a preview of what it will look like in the lower-

Figure 19 New frames pages. By selecting New under the File menu, then Page, and then clicking the Frames tab, you can see several choices of frame templates for your page. Click once on a selection to get a general idea, shown in the lower-right corner of the screen, of what the frames will look like; the example here shows two frames, one for a footer. If you double-click a selection, it will then appear in your page.

Figure 18 Orca page. This is the orca page as shown in the browser, the home page that a user would see.

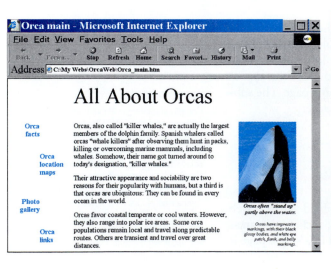

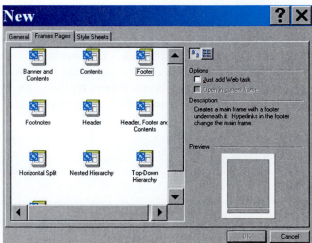

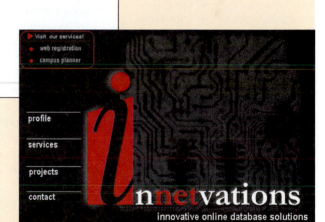

2000 and Beyond

FLEXIBLE HOURS, EARN BIG $$$!

BIG GREEN
WEB DESIGN

Big Green Web Design will provide a professional, cost-effective solution to your business or personal website needs.

Services   Pricing   Portfolio
                  Contact Us

See Our Town   The TownNH Network   NH Web Sites
Internet services by Communications 4NH

Big Green, whose web site is shown here, is run by Dartmouth College student Steve Margoun. He designs and builds web sites for people in the community, using the fees to supplement his tuition. On the opposite coast, Stanford students Esteban Morales and Luis Arellano are running their own business, Innetvations,

There are many time-honored ways to work your way through college, from flipping burgers to clerking to working in the college library. These jobs tend to have two disadvantages in common: a fixed schedule and low pay. But the job picture is changing for some students, and it involves what may be the preferred job of the future: writing web pages.

Visit our services!
web registration
campus planner

profile

services

projects

contact

innetvations
innovative online database solutions

whose site is shown here. Innetvations' service uses a database to handle and track online reservations for large conferences. In both situations, the students are earning money and also developing valuable business skills.

In his freshman year at Harvard, golfer Amar Goel decided to write a web page to sell customized golf clubs at a discount. He combined his own economics and computer science skills with the graphics skills of Edwin Chong, a Dartmouth student, to produce the sophisticated Chipshot page shown here.

InfoBit

Afraid people won't be able to find your newly created pages? If you wait long enough, usually two weeks to a month, the roving "spiders" (software) run by the search engine providers likely will find and index your page. If you are impatient, most of the major search engines like Metacrawler, AltaVista and Lycos will let you add your web page to their engines just by clicking on a link and typing your URL.

Critical Thinking

Have students examine several web pages using frames. What do you see as the Pros and Cons of frames? (Pros: No need to add navigation buttons on every page you make. Images in a frame only have to load once. It is easy to indicate visually where the user is in your pages. Cons: Older browsers may not support frames. Frames take longer to load than simpler pages. Printing may not work as you expect since your browser may automatically select the navigation frame and not the frame you are reading when you print. Advertisements in frames can't be avoided; even scrolling down the page leaves the ad exposed.)

right corner of the window. If you double-click a template, it will appear in the usual page view and you can begin to work with it. You can take a closer look at some of the popular frame arrangements in Figure 20.

Some of the frame templates include a frame called **contents.** The contents frame contains links to subpages that will be shown, one at a time, in the **target** frame. That is, when a link is clicked from the content frame, its associated page shows up in the target frame. This kind of configuration is popular for many applications, such as a retail site showing types of products in the target frame from a list in the contents frame, or even a business delivering a report with a table of contents in the contents frame and the various report sections in the target frame.

Orca Redux

We will redo the orca example, with a few variations, using frames. Notice the different sets of frames shown in Figure 20. Most professionally-made sites, especially commercial sites, use frames. This fact may not be obvious because the sites often do not have borders around the frames. But once you are aware of frame configurations, such as those shown in Figure 20, it is easier to see how they have been used.

We will use the frame template called "Banner and Contents" for our orca example; we double-click that selection in the new frames page menu (Figure 19). The general shape of that template is shown in Figure 20a. The actual template—frames but no content—appears in page view (Figure 21a). (*Aside:* Figure 21 also shows the list of page files under Folders; we will talk about creating these pages momentarily.) We are aiming for a page that looks something like the result shown in Figure 21b. The top frame, called the banner frame, will contain a heading. The frame on the left is the contents frame; it will have six links: Orca facts, Orca maps, Orca tracking,

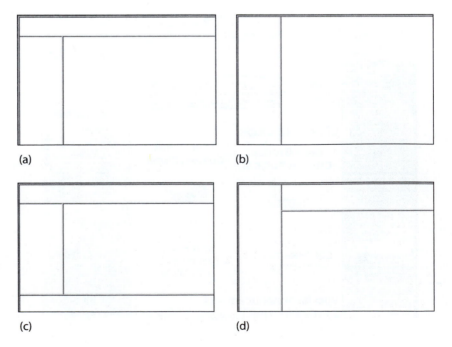

(a)

(b)

(c)

(d)

Figure 20 Sample frame configurations. Shown here are four possible frame configurations, referred to by FrontPage as (a) Banner and Contents; (b) Contents; (c) Header, Footer, and Contents; and (d) Nested Hierarchy. "Contents" is a reference to the content of the web site, with the content frame on the left having links to subpages that will show up, when their links are clicked, in the target frame on the right.

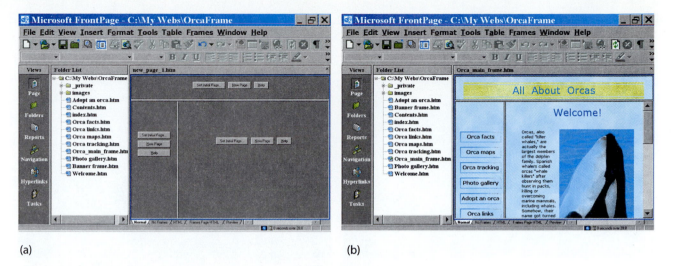

(a)

(b)

Figure 21 Frameset. A frameset holds several frames on the same page.
(a) This is the way the frameset template called "Banner and Contents" looks when first selected for use. The top frame is called the banner frame, the left frame is for contents, and the right frame is the target frame. When clicked, a link in the contents frame will cause the corresponding frame to appear in the target frame.
(b) This is the same frameset filled in with its initial pages. There are several steps to get from (a) to (b).

Photo gallery, Adopt an orca, and Orca links. Each of these links has a corresponding page that will show up in the target frame, to the right, when the link is clicked. The initial page in the target frame is the Welcome page, as shown in Figure 21b.

Keep in mind that each frame holds a separate page. Before the frames can be filled, the pages must be created. We will make one page each for the banner and contents frames. We will make seven pages for the target frame to the right, the initial Welcome page and the six pages—Orca facts, Orca maps, Orca tracking, Photo gallery, Adopt an orca, and Orca links—to which the contents frame links. Some of these pages are shown in Figure 22. Notice that they all look a bit alike; this is because they were each given the same theme, Clear Day, to promote a unified look.

We will not go into the details about how to make the pages, since the procedures are similar to what we discussed in the earlier examples. To summarize generally, the Welcome page was created with the "one-column body with two sidebars" page template (the link text was deleted), the contents page is just a plain new page with a vertical navigation bar (the links will show up as buttons, a look from the Clear Day theme), and all the other pages are plain pages to which content was added. One more thing: The banner page has a banner added to the text; its appearance is part of the Clear Day theme.

Adding Pages to the Frames

Look again at Figure 21a. This is the yet-unused frameset and we now have content—pages—to place in the frames. One way of doing so is to click a frame (its border will light up) and then click Frames Properties under the

InfoBit

Studies have shown that most people will wait only a short time for graphics to load on your page before switching away. In light of this, you should probably consider any image over 25KB too large. One alternative is to show small "thumbnail" preview images, and download the full image only when the user clicks on the preview.

InfoBit

One way of making your web page more interesting for Internet surfers is to provide a "freebie" on the page to draw interest. Examples include free "wallpaper" images, links to free games, free sewing patterns, a joke of the day, recipes, quotations, and so on.

InfoBit

Although not covered in the chapter, it is worth noting that tables allow users to organize ideas and information on a page almost like a spreadsheet. Almost all browsers support tables, and they are easy to create.

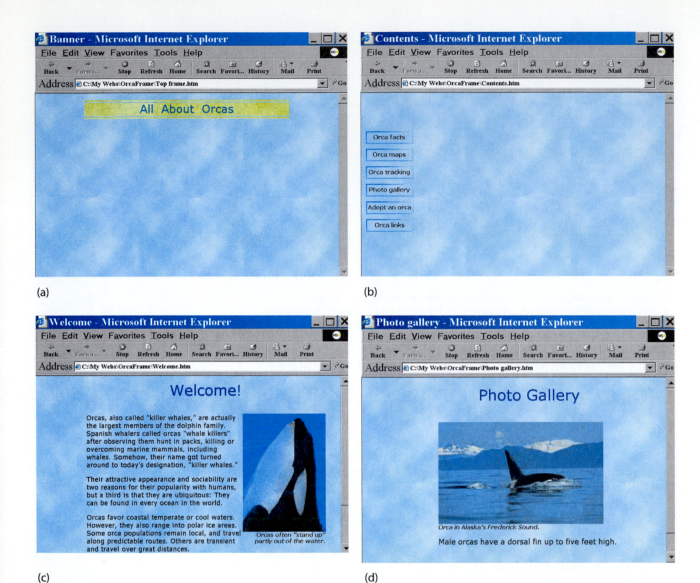

(a)

(b)

(c)

(d)

Figure 22 Pages to be used in the frameset. Before a frameset can be put together, at least the initial page for each frame must be created. Shown here are some of the pages: (a) banner, (b) contents, (c) Welcome, and (d) Photo gallery.

Frames menu. Within the Frames Properties window you will be able to select the file name of the initial page for the frame, change the width of the frame margins (or accept the defaults), and decide whether scroll bars are needed for the frame (If Needed, Never, or Always). In the orca example, scroll bars will never be needed for the banner and contents frames, but they should be used as needed in the target frame because some pages will be longer than can fit on a screen. You can create borders between frames that are thick or thin or, as many professional sites do, display frames without borders. We will leave our frame borders medium size. Complete the Frames Properties for each frame. Now save the page as Orca_main_frame. Set up the Navigation view with the banner, contents, and Welcome pages under the home page and the other pages under contents. Now use the button to preview in the web browser 🔍 to display the Orca_main_frame page. Figure 23a shows how it would first appear to a visitor to the site. Any link in the contents frame can be clicked to bring up the corresponding page in the

Figure 23 **Frames in the browser.** This is how the completed page will appear to a visitor to the web site. (a) The page as it first appears, with the Welcome page initially in the target frame to the right. Notice that only the target frame has a scroll bar, indicating that there is more to the page in that frame. (b) When the *Orca links* link is clicked (note the hand pointer over it and its changed color), it causes the Orca links page to appear in the target frame.

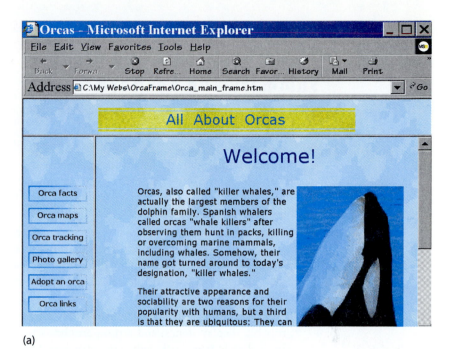

(a)

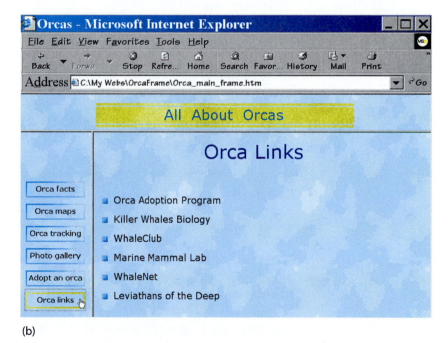

(b)

target frame. Figure 23b shows that the *Orca links* link has been clicked and that the links page is in the target frame.

There is so much more. We have only scratched the surface of what FrontPage can do. But even this much demonstrates its power and ease of use. If you want to know more, purchase one or two of the many books that are available in any bookstore.

CHAPTER REVIEW

Summary and Key Terms

- The language called **HTML,** which stands for **HyperText Markup Language,** is used to write pages for the Web.

- HTML consists of a set of **tags,** commands that tell the browser to perform specific functions.

- The HTML tags go at the beginning and end of the HTML file, the **head tags** enclose the page **title tags,** and the **body tags** enclose the content of the page. Tags enclosed within another set of tags are called **nested tags. Heading tags** cause text to be printed in six sizes, **paragraph tags** enclose a paragraph of text, and the **line break tag** starts a new line.

- The two kinds of **lists** used most often are unordered lists and ordered lists. The **unordered list tags** produce an indented list with a browser-supplied character in front of each item, probably a small circle or square. The **ordered list tags** cause the browser to number the indented list items in order, usually 1., 2., and so forth. Each item in a list is preceded by a single **list item tag.**

- **Logical style tags** leave it up to the browser to format text in its own way. **Emphasis tags** will probably display italics, and **strong emphasis tags** will likely display the text as boldface. **Physical style tags** work with most browsers; some commonly used ones are the **italic tag,** the **boldface tag,** and the **center tag.**

- For the foreseeable future, the standard file format for images on the Internet are **GIF,** for **Graphic Interchange Format; JPG,** for **Joint Photographic Experts Group;** and **PNG,** for **Portable Network Graphics.**

- An image that is referenced right in the HTML code and whose file is loaded with the HTML code is called an **inline image.** An image can be included in a page by using the **image tag,** which offers several **attributes** within the tag, including SRC to define the location of the file, ALT to permit alternative text, HEIGHT and WIDTH for sizing, and ALIGN for placement.

- Links are accomplished by using the **anchor tag.** The key attribute is HREF, which indicates a link destination, an URL or a file name. The anchor tag also includes the name of the word or words—the **hypertext**—that will be clicked to initiate the move to the new site.

- **Background** refers to the screen appearance behind the text and images. Backgrounds are added using an attribute of the body tag. The attribute BGCOLOR uses a six-digit hexadecimal code that signifies the desired background color, two digits each for red, green, and blue. The attribute BACKGROUND uses a graphic that is a small square that is **tiled** by the browser—spread down and across the screen to make a complete background.

- **Authoring software** lets you make a web page without any having knowledge of HTML; the software converts your specifications to HTML for you. One brand of authoring software is FrontPage 2000, designed to interface with the Office 2000 suite.

- FrontPage calls a web site a **web;** a web is a set of related web pages. FrontPage uses **WYSIWYG,** for **what you see is what you get.**

- FrontPage offers several views of a web: **Page view,** showing the web page in progress; **Navigation view,** the structure showing the relationships among the pages; **Folders view,** listing the files in detail; **Reports view,** giving detailed information about the site; **Hyperlinks view,** giving a graphic picture of link relationships; and **Tasks view,** showing a list of items to be completed on the web and who is responsible for each item.

- A **Navigation bar** is a set of links on a web page.

- The **page tabs** at the bottom of a page are the **Normal tab,** to use or view the page in the usual WYSIWYG mode; the **HTML tab,** to see the HTML version of the current page; and the **Preview tab,** to see how the page will look when it is displayed in the browser. Also below the page is **estimated loading time,** the time it will take a page to load in a user's browser.

- A **theme** is a unified set of design elements and color schemes that you can apply to a page to give it a consistent and attractive appearance. A **banner** is a pictorial heading that can be included as part of a theme. A **page template** is a predesigned page that can contain page settings, formatting, and page elements.

- A **frame** is a rectangular area on a page that can that hold a separate page. A collection of frames displayed on a single page is called a **frameset.** Some of the frame templates include a frame called **contents,** which can hold links to subpages that will be shown, one at a time, in another frame called the **target** frame.

Discussion Questions

1. Themes have proven quite popular in authoring languages. Discuss their advantages. Are there any disadvantages?

2. How might you set up a frames home page for the following types of web pages? (a) an online tour of a museum, (b) a photo gallery of animals in a zoo, (c) a store selling auto parts.

Student Study Guide

True/False

T F 1. It is permissible to use nested tags as long as they overlap.

T F 2. Once you begin coding with authoring software, it is not possible to insert any code in HTML.

T F 3. A template is a set of themes.

T F 4. Background graphics are tiled by the browser.

T F 5. The two most common formats for images on the Internet are GIF and JIF.

T F 6. Web page lists can be ordered or unordered.

T F 7. In HTML, links are created using the anchor tag.

T F 8. Authoring software requires some background knowledge of HTML.

T F 9. Text within strong emphasis tags probably will display as boldface.

T F 10. Some HTML commands have attributes.

Fill-In

1. A unified set of design elements and color schemes for a page is called a(n) _____ .

2. A type of software that lets you make a web page without any knowledge of HTML is called _____ .

3. A pictorial heading that can be included as part of a theme is called a(n) _____ .

4. HTML stands for _____ .

5. HTML commands are executed by a series of _____ .

6. FrontPage refers to a set of related pages as a(n) _____ .

7. WYSIWYG stands for _____ .

8. A rectangular area on a page that can hold a separate page is called a(n) _____ .

9. A predesigned web page that can contain page settings, formats, and elements is called a(n) _____ .

10. The screen appearance behind the text and images is called the _____ .

Answers

True/False

1.	F	3.	F	5.	F	7.	T	9.	T
2.	F	4.	T	6.	T	8.	F	10.	T

Fill-In

1. theme
2. authoring software
3. banner
4. HyperText Markup Language
5. tags
6. web
7. what you see is what you get
8. frame
9. page template
10. background

ETHICS AND THE INTERNET

Ethics refers to judgment, of what is wrong and what is right. At first, it may seem strange that ethics issues would be attached to something as new and different and ethereal as the Internet. How can the Internet be right or wrong? As it turns out, the issues are many, and they are not so very different from ethical issues in other parts of society. Consider also that any ethics issue may or may not have legal ramifications.

Many people and many organizations have raised concerns about ethics and the Internet. They often make their positions known on their web sites. We will take a brief glance at some of the issues. As with many ethics issues, it is easier to raise questions than to provide answers.

User behavior. There are many netiquette sites proposing a certain code of conduct of behavior for Internet users. Chat rooms, where a number of users can communicate in real time, are a particular focus of behavior standards; participants are expected to refrain from offensive communications, from being rude to others, from hogging the chat, and so forth. Some people consider these to be ethical issues, especially if a user is being annoying and thus ruining the Internet experiences of other users. Others, instead of raising these to the level of ethical issues, prefer to think of them in terms of expected courtesy.

Hacking. Is it ethical to give tips to hackers so that they can then proceed to invade computers? Many sites do just that. However, some carefully state that their purpose is only to "increase awareness" and alert security employees to the potential problems they face. There are hundreds of hacker sites, most of them "how-to" sites, loaded with hacking tips and gleeful bragging. Astonishingly, there are developer sites with "challenges" (their word) to hackers: They are invited to try to break an encryption code or penetrate a firewall, with thousands of dollars in prizes for those who are successful. Try sorting out those ethics!

Intellectual property. Some people have the notion that "if I can connect to it, I can treat it as if it's mine to do with as I please." That attitude overlooks federal copyright laws, which protect an individual's original expressions, whether they are a book or a song or a work of art. The originator has exclusive

rights to his or her works. Their presence on an Internet site does not alter the law. Many sites include a phrase such as *All rights reserved,* but this is really just a reminder. Such a warning could be compared with putting a sign on your bike, saying "Don't steal this bike"—a theft is a theft with or without the sign. Similarly, rights to material on web sites belong to the originator, regardless of warnings.

Privacy. A little tug-of-war is going on between business interests, who want your e-mail address and any other demographic information they can persuade you to hand over, and site visitors who prefer to maintain their privacy. People sometimes readily give up their addresses for some enticement such as a contest, only to be surprised when they get junk e-mail (and often junk snail mail as well). One approach is to use a site like Switchboard as a go-between, to camouflage your identity.

Many business sites record cookie files related to site usage on a visitor's hard disk; some even insist on acceptance of cookies as a requirement of doing business with them. Some groups are objecting to this practice, both on privacy and property bases. The Internet Engineering Task Force, for example, wrote to several industry and government leaders, promoting "the ability of users to see and exercise control over the disclosure of personally identifiable information."

Get off of my site! Can your site be considered your property and an unwanted visitor thus be considered a trespasser? If this makes your head spin, be assured that some legal scholars are pondering this very issue. It can be argued, of course, that it is already possible, using current technology, to admit only selected people to a site or to reject certain others. Businesses do this all the time with their internal sites.

Fraud. The warnings are the same on the Internet as they are in other parts of society: Look out for scams. A rather famous fraud was the successful promotion of SoftRAM, a software product that allegedly doubled memory without the purchase of new memory chips. Many people liked that idea a lot and continued to buy the product long after it was exposed as a fraud. Interestingly, the bad news came from users across the Internet

long before the traditional press caught up with the story. Fraud, of course, is never ethical and is well covered by law.

New laws? Many people argue that no new laws are needed for the Internet, because the problems related to the Internet—fraud, theft, copyright infringement, and so forth—are covered by pre-Internet laws. This argument has been applied to the regulation of pornography on the Internet. Why should material that is legally permissible in a bookstore, some argue, not be permissible in a different forum, the Internet? People who take the opposite view argue that the immediacy and availability of Internet materials, especially to children, paint a different and scarier scenario. Each side sees this as an ethical issue. The Communications Decency Act of 1996 proposed penalties for placing indecent materials on the Internet, but it was struck down for vagueness by the United States Supreme Court.

Service. Lest we see nothing but problems, it is appropriate to note that some Internet sites perform a service by proposing ethical codes and behaviors. Others publish the pre-Internet codes of ethics for particular professions and organizations, including medical, business, computer, and sports organizations.

Universal access. An organization called Computer Professionals for Social Responsibility has a comprehensive and serious site representing its members' concerns. A key ethical issue for them is the right of everyone to Internet access. They express this in terms that look not unlike a set of existing non-Internet rights: the right to assemble in online communities; the right to speak freely; the right to privacy; and the right to access regardless of income, location, or disability. They look to the government to make this happen.

Internet Exercises

1. **Structured exercise.** Begin with the URL http://www.prenhall.com/capron and link to the Computer Professionals for Social Responsibility site.

2. **Freeform exercise.** Put the words *computer* and *ethics* through a search engine and check out a few sites that look promising.

CHAPTER TEN

SECURITY AND PRIVACY

Computers and the Internet

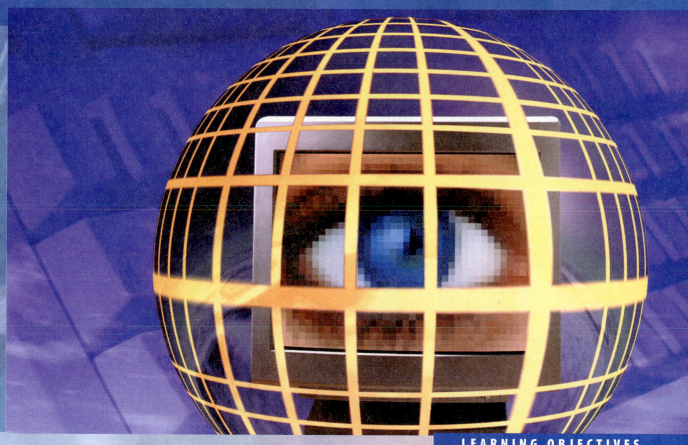

LEARNING OBJECTIVES

- Become aware of the problem of computer crime, including its changing nature and the difficulties of discovery and prosecution
- Become aware of the need for security, including disaster recovery plans, software and data security, and security legislation
- Understand the importance of privacy and how it is affected by the computer age
- Understand your own privacy vulnerability in the workplace and on the Internet

At Wolfe-Straus, a company that manufactures particle board, they have a high awareness of computer security. Potential hires are carefully screened. Employees know better than to reveal their computer passwords. Diskettes holding data are never left lying around. Important files are backed up on a regular basis. Outdated reports with sensitive data are fed to the shredder. And so forth and so on.

How it is, then, that a thief was able to walk off with the entire employee personnel file? Stolen reports? Illicit Internet access? No,

it was really a simple matter. Using a screwdriver, the thief was able to remove and steal the entire hard drive from a personal computer.

The file contained employee names, addresses, birth dates, Social Security numbers, salaries, and home phone numbers. The company had to warn its 577 employees that their personal data had been compromised. That information could be used to apply for fraudulent credit cards in the employees' names or to gain access to other information about them. Even worse, the stolen hard disk contained the bank account numbers of retired workers who opted for direct-deposit pension checks. Managers could only shake their heads and hope they were faced with a

"dumb" criminal who wanted only the $200 hardware, as opposed to a "smart" criminal who would recognize that the data could be worth hundreds of thousands of dollars.

Security personnel considered several options to prevent such incidents in the future, including keeping all data on server disks in locked rooms, passwording all files, using hard drives that required special tools for detachment, and placing cages around desktop machines when not in use. They settled on a triple plan: using file passwords, placing important files on servers only, and placing other personal computer files on removable hard drives that could be locked away at night.

A First Look at Security and Privacy

There was a time when security and privacy issues related to computers were easily managed: You simply locked the computer room door. Those centralized days are, of course, long gone. Now, in theory, anyone can hook up to any computer from any location. In light of data communications access, the first issue is security. The vast files of computer-stored information must be kept secure—safe from destruction, accidental damage, theft, and even espionage.

A second issue is privacy. Private data—salaries, medical information, Social Security numbers, bank balances, and much more—must be kept from prying eyes. The problems are many and the solutions complex. The escalating expansion of the Internet has only heightened the existing problems and added new problems of its own.

These issues and more will be addressed in this chapter as we march through security, privacy, and the specific problems associated with the Internet. However, we begin with a fascinating aspect of the security problem: computer crime.

Computer Crime

It was 5 o'clock in the morning, and 14-year-old Randy Miller was startled to see a man climbing in his bedroom window. "FBI," the man announced, "and that computer is mine." So ended the computer caper in San Diego where 23 teenagers, ages 13 to 17, had used their home computers to invade computer systems as far away as Massachusetts. The teenagers were **hackers,** people who attempt to gain access to computer systems illegally, usually from a personal computer, via a data communications network.

The term *hacker* used to mean a person with significant computer expertise, but the term has taken on the more sinister meaning with the advent of computer miscreants. In this case the hackers did not use the system to steal money or property. But they did create fictitious accounts and destroyed or changed some data files. The FBI's entry through the bedroom window was calculated: The agents figured that, given even a moment's warning, the teenagers were clever enough to alert each other via computer.

This story—except for the name—is true. Hackers ply their craft for a variety of reasons but most often to show off for their peers or to harass people they do not like. A favorite trick, for example, is to turn a rival's telephone into a pay phone, so that when his or her parents try to dial a number an operator interrupts to say, "Please deposit 25¢." A hacker may have more sinister motives, such as getting computer services without paying for them or getting information to sell.

You will probably not be surprised to learn that hackers have invaded web sites. These vandals show up with what amounts to a digital spray can, defacing sites with taunting boasts, graffiti, and their own private jokes. Although the victims feel violated, the perpetrators view their activities as mere pranks. In reality, such activity is antisocial and can result in great expense.

Hackers and Other Miscreants

Hacking has long been thought the domain of teenagers with time on their hands. The pattern is changing, however. A recent government survey showed that the computer systems of over half of the largest U.S. corporations had been invaded, but not by teenagers. Most intruders were competitors attempting to steal proprietary information. Even more astounding, federal investigators told a U.S. Senate hearing that the U.S. Department of Defense computers are attacked more than 200,000 times per year. Most worrisome is the emerging computer attack abilities of other nations, which, in a worst-case scenario, could seriously degrade the nation's ability to deploy and sustain military forces.

Hackers ply their craft by surprisingly low-tech means. Using what is called **social engineering,** a tongue-in-cheek term for con artist actions,

InfoBit

In some cases, computer criminals need not even obtain the actual contents of electronic messages to benefit from eavesdropping. If, for instance, a competitor finds out that the number of e-mail messages between two corporations has increased by 100 percent in the last few weeks, he or she may be able to infer that a merger is in the offing.

hackers simply persuade unsuspecting people to give away their passwords over the phone. Recognizing the problem, employers are educating their employees to be alert to such scams.

Hackers are only a small fraction of the security problem. The most serious losses are caused by electronic pickpockets who are usually a good deal older and not so harmless. Consider these examples:

- A brokerage clerk sat at his terminal in Denver and, with a few taps of the keys, transformed 1700 shares of his own stock, worth $1.50 per share, to the same number of shares in another company worth 10 times that much.
- A Seattle bank employee used her electronic fund transfer code to move certain bank funds to an account held by her boyfriend as a "joke"; both the money and the boyfriend disappeared.
- A keyboard operator in Oakland, California, changed some delivery addresses to divert several thousand dollars' worth of department store goods into the hands of accomplices.
- A ticket clerk at the Arizona Veteran's Memorial Coliseum issued full-price basketball tickets for admission and then used her computer to record the sales as half-price tickets and pocketed the difference.

These stories point out that computer crime is not always the flashy, front-page news about geniuses getting away with millions of dollars. These people were ordinary employees in ordinary businesses—committing computer crimes.

The problems of computer crime have been aggravated in recent years by increased access to computers (Figure 1). More employees now have access to computers on their jobs. In fact, computer crime is often just white-collar crime with a new medium: Every time an employee is trained on the computer at work, he or she also gains knowledge that—potentially—could be used to harm the company.

The Changing Face of Computer Crime

Computer crime once fell into a few simple categories, such as theft of software or destruction of data. The dramatically increased access to networks has changed the focus to damage that can be done by unscrupulous people with online access. The most frequently reported computer crimes fall into these categories:

- **Credit-card fraud.** Customer numbers are floating all over public and private networks, in varying states of protection. Some are captured and used fraudulently.
- **Data communications fraud.** This category covers a broad spectrum, including piggybacking on someone else's network, the use of an office network for personal purposes, and computer-directed diversion of funds.
- **Unauthorized access to computer files.** This general snooping category covers everything from accessing confidential employee records to the theft of trade secrets and product pricing structures.
- **Unlawful copying of copyrighted software.** Whether the casual sharing of copyrighted software among friends or assembly-line copying by organized crime, unlawful copying incurs major losses for software vendors.

Disgruntled or militant employee could

- Sabotage equipment or programs
- Hold data or programs hostage

Competitor could

- Sabotage operations
- Engage in espionage
- Steal data or programs
- Photograph records, documentation, or CRT screen displays

Data control worker could

- Insert data
- Delete data
- Bypass controls
- Sell information

Clerk/supervisor could

- Forge or falsify data
- Embezzle funds
- Engage in collusion with people inside or outside the company

System user could

- Sell data to competitors
- Obtain unauthorized information

Operator could

- Copy files
- Destroy files

User requesting reports could

- Sell information to competitors
- Receive unauthorized information

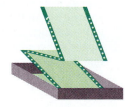

Engineer could

- Install "bugs"
- Sabotage system
- Access security information

Data conversion worker could

- Change codes
- Insert data
- Delete data

Programmer could

- Steal programs or data
- Embezzle via programming
- Bypass controls

Report distribution worker could

- Examine confidential reports
- Keep duplicates of reports

Trash collector could

- Sell reports or duplicates to competitors

Figure 1 The perils of increased access. By letting your imagination loose, you can visualize many ways in which people can compromise computer security. Computer-related crime would be far more rampant if all the people in these positions took advantage of their access to computers.

GETTING PRACTICAL

KEEPING A SECRET

Employers wish that computer passwords were better-kept secrets. Here are some hints on password use.

- Do not name your password after your child or car or pet, an important date, or your phone number. Passwords that are easy to remember are also easy to crack. If a hacker can find out personal details about a victim, he or she can deduce a password from this information about 40 percent of the time.
- Make passwords as random as possible. Include both letters and numbers. The more characters the better. Embed at least one nonalphabetic character, and consider mixing uppercase and lowercase letters. Example: Go*TOP6.
- Keep your password in your head or in a safe.

Astonishingly, an occasional thoughtless user will scribble the password on paper and stick it on the computer monitor where anyone can see it.

- Change your password often, at least once a month. In some installations, passwords are changed so seldom that they become known to many people, thus defeating the purpose.
- Do not fall for hacker phone scams—"social engineering"—to obtain your password. Typical ruses are callers posing as a neophyte employee ("Gosh, I'm so confused, could you talk me through it?"); a system expert ("We're checking a problem in the network that seems to be coming from your workstation. Could you please verify your password?"); a telephone company employee ("There seems to be a problem on your phone line"); or even an angry top manager ("This is outrageous! How do I get into these files anyway?").

Most people are naturally inclined to be helpful. Do not be inappropriately helpful. Keep in mind that you will be—at the very least—embarrassed if you are the source of information to a hacker who damages your company.

Some "Bad Guy" Tricks

Although the emphasis in this chapter is on preventing rather than committing crime, being familiar with the terms and methods computer criminals use is part of being a prudent computer user. Many of these words or phrases have made their way into the general vocabulary.

- **Bomb.** A "bomb" causes a program to trigger damage under certain conditions; it is usually set to go off at a later date—perhaps after the perpetrator has left the company. Bombs are sometimes planted in software to be used by the general public. Shareware, which is less rigorously monitored than commercial software, has been known as a source of bombs.
- **Data diddling.** This unattractive term refers to changing data before or as it enters the system, for example, a course grade or hours worked. Auditors who are monitoring a computer system are not limited to the

computer processing itself; they must verify the accuracy of the source data.

- **Piggybacking.** The term fits: An illicit user "rides" into the system on the back of another user. The original user gives some sort of identification, probably a password, to access the system. Then, if the legitimate user does not exit the system properly, the intruder may have access to systems and files by simply continuing where the original user has left off. Imagine this simple scenario: You are performing legitimate work on your office computer; you step out briefly to pick up some coffee, get waylaid by a colleague, and end up in a two-hour meeting. Could someone take advantage of your accessed computer in your absence? You bet.

- **Salami technique.** The name *salami,* as given to this embezzlement technique, reflects the small "slices" of money that may be squirreled away undetected from a large financial system. In one famous case, a bank employee commandeered the extra amounts when accounts were rounded to dollars and cents after interest was computed. If, for example, interest was computed to be $77.0829, the interest was reported as $77.08, and the $0.0029 added to the unauthorized salami account. Done hundreds of times over thousands of accounts, these small amounts add up. This scheme, by the way, would not work today; bank auditors are much too savvy for anything this overt.

- **Scavenging.** This simple approach, even in this day of shredders, is still all too common. Scavengers simply search company trash cans and dumpsters for printouts containing not-for-distribution information, perhaps even a gold mine of credit-card numbers. Further, it is not unusual for thieves to get account numbers and other information from the garbage and recycling bins of individuals, hence the popularity of personal home shredders.

- **Trapdoor.** This is an illicit program left within a completed legitimate program. A trapdoor allows subsequent unauthorized—and unknown—entry by the perpetrator, who then has the ability to make changes to the program. This technique is not available to the average person. The programmer who has the skills to do it can cause great damage, from altering the method of program processing to destroying records and files.

- **Trojan horse.** A "Trojan horse" refers to illegal instructions covertly placed in the middle of a legitimate program. The program does do something useful but also, via the Trojan horse instructions, does something destructive in the background.

- **Zapping.** This generic term refers to a variety of software, probably illicitly acquired, to bypass all security systems.

In summary, there are multiple opportunities for scoundrels to cause havoc in and around computer systems. It is up to employees and individuals at all levels to recognize the danger and protect their assets.

White-Hat Hackers

Perhaps you saw the movie *Sneakers,* in which Robert Redford, in the opening scene, appears to be in the process of robbing a bank. But, no, Mr. Redford is actually executing a test of the bank's security system. This is a common scene at today's banks and in any other organization that depends on computer networks.

Faced with threats on every side, most network-laced companies have chosen a proactive stance. Rather than waiting for the hackers and snoops and thieves to show up, they hire professionals to beat them to it. Called *white-hat hackers* or tiger teams, or sometimes "intrusion testers" or "hackers for hire," these highly trained technical people are paid to try to break into a computer system before anyone else does.

Using the same kind of finesse and tricks a hacker might, white-hat hackers exploit the system weaknesses. Once such chinks are revealed, they can be protected. The hacker's first approach, typically, is to access the company's system from the Internet. The quality of security varies from company to company. Sometimes security is fairly tight; other times, as one hacker put it, "It's a cakewalk."

Sometimes companies will hire one company to establish security and then hire white-hat hackers to try to defeat it. The company may not even alert its own employees to the hacker activities, preferring to see whether the intrusions are detected and, if so, how employees react.

Discovery and Prosecution

Prosecuting the computer criminal is difficult for several reasons. To begin with, discovery is often difficult. Many times the crime simply goes undetected. In addition, crimes that are detected are—an estimated 85 percent of the time—never reported to the authorities. By law, banks have to make a report when their computer systems have been compromised, but other businesses do not. Often these businesses choose not to report such crimes because they are worried about their reputations and credibility in the community.

Most computer crimes are discovered by accident. For example, a bank employee changed a program to add 10¢ to every customer service charge under $10 and $1 to every charge over $10. He then placed this overage into a bank account he opened himself in the name of Zzwicke. The system worked fairly well, generating several hundred dollars each month, until the bank initiated a new marketing campaign in which it singled out for special honors the very first depositor in the alphabet—and the very last.

Even if a computer crime is detected, prosecution is by no means assured. There are a number of reasons for this. First, some law enforcement agencies do not fully understand the complexities of computer-related fraud. Second, few attorneys are qualified to handle computer crime cases. Third, judges and juries are not always educated about computers and may not understand the nature of the violation or the seriousness of the crime.

In short, the chances of having a computer crime go undetected are, unfortunately, good. And the chances that, if detected, there will be no ramifications are also good: A computer criminal may not go to jail, may not be found guilty if prosecuted, and may not even be prosecuted.

But this situation is changing. Since Congress passed the **Computer Fraud and Abuse Act** in 1986, there has been a growing awareness of computer crime on the national level. This law is supplemented by state statutes; most states have passed some form of computer crime law. Computer criminals who are successfully prosecuted are subject to fines, jail time, and confiscation of their computer equipment.

Computer Forensics

"I'll lose my job if they find out what I sent you." Most companies keep copies of all e-mail sent and received, and most do spot checks of their contents. When the above statement was discovered among an employee's outgoing messages, a company security officer wondered if she had uncovered corporate espionage. Was the message sender, in fact, giving away—or perhaps selling—company secrets? In this case, it was easy to find out: The security officer simply extracted the attachment sent with the message. It turned out to be pornographic material—and the employee did indeed lose his job over this incident.

Checking an already-identified e-mail message stored on disk is relatively straightforward, but finding other kinds of data is trickier. The data of interest may be in a deleted file or stored with a phony file name or disguised in some other manner. But such data is not safely hidden from professionals known as forensic experts. A relatively new field, **computer forensics** refers to uncovering computer-stored information suitable for use in courts of law.

It would be expected that, in a business setting, just about every accountancy-related fraud involves a computer in some form. But computer forensics has been used in both criminal and civil cases, in applications as varied as murder, blackmail, and counterfeiting. Each computer forensic examination is unique in its purpose and, possibly, method of approach. One company may need to trace missing inventory while another may be responding to a court-ordered subpoena for e-mail messages containing sexual harassment language.

An unsophisticated perpetrator may get a tip that he or she is being investigated and delete the related files before anyone can examine the computer. This is a plaintiff's (or prosecutor's) delight: Not only can the deleted files be reconstructed; the accused party has displayed guilty behavior.

Some computer forensics experts have set up shop and are for hire, perhaps even advertising on their own web sites (Figure 2). But most such experts are on the staffs of police departments and law firms.

Security: Playing It Safe

As you can see from the previous sections, companies and organizations have been vulnerable in the matter of computer security. **Security** is a system of safeguards designed to protect a computer system and data from deliber-

Figure 2 Forensics experts. (a) Private firms offer their services to all comers. (b) This is the forensics page for a government site.

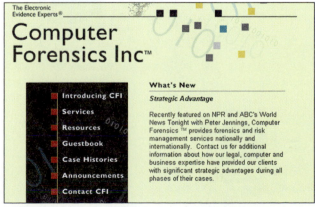

(a)

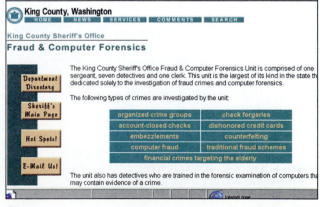

(b)

ate or accidental damage or access by unauthorized persons. That means safeguarding the system against such threats as natural disasters, fire, accidents, vandalism, theft or destruction of data, industrial espionage, and hackers (Figure 3).

Identification and Access: Who Goes There?

How does a computer system detect whether you are the person who should be allowed access to it? Various means have been devised to give access to authorized people without compromising the system. These means fall into four broad categories: what you have, what you know, what you do, and what you are.

■   **What you have.** You may have a key, badge, token, or plastic card to give you physical access to the computer room or to a locked-up terminal or personal computer. A card with a magnetized strip, for example, can give you access to your bank account via a remote cash machine. Taking this a step further, some employees begin each business day by donning an **active badge,** a clip-on identification card with an embedded com-

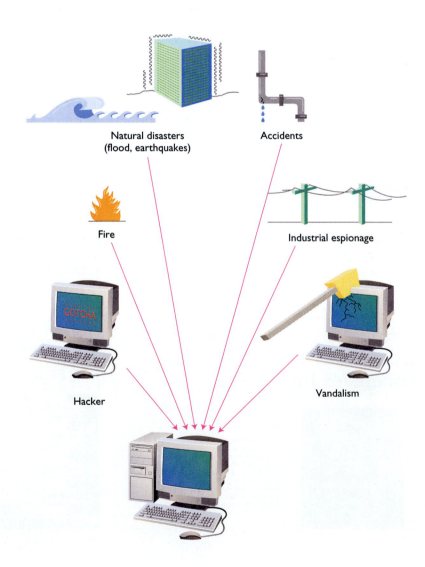

Natural disasters (flood, earthquakes)

Accidents

Fire

Industrial espionage

Hacker

Vandalism

Figure 3 Is your computer secure?
The computer industry is vulnerable to both natural disasters and disasters of human origin.

puter chip. The badge signals its wearer's location—legal or otherwise—by sending out infrared signals, which are read by sensors sprinkled throughout the building.

- **What you know.** Standard what-you-know items are a password or an identification number for your bank cash machine. Cipher locks on doors require that you know the correct combination of numbers.
- **What you do.** In their daily lives people often sign documents as a way of proving who they are. Though a signature is difficult to copy, forgery is not impossible. Today, software can verify both scanned and online signatures.
- **What you are.** Now it gets interesting. Some security systems use **biometrics,** the science of measuring individual body characteristics. Fingerprinting may seem to be old news, but not when you simply insert your finger into an identification machine (Figure 4). Some systems use the characteristics of the entire hand. Another approach is identification by voice pattern. Even newer is the concept of identification by the retina of the eye, which has a pattern that is harder to duplicate than a voiceprint, or by the entire face, which draws its uniqueness from heat radiating from blood vessels (Figure 5).

Some systems use a combination of the preceding four categories. For example, access to an automated teller machine requires both something you have—a plastic card—and something you know—a personal identification number (PIN).

When Disaster Strikes: What Do You Have to Lose?

In New York a power outage shut down computer operations and effectively halted business, air traffic, and transportation throughout the United States. In Italy armed terrorists singled out corporate and state computer centers as targets for attack and, during a 10-month period, bombed 10 such centers throughout the country. Computer installations of any kind can be struck by natural disasters or by disasters of human origin, which can lead to security violations. What kinds of problems might this cause an organization?

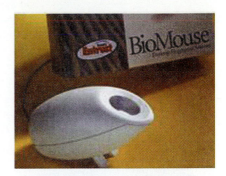

Figure 4 BioMouse. The BioMouse, a product of American Biometric, is a fingerprint authentication system. The system consists of a mouse/scanner, shown here, and related software. A user "trains" the mouse by inserting fingers, one at a time. The mouse is a scanner that saves not the fingerprint itself but a set of reference points for the fingerprint. After training, any of the saved fingerprints can be used to permit the computer to start. The BioMouse system, by the way, is not compatible with police systems, thus protecting the user's privacy.

Group Work

It should help to drive home some of the issues surrounding disaster planning if you have student teams develop a plan for disaster recovery at your college or university. As an example, you might ask each team to draft a plan that deals with the following questions and issues: What data should be backed up? What hardware and software are available to do this backup today? and What interim procedures for providing student records and processing college funds make sense in the event of a disaster?

Figure 5 Identification. A person's entire face is used for identification in some security systems. Identification is based on a unique pattern of heat radiating from an individual's facial blood vessels.

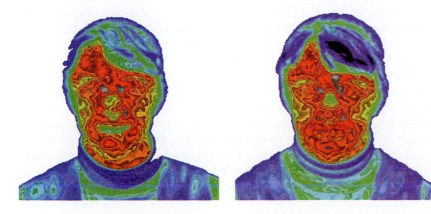

Losing Your Laptop

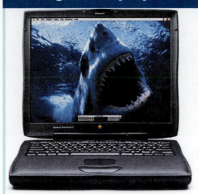

A laptop—or notebook—computer is an extremely attractive target for thieves. It is easy to steal, easy to hide, and easy to fence—exchange for money. Victims are especially vulnerable in airports and even on the airplane itself.

Experts offer hints on how to protect your laptop. Generally, these hints come down to being vigilant and inconspicuous.

- Carry your laptop in an ordinary briefcase or backpack, not in a case recognizably designed for a laptop.
- In a public place, never set your briefcase or backpack down. Hold it on your lap or beside you; if you must use a pay phone, place your foot firmly on the case.
- Never leave your laptop unattended, not even for a quick trip to the soda machine.
- Use the laptop software to set up a password so that anyone who steals it cannot even boot it up.

Finally, do not think your laptop is safe even in an office setting. Gangs of thieves dress in business suits and stroll into office buildings at lunch hour—and out with new laptops.

Your first thoughts might be of the hardware—the computer and its related equipment. But loss of hardware is not a major problem in itself; the loss will probably be covered by insurance, and the hardware can be replaced. The true problem with hardware loss is the diminished processing ability that exists while managers find a substitute facility and return the installation to its former state. The ability to continue processing data is critical. Some information industries, such as banking, would literally go out of business in a matter of days if their computer operations were suspended. Loss of software should not be a problem if the organization has heeded industry warnings—and used common sense—to make backup copies of program files.

A more important problem is the loss of data. Imagine trying to reassemble lost or destroyed files of customer records, accounts receivable, or design data for a new airplane. The costs would be staggering. Software and data security will be presented in more detail later in this chapter. First, however, consider an overview of disaster recovery, the steps to restoring processing ability.

Disaster Recovery Plan

A **disaster recovery plan** is a method of restoring computer processing operations and data files if operations are halted or files are damaged by major destruction. There are various approaches. Some organizations revert temporarily to manual services, but life without the computer can be difficult indeed. Others arrange to buy time at a service bureau, but this is inconvenient for companies in remote or rural areas. If a single act, such as a fire, destroys your computing facility, it is possible that a mutual aid pact will help you get back on your feet. In such a plan two or more companies agree to lend each other computing power if one of them has a problem. This would be of little help, however, if there were a regional disaster and many companies needed assistance.

Banks and other organizations with survival dependence on computers sometimes form a **consortium,** a joint venture to support a complete computer facility. Such a facility is completely available and routinely tested but used only in the event of a disaster. Among these facilities, a **hot site** is a fully equipped computer center, with hardware, environmental controls, security, and communications facilities. A **cold site** is an environmentally suitable empty shell in which a company can install its own computer system.

The use of such a facility or any type of recovery at all depends on advance planning—specifically, the disaster recovery plan. The idea of such a plan is that everything except the hardware has been stored in a safe place somewhere else. The storage location should be several miles away, so it will not be affected by local physical forces, such as a hurricane. Typical items stored at the backup site are program and data files, program listings, program and operating systems documentation, hardware inventory lists, output forms, and a copy of the disaster plan manual.

The disaster recovery plan should include a list of priorities identifying the programs that must be up and running first, plans for notifying employees of changes in locations and procedures, a list of needed equipment and where it can be obtained, a list of alternative computing facilities, and procedures for handling input and output data in a different environment.

Computer installations actually perform emergency drills. At some unexpected moment a notice is given that "disaster has struck," and the computer professionals must run the critical systems at some other site.

2000 and Beyond

CORPORATE CYBERSLEUTHS

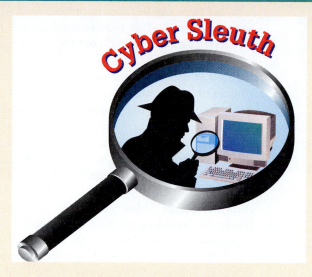

Corporate spying, each side trying to find a competitive advantage over the other, is an old story. So are laws that prohibit breaking and entering and snooping. Thus businesses have been limited to playing their hunches, perhaps picking up an occasional bone via the press or perhaps from mere gossip.

But what if you could scrutinize the competition in a legitimate way without ever leaving the comfort of your office? Make that a computer-equipped office, a *connected,* computer-equipped office. This is the direction of corporate spying in the twenty-first century.

Computers and the Internet offer opportunities to acquire information that has always been available, but not so readily available. Data that once sat quietly in corporate reports or academic research papers is now available on the

Internet, only a few clicks away. Further, computers can take data, combine it with other bits of data, and perform an analysis that reveals new information.

Enter the cybersleuth, who may even promote his or her services under that title. The cybersleuth is a professional who is knowledgeable about computers and also about a certain industry. The cybersleuth

knows not only where on the Internet to look for data, but also how to recognize patterns of data and to reach a conclusion.

As an example, over a period of time, a cybersleuth for a photo film manufacturer (1) saw conference papers about a new process for making a chemical compound called acetate, which is used in making photographic film,

(2) noted increased expenditures for research in the annual report of the company whose engineers wrote the papers, and (3) observed that the same company suddenly was hiring more chemical engineers. A knowledgeable cybersleuth could conclude from the data that the competition was onto a new film-making process. We need not linger over how valid this conclusion is; that is left to the company that hired the cybersleuth. The point here is that all kinds of information are available to outsiders for consideration.

A related issue is how companies respond to the dissemination of data that may seem innocuous but be ultimately to their detriment. To be brief, they are shoring up their defenses. In particular, they are hiring armies of security personnel to advise them on keeping their secrets secret.

Software Security

Software security has been an industry concern for years. Initially, there were many questions: Who owns custom-made software? Is the owner the person who wrote the program or the company for which the author wrote the program? What is to prevent a programmer from taking copies of programs from one job to another? The answer to these questions is well established. If the author of the software—the programmer—is in the employ of the organization, the software belongs to the organization, not the programmer. The programmer may not take the software along to the next job. If the programmer is a consultant, however, the ownership of the software produced should be spelled out specifically in the contract; otherwise, the parties enter extremely murky legal waters. According to a U.S. Supreme Court decision, software can be copyrighted.

Data Security

We have discussed the security of hardware and software. Now consider the security of data, which is one of an organization's most important assets. Here too there must be planning for security. Usually, this is done by security officers who are part of top management.

What steps can be taken to prevent theft or alteration of data? There are several data-protection techniques; these will not individually (or even collectively) guarantee security, but they make a good start.

Secured Waste   Discarded printouts, printer ribbons, and the like can be sources of information to unauthorized persons. This kind of waste can be made secure by the use of shredders or locked trash barrels.

Internal Controls   Internal controls are controls that are planned as part of the computer system. One example is a transaction log. This is a file of all accesses or attempted accesses to certain data.

Auditor Checks   Most companies have auditors go over the financial books. In the course of their duties, auditors frequently review computer programs and data. From a data security standpoint, auditors might also check to see who has accessed data during periods when that data is not usually used. Today auditors can use off-the-shelf audit software, programs that assess the validity and accuracy of the system's operations and output.

Applicant Screening   The weakest link in any computer security system is the people in it. At the very least, employers should verify the facts that job applicants list on their résumés to help weed out dishonest applicants before they are hired.

Passwords   A password is a secret word or number, or a combination of the two, that must be typed on the keyboard to gain access to a computer system. Cracking passwords is the most prevalent method of illicit entry to computer systems.

Built-in Software Protection   Software can be built into operating systems in ways that restrict access to the computer system. One form of software protection is a system that matches a user number against a number assigned to the data being accessed. If a person does not get access, it is recorded that he or she tried to tap into some area to which that person was not authorized. Another form of software protection is a user profile: Information is stored about each user, including the files to which the user has legitimate access. The profile also includes each person's job function, budget number, skills, areas of knowledge, access privileges, supervisor, and loss-causing potential. These profiles are available for checking by managers if there is any problem.

Personal Computer Security

One summer evening two men in coveralls with company logos backed a truck up to the building that housed a university computer lab. They showed the lab assistant, a part-time student, an authorization slip to move 23 personal computers to another lab on campus. The assistant was surprised but not shocked, since lab use was light in the summer quarter. The computers were moved, all right, but not to another lab. In another case a ring of thieves mingled with students in computer labs at various West Coast universities and stole hundreds of microprocessor chips from the campus computers.

There is an active market for stolen personal computers and their internal components. As these unfortunate tales indicate, personal computer security breaches can be pretty basic. One simple, though not foolproof, remedy is to secure personal computer hardware in place with locks and cables. Also, most personal computers have an individual cover lock that prevents access to internal components.

In addition to theft, personal computer users need to be concerned about the computer's environment. Personal computers in business are not coddled the way bigger computers are. They are designed, in fact, to withstand the wear and tear of the office environment, including temperatures set for the comfort of people. Most manufacturers discourage eating and smoking near computers and recommend some specific cleaning techniques, such as vacuuming the keyboard. The response to these recommendations is directly related to the awareness level of the users.

Several precautions can be taken to protect disk data. One is to use a **surge protector,** a device that prevents electrical problems from affecting computer data files. The computer is plugged into the surge protector, which is plugged into the outlet. Diskettes should be under lock and key. The most critical precaution, however, is to back up your files regularly and systematically.

Prepare for the Worst: Back Up Your Files

A computer expert, giving an impassioned speech, said, "If you are not backing up your files regularly, you deserve to lose them." Strong words. Although organizations recognize the value of data and have procedures in place for backing up data files on a regular basis, personal computer users are not as devoted to this activity. In fact, one wonders why, with continuous admonishments and readily available procedures, some people still leave their precious files unprotected.

What Could Go Wrong?   If you use software incorrectly or simply input data incorrectly, it may be some time before the resulting erroneous data is detected. You then need to go back to the time when the data files were still acceptable. Sometimes the software itself can harm data, or a hard disk could physically malfunction, making your files inaccessible. Although none of these mishaps are too likely, they certainly do happen. It is even less likely that you would lose your hard disk files to fire or flood, but this is also possible. The most likely scenario is that you will accidentally delete some files yourself. One fellow gave a command to delete all files with the file name extension BAK—there were four of them—but accidentally typed BAT instead, inadvertently wiping out 57 files. (Deleted files, we should mention, can probably be recovered using utility software if the action is taken right away, before other data is written over the deleted files.) Finally, there is always the possibility of your files being infected with a virus. Experts estimate that average users experience a significant disk loss once every year.

Ways to Back Up Files   Some people simply make another copy of their hard disk files on diskette. This is not too laborious if you do so as you go

Critical Thinking
One major problem with passwords is that users are reluctant to change them and often write them down. In what way may increased password security rules actually increase the likelihood that users will write down their passwords? (Just about everything a computer security administrator can do to decrease the probability that an intruder will be successful in a "password guessing" attack will actually increase the probability that users will resort to writing their passwords down. Longer passwords, random passwords, frequently changing passwords, and passwords containing numbers as well as letters all encourage forgetful users to rely on the crutch of writing down—and thus exposing—their passwords.)

Good Times

The Good Times virus is probably the most widespread of all virus hoaxes. That is, it is not a virus at all, but it scares people to death anyway. The perpetrators tell people that if they open an e-mail message with the words *Good Times* in the subject line, their hard disk will be destroyed.

Hoaxers prey on people's healthy fear of real viruses by spreading rumors of nonexistent ones. To make matters worse, innocent people perpetuate the hoax by warning all their friends, usually by e-mail. When they find out that the so-called virus was a hoax, they may become a bit jaded and be less cautious about the real threats.

Critical Thinking
Why would anyone write a computer virus? (Reasons include a desire to show off programming prowess, a desire for revenge, sabotage, intellectual curiosity about how far it could spread, and a desire for notoriety.)

InfoBit
Unleashing a computer virus may no longer require a lot of programming talent. A mail-order advertisement in a recent hacker magazine offers a "virus do-it-yourself kit" for $29.95, with "no programming knowledge required."

along. If you are at all vulnerable to viruses, you should back up all your files on a regular basis.

A better way is to back up all your files on a tape. Backing up to a tape drive is safer and faster. You can also use software that will automatically back up all your files at a certain time of day, or on command. Sophisticated users place their files on a mirror hard disk, which simply makes a second copy of everything you put on the original disk; this approach, as you might expect, is expensive.

Keep backed-up files in a cool, dry place off-site. For those of you with a home computer, this may mean keeping copies of your important files at a friend's house; some people even use a bank safety deposit box for this purpose.

Viruses: Notorious Pests

Worms and *viruses* are rather unpleasant terms that have entered the jargon of the computer industry to describe some of the insidious ways that computer systems can be invaded.

A **worm** is a program that transfers itself from computer to computer over a network and plants itself as a separate file on the target computer's disks. One newsworthy worm, originated by a student at Cornell University, traveled the length and breadth of the land through an electronic mail network, shutting down thousands of computers. The worm was injected into the network and multiplied uncontrollably, clogging the memories of infected computers until they could no longer function.

Worms, however, are rare. The ongoing nuisance is the virus, which, as its name suggests, is contagious. A **virus** is a set of illicit instructions that passes itself on to other programs with which it comes in contact. In its most basic form, a virus is the digital equivalent of vandalism. It can change or delete files, display words or obscene messages, or produce bizarre screen effects. In its most vindictive form, a virus can slowly sabotage a computer system and remain undetected for months, contaminating data or, in the case of the famous Michelangelo virus, wiping out your entire hard drive. A virus may be dealt with by means of a **vaccine,** or **antivirus,** a computer program that stops the spread of and often eradicates the virus. However, a **retrovirus** has the ability to fight back and may even delete antivirus software.

Viruses seem to show up when least expected. In one instance a call came to a company's information center at about 5 p.m. The caller's computer was making a strange noise. With the exception of an occasional beep, computers performing routine business chores do not usually make noises. Soon employees were calling from all over the company, all with "noisy" computers. One caller said that it might be a tune coming from the computer's small internal speaker. Finally, one caller recognized a tinny rendition of "Yankee Doodle," confirmation that an old virus had struck once again. The Yankee Doodle virus, once attached to a system, is scheduled to go off at 5 p.m. every eight days. Viruses, once considered merely a nuisance, are costing American businesses billions of dollars a year. In addition, they cause serious aggravation for countless individual users, especially college students, who may be subjected to damage inflicted by devious fellow students.

You may wonder who produces viruses. At one point, the mischief makers were mostly curious young men. Now, virus makers are older and actually trade notes and tips on the Internet. They do what they do, psychologists say, mostly to impress their friends. Experts have estimated that there are hundreds of virus writers worldwide. However, although there are thousands of known viruses, most of the damage is caused by only a dozen or so (Table 1).

Transmitting a Virus

Consider this typical example. A programmer secretly inserts a few viral instructions into a game called Kriss-Kross, which she then offers free to others via the Internet. Any takers download the game to their own computers. Now, each time a user runs Kriss-Kross—that is, loads it into memory—the virus is loaded too. The virus stays in memory, infecting any other program loaded until the computer is turned off. The virus now has spread to other programs, and the process can be repeated again and again. In fact, each

InfoBit

As antivirus software has gotten "smarter" about detecting and removing viruses, so have some of the viruses been improved by their authors. Recent developments include "stealth" viruses that actually modify themselves as they are transferred from machine to machine, making it much harder for the antiviral software to detect their familiar "signature" on disk.

Table 1 Typical Viruses

Name	Unpleasant consequences
Form	Causes a clicking noise in the computer's keyboard on the 18th day of the month; it may also corrupt data on diskettes.
Melissa	A macro virus distributed as an e-mail attachment that, when opened, disables a number of safeguards in Word 97 or Word 2000, and, if the user has the Microsoft Outlook e-mail program, causes the virus to be re-sent to the first 50 people in each of the user's address books.
Ripper	Corrupts data written to a hard disk approximately one time out of a thousand.
Junkie	Infects disk files and also causes memory conflicts.
MDMA	Affects Microsoft Word files; can delete files.
Anti-CMOS	Wipes out information stored on the chip containing the computer's configuration data; however, the data can be restored.
Concept	Transferred from one Microsoft Word file to another if both are in memory at the same time; also transferred by e-mail attachments. Causes a file to be saved in the template directory instead of where it belongs; confuses users, who do not know what happened to the most recent version of the file.
Monkey	Makes it appear as if your hard disk has crashed, even though it has not. If you try to boot a Windows machine it locks up; you can boot from a diskette but then it cannot find the hard drive.
Cookie monster	Shows screen message I WANT A COOKIE! and locks up the computer until you type FIG NEWTON.
One_Half	Encrypts the hard disk so that only the virus can read the data there; when the encryption is half-completed, it flashes One_Half on the screen. If you try to remove the virus without the proper antivirus software, you lose the encryption key and thus your data.
Wazzu	Benign versions merely reset screen colors; more destructive ones reformat the hard drive, thus losing all file data.
Michelangelo	Destroys all data on the hard disk on March 6, Michelangelo's birthday.
Cascade	Picks random text characters and drops them to the bottom of the screen.
Jerusalem	Deletes any program executed on Friday the 13th.

Figure 6 An example of a virus invasion.

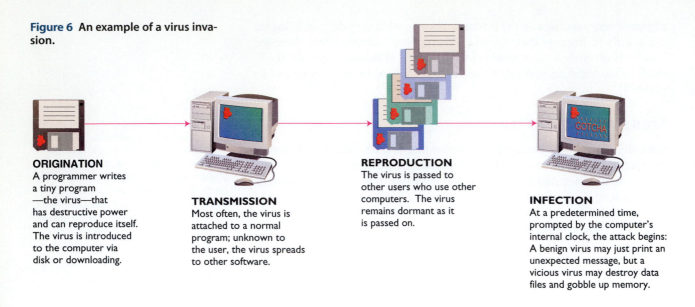

ORIGINATION
A programmer writes a tiny program —the virus—that has destructive power and can reproduce itself. The virus is introduced to the computer via disk or downloading.

TRANSMISSION
Most often, the virus is attached to a normal program; unknown to the user, the virus spreads to other software.

REPRODUCTION
The virus is passed to other users who use other computers. The virus remains dormant as it is passed on.

INFECTION
At a predetermined time, prompted by the computer's internal clock, the attack begins: A benign virus may just print an unexpected message, but a vicious virus may destroy data files and gobble up memory.

newly infected program becomes a virus carrier. Although many viruses are transmitted just this way via networks, another common method is by passing diskettes from computer to computer (Figure 6).

Here is another typical scenario. An office worker puts a copy of a report on a diskette and slips it into her briefcase to take home. After shooing her children away from the new game they are playing on the computer, she sits down to work on the report. She does not know that a virus, borne by the kids' new software, has infected the diskette. When she takes the disk back to work, the virus is transmitted from her computer to the entire office network.

The most insidious viruses attach to the operating system. One virus, called Cascade, causes random text letters to "drop" to a pile at the bottom of the screen (Figure 7). Viruses attached to the operating system itself have greater potential for mischief.

A relative newcomer to the virus scene is the macro virus, which uses a program's own macro programming language, typically Microsoft Word, to distribute itself. A macro virus infects a document by being carried as a macro program. When you open the document that has the virus, any other documents opened in the same session may become infected by the virus. This also applies to an infected document that you may have received as an e-mail attachment.

Damage from Viruses

Some viruses are benign, more on the order of pranks, but many cause serious damage. Even those that are benign can cause confusion and possibly panic, leading to lost time and effort. Many viruses remain dormant until triggered by some activity. For example, a virus called Jerusalem B activates itself every Friday the 13th and proceeds to erase any file you may try to load from your disk. Another virus includes instructions to add 1 to a counter each time the virus is copied to another disk. When the counter reaches 4, the virus erases all data files. But this is not the end of the destruction, of course; the three copied disks have also been infected.

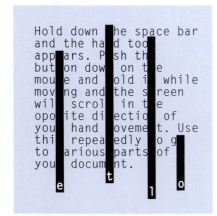

Figure 7 The Cascade virus. This virus attaches itself to the operating system and causes random letters in text to "drop" to a pile at the bottom of the screen display.

Virus Myths

Viruses are merely programs written to create copies of themselves and to attach these copies to other programs. The only way any virus can infect your computer is by executing one of these programs or by booting from a diskette containing an infected boot sector. Almost no one boots from a diskette, preferring instead to use the operating system on the hard disk. However, it is fairly common to boot the computer when a diskette is accidentally left in the drive. Even though you receive the "Non-system disk" error message and remove the diskette, the damage may have been done.

Keeping in mind that a virus must be in an executable program (including an executable macro program within a document) or booted from a diskette, it is possible to debunk some virus myths:

- You cannot get a virus by simply being online, not by surfing the Internet or even from your own local area network. You could, of course, download a program and then, by executing it, get a virus.
- You cannot get a virus by opening and reading e-mail. (Distinguish "opening and reading" the actual mail from opening an attached document that contains a macro virus.)
- Data is not executed, so you cannot get a virus from data, including graphics files. However, beware of graphics files that include a viewer program; that program could contain a virus.

Virus Prevention

A word about prevention is in order. The most powerful weapon at your disposal is antivirus software. But it is not sufficient to pick up an antivirus package from the store and install it on your computer. That is just the beginning. New viruses appear regularly. Companies that specialize in virus detection, such as Symantec and McAfee, maintain web sites from which you can download prevention measures and fixes for the most recently discovered viruses. Antivirus software will scan your hard disk every time you boot the computer or, if you prefer, at regularly scheduled intervals.

Although there have been isolated instances of viruses in commercial software, viruses tend to show up on free software or software acquired from friends or the Internet. Use a commonsense approach to new files. Never install a program unless the diskette comes in a sealed package. Be especially wary of software that arrives unexpectedly from companies with whom you have not done business. Use virus-scanning software to check any file or document, no matter what the source, before loading it onto your hard disk. If your own diskette was used in another computer, scan it to see if it caught a virus. Avoid use of programs that may be stolen or whose origin is unclear.

Privacy: Keeping Personal Information Personal

Think about the forms you have willingly filled out: paperwork for loans or charge accounts, orders for merchandise through the mail, magazine subscription orders, applications for schools and jobs and clubs, and on and on. There may be some forms you filled out with less delight—for taxes, military

Critical Thinking

Imagine that your job is that of an "electronic privacy advocate." What criteria do you think are important for privacy and electronic data processing rules and regulations? (Examples include no "secret" databases, the right to inspect your own data, the right to correct errors, freedom from unauthorized distribution and disclosure, the right to know that personal data is being collected, and the right to know that important personal data—like Social Security and immigration records—will not be subject to damage, alteration, or loss.)

draft registration, a court petition, an insurance claim, or a stay in the hospital. And remember all the people who got your name and address from your check—fund-raisers, advertisers, and petitioners. These lists may not have covered all the ways you have supplied data, but you can know with certainty where it all goes: straight to computer files.

Passing Your Data Around

Where is that data now? Is it shared, rented, sold? Who sees it? Will it ever be deleted? Or, to put it more bluntly, is *anything* private anymore? In some cases one can only guess at the answers. It is difficult to say where your data is now, and bureaucracies are not eager to enlighten you. The data may have been moved to other files without your knowledge. In fact, much of the data is most definitely passed around, as anyone with a mailbox can attest. Even online services sell their subscriber lists, neatly ordered by zip code and computer type.

As for who sees your personal data, the answers are not comforting. Government agencies, for example, regularly share data that was originally filed for some other purpose. Consider IRS records, which are compared with student loan records to intercept refunds to former students who have defaulted on their loans. The IRS created a storm of controversy by announcing a plan to use commercial direct-mail lists to locate tax evaders. Many people are worried about the consequences of this kind of sharing (Figure 8). For one thing, few of us can be certain that data about us, good or bad, is deleted when it has served its legitimate purpose.

Figure 8 Potential paths of data.
When an organization acquires data about you, it is often shared with—or sold to—other organizations.

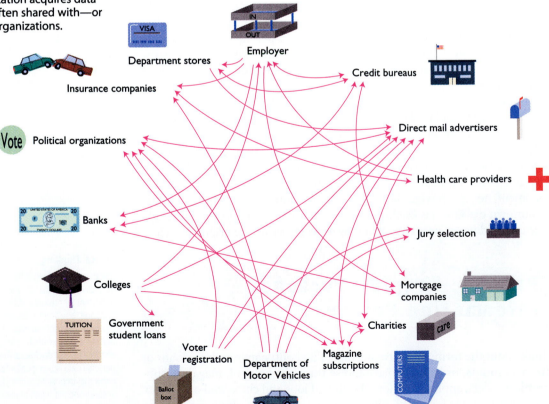

The unfortunate fact is that, for very little money, anybody can learn anything about anybody—through massive databases. There are matters you want to keep private. You have the right to do so. Although you can do little to stop data about you from circulating through computers, there are some laws that give you access to some of it. Let us see what kind of protection is available to help preserve privacy.

Privacy Legislation

Significant legislation relating to privacy began with the **Fair Credit Reporting Act** in 1970. This law allows you to have access to and gives you the right to challenge your credit records. In fact, this access must be given to you free of charge if you have been denied credit. Businesses usually contribute financial information about their customers to a community credit bureau, which gives them the right to review a person's prior credit record with other companies. Before the Fair Credit Reporting Act, many people were—without explanation—turned down for credit because of inaccurate financial records about them. Because of the act, people may now check their records to make sure they are accurate.

The **Freedom of Information Act** was also passed in 1970. This landmark legislation allows ordinary citizens to have access to data about them that was gathered by federal agencies (although sometimes a lawsuit has been necessary to pry data loose).

The most significant legislation protecting the privacy of individuals is the **Federal Privacy Act** of 1974. This act stipulates that there can be no secret personnel files; individuals must be allowed to know what is stored in files about them and how the data is used, and they must be able to correct it. The law applies not only to government agencies but also to private contractors dealing with government agencies. These organizations cannot obtain data willy-nilly, for no specific purpose; they must justify the need to obtain it.

A more recent law is the **Video Privacy Protection Act** of 1988, which prevents retailers from disclosing a person's video rental records without a court order; privacy supporters want the same rule for medical and insurance files. Another step in that direction is the **Computer Matching and Privacy Protection Act** of 1988, which prevents the government from comparing certain records in an attempt to find a match. However, most comparisons are still unregulated.

The Internet: Security and Privacy Problems

Networks, whether connected to the Internet or not, pose unique security and privacy problems. Many people have access to the system, often from remote locations. Clearly, questions arise: If it is so easy for authorized people to get data, what is to stop unauthorized people from tapping it? Organizations must be concerned about unauthorized people intercepting data in transit, whether hackers or thieves or industrial spies.

One fundamental approach to network security is to dedicate a computer, called a **firewall,** whose sole purpose is to talk to the outside world. A firewall will provide an organization with greatly increased security because only one

TRUSTe

To assure users of privacy, many sites have adopted the TRUSTe standard. TRUSTe is a nonprofit organization whose mission is to build users' trust in the Internet by promoting disclosure and informed consent. A site supporting TRUSTe agrees to certain principles. When you visit a web site displaying the TRUSTe mark, shown here, you can expect to be notified as to

- What information is gathered/tracked
- How the information is used
- With whom information is shared
- This site's opt-out policy
- This site's correct/update policy
- This site's delete/delist policy

network computer is accessible to people outside the network, and that one computer accepts only appropriate access.

Encryption

Data being sent over communications lines may be protected by scrambling the messages—that is, putting them in code that can be broken only by the person receiving the message. The process of scrambling messages is called **encryption.** The American National Standards Institute has endorsed a process called the **Data Encryption Standard (DES),** a standardized public key by which senders and receivers can scramble and unscramble their messages. Although the DES code is well known, and breakable even with a personal computer, companies still use it because the method makes it quite expensive to intercept coded messages. Thus interlopers are forced to use other methods of gathering data—methods that carry greater risk of detection. Encryption software is available for personal computers. A typical package, for example, offers a variety of security features: file encryption, keyboard lock, and password protection.

Privacy Problems for Networked Employees

Although employees do not have expectations of total privacy at the office, they are often shocked when they discover that the boss has been spying on them via the network, even their comings and goings on the Internet. The boss, of course, is not spying at all, merely "monitoring." This debate has been heightened by the advent of software that lets managers check up on networked employees without their ever knowing that they are under surveillance. With a flick of a mouse button, the boss can silently pull up an employee's current computer screen.

Surveillance software is not limited to checking screens. It can also check on e-mail, count the number of keystrokes per minute, note the length of a worker's breaks, and monitor what computer files are used and for how long.

Worker associations complain that workers who are monitored suffer much higher degrees of stress and anxiety than nonmonitored workers. However, vendors defend their products by saying that they are not "spy software" but rather products designed for training, monitoring resources, and helping employees. Privacy groups are lobbying legislators at both the state and federal levels to enact legislation that requires employers to at least alert employees that they are being monitored.

People who feel invaded at work may be shocked to find out that they are also being watched when online—from the privacy of their homes. This time it is not the boss but the web site owners who are watching.

You Are Being Watched

It may seem to be the ultimate in privacy invasion. When you visit a web site, it can easily collect the city you are calling from, the site from which you just came, and, of course, everything you do while you are at the site. Software can also discover and record the hardware and software you use. That's the good part. Software can even monitor a user's **click stream,** the series of mouse clicks that link from site to site. Thus a history of what a user chooses to view on the Web can be recorded and used for a variety of purposes by managers and marketers.

MAKING THE RIGHT CONNECTIONS

YOU HAVE NO PRIVACY WHATEVER

No privacy on the company e-mail, that is. Your employer can snoop into messages you send or receive even if you think you erased them. You have only erased them from their current hard drive location; copies are still in the company computer files. In fact, most companies archive all such files on tape and store them for the foreseeable future. Companies may fail to convey the message that e-mail, as a company conduit, is not private. Employees are often startled, after the fact, to discover that their messages have been invaded.

Furthermore, some people specialize in extracting deleted messages for use as evidence in court. E-mail can be a dangerous time bomb because litigators argue that, more than any other kind of written communication, e-mail reflects the real, unedited thoughts of the writer. This candid form of corporate communication increasingly is providing the most

incriminating evidence used against companies in litigation.

What to do? It is certainly degrading to have something you thought was private waved in front of you as evidence of malingering. As one computer expert put it, if noth-

ing is private, just say so. Companies have begun doing exactly that. The company policy on e-mail is—or should be—expressed in a clear, written document and routinely disseminated to all employees. However, even that step is probably insufficient. People tend to forget or get complacent. Reminders should be given through the usual company conduits—bulletin boards, posters, and so forth.

What about the e-mail you send and receive at home—do you at least have privacy in your own home? Maybe not. You certainly cannot count on it if the computer of the party at the other end is in an office. Further, keep in mind that messages sent across the Internet hop from computer to computer, with (depending on the service used) the sender having little say about its route. There are many vulnerable spots along the way.

If your computer is identifiable, presumably by an e-mail address, then the web site adds a record to a special file called a **cookie**. To add insult to injury, the file—actually called *cookie*—is kept right on your own computer, without your permission and possibly without your knowledge. (Go ahead, check your computer's files.) The next time you show up at that web site, it checks what it knows about you on your cookie file.

In true computer industry style, however, anonymity software can now defeat the snooping software. The anonymous software, where you must begin each web session, acts as a middleman, retrieving sites and documents without revealing your identity.

Guard Dog

What about those cookies being put on your hard drive? Are you just going to sit still for this kind of invasion? Not if Guard Dog has anything to say about it. Once installed, Guard Dog software is ever vigilant and informs you (*woofs,* actually) whenever a web site you are visiting tries to put a cookie file on your hard drive. You may not only decline, you may inform Guard Dog that you will *never* accept a cookie from that site.

Guard Dog offers other functions, such as cleaning up your URL history and guarding against incoming viruses. Guard Dog cannot protect against everything, but it can take a healthy bite out of security invasions.

Critical Thinking

It is possible to send e-mail or newsgroup postings anonymously, using a "remailer"—a special e-mail server, a web site, or a Java applet that disguises the originator's e-mail address, often substituting "nobody@nowhere.com" or the like. What issues do you see—pro and con—for these services? (Pro: There may be legitimate reasons for disguising one's e-mail address—to avoid "junk" e-mail; to participate in discussions on topics where disclosure of identity could lead to negative personal consequences, such as a forum for recovering alcoholics; and for reporting waste or corruption as a "whistle-blower." Con: Anonymity could be used for sending harassing e-mail, transmitting stolen information, or augmenting other criminal activity. Also "spammers," "flamers," and other undesirable elements might be encouraged by anonymity.)

A similar but unrelated approach is the cupcake. A **cupcake** is based on a technology that allows a Web user to create personal information (name, occupation, professional interests, and so forth) that can be shared with any web site the user wants to share it with. Like a cookie, a cupcake keeps the information on your computer's hard disk. However, unlike cookies, you create the file yourself and are always aware of who has permission to look at your personal information and how much they can look at.

Junk E-mail

Privacy invasion in the form of junk e-mail has become, unfortunately, a common event. The volume of junk e-mail will only soar as more marketers discover how cheap it is. A postal mailing to a million people costs about $800,000, including postage and printing. Internet marketers can reach the same number of people by making a phone call and paying a few hundred dollars for time spent online. The software that makes mass advertising—called **spamming**—possible both gathers e-mail addresses and sends e-mail messages for marketers, thousands and thousands every day. One of the most annoying aspects of e-mail is that, unlike postal junk mail, which at least arrives at no cost to you, a user who pays for online usage may be paying for part of the cost of junk e-mail delivery. Furthermore, the spammers are often devious, using subject lines such as "Do I have the right e-mail address?" or, supposedly, replying to "Your request for information."

Enraged spam recipients sometimes respond to the perpetrator by **flaming,** sending insulting messages in return. Experienced spammers, however, probably have already abandoned the originating site and, most likely, moved to another one. If you want to maximize your privacy and reduce your chances of getting junk e-mail, be careful where you leave your e-mail address. A prime source of e-mail addresses is newsgroup messages, whose e-mail addresses will likely be gathered up and sold. Further, Internet business sites entice visitors to supply personal data that can be used for marketing and promotion. An e-mail address is their most treasured commodity.

There is no sure protection from junk e-mail, but there are ways to minimize it. One approach is to use **filter software,** which gives you some control over what messages will be accepted. The filter software already knows that you do not want messages whose titles are "Lose 30 pounds in 10 days!!!" or "Earn $$$$ at home!" In addition to eliminating the obvious, you may add your own list of screening words. You may even state the exact e-mail addresses from which you will accept mail.

Your online service will let you make up several online names if you wish. Most experts recommend that you use a separate name for surfing the Internet, then simply ignore any mail that comes in for that name. More spam-fighting advice from experts includes never filing a "member's profile" with your online service, not filling in registration sites at web sites unless the purveyor promises not to sell or exchange your information, and never, never responding to a spammer.

The federal government has been unable to produce anti-spamming legislation, but the individual states are starting to take up the slack. The first such law with teeth was passed by the state of Washington in 1998. The law specifically bans unsolicited commercial e-mail that has misleading information in the subject line, disguises the path it took across the Internet, or contains an invalid reply address. Suits brought by the state have sought $2000 for each piece of unsolicited commercial e-mail sent to Washington residents in violation of the law.

Protecting Children

The Internet has opened up wonderful new opportunities for children— help with homework, dazzling new adventure games, and a chance to strike up conversations with new friends in another country. Millions of youngsters are surfing and chatting and e-mailing. But cyberspace can be a mixed blessing for children, who may also be exposed to its less savory elements. Concerned parents are taking steps to monitor their children's use of the Internet.

The most widely used online service, America Online, gives parents control of usage. The parent can create extra sign-in names and tailor privileges to each child. Younger children, for example, can be limited to AOL's kids' area, which includes its own kids' Web browser. Another possibility is blocking software, a product that tries to act as a high-tech chaperone (Figure 9). **Blocking software** typically keeps children away from its own updatable list of objectionable sites and avoids sites with other objectionable material such as foul language or sites requesting name, phone number, or credit-card number. Blocking software cannot be totally effective because the Web changes too fast for any software staff to maintain a complete list of objectionable sites.

Other oversight techniques available to parents are examining their browser's history files (which show recent visits) and searching their computer's files for files that may contain images, with extensions such as .gif, .jpg, .tif, or .zip. The best monitoring technique, however, may to avoid computers in a child's bedroom. That is, the computer might be located in a semipublic, high-traffic location, such as the family room or kitchen.

Government Intervention?

The invasion of privacy online, especially through the Internet, may be that rare problem that, in the opinion of some communications experts, requires government intervention. Such laws would have to carefully carve out a middle ground between preserving new opportunities for the legitimate needs of business people, researchers, and investigators on the one hand and preserving the right to privacy on the other.

Congress passed the Communications Decency Act in 1996, attempting to target, in particular, people who preyed on children on the Internet. The

Figure 9 Blocking software. Both (a) Cyber Patrol and (b) Net Nanny software let parents control online access and block entry to objectionable sites.

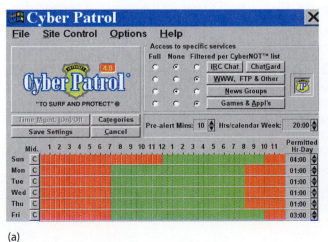

(a)

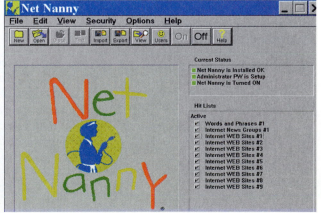

(b)

law caused a firestorm on the Internet, with many sites displaying the "blue ribbon" of free speech. The U.S. Supreme Court struck down the law for vagueness.

But more laws have been passed since that time, and others are likely to follow. The Children's Online Privacy Act requires web sites to get parental consent before gathering information from children 12 or younger. The bill directs the Federal Trade Commission to establish online privacy protections.

Ethics and Privacy

Snooping did not begin with computers. Neither did improper dissemination of personal information. But computers have elevated those problems to a much more serious level. As we have already noted, just about everything there is to know about you is already on a computer file, more likely several computer files. The thorny issues center around appropriate ethical treatment of that data by those who control it or merely have access to it. It is not unlikely that, in the course of your career, you yourself will see personal data about other people. Consider these scenarios:

- Suppose that, as a programmer, you work on software that uses the company personnel files. Is it legitimate to look up salary data for people you know? If you see such data in the normal course of your work, is it appropriate to let those individuals know that you saw it?
- Suppose that you had access to data about bank loan applications, some of which appeared in test reports on which you are working. If someone takes these from your desktop while you are on your lunch break, is this an ethical breach on your part?
- Suppose that you are a programmer for a medical organization, and in the normal course of your work, you see records about a celebrity. Is it ethical to describe the medical treatment to your friends, saying that it is a celebrity but not giving the name? Is it ethical to mention that the named celebrity uses your clinic without giving any medical details?

The above descriptions involve programmers, who are likely to see considerable private data over the course of a career. But people in many walks of life—accountants, tellers, nurses, contractors, and more—see data that resides on a computer. All of us need to respect the privacy of personal data.

The issues raised in this chapter are often the ones we think of after the fact—that is, when it is too late. Security and privacy factors are somewhat like insurance that we wish we did not have to buy. But we do buy insurance for our homes and cars and lives because we know we cannot risk being without it. The computer industry also knows that it cannot risk being without safeguards for security and privacy. As a computer user, you will share responsibility for addressing these issues.

Global Perspective

The scope and extent of international electronic privacy protection varies widely from the standards of the United States. In 1995, the European Union began implementing the European Data Protection Directive, a stringent series of regulations that attempts to define those circumstances under which computer processing of personal data is "legitimate." One set of provisions requires prior, informed consent from citizens of European nations before information collected about them can be redistributed or subjected to other electronic data processing.

CHAPTER REVIEW

Summary and Key Terms

- The word **hacker** originally referred to an enthusiastic, self-taught computer user, but now the term usually describes a person who gains access to computer systems illegally. Using **social engineering,** a tongue-in-cheek term for con artist actions, hackers persuade unsuspecting people to give away their passwords over the phone.

- Tricks employed by unscrupulous computer users can involve various devices, including a **bomb,** which causes a program to trigger damage under certain conditions; **data diddling,** or changing data before or as it enters the system; **piggybacking,** which is accessing a system via a legitimate user; **salami,** or embezzling small "slices" of money; **scavenging,** or searching company trash cans and dumpsters; a **trapdoor,** which allows subsequent unauthorized entry to a legitimate program; a **Trojan horse,** which places illegal instructions in the middle of a legitimate program; and **zapping,** or using software to bypass security systems.

- **Computer forensics** refers to uncovering computer-stored information suitable for use in courts of law.

- Prosecution of computer crime is often difficult because law enforcement officers, attorneys, and judges are unfamiliar with the issues involved. However, in 1986 Congress passed the latest version of the **Computer Fraud and Abuse Act,** and most states have passed some form of computer crime law.

- **Security** is a system of safeguards designed to protect a computer system and data from deliberate or accidental damage or access by unauthorized persons.

- The means of giving access to authorized people are divided into four general categories: (1) **what you have** (a key, badge, or plastic card); (2) **what you know** (a system password or identification number); (3) **what you do** (such as signing your name); and (4) **what you are** (your fingerprints, voice, and retina, as known through **biometrics,** the science of measuring individual body characteristics). An **active badge,** a clip-on employee identification card with an embedded computer chip, signals its wearer's location—legal or otherwise—by sending out infrared signals, which are read by sensors throughout the building.

- A **disaster recovery plan** is a method of restoring data processing operations if they are halted by major damage or destruction. Common approaches to disaster recovery include relying temporarily on manual services; buying time at a computer service bureau; making mutual assistance agreements with other companies; or forming a **consortium,** a joint venture with other organizations to support a complete computer facility to be used only in the event of a disaster.

- A **hot site** is a fully equipped computer facility with hardware, environmental controls, security, and communications equipment in place. A **cold site** is an environmentally suitable empty shell in which a company can install its own computer system.

- Personal computer security is based on such measures as locking hardware in place; providing an appropriate physical environment; and using a **surge protector,** a device that prevents electrical problems from affecting computer data files.

- A **worm** is a program that transfers itself from computer to computer over a network, planting itself as a separate file on the target computer's disks. A **virus** is a set of illicit instructions that passes itself on to other programs with which it comes in contact. A **vaccine,** or **antivirus,** is a computer program that stops the spread of the virus and eradicates it. A **retrovirus** can fight back and may delete antivirus software.

- The security issue extends to the use of information about individuals that is stored in the computer files of credit bureaus and government agencies. The **Fair Credit Reporting Act** allows individuals to check the accuracy of credit information about them. The **Freedom of**

Information Act allows people access to data that federal agencies have gathered about them. The **Federal Privacy Act** allows individuals access to information about them that is held not only by government agencies but also by private contractors working for the government. Individuals are also entitled to know how that information is being used. The **Video Privacy Protection Act** and the **Computer Matching and Privacy Protection Act** have extended federal protections.

■ A **firewall** is a dedicated computer whose sole purpose is to talk to the outside world and decide who gains entry to a computer network.

■ The process of scrambling messages is called **encryption.** The American National Standards Institute has endorsed a process called the **Data Encryption Standard (DES)**, a standardized public key by which senders and receivers can scramble and unscramble their messages.

■ Software can monitor a user's **click stream,** the series of mouse clicks that link from site to site and provide a history of what that user chooses to view on the Web.

■ If your computer is identifiable, the web site can add a record of your activity to a **cookie** file that is stored on your computer. A **cupcake** is a personal profile created by the individual, stored on disk, and shared only at his or her discretion.

■ Privacy invasion in the form of junk e-mail has become a common event and will get worse because junk e-mail is inexpensive to send. Mass advertising on the Internet is called **spamming.** Enraged spam recipients sometimes respond to the perpetrator by **flaming,** sending insulting messages in return. **Filter software** offers some control over what e-mail messages will be accepted.

■ **Blocking software** helps parents monitor children's Internet access to objectionable web sites.

Discussion Questions

1. Before accepting a particular patient, a doctor might like access to a computer file listing patients who have been involved in malpractice suits. Before accepting a tenant, the owner of an apartment building might want to check a file that lists people who have previously sued landlords. Should computer files be available for such purposes?

2. Discuss the following statement: An active badge may help an organization maintain security, but it also erodes the employee's privacy.

Student Study Guide

Multiple Choice

1. Persuading people to tell their passwords is called
   a. social engineering   c. biometrics
   b. flaming   d. encryption

2. The history of a user's movements from site to site is in the
   a. worm   c. consortium
   b. vaccine   d. click stream

3. One safeguard against theft or alteration of data is the use of
   a. DES   c. identical passwords
   b. the Trojan horse   d. data diddling

4. The legislation that prohibits government agencies and contractors from keeping secret personal files on individuals is the
   a. Federal Privacy Act   c. Fair Credit Reporting Act
   b. Computer Abuse Act   d. Freedom of Information Act

5. Uncovering computer data useful in a court of law is called
   a. spamming   c. social engineering
   b. computer forensics   d. flaming

6. Computer crimes are usually
   a. easy to detect   c. prosecuted
   b. blue-collar crimes   d. discovered accidentally

7. The "what you are" criterion for computer system access involves
   a. a badge   c. biometrics
   b. a password   d. a magnetized card

8. The key problem for a computer installation that has met with disaster is generally
   a. equipment replacement c. loss of hardware
   b. insurance coverage   d. loss of processing ability

9. In anticipation of physical destruction, every computer organization should have a
   a. biometric scheme   c. disaster recovery plan
   b. DES   d. set of active badges

10. A file with a record of web site activity is called a(n)
    a. hot file   c. filter file
    b. cookie file   d. active file

True/False

T F 1. Most computer organizations cannot afford consortiums.

T F 2. Vaccine is another name for antivirus software.

T F 3. The Trojan horse is an embezzling technique.

T F 4. If a computer crime is detected, prosecution is assured.

T F 5. Blocking software prevents all users from accessing the Internet.

T F 6. Fingerprints are an example of biometrics.

T F 7. The actual loss of hardware is a major security problem because of its expense.

T F 8. If a user is identifiable, a web site may add a record to the user's spam file.

T F 9. A victim of mass advertising may respond by flaming.

T F 10. Most computer crimes are not detected.

Fill-In

1. An environmentally suitable empty shell into which a computer organization can put its computer system is known as a(n)

    _____.

2. A system of safeguards to protect a computer system and data from damage or unauthorized access: is called a(n)_____ system.

3. Bypassing security systems with an illicitly acquired software package is called

    _____.

4. The field concerned with the measurement of individual body characteristics is known as

    _____.

5. A fully equipped computer center to be used in the event of a disaster is called a(n)

    _____.

6. The assurance to individuals that personal property is used properly is called

    _____.

7. A person who gains access to a computer system illegally is called a(n) _____.

8. A standardized public key by which senders and receivers can scramble and unscramble their messages is the _____.

9. A device that prevents electrical problems from affecting computer files is the

    _____.

10. The file on your own computer that has records of Web activity is called a(n) _____.

Answers

Multiple Choice
1. a   6. d
2. d   7. c
3. a   8. d
4. a   9. c
5. b   10. b

True/False
1. T   6. T
2. T   7. F
3. F   8. F
4. F   9. T
5. F   10. T

Fill-In
1. cold site
2. security
3. zapping
4. biometrics
5. hot site
6. privacy
7. hacker
8. Data Encryption Standard (DES)
9. surge protector
10. cookie

PLANET INTERNET

You never know what you might find on the Internet. If you deliberately put provocative words, even something as tame as *strange*, through a search engine, you may find some of the sites returned to be disconcerting or even alarming. But it is pretty easy to stay away from such sites if you tread the beaten paths.

Unexpected. Even so, you can easily come across sites that feature subjects you never expected to find on the Web. For example, few would expect to come across a site that tells you more about New York City underground than you ever thought you needed

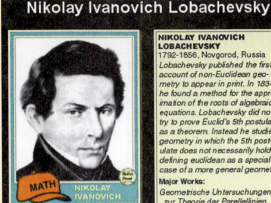

Nikolay Ivanovich Lobachevsky

NIKOLAY IVANOVICH LOBACHEVSKY
1792-1856, Novgorod, Russia
Lobachevsky published the first account of non-Euclidean geometry to appear in print. In 1834 he found a method for the approximation of the roots of algebraic equations. Lobachevsky did not try to prove Euclid's 5th postulate as a theorem. Instead he studied geometry in which the 5th postulate does not necessarily hold, defining euclidean as a special case of a more general geometry.

Major Works:
Geometrische Untersuchungen zur Theorie der Parellellinien

NIKOLAY
IVANOVICH
LOBACHEVSKY

MATH

to know. Or you could come across the Found Money site, which suggests that "you may be rich and not even know it!" You can check their database to see if you have any money lying around.

Not your everyday pursuit. Been thinking about prisons lately? Probably not. But there it is, the Alcatraz prison site. An even more somber site is the World Wide Cemetery, in which

you can post dedications to departed loved ones. You might whip up more interest in your math course if you check out the math trading cards site; collect them all. Or perhaps you would prefer to collect toasters; as you may imagine, there is more than one site devoted to this activity.

You didn't know you needed this. Watch the robot dance. Check out the driveways of the rich and famous (Dolly Parton's driveway is shown here). See what the flying pigs are about. See if you can tell which candy bar is which from cross sections of candy bars.

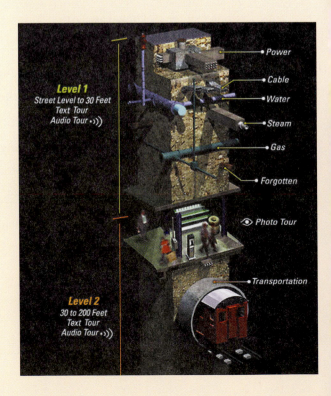

Level 1
Street Level to 30 Feet
Text Tour
Audio Tour •))

Level 2
30 to 200 Feet
Text Tour
Audio Tour •))

Power
Cable
Water
Steam
Gas
Forgotten
Photo Tour
Transportation

Finally, if you really have a lot of time on your hands, go to the SuperBad site. The bear shown here is more benign than other graphics found on the multileveled site, which goes on and on, deeper and deeper, with many options at every turn.

Internet Exercises

1. **Structured exercise.** Begin with the URL http://www.prenhall.com/capron and take a tour of Alcatraz. Visit the prison bookstore.

2. **Freeform exercise.** Use the WebCrawler's Search Ticker to check out a few of its randomly selected sites.

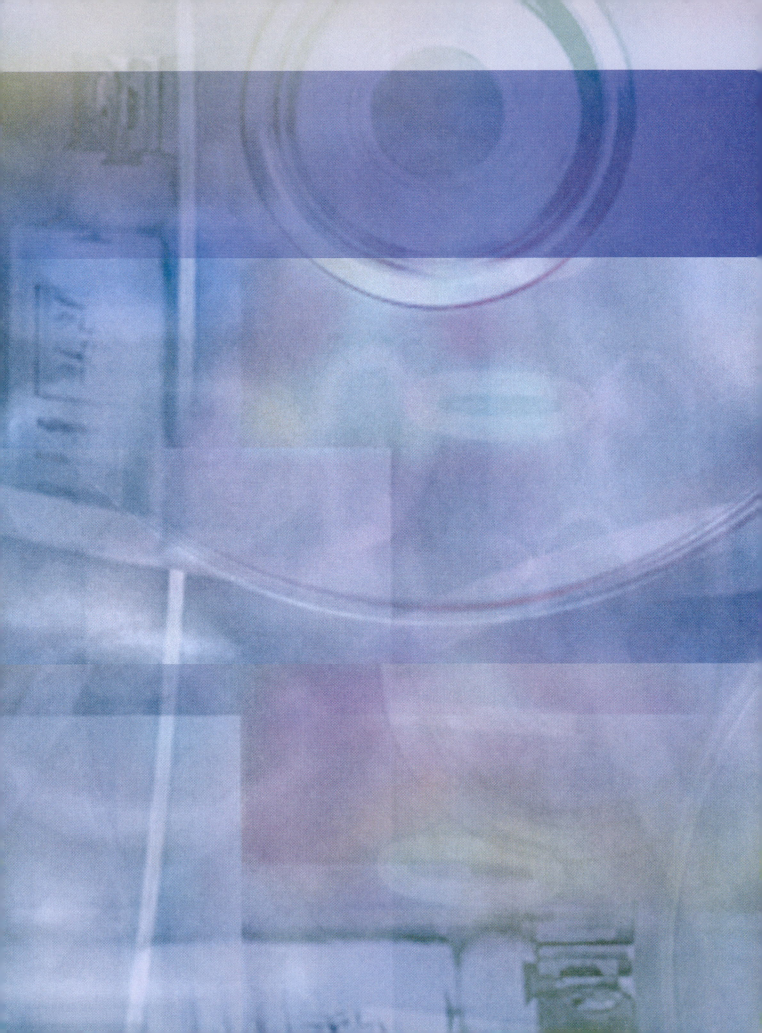

CHAPTER ELEVEN

WORD PROCESSING AND DESKTOP PUBLISHING

Printing It

LEARNING OBJECTIVES

- Appreciate the need for word processing
- List the basic features of word processing programs
- Describe spelling checkers and thesaurus programs
- Understand the value of collaboration using word processing and the Web
- Appreciate the advantages of desktop publishing
- Understand desktop publishing terminology

Jane Duffin, a physical therapist in the Mount Tahoma School District, appreciates the interaction between her students and computers. In particular, she has observed them using software specially designed to help physically challenged students communicate.

Until recently, however, Jane has done most of her own paperwork by hand. Other papers, primarily the dreaded end-of-year reports, were typed and retyped by a secretary using a typewriter. For Jane, everything changed the day the district administrators announced that professional employees would get their own computers to take home with them. The administrators also required a series of classes on how to use the computer software.

Jane learned word processing, software that let her prepare and print text documents such as memos and reports. She made her first tentative foray into word processing by typing a memo. She was not concerned about typing mistakes she made but simply corrected them on-screen before she printed the memo.

That was the beginning. With a speed that surprised her, Jane found herself moving all her paperwork to the computer: individualized child service plans, bus schedules, academic and physical progress reports, and her own time records for each child. At first Jane composed what she wanted to communicate on paper and then keyed it into the word processing program. Before long she became comfortable enough to compose directly on the computer. Furthermore, she saw her overall communication improve as she wrote memos to parents, teachers, doctors, and staff members.

A few months later Jane decided to use her word process-ing skills to tackle the annual grant proposal document. In past years the entire proposal, running some 40 pages, had to be typed from scratch. This was true even though much of the proposal was the same from year to year. A word-processed document can be handled differently: Only the new or changed material has to be keyed, and then the entire document can be printed as if new. Relishing the thought of how easy it was going to be next year, Jane set out to produce the grant proposal in word-processed form.

Jane could also improve the document's attractiveness by using features such as boldface, underlining, and even drawings. Best of all, she could make the document look professionally printed by choosing an attractive typeface—font—from her word processing package.

Jane is still a busy physical therapist. But thanks to her computer and its word processing software, she has more time for her first love: children.

2000 and Beyond

DIGITAL ART

Imagine the day when, instead of a minimalist collection of clip art, you have the works of the masters at your disposal—Matisse, van Gogh, and Renoir (Renoir's In a Dinghy is shown here). Now add the works of famous photographers such as Ansel Adams. If we had such collections available at the click of a mouse, we could indeed produce impressive output.

A company called Corbis Publishing is taking major steps in this direction. Corbis is not the usual high-tech company; art history majors and librarians outnumber techies. Founded in 1989, Corbis is a leading provider of photography and fine art on the Internet. Corbis's offerings include a broad spectrum of products and services for both professionals and everyday online consumers.

The company has acquired the digital rights—usually nonexclusive—to several collections. The Corbis col-lection currently contains more than 25 million fine art and photographs from yesterday and today. Of those images, about one and a half million are available online in a high-resolu-tion digitized format. These images are stored in searchable databases, making the collection an accessible reservoir of quality digital images. Thus these works in digital form can be a primary visual resource for the consumer, education, and publishing markets.

Perhaps the most renowned image library acquired by Corbis is the Bettmann Archive, a collection that illustrates the entire history of mankind, from prehistoric cave paintings to modern-day photojour-nalism. But Bettmann is most noted for its World War II vintage black and white photography.

It should be noted that digitized images from Corbis and similar com-panies are available for a fee. However, most word processing and desktop publishing packages also offer a limited a set of photographs and artwork, along with the usual clip art. These images are freely available for use as part of the cost of the soft-ware package. It seems likely that, in the near future, these attached collec-tions will continue to expand.

Word Processing as a Tool

Word processing software lets you create, edit, format, store, retrieve, and print a *text document*. Let us examine each part of the definition. A text doc-ument is any text that can be keyed in, such as a memo. *Creation* is the orig-inal composing and keying in of the document. *Editing* is making changes to the document to fix errors or improve its content—for example, deleting a sentence, correcting a misspelled name, or moving a paragraph. *Formatting* refers to adjusting the appearance of the document to make it look appropriate and attractive. For example, you might want to center a heading, make wider margins, or use double spacing. *Storing* the document means saving it on disk so that it can be accessed on demand. (Although beginners usually think only in terms of saving the completed document, all users, whether experienced or inexperienced, should save a document at regular intervals as it is being keyed to avoid losing work if something should go wrong.) *Retrieving* the document means bringing the stored document from disk back into computer memory so that it can be used again or changed in some way. *Printing* is producing the document on paper, using a printer connected to the computer.

A word processing package is a sophisticated tool with many options. This chapter discusses several of them. First, here is an overview of how word processing works.

An Overview: How Word Processing Works

Think of the computer's screen as a page of typing paper. When you type, you can see the line of text you are typing on the screen—it looks just like a line of typing on paper. You are not really typing on the screen, of course; the screen merely displays what you are entering into memory. As you type, the program displays the **insertion point,** or **cursor,** to show where the next character you type will appear on the screen. The insertion point is usually a blinking dash or line or rectangle that you can easily see. Although this chapter examines word processing in a general way that applies to any word processing software, occasionally, as here, a point will be demonstrated with Microsoft Word 2000 (Figure 1).

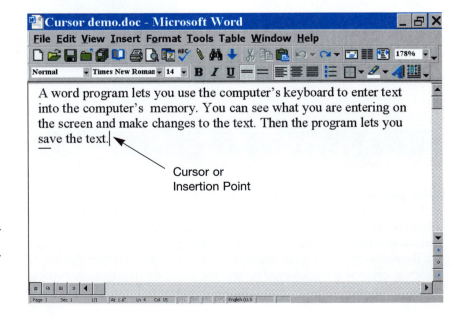

Figure 1 Entering text with word processing software. As you type in your text, the position of the cursor (the vertical line just to the right of the last word on the screen) shows where the next character will be placed.

Scrolling

A word processing program lets you type page after page of material. Most programs show a horizontal line on the screen to mark where one printed page will end and another will begin; this line does not appear on the printed document. Most word processing programs also display, at the bottom of the screen, the number of the page on which you are currently typing and also an indicator of the line, either by line number or by inches from the top of the printed page. Although the screen display size is limited, your document size is not. As you add new lines at the bottom of the screen, the lines you typed earlier move up the screen. Eventually, the first line you typed disappears off the top of the screen. The line has not disappeared from the document or from the computer's memory.

To see lines that have disappeared from the top, you can move the cursor up to the top of the screen and press the up arrow key; lines that had disappeared drop back down onto the screen. You can also use a mouse to accomplish the same thing by clicking over the up arrow of the scroll bar to the right of the screen. You can use opposite movements to send screen lines in the upward direction. This process, called **scrolling,** lets you see any part of the document—but only one screen at a time.

No Need to Worry about the Right Side

After you start to type the first line of a document, you will eventually get to the right edge of the screen. If there is not enough room at the end of a line to complete the word you are typing, the program automatically starts that word at the left margin of the next line down. This feature is called **word wrap.** With word wrap you do not have to push a carriage return key (on the computer, the *Enter* key) at the end of each line as you would with a typewriter; in fact, you should *not* press *Enter* at the end of a line, or the word wrap feature will not work properly. You should only press *Enter* when you want a blank line or to signal the end of a paragraph.

Easy Corrections

What if you make a mistake while you are keying? No problem: Move the cursor to the position of the error and make the correction. Use the **Backspace key** to delete characters to the left of the cursor, or use the **Delete key** to delete the character under the cursor or just to the right of the cursor. Word processing programs let you delete characters or whole words or lines that you have already typed; the resulting spaces are closed up automatically.

Sometimes people delete parts of a document and immediately regret it. Accidental or incorrect deletions can usually be repaired with the **undo command,** usually shown as a reverse arrow on the toolbar. Undo reverses the effect of the previous action and returns the document to its condition just prior to that operation. High-performance word processing programs offer the ability to undo more than one previous operation.

You can also insert new characters in the middle of a line or a word without typing over (and erasing) the characters that are already there. The program automatically moves the existing characters to the right of the insertion as you type the new characters and rewraps the text. However, if you wish, the word processing program also lets you *overtype* (replace) characters you typed before.

InfoBit

Small Office and Home Office word processing users will can find now find a wide variety of special papers, forms, envelopes and business cards designed to improve the appearance of their output. As an example, the SOHO user needn't worry about purchasing and trying to give out thousands of business cards. Using readily-available sheets of blank business cards, an ink-jet or laser printer and a word processor, SOHO users can produce a few dozen attractive business cards "on-demand."

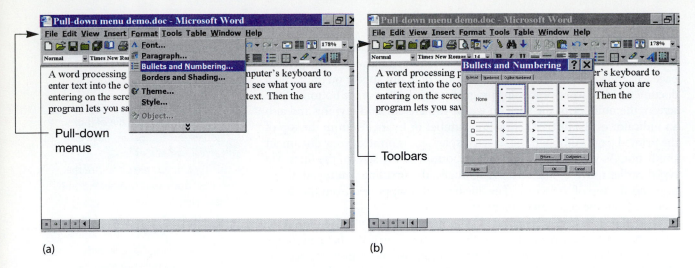

(a)   (b)

Figure 2 Pull-down menus. (a) When the Format menu is clicked with a mouse, a submenu of choices appears. The submenu Bullets and Numbering is highlighted. If it is clicked, the submenu shown in (b) appears. (b) Some submenus have their own submenus; here, the submenu Bullets and Numbering has further selections. Note also the vertical scroll bar on the right side of the screen. When a mouse is used to click one of the large up or down arrows on the scroll bar, the document moves up or down, respectively. A mouse can also move the square within the scroll bar, and the document will move up or down.

Menus and Buttons: At Your Command

Most word processing packages permit commands to be given via **menus,** a set of choices normally laid out across the top of the screen. The menus are called **pull-down menus** because each initial choice, when clicked with a mouse, reveals lower-level choices that pull down like a window shade from the initial selection at the top of the screen. For example, an initial selection of Format may reveal several submenus; the submenu Bullets and Numbering has its own set of selections (Figure 2). A mouse user can also invoke commands using **buttons.** A **toolbar** is a collection of such buttons, usually shown across the top of the screen just below the pull-down menus (Figure 2). There are different kinds of toolbars for different application programs, and even a variety of toolbars within the same software. As an example of button functions, the top leftmost buttons on the screen in Figure 2b let you begin a new document (the white paper button), open an existing document (the file folder button), or save a document (the diskette button). You can discover the meaning of any button by resting your mouse on it; a printed phrase will soon appear.

Word Processing Features

All word processing users begin by learning the basics: Invoke the word processing software, key in the document, change the document, and save and print the document. However, most users also come to appreciate the various features offered by word processing software (Figure 3).

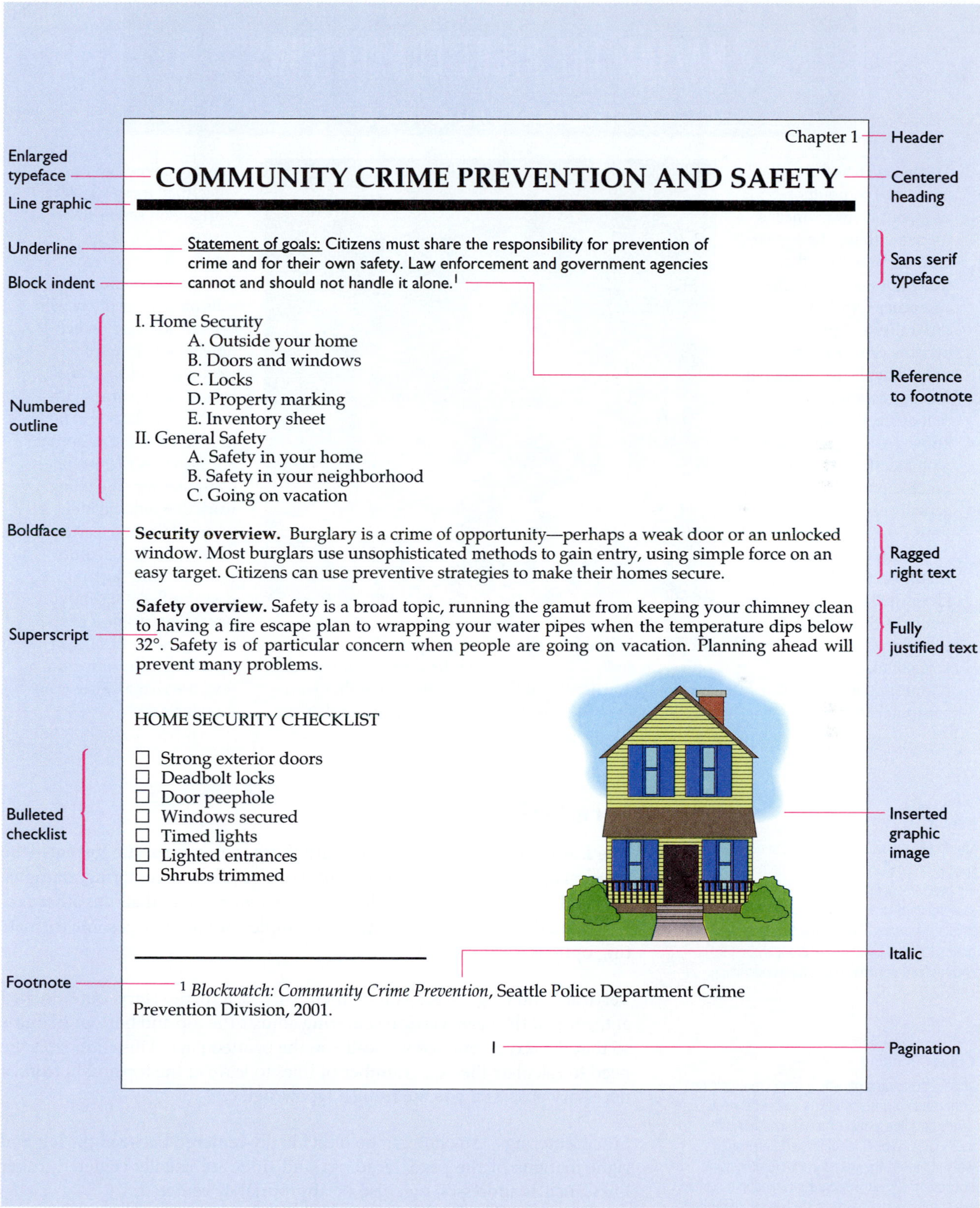

Chapter 1
Header
Enlarged typeface
COMMUNITY CRIME PREVENTION AND SAFETY
Centered heading
Line graphic
Underline
Statement of goals: Citizens must share the responsibility for prevention of crime and for their own safety. Law enforcement and government agencies cannot and should not handle it alone.[1]
Block indent
Sans serif typeface
Numbered outline
I. Home Security
A. Outside your home
B. Doors and windows
C. Locks
D. Property marking
E. Inventory sheet
II. General Safety
A. Safety in your home
B. Safety in your neighborhood
C. Going on vacation
Reference to footnote
Boldface
Security overview. Burglary is a crime of opportunity—perhaps a weak door or an unlocked window. Most burglars use unsophisticated methods to gain entry, using simple force on an easy target. Citizens can use preventive strategies to make their homes secure.
Ragged right text
Superscript
Safety overview. Safety is a broad topic, running the gamut from keeping your chimney clean to having a fire escape plan to wrapping your water pipes when the temperature dips below 32°. Safety is of particular concern when people are going on vacation. Planning ahead will prevent many problems.
Fully justified text
HOME SECURITY CHECKLIST
Bulleted checklist
☐ Strong exterior doors
☐ Deadbolt locks
☐ Door peephole
☐ Windows secured
☐ Timed lights
☐ Lighted entrances
☐ Shrubs trimmed
Inserted graphic image
Italic
Footnote
1 Blockwatch: Community Crime Prevention, Seattle Police Department Crime Prevention Division, 2001.
1
Pagination

Figure 3 Word processing features. Although it is not possible to show all word processing features on a single page, this page illustrates many of the capabilities available.

MAKING THE RIGHT CONNECTIONS
THE VIRTUAL OFFICE

The word *virtual* is applied in various computer settings, but it always means the same thing: the appearance of something that really does not exist. The computer somehow masks the reality and permits benefits similar to those offered by the real thing. In this discussion of the virtual office, the office as we know it—a physical place with a desk and a chair and office supplies—does not actually exist. But its functions do exist.

Consider the way Nora Mathison runs her sprinkler installation business in Phoenix. She relies on a toll-free phone number, voice mail, a cellular phone, and a notebook computer with a fax modem. No building, no office, no desk.

Nora advertises her toll-free number in the Yellow Pages; potential customers in the urban/suburban area can call the number without charge. When they do, they are advised to leave a voice-mail message. Nora, working on site in some customer's yard, can retrieve her voice-mail messages and return the calls on her cell phone. She can use software on her notebook computer to work up a bid right at a customer site, or she can do the work later and fax the results to the customer. She also uses the notebook computer for scheduling, work flow, and billing.

In addition to convenience, the virtual office can minimize start-up costs for fledgling entrepreneurs. For business people who spend most of their time out of the office anyway, the virtual office is an ongoing asset.

Formatting

The most commonly used features are those that control the **format**—the physical appearance of the document. Format refers to centering, margins, tabs and indents, justification, line spacing, emphasis, and all the other factors that affect appearance. Note the examples in Figure 3 as some formatting options are described.

Vertical Centering   A short document such as a memo starts out bunched at the top of the page. **Vertical centering** adjusts the top and bottom margins so that the text is centered vertically on the printed page. This eliminates the need to calculate the exact number of lines to leave at the top and bottom, a necessary process if you are using a typewriter.

Line Centering   Any line can be individually **centered** between the left and right margins of the page. Headings and titles are usually centered; other lines, such as addresses, may also be appropriately centered.

Margins   Some settings, called **default settings,** are used automatically by the word processing program; they can be overridden by the user. The default left and right margins are usually 1 1/4 inches wide. Documents are often typed using the default margin settings. However, if the document would look better with narrower or wider margins, the margin settings can be changed accordingly. When the margin settings are changed, word processing software automatically adjusts the text to fit the new margins. This process is called **automatic reformatting.**

Tabs and Indentation   It is common to **tab** just once to begin a paragraph. Some users need a set of tab positions across the page to make items align. It is also possible to indent an entire paragraph, and even to **indent** it from two sides, so that it stands out.

Justification   The evenness of text at the side margins is called **justification.** A document of several paragraphs is often most attractive if it is **fully justified,** that is, has an even margin down each side. The program adjusts each line so that it ends exactly at the right margin, spacing the words evenly. There are occasions, perhaps to spot any unintentional spaces, when only left justification is desired; this is referred to as **ragged-right** text because of the uneven appearance of the unjustified right side.

Line Spacing   Most of the time you will want your documents—letters, memos, reports—to be single-spaced. But on occasion you will find it is convenient or necessary to double-space or even triple-space a document. Word processing lets you do this with ease.

Boldface, Italic, and Underlining   Certain words or phrases, or even entire paragraphs, can be given emphasis by using a darker text known as **boldface** text, or by using the slanted type called *italic,* or by <u>underlining</u> important words. Some style guidelines still require underlining in special circumstances, and all modern word processing programs support it. However, underlining is something of an anachronism, given the italics, boldface, and special font features of modern word processing programs. Italics or boldface are probably better choices than underlining for emphasizing text.

Fonts   Most word processing packages offer dozens of fonts. In fact, you can easily see what they look like by using a pull-down menu (Figure 4). A

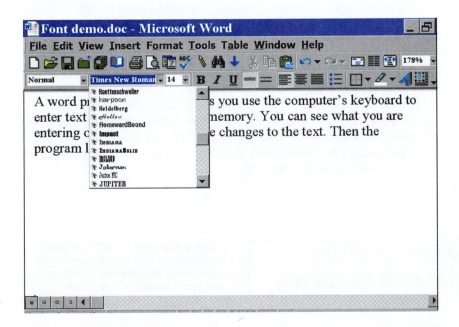

Figure 4 Pull-down fonts. Notice that the font name is written in the style of the font, an easy way to see what you are getting.

this font is called *Hogarth*

this font is called *Surf Style*

this font is called City

this font is called Commerce Lean

this font is called *Rage*

this font is called Arriba Arriba

THIS FONT IS CALLED BANG

this font is called Laser Chrome

this font is called Gotisch

this font is called Journal Ultra

Figure 5 Various fonts. These fonts, just ten of hundreds of possibilities, can serve a purpose or just whimsy. As you can see, some are more easily read than others.

Global Perspective

Most word processing programs can be set to support working with foreign languages, including non-Roman alphabets such as Greek, Cyrillic (Russian), and Hebrew. In addition to changing the character set to match the letters of the selected language, the word processing software will automatically alter how dates are printed, how tables are formatted, how words are sorted, and how spelling checkers and the thesaurus function.

font is a set of characters—letters, punctuation, and numbers—of the same design. Figure 5 shows some fonts in large enough size that you can get a better idea of the variety. Everyday fonts can generally be grouped into serif and sans serif fonts (*sans* means without). On a **serif** font, each character includes small marks called serifs, thought to help the eye travel more easily from character to character, making reading easier. A **sans serif** font is clean and stark, with no serif marks (Figure 6). In this book, the main text uses a serif font, but the margin notes use a sans serif font.

Most fonts available today are **scalable** fonts. This means that they can be set to almost any size without the individual letters appearing ragged or irregular. Fonts that use the trade name TrueType are always scalable. Most word processing programs let you "dress up" your text by adding color and three-dimensional effects (Figure 7).

(a) The quick brown fox jumped over the lazy dog.

(b) The quick brown fox jumped over the lazy dog.

Figure 6 Comparing serif and sans serif fonts. (a) This popular serif font is called Times New Roman. (b) This sans serif font is called Helvetica Light.

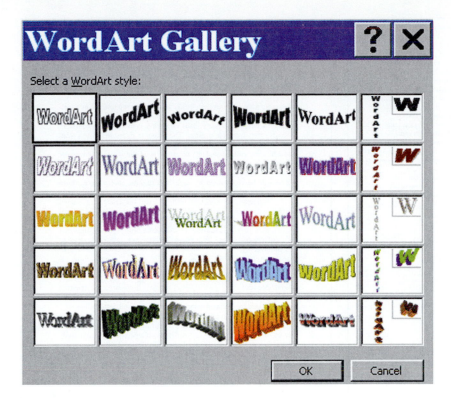

Figure 7 Three-dimensional fonts.
Using one of several choices from Microsoft Word's WordArt menu, shown here, a user can turn ordinary text into something special.

Squeezing or Stretching a Document

There are times when you want certain text to fit into a certain space. For example, an instructor could suggest that a term paper be at least ten double-spaced pages, or a potential employer could suggest a résumé of no more than two pages. Or perhaps the problem is something as simple as reducing a memo that runs three pages plus two lines to just three pages. There are several ways to use word processing features to adjust the length of a document:

- Adjust the margins, both sides and top and bottom, larger to stretch the number of pages, smaller to reduce the number.
- Try different line spacing. One-and-a-half line spacing, available with most word processing programs, looks quite similar to double spacing.
- Experiment with fonts. Some take up much less room than others at the same point size. And, of course, point size is a variable that you can adjust.

Note the variation in size in the two versions of the letter in Figure 8.

Printing Envelopes

After printing your computer-produced letter, you carefully fold it in thirds with nice even creases, slip it into an envelope that matches the paper, and then proceed to chicken-scratch the address onto it. The professional look falls through in this scenario. Using your computer to address and print the envelope adds that finishing touch.

It is not that difficult to do. Every word processing program offers a way to produce envelopes that look as good as the letters they contain. Here, gen-

Internet University

Learning from a distance is already available on the Internet in a variety of forms. But there is also something different, something more grand: a virtual university. This university goes beyond a course or two; it offers four-year degrees. The school is sponsored by ten western states (excluding California), created in response to the high costs of educating college students on-site. Called the Western Governors University, the school is an accredited regional university that exists solely in cyberspace. The key here is *accredited*, meaning that the degree will be recognized by other institutions, including graduate schools, throughout the country.

Western Governors University is a real university, just without a physical campus. The school is based on a simple idea: In the real world, people have jobs and lives and responsibilities that do not always allow them to sit in a university classroom. Students can take courses from institutions all across the country without ever leaving home. WGU does not offer instruction itself. Rather, it brokers instruction provided by affiliated colleges, universities, and corporations.

Using technology like the World Wide Web, e-mail, satellite broadcasts and more, WGU makes it possible for students to earn degrees or certificates in several different college and university study programs, no matter where they live or what their schedules.

As the WGU site, shown here, notes: WGU isn't your average university. But then again, who ever wanted to be average?

(a)

Internet University

Learning from a distance is already available on the Internet in a variety of forms. But there is also something different, something more grand: a virtual university. This university goes beyond a course or two; it offers four-year degrees. The school is sponsored by ten western states (excluding California), created in response to the high costs of educating college students on-site. Called the Western Governors University, the school is an accredited regional university that exists solely in cyberspace. The key here is *accredited*, meaning that the degree will be recognized by other institutions, including graduate schools, throughout the country.

Western Governors University is a real university, just without a physical campus. The school is based on a simple idea: In the real world, people have jobs and lives and responsibilities that do not always allow them to sit in a university classroom. Students can take courses from institutions all across the country without ever leaving home. WGU does not offer instruction itself. Rather, it brokers instruction provided by affiliated colleges, universities, and corporations.

Using technology like the World Wide Web, e-mail, satellite broadcasts and more, WGU makes it possible for students to earn degrees or certificates in several different college and university study programs, no matter where they live or what their schedules.

As the WGU site, shown here, notes: WGU isn't your average university. But then again, who ever wanted to be average?

(b)

Figure 8 Stretching a document. It is fairly easy to stretch or compress a document by varying margins, fonts, and line spacing. (a) This document is bunched at the top and poorly presented altogether. (b) The same document has been arranged more suitably on the page by making the side and top margins wider and increasing the font size from 12 to 14. While we were at it, we used full justification, moved the image to the center of the document, and made the title more attractive using the program's WordArt feature. We also centered the title.

erally, is how it is done. Find the command *Envelope* on one of your program's pull-down menus (Figure 9a). That menu will cause a window to be displayed (Figure 9b), giving you the opportunity to type in the recipient's address; the address will be there automatically if you highlighted it in the letter before you invoked the *Envelope* command. There is also space to type your return address. You can set your address as the default return address and not have to type it each time; this can, of course, be overridden. The return address can be omitted altogether if you are using an envelope with a preprinted return address.

The software will offer a variety of options, such as different fonts and font sizes, envelope size, and the manner in which the envelope is fed into the printer. The tricky part is getting the envelope into the printer correctly; we must refer you to the manual that matches your printer—or, even better, suggest that you have someone show you. When everything is ready, click the *Print* button in the Envelope window shown in Figure 9b. The envelope comes out of the printer ready to be stamped and mailed.

Other Important Features

Popular word processing packages offer more features than most people use. Although it is not possible to discuss every feature here, this list contains a few that you may find handy.

Search   Imagine working with a 97-page study called *Western Shorebirds,* all nicely prepared as a word-processed document. There has been an addi-

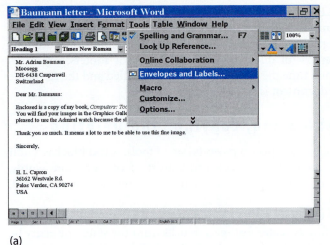
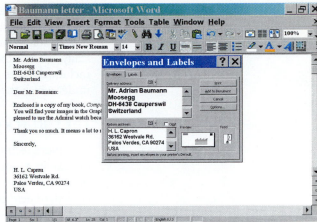

(a) (b)

tional sighting of the white-rumped sandpiper, and it has fallen to you to make a change in the report. You could, of course, leaf through the printed report to find out where to put the change. Alternatively, you could scroll the report on the screen, hoping to see the words *white-rumped sandpiper* pass by. The fast and easy way, however, is to use the **search command,** also called the **find command.** Just invoke the search command, key in the word or words you are looking for, and the exact page and place where it is located will appear on the screen.

Find and Replace   Suppose you type a long report in which you repeatedly and incorrectly spell the name of a client as *Mr. McDonald.* To make a change, you could search for each individual occurrence of *McDonald,* replacing each incorrect *Mc* with the correct *Mac.* There is, however, a more efficient way—using the **find-and-replace function.** You make a single request to replace one word or phrase with another. Then the find-and-replace command quickly searches through the entire document, finding each instance of the word or phrase and replacing it with the word or phrase you designated. Most word processing programs also offer **conditional replace,** which asks you to verify each replacement before it is carried out.

Pagination   Displaying page numbers in a document is a normal need for most users. Word processing programs offer every imaginable paging option, permitting the page number to be located at the top or bottom of the page and to the left, right, or center, or even alternating left and right.

Print Preview   Many users call this their favorite feature. With a single command a user can view on the screen in reduced size an entire page or two facing pages or even several consecutive pages. This gives a better overall view than the limited number of lines available on a screen.

Footnotes   A user need only give the footnote command and type the footnote. The word processing program keeps track of space needed and automatically renumbers if a new footnote is added.

Headers and Footers   Unlike footnotes, which appear just once, **headers** (top of the page) and **footers** (bottom of the page) appear on every page of

Figure 9 Printing an envelope. To print an envelope, (a) find the *Envelope* command on a menu, (b) invoke the command to see the window for addresses and options, and after completing the necessary steps, click *Print* to produce the printed envelope.

InfoBit

Since much of word processing is done for stylized documents, most word processors come with a variety of empty, formatted documents known as "templates." Although you have to fill them in with text, these templates greatly ease creating documents in a particular style and in a particular layout. Examples of templates provided include legal forms, agenda, balance sheets, business cards, term paper formats and many more.

Critical Thinking

Imagine that you are a writer, working on the manuscript for a book. What features of word processing software do you think would be most helpful? (Particularly helpful features include cut and paste, spell-checking, and the ability to deliver the manuscript on disk so that it need not be re-keyed into page composition programs by the publisher.)

a document (see Figure 3). A number of variations are available, including placement, size, and font. Footers commonly are used for the page number. In addition to page numbers, most word processing programs can automatically insert other useful information into headers or footers. Examples include the date and time the document was last modified and the file name under which the document is stored on disk.

Text Blocks: Moving, Copying, and Deleting

Text-block techniques comprise a powerful set of tools. A **text block** is a unit of text in a document. A text block can consist of one or more words, phrases, sentences, paragraphs, or even pages. Text blocks can be moved, copied, or deleted.

Consider this example. Robert Merino is the manager of the Warren Nautilus Club, a fitness center just seven blocks from the state university he attends. Last December, just before the student holidays, Robert used word processing to dash off a notice to the members, informing them of changes in the holiday schedule (Figure 10a).

Now, four months later, Robert wants to produce a similar notice regarding schedule changes during spring break. Rather than beginning anew, Robert will retrieve his old document from the disk and key in the changes. After Robert has given the command to retrieve the document, the current version of the notice, just as he saved it on disk, is loaded into memory and displayed on the screen. Robert plans to make changes so that the new notice will be as shown in Figure 10b. In particular, Robert uses text-block commands to move a paragraph.

Marking a Text Block Whenever action is to be taken on a block of text, that block must first be **marked,** which is a form of identification. Marking a block is sometimes called **selection,** since you are selecting text with which to work. A block usually is marked by placing the mouse at the beginning of the block, holding the mouse button down, and dragging the mouse to the end of the block. In Robert's memo the block to be marked is the paragraph with the special offer. On the screen the marked block is now highlighted, probably by **reverse video**—the print in the marked text is the color of the

Figure 10 Moving a text block.
(a) Robert's original memo. (b) Robert begins by deleting "assistant" so that his title reflects his recent promotion to manager. He next uses the find-and-replace command to change each mention of December to March. He takes a few moments to delete the old dates and times, add the new ones, and add April 1st as the deadline for the new member promotion. Finally, since the notice is supposed to be about the changed schedule, he uses text-block commands to move the *special offer* paragraph to the end of the notice. The result is the revised memo shown here.

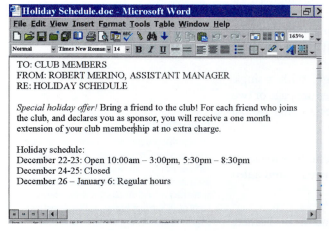

(a)

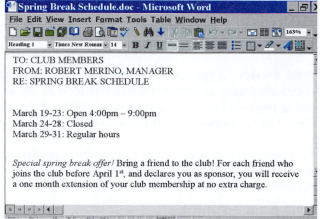

(b)

normal background and the background is the color of the normal text. Once the block is marked, it can be moved, copied, or deleted.

Moving a Text Block   Moving a block of text removes it from its original location and places it in another location. The block still appears only once in the document. Moving a block from one location to another is also called **cutting and pasting**, a reference to what you literally would have to do if you were working with a document on paper. Most word processing programs use the actual words *cut* and *paste* as command names: The cut command removes the block from its old location, and the paste command places the block in its new location, as indicated by the cursor location. To summarize the move operation: (1) mark the block, (2) cut, (3) move the cursor to the new destination, and (4) paste.

Copying a Text Block   The copy command leaves the block intact in its original location but also inserts it in a designated new location; now there are two copies of the block. Typical commands for copying a block are copy and paste. To summarize the copy operation: (1) mark the block, (2) copy, (3) move the cursor to the new destination, and (4) paste.

Deleting a Text Block   Deleting a block of text is easy. In fact, it has already been described. Once a block is marked and cut, it is effectively deleted. An easy alternative is to mark a block and then press the *Delete* key.

Spelling Checker and Thesaurus Programs

A **spelling checker** program finds spelling errors you may have made when typing a document. The program compares each word in your document to the words it has in its dictionary. If the spelling checker program finds a word that is not in its list, it assumes that you have misspelled or mistyped that word. The spelling checker draws attention to the offending word in some way, perhaps by reversing the screen colors. Then it displays words from its dictionary that are close in spelling or sound to the word you typed (Figure 11). If you recognize the correct spelling of the highlighted word in the list you are given, you can replace the incorrect word with the correct word from the list.

Spelling checkers often do not recognize proper names (such as *Ms. Verwys*) or acronyms (*NASA*) or technical words specific to some disciplines (*orthotroid*). So you must decide whether the word is actually misspelled. If it is, you can correct it easily with the word processing software. If the word is correct, the software lets you signal that the word is acceptable and, if you wish, even add it to the dictionary.

A **thesaurus program** offers synonyms (words with the same meaning) and antonyms (words with the opposite meaning) for common words. Suppose you find a word in your document that you have used too frequently or that does not seem suitable. Place the cursor on the word. Then click the menu or button that activates the thesaurus program. The program provides a list of synonyms for the word you want to replace (Figure 12). A click on the chosen new word replaces the word in your document with the synonym you prefer. It is easy, and even painlessly educational.

Figure 11 Spelling checker. The highlighted word, *associatiom,* is misspelled, so the spelling checker offers an alternative—*association*—in the suggestion window. In this case, selecting Change replaces the misspelled word with the correct spelling.

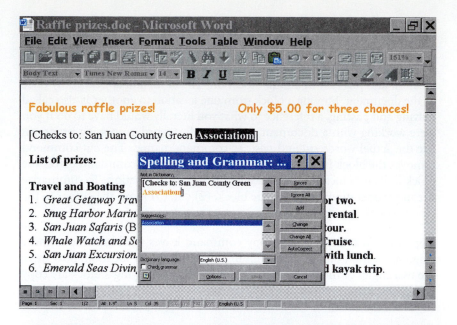

Figure 12 A thesaurus program. The words on the list are synonyms for the highlighted word, *exclusively.*

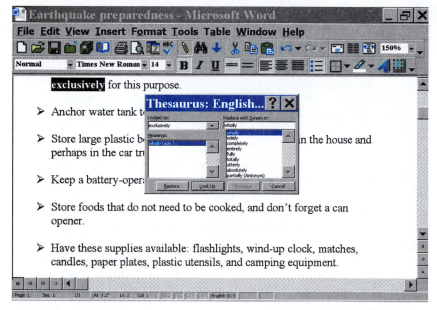

Word Processing and the Web

The World Wide Web can be used as a universal communications vehicle because all computers use the same protocol. Users can send messages to one another despite differences among their computers. However, instead of just relaying messages, users have taken the next logical step, collaboration on the same document by using the Web.

Suppose, for example, that three nutritionists, in different offices, are working on a paper to show the results of their joint study. They want to be able to massage the document as it is passed among them over the Web. They

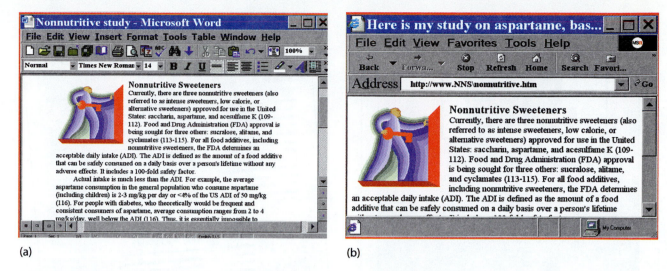

(a)   (b)

Figure 13 Word processing and the Web. Look-alikes? Not quite. Look in the upper-left corners for the clue, and then compare the toolbars. (a) This is the original text, saved as a word-processed document. (b) This is the same document, saved as a web page.

do not want to learn HTML, the language of web pages. They just want to work in the usual way, writing a word-processed document. There are ways to bend e-mail to collaborate on word-processed documents, but an easier way is to use the HTML feature provided by the word-processing programs themselves. In short, write the text in the usual way, but click a couple of extra buttons to save it as a web page that can be accessed by others.

Figure 13a shows a word-processed document. With a different save option, the document can be saved as a web page (Figure 13b). When the document is made available on a web page, others can access it and view it as a regular word-processed document while making changes or adding comments. One approach is to have the originator password the document in such a way that viewers can add comments but not change the original content.

Web options in word processing and other applications programs can be quite powerful. The details of the topic are beyond the scope of this book. For now, you simply need to be aware of the possibilities.

Desktop Publishing: An Overview

Would you like to be able to produce well-designed pages that combine elaborate charts and graphics with text and headlines in a variety of fonts? You can, with a technology called **desktop publishing.** You can use desktop publishing software to design sophisticated pages and, with a high-quality printer, print a professional-looking final document (Figure 14).

Unlike word processing, desktop publishing gives you the ability to do **page composition,** deciding where you want text and pictures on a page, what fonts to use, and what other design elements to include. Desktop pub-

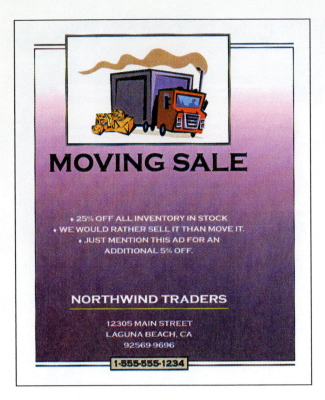

Figure 14 **Desktop publishing.** With desktop publishing software and a high-quality laser printer, you can create professional-looking newsletters and documents.

lishing fills the gap between word processing and professional typesetting (Figure 15).

The Publishing Process

Desktop publishing gives the user full control over the editing and design of the document. Desktop publishing also eliminates the time-consuming measuring and cutting and pasting involved in traditional production techniques.

The Art of Design

One part of the design of a document is **page layout**—how the text and pictures are arranged on the page. For example, magazine publishers have found that text organized in columns and separated by a solid vertical line is an effective page layout. If pictures are used, they must be inserted into the text. Picture size needs to be adjusted for proper fit on the page. In addition to page layout, designers must take into account such factors as headings, type sizes, and fonts. Are general headings used? Do separate sections or articles need their own subheadings? Does the size of the type need to be increased or decreased to fit a story into a predetermined space? What is the best font to use? Should more than one kind of font be used on a page?

To help you understand how some of these decisions are made, it is necessary to discuss some of the publishing terminology involved.

Fonts: Sizes and Styles

The type that a printer uses is described by its size, font, weight, and style. **Type size** is measured by a standard system that uses points. A **point** equals about 1/72 inch. Point size is measured from the top of the letter that rises the highest above the baseline (a letter such as *h* or *l*) to the bottom of the letter that descends the lowest (a letter such as *g* or *y*). Figure 16 shows type in different sizes.

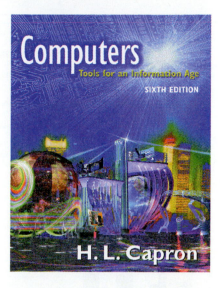

Figure 15 High-end desktop publishing. The cover of this book was produced with the latest computer technology. Using cross-country conference calls, e-mail, and modem file transfers, the Santa Rosa, California, artist developed his ideas in collaboration with the art director in Massachusetts. The image was rendered using 3-D modeling software. Drawn elements were seamlessly blended with textures, light effects, and shadows. A final high-resolution file was imported into a page layout program, then sent to Massachusetts to be converted to film.

Figure 16 Different point sizes. This figure shows a variety of different point sizes in a popular font called Times New Roman. The smallest shown here, point size 12, is often used for long text passages, such as correspondence. The larger sizes probably would be used only for headings or titles.

Times New Roman (12)

Times New Roman (18)

Times New Roman (24)

Times New Roman (36)

Times New Roman (48)

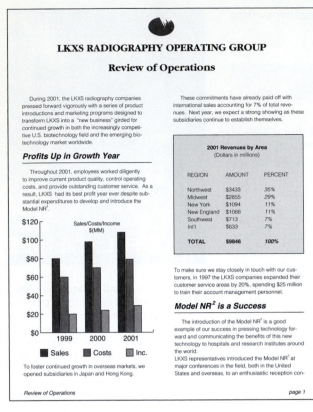

(a)

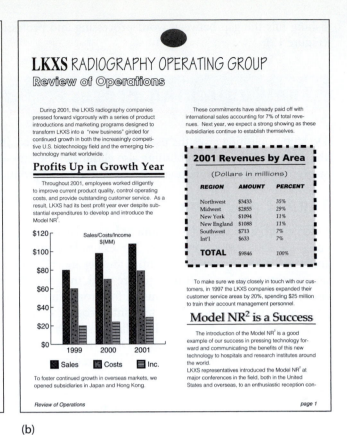

(b)

Figure 17 Sample designs. (a) This example uses complementary fonts to produce a professional-looking document. (b) The same page created with clashing fonts and other distractions.

The shapes of the letters and numbers in a published document are determined by the font selected. Recall that a **font** is a set of characters of the same design. A font can be printed in a specific **weight,** such as boldface, which is darker than usual, or in a specific **style,** such as italic. Changes in font provide emphasis and variety.

As shown in Figure 17a, varying the size and style of the type used in a publication can improve the appearance of a page and draw attention to the most important sections. However, using too many different fonts or using clashing fonts can create a page that is unattractive and hard to read (Figure 17b). Combine fonts with discretion.

Most printers used in desktop publishing store a selection of fonts in a ROM chip in the printer. These are called the printer's **internal fonts.** Also, most desktop publishing programs provide a **font library** on a disk. A font library contains a wide selection of type fonts called **soft fonts.** A soft font can be sent, or downloaded, from the library disk in the computer's disk drive to the computer, from which it then can be sent to the printer.

Principles of Good Typography

Word processing and desktop publishing programs put many different fonts at your disposal, but you can overwhelm a document if you use overly fancy fonts or too many fonts. A general rule is "less is better." The guidelines that follow promote a clean and attractive look for your document.

- Use only two or three fonts in a document.
- Be conservative: Limit the use of decorative or unusual fonts. In particular, use stylized fonts such as **Benguiat** or *Brush* or Lemonade only for signs and titles, never for passages of text.
- Use different sizes and styles of one font to distinguish between different heading levels, rather than using several different fonts.
- Never type text body in all capital letters.
- Do not use type that is too small to read easily just to fit everything on one page.
- Use a sans serif font only for short text passages; for long passages use a serif font, which is easier to read.
- Use italic or boldface, rather than underlining, for emphasis.

These simple guidelines almost guarantee an attractive document.

Leading and Kerning

Two terms you will encounter when you begin desktop publishing are *leading* and *kerning*. **Leading** (pronounced "ledding") refers to the spacing between the lines of type on a page. Leading is measured vertically from the base of one line of type to the base of the line above it. The greater the leading, the more white space between lines. Leading, just like type size, is measured in points.

Kerning refers to adjusting the space between the characters in a word. In desktop publishing software, each font has a default kerning. An example of kerning is shown in Figure 18.

Halftones

Halftones, which resemble photographs, appear in newspapers, magazines, books, and documents produced by desktop publishing. Halftones are representations made up of black dots printed on white paper. Varying the number and size of dots in a given space produces shades of gray. As you can see in Figure 19, the smaller the dot pattern used, the clearer the halftone.

(a) Unkerned: (b) Kerned:

WAVE   WAVE

Figure 18 **Kerning.** (a) In this example the space between the characters is not altered. (b) Kerning, or adjusting the space between the characters, can improve the overall appearance of the word.

Figure 19 **Halftones.** Halftones consist of a series of dots. Reducing the size of the dots makes the resulting halftone clearer.

GETTING PRACTICAL

GETTING HELP

Sooner or later most computer users need some help with hardware or software. Help is usually available in a variety of forms. All reputable vendors, whether of hardware or software, have their own web sites to offer support, such as those shown here for Intel and Dell. Vendors encourage users to go first for help to their web sites. A support site typically offers lists of frequently asked questions (with answers), software fixes that can be downloaded, and an e-mail service you can use to send

specific questions to their technical staff.

Many users prefer to get help directly over the phone from staff employed by the hardware or software maker. Typically, assistance is free for a certain time period, perhaps 90 days from the first phone call, but later there is a charge to the user. However, if the help line is not a toll-free number, then you may run up long-distance charges. To make the best use of your time on the phone, do some advance preparation. Before you call,

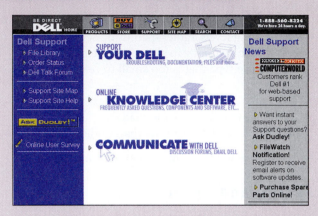

- Place your phone near your computer and be sitting at your computer as you call.
- If you are an established customer, have your customer number handy.
- Know your computer type, model, and serial number and the version of your software package.
- Write down the exact wording of any error messages.
- Be prepared to press phone buttons in

response to directions and then to wait—perhaps many minutes—to be connected to a live person who can help you.

When you call,

- Give identifying information when asked.
- State the problem clearly.
- Tell the technician what you have already tried.
- Be ready to explore solutions on the computer as you talk.

Using Desktop Publishing Software

The page composition program is the key ingredient of a desktop publishing system. **Page composition programs,** also called **page makeup programs,** let you design each page on the computer screen. You can determine the number and the width of the columns of text to be printed on the page. You can also indicate where pictures, charts, graphs, and headlines are to be placed. Once you have created the page design, you can use the page composition program to insert text and graphics into it. Text may be keyed as you prepare the page or imported as a file created by a word processing program. Page composition programs also let you move blocks of text and pictures around on your page. If you are not satisfied with the way the page looks, you can change the size of the type or the pictures.

Most desktop publishing programs offer **templates,** predetermined page designs that you can use quickly by filling in your own text. Templates typically offered include those for newsletters, flyers, greeting cards, banners, calendars, and even business forms. Page composition programs can also integrate **clip art**—images available for public use—into your publication to enliven your text. Most desktop publishing programs include a library of clip art. You can purchase disks of additional clip art. Figure 20 shows examples of illustrations in a clip-art library.

Ergonomic Considerations

Can all this computing be good for you? Are there any unhealthy side effects? The computer seems harmless enough. How bad can it be, sitting in a padded chair in a climate-controlled office? Health questions have been raised by the people who sit all day in front of computer screens. What about eyestrain? And what about the age-old back problem? Then there is repetitive strain injury (RSI), related to workers who hold their hands over a keyboard. RSI is caused by speed, repetition, awkward positioning, and holding a static position for a long period of time.

Ergonomic equipment　Workers can do a number of things to take care of themselves. A good place to begin is with an ergonomically designed workstation. In its formal sense, ergonomics is the use of research in designing systems, programs, or devices that are appropriate to use for their intended purposes. In the context of computers, **ergonomics** refers to human factors related to the use of computers. Begin with a pneumatically adjustable chair with five feet at its base and a monitor that can be tilted and swiveled to suit the user. A properly designed workstation takes a variety of factors into account, such as the distance from the eyes to the screen and the angle of the arms and wrists (Figure 21).

Ergonomic behavior　Experts recommend these steps to prevent injury:

- Turn the screen away from the window to reduce glare, and cover your screen with a glare deflector. Turn off overhead lights; illuminate your work area with a lamp.
- Place the keyboard low enough to avoid arm and wrist fatigue. Do not bend your wrists when you type. Use an inexpensive raised wrist rest. Do not rest your wrists on a sharp edge.
- Position the seat back so that your lower back is supported.
- Sit with your feet firmly on the floor.
- Enlarge fonts so that they are easier to see; you can return them to their normal size before printing the document.
- Most important of all: Take a break. At the least, exercise at your desk, occasionally rotating your wrists, rolling your shoulders, and stretching. Better yet, get up and walk around at regular intervals.
- Finally, keep your fingernails short, or at least not long.

Personal Greetings

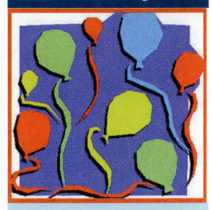

Computers have opened up all sorts of possibilities for "home-made" personal greetings. Several software packages are available to help you make banners, flyers, calendars, and greeting cards. You need not have any artistic talent—many images and preplanned designs are available as part of the software. In fact, all you really need in addition to a computer is some software and a color printer.

Even more popular are the many web sites that offer postcards and greetings cards that you can send online to a friend. These free services let you choose a card (such as the balloons shown here, from the Postcard Place site), select a message from their list (Happy Birthday, Congratulations, and so forth), and personalize it with your own message. Most sites will also let you include music to be delivered with the card.

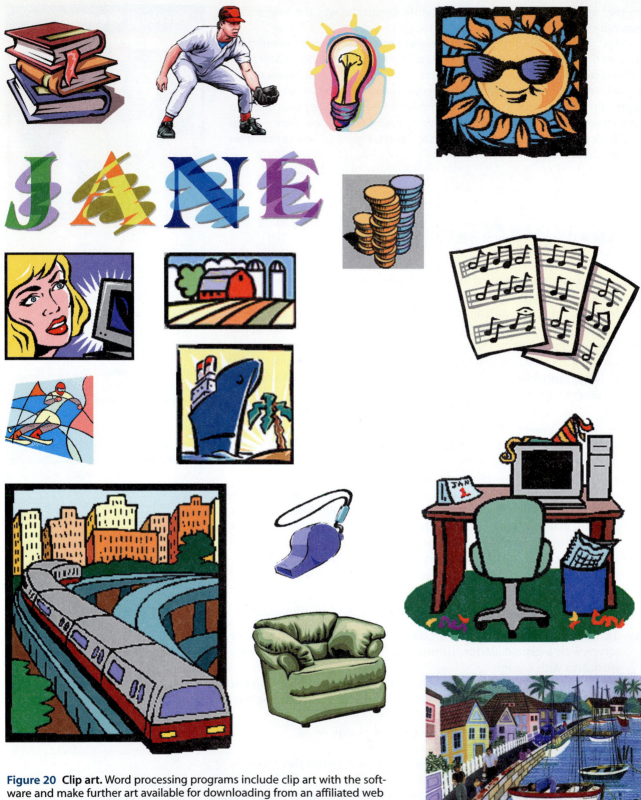

Figure 20 Clip art. Word processing programs include clip art with the software and make further art available for downloading from an affiliated web site. Clip art can also be purchased separately from other vendors. Much clip art is mundane—primitive sketches of familiar items such as pencils, stars, and grinning pumpkins. However, software makers have hired commercial artists to improve the look of clip art, resulting in a greater sophistication and variety.

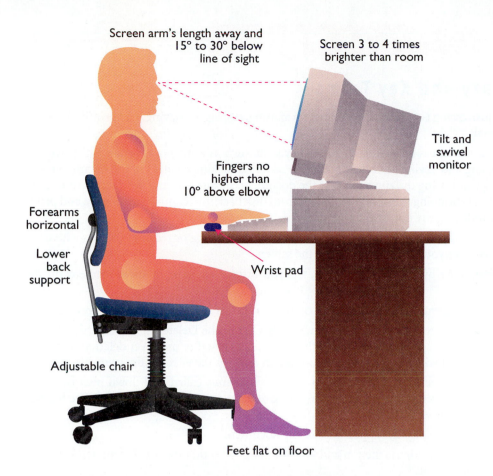

Screen arm's length away and 15° to 30° below line of sight

Screen 3 to 4 times brighter than room

Tilt and swivel monitor

Fingers no higher than 10° above elbow

Forearms horizontal

Lower back support

Wrist pad

Adjustable chair

Feet flat on floor

Figure 21 An ergonomically designed workstation. Start with the right equipment, such as an adjustable chair and a monitor that can be tilted and swiveled. It is up to the worker to sit in the proper manner—back supported, feet flat on the floor, and so forth.

Global Perspective

Europe, particularly Sweden and Germany, leads the U.S. in the development and promulgation of ergonomic standards for Video Display Terminals and keyboards. Germany makes ergonomic requirements part of the electrical safety certification of computers and Sweden has strict regulations on the amount of energy that may be radiated by computer monitors.

Repetitive strain injuries seem to be aggravated by overall job stress. Among the psychological and environmental factors that increase risk are long commutes, dissatisfaction with management, and the occurrence of stressful events in one's personal life. Even so, most computer-related health problems can be avoided with proper attention to your physical well-being at the computer.

▲

By now you should be convinced that word processing is probably essential for your career and, further, that desktop publishing is a valuable tool for individuals as well as businesses.

CHAPTER REVIEW

Summary and Key Terms

- **Word processing** is the creating, editing, formatting, storing, retrieving, and printing of a text document.

- A text document is any text that can be keyed in, such as a memo. *Creation* is the original composing and keying in of the document, *editing* is making changes to the document, *formatting* is adjusting the appearance of the document, *storing* is saving the document to disk, *retrieving* is bringing the stored document from disk back into computer memory, and *printing* is producing the document on paper.

- The **insertion point,** or **cursor,** usually a blinking dash or line or rectangle, shows where the next character you type will appear on the screen.

- **Scrolling,** done by moving the cursor, lets you display any part of the document on the screen.

- **Word wrap** automatically starts a word on the next line if it does not fit on the previous line.

- Use the **Backspace key** to delete characters to the left or the **Delete key** to delete the character under the cursor or to the right of the cursor. Accidental or incorrect deletions can usually be repaired with the **undo command,** which reverses the effect of the previous action.

- Mouse users issue commands through a series of **menus,** called **pull-down menus,** which offer initial choices and submenus, or by using **buttons** at the top of the screen. The **toolbar** is a collection of such buttons.

- The **format** is the physical appearance of the document.

- **Vertical centering** adjusts the top and bottom margins so that the text is centered vertically on the printed page.

- Any line can be individually **centered** between the left and right margins of the page.

- Settings automatically used by the word processing program are called **default settings.**

- When the margin settings are changed, word processing software adjusts the text to fit the new margins; this process is called **automatic reformatting.**

- Users can **tab** just once to begin a paragraph or can **indent** an entire paragraph.

- **Justification** refers to the evenness of the text at the side margins. A document is **fully justified** when it has an even margin down each side. Left justification causes an unjustified right side, which is referred to as **ragged-right** text.

- **Line spacing** variations include single-spaced, double-spaced, and even triple-spaced.

- Certain words or phrases or even entire paragraphs can be given special emphasis by using a darker text known as **boldface** text, or by using the slanted type called *italic,* or by underlining.

- A **font** is a set of characters—letters, punctuation, and numbers—of the same design. On a **serif** font, each character includes small marks, known as serifs. A **sans serif** font is clean and stark, with no serif marks. Most fonts available today are **scalable** fonts, meaning that they can be set to almost any size.

- The **search command,** also called the **find command,** displays on the screen the exact page and place where a word or phrase is located. The **find-and-replace function** finds each instance of a certain word or phrase and replaces it with another word or phrase. A **conditional replace** asks you to verify each replacement.

- Word processing programs offer **pagination** options, permitting the page number to be located at the top or bottom of the page and to the left, right, or center, or even alternating left and right.

- With a single command, a user can see in reduced size a **print preview** of an entire page or two facing pages or even several consecutive pages.

- A word processing program keeps track of space needed for a **footnote** and automatically renumbers if a new footnote is added.

- **Headers** (top) and **footers** (bottom) appear on every page of a document. A number of variations are available, including placement, size, and font.

- A **text block** can be moved, copied, or deleted. To manipulate a block of text, you must first **mark** (or **select**) the block, which then usually appears in **reverse video** (in which the background color becomes the text color and vice versa). The block move command, also known as **cut and paste,** moves the text to a different location. The block copy command copies the block of text into a new location, leaving the text in its original location as well. Block delete removes the block entirely.

- A **spelling checker** program includes a built-in dictionary. A **thesaurus** program supplies synonyms and antonyms.

- A **desktop publishing program** lets you produce professional-looking documents containing both text and graphics.

- One part of the overall design of a document is **page layout**—how text and pictures are arranged on the page. Adding text to a layout is called **page composition.**

- Type is described by **type size, font, weight,** and **style.** Type size is measured by a standard system based on the **point.**

- Most printers used in desktop publishing contain **internal fonts** stored in a ROM chip. Most desktop publishing programs provide a **font library** on disk, containing additional fonts called **soft fonts.**

- **Leading** refers to the spacing between the lines of type on a page. **Kerning** refers to adjusting the space between the characters in a word.

- A **halftone** is a photographic representation made up of dots.

- **Page composition programs,** also called **page makeup programs,** let the user design the page layout. Most desktop program packages offer **templates,** predetermined page designs. Page composition programs also allow the incorporation of electronically stored **clip art**—professionally produced images for public use.

- **Ergonomics** refers to human factors related to the use of computers.

Discussion Questions

1. You are producing a monthly newsletter for your volunteer organization, which helps illiterate adults learn to read. You prepare the first two issues using word processing, and these seem adequate. But you have seen newsletters that are more sophisticated and discover that they are made with desktop publishing software, something with which you are not familiar. Assuming that the cost of the software is not a problem, what would it take for you to make the switch?

2. List all the uses you might make of desktop publishing at home. Consider, for example, items such as birthday cards and banners.

3. Suppose you are an editorial assistant at a publishing house. As part of your job, you prepare the schedule for book development and production. You circulate your first cut of the schedule to various editors and designers (usually about six people), who return their copies with changes for you to incorporate. Contrast the differences in this process between using simple word processing and using the word processing feature that makes the shared papers into web pages.

Student Study Guide

Multiple Choice

1. A set of choices on the screen is called a(n)
   a. menu
   b. reverse video
   c. editor
   d. template

2. A program that provides synonyms is called a(n)
   a. indexing program
   b. form letter program
   c. editing program
   d. thesaurus program

3. An image made up of dots is called a
   a. pull-down menu
   b. block
   c. header
   d. halftone

4. A type of menu that shows further subchoices is a
   a. reverse menu
   b. scrolled menu
   c. pull-down menu
   d. wrapped menu

5. The feature that keeps track of the right margin is called
   a. find and replace
   b. word wrap
   c. ragged right
   d. right-justified

6. Verification with the find-and-replace feature is called
   a. verified replace
   b. conditional replace
   c. questionable replace
   d. "what-if" replace

7. The feature that allows viewing of any part of a document on the screen is called
   a. searching
   b. scrolling
   c. pasting
   d. editing

8. Transferring text to another location without deleting it from its original location is called
   a. scrolling
   b. searching
   c. copying
   d. moving

9. Ragged right means the right margin is set to be
   a. uneven
   b. variable
   c. even
   d. wide

10. Spelling checker programs use
    a. tab settings
    b. pasting
    c. pagination
    d. a dictionary

True/False

T F   1. Formatting refers to the physical appearance of a document.

T F   2. A thesaurus program supplies both synonyms and antonyms.

T F   3. A spelling checker program can detect spelling errors and improper use of language.

T F   4. Right-justified means that the right margin will be ragged right.

T F   5. The move command moves text to another place and deletes it from its original place.

T F   6. A footer appears on the bottom of each page of the document.

T F   7. The feature that word processing and typing have in common is that permanent marks are made on paper as the document is keyed.

T F   8. When margin settings are changed, automatic reformatting adjusts the text to fit the new margins.

T F   9. The copy command moves text to another place and deletes it from its original place.

T F 10. A template is a set of clip art.

T F 11. A pull-down menu can be clicked with a mouse to show submenus.

T F 12. Text is centered vertically by adjusting the right margin.

T F 13. Clip art is art that is designed by the user of a desktop publishing program.

T F 14. A conditional replace asks a user to verify each replacement.

T F 15. Another phrase for marking a text block is selecting a text block.

T F 16. Print preview permits a user to view one or more pages on-screen before printing.

T F 17. A sans serif font is clean, with no serif marks.

T F 18. Another name for the search command is the find command.

T F 19. Internal fonts are stored on hard disk.

T F 20. The cursor is usually a blinking dash or line or rectangle.

Fill-In

1. Settings automatically used by the word processing program unless overridden by the user are called

   _____.

2. A line that appears on the top of each page of the document is called the _____.

3. Copy and move commands are generally known as _____.

4. Which feature permits a user to view any part of a document, about 20 lines at a time?

   _____

5. Resetting what will make a document shorter and wider? _____

6. Which feature finds and changes text?

   _____

7. What are words printed in darker type said to be?

   _____

8. Before a block of text can be copied or moved, the user must _____.

9. An even right margin is said to be

   _____.

10. What is the verification feature with find and replace called? _____

11. Synonyms and antonyms can be supplied by

    _____.

12. A set of drawings stored on disk is called

    _____.

13. Printers used for desktop publishing must have what software on a ROM chip?

    _____

14. The fonts stored in the printer are called

    _____.

15. Adding type to a layout is called

    _____.

16. Adjusting the space between characters in a word is called _____.

17. Italic is an example of what font characteristic?

    _____

18. Boldface is an example of what font characteristic?

    _____

19. A set of characters of the same design comprise a(n) _____.

20. The feature that automatically moves a word to the next line if it does not fit on the previous line is known as _____.

Answers

Multiple Choice

1. a	6. b
2. d	7. b
3. d	8. c
4. c	9. a
5. b	10. d

True/False

1. T	6. T	11. T	16. T
2. T	7. F	12. F	17. T
3. F	8. T	13. F	18. T
4. F	9. F	14. T	19. F
5. T	10. F	15. T	20. T

Fill-In

1. default settings
2. header
3. cut and paste
4. scrolling
5. margins
6. find and replace
7. boldface
8. mark the text
9. justified
10. conditional replace
11. a thesaurus program
12. clip art
13. internal fonts
14. soft fonts
15. page composition
16. kerning
17. style
18. weight
19. font
20. word wrap

PLANET INTERNET

It seems a bit ironic to think of the Internet in terms of the great outdoors when, in fact, we are probably very much indoors checking it out. But, in fact, the very people who are Internet-literate are often the same ones who are active in a variety of ways, including ways that take them outdoors. It makes sense to use the resources on the Internet in pursuit of the outdoors in all its varieties.

And varieties there are. The outdoors can mean scenery, nature, the environment, travel, summer and winter outdoor sports, and that greatest of all outdoor places—outer space. The Internet covers these topics in, literally, hundreds of thousands of sites.

Nature. The South Florida Birding site is an interesting combination of commercial venture and

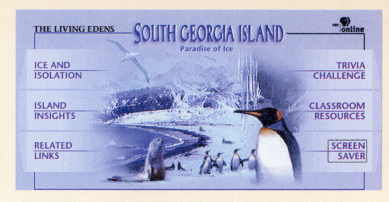

environmental concern. If you have an interest in birds, you can spend some time looking at the hundreds of images, such as the anhinga shown here, offered on the site. You can sign up for a trip too. The Butterfly Web Site also has collections of images and much information.

Environment. All sorts of nonprofit organizations benefit from a Web presence, but possibly none more so than environmental organizations. Some examples are the World Wildlife Fund and the Nature Conservancy. We chose the Rainforest Action Network to show here. We also could not resist the optional Florida license plate that lets people promote saving sea turtles.

Travel. Wondering about those infamous crop circles? See the CircleMakers site. Other possibilities for armchair travelers or those considering a trip are the sites for 360 Alaska, Covered Bridges, the Hamptons, All about Rio, Fall in Pennsylvania, 10 Downing Street, Legendary Lighthouses (the Limekiln Point lighthouse is shown here), and South Georgia Island.

Sports. From the Olympic Games to local ball scores, from tennis to tobogganing—it is all on the Internet. There are also a number on online magazines—"zines"—to cover the action. Surfer Magazine, shown here, is but one example.

Space. The government takes wonderful advantage of the Internet to disseminate information about the space program. The image shown here is of Orion Nebula. There are many space sites; we will list several on our site for your easy access.

Internet Exercises

1. **Structured exercise.** Hook up to the site through the URL http://www.prenhall.com/capron and take a look at the South Florida Birding site. Enjoy the hundreds of pictures provided here.

2. **Freeform exercise.** Choose an outdoor activity that interests you—tennis, surfing, skiing, whatever. Put those words through a search engine and follow up a half-dozen sites on that topic.

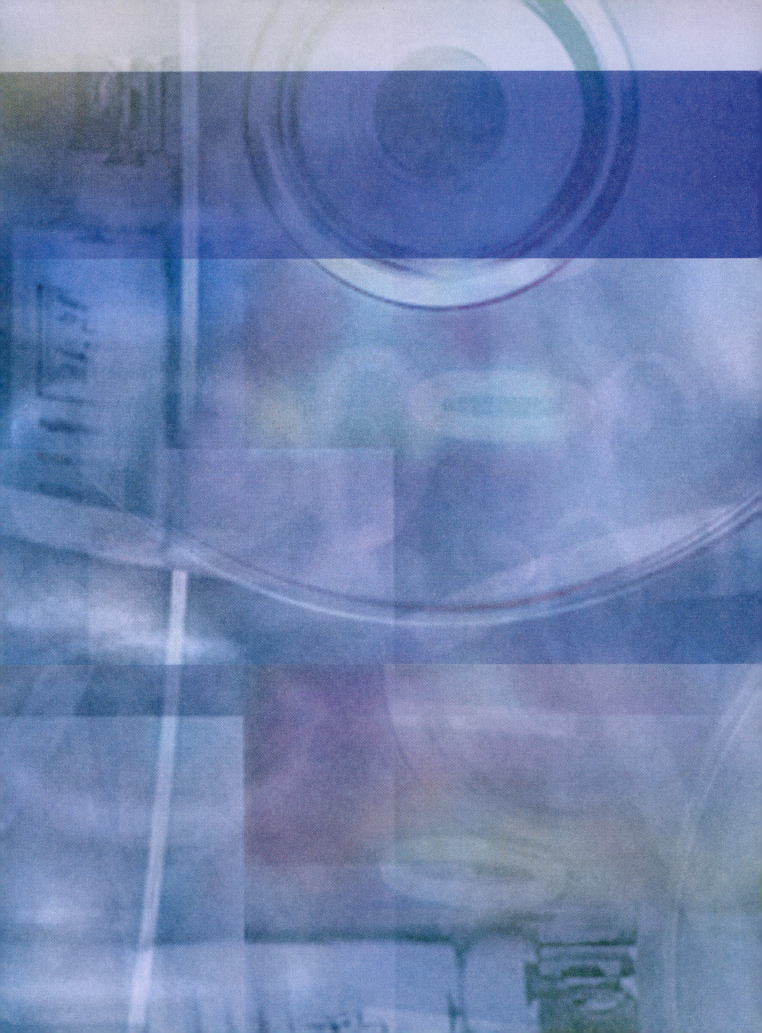

CHAPTER TWELVE

SPREADSHEETS AND BUSINESS GRAPHICS

Facts and Figures

LEARNING OBJECTIVES

- Appreciate the advantages of spreadsheets
- List several applications for spreadsheets
- Understand the underlying principles of electronic spreadsheet use
- Become acquainted with setting up and modifying a spreadsheet
- Appreciate the advantages of business graphics
- Differentiate analytical and presentation graphics

In his first year in college, Tom Ziolkowski took an introductory computer class that included a hands-on component for word processing, spreadsheets, and databases. He breezed through the word processing part, but he didn't "get" spreadsheets at first. What did rows and columns of numbers have to do with anything in the real world? Further, who wants to key in a whole bunch of numbers?

Tom came to understand two important notions. The first was that spreadsheets were good for helping to plan ahead because numbers in a spreadsheet can be changed in order to see what results the changes might cause—the famous "What if . . ." approach. The second, and even more attractive, fact was that he could get the computer to do some of the work.

Tom needed a secondhand car. He decided to see how the spreadsheet could help him predict how much money he would have, varying the amount he might use from his current bank savings, the amount he might put away per month, and the number of months he would have to save. The spreadsheet here shows the results. Tom typed in the first two columns and the computer produced the results in the last two columns, based on formulas that Tom supplied.

Savings in bank	Savings per month	Total in 12 mo.	Total in 24 mo.
$2,000	$100	$3,200	$4,400
$2,000	$200	$4,400	$6,800
$3,000	$100	$4,200	$5,400
$3,000	$200	$5,400	$7,800

This example is so trivial that it probably could be completed with a pencil in a shorter time than it would take to submit the spreadsheet to the computer. Nevertheless, it shows that you can use a spreadsheet to show the results of changes and to make the computer do some of the work. This chapter provides some information on how that happens.

The Nature of Spreadsheets

A worksheet that presents data in a grid of rows and columns is called a **spreadsheet** (Figure 1a). The manually constructed spreadsheet, on paper, has been used as a business tool for centuries. Spreadsheets can be used to organize and present business data, thus aiding managerial decisions. However, spreadsheets are not limited to businesses. Personal and family budgets, for example, are often organized on spreadsheets. Furthermore, nonfinancial or even nonnumeric data can be presented and analyzed in a spreadsheet format.

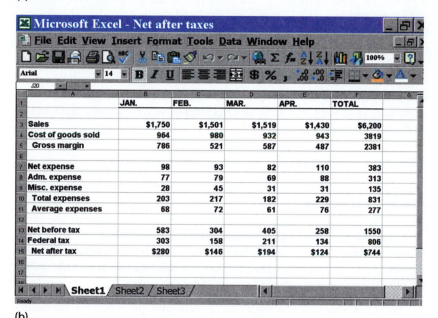

	JAN.	FEB.	MAR.	APR.	TOTAL
SALES	1750	1501	1519	1430	6200
COST OF GOODS SOLD	964	980	932	943	3819
GROSS MARGIN	786	521	587	487	2381
NET EXPENSE	98	93	82	110	383
ADM EXPENSE	77	79	69	88	313
MISC EXPENSE	28	45	31	31	135
TOTAL EXPENSES	203	217	182	229	831
AVERAGE EXPENSE	68	72	61	76	277
NET BEFORE TAXES	583	304	405	258	1550
FEDERAL TAXES	303	158	211	134	806
NET AFTER TAX	280	146	194	124	744

(a)

Figure 1 Manual versus electronic spreadsheets. (a) This manual spreadsheet is a typical spreadsheet consisting of rows and columns. (b) The same spreadsheet created with a spreadsheet program.

Unfortunately, creating a large spreadsheet manually is time-consuming and tedious, even when you use a calculator or copy results from a computer printout. Another problem with manual spreadsheets is that making a mistake is too easy. If you do not discover the mistake, the consequences can be serious. If you discover the mistake after the spreadsheet is finished, you must manually redo all the calculations that used the wrong number.

Electronic Spreadsheets

An **electronic spreadsheet,** or **worksheet,** is a computerized version of a paper spreadsheet (Figure 1b). Working with a spreadsheet on a computer eliminates much of the toil of setting up a manual spreadsheet. In general, an electronic spreadsheet works like this: You enter the data you want on your spreadsheet and then key in the types of calculations you need. The electronic spreadsheet program automatically does all the calculations for you, completely error-free, and produces the results in your spreadsheet. You can print a copy of the spreadsheet and store the data on your disk so that the spreadsheet can be used again. By the way, although this chapter examines spreadsheets in a general way, we will illustrate spreadsheets using software called Microsoft Excel 2000, as shown here in Figure 1b. Thus, although the screen is realistic, our area of concern is merely the spreadsheet, not the various menus and buttons that come with this specific software.

By far the greatest labor-saving aspect of the electronic spreadsheet is **automatic recalculation:** When you change one value or calculation on your spreadsheet, all dependent values on the spreadsheet are automatically recalculated to reflect the change. Suppose, to use a common example, that one entry on a spreadsheet is RATE, another is HOURS, and another is SALARY, which is the product of RATE and HOURS. Values for RATE and HOURS will be entered, but SALARY will be calculated by the spreadsheet software. But what if RATE changes? RATE can be entered anew, but the person entering the data need not worry about SALARY because the spreadsheet will recalculate SALARY using the new value for RATE. Although this example may seem trivial, the automatic recalculation principle has significant consequences for large, complex spreadsheets. A change in a single value could affect dozens or even hundreds of calculations, which, happily, the spreadsheet will perform.

"What-If" Analysis

Automatic recalculation is valuable for more than just fixing mistakes. If a number is changed—not because it is incorrect but because a user wants to see different results—related calculations will also be changed at the same time. This ability to change a number and have the change automatically reflected throughout the spreadsheet is the foundation of **"what-if" analysis**—the process of changing one or more spreadsheet values and observing the resulting calculated effect. Consider these examples:

- What if a soap manufacturer was to reduce the price of a certain brand by 5 percent; how would the net profit be affected? How about 10 percent? 15 percent?
- What if a general contractor was to subcontract with several workers, but one of them reneged and the contractor had to hire someone more expensive; how would that affect the total cost?
- What if the prime lending rate was raised or lowered; how would this affect interest moneys for the bank or the cost of a loan for bank customers?

Once the initial spreadsheet is set up, any of these "what-if" scenarios can be answered by changing one value and examining the new, recalculated results.

Spreadsheet Fundamentals

Before you can learn how to use a spreadsheet, you must understand some basic spreadsheet features. The characteristics and definitions that follow are common to all spreadsheet programs.

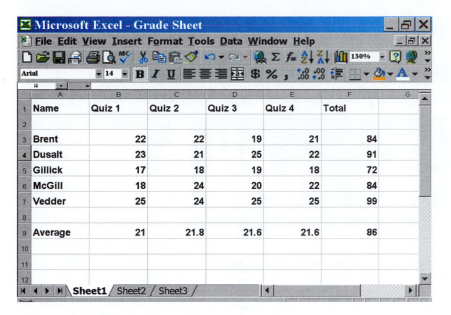

Figure 2 Anatomy of a spreadsheet screen. This screen shows a typical spreadsheet—a teacher's grade sheet. It shows space for 12 rows numbered down the side and 7 columns labeled A through G. The intersection of a row and column forms a cell. Here, cell A1 is the active cell—the cell into which a user may key data. Only one cell may be active at a given time.

Cells and Cell Addresses

Figure 2 shows one type of spreadsheet—a teacher's grade sheet. Notice that the spreadsheet is divided into rows (horizontal) and columns (vertical). The rows have *numeric labels* and the columns have *alphabetic labels*. There are actually more rows and columns than you can see on the screen. Some spreadsheets have thousands of rows and hundreds of columns—probably more than you will ever need to use.

The intersection of a row and column forms a cell. A **cell** is a storage area on a spreadsheet. When referring to a cell, you use the letter and number of the intersecting column and row. For example, in Figure 2, cell B7 is the intersection of column B and row 7—the grade of 25 for Vedder on Quiz 1. This reference name is known as the **cell address,** or **cell reference.** Notice that the alphabetic column designation always precedes the row number: B7, not 7B.

On a spreadsheet one cell is always known as the **active cell,** or **current cell.** When a cell is active you can enter data or edit that cell's contents. Typically, the active cell is marked by highlighting in reverse video or with a heavy border drawn around it. The active cell in Figure 2 is cell A1.

You can use a mouse or the cursor-movement (arrow) keys to scroll through a spreadsheet both vertically and horizontally.

Contents of Cells: Labels, Values, and Formulas

Each cell can contain one of three types of information: a label, a value, or a formula. A **label** provides descriptive text information about entries in the spreadsheet, such as a person's name. A cell that contains a label is not generally used to perform mathematical calculations. For example, in Figure 2,

MAKING THE RIGHT CONNECTIONS
UPDATING SOFTWARE ONLINE

When you buy packaged software from a store, it may have been on the shelf for some time. Even if you download software from the Internet, it will soon be out of date, or at least it will not benefit from subsequent improvements such as fixes and the latest upgrades. These changes, almost always free, are available on web sites associated with the software. What to do?

Well, you could check out the web site for each of your software packages on a regular basis and see if they offer any extra downloads. They probably do. But, even more probably, you will not get around to doing checking and downloading. One solution is to use software to do the looking and downloading for you. Oil Change is such a program.

Oil Change identifies all the applications software on your hard disk, hunts down the latest updates, and provides a list of possible changes. Once you select which ones you want, or simply accept them all, Oil Change downloads and makes the changes.

cells A1, A9, and F1, among others, contain labels. A **value** is an actual number entered into a cell to be used in calculations. In Figure 2, for example, cell B3 contains a value.

A **formula** is an instruction to the program to calculate a number. A formula generally contains cell addresses and one or more arithmetic operators: a plus sign (+) to add, a minus sign (-) to subtract, an asterisk (*) to multiply, and a slash (/) to divide. When you use a formula rather than entering the calculated result, the software can automatically recalculate the result if you need to change any of the values on which the formula is based.

In addition to the types of calculations just mentioned, a formula can include one or more functions. A **function** is like a preprogrammed formula. Two common functions are the SUM function, which adds numbers together, and the AVG function, which calculates the average of a group of numbers. Most spreadsheet programs contain many functions for a variety of uses, from mathematics to statistics to financial applications. A formula or function does not appear in the cell; instead, the cell shows the result of the formula or function. The result is called the **displayed value** of the cell. The formula or function is the **content** of the cell.

Ranges

Sometimes it is necessary to specify a range of cells in order to build a formula or perform a function. A **range** is a group of one or more adjacent cells occurring in a rectangular shape; the program treats the range as a unit during an operation. Figure 3 shows some ranges. To define a range, you must indicate the upper-left and lower-right cells of the block. Depending on the particular spreadsheet software you are using, the cell addresses are sepa-

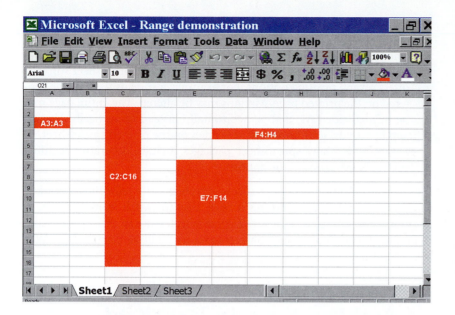

Figure 3 Ranges. A range is a group of one or more cells arranged in a rectangle. You can name a range or refer to it by using the addresses of the upper-left and lower-right cells in the group.

rated by a colon or by two periods. For example, in Figure 2, the Quiz 1 range is B3:B7 (or B3..B7), and the Brent quiz range is B3:E3 (or B3..E3).

Spreadsheet Features

Once spreadsheet users master the basics, they are usually eager to learn the extra features, especially formatting and graphics, that make their work more useful or attractive. Formatting features take a worksheet beyond the historically plain page full of numbers. Here is a partial list of features you will probably find included with spreadsheet software:

- **Column width.** Columns containing labels—words—usually need to be wider than columns for numbers. Note, for example, that the leftmost column in Figure 1 is wider than the other columns to accommodate the data. Columns can also be made narrower. (Incidentally, although less common, it is also possible to alter the height of a row.)
- **Headings.** If a heading is desired, it can be invoked as a wide column and can even be centered.
- **Number symbols.** If appropriate, a number value can be shown with a dollar sign ($), a percent sign (%), and commas and decimal places, as desired.
- **Appearance of data.** Spreadsheet data can be presented in one of many proffered fonts and in boldface or italic. Furthermore, data can be centered within the cell or can be justified right or left within the cell. Often an entire column of cells will be justified right or left. In Figure 2, for example, all data in column A is left-justified, whereas data in columns B through F are right-justified.

Learn By Doing

Students may find it interesting to examine a sample printout from an electronic spreadsheet. If the spreadsheet software that produced the printout can print out formulas, as well as values, you may wish to provide two copies, one with the results and one showing the formulas used to get those results.

Spreadsheets in the Home

Family budgeting is the most common home use for spreadsheets. However, some people are more interested in "what-if" scenarios, for which spreadsheets are the perfect tool. Here are some examples users have dreamed up:

- What if I go back to work ... is it really worth it? You can factor in all the expenses of employment—travel, wardrobe, child care, taxes, and other disbursements—and compare the total against the income received.
- What if I start my own business ... can I make a go of it? Although estimates may be sketchy at best, a budding entrepreneur can approximate expenses (for materials, tools, equipment, office rental, and so forth) and compare them with anticipated revenues from clients over different periods of time.
- What if I jump into the stock market ... or stick to a more conservative investment approach? A popular sport among investors is running dollar amounts and anticipated growth rates of various investment opportunities through spreadsheets. The results may give them a glimpse of their future financial picture.
- What if I save $50 per month for my child's education ... how much money would be saved (with accumulated interest) by the time the child is 18? What if I was to save $75 or $100 per month?

- **Printing.** When a user is developing and experimenting with a spreadsheet, he or she is looking at the spreadsheet on the screen. But the finished product, or even a series of variations of the product, will probably be printed for distribution and examination. Spreadsheet software offers several printing options. For example, a spreadsheet may be centered on the printed page. Margins may be altered. The entire page may be printed sideways, that is, horizontally instead of vertically. Vertical and horizontal grid lines may be hidden on the printed spreadsheet.
- **Decoration.** Many spreadsheet packages include decorative features, such as borders and color options.

The change from numbers to pictures—graphics—is a refreshing variation. Most spreadsheet software makes it fairly easy to switch from numbers to pictures. That is, once you prepare a spreadsheet, you can show your results in graphic form. The value of business graphics will be discussed in detail later in the chapter.

A Problem for a Spreadsheet

Gina Hagen, at age eight, was an entrepreneur. One hot summer day she borrowed some sugar and lemons from the kitchen and stirred up a pitcher of lemonade, which she proceeded to sell from a stand in front of her house. By the end of the day, she had gone through three pitchers and had taken in $6.25. Her joy, however, subsided when her mother explained that a business person has to pay for supplies—in this case, the sugar and lemons. But Gina was not deterred for long. In her growing-up years, she sold bird houses, a neighborhood newsletter, and sequined hair barrettes. In the process, she learned that it was important to keep good business records.

A New Business

When Gina attended Ballard Community College, she noticed that the only beverages available were milk, coffee, and canned soft drinks. Thinking back to her early days, Gina got permission to set up a lemonade stand on campus. In addition to fresh lemonade, she sold bagels and homemade cookies. The stand was soon successful, and eventually Gina hired other students to manage stands on nearby campuses: Aurora, Eastlake, and Phinney.

Using Spreadsheets for the Business

When Gina took a computer applications course at the college, she decided that spreadsheets were appropriate for keeping track of her business. She began by comparing sales for the four campuses for the fourth quarter of the year. She sketched her spreadsheet on paper (Figure 4). As she invoked the spreadsheet software, Gina decided that she also would add some headings. In her first cut at the spreadsheet, Gina keyed in the campus names in column A and the campus sales for each of the three months in columns B, C, and D.

Gina does not, of course, have to compute totals—the spreadsheet software will do that. In fact, the obvious solution is to key formulas using the SUM function to compute both column and row totals. In cell E6, for

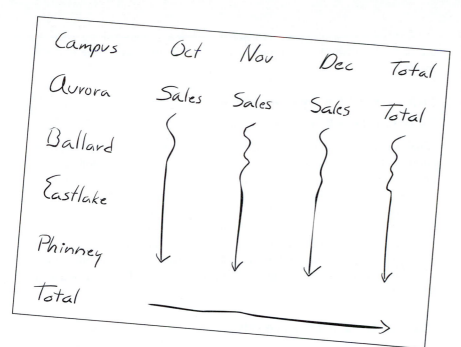

Figure 4 Spreadsheet planning. A sketch of a spreadsheet is useful before invoking the software. This plan includes one row per campus and the monthly totals, and one column for the campus names, each month's sales, and the campus totals.

	A	B	C	D	E	F
1	GINA'S LEMONADE					
2	4th Quarter Sales Report					
3	CAMPUS	OCT	NOV	DEC	TOTAL	
4						
5	Aurora	1006	978	956	2940	
6	Ballard	1675	1566	1430	4671	
7	Eastlake	1378	1340	1198	3916	
8	Phinney	1312	1390	1150	3852	
9						
10	TOTAL	5371	5274	4734	15379	

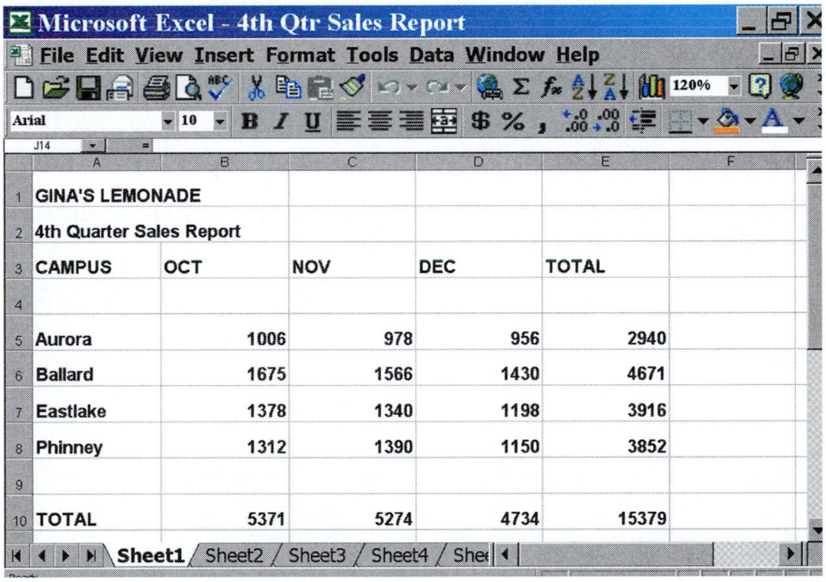

Figure 5 First draft of sales spreadsheet. This initial look at Gina's spreadsheet shows the headings and data keyed into the spreadsheet. Gina keyed formulas that include the SUM function in cells E5, E6, E7, E8, B10, C10, D10, and E10. Later, Gina will make a change to a data item. She will also format the spreadsheet to improve its appearance; for example, the month headings (OCT, NOV, and so forth) need to be centered over their appropriate columns.

example, Gina keys =SUM(B6:D6). This instructs the software to sum the values in cells B6, C6, and D6 and place the resulting sum in cell E6. Even though she typed a formula in the cell, the result is a value, in this case 4671 (Figure 5). Keep in mind that the resulting value in any cell containing a formula will change if any of the values in the cells in the formula change. For cell E6 the resulting value would change if there was a change to the values in cell B6, C6, or D6. The other cells containing totals (E5, E7, E8, B10, C10, D10, and E10) also contain formulas that will calculate values. Cell E10, by the way, could sum up either column E (=SUM(E5:E8)) or row 10 (=SUM(B10:D10)). The result is the same either way.

Gina has been saving her spreadsheet on disk as she goes along. Now that the basic spreadsheet is complete, Gina saves it one more time and then prints it.

Changing the Spreadsheet: Automatic Recalculation

Gina has discovered an error in her spreadsheet: Cell D6, rather than containing 1430, should be 1502. Again using her spreadsheet software, she needs merely to retrieve the spreadsheet from disk and make the single change to cell D6 (Figure 6). Note, however, that cell D6 is used for the totals calculations in cells E6 and D10. Furthermore, because either column E or row 10 is used to compute the final total in E10, either changed cell E6 or changed cell D10 will cause a change in the value calculated in cell E10. All these changes are made by the spreadsheet software automatically. Indeed, note the changed values in cells E6, D10, and E10—all the result of a single change to cell D6.

Formatting and Printing

Now that Gina is satisfied with her spreadsheet calculations, she decides to make some formatting changes and then print the spreadsheet. She uses the spreadsheet software to make the changes (to see the changes, you can look ahead to Figure 7a). Here is a list of the changes she wants to make:

- Center the two major headings.
- Use a different font on the two major headings and change them to boldface.
- Center CAMPUS, OCT, NOV, DEC, and both TOTAL labels, each within its own cell, and boldface each label.
- Put each campus name in italic.
- Present the sales figures as currency by adding dollar signs ($) and decimal points.

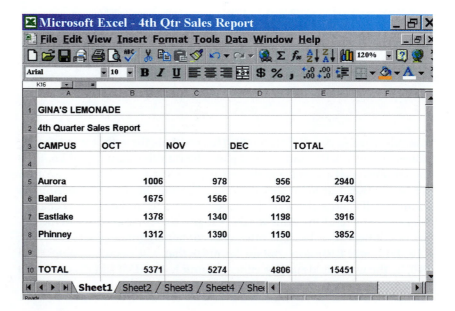

Figure 6 The altered spreadsheet, reflecting automatic recalculations. Gina changed the value in cell D6, causing an automatic change to calculated values in cells E6, D10, and E10.

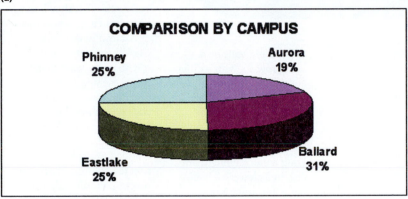

GINA'S LEMONADE				
4th Quarter Sales Report				
CAMPUS	OCT	NOV	DEC	TOTAL
Aurora	$ 1,006.00	$ 978.00	$ 956.00	$ 2,940.00
Ballard	$ 1,675.00	$ 1,566.00	$ 1,502.00	$ 4,743.00
Eastlake	$ 1,378.00	$ 1,340.00	$ 1,198.00	$ 3,916.00
Phinney	$ 1,312.00	$ 1,390.00	$ 1,150.00	$ 3,852.00
TOTAL	$ 5,371.00	$ 5,274.00	$ 4,806.00	$ 15,451.00

(a)

COMPARISON BY CAMPUS

(b)

Figure 7 The finished spreadsheet and a matching graph. (a) On the final version of her spreadsheet, printed here, Gina has boldfaced and centered the headings and changed their fonts, added vertical and horizontal borders, used italics and boldface on certain cells, and expressed the sales figures as currency. **(b)** This simple pie chart shows the figures from the rightmost column of the spreadsheet, the campus totals, as percentages of total sales.

- Use a vertical double border to separate the campus names from the sales figures, a horizontal double border to separate the headings from the sales figures, and a single horizontal border to separate the top two heading rows from the rest of the spreadsheet.
- Remove the spreadsheet grid lines.

Note that the printed result need not include the alphabetic column labels or the numeric row labels (Figure 7a).

A Graph from Spreadsheet Data

Gina decides to make a chart to contrast the sales totals among the four campuses. These figures already exist in the last column of the spreadsheet, cells E5 through E8. Using the software's charting capability, Gina can select those cells and then request a three-dimensional pie chart to display them. She decides to specify that the sales figures be shown as percentages of total sales and that each pie wedge be further labeled with the campus name, supplied from column A on the spreadsheet. After adding a title, Comparison by Campus, Gina saves and prints the finished chart (Figure 7b).

InfoBit

Every graph should have a title. It is surprising difficult to recall the exact meaning of an untitled chart produced last quarter. For this reason, most programs support not only titling the entire graph, but adding separate titles to the individual axes as well.

Global Perspective

Spreadsheet users who work extensively with foreign currencies and exchange rates have a new challenge—the Euro. Not only is there a new column or row of formulas contrasting the value of dollars into Euros, but users will also need to download a new font consisting of one character—the special Euro symbol. The Euro symbol is €.

InfoBit

Graphs are easy to produce with spreadsheets and often convey numbers more clearly than tables. However, experts point out that if you have only a few numbers to display, a simple table with a handful of numbers in a large, attractive font may actually be easier to read than a graph of the same information.

GETTING PRACTICAL

SPREADSHEET TIPS

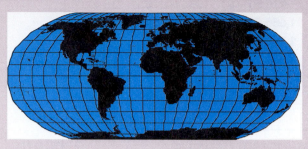

Serious users of spreadsheets employ many, or even most, of the hundreds of options available with spreadsheet software. More ordinary mortals probably use only the basic features. But even minimalists like to use an extra gimmick now and again. Here are a few that are easy and handy.

Do it all at once. If you have an action to apply to the entire spreadsheet, such as changing row height or adding background color, select the entire sheet by clicking the upper-left-hand cell-like space where the row designation meets the column designation (above 1, to the left of A). Then the action you choose will apply to the entire spreadsheet. Similarly, you can click on the row number to select the entire row or the column letter to designate an entire column.

Taller and wider. Spreadsheets look better if they are not crowded. So find the Format menu and change the row height and perhaps the column width. This is especially helpful if you selected the entire spreadsheet first. A common scenario, however, is to improve the row height for the entire spreadsheet but to set column width according to the width of the data content. You can, of course, make everything smaller instead if you must fit a lot of data on a page.

Go the max. Use the MAX function to find the highest, the longest, the most expensive, and so forth—the maximum. Suppose, for example, that an expense spreadsheet lists the cost of meals by day along row 15, with a different column, B through F, for Monday through Friday. To determine the most expensive meal, use = MAX(B15:F15).

Drag data. Highlight any cell. In its lower-right corner you can see a tiny square, called the fill handle. If you wish to duplicate data from one cell to any adjacent cell, simply drag its fill handle to the cell you want to fill with duplicate data. Suppose, for example, you are making calculations on each row that always include 40 in one cell. Place 40 in the cell at the top of the appropriate column. Now drag it down the column to the other rows. Now all cells in that column have the value 40 in them.

Add a new row or column. Sometimes people get part way through a spreadsheet and realize that they forgot, or want to add, a new row or column in the middle. Click the number of the row that you want to be below the new blank row. Find the Insert menu and click row; a new blank row appears above the row you designated. A new column is added to the left of the selected column. With each row or column addition, all rows or columns, and all calculations based on cells, are renumbered automatically.

Map it. Spreadsheet software offers a variety of maps, such as the one of the countries of the world shown here. You can add extras, such as marking regions by name and color and adding "pins" for points of interest.

Business Graphics

Graphics can show words and numbers and data in ways that are meaningful and quickly understood. This is the key reason they are valuable. Personal computers give people the capability to store and use data about their businesses. These same users, however, sometimes find it difficult to convey this information to others—managers or clients—in a meaningful way. **Business graphics**—graphics that represent data in a visual, easily understood format—provide an answer to this problem.

Why Use Graphics?

Graphics generate and sustain the interest of an audience by brightening up any lesson, report, or business document. In addition, graphics can help get a point across by presenting numeric data (Figure 8a) in one simple, clear graph (Figure 8b). What is more, that simple graph can reveal a trend that could be lost if buried in long columns of numbers. In addition, a presenter who uses graphics often appears more prepared and organized than one who does not. To sum up, most people use business graphics software for two reasons: (1) to view and analyze data and (2) to make a positive impression during a presentation. To satisfy these different needs, two types of business graphics programs have been developed: analytical graphics and presentation graphics.

Analytical Graphics

Analytical graphics programs are designed to help users analyze and understand specific data. Sometimes called analysis-oriented graphics programs, these programs use already-entered spreadsheet or database data to con-

InfoBit

There are ethical considerations to developing spreadsheet graphics. Spreadsheet software can produce accurate, informative charts, or—if used incorrectly—misleading and confusing output. Among the problems to watch out for are exaggerated vertical scales (making the 1/2% increase in profit a bar three inches high), misleading comparisons (a chart with a scale of $1 million side-by-side with a chart whose scale is $100 million), and charts that use 3D-effects and colors to camouflage bogus numbers.

Critical Thinking

For what kind of presentations would a table of numbers be more understandable than a chart? (Two examples—the case where the precise numbers themselves are more important than trends or comparisons, as in a tax table, and the case where the numbers vary so widely that some elements would dwarf others, as in a bar chart comparing executive compensation with teacher salaries.)

Figure 8 Business graphics. (a) A large amount of data can be translated into (b) one simple, clear bar graph.

	Units Sold Each Month			
Material	**Jan.**	**Feb.**	**Mar.**	**Apr.**
Copper	6	10	13	22
Bronze	18	28	36	60
Iron	9	15	19	32
Gold	32	52	64	110
Silver	20	32	40	68
Totals:	85	137	172	292

(a)

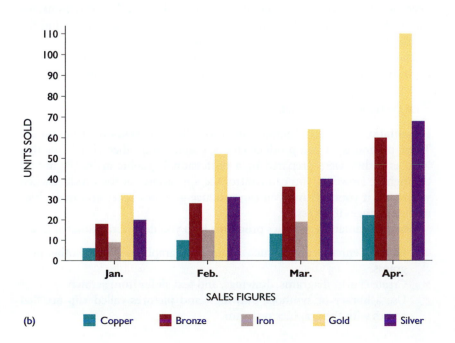

(b)   Copper   Bronze   Iron   Gold   Silver

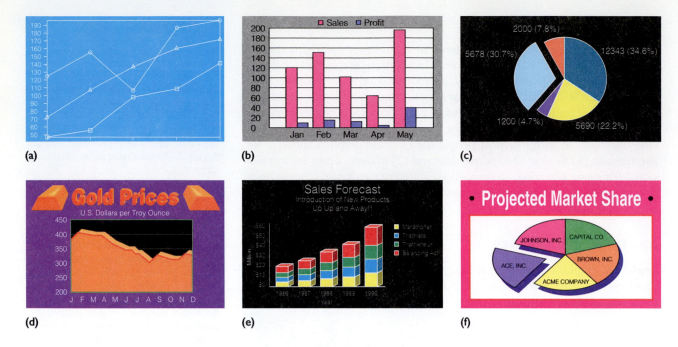

Figure 9 Analytical graphics compared with presentation graphics. Analytical graphics (a, b, and c) are certainly serviceable, but they lack the clarity and appeal of presentation graphics (d, e, and f). Compare the line graphs (a and d), bar graphs (b and e), and pie charts (c and f).

struct and display line, bar, and pie chart graphs (Figure 9a through c). Spreadsheet software usually provides this option.

Although analytical graphics programs do a good job of producing simple graphs, these programs are too limited and inflexible for a user who needs to prepare elaborate presentations. Analytical graphics programs, for example, let you choose from only a small number of graph types, and the formatting features—graph size, color, and lettering—are limited. These restrictions may be of little concern to some users, but those who require sophisticated graphics will want to consider presentation graphics.

Presentation Graphics

Presentation graphics programs are also called **business-quality graphics.** These programs let you produce charts, graphs, and other visual aids that look as if they were prepared by a professional graphic artist (Figure 9d through f). However, you can control the appearance of the product when you create it yourself, and you can produce graphics faster and make last-minute changes if necessary.

Most presentation graphics programs help you do several kinds of tasks:

- Edit and enhance charts, such as analytical graphs, created by other programs.
- Create charts, diagrams, drawings, and text slides from scratch.
- Use a library of symbols, drawings, and pictures called **clip art** that comes with the graphics program.

- Permit an animated presentation so that, for example, letters of a title can swoop in one by one to create a dynamic effect.
- Use small files that come with the program to add sounds—chimes, applause, swoosh, and even thunk—to your presentation.

Although graphics hardware requirements vary, be aware that to use presentation graphics you will need a high-resolution color monitor, possibly a color printer, and perhaps some method of transferring your computer-produced results to slides or transparencies or to a projector that can show computer screen output on a wall screen.

Some Graphics Terminology

To use a graphics program successfully, you should know some basic concepts and design principles. Let us begin by exploring the types of graphs you can create.

Line Graphs

One of the most useful ways of showing trends or cycles over a period of time is to use a **line graph.** For example, the graph in Figure 10 shows com-

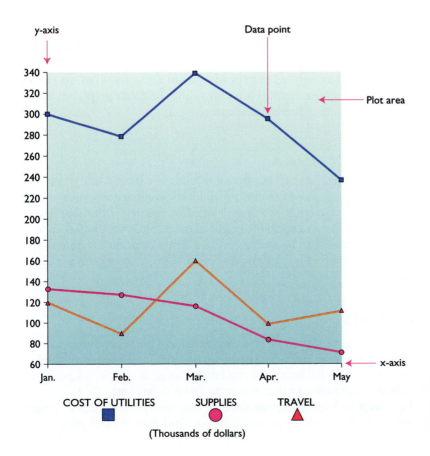

Figure 10 A line graph. Line graphs are useful for showing trends over a period of time. In many analytical programs, different symbols are used to show the different types of data being plotted.

pany costs for utilities, supplies, and travel during a five-month period. Line graphs are appropriate when there are many values or complex data. In the business section of a newspaper, line graphs are used to show complex trends in gross national product, stock prices, or employment changes over a period of time. Also, corporate profits and losses are often illustrated by line graphs.

Notice, in Figure 10, the line that runs vertically on the left and the one that runs horizontally across the bottom; each line is called an **axis.** (The plural of *axis* is *axes.*) The horizontal line, called the **x-axis,** often represents units of time, such as days, months, or years; it can also represent characteristics, such as model number, brand name, or country. The vertical line, called the **y-axis,** usually shows measured values or amounts, such as dollars, staffing levels, units sold, and so on. The area above and to the right of the axes is called the **plot area**—the space in which the graph is plotted, or drawn.

Graphics programs automatically scale (arrange the units or numbers on) the x-axis and y-axis so that the graph of your data is nicely proportioned and easy to read. When you become proficient with a graphics program, you can select your own scaling for the axes. Each dot or symbol on a line graph represents a single numeric quantity called a **data point.** You must specify the data to be plotted on the graph; many graphs are produced from the data stored in the rows and columns of spreadsheet files. This data is usually referred to as the set of **values.** The items that the data points describe are called **variables.** For example, in Figure 10 the variable Utilities includes the values 300, 280, 340, 300, and 240; the top line in the plot area shows how these values are graphed.

To make the graph easier to read and understand, **labels** are used to identify the categories along the x-axis and the units along the y-axis. **Titles** summarize the information in the graph and are used to increase comprehension. Every graph should have a title. It is surprisingly difficult to recall the exact meaning of an untitled chart produced just a few weeks before. For this reason, most programs support not only titling the entire graph but adding separate titles to the individual axes as well.

Bar Graphs

Bar graphs are used for graphing the same kinds of data that line graphs represent. They are often used to illustrate multiple comparisons, such as sales, expenses, and production activities. Notice in Figure 9b that **bar graphs** shade a rectangular area up to the height of the point being plotted, creating a bar. These graphs can be striking and informative when they are simple. Bar graphs are useful for presentations because the comparisons are easy to absorb.

Pie Charts

Representing just a single value for each variable, a **pie chart** shows how various values make up a whole. These charts really look like pies; the whole amount is represented by a circle, and each wedge of the pie—a portion of the whole—represents a value. Figure 9c shows a pie chart.

Pie charts can show only the data for one time period, such as a single month. However, of all the graphics, the pie chart does the best job of show-

2000 and Beyond

READY AND ENABLED

Technology is helping to level the playing field for the disabled in the twenty-first century. This is especially true for workers using computers, where technology means that disabled employees can take on jobs that move them into the mainstream workforce. In particular, workers who have computer access also can get access to the Internet, a focal point for all sorts of business endeavors.

Assistive hardware devices and software packages are helping to make the difference. Workers who are visually impaired can use voice input and output packages. For those who just need greater screen readability, Windows offers, as shown here, the option of enlarged letters and high-contrast colors. There is also software that produces greatly magnified screens. To use the related software manuals, a worker can use a camera-based system that enlarges and projects print onto the computer screen.

Improved visibility is only part of the story. Software typically offers aids for seeing, hearing, and touching.

A hearing-impaired individual can elect to have any computer sound show up as a visual indicator on the screen. Furthermore, spoken words and other sounds can be shown on the screen as captions. For those who cannot use two hands, options permit keys that normally must be pressed at the same time in order to invoke a command, such as Ctrl-Alt-Del, to be pressed separately but still achieve the same effect.

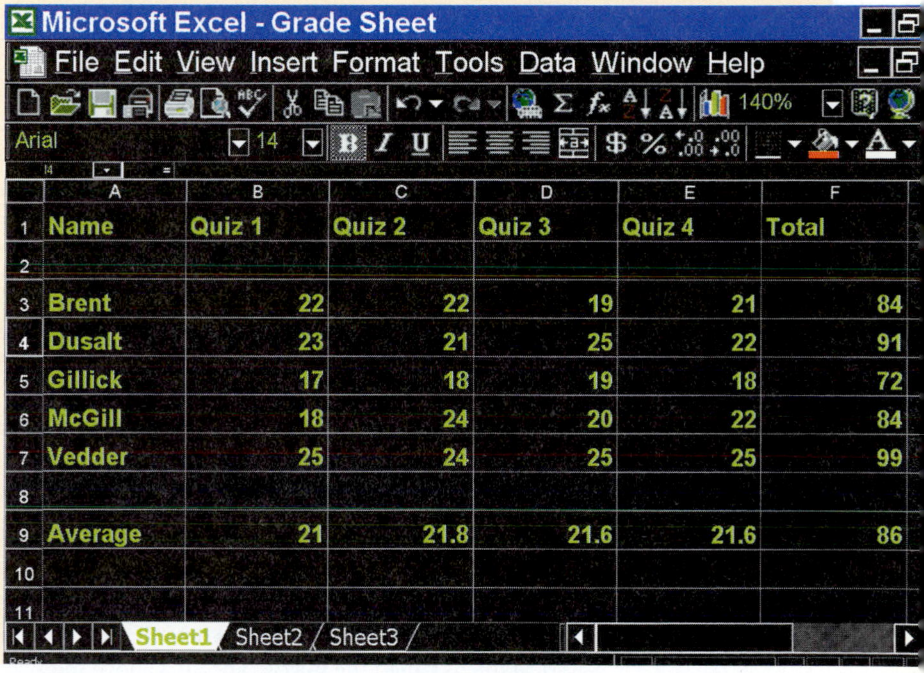

Microsoft Excel - Grade Sheet

File Edit View Insert Format Tools Data Window Help

Arial 14

	A	B	C	D	E	F
1	Name	Quiz 1	Quiz 2	Quiz 3	Quiz 4	Total
2						
3	Brent	22	22	19	21	84
4	Dusalt	23	21	25	22	91
5	Gillick	17	18	19	18	72
6	McGill	18	24	20	22	84
7	Vedder	25	24	25	25	99
8						
9	Average	21	21.8	21.6	21.6	86
10						
11						

Sheet1　Sheet2　Sheet3

ing the proportions for different variables. If a pie chart for expenses, for example, showed that more than half went for rent, that half-pie is easy to spot. Figure 9f shows one of the wedges pulled slightly away from the pie for emphasis. This type of pie chart is called an **exploded pie chart.**

▲

The most common applications software, word processing, deals with communicating with words. This chapter has addressed a subject of more interest to business than to individuals: analyzing and communicating with numbers.

Summary and Key Terms

■ Forms that are used to organize business data into rows and columns are called **spreadsheets.** An **electronic spreadsheet,** or **worksheet,** is a computerized version of a manual spreadsheet.

■ The greatest labor-saving aspect of the electronic spreadsheet is **automatic recalculation:** When one value or calculation in a spreadsheet is changed, all dependent values on the spreadsheet are automatically recalculated to reflect the change.

■ **"What-if" analysis** is the process of changing one or more spreadsheet values and observing the resulting calculated effect.

■ The intersection of a row and column forms a **cell.** The letter and number of the intersecting column and row is the **cell address,** or **cell reference.**

■ The **active cell,** or **current cell,** is the cell in which you can type data.

■ Each cell can contain one of three types of information: A **label** provides descriptive information about entries in the spreadsheet; a **value** is an actual number entered into a cell; and a **formula** is an instruction to the program to perform a calculation. A **function** is like a pre-programmed formula. Sometimes you must specify a **range** of cells, a group of adjacent cells in a rectangular area, to build a formula or perform a function.

■ To create a spreadsheet you enter labels, values, formulas, and functions into the cells. Formulas and functions do not appear in the cells; instead, the cell shows the result of the formula or function. The result is called the **displayed value** of the cell. The formula or function is the **content** of the cell, or the **cell content.**

■ **Business graphics** represent business data in a visual, easily understood format.

■ **Analytical graphics** programs help users analyze and understand specific data by presenting data in visual form. **Presentation graphics** programs, or **business-quality graphics** programs, produce sophisticated graphics. Presentation graphics programs contain a library of symbols and drawings called **clip art** and also offer animation and sounds.

■ A **line graph,** which uses a line to represent data, is useful for showing trends over time. A reference line on a line graph is an **axis.** The horizontal line is called the **x-axis,** and the vertical line is called the **y-axis.** The area above the x-axis and to the right of the y-axis is the **plot area.** Each dot or symbol on a line graph is a **data point.** Each data point represents a **value.** The items that the data points describe are called **variables. Labels** identify the categories along the x-axis and the units along the y-axis. **Titles** summarize the information in the graph.

■ **Bar graphs** show data comparisons by the lengths or heights of bars.

■ A **pie chart** represents a single value for each variable. A wedge of an **exploded pie chart** is pulled slightly away from the pie, to emphasize that share of the whole.

Discussion Questions

1. Consider more "what-if" scenarios. What if I save $100 a month . . . how soon can I buy a car? What if I save $125 or $150 per month? If you have a price in mind for a car, what information could such a spreadsheet give you? What information could you get by varying interest rates and the price of the car? What if I buy the house by the lake . . . instead of the house near work? The houses have different price tags and different expenses. These factors and others can be built into a spreadsheet and used to calculate monthly payments and other factors that might affect your budget. What factors might you include in your spreadsheet? *Hint:* One fac-

tor may be reduced transportation costs for the house near work.

2. How might you use a spreadsheet in your career? What use might these workers have for a spreadsheet: a video store manager, a dietitian, a civil engineer who designs bridges, a day-care supervisor?

3. Business people who only occasionally give presentations say that one reason they prefer using graphics is that graphics focus the audience on the screen and thus reduce the nervousness of the speaker. What other advantages do graphics offer to the speaker?

4. In addition to standing on their own, spreadsheets are often used back up a discussion or illuminate a point in a text report. With this is mind, word processing programs let users import spreadsheets into text documents, such as reports or memos. This is just the sort of thing that give software suites value; the word processing and spreadsheet programs are compatible and can exchange data easily. What scenarios can you imagine for a report with an embedded spreadsheet, even a small one, for these types of workers: a roofing subcontractor, a visiting nurse, an office project manager.

Student Study Guide

Multiple Choice

1. The active cell is the
   - a. current cell
   - b. range
   - c. formula
   - d. cell address

2. A preprogrammed formula is called a
   - a. function
   - b. graph
   - c. range
   - d. cell

3. A chart that represents only one value for each variable is known as a
   - a. function
   - b. line graph
   - c. pie chart
   - d. bar graph

4. Business-quality graphics is another name for
   - a. a recalculation
   - b. a range
   - c. analytical graphics
   - d. presentation graphics

5. The intersection of a row and column creates a(n)
   - a. active address
   - b. formula
   - c. cursor
   - d. cell

6. The result of a formula in a cell is known as the
   - a. label
   - b. value
   - c. range
   - d. displayed value

7. Text information in a cell is called a
   - a. label
   - b. value
   - c. formula
   - d. cell address

8. A dot or symbol on a line graph is called a(n)
   - a. label
   - b. data point
   - c. variable
   - d. axis

9. The element that summarizes information related to a graph is called the
   - a. plot area
   - b. title
   - c. label
   - d. axis

10. Computer-prepared art is called
    - a. a cell
    - b. analytical
    - c. clip art
    - d. a range

11. As opposed to analytical graphics, presentation graphics are
    - a. more sophisticated
    - b. larger
    - c. more accurate
    - d. not used in business

12. When a wedge is made separate, the pie chart is referred to as
    - a. exploded
    - b. active
    - c. referenced
    - d. displayed

13. A cell entry that provides descriptive information is called a
    - a. value
    - b. data point
    - c. label
    - d. title

14. Automatic recalculation refers to the changes to values dependent on
    - a. what if
    - b. the axis
    - c. a function
    - d. a changed value

15. SUM is an example of a
    - a. displayed value
    - b. range
    - c. label
    - d. function

16. Each data point on a line graph represents a
    - a. function
    - b. pie wedge
    - c. cell
    - d. value

17. A reference line on a line graph is called a(n)
    - a. axis
    - b. label
    - c. title
    - d. data point

18. F2:G6 is an example of a
    - a. function
    - b. range
    - c. value
    - d. cell address

19. Which of these is a correct cell address?
    a. DD
    b. B6
    c. 2C
    d. F0

20. A set of adjacent cells that form a rectangle is called a
    a. data point
    b. function
    c. range
    d. cell reference

True/False

T F 1. Another name for the content of a cell is the displayed value.

T F 2. A group of cells in a rectangular form is called a range.

T F 3. Another name for the active cell is the cell reference.

T F 4. A manual spreadsheet is capable of automatically recalculating totals when changes are made to figures in the spreadsheet.

T F 5. A disadvantage of business graphics is that they depict data in a manner that is hard to grasp.

T F 6. The displayed value of a cell is called its formula or function.

T F 7. The shape of the set-apart portion of an exploded pie chart is a wedge.

T F 8. A function is like a preprogrammed formula.

T F 9. Another name for the current cell is a labeled cell.

T F 10. In a spreadsheet, both column width and row height can be altered.

T F 11. Analytical graphics let you construct line, bar, and pie chart graphs.

T F 12. Many presentation graphics programs can edit and enhance charts created by other programs.

T F 13. Presentation graphics appear professionally produced.

T F 14. Column widths in spreadsheets are fixed.

T F 15. Analytical graphics use a library of symbols to enhance output.

T F 16. The active spreadsheet cell is marked by the pointer.

T F 17. Labels identify categories along graph axes.

T F 18. On an exploded pie chart, one wedge is slightly removed from the pie for emphasis.

T F 19. The greatest labor-saving aspect of an electronic spreadsheet is its ability to recalculate dependent values when the value it depends on is changed.

T F 20. In a spreadsheet a label cannot be used for calculations.

Fill-In

1. The actual number entered into a cell is the _____.

2. What is the name of the kind of analysis that lets a user change spreadsheet values and then observe the resulting effect? _____

3. What are enhanced graphics called? _____

4. In a spreadsheet a formula or function is called the cell content; what is the calculated result called? _____

5. What is the intersection of a row and column on a spreadsheet called? _____

6. Plain line graphs are an example of what kind of graphics? _____

7. Another name for a cell address is the _____.

8. Another name for the active cell is the _____.

9. In a line graph the horizontal axis is called the _____.

10. A preprogrammed formula is called a _____.

11. A group of cells in a rectangular form is called a _____.

12. The type of chart that has a single wedge separate from the rest of the chart is called _____.

13. When one value or calculation on a spreadsheet is changed, all dependent calculations are also changed by the software. This is called

    _____ .

14. The letter and number of the intersecting column and row of a cell is called

    _____ .

15. Another name for an electronic spreadsheet is

    _____ .

16. The type of cell that contains descriptive information is called a _____ .

17. A library of usable symbols and drawings is called

    _____ .

18. In a line graph the vertical axis is called the

    _____ .

19. How many values can a pie chart represent for each value? _____ .

20. The type of graph used to show a trend over time is called a _____ .

Answers

Multiple Choice

1.	a	11.	a
2.	a	12.	a
3.	c	13.	c
4.	d	14.	d
5.	d	15.	d
6.	d	16.	d
7.	a	17.	a
8.	b	18.	b
9.	b	19.	b
10.	c	20.	c

True/False

1.	F	11.	T
2.	T	12.	T
3.	F	13.	T
4.	F	14.	F
5.	F	15.	F
6.	F	16.	F
7.	T	17.	T
8.	T	18.	T
9.	F	19.	T
10.	T	20.	T

Fill-In

1. value
2. "what-if" analysis
3. presentation graphics
4. displayed value
5. cell
6. analytical
7. cell reference
8. current cell
9. x-axis
10. function
11. range
12. exploded pie chart
13. automatic recalculation
14. cell address
15. worksheet
16. label
17. clip art
18. y-axis
19. one
20. line graph

PLANET INTERNET

The Internet was started by the military and long remained the province of the government and educational institutions. Businesses wondered if commercial enterprises were even permitted on the Internet. The answer, a resounding yes, has led to an explosion of activity.

Big and small. You may have heard about individuals starting their own small businesses on the Internet. There are many thousands of them. But what about the big companies that have been established for decades? Are serious businesses interested in the Internet? You bet. Much of the Internet is embraced—and supported—by business. More than half of Internet sites are business-related.

A Web presence. Just being "on the Web" is probably not enough. The issue is whether a business site has established a Web presence —that is, has an oft-visited site respected for its value and content. Notice that the web sites shown here for Boeing, Kellogg, and FedEx are both attractive and useful; each has many clickable icons as links to informational parts of their sites. But companies use their sites in different ways. No one, for example, expects to drop by the Boeing site to buy an airplane. Nor, for that matter, is anyone visiting the Kellogg site to pick up a box of cereal. The sites are used mainly for company information and to make visitors comfortable with their corporate presence. FedEx, on the other

hand, offers a functional, interactive site that encourages visitors to do business right on the site. Thus a visitor can, for example, order a package pickup or track the progress of a package in transit.

Success factors. The secret to a successful page is that users accept the invitation to visit the site and, more importantly, keep coming back to it. If they form a habit of visiting a page, they will be more disposed toward that company's products and services. The primary reason users come back is that they know they can expect some useful content. Selling food? Include recipes at your site. Offering golf equipment? Report the latest information on tournaments and courses. In fact, many retail sites begin by offering useful information; only when an audience is established do they start offering products.

Advertising. There are different approaches to advertising on the Internet. A business can, of course, pitch its products or services on its own site. Many businesses now trumpet their web sites by including their Internet address in their television or print advertisements. In another approach, they buy advertising on a popular site—perhaps Yahoo! or ESPNET SportsZone. The point is, they pick a site known to have a lot of traffic, where a click on their specific advertising banner or icon takes the user to their site.

Targeting users. What business people on the Internet desperately want is measurements.

stakes, drawings, and prizes. Whether or not the user chooses to participate is another matter.

Sending mail. An obvious interactive technique for a business site is to offer an e-mail option. Users who take the trouble to write, to ask questions, or even to complain supply valuable marketing data to the company. The business, of course, must respond to all e-mail messages promptly.

The future. The Internet has both short-term and long-term benefits for businesses and for their users. For business people, in the short term there is e-mail, information gathering, and even direct marketing. For users, business sites provide information and convenience. Long term, the most compelling benefit for both groups is that the Internet represents the way business is going to be transacted in the future.

How many people visit the site? Who are they? What hardware and software do they have? Is this their first time, or are they repeat visitors? If they have been here before, what parts of the site did they visit? If businesses had the answers to these questions, they could tailor their sites to the user and improve their prospects. Some information is relatively easy to gather; even a novice can include a counter on a web page so that the number of visits—if not visitors—can easily be known. Web site analysis software, available for a fee or via consultants, can track other data.

One on one. Successful business sites take advantage of the Internet's unique characteristic, its interactivity. A business that prepares a television commercial is pitching to a passive audience. But an ad on the Internet can be a two-way activity between the business, as represented by the site, and the user. The most straightforward way to take advantage of interactivity is to ask users to voluntarily give some information about themselves and their preferences, a process called registration. A more likely method is to offer something of value in return for the user's name, e-mail address, and other information. For this reason, the Internet abounds with contests, sweep-

Internet Exercises

1. **Structured exercise.** Begin with the URL http://www.prenhall.com/capron. Choose a business directory to see what kinds of sites are on the Internet.

2. **Freeform exercise.** Think of a business product or service that interests you—computers, chocolate, motorcycles, whatever. Feed that word to a search engine and see what business sites you find.

Pictures Do Lie

The works on this page show how photographs can be manipulated by the computer. Begin with 1. a photo of a building interior. Then consider 2., photos of strolling tourists, a statue, and a painting. These four photos have been scanned into the computer and manipulated to become 3., a museum with artworks and tourists to view them. Note in particular the adjusted shape of the painting and the computer artist's addition of clouds in the skylight.
4. Here is the intriguing result of computer imaging of four photos. The original photos were of trees, a sunset, a swan, and a red world logo.
5. Here the artist has produced various computer-manipulated versions of an original photo of a child.

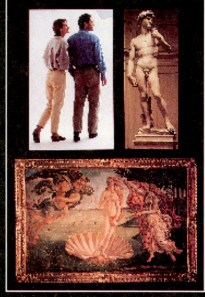

2

1

3

4

5

COMPUTER GRAPHICS

6

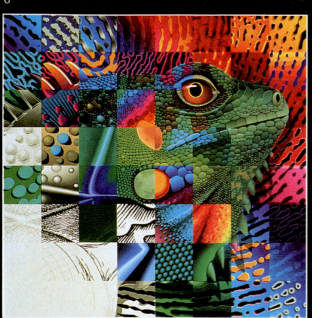

Computer Graphics as Art

The computer artwork on the title page of this gallery, by Dave Martland, won best of the month in the abstract category in the annual contest sponsored by CorelDraw software.

6. Bill Frymire produced this work, which is something of a classic in graphics circles. The artist scanned his own thumb print to be used as the background. But all eyes are on Rex, his pet iguana.

7. This cathedral ceiling artwork, which Italian artist Antonio De Leo calls Duomo, won Best of Show in the CorelDraw contest.

8. Karin Kuhlmann won best of the month in the landscape category in the CorelDraw contest.

9. Joseph Maas, who also did the illustration for the cover for this book, calls this work Chess Mystery.

10. This image, by Huan Le Tran, won best of the month in the abstract category in the CorelDraw contest.

7

11

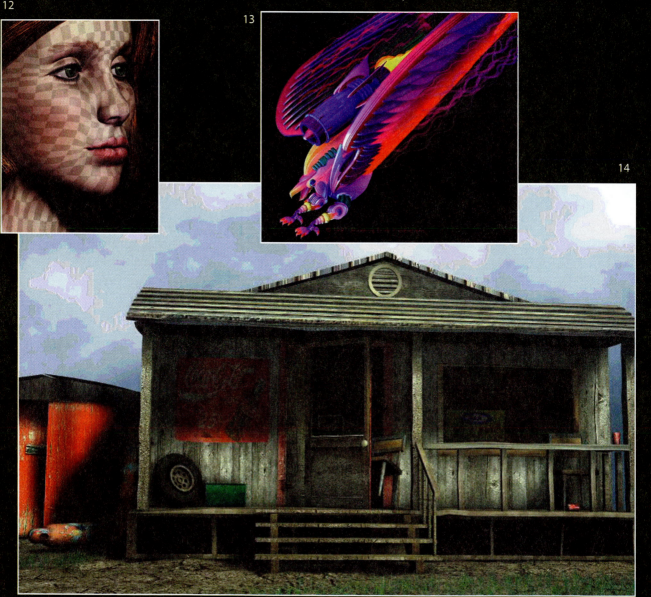

Graphic Artists and Their Tools

We mentioned CorelDraw on the two prior pages; it is one of many software tools that graphic artists may use. Other popular software graphics packages are Studio Max, Ray Dream, Lightwave, POV Ray, and Bryce. Artists may use tools from different software on the same artwork. The artists whose work is shown on these two pages all use three-dimensional versions of the software. 11. Marcus Benko calls this work Intruder; 12. this is called simply Head Test, according to Jeremy Birn; 13. David Brickley names his work Eagle. 14. Kyle Nau, with this work called Country Store, won the grand prize in a contest sponsored by Marlin Studios, which encouraged entrants to use as many of the Marlin textures as possible. Marlin offers a CD-ROM with photorealistic real-world textures such as peeling paint, rust, corrosion, aged wooden planks, rusted metals, metal grates, concretes, windows, and doors.

More images from the artists' imagination: 15. Fountain Pens by Kris Lazoore; 16. Bug and Dolphin by Alberto Giorgi; and 17. Pocketwatch by Kevin Odhner.

12

13

14

Ray Tracing

An important aspect of realistic perspective is the use of light and shadow. Rather than adding these elements individually, graphic artists can use software to enhance their works. The "ray" in ray tracing refers to light rays, whose direction can be "traced" by the software. For example, a user can specify the location—point of view—of a light element, such as light from the sun or a nearby window or a lamp, and the software will add appropriate shadows. The light source need not actually be included in the image; it could be "off screen" but still cause shadows.

The works shown here were all entries in the Internet Ray Tracing Competition, which has a new contest every few months on a different theme. Examine them carefully to see how the artists made use of light and shadow.

18. Steve Gowers won first prize in the Summer theme contest with his rendition of a bucket of seashells.
19. Nathan O'Brien took second place in the contest with the theme Elements.
20. Gautam Lad submitted this entry, called Grade One, to the contest with the theme School.
21. Ian Armstrong won honorable mention in the Flight category.
22. In the competition with a Time theme, Adrian Baumann won second place with this Admiral watch.
23. Nathan O'Brien won second place with this image, called Ode to Prianesi, in the Imaginary Worlds contest.

18

19

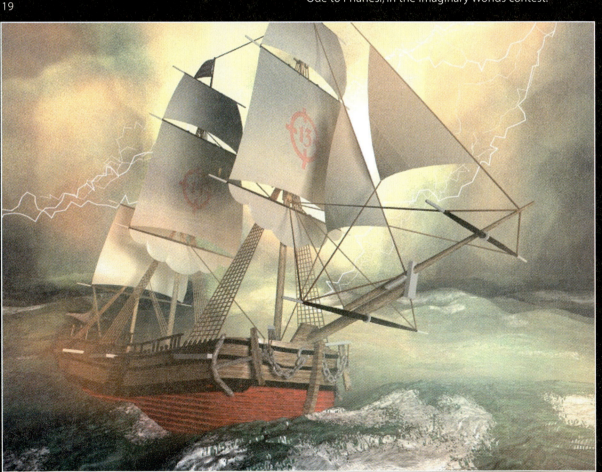

20

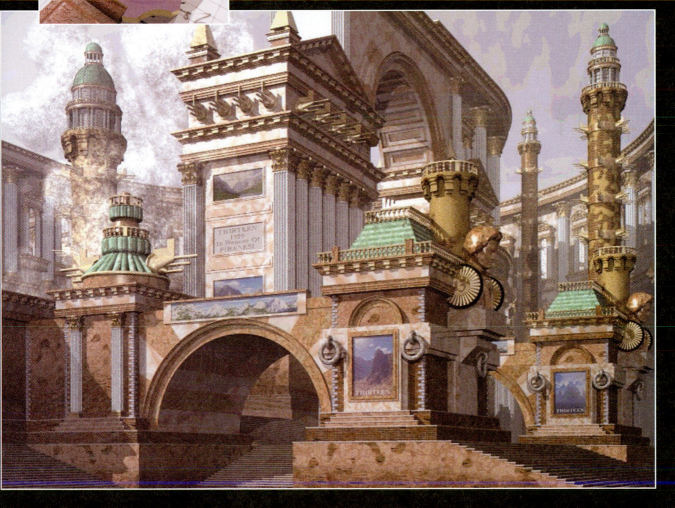

21

22

23

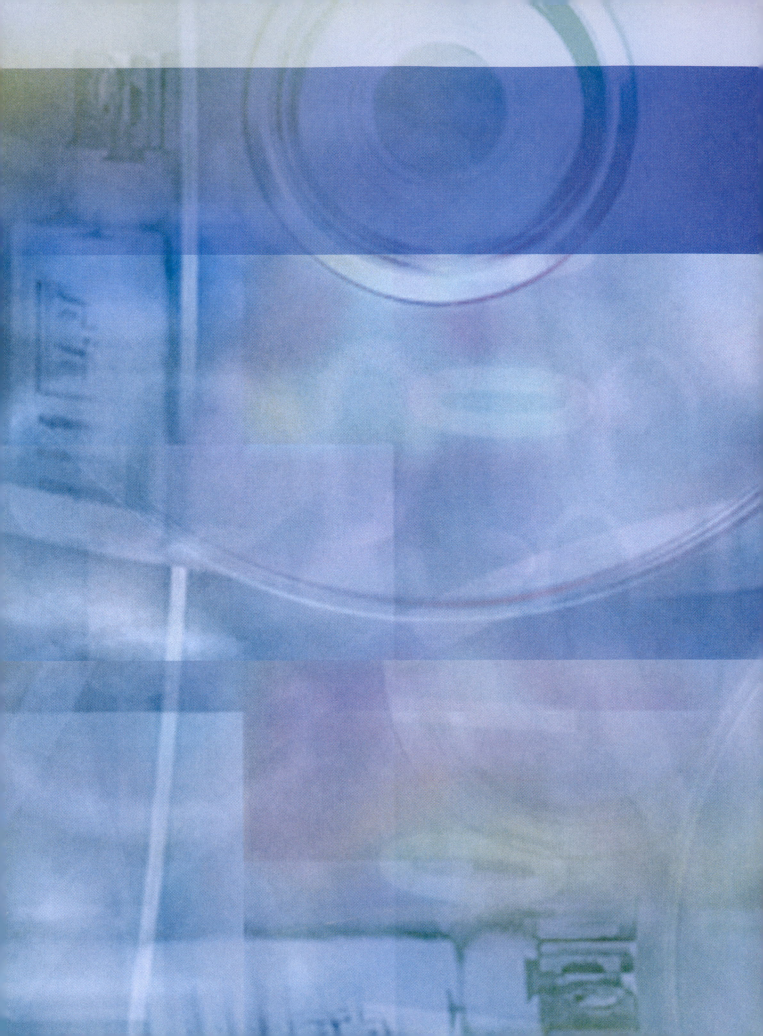

CHAPTER THIRTEEN

DATABASE MANAGEMENT SYSTEMS

Getting Data Together

LEARNING OBJECTIVES

- Appreciate the advantages of databases
- Understand how databases are organized
- Become familiar with database terminology
- Understand, in general, how to build and change a database

Suppose you had a really terrific recipe for chocolate chip cookies. In fact, your friends and family rave about your oatmeal-raisin cookies too, not to mention your snickerdoodles and macadamia nut specials. Thus encouraged, you open a small cookie shop. Just one. It is not too difficult to keep track of supplies—just multiply the ingredients of a few recipes.

But that simplicity has changed for Debbi Fields, whose Mrs. Fields Cookies has blossomed from a single store in Palo Alto, California, to a chain of more than 600 stores in almost every state and several foreign countries. Fortunately, her husband, Randy Fields, a computer programmer, put together a team of technicians to provide databases with every kind of information a store might need.

Recipes and ingredients are just the beginning. The databases specialize in planning and marketing strategies. For example, from data gathered and stored over a period of time, the database knows how meteorological conditions affect sales at each store. In Seattle, rain means more cookie sales; in Los Angeles, rain means fewer cookie sales. Stores in either city can plan the amount of cookies to bake accordingly. But the weather is only one factor. Cookies sold and dollars generated are updated at each store hourly. These records can be accessed in the future to predict sales. If, for example, a store sees that its sales are below predictions, workers are authorized to offer specials—say, a free soft drink or "buy 5 get 2 free."

Employees at Mrs. Fields Cookies find it easy to learn to use the database software. The databases have many advantages—in particular, keeping consistent standards at each store. But the bottom line is that the computer databases squeeze out higher productivity.

Getting It Together: Database Systems

A **database** is an organized collection of related data. In a loose sense you are using a database when you use a phone book or when you take papers from a file cabinet. Unfortunately, as the amount of data increases, creating, storing, changing, sorting, and retrieving data become overwhelming tasks.

Suppose you had a collection of names and addresses, each on a separate index card, stored in an index-card file (Figure 1). If you had only 25 cards, sorting the cards into alphabetical order or even finding all the people who have the same zip code would be fairly easy. But what if you had 100, or 1000, or 10,000 cards? What if you had several different boxes, one organized by names, one by cities, and one by zip codes? What if different file clerks added more cards each day, not knowing whether they were duplicating cards already in the file? And what if another set of clerks was trying to update the data on the same cards? As you can see, things might get out of hand. Enter computers and database management software.

A **database management system** (DBMS) is software that helps you organize data in a way that allows fast and easy access to the data. In essence, the program acts as an efficient and elaborate file system. With a database program you can enter, modify, store, and retrieve data in a variety of ways.

Databases Are Different

Before we proceed further, it should be noted that database systems are different from word processing or spreadsheet software. Generally, most users have a good understanding of both word processing and spreadsheets. They enter and use the data in the same form as that in which it resides on disk. Data in databases, however, can reside on the disk in ways unknown to a user. In particular, sophisticated database systems, particularly those designed for a mainframe computer environment, are complex and must be planned and managed by computer professionals.

However, even though the underlying technology may be complex, such databases are available to the average user. Users are trained to input data to and retrieve data from the database system by using appropriate software; they can do this successfully without ever having to understand the underlying technology.

On the other hand, database software that a novice user can apply to simple or moderately complex problems is available for personal computers. That is, in contrast to complex databases that must be set up by professionals, a user could both set up and use a database on a personal computer. That is the kind of database we will be examining in this chapter.

Advantages of Databases

Several advantages are generally associated with databases.

- **Reduced redundancy.** Data stored in separate files, as opposed to in a database, tends to repeat some of the same data over and over. A college, for example, needs to have various kinds of information for a student—perhaps financial, academic, and career data. If each of these sets of data is in a separate file, some repetition is inevitable—such as each student's name, address, and Social Security number or other identification. In a database most of this information would appear just once.

- **Integrated data.** Rather than being in separate and independent files, data in a database is considered integrated because any item of data can be used to satisfy an inquiry or a report. This advantage is related to the reduced redundancy advantage: Since data can be retrieved from any place in the database, many specific data items need not be repeated.

- **Integrity.** People who maintain any kind of file hope that it has integrity, that is, that the file is accurate and up-to-date. Integrity concerns increase as the sophistication of the data increases. Reduced redundancy increases the likelihood of data integrity.

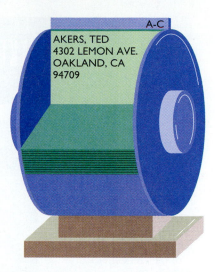

Figure 1 An index-card database. Each card in this index-card file contains one person's name and address. The cards are arranged alphabetically by last name.

InfoBit

Actually, sorting those index cards by hand might be even worse than you imagine. Before electronic computers, mechanical card sorting machines were used. A good machine with a smart operator still took about two hours to sort 10,000 cards.

Critical Thinking

What practices and procedure do you think are important for ensuring data integrity? (Some possibilities—running exception report programs to look for inaccurate values, program "edit-checks" to ensure that appropriate kinds of data—numbers only in numeric fields, for example—are entered, frequent backups to prevent data loss, physical and password security against unauthorized access or alteration, and storage of backup copies off-site or in fire-resistant safes).

Critical Thinking

What problems could redundancy in data cause? (Wasted storage space from having the same data replicated, problems with altering or updating data causing inconsistencies when one copy is updated and another may not be, the need to add new data to more than one file, and the possibility of incompletely deleting records by removing the information from one file, but not others.)

MAKING THE RIGHT CONNECTIONS
TERRASERVER

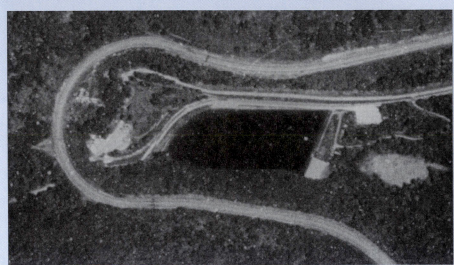

At the Microsoft Terra-Server site you can find a collection of satellite images of just about any place on earth. The images are cataloged in a massive database and can be viewed online or purchased for a modest fee. The image shown here is of the Horseshoe Curve Railway, famous for its 180-degree turnaround, near Altoona, Pennsylvania. The TerraServer site is popular around the clock, receiving over 30 million hits per day.

Global Perspective

As corporate databases become truly international, problems arise in scheduling needed "downtime" for maintenance and updates. With users in widely differing time-zones, it is no longer possible for database programmers to take an entire database system "down" between midnight and dawn. Instead, international database systems must provide redundancy and backup so that is one system is down for repair during that country's off-hours, other worldwide users are not disrupted.

InfoBit

Although the most obvious reason to minimize redundancy in databases is to save on storage space, a more important reason is to enhance database integrity and ease maintenance of records. Data stored in more than one location can quickly become inconsistent and it requires a lot of extra care and effort to retain accuracy under these circumstances.

Global Perspective

Perhaps the most far-flung, and truly international, database is the Domain Name Server (DNS) system used on the Internet. In the DNS database, thousands of computers collaborate across the Internet to share information about how a millions of URLs—like http://www.awl.com—get turned into network addresses like 192.168.16.1.

Database Concepts

There are many DBMS programs on the market today. Covering all the operations, features, and functions of each package would be impossible. Instead, this chapter examines database management in a generic way. The features discussed are common to most database software packages.

Database Models

The way a database organizes data depends on the type, or **model,** of the database. There are three main database models: hierarchical, network, and relational. Each type structures, organizes, and uses data differently. Hierarchical and network databases are usually used with large computers and will not be discussed here. However, relational databases are used with personal computers as well as mainframes. A **relational database** organizes data in a table format consisting of related rows and columns. Figure 2a shows an address list; in Figure 2b this data is laid out as a table.

Fields, Records, and Files

Notice in Figure 2b that each box in the table contains a single piece of data, known as a **data item,** such as the name of one city. Each column of the table represents a **field,** which is a type of data item. The specific data items in a field may vary, but each field contains the same type of data item—for example, first names or zip codes. The full set of data in any given row is called a **record.** Each record has a fixed number of fields. The fields in a particular

Akers, Ted
4302 Lemon Ave.
Oakland, CA 94709

Brown, Ann
345 Willow Rd.
Palo Alto, CA 94025

Chandler, Joy
4572 College Ave.
Berkeley, CA 94705

James, Susan
822 York St.
San Francisco, CA 94103

Mead, Ken
8 Rocklyn Ave.
Tiburon, CA 94903

(a)

Figure 2 A relational database. In this example the address list in (a) is organized as a relational database in (b). Note that the data is laid out in rows and columns; each field is equivalent to a column, and each record is equivalent to a row.

Field

LAST NAME	FIRST NAME	STREET	CITY	STATE	ZIPCODE
AKERS	TED	4302 LEMON AVE.	OAKLAND	CA	94709
BROWN	ANN	345 WILLOW RD.	PALO ALTO	CA	94025
CHANDLER	JOY	4572 COLLEGE AVE.	BERKELEY	CA	94705
JAMES	SUSAN	822 YORK ST.	SAN FRANCISCO	CA	94103
MEAD	KEN	8 ROCKLYN AVE.	TIBURON	CA	94903

(b)

Data item

record contain related data—for example, the name and address of a person. A collection of related records makes up a **file.** In a relational database a file is also called a **relation.** There can be a variable number of records in a given relation; Figure 2b shows five records—one for each person. There can also be more than one file in a database.

Database Power

Now that you know what *field, record, file,* and *relation* mean, you are ready to glimpse the real power of databases. The power is in the connection: A relational system can relate data in one file to data in another file, allowing a user to tie together data from several files. To understand how this works, consider the database called MOORE that uses a set of four related files—four relations—to constitute one database. These four files have some fields in common (Figure 3). The files are part of a database for Moore Contax, Inc., a company that warehouses computer equipment and supplies. Moore needs to keep track of its sales representatives, customers, orders, and inventory.

Now look at a detailed version of these relations (Figure 4). The Sales Representative file has six fields: REP-ID (representative identification), LNAME (last name), FNAME (first name), REGION (geographic area), HDATE (hire date), and PHONE. Similarly, the Customer file has four fields, the Order file has four fields, and the Inventory file has three fields (QOH stands for quantity on hand). The interesting point about these relations is that they are connected. Both the Sales Representative file and the Customer file have a REP-ID field. The Customer file and the Order file are connected by the field CUST-

Figure 3 Conceptual diagram of the files in the MOORE database. The files are Sales Representative, Customer, Order, and Inventory. Note the common fields.

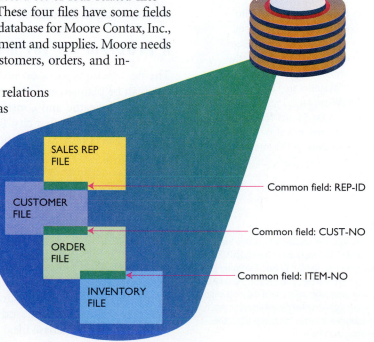

Database on disk

SALES REP FILE

CUSTOMER FILE

ORDER FILE

INVENTORY FILE

Common field: REP-ID

Common field: CUST-NO

Common field: ITEM-NO

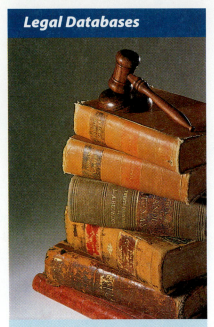

You have seen the formal photograph of the judge, the attorney, the politician—each with a solid wall of law books in the background. Those books are not just decoration, however. Workers in any law office need to be able to research legal precedents and related matters.

But why not take the information in those books and just "drop it" into a computer? That is, in essence, what has been done. The books have been converted into computer-accessible databases, and the result is that legal research time has decreased significantly. Two common computerized legal research systems are LEXIS and WESTLAW, available in most law libraries and law firms. Much of the same information is also available on various sites on the Internet.

InfoBit

In the terminology of relational databases, the SALES REPRESENTATIVE FILE and the CUSTOMER FILE are "joined" on the REP-ID field. The power and flexibility inherent in being able to join separate files into one or more relations is one of the most important reasons that relational databases are so much more popular on personal computers than other database organizations.

NO. The Order file and the Inventory file are connected by the field ITEM-NO. These sample files are, of course, rather primitive, but they illustrate the point of connectivity.

These connections allow users to extract information across several relations, something that would not be possible if each relation were an independent file instead of a file within a database. Suppose, for example, that Anthony Harl, an employee for Moore Contax, receives a phone call inquiring about an order for Computer City. The folks at Computer City are concerned because a promised order is overdue and they have not heard from their sales representative. Anthony has, of course, a computer on his desk. Keep in mind that Anthony need not be concerned with how the relations are set up and may not even know what a relation is. From his training, however, he has a pretty good idea of what information he can get from the database system.

Anthony can, by using commands appropriate to his database software, ask a question that is the equivalent of this: What is the status of Computer City's order? The database software would look to the Customer file (follow along in Figure 4), find CUST-NO 3007 for Computer City, and then go to the Order file and look up the order lines for CUST-NO 3007. From the 3007 line in the Order file, the software could pick up ITEM-NO data 7639; using that data and now moving to the Inventory file, it can be seen that item 7639, a sound card, is out of stock. All this scrambling around is **transparent** to the user; that is, the user is not aware of the specific searches through the files but is merely given a response to the request. Anthony gets a message back on his screen with the net result: On Computer City's order, item 7639, sound card, is out of stock. Anthony can convey this information to the customer waiting on the line.

Furthermore, Anthony can, again by using commands appropriate to his database software, ask about Computer City's sales representative. The database software, looking in the Customer file, can see that Computer City's REP-ID is 230. Moving now to the Sales Representative file, REP-ID 230 is Pat Sullivan, whose phone number is (305) 734-2987. When a message to this effect comes back on the screen, Anthony can pass this information along to the customer on the phone line.

A Problem Fit for a Database

The next sections focus on just one database file and show, generally, how data can be planned and entered. Patricia Mahtani is a convention planner. She lives in Seattle and contracts with various organizations who plan to hold conventions in that city. Patricia and her staff of five coordinate every physical aspect of the convention, including transportation, housing, catering, meeting rooms, services, tours, and entertainment.

Patricia began moving her files to a computer three years ago. She has found database software useful because of its ability to cross-reference several files and, in particular, to answer inquiries about the data. Patricia thinks the time is ripe to set up a database file for the tours she offers. She has noticed that clients ask many questions about the tours available, including times, costs, and whether or not food is included. Also, clients want to know if much walking is included on the tour and whether or not there are stairs.

In answer to these kinds of questions, Patricia or one of her staff now has to shuffle through a thick folder of brochures and price lists. Patricia knows that she will be able to respond more quickly to client inquiries if this information is in her database file.

SALES REPRESENTATIVE FILE

REP-ID	LNAME	FNAME	REGION	HDATE	PHONE
114	Abele	Lori	SW	10-15-86	(602) 624-9384
159	Higgins	Heatheryn	SE	12-16-91	(404) 524-8472
230	Sullivan	Pat	SE	2-21-88	(305) 734-2987
386	Speed	Kristen	MW	6-14-90	(708) 823-8222
349	Demaree	Donn	NW	7-10-93	(206) 634-1955

CUSTOMER FILE

CUST-NO	CNAME	CITY	REP-ID
2934	Ballard Computer	Seattle	349
3007	Computer City	Miami	230
4987	Laser Systems	Atlanta	159
8987	Varner User Systems	Naperville	386
9185	CGI Computers	Spokane	349
9876	Computing Solutions	Tucson	114

ORDER FILE

CUST-NO	DATE	ITEM-NO	QTY
3007	8-12-99	7639	11
4987	8-12-99	6720	15
8987	8-13-99	2378	14
9185	8-10-99	1628	10
9876	8-14-99	6720	20

INVENTORY FILE

ITEM-NO	DESCR	QOH
1628	Hand scanner	191
2378	Modem	453
3457	Hard drive	294
5647	Printer pack	676
6720	3 1/2" disk holder	982
6599	CD-ROM drive	817
7639	Sound card	0
8870	Mouse	296
9037	Monitor	152

Figure 4 Records in the four files in the MOORE database. Observe that there are common fields among the files, enabling the files to reference one another.

Focus on Ethics

Who Gets to Know All about You?

Ethical use of databases is a recurring matter requiring careful examination. Consider a medical database containing the following information for each individual: blood type, allergies, medical history, date of birth, marital status, next of kin, home address, employer, financial responsibility figures, DNA data, and a set of fingerprint images. Many people would agree that it is ethical and appropriate for emergency room personnel to have access to such information.

The premise, of course, is that the information is used for medical purposes. Would it be ethical to let insurance companies access that database? Should an attorney be able to subpoena the database information in relation to a civil suit?

Creating and Using a Database

After you have considered your needs, such as what reports and inquiries you will want to make, there are two steps to creating a database file: (1) designing the structure of the file and (2) entering the data into the file. Look ahead to Figure 7 if you want to see what Patricia's final database will look like.

Determining the File Structure

Patricia begins creating what will be called the TOUR database by sketching on paper the **file structure**—what kind of data she wants in each column

2000 and Beyond

BUSTING LOOSE: DATA IN THE 21ST CENTURY

Before long, it is going to seem old-fashioned to call it data. Traditional data is making room for audio, video, text, and images. The idea, in theory, is simple: Anything that can be conceived can be defined and captured. Once captured, it then can be converted to the basic 0s and 1s required for computer processing.

Working with a database will change too. The vehicle of choice will likely be an Internet site connected to a database in a way that is trans-

parent—not obvious—to the user. For example, the screen could show a shiny car, say a red Corvette. By clicking on the car, a General Motors marketer could bring up a profile of Corvette buyers.

Future thinkers wonder if the name *database* is too mundane to convey the source of all this information. Perhaps. But the concepts of data storage and retrieval are still the same. Only the kinds of data and the elaborate retrieval methods will change.

Learn By Doing

Try challenging students to come up with names and descriptions of fields that would be appropriate for connections between files. You can have the students indicate the name for the field, and which particular files it could link. (Possible suggestions are various personal identifiers like Social Security Number linking credit history and school transcript, or Vehicle Identification Number linking to both a car dealers sales records and a state's licensing program.)

(Figure 5). To create the file structure, she must choose meaningful fields. The fields she chooses should be based on the data she will want to retrieve from the database. Let us take a look at each type.

Field Name   Names of the types of data you want to use are called **field names.** Each field must have a unique name. Patricia plans to use these field names for her TOUR database: Tour-ID (identifying number for the tour), Description (description of the tour), Cost (cost of the tour), Hours (number of hours the tour takes), Food (yes or no on whether food is included in the tour), Walk (yes or no regarding much walking on the tour), and Stairs (yes or no on whether there are stairs on the tour).

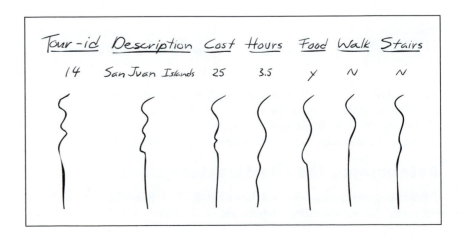

Figure 5 Sketch of the structure of the TOUR database.

Field Type   Although different software packages offer different field types, there are four commonly used types of fields: character fields, numeric fields, date fields, and logical fields. **Character fields** contain descriptive data, such as names, addresses, and telephone numbers. **Numeric fields** contain numbers used for calculations, such as rate of pay. When you enter a numeric field, you must specify the number of decimal places you wish to use. Patricia will use two decimal places for Cost and one decimal place for Hours. **Date fields** are usually limited to eight characters, including the slashes used to separate the month, day, and year. **Logical fields** are used to keep track of true/false, yes/no conditions. For example, Patricia can keep track of which tours include food by making Food a logical field; when entering data for that field, she indicates Yes or No. Note that in Microsoft Access 2000, the software used here, this is indicated by checking (Yes) or not checking (No) a box.

Field Widths   The **field width** determines the maximum number of characters or digits to be contained in the field, including decimal points.

Key Fields   One or more **key fields** can be designated as a field on which an inquiry to the database can be based. A key field is sometimes called an *index field.* For example, if Patricia will want to ask the database to list all tours that take less than two hours, she will declare the Hours field to be a key field.

Setting Up the File Structure

We have used Microsoft Access to demonstrate how database software can accept a database file structure (Figure 6). Access presents the *design view* to accept the file structure. Patricia will type one line for each field in her database. At a glance, the line consists of the field name (Tour-ID for the first field), Data Type (Text), and an optional Description.

Furthermore, when typing in the Date field, Patricia can click an arrow in the right of the field to provide many choices for the Date field. In the example shown in Figure 6, working on the line for the field Food (as indicated by the arrow on the left), she has selected the Yes/No choice for the Data Type, indicating that Food is a logical field requiring Yes/No data. Patricia proceeds to enter one line for each field in her database on the design view screen.

Entering the Data

When it is time to key in the records in the file, Access presents a table called *datasheet view.* The fields that Patricia defined in the file structure—the design view—are presented as headings across the datasheet (Figure 7). Patricia keys the appropriate data under each name—14 for Tour-ID, San Juan Islands for Description, and so on. The ID heading to the far left is generated automatically by Access.

After Patricia has filled in all the data for the first record, the database program automatically displays another blank input line so that she can enter the data items for the fields in the second record. She will continue this

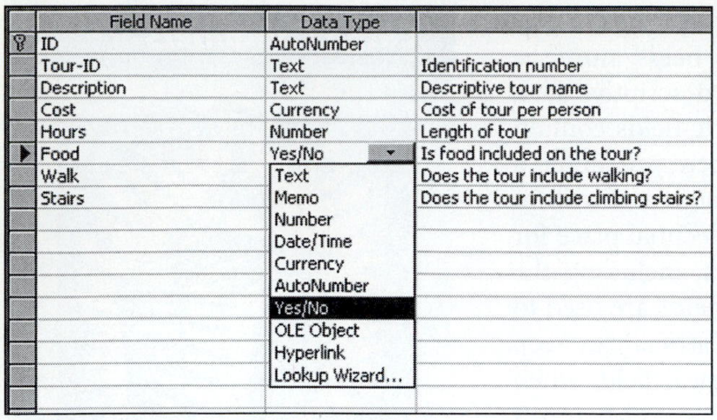

Figure 6 **File structure.** On the Microsoft Access design view, one line is entered for each field. These field entries establish the structure of the TOUR database. We have zoomed in on the main part of the screen, for readability. A submenu is shown for the Data Type for the Food entry. Keep in mind that the structure only describes what kind of data will be entered into the database; no actual data has been entered yet.

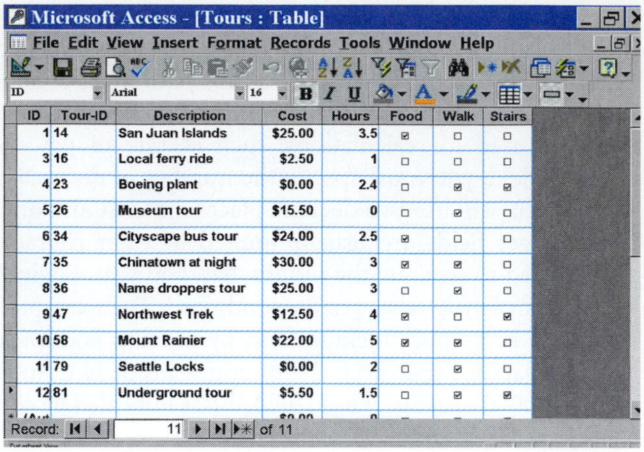

Figure 7 **The complete set of records for the TOUR database.** The field names are across the top of the datasheet. The data items are keyed in under the appropriate field name.

pattern for each record. Eventually, she will signal the database software that she has entered all the records.

Other Options

Since this chapter is not describing a specific software package, it is not practical to demonstrate options that are available to modify the database. The following are descriptions of operations available with any database software package.

- **List the records.** Patricia could ask for a list of all existing records, either displayed on the screen or printed out on paper. If she is displaying the records on-screen, the software displays only as many records as will fit on the screen. Scrolling up or down displays additional records. If there are a large number of fields in a record, Patricia could **pan**—scroll horizontally across the screen—to the left or right. Panning is a horizontal version of scrolling.
- **List specific fields.** In addition to printing all records, Patricia has the option of printing just certain fields of each record. Perhaps, to satisfy a customer request, she could print only the Description and Cost fields for each record. The software also offers the option of printing the fields in any order requested, not just the order in which they appear in the record. For example, Patricia could request a list of these fields in this order: Description, Tour-ID, Walk, and Hours.
- **Query.** Patricia can make a query—ask a question—about the records in the file. She will need to use a **relational operator** when entering instructions that involve making comparisons. Table 1 shows the rela-

GETTING PRACTICAL

CLEAN UP YOUR HARD DISK

Your computer constantly accumulates junk files and fragments that fill the disk and slow it down. Part of the reason is related to removing software from the hard drive, "uninstalling" it.

There are a number of reasons for uninstalling software. A user may want to uninstall software because it has lost value or because the disk is getting full. In a simpler time, a user would merely delete a

program file, and that would be the end of it.

Software installed under Microsoft Windows, how-

ever, involves the addition of several related files and changes to others. The average person does not know how to hunt them all down in order to do a complete uninstall. Thus, many useless odds and ends may be taking up space on the disk.

One solution is to use special uninstall software, such as the UnInstaller, shown here, that will take care of the task.

---

tional operators that are commonly used. These operators are particularly useful when you want to locate specific data items. Suppose, for example, that, on the basis of a client request, Patricia wants to find all the tours that cost less than $15. She could issue a query to the database software to find records that meet this requirement by using a command that includes the stipulation Cost < 15. Note that Cost is a key field. The software would respond with a list of all records that meet the requirement, in this case a local ferry ride, the Boeing plant, Northwest Trek, the Seattle Locks, and the underground tour.

■ **Add new records.** Patricia can add records for new tours at any time.

■ **Modify existing records.** Patricia may need to change an existing record. In the TOUR file, it would not be uncommon, for example, for the price of a tour to change.

■ **Delete records.** Sometimes a record must be removed, or deleted, from a database file. Perhaps a tour no longer exists or Patricia, for whatever reason, no longer wants to promote the tour; she would then want to delete that tour from the TOUR file. Database software provides this option.

There are many database options beyond the basic features this chapter has discussed. Those options are beyond the scope of this book, but you may have an opportunity in the future to learn all the bells and whistles of a database management package.

Group Work

Have students find out what the registration or records database at your institution "looks like" by interviewing local Information Services representatives about the basic file structure, fields, relationships, and forms used.

Learn By Doing

You might try having students sketch out the structure of a database file to keep track of their favorite music CDs. Example fields could include "ARTIST-NAME" and "RUNNING-TIME ." There should be one record in the file for each CD in the collection. An interesting variation might be to have each student bring in the information for one CD and enter this data into the database file.

Table 1   Relational Operators

Command	Explanation
<	Less than
>	Greater than
=	Equal to
<=	Less than or equal to
>=	Greater than or equal to
<>	Not equal to

CHAPTER REVIEW

Summary and Key Terms

- A **database** is an organized collection of related data. A **database management system** (**DBMS**) is software that creates, manages, protects, and provides access to a database.

- Advantages of databases are **reduced redundancy, integrated data,** and **integrity.**

- A database can store data relationships so that files can be integrated. The way the database organizes data depends on the type, or **model,** of database. There are three main database models—hierarchical, network, and relational.

- A **relational database** organizes data in a table format consisting of related rows and columns. Each location in the table contains a single piece of data, known as a **data item.** Each column of the table represents a **field,** which consists of data items. The full set of data in any given row is called a **record.** Related records make up a **file.** In a relational database, a file is also called a **relation.**

- Computer activities are considered **transparent** if a user is unaware of them as they are taking place.

- The power of databases is in the connection: A relational system can relate data in one file to data in another file, allowing a user to tie together data from several files.

- There are two steps to creating a database file: (1) designing the file structure and (2) entering the data.

- When a **file structure** is defined, many database programs require the user to identify the field types, field names, and field widths. **Field names** are used to describe the data you want to use. There are four commonly used types of fields: **character fields, numeric fields, date fields,** and **logical fields.** The **field width** determines the maximum number of letters, digits, or symbols to be contained in the field. One or more **key fields** can be designated as a field on which a query to the database can be based.

- Once a **file structure** is defined, it is presented to the user as an input form so that data for each record may be entered.

- At times you may have to **pan**—scroll horizontally across the screen—to view all the fields in a database record.

- A **relational operator** is needed when making comparisons or when entering instructions.

Discussion Questions

1. Consider these workers as possible users of a database: a crime lab technician handling evidence, a tulip-bulb grower who produces 47 varieties for more than 200 customers, a runners club that tracks meets and member data. What data might such users want to look up? What data would they need to store? What fields might be key fields?

2. An environmental organization concerned about preserving undeveloped land keeps a database of its donors with these fields: last name, first name, street address, city, state, zip code, phone number, amount of last donation, date of last donation, amount of highest donation, date of highest donation, amount of average donation, code for special interests (M for mountains, R for rivers, and so forth). The organization regularly sends out form letters soliciting donations. The form letters are keyed to a particular donor population, for example, those who have not sent a donation in six months or those who might want to give to a special shorebirds preserve. Among the fields listed, which might be key fields?

3. For the data mentioned in question 2, list some relational operators and appropriate fields that might be used for making a query to the database. Examples: Use the "equal to" operator to find donors in a certain zip code: ZIP = 22314; use "greater than" to find donors whose average donation is over $100: AVGDON > 100.

Student Study Guide

True/False

T   F   1. A logical operator, such as =, <, or >, is needed when making database comparisons.

T   F   2. There are two commonly used types of fields: character and index.

T   F   3. In a database, only one field can be designated as the key field.

T   F   4. A database is a collection of data prepared for a particular user in separate files.

T   F   5. Panning means to move across the screen to view all fields in a database.

T   F   6. Two key benefits of database processing are shared data and segregated files.

T   F   7. One disadvantage of databases is that they can be used by only a single user.

T   F   8. The two steps to creating a file are designing its structure and entering the data.

T   F   9. The power of a relational database is related to connections among files.

T   F   10. Database records may be entered and modified but not deleted.

T   F   11. The database model most commonly used on personal computers is the hierarchical model.

T   F   12. A record is made up of fields.

T   F   13. An advantage of databases is that redundancy is reduced.

T   F   14. A database is an organized collection of related data.

T   F   15. Computer activities are considered transparent if a user is unaware of them when they are taking place.

T   F   16. A user may request to print only certain fields of a database.

T   F   17. A DBMS is software.

T   F   18. Field widths may vary for character fields but are always the same for numeric fields.

T   F   19. Users can use a database successfully only if they understand the underlying technology.

T   F   20. A database is an unorganized collection of related data.

Fill-In

1. The abbreviation for a database management system is _____.

2. Advantages of databases include

_____.

3. A designated field on which a query to a database can be based is called the _____.

4. Symbols such as = , >, and < are called

_____.

5. As related to databases, network, hierarchical, and relational are each a type of _____.

6. In a relational database another name for a file is a(n) _____.

7. To move sideways across the screen is to

_____.

8. The kind of field that would hold only Yes or No is called a(n) _____ field.

9. When planning a database, the first step is to determine the rows and columns that together form the _____.

10. The database model usually used on personal computers is the _____ model.

Answers

True/False

1. F	6. F	11. F	16. T
2. F	7. F	12. T	17. T
3. F	8. T	13. T	18. F
4. F	9. T	14. T	19. F
5. T	10. F	15. T	20. F

Fill-In

1. DBMS
2. reduced redundancy, integrated data, integrity
3. key field
4. relational operators
5. model
6. relation
7. pan
8. logical
9. file structure
10. relational

ENTERTAINMENT

Entertainment on the Internet falls into two categories. The first and largest category comprises sites *about* entertainment—sports, music, television, movies, and more. The second category includes the sites that actually *provide* online entertainment, notably games, children's sites, and humor.

Sports and more sports. You can follow any sport that captures your interest. The sites for the most popular sports—basketball, football, and baseball—compete with one another to offer the most complete account of scores, player statistics, schedules, standings, and even player injuries. ESPNet

There are also many sports sites for fans of particular athletes, such as the Tim Duncan site shown here.

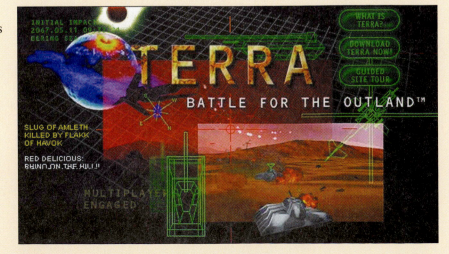

Music, music, music. Everything you could possibly want to know about music is on the Internet. Keep in mind that the multimedia capability of the Web means the potential for hearing as well as seeing the subject matter. The Rock and Roll Hall of Fame site has tourable exhibits and, among other things, a list of "500 songs that define rock and roll." Regardless of your taste—rock, classical, jazz, country, whatever—it's all on the Internet. Mary Chapin Carpenter is just one of several country stars featured on the Austin Cyber Limits site.

Online humor. The Internet has been a veritable hotbed of humor from the beginning. For a classic humor piece, see the purported news story about Microsoft acquiring the Vatican in

SportsZone is an example of a major sports presence on the Web; in fact, it is a good example of a site that offers free access to much of its content but that charges a fee to access some of its more popular services. Every manner of sport can be found on the Internet, from the Iditarod dog race in Alaska to the Tour de France cycling race in France.

exchange for stock. Other interesting humor sites are Chickenhead, The Onion, and Manic Media, whose trademark blender is shown here. The Humor Search site is a good place to start for everything else.

Armchair entertainment. Ever wondered whether your phone number spells something interesting? For example, 929-2665 spells WAY-COOL. Stop by the Phonetic site to check out your phone number. If you like kitchen table games, the Games Domain site has every kind of game—board, card, and (of course) computer games.

Kids and games. There are many, many sites geared to entertaining children online. A popular site, as shown here, is Yeeeoww. Games cross over to adults, as shown by Terra, a sophisticated action game. But the most charming and disconcerting game may be the Shockwaved Bali Highway, sponsored by the very unstuffy Boston Museum.

Go look. We have assembled a long list of entertainment links on our site. Click and enjoy.

Internet Exercises

1. **Structured exercise.** Beginning with the URL http://www.prenhall.com/capron go

to the Phonetic site and get a new name for your telephone number. *Hint:* Give the two parts of your phone number separately; for 634-8366, for example, submit first 634 and then 8366.

2. **Freeform exercise.** Pick an interest, say, music or sports, and compare offerings from the competing web sites.

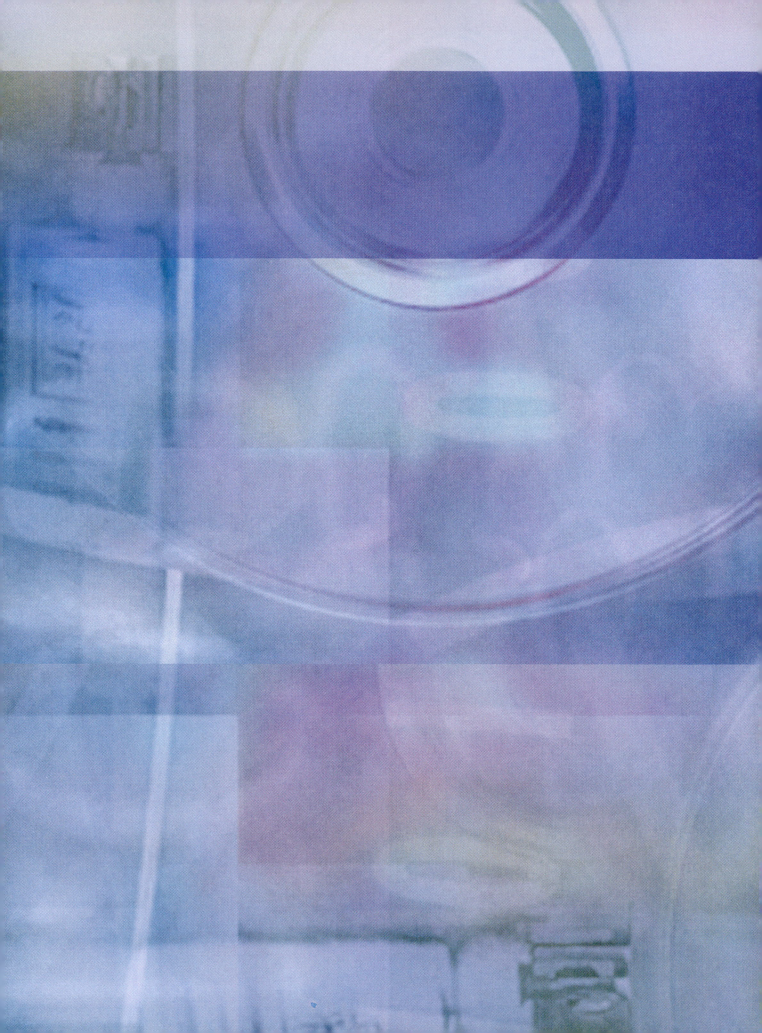

CHAPTER FOURTEEN

PROGRAMMING AND LANGUAGES

Telling the Computer What to Do

LEARNING OBJECTIVES

- Understand what programmers do and do not do
- Learn how programmers define a problem, plan the solution, and then code, test, and document the program
- Be able to list the levels of programming languages—machine, assembly, high level, very high level, and natural
- Become acquainted with some major programming languages
- Understand the concepts of object-oriented programming

oberta Matnick and Sean O'Connor met as freshmen at Oregon State University in an introductory business class. They became fast friends when they discovered that they were both majoring in accounting. The next semester they signed up for an introductory computer course to get a good foundation in computer technology and, in particular, to become proficient in the use of spreadsheets.

After studying what programmers do, however, Roberta recalled her rusty BASIC programming from high school and decided to take a closer look. She signed up for a learn-at-your-own-pace lab course in BASIC programming. From there she gravitated to the computer science department, where she studied more languages and took a variety of theoretical courses. Roberta eventually decided on a computer science major but minored in accounting. Sean was not as taken with computers, particularly with the details of programming, and he remained an accounting major.

After graduation, they found jobs in their respective fields. Their paths crossed again by chance seven years later when they began attending an evening M.B.A. program at a private university. Both accounting skills and computer skills were needed for various projects in the program. Roberta and Sean were able to help each other out, each contributing specific expertise. In particular, Sean came to appreciate the care and precision needed to write a computer program.

Why Programming?

InfoBit

Large companies may supply specialized personnel such as systems analysts to assist in gathering and documenting user requirements. In smaller companies, however, these problem-definition tasks often fall to the programmers themselves.

You may already have used software, perhaps for word processing or spreadsheets, to solve problems. Perhaps now you are curious to learn how programmers develop software. As noted earlier, a **program** is a set of step-by-step instructions that directs the computer to do the tasks you want it to do and produce the results you want. A set of rules that provides a way of telling a computer what operations to perform is called a **programming language.** There is not, however, just one programming language; there are many.

In this chapter you will learn about controlling a computer through the process of programming. An important point before proceeding: You will not be a programmer when you finish reading this chapter or even when you finish reading the final chapter. Programming proficiency takes practice and training beyond the scope of this book. However, you will become acquainted with how programmers develop solutions to a variety of problems.

What Programmers Do

In general, the programmer's job is to convert problem solutions into instructions for the computer. That is, the programmer prepares the instructions of a computer program and runs those instructions on the computer, tests the program to see if it is working properly, and makes corrections to the program. The programmer also writes a report on the program. These activities are all done for the purpose of helping a user fill a need, such as paying employees, billing customers, or admitting students to college.

The programming activities just described could be done, perhaps, as solo activities, but a programmer typically interacts with a variety of people. For example, if a program is part of a system of several programs, the programmer coordinates with other programmers to make sure that the programs fit together well. If you were a programmer, you might also have coordination meetings with users, managers, and systems analysts, as well as with peers who evaluate your work—just as you evaluate theirs.

The Programming Process

Developing a program involves steps similar to any problem-solving task. There are five main ingredients in the programming process: (1) defining the problem, (2) planning the solution, (3) coding the program, (4) testing the program, and (5) documenting the program.
Let us discuss each of these in turn.

1. Defining the Problem

Suppose that, as a programmer, you are contacted because your services are needed. You meet with users from the client organization to analyze the problem, or you meet with a systems analyst who outlines the project. Specifically, the task of defining the problem consists of identifying what it is you know (input—the data given) and what it is you want to obtain (output—the result). Eventually, you produce a written agreement that, among other things, specifies the kind of input, processing, and output required. This is not a simple process.

2. Planning the Solution

Two common ways of planning the solution to a problem are to draw a flowchart and to write pseudocode, or possibly both. Essentially, a **flowchart** is a pictorial representation of a step-by-step solution to a problem. It consists of arrows representing the direction the program takes and boxes and other symbols representing actions. It is a map of what your program is going to do and how it is going to do it. The American National Standards Institute (ANSI) has developed a standard set of flowchart symbols. Figure 1 shows the symbols and how they might be used in a simple flowchart of a common everyday act—like preparing a letter for mailing. As a practical matter, few programmers use flowcharting in their work, but flowcharting retains its value as a visual representation of the problem-solving process.

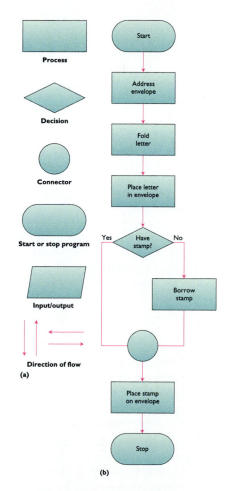

Figure 1 Flowchart symbols and a simple flowchart. (a) The ANSI standard flowchart symbols. (b) A flowchart shows how the standard symbols might be used to prepare a letter for mailing. There can be as many flowcharts to represent the task as there are ways of mailing a letter.

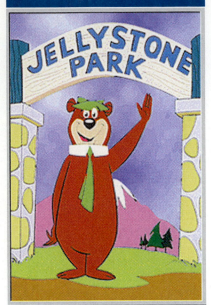
Pseudocode is an English-like nonstandard language that lets you state your solution with more precision than you can in plain English but with less precision than is required when using a formal programming language. Pseudocode permits you to focus on the program logic without having to be concerned just yet about the precise rules of a particular programming language. However, pseudocode is not executable on the computer.

These two approaches, flowcharting and pseudocode, will be illustrated later in this chapter, when focusing on language examples.

3. Coding the Program

As the programmer, your next step is to code the program—that is, to express your solution in a programming language. You will translate the logic from the flowchart or pseudocode or some other tool to a programming language. There are many programming languages: BASIC, COBOL, Pascal, FORTRAN, and C are some examples. The different types of languages will be discussed in detail later in this chapter.

Although programming languages operate grammatically, somewhat like the English language, they are much more precise. To get your program to work, you have to follow exactly the rules—the **syntax**—of the language you are using. Of course, using the language correctly is no guarantee that your program will work, any more than speaking grammatically correct English means you know what you are talking about. The point is that correct use of the language is the required first step. You will key your program as you compose it, using a terminal or personal computer.

One more note here: Programmers usually use a **text editor,** which is somewhat like a word processing program, to create a file that contains the program. However, as a beginner, you will probably want to write your program code on paper first.

4. Testing the Program

In theory, a well-designed program can be written correctly the first time. However, the imperfections of the world are still with us, so most programmers get used to the idea that their newly written programs will probably have a few errors. Therefore, after coding the program, you must prepare to test it on the computer. This step involves these phases:

■ **Desk-checking.** In **desk-checking** you simply sit down and mentally trace, or check, the logic of the program to attempt to ensure that it is error-free and workable. Many organizations take this phase a step further with a **walkthrough,** a process in which a group of programmers—your peers—review your program and offer suggestions in a collegial way.

■ **Translating.** A **translator** is a program that (1) checks the syntax of your program to make sure the programming language was used correctly, gives you syntax-error messages, called **diagnostics,** and then (2) translates your program into a form the computer can understand. The mistakes are called **syntax errors.** The translator produces descriptive error messages. For instance, if in FORTRAN you mistakenly write N = 2*(I + J))—with two closing parentheses instead of one—you will get an error message that might say, "UNMATCHED PARENTHESES." Programs are most commonly translated by a **compiler,** which translates your entire program at one time. As shown in Figure 2, the trans-

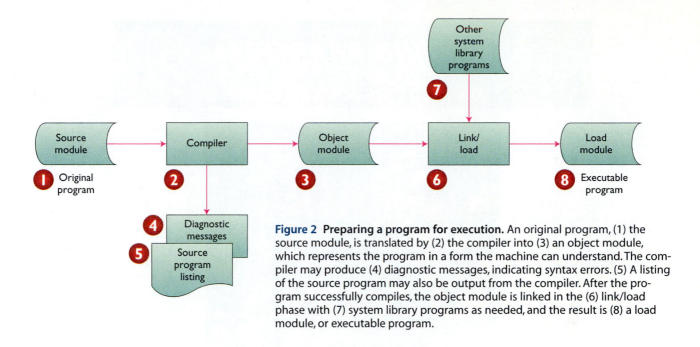

Figure 2 Preparing a program for execution. An original program, (1) the source module, is translated by (2) the compiler into (3) an object module, which represents the program in a form the machine can understand. The compiler may produce (4) diagnostic messages, indicating syntax errors. (5) A listing of the source program may also be output from the compiler. After the program successfully compiles, the object module is linked in the (6) link/load phase with (7) system library programs as needed, and the result is (8) a load module, or executable program.

lation involves your original program, called a **source module,** which is transformed by a compiler into an **object module.** Prewritten programs from a system library may be added during the **link/load** phase, resulting in a **load module,** which can be executed by the computer.

- **Debugging.** A term used extensively in programming, **debugging** means detecting, locating, and correcting bugs (mistakes), usually by running the program. These bugs are **logic errors,** such as telling a computer to repeat an operation but not telling it how to stop repeating. In the debugging phase you run the program using test data that you devise. You must plan the test data carefully to make sure you test every part of the program.

5. Documenting the Program

An ongoing process, **documentation** is a detailed written description of the programming cycle and specific facts about the program. Typical program documentation materials include the origin and nature of the problem, a brief narrative description of the program, logic tools such as flowcharts and pseudocode, data-record descriptions, program listings, and testing results. Comments in the program itself are also considered an essential part of documentation. Many programmers document as they code. In a broader sense, program documentation can be part of the documentation for an entire system.

Levels of Language

There are several programming languages in common use today. Before turning to specific languages, however, we need to discuss levels of language. Programming languages are said to be "lower" or "higher," depending on how close they are to the language the computer itself uses (0s and 1s—low)

InfoBit

Assembly language is sufficiently complex and tedious that, during the time when it was the primary way of writing software, average programmer productivity was estimated at a mere ten lines of tested, debugged code per day.

Critical Thinking

One important difference between programming languages and human languages is that in programming languages, the meaning of each word must be absolutely unambiguous. What examples can you think of in English where a word has more than one meaning or can be used as more than one part of speech? (Examples abound; one is green—a color, a part of a golf course, and an adjective meaning "new." Another is duck—a noun meaning a type of fowl, or a verb meaning "to stoop.")

GETTING PRACTICAL

ON BECOMING A PROGRAMMER

There is a shortage of qualified personnel in the computer field, but, paradoxically, there are many people at the front end trying to get entry-level programming jobs. Before you join their ranks, consider the advantages of the computer field and what it takes to succeed in it.

■ **The joys of the field.** Although many people make career changes that take them into the computer field, few choose to leave it. In fact, surveys of computer professionals, especially programmers, consistently report a high level of job satisfaction. There are several reasons for this contentment. One is the challenge; most jobs in the computer industry are not routine. Another is security: Established computer professionals can usually find work. And that work pays well—you should certainly be comfortable and, if you should happen to be part of an organization that offers stock options to all employees, possibly very comfortable. The computer industry has historically been a rewarding place for women and minorities. And finally, the industry holds endless fascination, since it is always changing.

■ **What it takes.** Although some people buy a book

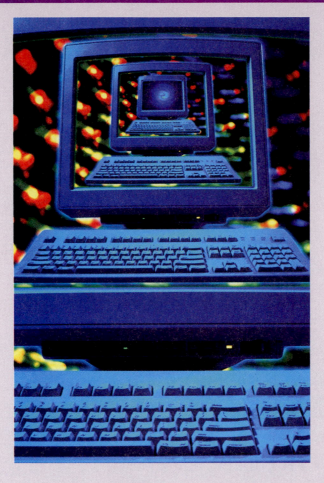

and teach themselves a programming language, this is unlikely to lead to a job. You need some credentials, most often a two- or four-year degree in computer information systems or computer science. (Note that this degree will require math and science courses.) The requirements and salaries vary by the organization and the region, so we will not dwell on these here. Beyond that, the person most likely to land a job

and move up the career ladder is one with excellent communication skills, both oral and written. These are also the qualities that can be observed by potential employers in an interview. Promotions are sometimes tied to advanced degrees (for example, an M.B.A. or an M.S. in computer science).

■ **Open doors.** The overall outlook for the computer field is promising. The Bureau of Labor Statistics projects,

through the 1990s, a 72 percent increase in the number of programmers and a 69 percent increase in the number of systems analysts. Further, these two professions are predicted to be the number two and number three high-growth jobs into the next century. (In case you are curious, the number one high-growth job area is predicted to be the paralegal profession.) The reasons for the continued job increase in the computer field are more computers, more applications of computers, and more computer users.

Traditionally, career progression in the computer field was a path from programmer to systems analyst to project manager. This is still a typical direction, but it is complicated by the large number of options open to computer professionals. Computer professionals sometimes specialize in some aspect of the industry, such as communications, database management, personal computers, graphics, or, most especially, the Internet. Others may specialize in the computer-related aspects of a particular industry, such as banking or insurance. Still others strike out on their own, becoming consultants or entrepreneurs.

or to the language people use (more English-like—high). There are five levels of language, numbered 1 through 5 to correspond to levels, or generations. In terms of ease of use and capabilities, each generation is an improvement over its predecessors. The five generations of languages are (1) machine language, (2) assembly languages, (3) high-level languages, (4) very high level languages, and (5) natural languages.

Machine Language

Humans do not like to deal in numbers alone; they prefer letters and words. But, strictly speaking, numbers are what machine language is. This lowest level of programming language, **machine language,** represents data and program instructions as 0s and 1s, binary digits corresponding to the on and off electrical states in the computer. This is really the only language the computer truly understands; all other languages must be translated to the machine language before execution (Figure 3). Each type of computer has its own machine language. Primitive by today's standards, machine language programs are not convenient for people to read and use. The computer industry quickly moved to develop assembly languages.

Assembly Languages

Today, **assembly languages** are considered very low level—that is, they are not as convenient for people to use as more recent languages. At the time they were developed, however, they were considered a great leap forward. To replace the 0s and 1s used in machine language, assembly languages use mnemonic codes, abbreviations that are easy to remember: A for add, C for compare, MP for multiply, STO for storing information in memory, and so on. Furthermore, assembly languages permit the use of names—perhaps RATE or TOTAL—for memory locations instead of actual address numbers. As with machine language, each type of computer has its own assembly language.

Since machine language is the only language the computer can actually execute, a translator, called an **assembly program,** is required to convert the assembly language program into machine language. Assembly language may be easier to read than machine language, but it is still tedious (Figure 4).

High-Level Languages

The first widespread use of **high-level languages** in the early 1960s transformed programming into something quite different from what it had been. Programs were written in an English-like manner, thus making them more convenient to use. As a result, a programmer could accomplish more with less effort, and programs could now direct much more complex tasks.

Of course, a translator is needed to translate the symbolic statements of a high-level language into computer-executable machine language; this translator is usually a compiler. There are many compilers for each language and at least one for each type of computer.

Very High-Level Languages

Languages called **very high-level languages** are often known by their generation number; that is, they are called **fourth-generation languages** or, more simply, **4GLs.** The 4GLs are essentially shorthand programming languages. An operation that requires hundreds of lines in a third-generation language

```
FD   71   431F   4153
F3   63   4267   4321
96   F0   426D
F9   10   41F3   438A
47   40   40DA
47   F0   4050
```

Figure 3 Machine language. True machine language is all binary—only 0s and 1s—but since an example would take too much space here, we are showing an example of machine language in the hexadecimal (base 16) numbering system. (The letters A through F in hexadecimal represent the numbers 10 through 15 in the decimal system.) The computer commands shown, taken from machine language for an IBM mainframe computer, are operation codes instructing the computer to divide two numbers, compare the quotient, move the result into the output area of the system, and set up the result so it can be printed.

InfoBit

The grammar of programming languages, while annoyingly exact and notoriously unforgiving, is actually vastly simpler than that of English or most other human languages. For instance, the "vocabulary" of most programming languages—called "reserved words"—rarely exceeds 50 words. Compare this to the size of a dictionary.

Critical Thinking

Since computers understand only a very low-level language—1s and 0s—how was it possible to write the language translator programs, the compilers and assemblers themselves? (Each generation was initially built from the preceding one. The first assemblers were written in machine language. The first high-level-language compilers were written in assembly language, and so forth.)

InfoBit

One reason that 4GLs are not as popular as third-generation languages for commercial applications is that 4GLs tend to generate programs that are bulky and slow to perform. Although third-generation languages are more difficult for the programmer, the result is a better-performing program for the consumer.

InfoBit

Although beginning programmers often find the many syntax errors disheartening, experienced programmers dread logic errors the most, because they are much more difficult to find and fix.

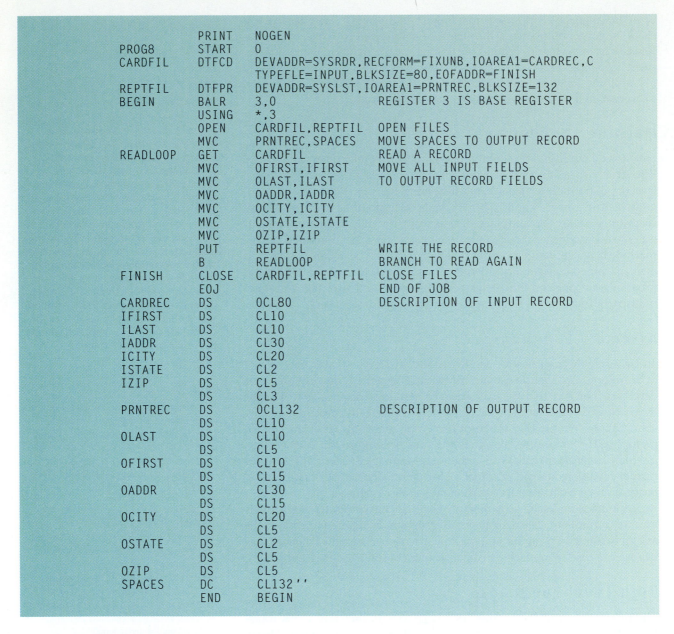

```
                   PRINT    NOGEN
PROG8              START    0
CARDFIL            DTFCD    DEVADDR=SYSRDR,RECFORM=FIXUNB,IOAREA1=CARDREC,C
                            TYPEFLE=INPUT,BLKSIZE=80,EOFADDR=FINISH
REPTFIL            DTFPR    DEVADDR=SYSLST,IOAREA1=PRNTREC,BLKSIZE=132
BEGIN              BALR     3,0                    REGISTER 3 IS BASE REGISTER
                   USING    *,3
                   OPEN     CARDFIL,REPTFIL        OPEN FILES
                   MVC      PRNTREC,SPACES         MOVE SPACES TO OUTPUT RECORD
READLOOP           GET      CARDFIL                READ A RECORD
                   MVC      OFIRST,IFIRST          MOVE ALL INPUT FIELDS
                   MVC      OLAST,ILAST            TO OUTPUT RECORD FIELDS
                   MVC      OADDR,IADDR
                   MVC      OCITY,ICITY
                   MVC      OSTATE,ISTATE
                   MVC      OZIP,IZIP
                   PUT      REPTFIL                WRITE THE RECORD
                   B        READLOOP               BRANCH TO READ AGAIN
FINISH             CLOSE    CARDFIL,REPTFIL        CLOSE FILES
                   EOJ                             END OF JOB
CARDREC            DS       0CL80                  DESCRIPTION OF INPUT RECORD
IFIRST             DS       CL10
ILAST              DS       CL10
IADDR              DS       CL30
ICITY              DS       CL20
ISTATE             DS       CL2
IZIP               DS       CL5
                   DS       CL3
PRNTREC            DS       0CL132                 DESCRIPTION OF OUTPUT RECORD
                   DS       CL10
OLAST              DS       CL10
                   DS       CL5
OFIRST             DS       CL10
                   DS       CL15
OADDR              DS       CL30
                   DS       CL15
OCITY              DS       CL20
                   DS       CL5
OSTATE             DS       CL2
                   DS       CL5
OZIP               DS       CL5
SPACES             DC       CL132' '
                   END      BEGIN
```

Figure 4 Assembly language. This example shows the IBM assembly language BAL used in a program for reading a record and writing it out again. The left column contains symbolic addresses of various instructions or data. The second column contains the actual operation codes to describe the kind of activity needed; for instance, MVC stands for "move characters." The third column describes the data on which the instructions are to act. The far-right column contains English-like comments related to the line or lines opposite. This entire page of instructions could be compressed to a few lines in a high-level language.

typically requires only 5 to 10 lines in a 4GL. However, beyond the basic criterion of conciseness, 4GLs are difficult to describe because there are so many different types.

Most experts say the average productivity improvement factor is about 10; that is, you can be 10 times more productive in a fourth-generation language than in a third-generation language. Consider this request: Produce a report showing the total units sold for each product, by customer, in each month and year, and with a subtotal for each customer. In addition, each new customer must start on a new page. A 4GL request looks something like this:

```
TABLE FILE SALES
SUM UNITS BY MONTH BY CUSTOMER BY PRODUCT
ON CUSTOMER SUBTOTAL PAGE BREAK
END
```

Even though some training is required to do even this much, you can see that it is pretty simple. The third-generation language COBOL, however, typically requires more than 500 statements to fulfill the same request. It would be naive, however, to assume that all programs should be written using 4GLs; a third-generation language makes more sense for commercial applications that require a high degree of precision.

A variation on fourth-generation languages is **query languages,** which can be used to retrieve information from databases. Data is usually added to databases according to a plan, and planned reports may also be produced. But what about a user who needs an unscheduled report or a report that differs somehow from the standard reports? A user can learn a query language fairly easily and then request and receive the resulting report on his or her own terminal or personal computer.

Natural Languages

The word *natural* has become almost as popular in computing circles as it has in the supermarket. The newest level of languages, called fifth-generation languages, is even more ill-defined than fourth-generation languages. They are most often called **natural languages** because of their resemblance to the "natural" spoken English language; that is, they resemble the way that you speak. A user of one of these languages can say the same thing in any number of ways. For example, "Get me tennis racket sales for January" works just as well as "I want January tennis racket revenues." The natural language translates human instructions—bad grammar, slang, and all—into code the computer understands. If it is not sure what the user has in mind, it politely asks for further explanation. An example of a natural language is shown in Figure 5.

Figure 5 A natural language. This package, called Cash Management System, uses a language that is so "natural" that some might think it a little too cute, as in "Just a sec." You can follow the dialogue more easily by noting that, in this demonstration, the command from the user is in reverse video and the response from the computer is not.

```
Hello
How may I help you?
Who are my customers in Chicago?
Just a sec.  I'll see.
The customers in that city are:
I.D.                 Name

Ballard          Ballard and Sons, Inc.
Fremont          Henry Fremont Associates
Greenlake        Greenlake Consortium
Wallingford      Wallingford, Inc.
What can I do for you now?
What is Fremont's balance?
Hang on.  I'll see.
Accounts Receivable    563.47
Unapplied Credit        79.16
          Balance      484.31
What else can I do for you?
Give me Fremont's phone number!
Please wait while I check the files.
   (312) 789-5562
What can I do for you now?
```

The First Bug Was Real

Computer literacy books are bursting with bits and bytes and disks and chips and lessons on writing memos using word processing. All this is to provide quick enlightenment for the computer illiterate. But the average newly computer-literate person has not been told about bugs.

It is a bit of a surprise, then, to find that the software you are using does not always work quite right. Or perhaps the programmer who is doing some work for you cannot seem to get the program to work correctly. Both problems are "bugs," errors that were introduced unintentionally into a program when it was written.

The term *bug* comes from an experience in the early days of computing. One summer day in 1945, according to computer pioneer Grace M. Hopper, the Mark I computer came to a halt. Working to find the problem, computer personnel actually found a moth inside the machine (see photo). They removed the offending bug, and the computer was fine. From that day forward, any mysterious problem or glitch was said to be a bug.

Learn by Doing
Try having students scan the pages of a software catalog or magazine advertisements in programming-related magazines, counting the number of different brands of compilers available for the following languages: C/C++, BASIC, COBOL, and "other."

Group Work
Consider having students work in teams to survey the shelves of local software retailers and bookstores to determine which high-level languages get the most interest in your area. Have them survey the number of feet of shelf space or count the number of books devoted to each of the following languages: C/C++, BASIC, COBOL, Java, and "other."

Choosing a Language

How do you choose the language with which to write your program? There are several possibilities. In a work environment, your company may decree that everyone on your project will use a certain language, possibly because there is a need to interface with other programs written in that language. If a program is to be run on different computers, it must be written in a language that is portable—suitable on each type of computer—so that the program need be written only once but will run on all of the various computers.

Perhaps the simplest reason for choosing a language, one that applies to many amateur programmers, is that they know the language called BASIC because it came with, or was inexpensively purchased with, their personal computers.

Major Programming Languages

The following sections on individual languages will give you an overview of some third-generation languages in use today: FORTRAN, COBOL, BASIC, Pascal, and C. You will see a program written in each of these languages, as well as the output produced by each program. Each program is designed to find the average of three numbers; the resulting average is shown in the sample output matching each program. Since all of the programs perform the same task, you will see some of the differences and similarities among the languages. You are not expected to understand these programs; they are here merely to let you glimpse each language. Figure 6 presents the flowchart and pseudocode for the task of averaging numbers. This logic will be used for each of the programs.

FORTRAN: The First High-Level Language

Developed by IBM and introduced in 1954, **FORTRAN**—for FORmula TRANslator—was the first high-level language. FORTRAN is a scientifically oriented language; in the early days, use of the computer was primarily associated with engineering, mathematical, and scientific research tasks.

FORTRAN is noted for its brevity, and this characteristic is part of the reason it remains popular. This language is very good at serving its primary purpose, which is the execution of complex formulas such as those used in economic analysis and engineering. Figure 7 shows a FORTRAN program and sample output from the program.

COBOL: The Language of Business

By the mid-1950s FORTRAN had been developed, but there was still no accepted high-level programming language appropriate for business. The U.S. Department of Defense in particular was interested in creating such a standardized language and called together a committee that, in 1959, introduced **COBOL**, for COmmon Business-Oriented Language.

COBOL is very good for processing large files and performing relatively simple business calculations, such as payroll or interest. COBOL is English-

(a)   Flowchart

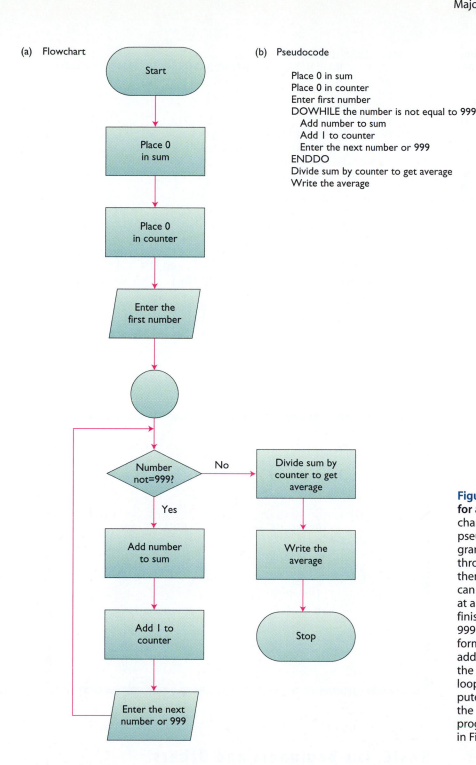

(b)   Pseudocode

Place 0 in sum
Place 0 in counter
Enter first number
DOWHILE the number is not equal to 999
  Add number to sum
  Add 1 to counter
  Enter the next number or 999
ENDDO
Divide sum by counter to get average
Write the average

Figure 6 Flowchart and pseudocode for averaging numbers. (a) This flowchart, along with (b) matching pseudocode, shows the logic for a program to let a user enter numbers through the keyboard; the program then averages the numbers. The user can make any number of entries, one at a time. To show when he or she is finished making entries, the user enters 999. The logic to enter the numbers forms a loop: entering the number, adding it to the sum, and adding 1 to the counter. When 999 is keyed, the loop is exited. Then the machine computes the average and displays it on the screen. This logic is used for the programs, in various languages, shown in Figures 7 through 11.

like; even if you know nothing about programming, you may still understand what the program does. However, the feature that makes COBOL so useful—its English-like appearance and easy readability—is also a weakness, because a COBOL program can be incredibly verbose (Figure 8).

Today, many consider COBOL old-fashioned and inelegant. In fact, many companies devoted to fast, nimble program development have converted to the language called C.

Figure 7 FORTRAN program and sample output. This program is interactive, prompting the user to supply data. (a) The first two lines are comments, as they are in the rest of the programs in this chapter. The WRITE statements send output to the screen in the format called for by the second numeral in the parentheses, which represents the line number containing the format. The READ statements accept data from the user and place it in location NUMBER, where it can be added to the accumulated total, SUM. The IF statement checks for 999 and, when 999 is received, diverts the program logic to statement 2, where the average is computed. The average is then displayed. (b) This screen display shows the interaction between program and user.

```
C       FORTRAN PROGRAM
C       AVERAGING INTEGERS ENTERED THROUGH THE KEYBOARD
        WRITE (6,10)
        SUM = 0
        COUNTER = 0
        WRITE (6,60)
        READ (5,40) NUMBER
   1    IF (NUMBER .EQ. 999) GOTO 2
        SUM = SUM + NUMBER
        COUNTER = COUNTER + 1
        WRITE (6,70)
        READ (5,40) NUMBER
        GO TO 1
   2    AVERAGE = SUM / COUNTER
        WRITE (6,80) AVERAGE
  10    FORMAT (1X, 'THIS PROGRAM WILL FIND THE AVERAGE OF',
      * 'INTEGERS YOU ENTER ',/1X, 'THROUGH THE ',
      * 'KEYBOARD. TYPE 999 TO INDICATE END OF DATA.',/)
  40    FORMAT (13)
  60    FORMAT (1X, 'PLEASE ENTER A NUMBER ')
  70    FORMAT (1X, 'PLEASE ENTER THE NEXT NUMBER ')
  80    FORMAT (1X, 'THE AVERAGE OF THE NUMBERS IS ',F6.2)
        STOP
        END
```

(a)

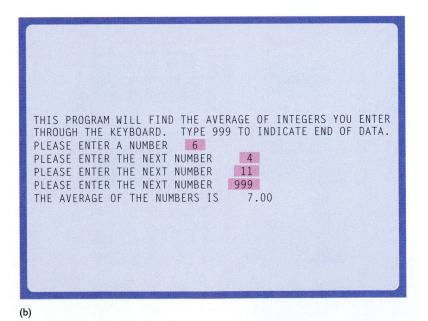

(b)

BASIC: For Beginners and Others

BASIC—Beginners' All-purpose Symbolic Instruction Code—is a common language that is easy to learn. Developed at Dartmouth College, BASIC was introduced by John Kemeny and Thomas Kurtz in 1965 and was originally intended for use by students in an academic environment. The use of BASIC has extended to business and personal computer systems.

The primary feature of BASIC is one that may be of interest to many readers of this book: BASIC is easy to learn, even for a person who has never programmed before. Thus the language is often used to train students in the

Learn by Doing

Demonstrate, or have students type in and run, the sample BASIC program given in this book.

```
****************************************************************
IDENTIFICATION DIVISION.
****************************************************************
PROGRAM-ID.  AVERAGE.
* COBOL PROGRAM
* AVERAGING INTEGERS ENTERED THROUGH THE KEYBOARD.
****************************************************************
ENVIRONMENT DIVISION.
****************************************************************
CONFIGURATION SECTION.
SOURCE-COMPUTER.              H-P 9000.
OBJECT-COMPUTER.              H-P 9000.
****************************************************************
DATA DIVISION.
****************************************************************
FILE SECTION.
WORKING-STORAGE SECTION.
01 AVERAGE        PIC ---9.99.
01 COUNTER        PIC 9(02)      VALUE ZERO.
01 NUMBER-ITEM    PIC S9(03).
01 SUM-ITEM       PIC S9(06)     VALUE ZERO.
01 BLANK-LINE     PIC X(80)      VALUE SPACES.
****************************************************************
PROCEDURE DIVISION.
****************************************************************
100-CONTROL-ROUTINE.
    PERFORM 200-DISPLAY-INSTRUCTIONS.
    PERFORM 300-INITIALIZATION-ROUTINE.
    PERFORM 400-ENTER-AND-ADD
            UNTIL NUMBER-ITEM = 999.
    PERFORM 500-CALCULATE-AVERAGE.
    PERFORM 600-DISPLAY-RESULTS.
    STOP RUN.
200-DISPLAY-INSTRUCTIONS.
    DISPLAY
      "THIS PROGRAM WILL FIND THE AVERAGE OF INTEGERS YOU ENTER".
    DISPLAY
      "THROUGH THE KEYBOARD. TYPE 999 TO INDICATE END OF DATA.".
    DISPLAY BLANK-LINE.
300-INITIALIZATION-ROUTINE.
    DISPLAY "PLEASE ENTER A NUMBER".
    ACCEPT NUMBER-ITEM.
400-ENTER-AND-ADD.
    ADD NUMBER-ITEM TO SUM-ITEM.
    ADD 1 TO COUNTER.
    DISPLAY "PLEASE ENTER THE NEXT NUMBER".
    ACCEPT NUMBER-ITEM.
500-CALCULATE-AVERAGE.
    DIVIDE SUM-ITEM BY COUNTER GIVING AVERAGE.
600-DISPLAY-RESULTS.
    DISPLAY "THE AVERAGE OF THE NUMBERS IS ".AVERAGE.
```
(a)

Figure 8 COBOL program and sample output. The purpose of the program and its results are the same as those of the FORTRAN program, but (a) the look of the COBOL program is very different. Note the four divisions: identification, environment, data, and procedure. In particular, note that the logic in the procedure division uses a series of PER-FORM statements, which divert action to other places in the program. After a prescribed action has been performed, the computer returns to the procedure division, to the statement after the one that was just completed. DISPLAY writes to the screen, and ACCEPT takes user input. (b) This screen display shows the interaction between program and user.

```
        THIS PROGRAM WILL FIND THE AVERAGE OF
        INTEGERS YOU ENTER THROUGH THE KEYBOARD.
        TYPE 999 TO INDICATE END OF DATA.

        PLEASE ENTER A NUMBER
        6
        PLEASE ENTER THE NEXT NUMBER
        4
        PLEASE ENTER THE NEXT NUMBER
        11
        PLEASE ENTER THE NEXT NUMBER
        999
        THE AVERAGE OF THE NUMBERS IS   7.00
```
(b)

Global Perspective

Pascal is an internationally popular programming language. Various foreign language versions have been produced, including one in French. The French version has the same syntax or grammar as the English version; however, all of the keywords—like BEGIN and END—have been translated into French. The real difficulty for programmers attempting to translate from French Pascal to English Pascal is that all of the variable names and the comments—elements vital for human understanding—also appear in French and require translation.

classroom. An example of a BASIC program and its output are shown in Figure 9.

Pascal: The Language of Simplicity

Named for Blaise Pascal, the seventeenth-century French mathematician, **Pascal** was developed as a teaching language by a Swiss computer scientist, Niklaus Wirth, and became available in 1971. Its use spread first in Europe and then in the United States, particularly in schools offering computer science programs, although its popularity is now in decline.

An attractive feature of Pascal is that it is simpler than other languages—it has fewer features and is less wordy than most. In addition to being popular in college computer science departments, the language has also made large inroads in the personal computer market as a simple yet sophisticated

```
'BASIC PROGRAM
'AVERAGING INTEGERS ENTERED THROUGH THE KEYBOARD
CLS
PRINT "THIS PROGRAM WILL FIND THE AVERAGE OF INTEGERS YOU ENTER"
PRINT "THROUGH THE KEYBOARD. TYPE 999 TO INDICATE END OF DATA."
PRINT
SUM=0
COUNTER=0
PRINT "PLEASE ENTER A NUMBER"
INPUT NUMBER
DO WHILE NUMBER <> 999
    SUM=SUM+NUMBER
    COUNTER=COUNTER+1
    PRINT "PLEASE ENTER THE NEXT NUMBER"
    INPUT NUMBER
LOOP
AVERAGE=SUM/COUNTER
PRINT "THE AVERAGE OF THE NUMBERS IS"; AVERAGE
END
```
(a)

```
THIS PROGRAM WILL FIND THE AVERAGE OF INTEGERS YOU ENTER
THROUGH THE KEYBOARD. TYPE 999 TO INDICATE END OF DATA.

PLEASE ENTER A NUMBER
?6
PLEASE ENTER THE NEXT NUMBER
?4
PLEASE ENTER THE NEXT NUMBER
?11
PLEASE ENTER THE NEXT NUMBER
?999
THE AVERAGE OF THE NUMBERS IS    7
```

Figure 9 BASIC program and sample output. (a) PRINT displays data right in the statement on the screen. INPUT accepts data from the user. (b) This screen display shows the interaction between program and user.

(b)

MAKING THE RIGHT CONNECTIONS

FOLLOW ME ANYWHERE

Yachting is not exactly a spectator sport. Even the celebrated America's Cup takes place far from shore, visible only in bits and pieces on television. How, then, could it be possible for a fan to follow day-to-day progress of a world-spanning sailing competition? The answer, of course, is computer connections. The onboard action is sent via satellite to onshore computers, which post the latest on a web site for all the world to see.

It is not an exaggeration to refer to a worldwide audience. When an Internet company called Quokka Sports decided to follow the Whitbread Round the World race, nearly a million people from 177 countries checked the site each day. The boats became an irresistible draw because the viewers were put virtually onboard, an experience so richly interactive that, as one wag put it, you could almost feel the spray on your face.

Hyperbole aside, the interaction is rather amazing. The boats become floating media labs, outfitted with powerful laptop computers, digital video cameras, microphones, and satellite telecommunications. On a regular basis,

when they are not grinding winches or changing sails, crew members send off reams of data about themselves—reports on the sea and weather conditions, their exact location on the ocean, their place in the race relative to other competitors, and video and still photos. The e-mail dispatches are especially compelling: *Weather cold and wet, wet, wet. Sleet storm yesterday and again today. Last night the bow dove into a wave, and tons of water sent me hurling back to the mast.* Other dispatches are more prosaic, telling of passing icebergs, lying becalmed, or juryrigging a damaged boom.

Quokka cut its teeth on the Whitbread race but that was just the beginning.

Their site lists a variety of events in preview, in progress, or in review. The events have one thing in common: They cannot easily be tracked by the average person.

Quokka's next Internetmonitored water event was the Around Alone: One person, on a sailboat, around the world. Alone. Held every four years, it is the longest race on earth for an individual in any sport, spanning 27,000 miles of the world's roughest and most remote oceans. It is a grueling singlehanded sailing race where competitors are both the captain and crew, and the finish line is literally a world away. The same communications paraphenalia is aboard but, the

sailor, operating the craft without assistance, does not get to it as readily.

A land-based example is the seven-day Marathon des Sables through the desert sands of Morocco, billed as the toughest foot race on earth. Another event was initiated by Quokka—a reconnaissance mission to Hidden Peak, the eleventh-highest mountain in the world. The climbers searched for a northern route up the 26,500-foot mountain, whose northeast face, the Chinese side, has never been climbed. Needless to say, Quokka makes sure that all such events have Internet-based coverage.

Pay Up or Else

What happens when a programmer writes a custom program in good faith but then is refused payment by the customer? Once the program is delivered, it may be impossible to recover it in the event of nonpayment. Some programmers protect themselves or their company by embedding self-destruct code in custom programs. If payment is not received in a timely manner and a countermanding instruction key loaded, the user suddenly finds the program inoperative. Is this a smart protective business action or an example of an unethical business practice? Does it make a difference if the customer is dissatisfied with the program, as opposed to simply a deadbeat bill payer?

Global Perspective

Java is the first major programming language to be designed from the ground up to support all human alphabets. Java uses a 16-bit representation of characters called Unicode that allows the complex characters of Japanese, Chinese, and other non-Western alphabets to be processed and printed.

---

alternative to BASIC. Today, Borland's Turbo Pascal is used by the business community and is often the choice of nonprofessional programmers who need to write their own programs. An example of a Turbo Pascal program and its output are shown in Figure 10.

C: A Portable Language

A language invented by Dennis Ritchie at Bell Labs in 1972, C produces code that approaches assembly language in efficiency while still offering the features of a high-level language. C was originally designed to write systems software but is now considered a general-purpose language. C contains some of the best features from other languages, including Pascal. C compilers are simple and compact. A key attraction is that there are C compilers available for different operating systems, a fact that contributes to the portability of C programs.

An interesting side note is that the availability of C on personal computers has greatly enhanced the value of personal computers for budding software entrepreneurs. Today C is fast being replaced by its enhanced cousin, C++, a language that will be discussed shortly. An example of a C++ program and its output are shown in Figure 11.

Java

Programming languages rarely attain media darling status. But it seems that the language called **Java**, from developers at Sun Microsystems, has had continuous hard-core coverage in the computer press. Java is a network-friendly programming language, derived from the C++ language, that permits a piece of software to run on many different platforms. A **platform** is the hardware and software combination that composes the basic functionality of a computer. For example, a popular platform today is based on some version of Microsoft's Windows operating system and Intel's processors, a combination nicknamed Wintel.

Traditionally, programmers have been limited to writing a program for a single platform. Coding has had to be redone for other platforms. But a programmer can write a program in Java, which operates across platforms, and have it run anywhere. So how does Java accomplish this cross-platform feat? Programs written in Java can be understood by a universal platform, called the Java platform, that sits atop a computer's regular platform. Essentially, then, this universal platform is an extra layer of software that has been accepted as a standard by most of the computer industry—no small feat. The Java platform translates Java instructions into instructions that the platform underneath can understand.

When you consider that Java can run across many platforms, it is easy to see why it is relevant to Internet development; in fact, Java's earliest incarnations were on web applications. Java has a good start on becoming the universal language of Internet computing.

Object-Oriented Programming

The approach called **object-oriented programming** (OOP) is relatively new and distinctly different. An important emerging trend, this development

```
PROGRAM AverageofNumbers;
(*Pascal Program
  averaging integers entered through the keyboard*)

USES
    crt;

VAR
    counter, number, sum : integer;
    average : real ;

BEGIN (*main*)
    WRITELN ('THIS PROGRAM WILL FIND THE AVERAGE OF INTEGERS YOU ENTER');
    WRITELN ('THROUGH THE KEYBOARD. TYPE 999 TO INDICATE END OF DATA.');
    WRITELN;
    sum :=0;
    counter :=0;
    WRITELN ('PLEASE ENTER A NUMBER');
    READLN (number);
    WHILE number <> 999 DO
        Begin  (*while loop*)
            sum := sum + number;
            counter := counter + 1;
            WRITELN ('PLEASE ENTER THE NEXT NUMBER');
            READ (number);
        END; (*while loop*)
    average := sum / counter;
    WRITELN ('THE AVERAGE OF THE NUMBERS IS ', average:6:2);
END.  (*main*)
```

(a)

```
THIS PROGRAM WILL FIND THE AVERAGE OF INTEGERS YOU ENTER
THROUGH THE KEYBOARD. TYPE 999 TO INDICATE END OF DATA.

PLEASE ENTER A NUMBER
6
PLEASE ENTER THE NEXT NUMBER
4
PLEASE ENTER THE NEXT NUMBER
11
PLEASE ENTER THE NEXT NUMBER
999
THE AVERAGE OF THE NUMBERS IS   7.00
```

(b)

Figure 10 Pascal program and sample output. (a) Comments are from (* to *). Each variable name must be declared. The symbol := assigns a value to the variable to its left; the symbol <> means "not equal to." WRITELN by itself puts a blank line on the screen. (b) This screen display shows the interaction between program and user. The program was written in Turbo Pascal.

```
// C++ PROGRAM
// AVERAGING INTEGERS ENTERED THROUGH THE KEYBOARD

#include <iostream.h>
main ()
{
  float average;
  int number, counter = 0; int sum = 0;
  cout << "THIS PROGRAM WILL FIND THE AVERAGE OF INTEGERS YOU ENTER \ n";
  cout << "THROUGH THE KEYBOARD.  TYPE 999 TO INDICATE END OF DATA. \ n";
  cout << "PLEASE ENTER A NUMBER";
  cin >> number;
  while (number !=999)
    {
      sum := sum + number;
      counter ++;
      cout << "\nPLEASE ENTER THE NEXT NUMBER";
      cin >> number;
    }
  average = sum / counter;
  cout << "\nTHE AVERAGE OF THE NUMBERS IS " << average
}
```
(a)

```
THIS PROGRAM WILL FIND THE AVERAGE OF INTEGERS YOU ENTER
THROUGH THE KEYBOARD.  TYPE 999 TO INDICATE END OF DATA.
PLEASE ENTER A NUMBER       6
PLEASE ENTER THE NEXT NUMBER       4
PLEASE ENTER THE NEXT NUMBER       11
PLEASE ENTER THE NEXT NUMBER       999
THE AVERAGE OF THE NUMBERS IS       7.00
```
(b)

Figure 11 C++ program and sample output. (a) The symbol // marks comment lines. All variable names, such as number, must be declared. The command cout sends output to the screen, and cin takes data from the user. (b) This screen display shows the interaction between program and user. The program was written in Turbo C++.

deserves its own section. It is possible here only to introduce the concepts and terminology of object technology. There is no expectation that you will understand exactly how object-oriented programming works; even professional programmers can take months to gain that knowledge.

What Is an Object?

Consider items that, in everyday parlance, might be called objects—for instance, a tire or a cat. Now affix known facts to those everyday objects. Without trying to be exhaustive, it can be said that a tire may be round and black and that a cat has four feet and fur. Taking this further, each object also has functions: A tire can roll or stop or go flat, and a cat can eat or purr or howl. In the world of object orientation, an object includes the item itself and also related facts and functions. More formally, in a programming environment, an **object** is a self-contained unit that contains both data and related facts and functions—the instructions to act on that data. This is in direct contrast to traditional programming, in which procedures are defined in the program separate from the data.

The word that is used to describe an object's self-containment is *encapsulation:* An object **encapsulates** both data and its related instructions. In an object, related facts are called **attributes,** and the instructions that tell the data what to do are called **methods** or **operations.** A specific occurrence of an object is called an **instance;** your pet kitty Tschugar is an instance of the object Cat.

Beginnings: Boats as Objects

Object orientation was first conceived in 1969 by Dr. Kristin Nygaard, who was trying to develop a computer model of boats passing through Norwegian fjords. As Dr. Nygaard wrestled with the complex components of waves, tides, an irregular coastline, and moving boats, he hit upon the idea of isolating each component into autonomous elements—objects—and then modeling the relationships among the elements. Consider the object Boat, shown in Figure 12. The object called Boat consists of the boat itself, its attributes, and its methods—descriptions of the things it does, such as float or sink. It should be noted, however, that in practice few objects have an inner life and can invoke their own methods spontaneously. Thus, methods in most cases are actions from the outside that change the state of the object.

Using object-oriented programming, programmers define classes of objects. Each **class** contains the characteristics that are unique to objects of that class. In Figure 12, for example, a Boat object is an instance of the Boats class. In addition to classes, objects may be formed from subclasses. Objects

Figure 12 Object classes and subclasses. The subclasses Sailboat, Powerboat, and Canoe inherit the characteristics float and sink from the higher-class object Boat. Furthermore, each subclass, under the property of polymorphism, can respond to the message "move" by using its own methods.

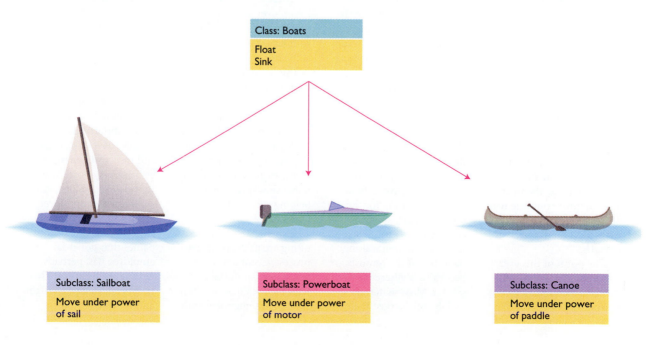

Class: Boats
Float
Sink

Subclass: Sailboat
Move under power of sail

Subclass: Powerboat
Move under power of motor

Subclass: Canoe
Move under power of paddle

2000 and Beyond

THE ALL-DAY, ALL-NIGHT, NO-TROUBLE JOB SEARCH

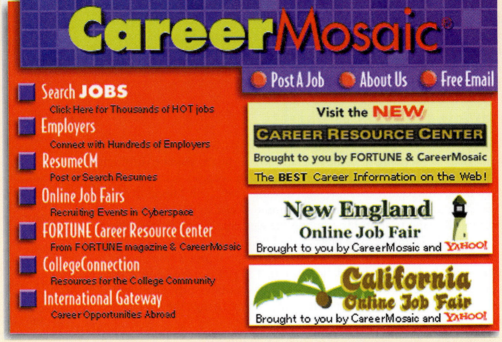

Carolyn Butler, the human resources manager for a 47-unit nationwide chain based in New York, needed corporate sales managers in three different cities: Newark, San Antonio, and Portland. In the past, Carolyn would have placed ads in the local newspapers and then waited a month before sifting through the hundreds of resumés that landed on her desk. This time she tried another approach: Let the computer do the searching.

For a fee, Carolyn signed on with a web service that offers thousands of job candidates in its database. The service quickly found 452 potential matchups. Within two days, using particular keywords—job titles or specific skills—to zero in on the candidates with the best fit, the list had been culled to 37. This initial search is just the beginning, of course; the hiring process must continue with initial interviews, interviews with managers, and so forth.

The point of this exercise is that, for employers, at least a month can be cut from the front end of the

hiring process. Carolyn plans to continue using the computer for the first cut. Other employers are having the same thoughts. As the twenty-first century evolves, traditional job candidate searches via newspaper classifieds or job placement services are being replaced by web-based database searches.

These changes also affect job seekers. Happily, the days of stuffing dozens of envelopes with your resumé and cover letter, and then waiting for the phone to ring, are fast coming to an end. The job seeker is still in a waiting pattern, but the rewards are becoming swifter and greater. Most match sites let job seekers post their

resumés free; in fact, many sites offer resumé assistance.

There are, in a recent count, over a thousand web sites that match employers with future employees. Some are niche sites, such as a site offering Pacific Rim opportunities for those who speak Asian languages. Nearly every profession, from architects to zoologists, has its own special sites that post jobs and career management advice. Some sites specialize in helping college students get that first job.

Other changes in the offing are in the interview process. Companies are becoming comfortable with the idea that they can conduct an interview with

a job candidate using teleconferencing from the candidate's personal computer.

The web sites have spawned yet another phenomenon: the passive job seeker. Some workers, although happy in their jobs and not actively seeking other employment, will post their resumés on a few web sites just to troll for a better opportunity. In fact, in these days of downsizing and insecurity, many workers routinely post their resumes on job sites just to see if another employer will find them. The resume sites are available to companies that potential employee has, perhaps, never even heard of. That is, indeed, all day, all night, and no trouble.

are arranged hierarchically in classes and subclasses by their dominant characteristics. In Figure 12, some kinds of boats—sailboats, powerboats, and canoes—are subclasses of the object Boat.

An object in a subclass automatically possesses all the characteristics of the class from which it is derived; this property is called **inheritance.** The subclass object Canoe, for example, contains not only its own characteristics, such as a need to be paddled, but also characteristics such as the ability to float or sink inherited from the higher object class called Boats. The characteristics of the class that a subclass is derived from need not be repeated in each subclass. This means that, in a programming environment, a programmer would not have to repeat the instructions for characteristics that are inherited, saving both time and money.

Even more savings accrue from the ability to reuse objects. As object technology is used by an organization, the organization gradually builds a library of classes. Once a class has been created, tested, and found useful, it can be used again. In fact, classes may be used and reused in future program applications. Because each class is self-contained, it need not be altered for use in future applications. This reduces errors significantly, since new programs can be constructed largely of pretested error-free classes. Of course, organizations will not reap the benefits of reuse until they are a few projects down the line.

Activating the Object

Since an object is self-contained, how do you get it to do something? A command, called a **message,** is sent to the object from outside it. The message tells the object what needs to be done, and just how it is done may be contained in the object's methods. For example, the message "move" could be sent to objects belonging to any subclass of the Boats class—Sailboat, Powerboat, or Canoe. This brings up a fancy word that goes a long way toward revealing the value of object technology: *polymorphism.* When a message is sent, the property of **polymorphism** allows an individual object receiving the message to know how, using its own methods, to process the message in the appropriate way for that particular object. For example, when the message "move" is received, the object Sailboat knows it is supposed to move under power of sail, the object Powerboat knows that it moves by means of a motor, and the object Canoe knows that it moves by being paddled. In each case the object merely has to be told to move and it moves, using its own built-in methods.

Object-Oriented Languages: C++, Smalltalk, and Visual Basic

The object-oriented language that currently dominates the market is C++, which is an enhanced version of the C language. C++ includes everything that is part of C and adds support for object-oriented programming. In addition, C++ also contains many improvements and features that make it a "better C," independent of object oriented programming. However, if you just use C++ as a better C, you will not be using all of its power. Like any quality tool, C++ must be used the way it was designed to be used to exploit its richness. Versions of C++ are available for large systems and personal computers.

Smalltalk, which was one of the first object-oriented languages on the market, is making inroads. Smalltalk signaled a dramatic departure from

Critical Thinking

If the ability to reuse program elements is so valuable, why don't more companies already reuse significant amounts of previously written software? (Although the amount of reuse does vary from one company to another, a major problem is that developing software that is easily reused adds extra expense and complexity. Also, business requirements seem to change at an ever-increasing pace, and much of the software developed a few years ago may already be obsolete.)

InfoBit

Object-oriented technology is such a powerful concept that a number of books have been written suggesting that modeling an entire business in terms of objects rather than functions or divisions is an effective approach to business reengineering and development.

Critical Thinking

What business objects can you think of in a mail-order catalog business? (Possible objects include customers, orders—divided into filled, open, and back orders—phone logs, shippers, vendors, clerks, supervisors, warehouse shelves, and many others.)

InfoBit

One factor that is driving the migration from C to C++ is that C++ is truly a "superset" of C. This means that almost every C program can be recompiled with C++ and will run without modification. If a developer wishes gradually to take advantage of the advanced object-oriented features of C++, he or she can begin by simply reusing any C programs already written.

Figure 13 Visual Basic. On this screen you can see part of the program as well as the visual result being achieved.

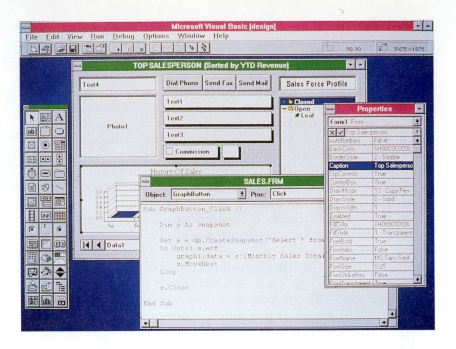

traditional computer languages because it supports an especially visual system. Smalltalk works by using a keyboard to enter text, but all other interaction takes place through a mouse and icons. There are other languages that have object-oriented versions, notably Pascal and Microsoft's Visual Basic (Figure 13).

Object Technology in Business

When businesses approach object technology, they are more likely to be interested in invoices and payroll checks than cats or boats. Business items have their own attributes and methods, which can be coded into objects. Once the objects exist, they can inherit characteristics from objects in higher classes. For example, subclass objects relating to a customer account could inherit the address of the customer, which need not then be repeated in each subclass object. In the fashion of object technology, business objects can also respond to messages and, of course, can be reused.

Getting Serious and Getting Started

Would-be programmers often ask the same question: How do I get started? In addition to the obvious answer of taking a set of courses via an academic program, it is possible to take some steps on your own.

Languages

Complex applications these days are usually written in C++ or Visual Basic. In particular, such applications are often written using Microsoft Visual C++ or Microsoft Visual Basic. We do not promote any particular brand or vendor; we are merely reporting the pervasiveness of these products in the marketplace. These tools support applications in Microsoft Windows, the operating system in place on the majority of personal computers. These are the languages most often used to create sophisticated software, such as dynamic Web applications and mission-critical corporate applications. They are considered by many to be the most productive tools for development for Windows and the Web. Further, both languages support HTML. Visual C++ has built industrial-strength e-commerce applications at some of the busiest sites on the Web, such as Dell and Barnes and Noble.

Although there are major differences, Visual Basic is founded on the original BASIC language. That is, you use BASIC-like code to implement Visual Basic concepts. If you are not familiar with the BASIC language, pick up a book on QBASIC. QBASIC uses roughly the same commands as Visual Basic, so once you feel comfortable with QBASIC you can start coding in Visual Basic right away. Similarly, if you know the C language, you can code in C++ right away. In either language, Visual Basic or Visual C++, the model and concepts are new, if you know the underlying language then you know the fundamental commands.

Some Beginning Steps

The overall advice can be summed up as "study and practice." But that can be broken down into smaller steps:

- **Read.** Good sources for beginners are the Visual C++ Programmer's Guide and Visual Basic Programmer's Guide, both available directly from the Microsoft Press site and from most book sites and bookstores. Be sure to get the latest version.
- **Use the tutorials.** These online lessons are valuable and convenient. Since they come with the software, you can peruse them at your leisure.
- **Study sample code.** Coding examples are included in the software package; these are well worth the time you spend to examine and study them. Further, many web sites offer sample code. In fact, all sorts of code is available free, for both study and for use.
- **Code.** You must write code, early and often. Reading and studying are important, but the most effective learning tool is the act of coding.
- **Start small.** Start with small coding projects and work your way up to more complex ones. Examples that come with your language documentation are a good place to begin. You will get more feedback and knowledge from several small projects than one or two big ones.
- **Use the Help file**. Instead of making occasional visits when you have a problem or need information, go through the Help file as you would a manual. Pay close attention to the examples.
- **Use your time productively.** Translation: Do not spend all day hanging out on Internet newsgroups or with user groups devoted to your favorite language. At best, you will not understand much of what is said and at worst you will (possibly because you did not understand) get bad information. Wait until you know more, or at least have a specific question.

Others have gone before you and been successful. Perhaps the greatest advantage to a beginning programmer today is that there is a large support community, with dozens of supportive sites, on the Internet.

▲

There will always be a need for programming and always be a need for programmers. The future of both is bright.

Getting to the Top: A Dozen Tips from Successful Programmers

1. **Seek out training opportunities in the workplace.** Training is sometimes offered right in the workplace or perhaps elsewhere with company sponsorship. Managers are impressed by employees who want to learn.

2. **Form alliances with key players.** Think you do not want to "play politics"? Think again. Many people think that they can get ahead by simply doing a good job. That is not likely to be enough. You must build trust. Go out of your way to get to know people and show them you share the same work goals.

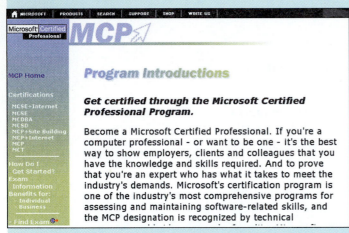

3. **Think and act like a leader.** Take the initiative, be responsible, take control when appropriate.

4. **Demonstrate that you have endurance.** Put in the long hours to help the team get the job done. In the computer field, you will have many such opportunities. In most places it will not go over well if you can *never* stay late or work weekends.

5. **If you have a major good idea that is accepted, try to attach your name to it.** That information would probably be in a report or in meeting minutes or perhaps in a memo. Keep a copy. A really good idea is uncommon and will draw many sponsors. If it really is yours, then you deserve credit.

6. **Share credit and blame.** Although your major good idea should be credited to you, most credit should be shared, at least for a while. For example, if you could truthfully take credit for most of

the work on some team subproject, deflecting praise to lesser players will win supporters. Similarly, you can, at least occasionally, say *we* when a team member botches something along the way.

7. **Do not be discouraged if you fail to sell an idea.** Figure out how to refine or repackage the idea and try again.

8. **Keep a positive attitude.** Attitude counts. See your job as filled with prospects rather than obstacles.

9. **Keep personal stories out of the workplace.** If you confide your woes to colleagues you will be taken less seriously and may even become defined by your problems.

10. **Do not underestimate yourself.** Push through initial discomfort so that you can take risks and seize opportunities.

11. **Pick your boss, insofar as you are able, carefully.** Find someone who will assign you interesting work and give you visibility.

12. **Seek out certifications that will enhance your job performance.** Many high-tech companies offer training, both at their own headquarters and at authorized locations worldwide. Some offer home study courses. These are major programs requiring many months of study and expense, culminating in testing. Seek information on their web sites. The Microsoft Certified Professional Program and Sun Microsystems Certification are shown here.

CHAPTER REVIEW

Summary and Key Terms

- A **programming language** is a set of rules for telling the computer what operations to perform.

- A programmer converts solutions to the user's problems into instructions for the computer. These instructions are called a **program.** Writing a program involves defining the problem, planning the solution, coding the program, testing the program, and documenting the program.

- Defining the problem means discussing it with the users or a systems analyst to determine the necessary input, processing, and output.

- Planning can be done by using a **flowchart,** which is a pictorial representation of the step-by-step solution, and by using **pseudocode,** which is an English-like outline of the solution. Pseudocode is not executable on the computer.

- Coding the program means expressing the solution in a programming language. Programmers usually use a **text editor,** which is somewhat like a word processing program, to create a file that contains the program.

- Testing the program consists of desk-checking, translating, and debugging. The rules of a programming language are referred to as its **syntax. Desk-checking** is a mental checking or proofreading of the program before it is run. A **walkthrough** is a process in which a group of programmers—your peers—review your program and offer suggestions in a collegial way. In translating, a **translator** program converts the program into a form the computer can understand and in the process detects programming language errors, which are called **syntax errors.** A common translator is a **compiler,** which translates the entire program at one time and gives error messages called **diagnostics.** The original program, called a **source module,** is translated to an **object module,** to which prewritten programs may be added during the **link/load phase** to create an executable **load module. Debugging** involves running the program to detect, locate, and correct mistakes known as **logic errors.**

- Typical **documentation** contains a detailed written description of the programming cycle and the program along with the test results and a printout of the program.

- Programming languages are described as being lower level or higher level, depending on how close they are to the language the computer itself uses (0s and 1s—low) or to the language people use (more English-like—high). There are five main levels, or generations, of languages: (1) machine language, (2) assembly languages, (3) high-level languages, (4) very high level languages, and (5) natural languages.

- **Machine language,** the lowest level, represents data as 0s and 1s, binary digits corresponding to the on and off electrical states in the computer.

- **Assembly languages** use letters as mnemonic codes to replace the 0s and 1s of machine language. An **assembly program** is used to translate the assembly language into machine language.

- **High-level languages** are written in an English-like manner. Each high-level language requires a different compiler, or translator program, for each type of computer on which it is run.

- **Very high level languages,** also called **fourth-generation languages (4GLs),** are basically shorthand languages. A variation on 4GLs are **query languages,** which can be used to retrieve data from databases.

- Fifth-generation languages are often called **natural languages** because they resemble "natural" spoken language.

- The first high-level language, **FORTRAN** (FORmula TRANslator), is a scientifically oriented language that was introduced by IBM in 1954. Its brevity makes it suitable for executing complex formulas.

- **COBOL** (COmmon Business-Oriented Language) was introduced in 1959 as a standard programming language for business.

- When **BASIC** (Beginners' All-purpose Symbolic Instruction Code) was developed at Dartmouth and introduced in 1965, it was intended for instruction in programming. Now its uses include business and personal computer applications.

- **Pascal,** named for the French mathematician Blaise Pascal, first became available in 1971. It is popular in college computer courses.

- Invented at Bell Labs, **C** offers high-level language features such as structured programming. C code is almost as efficient as assembly language, and it is suitable for writing portable programs that can run on more than one type of computer.

- **Java** is a network-friendly programming language, derived from the C++ language, that permits a piece of software to run on many different **platforms,** the hardware and software combination that composes the basic functionality of a computer.

- The approach called **object-oriented programming (OOP)** uses **objects,** self-contained units that hold both data and related facts and functions—the instructions to act on that data. An object **encapsulates** both data and its related instructions. In an object, related facts are called **attributes,** and the instructions that tell the data what to do are called **methods** or **operations.** A specific occurrence of an object is called an instance.

- An object **class** contains the characteristics that are unique to that class. Objects are arranged hierarchically in classes and subclasses by their dominant characteristics. An object in a subclass automatically possesses all the characteristics of the class to which it belongs; this property is called **inheritance.**

- Once an object has been created, tested, and found useful, it can be used and reused in future program applications.

- A command called a **message,** telling what—not how—something is to be done, activates the object. **Polymorphism** means that an individual object receiving a message knows how, using its own methods, to process the message in the appropriate way for that particular object.

- The object-oriented language that currently dominates the market is **C++,** which is the object-oriented version of the programming language C. Versions of C++ are available for large systems and personal computers. The language called **Smalltalk,** which supports an especially visual system, is making inroads.

Discussion Questions

1. It has been noted that, among other qualities, good programmers are detail-oriented. Why might attention to detail be important in the programming process?

2. In addition to insisting on proper documentation, managers encourage programmers to write straightforward programs that another programmer can easily follow. Discuss occasions in which a programmer may have to work with a program written by another programmer. Under what circumstances might a programmer completely take over the care of a program written by another? If you inherited someone else's program, about which you knew nothing, would you be dismayed to discover minimal documentation?

3. Should students taking a computer literacy course be required to learn some programming?

Student Study Guide

Multiple Choice

1. The presence of both data and its related instructions in an object is called
   a. C++
   b. orientation
   c. encapsulation
   d. inheritance

2. In preparing a program, one should first
   a. plan the solution
   b. document the program
   c. code the program
   d. define the problem

3. During the development of a program, drawing a flowchart is a means to
   a. plan the solution
   b. define the problem
   c. code the program
   d. analyze the problem

4. An English-like language that one can use as a program design tool is
   a. BASIC
   b. Cobol
   c. pseudocode
   d. Pascal

5. In preparing a program, desk-checking and translating are examples of
   a. coding
   b. testing
   c. planning
   d. documenting

6. The process of detecting, locating, and correcting logic errors is called
   a. desk-checking
   b. debugging
   c. translating
   d. documenting

7. Comments in the program itself are part of
   a. compiling
   b. linking
   c. translating
   d. documenting

8. The hardware/software combination that composes a computer's functionality is its
   a. platform
   b. pseudocode
   c. class
   d. syntax

9. The first high-level language to be introduced was
   a. COBOL
   b. Pascal
   c. FORTRAN
   d. BASIC

10. The ability of an object to interpret a message using its own methods is known as
    a. polymorphism
    b. inheritance
    c. encapsulation
    d. messaging

11. The language named for a French mathematician is
    a. C
    b. Pascal
    c. FORTRAN
    d. COBOL

12. Specifying the kind of input, processing, and output required for a program occurs when
    a. planning the solution
    b. coding the program
    c. flowcharting the problem
    d. defining the problem

13. Error messages provided by a compiler are called
    a. bugs
    b. translations
    c. diagnostics
    d. mistakes

14. After stating a solution in pseudocode, you would next
    a. test the program
    b. implement the program
    c. code the program
    d. translate the program

15. The highest-level languages are called
    a. 4GLs
    b. assembly languages
    c. high-level languages
    d. natural languages

16. To activate an object, send a(n)
    a. message
    b. method
    c. instance
    d. attribute

17. Popular object-oriented languages are
    a. Pascal, COBOL
    b. C++, FORTRAN
    c. C++, Smalltalk
    d. COBOL, BASIC

18. Software that translates assembly language into machine language is a(n)
    a. binary translator
    b. assembler
    c. compiler
    d. link-loader

19. A standardized business language is
    a. Pascal
    b. COBOL
    c. BASIC
    d. FORTRAN

20. In developing a program, documentation should be done
    a. as the last step
    b. only to explain errors
    c. throughout the process
    d. only during the design phase

21. A fourth-generation language used for database retrieval is a(n)
    a. high-level language
    b. query language
    c. assembly language
    d. machine language

22. The network-friendly language derived from C++ is
    a. Java   c. Smalltalk
    b. Pascal   d. BASIC

23. The lowest level of programming language is
    a. natural language   c. assembly language
    b. BASIC   d. machine language

24. An assembly language uses
    a. English words   c. mnemonic codes
    b. 0s and 1s   d. binary digits

25. The language Smalltalk is
    a. machine-oriented   c. document-oriented
    b. problem-oriented   d. object-oriented

True/False

T F 1. The usual reason for choosing a programming language is simply that it is the one the programmer likes best.

T F 2. Developing a program requires just two steps, coding and testing.

T F 3. A flowchart is an example of pseudocode.

T F 4. Desk-checking is the first phase of testing a program.

T F 5. A translator is a form of hardware that translates a program into language the computer can understand.

T F 6. Wintel is an example of a platform.

T F 7. Debugging is the process of locating program logic errors.

T F 8. The highest level of language is natural language.

T F 9. Pseudocode can be used to plan and execute a program.

T F 10. 4GLs increase clarity but reduce user productivity.

T F 11. An object encapsulates both data and its related instructions.

T F 12. Pascal is particularly easy to use because it has fewer features than most languages.

T F 13. COBOL is divided into four parts called areas.

T F 14. BASIC is especially suited for large and complex programs.

T F 15. FORTRAN stands for FORms TRANsfer.

T F 16. Expressing a problem solution in Pascal is an example of coding a program.

T F 17. Diagnostic messages are concerned with improper use of the programming language.

T F 18. An assembly program translates high-level language into assembly language.

T F 19. An object subclass inherits characteristics from higher object classes.

T F 20. A specific occurrence of an object is called an instance.

T F 21. Polymorphism means that an object knows how, using its own methods, to act on an incoming message.

T F 22. Another name for a high-level language is 4GL.

T F 23. A query language is a type of assembly language.

T F 24. FORTRAN is used primarily in scientific environments.

T F 25. Low-level languages are tied more closely to the computer than are high-level languages.

Fill-In

1. The type of language used to access databases is called a(n) _____ language.

2. The type of language that replaced machine language by using mnemonic codes is called a(n) _____ language.

3. The object orientation property that permits a subclass to retain the characteristics of a higher class is called _____.

4. A query language is what level of language? _____

5. The name for a translator that translates high-level languages into machine language is _____.

6. The rules of a programming language are called its _____.

7. How many levels of language were described in the chapter? _____

8. A source module is translated into a(n)
_____.

9. The object orientation property that permits an object to use its own methods to act on a message is called _____.

10. Two commonly used OOP languages are

a. _____

b. _____

11. The hardware and software combination that composes the basic functionality of a computer is called a(n) _____.

12. An object module is link-loaded into a(n)
_____.

13. Languages that resemble spoken languages are called _____.

14. The high-level language that is scientifically oriented is _____.

15. The command that activates an object is a(n)
_____.

16. The programming process step that is best done throughout the process is_____.

17. Two common methods of planning the solution to a problem are

a. _____

b. _____

18. List the three phases of testing a program:

a. _____

b. _____

c. _____

19. The next step after a programmer has planned the solution is to: _____
_____.

20. The term for the error messages that a translator provides is: _____.

Answers

Multiple Choice

1. c	6. b	11. b	16. a	21. b
2. d	7. d	12. d	17. c	22. a
3. a	8. a	13. c	18. b	23. d
4. c	9. c	14. c	19. b	24. c
5. b	10. a	15. d	20. c	25. d

True/False

1. F	6. T	11. T	16. T	21. T
2. F	7. T	12. T	17. T	22. F
3. F	8. T	13. F	18. F	23. F
4. T	9. F	14. F	19. T	24. T
5. F	10. F	15. F	20. T	25. T

Fill-In

1. query
2. assembly language
3. inheritance
4. very high level language
5. compiler
6. syntax
7. five
8. object module
9. polymorphism
10. C++, Smalltalk
11. platform
12. load module
13. natural languages
14. FORTRAN
15. message
16. documentation
17. a. flowcharting
    b. writing pseudocode
18. a. desk-checking
    b. translating
    c. debugging
19. code the program
20. diagnostics

Although sociologists fret over the potential isolation of people focused on their personal computers, several sites cater to togetherness among online folks, going so far as to call their sites communities. Beyond this, the Internet caters to people-to-people connections by offering searches for lost friends or colleagues, advocating for missing or adoptable children, providing parent-to-parent support, listing class reunions, and even chronicling celebrities.

Virtual communities. The Well is the oldest and perhaps best-known virtual community, and they describe themselves as literate and iconoclastic. The Well has more than 200 "conferences" on topics as varied as parenting, the future, current events, and the Rockies.

Most communities offer live chat, with members contributing to the discussion, which scrolls down the screen, from their individual computers. Another virtual community site shown here is called Cybertown. The site is easy to navigate—just click on an icon—and full of content.

People search. Whatever happened to Lowell? Lowell can possibly be found by using the Internet, even if he never heard of it. In fact *possibly* will soon become *probably*. Two forces are coming together to make this likely. One is the steadily growing number of computers connected to the Internet. The other is the increasing amount of information about people being stored in computer databases. The Internet provides fast access to those databases.

Standard search engines can find the name of a person if the name is mentioned in a web page or in a newsgroup. More-specialized people searchers, such as WhoWhere? or Switchboard, may be able to provide an individual's address, phone number, and e-mail address. Note the WhoWhere? form shown here; simply fill in the person's name and await the return of more detailed information. However, if the name is insufficient input, you will be prompted for more details, such as city and state. Different search sites use different databases, so if you strike out with one, try others.

Specialized people-to-people. Many people want to connect with their own kind. Typical affinity groups involve a nationality, school, hobby, common interest, set of shared values, profession, or family name. There are numerous sites in all of these categories and many more. The Tribal Voice logo shown here highlights the home page for certain Native Americans. The Faces of Adoption image represents a site where adopters and children who can be adopted may come together. Reunion sites, listing gatherings by school and class, abound. If you are interested in tracking your family, look up some of the many

you'd be surprised who you know

sixdegrees®

genealogy sites. Finally, if you want to discover how you may be related to someone else, the Six Degrees site operates on the premise that we are all connected by no more than six degrees of separation—that is, through no more than six people who have some connection to each other.

Internet Exercises

1. **Structured exercise.** Begin with the URL http://www.prenhall.com/capron and use both the WhoWhere? and Switchboard sites to try to locate an old friend.

2. **Freeform exercise.** Hang out in one or more virtual communities and join in the live chat.

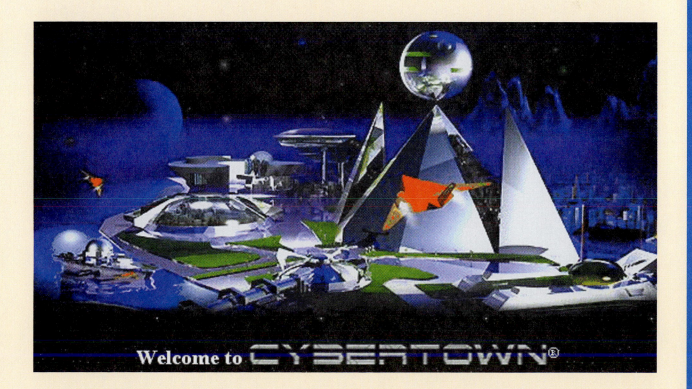

Welcome to CYBERTOWN®

SYSTEMS ANALYSIS AND DESIGN

The Big Picture

LEARNING OBJECTIVES

- Be able to define the terms *system, analysis,* and *design*
- Know the principal functions of the systems analyst
- Be able to list and describe the phases of the systems development life cycle
- Become acquainted with data gathering and analysis tools
- Become acquainted with systems design tools
- Understand the concept of prototyping
- Appreciate the predominance of maintenance

Tomina Edmark was enjoying a successful career as large-systems salesperson at IBM. One evening, as she was standing in line waiting to get into a movie, a curious question popped into her mind: Was it possible to turn a ponytail inside out? To greatly compress this success story, Tomina went on to invent the now-famous TopsyTail, a kind of hair barrette.

TopsyTail was widely imitated, forcing Ms. Edmark into litigation to defend her product rights. It is understandable that she would want to keep her new company's information—product designs, financial data, client list—under wraps. It helps, of course, that Ms. Edmark is computer-savvy herself.

Even so, Ms. Edmark shines as a hallmark of *outsourcing,* the practice of contracting out almost all company functions—forecasting, manufacturing, packaging, shipping, advertising, and customer service. Despite the fact that her company rings up millions of dollars of sales annually,

the TopsyTail company has only a handful of employees. As Ms. Edmark notes, outsourcing lets her focus on researching and developing new products.

This true story is notable in that it is almost the reverse of what happens in many organizations, which mostly do their own product manufacturing and other related tasks but outsource the computing functions. As this chapter shows, the planning and maintenance required for computer systems is detailed and complex.

The Systems Analyst

People are often nervous when they are about to be visited by a systems analyst. A systems analyst with any experience, however, knows that people are uneasy about having a stranger pry into their job situations and that they may be equally nervous about computers. Before discussing how the systems analyst helps people address change, let us begin with a few basic definitions.

The Analyst and the System

Although a systems project will be described more formally later in the chapter, let us start by defining the words *system, analysis,* and *design.* A **system** is an organized set of related components established to accomplish a certain task. There are natural systems, such as the cardiovascular system, but many systems have been planned and deliberately put into place by people. For example, a fast-food franchise has a system for serving a customer, including taking an order, assembling the food, and collecting the amount due. A **computer system** is a system that has a computer as one of its components.

Systems analysis is the process of studying an existing system to determine how it works and how it meets user needs. Systems analysis lays the groundwork for improvements to the system. The analysis involves an investigation, which in turn usually involves establishing a relationship with the client for whom the analysis is being done and with the users of the system. The **client** is the person or organization contracting to have the work done. The **users** are people who will have contact with the system, usually employees and customers. For instance, in a fast-food system, the client is probably the franchise owner or manager, and the users are both the franchise employees and the customers.

Systems design is the process of developing a plan for an improved system, based on the results of the systems analysis. For instance, an analysis of a fast-food franchise may reveal that customers stand in unacceptably long lines waiting to order. A new system design might involve plans to have employees press buttons that match ordered items, causing a display on an overhead screen that can be seen by other employees who can quickly assemble the order.

The **systems analyst** normally performs both analysis and design. (The term *systems designer* is used in some places.) In some computer installations a person who is mostly a programmer may also do some systems analysis and thus have the title **programmer/analyst.** Traditionally, most people who have become systems analysts started out as programmers.

A systems analysis and design project does not spring out of thin air. There must be an *impetus*—motivation—for change and related *authority* for the change. The impetus for change may be the result of an internal force, such as the organization's management deciding that a computer could be useful in warehousing and inventory, or an external force, such as government reporting requirements or customer complaints about billing (Figure 1). Authority for the change, of course, comes from higher management.

The Systems Analyst as Change Agent

The systems analyst fills the role of **change agent,** the catalyst or persuader who overcomes the natural reluctance to change within an organization. The key to success is to involve the people of the client organization in the development of the new system. The common industry phrase is **user involvement,** and nothing could be more important to the success of the system. Some analysts like to think in terms of who "owns" the system. If efforts

InfoBit

The distinction between client and user is crucial to successful systems analysis, and this is particularly true for external consultants. While it is understandable that consultants tend to focus on those who are responsible for hiring and paying them—the clients—the eventual success of the system depends on satisfying the needs quite another constituency—the users. The end-users of the system probably have no say in hiring or rewarding systems analysts, but if the new system doesn't work for them, it will have been a waste of the client's funds.

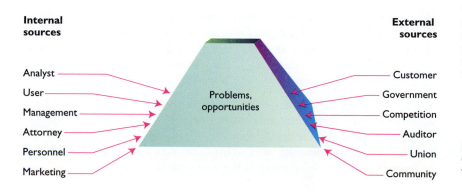

Figure 1 Impetus for change. Internal or external sources can initiate a system change.

InfoBit

Increasingly, communication among the analyst, client and users is likely to take graphical form. While it is very difficult to get some clients and many users to read a thick design or analysis document, it is often possible to create visual overviews using drawing programs and presentation software. A diagram showing the components of the proposed system and their relationship at a high level is crucial to achieving user and client understanding of what is being proposed.

Critical Thinking

Imagine that you are a business person who must hire a systems analyst to help design a new system for automating your business. What questions could you ask or skills could you get the candidates to demonstrate that would increase your confidence that they could do a good job for you? (Demonstrated knowledge and experience in systems design is important, but communication skills, organization ability, and effective listening are also important. Among the activities you could use to select these individuals are asking for writing samples, watching them interview one of your system's users, and asking them to make a short, impromptu presentation.)

toward user involvement are successful, the user begins to think of the system as *my* system, rather than *their* system. Once that happens, the analyst's job becomes much easier.

What It Takes to Be a Systems Analyst

Before one can understand what kind of person might make a good systems analyst, it is necessary to look at the kinds of things an analyst does. The systems analyst has three principal functions:

- **Coordination.** An analyst must coordinate schedules and system-related tasks with a number of people: the analyst's own manager; the programmers working with the system; the system's users, from clerks to top management; the vendors selling the computer equipment; and a host of others, such as mail-room employees handling mailings and carpenters doing installation.
- **Communication, both oral and written.** The analyst may be called upon to make oral presentations to clients, users, and others involved with the system. The analyst provides written reports—documentation—on the results of the analysis and the goals and means of the design. These documents may range from a few pages long to a few inches thick.
- **Planning and design.** The systems analyst, with the participation of members of the client organization, plans and designs the new system. This function involves all the activities from the beginning of the project until the final implementation of the system.

In light of these principal functions, the kinds of personal qualities that are desirable in a systems analyst become apparent: an *analytical mind* and *good communication skills.* Perhaps not so obvious, however, are qualities such as *self-discipline* and *self-direction,* since a systems analyst often works without close supervision. An analyst must have good *organizational skills* to be able to keep track of all the facts about the system. An analyst also needs *creativity* to envision the new system. Finally, an analyst needs the *ability to work without tangible results.* There can be long dry spells when the analyst moves numbly from meeting to meeting and it can seem that little is being accomplished.

How a Systems Analyst Works: Overview of the Systems Development Life Cycle

Whether you are investigating how to improve a bank's customer relations, how to track inventory for a jeans warehouse, how to manage egg production on a chicken ranch, or any other task, you will proceed by using the **systems development life cycle (SDLC).** The systems development life cycle can be described in five phases:

1. Preliminary investigation—determining the problem
2. Analysis—understanding the existing system
3. Design—planning the new system
4. Development—doing the work to bring the new system into being
5. Implementation—converting to the new system

GETTING PRACTICAL

CRANKING UP YOUR SKILL LIST

When Althea Burgess was an adolescent she wanted to be a doctor. However, she gradually realized that the ever-changing medical field meant that she would have to spend her entire career trying to keep up with the latest developments. So she went into the computer field instead.

This true little story is still amusing to Althea's family. Today everyone knows that the computer field is also ever-changing. Indeed, computer professionals soon discover that their original training is just the beginning. Many employers actually put a monetary premium on certain skills. It is out of the question for an individual to have every skill. But a look at the "most wanted" skills, by category, may give you an idea of a direction in which to go: for the Internet, learn HTML and Java; in languages, C++; in development tools, Microsoft Visual BASIC, Visual C++, and PowerBuilder; for networking, TCP/IP, IPX; as a database, Oracle, DB2, Microsoft SQL; in operating systems, Windows, Unix; for internetworking, Ethernet, ATM; for LAN administration, Windows NT Server, Novell Netware; and in client/server applications, Oracle, SAP.

Some of the names mentioned above may be unfamiliar, since some of them are brand names. But you can find them on the Internet. SAP AG, for example, makes software to manage accounting, human resources, materials management, and manufacturing. To give you an idea of the potency of training in SAP applications, both IBM and Microsoft use software from SAP to run their companies.

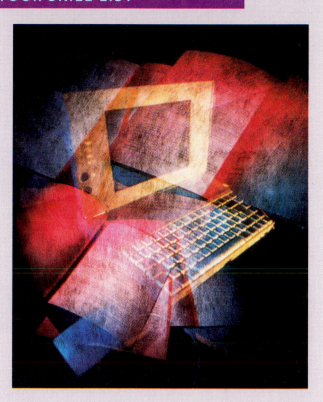

These simple explanations for each phase will be expanded to full-blown discussions in subsequent sections. It is important to note at this point that moving through these five phases is not necessarily a straightforward, linear process; that is, there will doubtless be adjustments to previous phases as you move along.

As you read about the phases of a systems project, follow the Swift Sport Shoes inventory case study, which is presented in accompanying boxes. Although space limitations prohibit us from presenting a complete analysis and design project, this case study gives the flavor of the real thing.

Phase 1: Preliminary Investigation

The **preliminary investigation,** often called the **feasibility study** or **system survey,** is the initial investigation, a brief study of the problem to determine whether the systems project should be pursued. You, as the systems analyst, need to determine what the problem is and what to do about it. The net result will be a rough plan for how—and whether—to proceed with the project.

Before you can decide whether to proceed, you must be able to describe the problem. To do this, you will work with the users. One of your tools will be an **organization chart,** which is a hierarchical drawing showing the organization's management by name and title. Figure 2 shows an example of an organization chart. Many organizations already have such a chart and can give you a copy. If the chart does not exist, you must ask some questions and then make it yourself. Constructing such a chart is not an idle task. If you are to work effectively within the organization, you need to understand the lines of authority through the formal communication channels.

Problem Definition: Nature, Scope, Objectives

Your initial aim is to define the problem. You and the users must come to an agreement on these points: You must agree on the nature of the problem and then designate a limited scope. In the process you will also determine what the objectives of the project are. Figure 3 shows an overview of the problem definition process, and Figure 4 gives an example related to the Swift Sport Shoes project.

Figure 2 An organization chart. The chart shows the lines of authority and formal communication channels. This example shows the organizational setup for Swift Sport Shoes, a chain of stores.

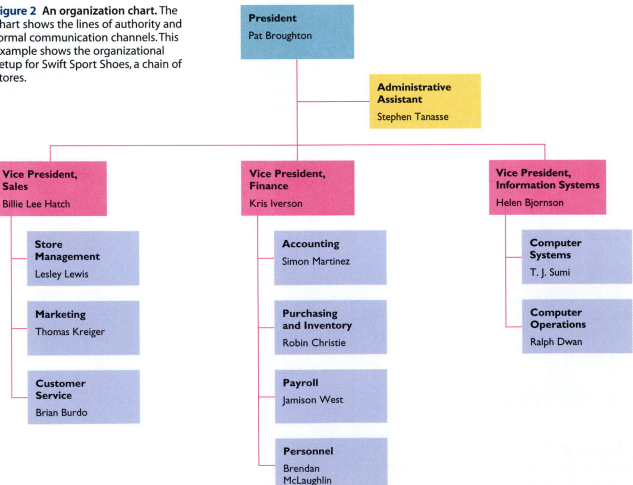

Nature of the Problem   Begin by determining the true nature of the problem. Sometimes what appears to be the problem turns out to be, on a closer look, only a symptom. For example, suppose that you are examining customer complaints of late deliveries. Your brief study may reveal that the problem is not in the shipping department, as you first thought, but in the original ordering process.

Scope   Establishing the scope of the problem is critical because problems tend to expand if no firm boundaries are established. Limitations are also necessary to stay within the eventual budget and schedule. So in the beginning the analyst and user must agree on the scope of the project: what the new or revised system is supposed to do—and not do.

Objectives   You will soon come to understand what the user needs—that is, what the user thinks the system should be able to do. You will want to express these needs as objectives. Examine the objectives for the Swift inventory process. The people who run the existing inventory system already know what such a system must do. It remains for you and them to work out how this can be achieved on a computer system. In the next phase, the systems analysis phase, you will produce a more specific list of system requirements based on these objectives.

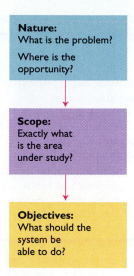

Figure 3 **Problem definition overview.**

SWIFT SPORT SHOES: PROBLEM DEFINITION

True Nature of the Problem

The nature of the problem is the existing manual inventory system. In particular:
■ Products are frequently out of stock
■ There is little interstore communication about stock items
■ Store managers have no information about stock levels on a day-to-day basis
■ Ordering is done haphazardly

Scope

The scope of the project will be limited to the development of an inventory system using appropriate computer technology.

Objectives

The new automated inventory system should provide the following:
■ Adequate stock maintained in stores
■ Automatic stock reordering
■ Stock distribution among stores
■ Management access to current inventory information
■ Ease of use
■ Reduced operating costs of the inventory function

Figure 4 **Problem definition.** The nature and scope of the problem along with system objectives are shown for the Swift Sport Shoes system.

CASE STUDY   *Preliminary Investigation*

You are employed as a systems analyst by Software Systems, Inc., a company offering packaged software as well as consulting and outsourcing services. Software Systems has received a request for a consultant; the client is Swift Sport Shoes, a chain of stores carrying a huge selection of footwear for every kind of sport. Your boss hands you, a systems analyst, this assignment, telling you to contact company officer Kris Iverson.

In your initial meeting with Mr. Iverson, who is vice president of finance, you learn that the first Swift store opened in San Francisco in 1984. The store has been profitable since the second year. Nine new stores have been added in the metropolitan area and outlying shopping malls. These stores also

show a net profit; Swift has been riding the crest of the fitness boom. But even though sales have been gratifying, Mr. Iverson is convinced that costs are higher than they should be and that customer service has never been adequate.

In particular, Mr. Iverson is disturbed about inventory problems, which are causing frequent stock shortages and increasing customer dissatisfaction. The company has a low-end mainframe computer at headquarters, where management offices are. Although there is a small information systems staff, their experience is mainly in batch processing for financial systems. Mr. Iverson envisions more sophisticated technology for an inventory system and figures that outside expertise is needed to design it.

He introduces you to Robin Christie, who is in charge of purchasing and inventory. Mr. Iverson also tells you that he has sent a memo to all company officers and store managers indicating the purpose of your presence and his support of a study of the current system. Before the end of your visit with Mr. Iverson, the two of you construct the organization chart shown in Figure 2.

In subsequent interviews with Ms. Christie and other Swift personnel, you find that deteriorating customer service seems to be due to a lack of information about inventory supplies. Together, you and Ms. Christie determine the problem definition, as shown in Figure 4. Mr. Iverson accepts your report, in which you outline the problem definition and suggest a full analysis.

Wrapping Up the Preliminary Investigation

The preliminary investigation, which is necessarily brief, should result in some sort of report, perhaps only a few pages long, telling management what you have found and listing your recommendations. Furthermore, money is always a factor in go/no-go decisions: Is the project financially feasible? At this point management has three choices: They can (1) drop the matter; (2) fix the problem immediately if it is simple; or (3) authorize you to go on to the next phase for a closer look.

Phase 2: Systems Analysis

Let us suppose that management has decided to continue. Remember that the purpose of systems analysis is to understand the existing system. A related goal is to establish the system requirements. The best way to understand a system is to gather all the data you can about it; this data must then be organized and analyzed. During the systems analysis phase you will be concerned with (1) data gathering and (2) data analysis. Keep in mind that the system being analyzed may or may not already be a computerized system.

Data Gathering

Data gathering is expensive and requires a lot of legwork and time. There is no standard procedure for gathering data because each system is unique. But there are certain sources that are commonly used: written documents, interviews, questionnaires, observation, and sampling. Sometimes you will use all of these sources, but in most cases it will be appropriate to use some and not others.

Written Documents   These include procedures manuals, reports, forms, and any other kind of material bearing on the problem that you find in the organization. Take time to get a copy of each form an organization uses.

Interviews   A key advantage of interviews is their flexibility; as the interviewer, you can change the direction of your questions if you discover a productive area of investigation. Another bonus is that you can probe with open-ended questions that people would balk at answering on paper. You can also observe the respondent's voice inflection and body motions, which may tell you more than words alone. Finally, of course, there is the bonus of getting to know clients better and establishing a rapport with them, an important factor in promoting user involvement in the system from the beginning. Interviews have certain drawbacks: They are time-consuming and therefore expensive. If you need to find out about procedures from 40 mail clerks, you are better off using a questionnaire.

There are two types of interviews, structured and unstructured. A **structured interview** includes only questions that have been planned and written out in advance. A structured interview is useful when it is desirable—or required by law—to ask identical questions of several people. However, the **unstructured interview** is often more productive, since the interviewer may stray from the line of questioning.

Questionnaires   Unlike interviews, questionnaires can be used to get information from large groups. Also, because of the large number of respondents, sometimes a trend or problem pattern emerges that would not be evident from a small number of interviews. Questionnaires allow people to respond anonymously and, presumably, more truthfully. Questionnaires do have disadvantages, however, including the problem of getting them returned and the possibility of biased answers.

InfoBit

A problem that may limit the usefulness of an unstructured interview is the analyst's natural tendency to do more talking than listening. One way to address this problem is to provide interviewees with a list of questions in advance. Rather than asking each question in turn, the analyst lets the user pick which questions to answer and in what order to proceed. This approach combines the better aspects of both structured and unstructured interview techniques.

CASE STUDY   *Systems Analysis*

With the assistance of Ms. Christie, you learn more about the current inventory system. She helps set up interviews with store managers and arranges to have you observe procedures in the stores and at the warehouse. As the number of stores has increased, significant expansion has taken place in all inventory-related areas: sales, scope of merchandise, and number of vendors.

Out-of-stock situations are common. The stock shortages are not uniform across all 10 stores, however; frequently, one store will be out of an item that the

central warehouse or another store has on hand. The present system is not able to recognize this situation and transfer merchandise on a timely basis. There is a tendency for stock to be reordered only when the shelf is empty or nearly so. Inventory-related costs are significant, especially those for special orders of some stock items. Reports to management are minimal and often too late to be useful. Finally, there is no way to correlate order quantities with past sales records, future projections, or inventory situations.

During this period you also analyze the data as it is gathered. You prepare data flow diagrams of the various activities relating to inventory. Figure 6 shows the general flow of data to handle purchasing in the existing system. You prepare various decision tables, such as the one shown in Figure 7b.

Your written report to Mr. Iverson includes the list of system requirements in Figure 8.

InfoBit

If questionnaire data is extensive, Optical Mark Reading equipment can be used to scan questionnaires, Statistical software packages or spreadsheets can be used for analyzing and reporting the results. Sampling too can be accomplished with special software. A laptop or palm-top computer is handy for recording the results of observations in real time.

InfoBit

The challenge of sampling is to get a representative sample. Because attitudes, beliefs, and practice vary so widely even within the same organization, interviewing only those users in a particular building or unit or even city may give a misleading picture of the overall system requirements. Statistical random sampling is one way to obtain a representative sample.

Observation   As an analyst and observer, you go into the organization and watch who interrelates with whom. In particular, you observe how data flows: from desk to desk, fax to fax, or computer to computer. Note how data comes into and leaves the organization. Initially, you make arrangements with a group supervisor and make everyone aware of the purpose of your visit. Be sure to return on more than one occasion so that the people under observation become used to your presence. One form of observation is **participant observation;** in this form the analyst temporarily joins the activities of the group.

Sampling   You may need to collect data about quantities, costs, time periods, and other factors relevant to the system. For example, how many phone orders can be taken by an order entry clerk in an hour? If you are dealing with a major mail-order organization, such as L. L. Bean in Maine, this type of question may be best answered through a procedure called sampling: Instead of observing all 125 clerks filling orders for an hour, you pick a sample of 3 or 4 clerks. Or, in a case involving a high volume of paper output, such as customer bills, you could collect a random sample of a few dozen bills. Although actual sampling methods are beyond the scope of this book, it should be mentioned that there are statistical techniques that can determine exactly what sample size will yield accurate results.

Data Analysis

Your data-gathering processes will probably produce an alarming amount of paper and a strong need to get organized. It is now time to turn your attention to the second activity of this phase, data analysis. A variety of tools—charts and diagrams—are used to analyze data, not all of them appropriate for every system. You should become familiar with the techniques favored by your organization and then use the tools that suit you at the time. Two typical tools are data flow diagrams and decision tables. Data analysis shows how the current system works and helps determine the system requirements. In addition, data analysis materials will serve as the basis for documentation of the system.

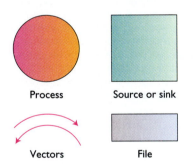

Figure 5 Symbols used in data flow diagrams. Circles represent processes, the actions taken on the data—comparing, checking, stamping, authorizing, filing, and so forth. An open-ended box represents a file, a repository of data; this can be a disk file, a set of papers in a file cabinet, or even mail in an in-basket or blank envelopes in a supply bin. Sources and sinks are represented by a square. A source is a data origin outside the system under study. An example is a payment sent to a department store by a charge customer; the customer is a source of data. A sink is a destination for data going outside the system; an example is the bank that receives money deposits from the accounts receivable department. The flow of data is shown using vectors, or arrows.

Data Flow Diagrams

A **data flow diagram (DFD)** is a sort of road map that graphically shows the flow of data through a system. It is a valuable tool for depicting present procedures and data flow. Although data flow diagrams can be used in the design process, they are particularly useful for facilitating communication between you and the users during the analysis phase. Suppose, for example, you spend a couple of hours with a McDonald's franchise manager, talking about the paperwork that keeps the burgers and the customers flowing. You would probably make copious notes about what goes on where. But that is only the data gathering function; now you must somehow analyze your findings. You could come back on another day with pages of narrative for the manager to review or, instead, with an easy-to-follow picture. Most users would prefer the picture.

There are a variety of notations for data flow diagrams. The notation used here has been chosen because it is informal and easy to draw and read. The elements of a data flow diagram are processes, files, sources and sinks, and vectors, as shown in Figure 5. Note also the DFD for Swift Sport Shoes (Figure 6) as you follow this discussion.

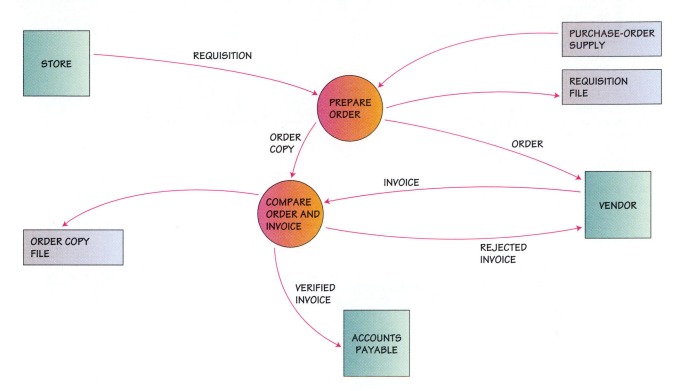

Figure 6 A data flow diagram. This "map" shows the current flow of data in the purchasing department at Swift Sport Shoes. The diagram (greatly simplified) includes authorization for purchases of goods, purchase-order preparation, and verification of the vendor's invoice against the purchase order. Note that the stores, vendors, and accounts payable are in square boxes because they are outside the purchasing department.

Decision Tables   A **decision table,** also called a **decision logic table,** is a standard table of the logical decisions that must be made regarding potential conditions in a given system. Decision tables are useful in cases that involve a series of interrelated decisions; their use helps to ensure that no alternatives are overlooked. Programmers can code portions of a program right from a decision table. Figure 7a shows the format of a decision table; Figure 7b gives an example of a decision table that applies to the Swift Sport Shoes system.

System Requirements

As noted earlier, the purpose of gathering and analyzing data is twofold: to understand the system and, as a by-product of that understanding, to establish the **system requirements,** a detailed list of the things the system must be able to do. You need to determine and document specific user needs. A system that a bank teller uses, for example, needs to be able to retrieve a customer record and display it on a screen within five seconds.

The importance of accurate requirements cannot be overemphasized, because the design of the new system will be based on the system requirements. Furthermore, the analyst and management must come to clear agreement on the system requirements, since a misunderstanding can result in a poor evaluation of the new system and even cause a delay in project completion. Note the requirements for the Swift system shown in Figure 8.

Report to Management

When you have finished the systems analysis phase, you present a report to management. This report summarizes the problems you found in the current system, describes the requirements for the new system, includes a cost analysis, and makes recommendations on what course to take next. If the

InfoBit

It takes considerable subject matter knowledge and a bit of political savvy for the systems analyst to separate what the users want from what they need. Still, this is a critical distinction that can save the client substantial amounts of money in the long run, provided that the systems analyst has the diplomatic skills to get the users to agree.

InfoBit

A systems analyst needs to focus not just on how the proposed system can automate the current business practice, but how a new system could actually improve the underlying business process. As an example, consider a process that requires five signatures on purchases under one thousand dollars. The proposed system could be designed to support e-mail and electronic signatures for all five levels of authority. It might be more reasonable, however, to take the opportunity provided by the new system to reduce the number of signatures required.

Figure 7 Decision tables. (a) The format of a decision table. The table is organized according to the logic that "If this condition exists or is met, then do this." (b) A decision table example. This decision table, which describes the current ordering procedure at Swift Sport Shoes, takes into consideration whether a requisition for goods from a store is valid, the availability of the wanted goods in the warehouse or some other Swift store, whether the quantity ordered warrants an inventory order, and whether the order is a special order for a customer. Examine rule 4. The requisition is valid, so proceed. The desired goods are not available in either the warehouse or in another store, so they must be ordered. However, there is not the required volume of customer demand to place a standard inventory order now, so the requisition is put on hold until there is. (In other words, this order will be joined with others.) And finally, since this is a special customer order and the order is on hold, a back order notice is sent.

(a)

Order procedure	Rules					
	1	2	3	4	5	6
Valid requisition	Y	Y	Y	Y	Y	N
Available warehouse	Y	N	N	N	N	—
Available another store	—	Y	N	N	N	—
Required order volume	—	—	Y	N	N	—
Special customer order	—	—	—	Y	N	—
Transfer goods from warehouse	X					
Transfer goods from store		X				
Determine vendor			X			
Send purchase order			X			
Hold requisition				X	X	
Send back order notice				X		
Reject requisition						X

(b)

InfoBit

One reason requirements are so difficult to set firmly is that the prospect of a new system forces users to rethink their former requirements. After users actually see what an automated system can do, they may think of new ways the system could help business, and that leads to new requirements. If the intention was to practice some sort of incremental or prototype-based development all along, changing requirements can be treated as a natural part of the life cycle, and need not cause serious repercussions.

SWIFT SPORT SHOES: REQUIREMENTS

The requirements for the Swift Sport Shoes inventory system are as follows:

- Capture inventory data from sales transactions
- Implement automatic inventory reordering
- Implement a standardized interstore transfer system
- Provide both on-demand and scheduled management reports
- Provide security and accounting controls throughout the system
- Provide a user-oriented system whose online usage can be learned by a new user in one training class
- Reduce operating costs of the inventory function by 20%

Figure 8 System requirements. These are the requirements for an inventory system for Swift Sport Shoes.

project is significant, you may also make a formal presentation, including visual displays. If management decides to pursue the project, you move on to phase 3.

Phase 3: Systems Design

The **systems design phase** is the phase in which you actually plan the new system. This phase is divided into two subphases: **preliminary design,** in which the analyst establishes the new system concept, followed by **detail design,** in which the analyst determines exact design specifications. The reason this phase is divided into two parts is that an analyst wants to make sure management approves the overall plan before spending time and money on the details of the new system.

Preliminary Design

The first task of preliminary design is to review the system requirements and then consider some of the major aspects of a system. Should the system be centralized or distributed? Should the system be online? Can the system be run on the users' personal computers? How will input data be captured? What kind of reports will be needed? The questions can go on and on.

A key question that should be answered early on is whether packaged software should be purchased, as opposed to having programmers write custom software. That is, instead of designing, developing, and implementing a new system from scratch, you may be able to obtain an existing system—**acquisition by purchase**—that meets your client's requirements. This may be tricky because clients often think that their problems are unique. However, if the new system falls into one of several major categories, such as accounting or inventory control, you will find that many software vendors offer packaged solutions. A packaged solution should meet at least 75 percent of client requirements. For the remaining 25 percent, the client can adjust ways of doing business to match the package software or, more expensively, the packaged software can be **customized,** or altered, to meet the client's special needs.

Another possibility is **outsourcing,** which means turning the system over to an outside agency to develop. Large organizations that employ their own computer professionals may outsource certain projects, especially if the subject matter is one in which a reputable outsourcing firm specializes. The outsourcing company then turns the completed system over to the client. Some organizations outsource most or all of their computer projects, preferring to avoid bearing the costs of keeping their own staff. (In fact, organizations that do not retain their own computer professionals usually outsource the entire project from its inception; this is the case, for example, in the accompanying case study, in which Swift Sport Shoes engages Software Systems, Inc.)

If you proceed with an in-house design, then, together with key personnel from the client organization, you determine an overall plan. In fact, it is common to offer alternative plans, called **candidates.** Each candidate meets the client's requirements but with variations in features and costs. The chosen candidate is usually the one that best meets the client's current needs and is flexible enough to meet future needs.

At this stage it is wise to make a formal presentation of the selected plan, or possibly of all the alternatives. The point is that you do not want to com-

CASE STUDY   *Systems Design*

The store managers, who were uneasy at the beginning of the study, are by now enthusiastic participants in the design of the new system they are counting on for better control of their inventory. As part of the preliminary design phase, you offer three alternative system candidates for consideration.

The first is a centralized system, with all processing done on the headquarters computer and batch reports generated on a daily basis and delivered by messenger to the stores. This system would provide little control in the stores and thus it is not considered seriously, being mentioned only because of its relatively low cost. The third candidate takes the opposite approach, placing all processing in the stores on their own computers. This approach proves attractive to the store managers but does not give the headquarters staff as much control or vision as they need.

The second candidate, the one eventually selected, is a client/server network system that uses point-of-sale (POS) terminals and a server in each store, with a larger server at the headquarters office. The POS terminals will be connected to the in-store server, which supplies prices and also captures sales transaction data. The captured sales data will be sent to the main server at the end of the day, where it will be used to update the inventory file and to produce inventory transfer reports that will be sent to the

warehouse and reorder reports that will be sent to purchasing. A key ingredient of the proposed solution is an automatic reorder procedure: The computer generates orders for any product shown to be below the preset reorder mark. A further enhancement is that each store will have a terminal devoted to inquiries, via a server program, about product availability, with the capability of ordering product transfers from another store. This fairly simple system is appropriate for the present size of the organization, with only 10 stores, but will continue to be workable for growth to 20 stores. Figure 9 shows the overall design from a user's viewpoint.

You make a formal presentation to Mr. Iverson and other members of company management. Slides you prepared on a personal computer (with special presentation software) accent your points visually. After a brief statement of the problem, you list anticipated benefits to the company; these are listed in Figure 10. You explain the design in general terms and describe the expected costs and schedules. With the money saved from the reduced inventory expenses, you project that the system development costs will be repaid in four years. Swift Sport Shoes management accepts your recommendations, and you proceed with the detail design phase. You then design printed reports

and screen displays for managers; samples are shown in Figures 11 and 12.

There are many other exacting and time-consuming activities associated with detail design. Although space prohibits discussing them, here is a list of some of these tasks, to give you the flavor of the complexity: You must plan the use of wand readers to read stock codes from merchandise tags, plan to download the price file daily to be available to the store sever and thus the POS terminals, plan all files on disk with regular backups on tape, design the records in each file and the methods to access the files, design the data communications system, draw diagrams to show the flow of the data in the system, and prepare structure charts of program modules. (Figure 14 shows a skeleton version of a systems flowchart that represents part of the inventory processing.) Some of these activities, such as design of a data communications system, require certain expertise, so you may be coordinating with specialists. Several systems controls are planned, among them a unique numbering system for stock items and validation of all data input at the terminal.

You make another presentation to managers and more technical people, including representatives from information systems. You are given the go-ahead.

mit time and energy to—nor does the client want to pay for—a detailed design until you and the client agree on the basic design. Such presentations often include a drawing of the system from a user's perspective, such as the one shown in Figure 9 for the Swift Sport Shoes system. This is the time to emphasize system benefits; see the list in Figure 10.

Prototyping

Building a prototype—a sort of guinea-pig model of the system—has become a standard approach in many organizations. Considered from a systems viewpoint, a **prototype** is a limited working system, or a subset of a system, that is developed quickly, sometimes in just a few days. Some organizations use prototyping very loosely, so that it has no true functionality but can

InfoBit

The value of the linear model of software development—the standard life cycle—versus variations using repetition and prototyping have been widely debated in the literature of software engineering. In fact, the linear model is often termed the "waterfall model" and iterative alternatives are termed "whirlpool models."

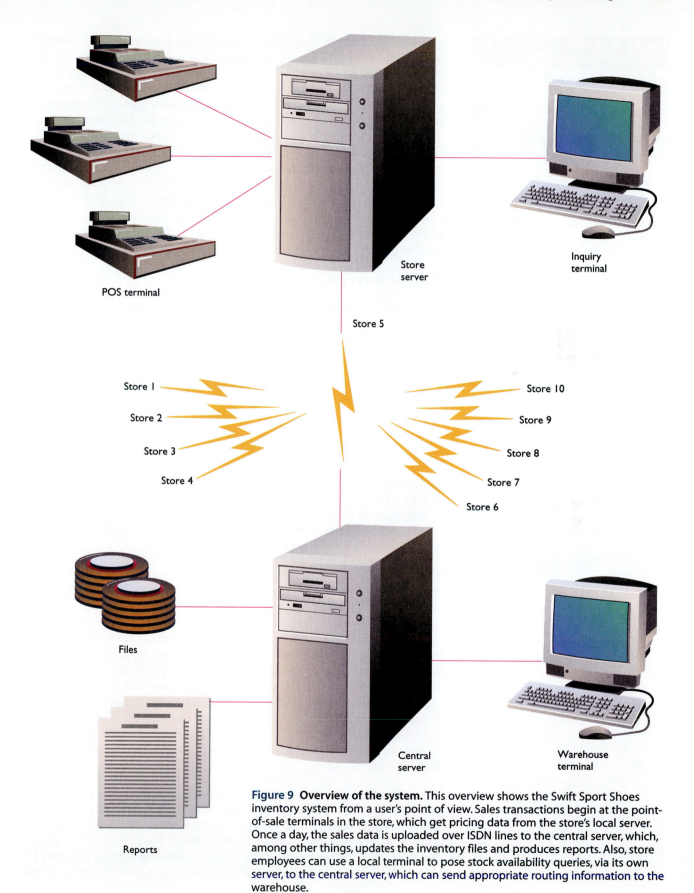

POS terminal

Store server

Inquiry terminal

Store 5

Store 1
Store 2
Store 3
Store 4

Store 10
Store 9
Store 8
Store 7
Store 6

Files

Central server

Warehouse terminal

Reports

Figure 9 Overview of the system. This overview shows the Swift Sport Shoes inventory system from a user's point of view. Sales transactions begin at the point-of-sale terminals in the store, which get pricing data from the store's local server. Once a day, the sales data is uploaded over ISDN lines to the central server, which, among other things, updates the inventory files and produces reports. Also, store employees can use a local terminal to pose stock availability queries, via its own server, to the central server, which can send appropriate routing information to the warehouse.

SWIFT SPORT SHOES: ANTICIPATED BENEFITS

- Better inventory control
- Improved customer service
- Improved management information
- Reduced inventory costs
- Improved employee morale

Figure 10 Benefits. Benefits are usually closely tied to the system objectives. These are the anticipated benefits of the new Swift Sport Shoes inventory system.

InfoBit

For some contemporary, highly graphical applications, an analyst may enlist the services of a graphical artist to help with the layout, color choice, icon design, images and logos required.

InfoBit

Another purpose of detailed design is to ease maintenance of the product after it is built. Those who will modify and correct the system in the future need good documentation of the detail design. This is particularly true in most software companies where programmer turnover is high. Design documentation reduces the training costs and shortens the learning curve for newly hired programmers who will maintain an existing system.

InfoBit

Planning for input requirements may sound obvious, but a number of systems have actually been designed and built only to fail to perform adequately because the misunderstood the volume of input data. In these cases simple arithmetic (number of users times number of keystrokes per hour times messages) would have shown that the system was infeasible from the very beginning.

produce output that *looks like* output of the finished system, enabling users to see and evaluate it. The idea is that users can get an idea of what the system might be like before it is fully developed. Many organizations develop a prototype as a working model, one that can be tinkered with and fine-tuned. No one expects users to be completely satisfied with a prototype, so requirements can be revised before a lot has been invested in developing the new system.

Could you adopt this approach to systems development? It seems at odds with this chapter's systems development life cycle, which promotes doing steps in the proper order. And yet many analysts in the computer industry are making good use of prototypes. The prototype approach exploits advances in computer technology and uses powerful, high-level software tools. These software packages allow analysts to build systems quickly in response to user needs. The systems produced can then be refined as they are used until the fit between user and system is acceptable.

Detail Design

Let us say that the users have accepted your design proposal and you are on your way. You must now develop detailed design specifications, or a **detail design.** This is a time-consuming part of the project, but it is relatively straightforward.

In this phase every facet of the system is considered in detail. Here is a list of some detail design activities: designing output forms and screens, planning input data forms and procedures, drawing system flowcharts, planning file access methods and record formats, planning database interfaces, planning data communications interfaces, designing system security controls, and considering human factors. This list is not comprehensive, nor will all activities listed be used for all systems. Some analysts choose to plan the overall logic at this stage, preparing program structure charts, pseudocode, and the like.

Normally, in the detail design phase, parts of the system are considered in this order: output requirements, input requirements, files and databases, systems processing, and systems controls and backup.

Output Requirements Before you can do anything, you must know exactly what the client wants the system to produce—the output. As an analyst, you must also consider the *medium* of the output—paper, computer screen, and so on. In addition, you must determine the *type* of reports needed (summary, exception, and so on) and the *contents* of the output—what data is needed for the reports. The *forms* that the output will be printed on are also a consideration; they may need to be custom-printed if they go outside the organization to customers or stockholders. You may wish to determine the report format by using a **printer spacing chart,** which shows the position of headings, the spacing between columns, and the location of date and page numbers (Figure 11). You may also use screen reports, mock-ups on paper of how the screen will respond to user queries. A sample screen report is shown in Figure 12.

Input Requirements Once your desired output is determined, you must consider what kind of input is required to produce it. First you must consider the input *medium:* Will you try to capture data at the source via point-of-sale (POS) terminals? Must the input be keyed from a source document? Next you must consider *content* again—what fields are needed, the order in which they appear, and the like. This in turn may involve designing *forms*

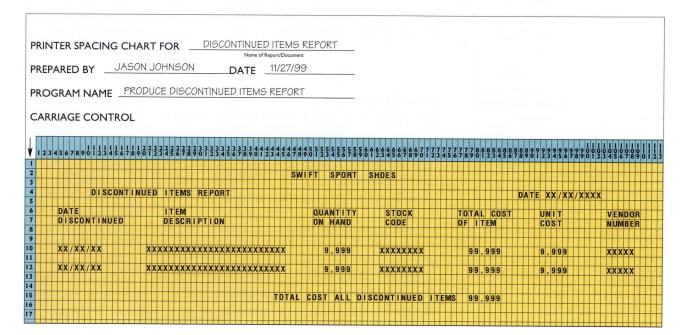

PRINTER SPACING CHART FOR   DISCONTINUED ITEMS REPORT
Name of Report/Document

PREPARED BY   JASON JOHNSON   DATE   11/27/99

PROGRAM NAME   PRODUCE DISCONTINUED ITEMS REPORT

CARRIAGE CONTROL

	SWIFT SPORT SHOES					
DISCONTINUED ITEMS REPORT					DATE XX/XX/XXXX	
DATE DISCONTINUED	ITEM DESCRIPTION	QUANTITY ON HAND	STOCK CODE	TOTAL COST OF ITEM	UNIT COST	VENDOR NUMBER
XX/XX/XX	XXXXXXXXXXXXXXXXXXXXXXX	9,999	XXXXXXXX	99,999	9,999	XXXXX
XX/XX/XX	XXXXXXXXXXXXXXXXXXXXXXX	9,999	XXXXXXXX	99,999	9,999	XXXXX
	TOTAL COST ALL DISCONTINUED ITEMS	99,999				

that will organize data before it is entered. You need to plan some kind of input *validation* process, a check that data is reasonable as well as accurate; you would not expect a six-figure salary, for example, for someone who works in the mail room. Finally, you need to consider input *volume*, particularly the volume at peak periods. Can the system handle it? A mail-order house, for instance, may have to be ready for higher sales of expensive toys during the December holiday season than at other times of the year.

Files and Databases   You need to consider how the files in your computer system will be organized: sequentially, directly, or by some other method. You also need to decide how the files should be accessed, as well as the for-

Figure 11 Example of a printer spacing chart. This chart shows how a systems analyst wishes the report format to look—headings, columns, and so on—when displayed on a printer. This example shows discontinued items, a report that is part of the new Swift Sport Shoes system. Xs represent alphabetic data, and 9s represent numeric data.

**SWIFT SPORT SHOES
INVENTORY QUERY**   XX/XX/XXXX

Enter stock code   XXXXXXXX
Item description: XXXXXXXXXXXX
Supplier code: XXXXX
Retail price: $9,999.99

Location	Qty on hand	Location	Qty on hand
XXX	99999	XXX	99999
XXX	99999	XXX	99999
XXX	99999	XXX	99999
XXX	99999	XXX	99999

Total Qty on hand: 999999
Total Qty on order: 999999
Print inventory report Y/N?   X

Figure 12 Example of a screen report. This screen report layout has been designed as part of the Swift Sport Shoes system. The purpose of the screen is to give information about how much of a given stock item is in each store. The report shows an approximation of what the user will see on the screen after entering a stock code.

InfoBit

Mission-critical business systems are expected to run non-stop and cannot tolerate failure due a journal file exceeding its limits. A typical approach is to keep two copies of a journal file, say JOURNAL.OLD and JOURNAL.NEW; when JOURNAL.NEW reaches the maximum size, JOURNAL.OLD is automatically overwritten and processing continues.

mat of records making up the data files. If the system has one or more databases or accesses databases used in other systems, you will have to coordinate your design efforts with the database administrator, the person responsible for controlling and updating databases.

Systems Processing   Just as you drew a data flow diagram to describe the old system, now you need to show the flow of data in the new system. One method is to use standard ANSI flowchart symbols (Figure 13) to illustrate what will be done and what files will be used. Figure 14 shows a resulting **systems flowchart.** Note that a systems flowchart is not the same as the logic flowchart used in programming. The systems flowchart describes only the big picture; a logic flowchart represents the flow of logic within a single program.

Systems Controls and Backup   To make sure that data is input and processed correctly, and to prevent fraud and tampering with the computer system, you will need to institute appropriate controls. In a batch system, in which data for the system is processed in groups, begin with the source documents, such as time cards or sales orders. Each document should be serially numbered so that the system can keep track of it. Documents are time-stamped when received and then grouped in batches. Each batch is labeled with the number of documents per batch; these counts are balanced against totals of the processed data. The input is controlled to make sure that the data is accurately converted from source documents to machine-processable form. Data input to online systems is backed up by **system journals,** files that record every transaction processed at each terminal, such as an account withdrawal through a bank teller. Processing controls include the data validation procedures mentioned in the section on input requirements.

Figure 13 ANSI systems flowchart symbols. These are some of the symbols recommended by the American National Standards Institute for systems flowcharts, which show the movement of data through a system.

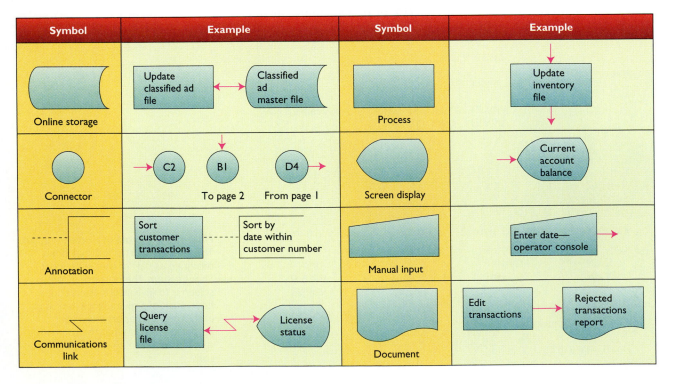

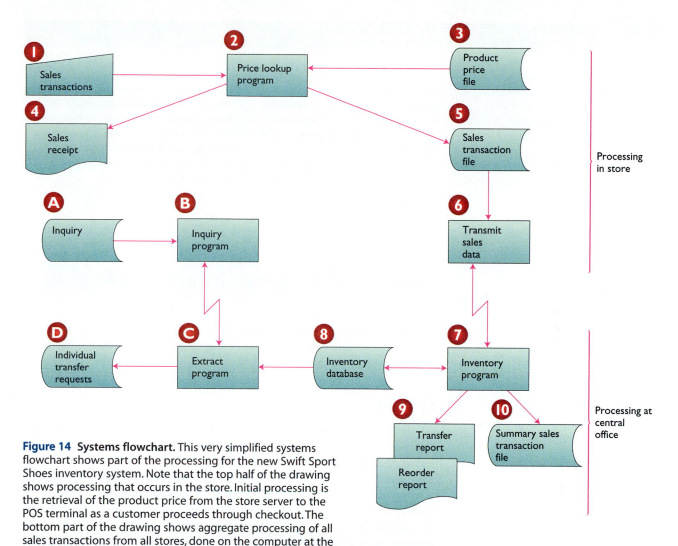

Figure 14 Systems flowchart. This very simplified systems flowchart shows part of the processing for the new Swift Sport Shoes inventory system. Note that the top half of the drawing shows processing that occurs in the store. Initial processing is the retrieval of the product price from the store server to the POS terminal as a customer proceeds through checkout. The bottom part of the drawing shows aggregate processing of all sales transactions from all stores, done on the computer at the central headquarters site. Also shown, on the left side of the chart, is an inquiry from a store to the central server. Step by step: The sales clerk (1) inputs sales transaction data, prompting (2) the POS terminal to look up the item price via an in-store server program that gets the information from (3) the product price file, and then (4) prints a sales receipt for the customer and also stores (5) the sales transaction data on a file. At the end of the sales day, (6) the store server runs a program to transmit the stored sales transactions over ISDN data communications lines to the central server, which (7) processes it for inventory purposes by updating the (8) inventory database, producing (9) transfer and reorder reports, and placing the sales transaction in (10) a file for subsequent auditing. In a separate process, in any store, an employee can use (A) a terminal to invoke (B) the store server program to send a product availability inquiry to (C) a program on the central server, which checks the inventory database and sends a response and possibly also sends (D) a message for action to the warehouse.

It is also important to plan for the backup of system files; copies of transaction and master files should be made on a regular basis. These file copies should then be stored temporarily in case the originals are inadvertently lost or damaged. Often the backup copies are stored off site for added security.

As before, the results of this phase are documented. The resulting report, usually referred to as the detail design specifications, is an outgrowth of the preliminary design document. The report is probably large and detailed. A presentation often accompanies the completion of this stage.

CASE STUDY *Systems Development*

Working with Dennis Harrington of the information systems department at Swift, you prepare a Gantt chart, as shown in Figure 15. This chart shows the schedule for the inventory project.

Program design specifications are prepared using pseudocode, the design tool Mr. Harrington thinks will be most useful to programmers. The programs will be written in C++, since that is the primary language of the installation and it is suitable for this application. Three programmers are assigned to the project.

You work with the programmers to develop a test plan. Some inventory data, both typical and atypical, is prepared to test the new system. You and the programmers continue to build on the documentation base by implementing the pseudocode and by preparing detailed data descriptions, logic narratives, program listings, test data results, and related material.

Phase 4: Systems Development

Finally, the system is actually going to be developed. As a systems analyst you prepare a schedule to monitor the principal activities in **systems development**—programming and testing.

Scheduling

Figure 15 shows what is known as a **Gantt chart,** a bar chart commonly used to depict schedule deadlines and milestones. In our example the chart shows the work to be accomplished over a given period. It does not, however, show the number of work hours required. If you were the supervisor, it would be common practice for you to ask others on the development team to produce individual Gantt charts of their own activities. Organizations that want further control may use **project management software,** which offers additional features, such as allocating people and resources to each task, monitoring schedules, and producing status reports.

Figure 15 Gantt chart. This bar chart shows the scheduled tasks and milestones of the Swift Sport Shoes project. Notice that some phases overlap.

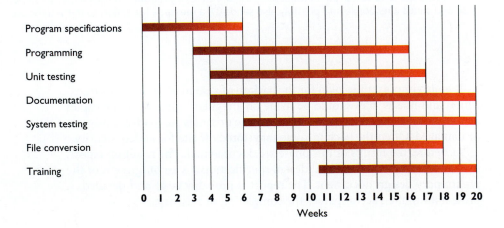

Programming

Until this point there has been no programming, unless, that is, some prototyping was done. So usually, before programming begins, you need to prepare program design specifications. Program development tools must be considered. Some of this work may already have been done as part of the design phase, but usually programmers participate in refining the design at this point. Program design specifications can be developed through detailed logic flowcharts and pseudocode, among other tools.

Testing

Would you write a program and then simply turn it over to the client without checking it over first? Of course not. Thus programmers perform **unit testing,** meaning that they individually test their own program pieces (units), using test data. Programmers even try bad data so that they can be confident that their program can handle it appropriately. This is followed by **system testing,** which determines whether all the program units work together satisfactorily. During this process the development team uses test data to test every part of the programs. Finally, **volume testing** uses real data in large amounts. Volume testing sometimes reveals errors that do not show up with test data, especially errors in storage or memory usage. In particular, volume testing of online systems will reveal problems that are likely to occur only under heavy use.

As in every phase of the project, documentation is required. In this phase documentation describes the program logic and detailed data formats.

Phase 5: Implementation

You may think that implementation means stopping the old system and starting the new system. You are not alone. Many companies believe that also, but they find out that there is much more to it. Even though **implementation** is the final phase, a good deal of effort is still required, including the following activities: training, equipment conversion, file conversion, system conversion, auditing, evaluation, and maintenance.

Training

Often systems analysts do not give **training** the attention it deserves, because they are so concerned about the computer system itself. But a system can be no better than the people using it. A good time to start training—for at least a few of the users—is at some point during the testing, so that people can begin to learn how to use the system even as the development team is checking it out. Do not be concerned that these users will see a not-yet-perfect system; users actually gain confidence in a budding system as errors get fixed and the system improves every day.

An important training tool is the user's manual, a document prepared to aid users not familiar with the computer system. Some organizations employ technical writers to create the user's manual while the system is being developed. But documentation for the user is just the beginning. Any teacher knows that students learn best by doing. Besides, users are as likely to read a

Where Can I Hide?

On November 2, 1998, ABC News published election results on its web site. The complete results of Senate and governors' races were on the web for anyone to see. There was just one problem: *No one had voted yet.* The election was to be on Tuesday, November 3.

It is certainly true that we all make mistakes, but some mistakes are more public than others. This particular story is so chilling that it is still being discussed in systems circles. The phony numbers on the web site had been for testing purposes only. Testing is, of course, an essential function of the system development process, but test results should not be seen by people who might mistake them for the real thing.

InfoBit

Unit testing can be more complete than system testing. A software module or unit has many fewer decisions, inputs and outputs than does the system as a whole; thus it can be much more thoroughly exercised than can the whole system. On the other hand, unit testing cannot take the place of system testing because some defects cannot be detected until all of the individual software units are required to work as a cohesive whole.

While the system is being developed, you take advantage of this time to write the user's manuals. This is done in conjunction with training store personnel and managers in the use of the system. The training is not a trivial task, but you do not have to do all of it yourself. Training on the new POS cash registers, for instance, will be done by the vendor, while you plan training classes for the people who will use the local computers to run programs and send data to the computer at headquarters.

You will have separate classes to teach managers to retrieve data from the system via terminal commands. In both cases training will be hands-on. Company personnel should find the training enjoyable if the on-screen dialogue is user-friendly—that is, the user is instructed clearly every step of the way.

File conversion is painful. One evening after closing time, the staff works into the night to take inventory in the stores. Temporary personnel are hired to key an inventory master file from this data. Transactions for the master file are accumulated as more purchases are made, up until the time the system is ready for use; then the master will be updated from these transactions. After discussing the relative merits of the various system conversion methods, you and Ms. Christie agree that a pilot conversion would be ideal. Together you decide to bring up the original store first, then add other stores to the system one or two at a time.

To evaluate the new system, Mr. Iverson puts together a local team consisting of Ms. Christie, a programmer, and an accountant. Since your documentation is comprehensive, it is relatively easy for the team to check the system completely to see if it is functioning according to specifications. The evaluation report notes several positive results: Out-of-stock conditions have almost disappeared (only two instances in one store in one month), inventory transfer among stores is a smooth operation, and store managers feel an increased sense of control. Negative outcomes are relatively minor and can be fixed in a system maintenance operation.

thick manual as they are to read a dictionary. The message is clear: Users must receive hands-on training to learn to use the system. The trainer must prepare exercises that simulate the tasks users will be required to do. For example, a hotel clerk learning a new online reservation system is given typical requests to fulfill—a family of four for three nights—and uses a terminal to practice. The user's manual is used as a reference guide. Setting all this up is not a trivial task. The trainer must consider class space, equipment, data, and the users' schedules.

Equipment Conversion

Equipment conversion can vary from almost none to installing a mainframe computer and all its peripheral equipment. If you are implementing a small- or medium-size system on established equipment in a major information systems department, your equipment considerations may simply involve negotiating scheduled run time and disk space. If you are purchasing a moderate amount of equipment, such as terminals or personal computers, you will be concerned primarily with delivery schedules, networking, and compatibility.

A major equipment purchase demands a large amount of time and attention. The planning for such a purchase, of course, must begin long before the implementation phase. For a major equipment purchase you will need site preparation advice from vendors and other equipment experts.

Personal computer systems are less demanding, but they too require site planning in terms of the availability of space, accessibility, and cleanliness. And, as the analyst, you may be the one who does the actual installation.

2000 and Beyond

DATA WAREHOUSING

Computer systems have been produced by companies large and small for decades. Many companies have dozens of systems—payroll, personnel, accounting, product design, inventory, sales, and more. In most cases, each system has its own data in files or databases. The data is useful for each system's tasks. For example, employee data such as name, pay rate, and hours worked is needed to produce paychecks and related reports.

What if a manager needs to base a decision on data from a variety of files? Can she, for example, combine data from product design and personnel files to find employees who might be suitable for a certain design team? Can a manager considering an acquisition quickly access and combine data from accounting, inventory, and sales files? Probably not. Generally, data is set up to work with its own system and is not in a format readily available for these kinds of cross-system questions. These systems are sometimes called *legacy systems* because they were probably developed long ago and have been "inherited" by today's employees. The data in a legacy system may not be available online and thus not subject to even the simplest kind of query from a networked manager.

The recent—and future—approach to this problem is data warehousing, the process of combining and reformatting data into a single system that can then be used as a basis for management queries. Companies that specialize in data warehousing offer software to set up and update a data warehouse from existing files and also easy-to-use software that managers can invoke to ask their questions. Data warehousing is neither easy nor inexpensive. But some companies are finding it necessary in order to give managers the information they need.

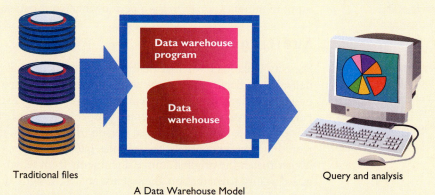

Traditional files

Data warehouse program

Data warehouse

A Data Warehouse Model

Query and analysis

File Conversion

File conversion may be very tricky if the existing files are being handled manually. The data must be prepared in such a way that it is accessible to computer systems. All of the contents of the file drawers in the personnel department, for instance, must be keyed, or possibly scanned, to be stored on disk. Some scheme must be used to input the data files and keep them updated. You may need to employ temporary help. The big headache during this process is keeping all file records up to date when some are still processed manually and some have been keyed in preparation for the new system.

If you are modifying an existing computer system and thus have files already in computer-accessible form, you may need to have a program written to convert the old files to the format needed for the new system. This is a much speedier process than having to key in data from scratch. Nevertheless, it is not unusual for file conversion to take a long time.

System Conversion

During the **system conversion** stage, you actually "pull the plug" on the old system and begin using the new one. There are four ways of handling the conversion.

Direct conversion means that the user simply stops using the old system and starts using the new one—a somewhat risky method, since there is no other system to fall back on if anything goes wrong. This procedure is best followed only if the old system is very small or in unusable condition. A **phased conversion** is one in which the organization eases into the new system one step at a time so that all the users are working with some of the system. In contrast, in a **pilot conversion** the entire system is used by a designated set of users and is extended to all users once it has proved successful. This works best when a company has several branch offices or separate divisions. In a **parallel conversion,** the most prolonged and expensive method, the old and new systems are operated simultaneously for some time, until users are satisfied that the new system performs to their standards.

System conversion is often a time of stress and confusion for all concerned. As the analyst, your credibility is on the line. During this time users are often doing double duty, trying to perform their regular jobs and simultaneously cope with a new computer system. Problems seem to appear in all areas, from input to output. Clearly, this is a period when your patience is needed.

Auditing

Security violations, whether deliberate or unintentional, can be difficult to detect. Data begins from some source, perhaps a written source document or a transaction, for which there must be a record log. Eventually, the data is part of the system on some medium, probably disk. Once the data is on disk, it is possible for an unauthorized person to alter it in some illicit way. How would anyone know that the disk files had been changed and, in fact, no longer match the original source documents from which the data came? To guard against this situation, the systems analyst designs an **audit trail** to trace output back to the source data. In real-time systems, security violations can be particularly elusive unless all transactions are recorded on disk for later reference by auditors. Modern auditors no longer shuffle mountains of paper; instead, they have computer programs of their own to monitor applications programs and data.

Evaluation

Is the system working? How well is it meeting the original requirements, benefits, and budgets? Out of such **evaluation** will come adjustments that will improve the system. Approaches to evaluation vary. Sometimes the systems analyst and someone from the client organization evaluate the system against preset criteria directly related to the requirements that were determined during the systems analysis phase. Some organizations prefer to bring in an independent evaluating team, on the assumption that independent members will be free from bias and expectations.

Maintenance

Many consider maintenance to be a separate phase, one that begins only when the initial system effort is implemented and complete. In any case

MAKING THE RIGHT CONNECTIONS

ACCESS TO RARE BOOKS

Rare books are so rare that, of course, they can be found only in one place. That works for scholars who live nearby or who can visit easily. Then there is the matter of proper authorization; the merely curious will not be allowed within touching range of a truly rare book. But many of us ordinary folk would be thrilled to peruse some rare books. Need we elaborate on who comes to the rescue? It is, of course, the computer and connectivity.

A superb example of such technology at work is the Beinecke Rare Book and Manuscript Library at Yale University. Thousands of photos and illuminated manuscripts have been digitized, stored, and made accessible—in content and view, at least—via the computer and the Internet. Shown here is a page from the Gutenberg Bible, published in 1455, the very first book ever printed.

maintenance is an ongoing activity, one that lasts the lifetime of the system. Monitoring must take place and necessary adjustments must be made if the computer is to continue to produce the expected results. Maintenance tasks also include making revisions and additions to the computer system.

The maintenance task poses interesting problems for programmers. New programmers, fresh from school, may have written only new programs to submit for academic credit. Others have also written programs for their own purposes. But on the first job they are likely to discover that their task is to make changes to programs written by others: maintenance. Some programmers like maintenance; in fact, sometimes a key programmer on development stays on the project to do maintenance, for both familiarity and job security reasons. Programmers who do not like maintenance must extricate themselves from each project as it nears completion and find a way to get on the next new project. The systems analyst, by the way, has long since left.

▲

The preceding discussion may leave the impression that, by simply following a formula, one can develop a system. In fact, novice analysts often believe this to be true. Each system is unique, however, so no one formula can fit every project. It would be more correct to say that there are merely guidelines.

CHAPTER REVIEW

Summary and Key Terms

- A **system** is an organized set of related components established to accomplish a certain task. A **computer system** has a computer as one of its components. A **client** requests a **systems analysis,** a study of an existing system, to determine both how it works and how well it meets the needs of its **users,** who are usually employees and customers. Systems analysis can lead to **systems design,** the development of a plan for an improved system. A **systems analyst** normally does both the analysis and design. Some people do both programming and analysis and have the title **programmer/analyst.** The success of the project requires both impetus and authority within the client organization to change the current system.

- The systems analyst must be a **change agent** who encourages user involvement in the development of a new system.

- The systems analyst has three main functions: (1) **coordinating** schedules and task assignments, (2) **communicating** analysis and design information to those involved with the system, and (3) **planning and designing** the system with the help of the client organization. A systems analyst should have an analytical mind, good communication skills, self-discipline and self-direction, good organizational skills, creativity, and the ability to work without tangible results.

- The **systems development life cycle (SDLC)** can be described in five phases: (1) preliminary investigation, (2) analysis, (3) design, (4) development, and (5) implementation.

- Phase 1, **preliminary investigation,** also known as the **feasibility study** or **system survey,** is the initial consideration of the problem to determine how—and whether—an analysis and design project should proceed. Aware of the importance of establishing a smooth working relationship, the analyst refers to an **organization chart** showing the lines of authority within the client organization. After determining the **nature of the problem** and its **scope,** the analyst expresses the users' needs as **objectives.**

- In phase 2, systems analysis, the analyst gathers and analyzes data from common sources such as written documents, interviews, questionnaires, observation, and sampling.

- The analyst must evaluate the relevance of **written documents** such as procedure manuals and reports. **Interview** options include the **structured interview,** in which all questions are planned and written in advance, and the **unstructured interview,** in which the questions can vary from the plan. **Questionnaires** can save time and expense and allow anonymous answers, but response rates are often low. Another method is simply **observing** how the organization functions, sometimes through **participant observation,** which is temporary participation in the organization's activities. Statistical sampling is also useful, especially when there is a large volume of data.

- The systems analyst may use a variety of charts and diagrams to analyze the data. A **data flow diagram** (DFD) provides an easy-to-follow picture of the flow of data through the system. Another common tool for data analysis is the **decision table,** or **decision logic table,** a standard table indicating alternative actions under particular conditions.

- The analysis phase also includes preparation of **system requirements,** a detailed list of the things the system must be able to do.

- Upon completion of the systems analysis phase, the analyst submits to the client a report that includes the current system's problems and requirements, a cost analysis, and recommendations about what course to take next.

- In phase 3, **systems design,** the analyst submits a general preliminary design for the client's approval before proceeding to the specific detail design.

- **Preliminary design** begins with reviewing the system requirements, followed by considering **acquisition by purchase** (perhaps to be **customized** for the client), **outsourcing** to an outside firm, or in-house development with, perhaps, alternative **candidates.** The analyst presents the plan in a form the users can understand.

- The analyst may also develop a **prototype,** a limited working system or part of a system that gives users a preview of how the new system will work.

- **Detail design** normally involves considering the parts of the system in the following order: output requirements, input requirements, files and databases, systems processing, and systems controls and backup. **Output requirements** include the medium of the output, the type of reports needed, the contents of the output, and the forms on which the output will be printed. The analyst might determine the report format by using a **printer spacing chart,** which shows the position of headings, columns, dates, and page numbers. **Input requirements** include the input medium, the content of the input, and the design of data entry forms. The analyst also plans an input validation process for checking whether the data is reasonable, and the analyst makes sure that the system can handle variations in input volume. The organization of **files and databases** must be specified. **Systems processing** must also be described, perhaps by using a **systems flowchart** that uses ANSI flowchart symbols to illustrate the flow of data or by using the hierarchical organization of a structure chart. The analyst must also spell out **systems controls and backup.** Data input to online systems must be backed up by **system journals,** files that record transactions made at the terminal. Processing controls involve data validation procedures. Finally, copies of transaction and master files should be made regularly.

- Phase 4, **systems development,** consists of scheduling, programming, and testing. Schedule deadlines and milestones are often shown on a **Gantt chart. Project management software** allocates people and resources, monitors schedules, and produces status reports. The programming effort involves selecting the program language and developing the program design specifications. Programmers then do **unit testing** (individual testing of their own programs), which is followed by **system testing** (assessing how the programs work together). **Volume testing** tests the entire system with real data. Documentation of phase 4 describes the program logic and the detailed data formats.

- Phase 5, **implementation,** includes **training** to prepare users of the new system; **equipment conversion,** which involves ensuring compatibility and providing enough space and electrical capacity; **file conversion** to make old files accessible to the new system; system conversion; **auditing,** the design of an **audit trail** to trace data from output back to the source documents; **evaluation,** the assessment of system performance; and **maintenance,** the monitoring and adjustment of the system.

- **System conversion** may be done in one of four ways: **direct conversion,** immediately replacing the old system with the new system; **phased conversion,** easing in the new system a step at a time; **pilot conversion,** testing the entire system with a few users and extending it to the rest when it proves successful; and **parallel conversion,** operating the old and new systems concurrently until the new system is proved successful.

Discussion Questions

1. Which qualities of a systems analyst do you consider to be the most important?

2. Would the following most likely be good projects for acquisition by purchase, for outsourcing, or for in-house development?

   a. An inventory control system for a pizza franchise

   b. A payroll system for a small retailer

   c. A system to network and provide basic software offerings for 13 office personal computers

d. A system to draw airplane-galley installation diagrams for an airline manufacturer

e. A system to process market research data gathered for new toys to be produced by the country's largest toy manufacturer

f. A system to permit networked artists to collaborate by computer on artistic ventures

g. A system to manage patient appointments, dental records, and billing for a clinic with four dentists

h. A system to track traffic tickets issued by the state highway patrol and convey this information to the state drivers' licensing agency

i. A system to perform automated check writing and expense tracking for a funeral home

j. A system to install a terminal in the field office of each franchisee, to be connected to the central headquarters of a truck rental company for the purpose of tracking truck locations

3. Should system evaluation be done by the analyst and client organization or by an independent evaluating team?

Student Study Guide

Multiple Choice

1. Testing of each individual program or module is called
   - a. program testing
   - b. system testing
   - c. volume testing
   - d. unit testing

2. The preliminary investigation of a systems project is also called a(n)
   - a. analysis survey
   - b. feasibility study
   - c. systems design
   - d. evaluation

3. The people who will have contact with the system, such as employees and customers, are referred to as
   - a. programmers
   - b. users
   - c. systems analysts
   - d. clients

4. The SDLC is defined as a project involving
   - a. two phases
   - b. three phases
   - c. four phases
   - d. five phases

5. Phase 1 of a systems project involves
   - a. a system survey
   - b. a systems analysis
   - c. data gathering
   - d. questionnaires

6. The person who fills the role of change agent is the
   - a. systems user
   - b. administrator
   - c. systems analyst
   - d. client

7. The scope and true nature of the problem is determined during
   - a. systems design
   - b. systems development
   - c. preliminary investigation
   - d. systems analysis

8. A chart of positions and departments within an organization is a(n)
   - a. data flow diagram
   - b. organization chart
   - c. project management report
   - d. Gantt chart

9. Testing the system with large quantities of real data is called
   - a. unit testing
   - b. system testing
   - c. parallel testing
   - d. volume testing

10. In the course of a systems project, systems design
    - a. follows systems analysis
    - b. precedes systems analysis
    - c. follows development
    - d. is the fourth phase

True/False

T F   1. Systems analysis is the process of developing a plan for an approved system.

T F   2. Users are people who will have contact with the system.

T F   3. A systems analyst normally performs both analysis and design.

T F   4. Documentation is the least important aspect of a systems project.

T F   5. A feasibility study needs to be conducted following data gathering.

T F   6. Questionnaires are usually a more expensive form of data gathering than are interviews.

T F   7. An organization chart shows the flow of data through an organization.

T F   8. A decision table can help ensure that no alternative is overlooked.

T F   9. In some cases it is possible to acquire a new system by purchasing it.

T F 10. Input requirements should be considered prior to considering output requirements.

Fill-In

1. The process that evaluates a currently existing system to determine how it works and how it meets user needs is called _____.

2. List the three principal functions of a systems analyst:

   a. _____

   b. _____

   c. _____

3. The data analysis tool used to illustrate information flow within a system is the

   _____.

4. As related to data, the two major steps of the systems analysis phase are

   a. _____

   b. _____

5. The overall name for the five phases involved in developing a new project is

   _____.

6. The person or organization that contracts to have a systems analysis done is called the

   _____.

7. The files whose records represent transactions processed by online systems are known as

   _____.

8. The type of interview that permits variation from planned questions is the _____ interview.

9. Since a systems analyst brings change to an organization, the analyst is often referred to as a(n)

   _____.

10. The by-product of understanding the system in the systems analysis phase is

   _____.

Answers

Multiple Choice

1.	d	6.	c
2.	b	7.	c
3.	b	8.	b
4.	d	9.	d
5.	a	10.	a

True/False

1.	F	6.	F
2.	T	7.	F
3.	T	8.	T
4.	F	9.	T
5.	F	10.	F

Fill-In

1. systems analysis
2. a. coordination
   b. communication
   c. planning and design
3. data flow diagram
4. a. data gathering
   b. data analysis
5. systems development life cycle
6. client
7. system journals
8. unstructured
9. change agent
10. system requirements

PLANET INTERNET

As in every other category, the Internet has much to offer to enrich our daily lives. Let's begin with art.

Artworks. Begin on the ArtWeb site to see both original physical works—oil, watercolor, and so forth—or computer graphics artworks. Many graphics images are available for viewing and, with permission, perhaps downloading. The Lightscape Technologies site will be of particular interest to those interested in the use of light effects in computer graphics images. Many images are shown as part of nonart sites, such as Planet Ketchup's "arty tomato" shown here. If you are interested in art as it applies to space, check out the NASA Cassini site, which includes art images of the Cassini mission, a multiyear project to send a two-

Spud Simple
Recipes for creamy mashed poatoes

story robotic spacecraft to Saturn. The image shown here is of the spacecraft landing on Titan, one of Saturn's moons, with Saturn looming in the background. For a more tactile adventure, check out the Antiques trunk.

A family affair. Check out the Kids' Web site, which has links to sites of interest to children so that parents and kids can explore together. Some kids might enjoy the Edible Insects site. They will certainly enjoy the game Fray, whose tall game image is shown here. The whole family will enjoy both CartooNet and the Electronic Zoo sites. Everyone can participate in the birthday site: Just input your name and birthday and it will show up on a list on your special day. If you mention an e-mail address, expect felicitations to roll in. Time to try a

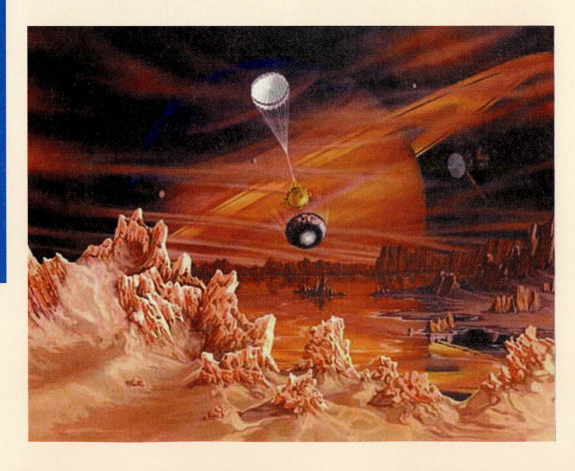

new mealtime experience? There are hundreds of cooking and recipe sites; they can be as simple as reinventing mashed potatoes or as adventurous as making your own sushi.

The stay-at-home tourist. If you'd like to take an electronic field trip, then check the sights and sounds of the Fantastic Forest, or visit Virtual Antarctica, or perhaps go Around the World in 80 Clicks. Another must-see site is Sobek Mountain Travel, whether or not you enjoy trekking. It features fascinating locations and exquisite graphics. If you are curious about New York City, visit the charming Central Park site. The United States of America site has a coast-to-coast map that can be clicked at a particular location to show more detailed information.

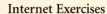

Internet Exercises

1. **Structured exercise.** Begin with the URL http://www.prenhall.com/capron and link to the United States home page. Click on your own home state to see what this site has to say about it.

2. **Freeform exercise.** Travel is just the thing to send you off in different directions worldwide. Begin with your favorite directory, click the travel menu, and link from site to glorious site.

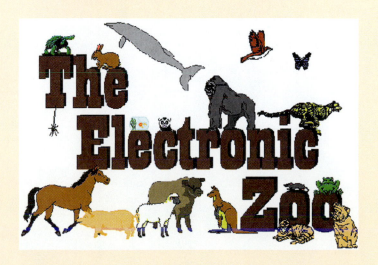

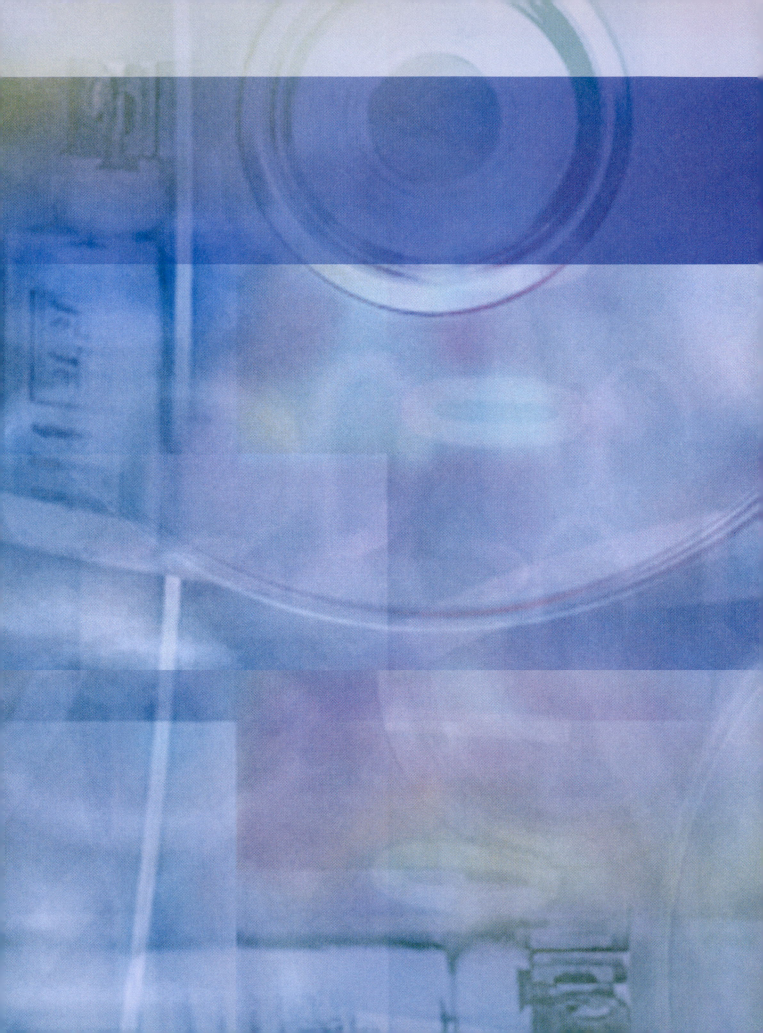

CHAPTER SIXTEEN

MANAGEMENT INFORMATION SYSTEMS

Classic Models and New Approaches

Lloyd Booker pursued a business degree with the goal of a career in management. He was uncertain, however, about his career ambitions. He thought that someday he would like to be at the very top of an organization, perhaps with an office with a stunning view. He thought it was more likely, however, that he would end up somewhere in the middle, reporting to the top bosses but with responsibilities for major activities below him. He assumed that his entry into management would be at the lowest rung on the ladder, where he would be in direct contact with the workers, supervising their operations and making sure they had what they needed to do the job.

As it happened, Lloyd did all these things, but not in the way he expected. While he was in college, he began a computer word processing service, typing up his classmates' term papers and resumés. He used part of his profits to buy a laser printer and desktop publishing software. Thus he was able to produce professional-looking documents and was able to offer his services to local small businesses. Lloyd's business-on-the-side grew beyond his expectations; he decided to go into business for himself full-time after graduation. Lloyd's company eventually specialized in the production end of publishing periodicals and paperback books. As the company grew, Lloyd managed at all levels and, eventually, did indeed have a corner office overlooking the cityscape.

Whether managing your own company or someone else's—whether at the top, middle, or bottom level—the challenge is the same: to use available resources to get the job done on time, within budget, and to the satisfaction of all concerned. Let us begin with a discussion of how managers do this, then see how computer systems can help them.

Classic Management Functions

Managers historically have had five main functions:

- **Planning,** or devising both short-range and long-range plans for the organization and setting goals to help achieve the plans
- **Organizing,** or deciding how to use resources, such as people and materials
- **Staffing,** or hiring and training workers
- **Directing,** or guiding employees to perform their work in a way that supports the organization's goals
- **Controlling,** or monitoring the organization's progress toward reaching its goals

All managers perform these functions as part of their jobs. The level of responsibility regarding these functions, however, varies with the level of the manager. The levels of management are traditionally represented as a pyramid, with the fewest managers at the top and the largest numbers at the lowest level (Figure 1). Often you will hear the terms *strategic, tactical,* and *operational* associated with high-level managers, middle-level managers, and low-level managers, respectively.

Whether the head of General Electric or of an electrical appliance store, a high-level manager must be concerned with the long-range view—the *strategic* level of management. For this manager, usually called an executive, the main focus is **planning.** Consider a survey showing that Americans want family vacations and want the flexibility and economy of a motor vehicle; however, they also want more space than the family car provides. To the president of a major auto company, this information may suggest further opportunities for expansion of the recreational vehicle line.

The middle-level manager of that same company must be able to take a somewhat different view because his or her main concern is the *tactical* level of management. The middle manager will prepare to carry out the visions of the top-level managers, assembling the material and personnel resources to do the job. Note that these tasks focus on **organizing** and **staffing.** Suppose the public is inclined to buy more recreational vehicles. To a production vice president, this may mean organizing production lines using people with the right skills at the right wage and perhaps farming out portions of the assembly that can be done by less expensive, less skilled labor.

The low-level manager, usually known as a supervisor, is primarily concerned with the *operational* level of management. For the supervisor, the focus is on **directing** and **controlling.** Workers must be directed to perform the planned activities, and the supervisor must monitor progress closely. The supervisor—an assembly line supervisor in our recreational vehicle example—is involved in a number of issues: making sure that workers have the parts they need, checking employee attendance, maintaining quality control,

Figure 1 The management pyramid. (a) The classic view of management functions involves a pyramid featuring top managers handling strategic long-range planning, middle managers focusing on the tactical issues of organization and personnel, and low-level managers directing and controlling day-to-day operations. (b) The increasing use of networked personal computers in business is squeezing out middle- and low-level managers, thus flattening the pyramid.

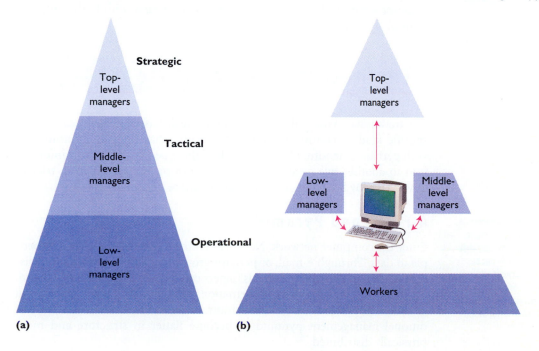

handling complaints, keeping a close watch on the schedule, tracking costs, and much more.

To make decisions about planning, organizing, staffing, directing, and controlling, managers need data that is organized in a way that is useful for them. An effective management information system can provide it.

MIS for Managers

A **management information system (MIS)** can be defined as a set of formal business systems designed to provide information for an organization. (Incidentally, you may hear the term *MIS system,* even though the S in the abbreviation stands for *system;* this is an accepted redundancy.) Whether or not such a system is called an MIS, every company has one. Even managers who make hunch-based decisions are operating with some sort of information system—one based on their experience. The kind of MIS we are concerned with here includes one or more computers as components. Information serves no purpose until it gets to its users. Timeliness is important, and the computer can act quickly to produce information.

The extent of a computerized MIS varies from company to company, but the most effective kinds are those that are integrated. An integrated MIS incorporates all five managerial functions—planning, organizing, staffing, directing, and controlling—throughout the company, from typing to top-executive forecasting. An integrated management computer system uses the computer to solve problems for an entire organization, instead of attacking them piecemeal. Although in many companies the complete integrated system is still only an idea, the functional aspects of an MIS are expanding rapidly in many organizations.

The **MIS manager** runs the MIS department. This person's position has been variously called information resource manager, director of information services, chief information officer, and a variety of other titles. In any case, whoever serves in this capacity should be comfortable with both computer technology and the organization's business.

The New Management Model

The traditional management pyramid that we discussed earlier means a very specific kind of communication. An executive has time to communicate with perhaps a handful of people. Each of these people can convey information to another five or six people below him or her. Information trickles down, layer by layer, either in meetings or more informally.

A Flattened Pyramid

Enter the computer network. Networks connect people to people and people to data. Through e-mail, or perhaps groupware, information can be disseminated companywide as fast as fingers can fly over a computer keyboard. So much for passing along information through traditional hierarchical channels. The dispersion of information via the network has caused the traditional management pyramid to become flatter in structure and more physically distributed.

2000 and Beyond

WORKING IN THE TWENTY-FIRST CENTURY

The millennium has inspired both deep thinkers and not-so-deep thinkers to contemplate our working lives in the twenty-first century. The ability to access information and services online will be a major factor. Here are some guesses about our future online tripping:

- Using a computer and online services will be akin to using a phone. Everyone in or out of an office will know how.
- Since most workers will telecommute most of the time, work will be less central to people's lives. Work will become less of a place to go and more of a thing to do. And, as the feet-up architect shown here can attest, the attire, and even the posture, will be casual.

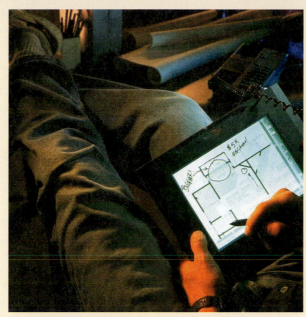

- A telecommuting society means we will stop building skyscrapers to house office workers. However, some people may go to a "work center" just to hang out with other humans and not feel isolated. Since most workers will be at home, the importance of family and community will increase.
- Large public companies will be replaced by hundreds of smaller entre-

preneurial companies that will survive nicely by ordering supplies online, advertising their goods and services online, and selling directly to their customers via the Internet and home computers.
- Workers will use their computers to access information and services related to accounting, the law, and medicine. Thus, since these services will become less labor-intensive, their prices to the consumer will drop significantly.

Eventually, people working at home will use their online computer services for activities beyond their work—to bank, vote, send gifts, get advice, download entertainment, and chat with friends.

What are managers, so long the keepers of information, supposed to do now that, via the network, information is so freely available to so many workers? A good part of a manager's job, communicating above and below, has been replaced by the flow of information through the network. Many industries are finding that, to some extent, they can do without middle managers and have eliminated certain positions. Managers on all levels still have plenty to do, but they are doing it a bit differently from the ways of the past. Networks irrevocably alter the nature of managerial authority and work.

The Impact of Groupware

Consider the impact of groupware on worker interaction. Groupware permits information to be assembled in central databases. People working on a project contribute information to a database and can see and use information contributed by others.

The introduction of groupware can be a searing experience for some managers. Two reasons for this are changes in the way information is shared and changes in managerial authority. People acquire power in an organiza-

Group Work

Interview some network managers at your institution or a local business by doing a "mini job-analysis." How much time does each spend on various activities related to network management (backups, restores, testing, security, adding and removing users, troubleshooting)?

tion by knowing things that others do not. Managers may feel threatened by groupware because they are not accustomed to unstructured information sharing. Studies have shown that groupware works best in organizations where there is already a fairly flexible corporate culture—that is, where an attitude of sharing and even egalitarianism already exists. Perhaps even more painful, managers may not enjoy being in the electronic spotlight when decisions that were once theirs alone are now fair game for comment and change by everyone involved. Furthermore, in contrast to organizations whose focal point is the manager, groupware supports organizations that are team-based and information-driven.

Consider another change from the old ways. Say a particular aspect of a project requires collaboration between two people, Jack and Jim, from different operational units under different management. The traditional way of doing business is for Jack to go to his manager and then for Jack's manager to talk to Jim's manager, who talks to Jim. Then the information flows in reverse, back to Jack. Up, across, down, and then back again. Now it is possible to accomplish the same communication using groupware. Information moves laterally, from worker to worker, saving a roundabout trip through the management maze.

As many managers have discovered, networks make leadership much harder. No longer able to look over their employees' shoulders, managers are learning to rely on other management techniques. They must first give careful attention to the selection and training of employees. Secondly, managers must set clear expectations for their employees. But most importantly, managers must use customer satisfaction as a measuring stick of employee performance in a networked environment.

Teamwork

The availability of networks and groupware coincides nicely with the concept of organizing employees into task-focused teams. Just as the manager is no longer the sole dispenser of wisdom and decisions, so the employee is no longer merely an individual in a static organization. Many companies are organizing their employees in teams. But a team has no permanence; work and people are organized around tasks. When a task is complete, the team is dispersed. When a new task is being tackled, a new team is assembled. Each team is composed of people whose skills are needed for the task at hand. In this kind of work environment, reorganization is a way of life.

Experts consider eight people an ideal team size. If a team gets much bigger than that, team members spend too much time communicating what is already inside their heads instead of applying that knowledge to their parts of the task. But what if the team is behind schedule? Imagine a status meeting in which it is revealed that a critical activity is behind schedule. The activity under scrutiny is to finalize product specifications for an electronic hoop, a toy that can be manipulated remotely and is expected to be a big hit for the upcoming holiday gift-buying season. This activity is critical because other activities down the line, including manufacturing and promotion, cannot begin until specifications are complete. The most common response to tardy projects is to add more people to the project, but this is exactly the wrong thing to do. If outsiders are belatedly added to an existing team, the project quickly comes to a halt in order to bring the new people up to speed. And, of course, from that moment forward, there are more people with whom one must communicate.

GETTING PRACTICAL

YOUR ELECTRONIC AGENT

You have an important job and an activity-packed life. You long ago stopped traipsing from store to store shopping for particular goods or services; instead you use catalogs or the Yellow Pages and the telephone. You even do some shopping at Internet retail sites. A new camera? Flowers for a birthday? A Mexican restaurant? A vacation? The next logical step is to dispatch your own electronic agent to track down the best deal and, if you wish, purchase it for you.

An electronic agent, sometimes called a software agent, is a piece of software to which a person can delegate some degree of responsibility. The agent

is given an order and goes shopping for you throughout the Internet. Suppose you have read some consumer articles and have decided that you want a camera weighing less than a pound with an automatic zoom lens for under $300. You type in these instructions to your computer and let your software agent do the work.

While you go on with other tasks, the agent goes to a directory, finds camera stores, and then sifts through their camera inventories, looking for the required features and price. Eventually, the agent accumulates a list of acceptable choices, which is presented on your personal computer screen at your convenience.

You can then choose which one, if any, to purchase. A variation on this option is available: You can give your agent advance authority to purchase a suitable camera with the best price, probably charging it to a credit card.

Someone eavesdropping on a discussion of agents might think that a real person was being described. The agent, of course, is just sophisticated software. Agent software is available today. What are slow in coming, however, are businesses that are willing to pay to make their list of goods and services available to the network. It is a chicken-and-egg problem: Users will not flock to an online agency until many

merchants and services are online, but the merchants and service providers will not sign up until there are many users.

Software agents are not limited to shopping. An agent is smarter than a standard search engine, partly because the agent indexes not the Web but the user. It knows its user's preferences and can, for example, find a list of appropriate restaurants in Phoenix for your next business trip. The list will include Mexican and Thai food (two of your favorites) but no fast-food joints or cafeterias (anathema).

1 Type instructions to your electronic agent about a camera you want

2 Your agent finds the correct directory, in this case, camera stores

3 The agent checks the inventories of cameras listed by the camera stores

4 When you check back, the agent displays suitable options

What is the proper solution? There is no ideal answer, other than to plan better in the first place, but most organizations find that the better part of wisdom is to rely on the commitment of the original team members. The good news, however, is that a properly composed team of an ideal size is less likely to get into trouble. Communication remains easy, and each member retains a strong sense of responsibility and participation while benefiting greatly from the contributions of teammates.

Top Managers and Computers

Since the early days of computing, managers at all levels have had computer support in the form of printed reports. In more recent times, most managers, even the most resistant executives, have succumbed to the personal computer. Managers have found personal computer software useful for every aspect of their jobs, from something as simple as sending an e-mail message to complex chores such as designing a compensation package for a thousand employees. For top managers, executives who must have the vision to guide the entire company, sophisticated software is needed.

Decision Support Systems

Imagine yourself as an executive trying to deal with a constantly changing environment, having to consider changes in competition, in technology, in consumer habits, in government regulations, in union demands, and so on. How are you going to make decisions about those matters for which there are no precedents? In fact, making one-of-a-kind decisions—decisions that no one has had to make before—is the real test of a manager's mettle. In such a situation you would probably wish you could turn to someone and ask a few "what-if" questions (Figure 2).

"What if. . . ?" That is the question business people want answered, especially when considering new situations. A **decision support system (DSS)** is a computer system that supports managers in nonroutine decision-making tasks. The key ingredient of a decision support system is a modeling process. A **model** is a mathematical representation of a real-life system. A mathematical model can be computerized. Like any computer program, the model can use inputs to produce outputs. The inputs to a model are called **independent variables** because they can change; the outputs are called **dependent variables** because they depend on the inputs.

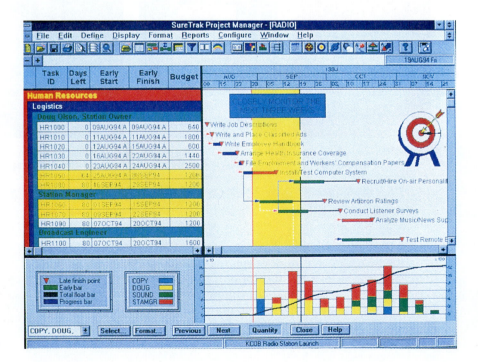

Figure 2 Making decisions with the help of a computer. Business people use computers to try out different scenarios without investing a great deal of time and money.

Consider this example. Suppose, as a manager, you have the task of deciding which property to purchase for one of your manufacturing plants. You have many factors to consider: the appraised value, asking price, interest rate, down payment required, and so on. These are all independent variables—the data that will be fed into the computer model of the purchase. The dependent variables, computed on the basis of the inputs, are the effect on your cash resources, long-term debt, and ability to make other investments. To increase complexity, we could add that the availability of workers and nearness to markets are also input factors. Increasing the complexity is appropriate, in fact, because decision support systems often work with problems that are more complex than any one individual can handle.

Using a computer model to reach a decision about a real-life situation is called **simulation.** It is a game of "let's pretend." You plan the independent variables—the inputs—and you examine how the model behaves based on the dependent variables—the outputs—it produces. If you wish, you can change the inputs and continue experimenting. This is a relatively inexpensive way to simulate business situations, and it is considerably faster than the real thing.

The decision-making process must be fast, so the DSS is interactive: The user is in direct communication with the computer system and can affect its activities. In addition, most DSSs cross departmental lines so that information can be pulled from the databases of a variety of sources, such as marketing and sales, accounting and finance, production, and research and development. A manager trying to make a decision about developing a new product, for example, needs information from all of these sources.

A decision support system does not replace an MIS; instead, a DSS supplements an MIS. There are distinct differences between them. MIS emphasizes planned reports on a variety of subjects; DSS focuses on decision making. MIS is standard, scheduled, structured, and routine; DSS is quite unstructured and available on request. MIS is constrained by the organizational system; DSS is immediate and friendly.

Executive Support Systems

Top-level executives and decision makers face unique decision-making problems and pressures. An **executive support system (ESS)** is a decision support system especially made for senior-level executives. An executive support system is concerned with how decisions affect an entire organization. An ESS must take into consideration

- The overall vision or broad view of company goals
- Strategic long-term planning and objectives
- Organizational structure
- Staffing and labor relations
- Crisis management
- Strategic control and monitoring of overall operations

Executive decision making also requires access to outside information from competitors, federal authorities, trade groups, consultants, and news-gathering agencies, among others. A high degree of uncertainty and a future orientation are involved in most executive decisions. Successful ESS software must therefore be easy to use, flexible, and customizable.

Several commercial software packages are available for specific modeling purposes. The purpose might be marketing, sales, or advertising. Other pack-

FOCUS ON Ethics

We Know What's on Your Hard Drive

Although it is clearly unethical—and illegal—for a worker to use pirated software, what ethical responsibility does a company have to keep tabs on software being used by employees? Most companies recognize that have not only an ethical responsibility but a practical one as well: If pirated software is discovered on an employee's computer, it is the company that will be held liable and be called upon to pay the legal penalties. Companies and organizations must protect themselves from employee ethics lapses by monitoring the software on each personal computer.

ages that are more general provide rudimentary modeling but let you customize the model for different purposes—budgeting, planning, or risk analysis.

Managing Personal Computers

Personal computers burst onto the business scene in the early 1980s with little warning and less planning. The experience of the Rayer International Paper Company is typical. One day a personal computer appeared on the desk of engineer Mike Burton—he had brought his in from home. Then accountants Sandy Dean and Mike Molyneaux got a pair of machines—they had squeezed the money for them out of the overhead budget. Nobuko Locke, the personnel manager, got personal computers for herself and her three assistants in the company's far-flung branch offices. And so it went, with personal computers popping up all over the company. Managers realized that the reason for runaway purchases was that personal computers were so affordable: Most departments could pay for them out of existing budgets, so the purchasers did not have to ask anyone's permission.

Managers, at first, were tolerant. There were no provisions for managing the purchase or use of personal computers, and there certainly was no rule against them. And it was soon apparent that these machines were more than toys. Pioneer users had no trouble justifying their purchases—their increased productivity said it all. In addition to mastering software for word processing, spreadsheets, and database access, these users declared their independence from the MIS department (Figure 3).

Managers, however, were soon faced with several problems. The first was that no one person was in charge of the headlong plunge into personal computers. The second problem was incompatibility—the new computers came in an assortment of brands and models and did not mesh well. Software that

Figure 3 Personal computers.
Managers must monitor the use of personal computers in the workplace.

worked on one machine did not necessarily work on another. Third, users were not as independent of the MIS department as they had thought—they needed assistance in a variety of ways. In particular, they needed data that was in the hands of the MIS department. In addition, companies were soon past the stage of the initial enthusiasts; they wanted all kinds of workers to have personal computers, and those workers needed training. Furthermore, in just a few years, most companies networked their computers together, bringing a whole new set of responsibilities and problems. Finally, many companies had so many personal computers that they did not know how many they had, or where they were, or what software was on them. Many organizations solved these management problems in the following ways:

- They corrected the management problem by creating a new position called the personal computer manager, which often evolved to the network manager.
- They addressed the compatibility problem by establishing acquisition policies.
- They solved the assistance problem by creating information centers and providing a variety of training opportunities.
- They used software to locate, count, and inventory their personal computers.
- They considered the total cost of ownership of personal computers.

Let us examine each of these solutions.

The Personal Computer Manager

The benefits of personal computers for the individual user have been clear almost from the beginning: increased productivity, worker enthusiasm, and easier access to information. But once personal computers move beyond entry status, standard corporate accountability becomes a factor. Large companies are spending millions of dollars on personal computers, and top-level managers want to know where all this money is going. Company auditors begin worrying about data security. The company legal department begins to worry about workers copying software illegally. Before long, everyone is involved, and it is clear that someone must be placed in charge of personal computer use. That person is the **personal computer manager.**

There are three prospective problem areas that need the attention of this manager:

- **Technology overload.** The personal computer manager must maintain a clear vision of company goals so that users are not overwhelmed by the massive and conflicting claims of aggressive vendors plying their wares. Users engulfed by phrases like *network topologies* and *file gateways* or a jumble of acronyms can turn to the personal computer manager for guidance.
- **Data security and integrity.** Access to corporate data is a touchy issue. Many personal computer users find they want to download (or access) data from the corporate mainframe to their own machines, and this presents an array of problems. Are they entitled to the data? Will they manipulate the data in new ways and then present it as the official version? Will they expect the MIS to take the data back after they have done who-knows-what with it? The answers to these perplexing questions are not always clear-cut, but at least the personal computer manager will be tuned in to the issues.

Critical Thinking

Why would employees use illegal copies of software on company computers? (Just as personal computer hardware was ushered in to many corporate environments in a series of "localized" purchases by individual users and managers, personal computer software is sometimes "sneaked" into corporations in violation of copyright restrictions. Employees may use their own personal copies of software on company computers because their employer has turned down their request for a particular software package. This situation poses an ethical problem for the user and potential legal problems for the employer.)

InfoBit

Clear and widely publicized policy is often as important in keeping corporate data secure as is technology. In spot checks and security audits of some companies, many security breaches were found to be the unintentional result of employees who did not realize the risk posed by their computer use. An example is the (legitimate) use of corporate credit cards to purchase work-related software or books over insecure links or from untrustworthy sources.

MAKING THE RIGHT CONNECTIONS
BLUETOOTH

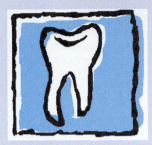

Notebook computers, cellular phones, and personal digital assistants have certainly been a boon for travelers, especially business professionals. No matter what your job is, or where it takes you, there is a device you can carry that will make connectivity easier. There is just one problem: For every device you add to your mobile computing arsenal, you must have another wire, cradle, or adapter of some sort to connect that device to your personal computer, as well as software to make the two devices talk to each other. But how much more can your briefcase take before it explodes in a mass of tangled wires?

Short-range radio technology
Instead, you could do away with the wires and insert small chips—radio chips. Suppose now that those devices in your briefcase can communicate with each other—wirelessly. The ability to have wireless connectivity around the globe is a powerful concept, but getting connected across a room is equally important. That is the premise behind Bluetooth, the code name for a low-cost, wireless communications solution based on short-range radio technology.

Scenarios
What could you actually do with Bluetooth? Here are some possibilities:

- Imagine that you are in a meeting with your notebook computer open in front of you. Suddenly the cursor begins to blink and a new e-mail message is displayed on the screen. Your computer is not plugged into anything, your cellular phone is in your briefcase under the table, but you are receiving e-mail over the wireless network. This is possible because your notebook is communicating with your cell phone, which in turn is communicating with the wireless network via the Bluetooth technology radio chip.
- You could walk into your office, put your briefcase down, and have the notebook computer inside it automatically sense that it is in range of your desktop and initiate the exchange of data to update both systems.
- You could walk into a meeting and automatically send copies of your presentation to the computers of everyone in the room.
- You could get off a plane with a cell phone in hand and a notebook computer in your carry-on luggage and transfer all the notebook's incoming and outgoing e-mail by simply pressing a couple of buttons on the phone. Data would be transferred between the notebook and the phone using Bluetooth; the phone would then transmit the notebook's data over

InfoBit

An effective personal computer manager may be able to channel the enthusiasm of the "computer junkie" into useful roles, among them tutor and localized "technical support" person for their own team.

Global Perspective

MIS manager efforts to standardize on a single set of manufacturers, software and configurations may be thwarted by international issues in global companies. Not only may foreign divisions prefer, or even be forced to, purchase different brands of computers, but some American software packages cannot be legally be exported because of copyright, patent, or encryption legal problems.

- **Computer junkies.** What about employees who are feverish with the new power and freedom offered by the computer? When they are in school, these user-abusers are sometimes called hackers; on the job they are often called junkies because their fascination with the computer seems like an addiction. Unable to resist the allure of the machine, they overuse it and neglect their other work. Personal computer managers usually respond to this problem by setting down guidelines for computer use.

The person selected to be the personal computer manager is usually from the MIS area. Ideally, this person has a broad technical background, understands both the potential and the limitations of personal computers, and is well known to a diverse group of users.

With the advent of networking, the personal computer manager is often the same person as the **network manager** or, if the network is a local area network, the **LAN manager.** The network manager must keep the network operational. The manager's basic task is to let network users share program and data files and resources such as printers. The network manager is

the cellular phone network. You would not even need to remove the notebook from the carry-on bag.

How it will work

Bluetooth technology will use integrated radio transceivers built on tiny microchips about a half-inch square. Bluetooth chips will be embedded into both computer and communication devices. Thus begins the long-anticipated convergence of computing and communications. Bluetooth technology will use—bear with us for a minute—the 2.45-GHz ISM (Industrial Scientific Medical) frequency band of the radio spectrum, which is free and is not licensed by the FCC. This means that you will not have to get permission from the FCC to use the band and that Bluetooth devices can be used globally. Equipped with the radio chip, Bluetooth devices will be able to talk

to one another—exchanging voice and data information—at data speeds up to 1 megabyte per second, within a range of about 30 feet. Unlike existing infrared networking, the radio-based technology of Bluetooth will work when line of sight is not available; the connecting devices need not even be in the same room. Each device will have a unique 48-bit address. Built-in encryption and verification will be provided.

The players

Founding members of the Bluetooth alliance are Intel, Ericsson, Nokia, Toshiba, and IBM; they were soon supported by nearly 100 companies, such as Motorola, Qualcomm, Compaq, Dell, 3COM Palm, VLSI, Xircom, and Lucent. The purpose of the alliance is to establish a de facto standard for the air interface and the software that controls it, thereby ensuring connectivity

between devices of different manufacturers. In addition to its simplicity, a major reason that analysts are high on Bluetooth technology is the list of big-name manufacturers integrating the technology into their products.

Win-win

Bluetooth appears to be a win for the computer industry. Most computer manufacturers have wanted to enable wireless communications but have been unable to determine which wide-area networks to support. The Bluetooth solution will eliminate this problem by leaving this decision to the makers of phones and modems and other wide-area network devices. Bluetooth also appears to be a win for the communications industry. Communications companies will no longer have to build external cables and PC cards so that their wireless phones and network cards can interface with

computers. A Bluetooth module built into the phone or wireless network connection points will enable it to send and receive information to and from any computer so equipped. The first Bluetooth-enabled products will include portable computers, personal digital assistants, digital cellular phones, printers, projectors, and hands-free headsets. Network access points will also support Bluetooth technology for local area and wide area networks.

A rose by any other name

Finally, what about that name, Bluetooth? It has nothing to do with teeth; the image shown here is just an attention-getter. No, Bluetooth was named, appropriately, after tenth-century Danish king Harald Bluetooth, noted for his unification talents: He is credited with joining all the provinces of Denmark under a single crown.

responsible for installing all software on the network and making sure that existing software runs smoothly. The network manager also must make sure that backup copies are made of all files at regular intervals. In addition, the network must be kept free from viruses and other illegal software intrusions. The greatest challenge may be to make sure that the network has no unauthorized users.

Company managers often underestimate the amount of work it takes to keep even a small network going. In a large company an individual or even an entire team of people may be dedicated to this task. In a small company the network may be managed by someone who already has a full-time job at the company.

Personal Computer Acquisition

As we noted, workers initially purchased personal computers before any companywide or even officewide policies had been set. The resulting compatibility problems meant that they could not easily communicate or share data.

InfoBit

One of the most vexing problems facing LAN managers who would like to streamline their operations by moving to a single networking environment is the problem of "island LANs." In existing companies, individual divisions or groups may already have a significant installed base of network applications and protocols incompatible with the emerging corporate standard. Building, maintaining, integrating or migrating these heterogeneous networks is one of the biggest challenges in corporate MIS network management.

Consider this example: A user's budgeting process calls for certain data that resides in the files of another worker's personal computer or perhaps involves figures output by the computer of a third person. If the software and machines these people use do not mesh, compatibility becomes a major problem.

In many companies MIS departments have now taken control of personal computer acquisition. The methods vary, but they often include establishing standards and restricting the number of vendors used. Most companies now have established standards for personal computers, for the software that will run on them, and for data communications. Commonly, users must stay within established standards so that they can tie into corporate resources. Some companies limit the number of vendors—sellers of hardware and software—from whom they allow purchases. Managers have discovered that they can prevent most user complaints about incompatibility, not to mention getting a volume discount, by allowing products from just a handful of vendors.

The Information Center

The **information center** is the place where workers can get help with software problems. In large organizations, the information center, often called by other names such as *support center,* offers help to users in several forms. The information center is devoted exclusively to giving users service. And best of all, user assistance is immediate, with little or no red tape.

Information center services often include the following:

- **Software selection.** The information center staff helps users determine which company-approved software packages suit their needs.
- **Data access.** If appropriate, the staff helps users get data from the large corporate computer systems for use on the users' computers.
- **Network access.** A staff typically offers information about using the network system, tells how to obtain passwords and authorization, disseminates security information, and probably offers regular classes on the Internet.
- **Training.** Education is a principal reason for an information center's existence. Classes are usually small, frequent, and on a variety of topics (Figure 4). Some information centers offer miniclasses, or a series of miniclasses, during lunch breaks; brown bags are welcome. The information center is not the only form of training, however; we will discuss training in more detail shortly.
- **Technical assistance.** Information center staff members stand ready to assist in any way possible, short of actually doing the users' work for them. That help includes advising on company standards for hardware purchases, aiding in the selection and use of software, finding errors, helping submit formal requests to the MIS department, and so forth.

To be successful, the information center must be placed in an easily accessible location. The center should be equipped with personal computers and terminals, a stockpile of software packages, and perhaps a library. It should be staffed with people who have a technical background but whose explanations feature plain English. Their mandate is "the user comes first."

Training: Pay Now or Pay Later

Any manager knows that simply "dumping" technology—hardware, software, networks, whatever—on workers in the hope of increased productivity would be a disaster. The first obvious approach is to provide training for the new technology, whatever it is.

Figure 4 The information center. Classes are held at the information center to teach managers and other employees how to use the company's computers.

InfoBit

The opportunity to practice training on real hardware and software is vital to successfully using these expensive resources. Research studies have shown that half of the technical knowledge covered in training is lost in the first two weeks to one month if there is not an opportunity to practice and apply it almost immediately.

InfoBit

It is important for supervisors and managers to properly reward and manage "office gurus." A friendly co-worker who is knowledgeable and accessible is a wonderful training resource for less skilled workers. However, if the guru does not receive any additional compensation, attention, or promotion for his or her efforts, and especially if they are still held to the same standards in their own work as those who are only infrequently interrupted with questions, their motivation and productivity are likely to suffer.

Organizations tend to be remiss about training. Years ago, vendors typically included training as part of the hardware or software package. Once training became a separate item with a separate price tag, organizations were more apt to think they could get along without it. Furthermore, although training was once needed for just a few technical workers, now training is needed for entire populations of workers companywide.

Those organizations that do offer training too often rely on the one-shot teacher-in-the-classroom model. This traditional approach, however, does not work well. To begin with, unless the classes are off-site or attendance is rigorously enforced, participation may be sporadic because employees are much more concerned about the real work that has to be abandoned on their desks. Furthermore, especially when new software is the topic, training lasting two days or two weeks, even hands-on in a computer-stocked classroom, yields minimal results.

Workers adopting new technology do need initial training, but they also need follow-up support. One approach that seems to work well is to cultivate home-grown gurus. When confronted with a computer problem, the first instinct of a baffled user is to consult a more knowledgeable friend or colleague. With this in mind, savvy companies, after the first round of train-

Laptop Lane

Laptop Lane sounds more like a place to frolic in the park than what it really is: a private suite at the airport with access to computer connections. You can bring your own laptop computer and hook up to a high-speed line, or you can use one of the offices with fully equipped desktop computers. A concierge will lead you to an individual office where you can close the door and, in complete privacy, write, print, fax, e-mail, surf the Net, make conference calls, or do whatever job you need to do all in one place, right at the airport. Office rental is by the half hour.

ing, ask for volunteers who would like to learn more. These users become the office gurus for that technology. Initially, they may not know a lot more than their colleagues, but they are usually a bit ahead and, by sheer numbers of consultations, accumulate more knowledge than other workers.

In-house support, such as an information center, can be a big factor in the success of new technology. The best guarantee that workers will absorb training, however, is prior motivation, achieved by getting them involved.

Involving the Workers   The catchphrase often used is *empowering the workers.* It is a variation on the systems analyst precept of user involvement. Rather than simply installing new technology and training the workers, begin with the workers—the people who will be using the technology. To put it another way, deal with the people at the same time you deal with the technology.

Paine Webber, a stock brokerage, offers a model approach. Paine Webber wanted to upgrade its brokers' 10-year-old computer system to a network that would offer far more information access and control. The systems analyst began by surveying the attitudes of the 5000-plus brokers. He discovered that approximately one-third of the brokers felt the current system met their needs, another third thought they would like some improvements, and the final third thought that the current system was hopelessly outmoded.

The company's response was to build a dazzling new system with the old system built into it. Paine Webber unfolded the new system branch by branch, emphasizing not the wonders of technology but what the system could do for brokers. The instructors were not technical types but specially trained Paine Webber employees who already knew the brokerage business. This worked well for everyone, even those who were initially reluctant. Workers whose comfort level was the old system could begin with that version, but most of them gradually picked up the features of the new system.

Another issue regarding worker involvement is the generation gap. Employees who grew up playing video games have a built-in advantage over their elders, who may show the foot-dragging signs of a precomputer upbringing. In fact, training experts recommend that big-time computerphobes loosen up by playing computer games. This way they will at least become comfortable with a mouse and with interactions that cause changes on the computer screen.

Enter the Web   Can we be surprised that, along with seemingly everything else, training is also moving to the Web? Text-based training has been in decline for some time, in favor of instructor-led training, but now the trend is to CD-ROMs and Web-based training (Figure 5). Since there is nothing to buy except the training software, computer-based training is an appealing option for small to medium-size businesses.

When convenience, interactivity, and affordability are high on the wish list for training, a Web-based approach may be the best answer. It promises training and collaboration that take place simultaneously at different locations, online mentoring and review, and customized lessons. A popular Web-based training site is ZD University, which offers training in mainstream business and Internet applications (Figure 6).

Do You Even Know Where Your PCs Are?

Many corporate administrators, when put to the test, are embarrassed to admit that they do not know where corporate personal computers are in use

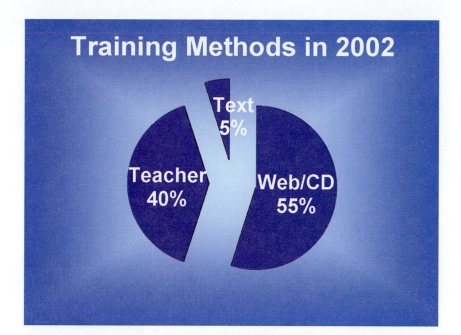

Training Methods in 2002

Text
5%

Teacher
40%

Web/CD
55%

Figure 5 Shift in training methods. By the year 2002, more than half of all computer training will be computer-based.

in the company; in fact, they do not even know how many there are. One manager, for example, was quite certain that the company had 600 personal computers and an average of 12 users per printer. The reality turned out to be quite different; there were 1100 computers and one printer per computer. To make matters even worse, managers may have no idea what software is on the computers—Microsoft Excel or WordPerfect or perhaps the latest incarnation of Doom.

This is a critical problem because administrators may have no idea how to budget for their personal computers. If the computers are hidden, then so are the costs of maintaining them. Clearly, administrators must confront the missing-computers problem.

Specialized computer services now offer a sort of lost-and-found for personal computers and related equipment. Corporate personal computers that are networked—and that means most of them—can be counted and interrogated by software set up on the network. The polling software not only counts computers but also determines their components and software.

Remote Users

Many companies want their sales representatives out of the office, both to reduce office costs and to make the sales effort more effective. But these representatives must have adequate access to computer data. Offering remote users access to data residing in computers in the office frees them from having to carry around large amounts of data. Sales people using laptop computers can connect to the home office to download pricing information from the mainframe to the laptop and to upload order entries from the field to the mainframe computer. The connection also manages electronic mail.

MIS managers have a variety of concerns about remote users and their access to information from the company's mainframe. The first concern is security. Remote users, at the least, should use a password when making connections. Training is a consistent problem because road warriors seldom come into the office for extended periods. Although it seems obvious, trav-

Figure 6 Web-based training. The site for ZD University, which offers training in mainstream business and Internet applications.

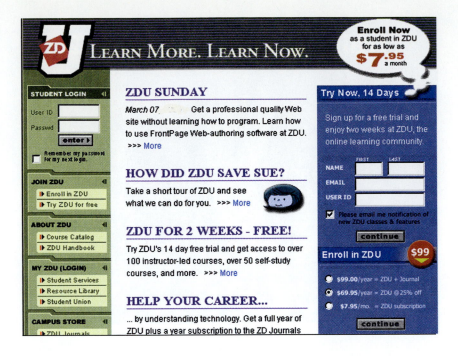

elers need to be trained about preserving their expensive equipment; laptop computers are extremely vulnerable to loss and theft.

Total Cost of Ownership

The **total cost of ownership**—of personal computers—has become such a pervasive concern that magazine articles routinely refer to it by its acronym, **TCO,** without even bothering to explain what the initials represent. TCO methodology for calculating costs of computer ownership in business was first developed in the early 1990s by a consulting company called the Gartner Group. Since then, dozens of consulting firms have helped clients apply TCO analysis to their operations. TCO was developed in response to perceived costs that missed the mark.

Early users thought that the costs of personal computers were paid back rapidly by increased productivity. If only the initial costs, hardware and perhaps some software, are considered, that observation might be true. But the real costs—the total cost—entail training, support, upgrading, maintenance, hardware and software extras, and communications networks. That is, the total cost goes far beyond the computer itself. Some professionals have estimated that the annual total cost of ownership of a personal computer is approximately four times the original cost of the hardware.

Many companies are eager to discover the total cost of ownership and, in particular, reduce those costs. The task is not a simple one. The main obstacle is the complex and nitty-gritty nature of the process itself. There is no simple answer or one-shot approach. Here are a few areas of concern.

Limited Options   A key factor was described above: Standardize the process of ordering hardware and create a very short list of standard options. Carrying this further, managers must define and enforce not only hardware standards, but also software and configuration standards. In essence, the less variation there is, the easier the system is to support—less training, fewer calls for help, and more fixes that help everyone. Defining standards takes an initial investment of time and then regular reviews to evaluate and update.

Helpful Software   A software category that has proven effective is desktop management software, which can perform a variety of functions. From the manager's point of view, the most valuable function is collecting inventory data—who has what version of what software, how often it is used, and so forth. This data can be collected automatically over the network. Other useful products provide automatic electronic distribution of software and software updates. Most such products also check for viruses on a regular basis.

Unhelpful Software   As one manager put it, "We have to limit users' abilities to get themselves in trouble." In effect, this manager was calling for standardized software. In addition to having official purchasing limitations, users must be prohibited from downloading shareware or installing games or other applications they bring from home. The added software can create complications that require extra troubleshooting. Minimizing those risks can reduce the total cost of ownership.

Hardware and Software Upgrades   This is a tricky one. It seems that as soon as the deployment of one upgrade wraps up, plans already are starting for the next. Many a manager has wondered if the benefits of an upgrade outweigh the costs. Does the worker really need faster computers when their tasks are limited to sending and receiving e-mail and the occasional memo? Will the new software enhancements really be used, or even noticed, by most workers? Increasingly, managers are minimizing hardware and software upgrades unless there is significant justification.

Tracking down TCO numbers can be hard work. Even worse, it may have political complications. For example, a staffer may not want to include the travel costs of a trip to a computer trade show. The TCO efforts, in the end, should pay off by giving managers a realistic picture of real computing costs. The net result should be better buying decisions and more efficient use of computer resources.

Leading Business into the Future

Who will manage businesses in the future? Someone once remarked, somewhat facetiously, that all top management—presidents, chief executive officers (CEOs), and so forth—should be drawn from the MIS ranks. After all, the argument goes, computers pervade the entire company, and people who work with computer systems can bring broad experience to the job. Today, most presidents and CEOs still come from legal, financial, or marketing backgrounds. But as the computer industry and its professionals mature, that pattern could change.

There are challenges for managers at every level. In addition to the ordinary technological changes for which they can be somewhat prepared, they face technology on the cutting edge, the subject of the next chapter.

InfoBit

Software, sometimes called *polling software,* can automatically check software inventories. The count of actual copies installed can be matched with the number of copies licensed to ensure that the company's software use remains legitimate. This procedure can help a company avoid legal and ethical entanglements associated with unlicensed or covertly copied software.

CHAPTER REVIEW

Summary and Key Terms

- All managers have five main functions: **planning, organizing, staffing, directing,** and **controlling.** A management pyramid shows that top-level managers focus primarily on strategic functions, especially long-range planning; middle-level managers focus on the tactical, especially the organizing and staffing required to implement plans; and low-level managers are concerned mainly with operational functions—controlling schedules, costs, and quality—as well as with directing personnel.

- A **management information system (MIS)** is a set of business systems designed to provide information for decision making. A computerized MIS is most effective if it is integrated.

- The **MIS manager,** a person familiar with both computer technology and the organization's business, runs the MIS department.

- The traditional management pyramid has been flattened by the dissemination and sharing of information over computer networks. The impact of groupware has removed exclusive manager access to information and has forced managers to share decision making. Some companies are organizing workers into teams around tasks.

- A **decision support system (DSS)** is a computer system that supports managers in nonroutine decision-making tasks. A DSS involves a **model,** a mathematical representation of a real-life situation. A computerized model allows a manager to try various "what-if" options by varying the inputs, or **independent variables,** to see how they affect the outputs, or **dependent variables.** The use of a computer model to reach a decision about a real-life situation is called **simulation.** Since the decision-making process must be fast, the DSS is interactive, allowing the user to communicate directly with the computer system and affect its activities.

- An **executive support system (ESS)** is a decision support system for senior-level executives, who make decisions that affect an entire company.

- When personal computers first became popular in the business world, most businesses did not have general policies regarding them, which led to several problems. Many businesses created the position of **personal computer manager** (later called the **network manager** or **LAN manager**) to ensure coordination of personal computers, established acquisition policies to solve the compatibility problem, established **information centers** to provide assistance to users, provided formal and informal training for users, and used software to monitor their existing personal computers.

Discussion Questions

1. Suppose a team of eight people in a construction firm is designing a new hospital. The team members, drawn from several departments, include two engineers, two architects, an electrician, a plumber, a graphic designer, and a planner. How and by whom might the classic management functions be carried out?

2. Describe a problem situation that could be simulated through a decision support system. Specify the input factors and the types of output.

3. What special pressures might there be on a network manager?

Student Study Guide

Multiple Choice

1. Which of the following is not one of the main functions of managers:
   a. controlling
   c. organizing
   b. pyramiding
   d. directing

2. A decision support system for senior-level executives is called a(n)
   a. model
   c. ESS
   b. MIS
   d. DSS

3. The inputs to a model are called
   a. dependent variables
   c. simulators
   b. spreadsheets
   d. independent variables

4. A mathematical representation of a real-world situation is called a(n)
   a. MIS
   c. network
   b. task
   d. model

5. A computer system that supports managers in non-routine decision-making tasks is called a(n)
   a. information center
   c. DSS
   b. variable
   d. model

6. Low-level managers are usually most concerned with
   a. long-range planning
   c. organizing and staffing
   b. scheduling and costs
   d. planning and organizing

7. Traditional management pyramids have been
   a. suspended
   c. expanded
   b. flattened
   d. eliminated

8. Internal company training is likely to be provided by the
   a. simulator
   c. information center
   b. MIS
   d. LAN manager

9. The MIS manager is likely to be familiar with both
   a. the network and the information center
   c. technology and business
   b. models and simulators
   d. ESS and DSS

10. MIS stands for
    a. Management Information System
    b. Management Internal Simulation
    c. Multiple Integrated System
    d. Model Independent Simulation

True/False

T F 1. The information center typically offers users training and assistance.

T F 2. The function of the network manager is to help executives with decision support systems.

T F 3. Communication of information is most efficient through the traditional management pyramid.

T F 4. Decision support systems help managers in nonroutine decision-making tasks.

T F 5. A model is a mathematical representation of an artificial situation.

T F 6. Middle-level managers focus on planning.

T F 7. Inputs to a model are called independent variables.

T F 8. Groupware is usually focused on groups of executives.

T F 9. The use of personal computers by managers is declining.

T F 10. Simulation is using a model to predict real-life situations.

T F 11. Part of the reason for changes in the classic management model is the increased use of networked computers.

T F 12. A personal computer manager is concerned only with technical issues.

T F 13. The use of groupware encourages workers in different organizations to communicate laterally, as opposed to going through the traditional management hierarchy.

T F 14. The use of networked computers in the organization has made information more unavailable than ever to workers.

T F 15. The flattened management pyramid has significantly increased the need for more mid-level managers.

Answers

Multiple Choice

1. b   6. b
2. c   7. b
3. d   8. c
4. d   9. c
5. c   10. a

True/False

1. T   6. F   11. T
2. F   7. T   12. F
3. F   8. F   13. T
4. T   9. F   14. F
5. F   10. T   15. F

PLANET INTERNET

Need information? Need it fast? Whether commonplace or rare, any information you need is probably somewhere on the Internet.

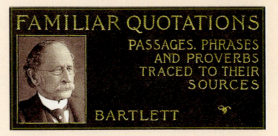

Government resources. The government had a head start and has made excellent use of the Internet. You can also use the resources of the Library of Congress, whose logo is the Stars and Stripes book shown here, or contact the U.S. House of Representatives or even the CIA. You may peruse recent Supreme Court decisions by topic or by case name.

Although you may have little inclination to do so, you can access the Internal Revenue Service site to get forms or advice. The U.S. Census Bureau has an enormous amount of information that is useful to businesses and organizations, large and small. The Smithsonian has searchable historic

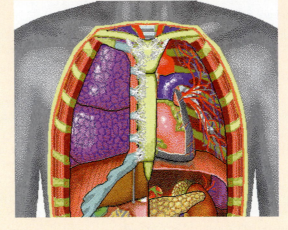

information and a significant online photo collection. The National Archives houses the Declaration of Independence, whose first draft is shown here, the Constitution (indexed), and a wonderful set of historic posters, such as the wartime propaganda image of Miss USA shown here.

Information you can use. Consider bits of information you might need in any given week. A weather forecast for your travel destination? Every sort of weather information is available, for regions and individual cities. The Old Farmer's Almanac supplies crop information and, notably, weather predictions. Buying a new or used car? Pricing information is just a computer away. Going camping? Check the National Parks Service for locations, entrance fees, and campground reservation information.

As you would expect, consumer information is available on the Internet on just about any topic. Need to know something about anatomy? Information, with detailed images, is available on several sites. Bartlett's Familiar Quotations lets you find that needed quote in a hurry. Some sites offer an entire comprehensive library online; others are devoted to information on fairly specific topics, such as the signal year 1968. Dr. Universe, geared to children but useful to anyone, has answers on just about any topic. Finally, would you just like a good book? Project Gutenberg makes books available online.

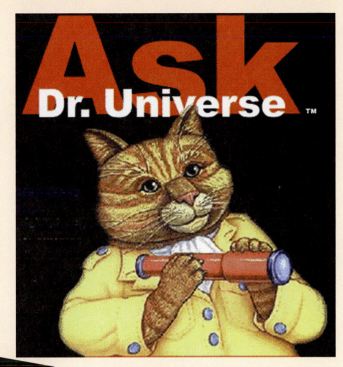

Internet Exercises

1. **Structured exercise.** Begin with the URL http://www.prenhall.com/capron and enjoy the historic posters at the National Archives.
2. **Freeform exercise.** Pick one topic at the Smithsonian to explore in depth.

Robots at Work

We begin with the best "computer workers" of all—robots. When most people think of robots, they probably have in mind the typical humanoid-shaped automaton of classic science fiction movies. But robots of all shapes and sizes are performing a variety of serious tasks—without looking much like people.

1. A multiple exposure of a computer-controlled robot doing arc welding on the pipework of a car exhaust.
2. This robotic arm is used in manufacturing microchips on wafers.

3. This pharmaceutical robot arm can accurately prepare an order of medicine.
4. This robot is guarding art objects at the Los Angeles County Museum of Art. The robot's computer has detailed maps of the museum; it travels on three wheels, using an ultrasonic navigation system. Its detectors can give warnings of smoke, fire, and increased humidity or gases. It can also detect movement and warn of an intruder.

1
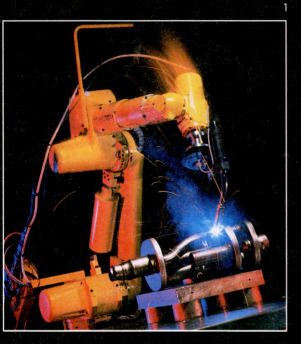

2

3

4
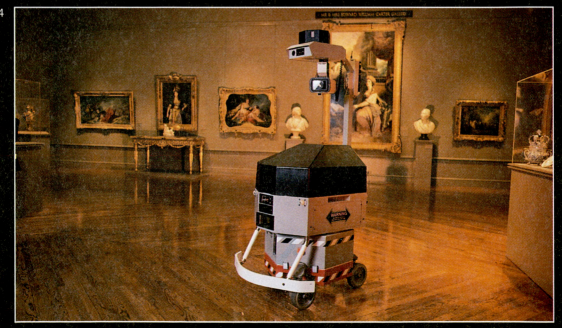

COMPUTERS AT WORK

5

6

Computers in a Variety of Settings

In this gallery we look at some of the ways in which workers put computers to use on the job. The photo on the title page of this gallery shows a lobsterman in Maine using his laptop computer to track schedules, locations, and various money matters.

We know that computers can be found in great numbers in offices. Further, we have become accustomed to seeing workers use computers in public place such as retail stores. But many workers use computers behind the scenes, in places as diverse as farms and chemistry labs and vacation getaways.

5. This Minnesota farmer keeps a small office on one side of the barn.
6. A technician uses a plasma emission spectrometer to check blood samples, and records his work on computer files.
7. Computers are regular tools of the trade on construction sites, as workers—among other things—check specifications and update progress reports.
8. This worker uses the computer to graph and monitor progress of biotechnological water quality control.
9. Just as many people have more than one television, some people have more than one computer. This writer keeps a computer at his main residence and another here, at his vacation home.
10. These architects, in the midst of designing changes to a warehouse, have discussions on site and make changes to their computer records as they go.
11. Aviation engineers work on an engine design.

7

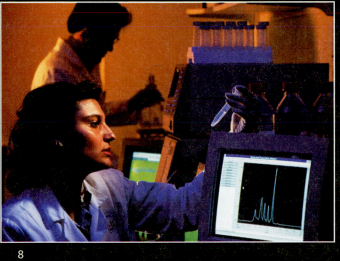

8

9

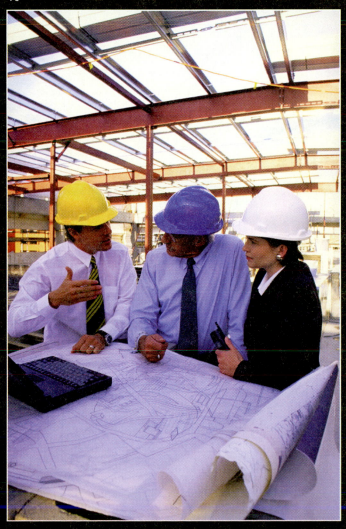

10

11

12

Computers on the Go

Many workers need computers on the job no matter where they are, so they simply take their computers with them.

12. Some workers catch up on work wherever they are, even during lunch hour in the park.

13. This repairman inputs data for each job as he moves from location to location. The data is later used for billing and marketing purposes.

14. This orchard man trucks daily among his trees and pauses on the tailgate to record status data.

15. Researchers studying an Adelie penguin rookery in Antarctica use their sturdy laptops to record and analyze data.

16. This Texas police officer uses her notebook computer to make reports from the field.

17. This marine biologist uses a laptop computer, wrapped to protect it from moisture, to record data he observes in various water-related environments.

18. Many realtors routinely keep information about house currently for sale or rent. They also use their computers to work up financing numbers for buyers.

19. A rancher carries his notebook computer to record field data and look up information about his acreage.

13

14

15

16

17

18

19

Computer Graphics at Work

Computer graphics software lets designers choose from a wide range of colors and styles to create just the image they need, whether for advertising, magazine covers, tourism, or some other useful purpose.

20. Diane Fenster made this illustration to accompany a magazine article comparing color monitors.
21. This stunning image was made by graphic artists to use as their own advertising logo.
22. Marc Yankus made this graphic to be used as a cover for a math book.
23. Matthias Gleirscher won top prize for Mosaic of Life in the good works category in the CorelDraw contest.

22

21

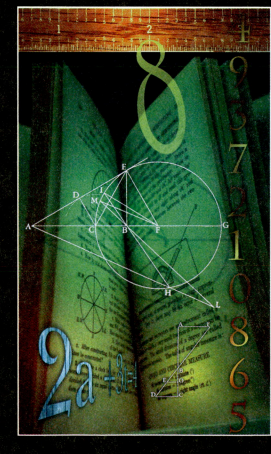

23

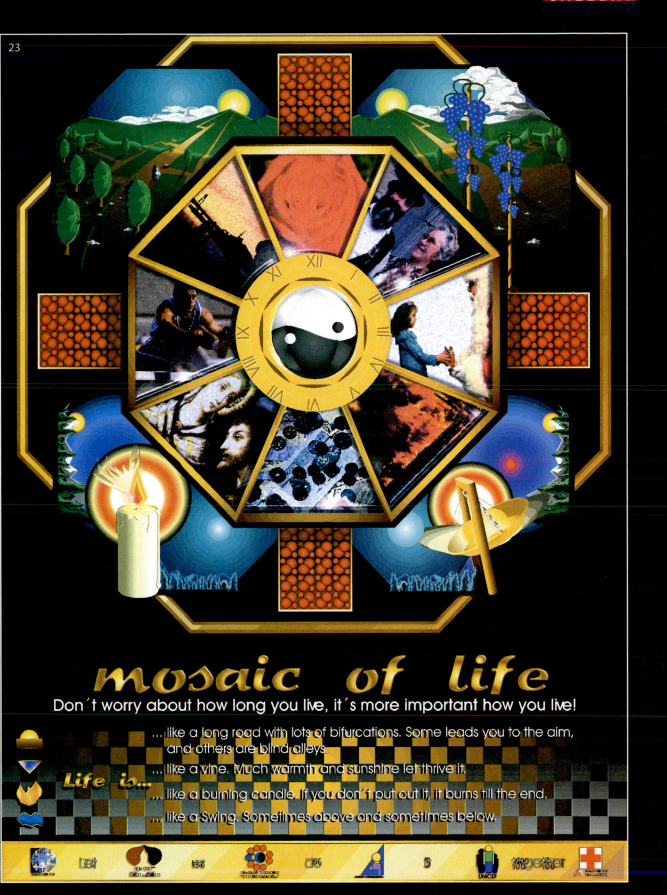

mosaic of life

Don´t worry about how long you live, it´s more important how you live!

Life is...

... like a long road with lots of bifurcations. Some leads you to the aim, and others are blind alleys.

... like a vine. Much warmth and sunshine let thrive it.

... like a burning candle. If you don´t put out it, it burns till the end.

... like a Swing. Sometimes above and sometimes below.

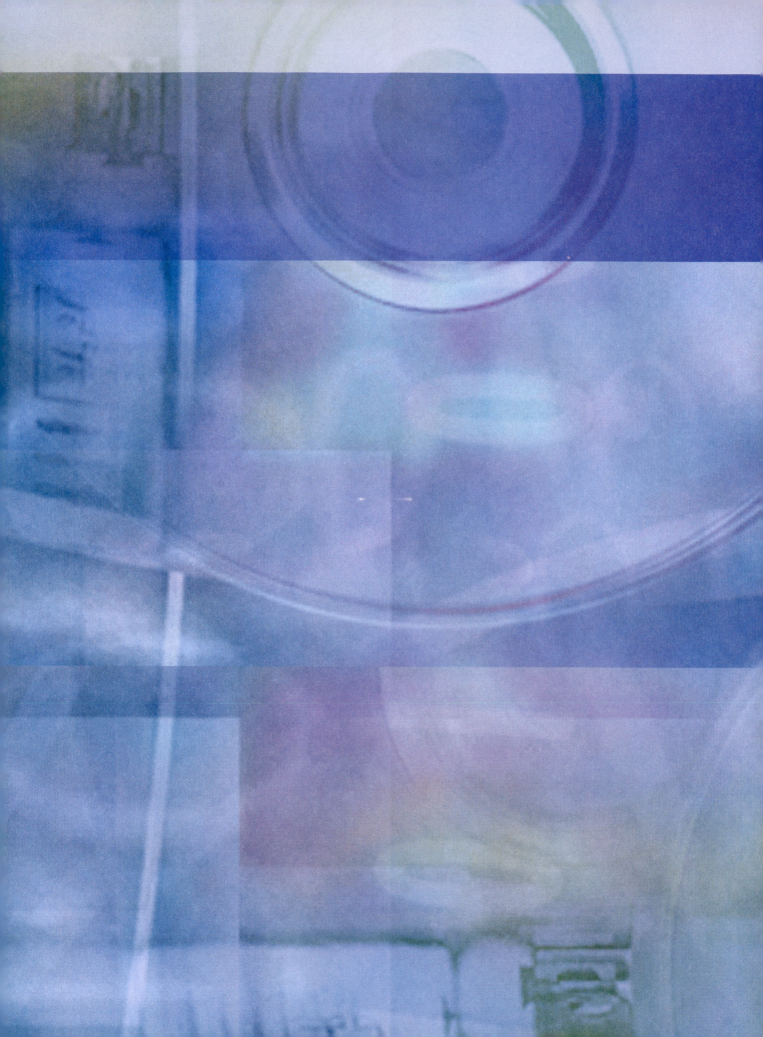

CHAPTER SEVENTEEN

THE CUTTING EDGE

Expert Systems, Robotics, and Virtual Reality

Anita Devine taught computer classes at Jackson Community College and worked on her master's degree in computer science on the side. She became quite interested in the artificial intelligence (AI) classes she was taking and thought her own students would be interested too. She did not want to teach a full-blown AI class but calculated that she could assemble an interesting introductory class that, for two Saturday sessions, would count as one credit.

Anita got the class approved. She then encouraged enrollment by posting flyers noting that there were no prerequisites and that the class included a demonstration of a home-built robot. She anticipated a good deal of interest and arranged for a large classroom, but was amazed when 247 students enrolled. One of them was Alex Martinez, who was majoring in computer information systems. He figured it could not hurt to have a class called Introduction to Artificial Intelligence on his resumé. Rather to his surprise, he enjoyed the class and came away with some idea of what artificial intelligence was all about.

Eighteen months later, as he was interviewing for his first job, Alex was startled to hear the interviewer say, "I see that you took an artificial intelligence class. Do you know what an expert system is?" Alex's first impulse was to protest that he really knew nothing at all about artificial intelligence, that it was just a little nothing class, but then—all this was in less than 10 seconds—he remembered what an expert system is. So he said, as calmly as possible, "An expert system is a computer system that lets the computer be an expert on some topic." The interviewer responded, "Well, you probably know more than I do."

As it happened, one of the groups managed by this interviewer had just been tagged to develop an expert system for an insurance waiver process. The AI professionals were already in place but some other technical folks were needed as a supporting cast. To his stunned delight, Alex was hired and added to the team. He was, in fact, no more than a gofer for a while, but it became an interesting experience. By the end of a year, he had moved within the company to a more traditional programming environment. But Alex remained bemused that artificial intelligence had been his ticket in the door.

The Artificial Intelligence Field

Artificial intelligence (AI) is a field of study that explores how computers can be used for tasks that require the human characteristics of intelligence, imagination, and intuition. Computer scientists sometimes prefer a looser definition, calling AI the study of how to make computers do things that—

at the present time—people can do better. The phrase *at the present time* is significant because artificial intelligence is an evolving science: As soon as a problem is solved, it is moved off the artificial intelligence agenda. A good example is the game of chess, once considered a mighty AI challenge. But now that most computer chess programs can beat most human competitors, chess is no longer an object of study by scientists and thus no longer on the artificial intelligence agenda.

Today the term *artificial intelligence* encompasses several subsets of interests (Figure 1):

- **Problem solving.** This area of AI includes a spectrum of activities, from playing games to planning military strategy.
- **Natural languages.** This facet involves the study of the person/computer interface in unconstrained native language.
- **Expert systems.** These AI systems present the computer as an expert on some particular topic.
- **Robotics.** This field involves endowing computer-controlled machines with electronic capabilities for vision, speech, and touch.

Although considerable progress has been made in these sophisticated fields of study, early successes did not come easily. Before examining current advances in these areas, let us pause to consider some moments in the development of artificial intelligence.

Early Mishaps

In the first days of artificial intelligence, scientists thought that the computer would experience something like an electronic childhood, in which it would gobble up the world's libraries and then begin generating new wisdom. Few people talk like this today because the problem of simulating intelligence is far more complex than just stuffing facts into the computer. Facts are useless without the ability to interpret and learn from them.

An artificial intelligence failure on a grand scale was the attempt to translate human languages via the computer. Although scientists were able to pour vocabulary and rules of grammar into the computer, the literal word-for-word translations often resulted in ludicrous output. In one infamous example the computer was supposed to demonstrate its prowess by translating a phrase from English to Russian and then back to English. Despite the computer's best efforts, the saying "The spirit is willing, but the flesh is weak" came back "The vodka is good, but the meat is spoiled."

An unfortunate result of this widely published experiment was the ridicule of artificial intelligence scientists, considered dreamers who could not accept the limitations of a machine. Funding for AI research disappeared, plunging the artificial intelligence community into a slump from which it did not recover until expert systems emerged in the 1980s. Nevertheless, a hardy band of scientists continued to explore artificial intelligence, focusing on how computers learn.

InfoBit

A *chatterbot* (sometimes called just *chatbot*) is a program that attempts to simulate the conversation or "chatter" of a human being. Chatterbots such as "Eliza" and "Parry" were well-known early attempts at creating programs that could at least temporarily fool a real human being into thinking they were talking to another person. A person at a computer, connected to another computer, would be fooled if he or she could not tell if responses were generated by a program or were from a real person typing replies.

Figure 1 The artificial intelligence family tree.

Robotics: *Machines that can move and relate to objects as humans can.*

Expert systems: *Programs that mimic the decision-making and problem-solving thought processes of human experts.*

Natural languages: *Systems that translate ordinary human commands into language computers can understand and act on.*

Problem solving: *Programs that cover a broad spectrum of problems, from games to military strategy.*

Artificial intelligence

MAKING THE RIGHT CONNECTIONS

STORM CHASING

People who want to witness awesome storms first-hand are called storm chasers. In particular, storm chasers are looking for a tornado, a violently rotating column of air in contact with the ground and extending from the base of a thunderstorm. More than a thousand tornadoes touch down in the United States each year, with the majority centered in western Oklahoma, the Texas panhandle, Kansas, and eastern Colorado.

Storm chasers usually fall into one of three categories: those who have advanced degrees in meteorology, engineers who are out to assess damage, and (the vast majority) tourists who like to take beautiful (or fearsome) pictures. Professional meteorologists speak comfortably of jet streams and isobars and outflow boundaries. At the other end of the spectrum, the folks who want to take pictures care little about the terminology; they just need someone to tell them where the storm is. Enter storm-chasing tourism. For one or two thousand dol-

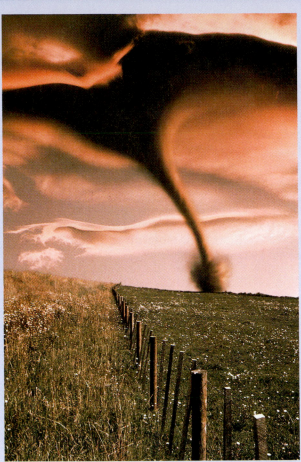

lars a pop, tourists are loaded into vans and driven hundreds of miles across the plains. If they are lucky, they will see a spectacular rotating tower, a gorgeous barrel in the sky, worthy of video and still photography.

But what about the dangers? Might these storm lookyloos be caught in the funnel? This is a possibility if they are on their own with no guidance. But storm tour guides are well equipped to stay out of harm's way. Professional storm chasers usually have cell phones or scanners and are in touch with other chasers who are in different locations and have a different view of the storm. They may be in contact with someone who is watching a radar screen or a television weathercast.

However, most importantly, they have laptop computers and access to Internet storm-watch sites. They even use their computers, via Real Audio software, to listen in to live reports from local radio stations. Storm watchers are able to use all this information to give the tornado a wide berth, staying more than a mile away, and often several miles. The Internet has led to a big breakthrough in storm chasing. Not only does it provide much-needed weather information, it also is the main medium to link chasers to each other.

InfoBit

The knowledge base for a conversation-simulating chatterbot could include client names, Internet addresses, geographic locations and other business-specific elements. There also may be a database of proper nouns to capitalize, a list of common acronyms, a few thousand categories of general knowledge "facts" and an additional file of "gossip" facts.

How Computers Learn

The study of artificial intelligence is predicated on the computer's ability to learn and to improve performance on the basis of past errors. The two key elements of this process are the knowledge base and the inference engine. A **knowledge base** is a set of facts and rules about those facts. An **inference engine** accesses, selects, and interprets a set of rules. The inference engine applies the rules to the facts to make up new facts—thus the computer has learned something new. Consider this simple example:

FACT: Amy is Ken's wife.
RULE: If X is Y's wife, then Y is X's husband.

The computer—the inference engine—can apply the rule to the fact and come up with a new fact: Ken is Amy's husband. Although the result of this simplistic example may seem of little value, it is indeed true that the computer now knows two facts instead of just one. Rules, of course, can be much more complex and facts more plentiful, yielding more sophisticated results. In fact, artificial intelligence software is capable of searching through long chains of related facts to reach a conclusion—a new fact.

Further explanation of the precise way in which computers learn is beyond the scope of this book. However, the learning discussion can be used as a springboard to the question that most people ask about artificial intelligence: Can a computer really think?

The Artificial Intelligence Debate

To imitate the functioning of the human mind, a machine with artificial intelligence would have to be able to examine a variety of facts, address multiple subjects, and devise a solution to a problem by comparing new facts to its existing storehouse of data from many fields. So far, artificial intelligence systems cannot match a person's ability to solve problems through original thought instead of by using familiar patterns as guides.

There are many arguments for and against crediting computers with the ability to think. Some say, for example, that computers cannot be considered intelligent because they do not compose like Beethoven or write like Shakespeare. The response is that neither do most ordinary human musicians or writers—you do not have to be a genius to be considered intelligent.

Look at it another way. Suppose you rack your brain over a problem and then—aha!—the solution comes to you all at once. Now, how did you do that? You do not know, and nobody else knows either. A big part of human problem solving seems to be that jolt of recognition, that ability to see things suddenly as a whole. Experiments have shown that people rarely solve problems by using step-by-step logic, the very thing that computers do best. Most modern computers still plod through problems one step at a time. The human brain beats computers at "aha!" problem solving because it has millions of neurons working simultaneously.

Back to the basic question: Can a computer think or not? One possible answer: Who cares? If a machine can perform a task really well, does it matter whether it actually thinks? Still another answer is, yes, machines can really think, but not as humans do. They lack the sensitivity, appreciation, and passion that are intrinsic to human thought.

Data Mining

Computer brainpower can also be brought to bear on stores of data through **data mining,** the process of extracting previously unknown information from existing data. You might think that once data has been gathered and made available, you could know everything about it, but this is not necessarily so.

The information stored in hundreds of thousands of records on disk can be tallied and summarized and perhaps even cross-referenced in some useful way by conventional computer programs. It is these traditional processes that produce the standard reports of business—bills and tax records and annual reports. But conventional processes are unlikely to discover the hidden infor-

Yes, We Have Bananas

You probably did not know that bananas are the most popular item in American shopping carts, more popular than bread or milk. But Wal-Mart knows. In fact, Wal-Mart, whose database is second in size only to that of the U.S. government, knows all sorts of things about customer buying habits.

Wal-Mart has found a new way to use the data it collects at cash registers. Using data mining techniques, it can peruse the data to discover popular items and, more importantly, find useful combinations. One key item they discovered was that people who bought bananas often bought cold cereal. Since bananas are so well liked, and some folks buy cereal too, it makes sense to encourage all buyers to buy both products. The answer: Place bananas, in addition to their usual produce location, in the cereal aisle. Sales of cereal jumped.

As a further result of data mining, other items now side by side on the shelf are bug spray and hunting gear, tissue and cold medicine, measuring spoons and baking oil, and flashlights and Halloween costumes.

InfoBit

Cellular carriers can use data mining to detect fraud. Cell phone systems generate huge amounts of data concerning the location, time, duration, and numbers for phone calls. Some cellular carriers regularly use data mining techniques to sift thorough this data to identify patterns of use indicating illegal or stolen cell phones.

InfoBit

The Royal Hospital for Women in Britain is using data mining techniques to reduce the risk of miscarriage or severe complications of pregnancy. By scanning the hospitals extensive medical records for patterns associated with fetal abnormalities, the system can help reduce the likelihood of complications in susceptible populations. The procedure involved mining the hospital records for over 20 fetal health measures from over 700 pregnancies.

mation that might give a competitive edge. The possible hidden information is just the sort of thing that a thinking person might uncover if the amount of data was a manageable size. But no human can find nuances in massive data stores. Data mining, however, in a somewhat humanlike manner, may uncover data relationships and trends that are not readily apparent.

Companies are indeed using data mining techniques to sift through their databases, looking for unnoticed relationships. Wal-Mart, for example, does this every day to optimize inventories. At the end of the day, all the sales data from every store comes into a single computer that then interprets the data. The computer might notice, for example, that a lot of green sweaters have been selling in Boston and that, in fact, the supplies were depleted. The same green sweater is hardly selling at all in Phoenix. A human can figure out the reason: It is St. Patrick's Day, and there are many more Irish in Boston than in Phoenix. For next St. Patrick's Day, the computer will order a larger supply of green sweaters for the Boston stores.

The Natural Language Factor

The language people use on a daily basis to write and speak is called a **natural language.** Natural languages are associated with artificial intelligence because humans can make the best use of artificial intelligence if they can communicate with computers in natural language. Furthermore, understanding natural language is a skill thought to require intelligence.

Some natural language words are easy to understand because they represent a definable item: *horse, chair, mountain.* Other words, however, are much too abstract to lend themselves to straightforward definitions: *justice, virtue, beauty.* But this kind of abstraction is just the beginning of the difficulty. Consider the word *hand* in these statements:

- Morgan had a hand in the robbery.
- Morgan had a hand in the cookie jar.
- Morgan is an old hand at chess.
- Morgan gave Sean a hand with his luggage.
- Morgan asked Marcia for her hand in marriage.
- All hands on deck!

As you can see, natural language abounds with ambiguities; the word *hand* has a different meaning in each statement. In contrast, sometimes statements that appear to be different really mean the same thing: "Alan sold Jim a book for five dollars" is equivalent to "Jim gave Alan five dollars in exchange for a book." It takes sophisticated software to unravel such statements and see them as equivalent.

Feeding computers the vocabulary and grammatical rules they need to know is a step in the right direction. However, as you saw earlier in the account of the language translation fiasco, true understanding requires more: Words must be taken in context. Humans start acquiring a context for words from the day they are born. Consider this statement: Jack cried when Alice said she loved Bill. From our own context, several possible conclusions can be drawn: Jack is sad, Jack probably loves Alice, Jack probably thinks Alice doesn't love him, and so on. These conclusions may not be correct, but they are reasonable interpretations based on the context the reader supplies. On the other hand, it would *not* be reasonable to conclude from the statement that Jack is a carpenter or that Alice has a new refrigerator.

One of the most frustrating tasks for AI scientists is providing the computer with the sense of context that humans have. Scientists have attempted to do this in regard to specific subjects and found the task daunting. For example, a scientist who wrote software so that the computer could have a dialogue about restaurants had to feed the computer hundreds of facts that any small child would know, such as the fact that restaurants have food and that you are expected to pay for it.

Expert Systems

An **expert system** is a software package used with an extensive set of organized data that presents the computer as an expert on a particular topic. For example, a computer could be an expert on where to drill oil wells, or on what stock purchase looks promising, or on how to cook soufflés. The user is the knowledge seeker, usually asking questions in a natural—that is, English-like—format. An expert system can respond to an inquiry about a problem with both an answer and an explanation of the answer. For example, an expert system specializing in stock purchases could be asked if stocks of the Milton Corporation are currently a good buy. A possible answer is no, with backup reasons such as a very high price/earnings ratio or a recent change in top management. The expert system works by figuring out what the question means and then matching it against the facts and rules that it "knows" (Figure 2). These facts and rules, which reside on disk, originally come from human experts.

But why go to all this trouble and expense? Why not just stick with human experts? Well, there are problems with human experts. They are typically expensive, subject to biases and emotions, and they may even be inconsistent. Finally, there have been occasions when experts have resigned or retired, leaving the company in a state of crisis. If there is just one expert, or even just a few experts, there may not be enough to satisfy the needs of the system. The computer, however, is ever present and just as available as the telephone.

InfoBit

Business schools are aware of the potential that expert systems and artificial intelligence pose for their students. A recent survey showed that almost 90% of business schools either offered or planned to offer some instruction about expert systems in their curricula.

InfoBit

A survey of accounting professionals by the American Institute of Certified Public Accountants has consistently shown that CPAs rate expert systems as one of the technologies "expected to have the most impact" on their profession in the next few years.

Figure 2 An expert system on the job. This expert system helps Ford mechanics track down and fix engine problems.

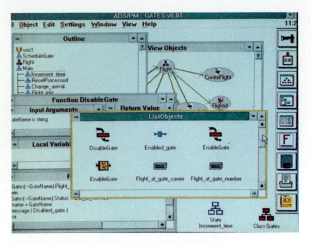

(a)

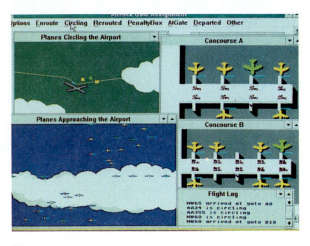

(b)

Figure 3 Airline scheduling program produced with the aid of an expert system. This system offers a graphical user interface to help solve a complex airport scheduling problem. (a) This screen illustrates the system's ability to display multiple views of objects and the relationships between them. (b) Various screen windows show planes circling the airport, the number of planes approaching the airport, gate information, and two concourses with planes at their gates.

Expert Systems in Business

In the early 1980s expert systems began to make their way into commercial environments. Consider these examples:

■ The Campbell Soup Company has an expert system nicknamed Aldo, for Aldo Cimino, the human expert who knows how to fix the company's cooking machines. Aldo was getting on in years and was being run ragged, flying from plant to plant whenever a cooker went on the blink. Besides, how would the company manage when he retired? Now Aldo's knowledge has been distilled into an expert system that can be used by workers in any location.

■ Factory workers at the Boeing Company use an expert system to assemble electrical connectors for airplanes. In the old days workers had to hunt through 20,000 pages of cross-referenced specifications to find the right parts, tools, and techniques for the job—approximately 42 minutes per search. The expert system lets them do the same thing in about 5 minutes.

■ The United Airlines terminal at O'Hare Airport in Chicago handles hundreds of flights per day, which must be distributed among 50 gates. Complications include the limitations of jumbo jets, which do not maneuver easily into some gates. Furthermore, both the weather and heavy runway traffic can affect how quickly planes can get in and out. Airline employees, who used to track planes on a gigantic magnetic board, now keep track of gate positions with an expert system that takes all factors into account (Figure 3).

■ Nordstrom is a chain of stores selling high-quality clothing. Suppose that a customer wants to charge a $300 coat on her Nordstrom account, but her credit limit is just $1000 and she has existing unpaid credit of $875. Should the customer be allowed to charge the coat anyway, or should the clerk adhere strictly to the credit limit? This ticklish question could be turned over to an in-store credit consultant who, after quickly reviewing the customer's records, would grant (or possibly refuse) the extra charge. Nordstrom recently converted the whole process to an expert system. The most compelling reason for the switch is that the expertise of one individual is not readily available to multiple users at the same time. The new expert system is available to any clerk at any time.

The cost of an expert system can usually be justified in situations where there are few experts but great demand for knowledge. It is also worthwhile to have a system that is not subject to human failings, such as fatigue.

Building an Expert System

Few organizations are capable of building an expert system from scratch. The sensible alternative is to buy an **expert system shell,** a software package that consists of the basic structure used to find answers to questions. It is up to the buyer to fill in the actual knowledge on the chosen subject. You could think of the expert system shell as an empty cup that becomes a new entity once it is filled—a cup of coffee, for instance, or a cup of sugar.

The most challenging task of building an expert system often is deciding who the appropriate expert is and then trying to pin down his or her knowledge. Experts often believe that much of their expertise is instinctive and thus find it difficult to articulate just why they do what they do. However, the expert is usually following a set of rules, even if the rules are only in his or her head. The person ferreting out the information, sometimes called a **knowledge engineer,** must have a keen eye and the skills of a diplomat.

Once the rules are uncovered, they are formed into a set of IF-THEN rules. For example, IF the customer has exceeded a credit limit by no more than 20 percent and has paid the monthly bill on time for six months, THEN extend further credit. After the system is translated into a computerized version, it is reviewed, changed, tested, and changed some more. This repetitive process can take months or even years. Finally, it is put into the same situations as the human expert would face, where it should give equal or better service but much more quickly.

Robotics

Many people smile at the thought of robots, perhaps remembering the endearing C-3PO of *Star Wars* fame and its "personal" relationship with humans. But vendors have not made even a small dent in the personal robot market—the much-heralded domestic robots who wash windows have not yet become household staples. So where are the robots today? Mainly in factories.

Robots in the Factory

Most robots are in factories, spray-painting and welding—and taking away jobs. The Census Bureau, after two centuries of counting people, has now branched out and today is counting robots as well. About 15,000 robots existed in 1985, a number that jumped to 50,000 just ten years later. What do robots do that merits all this attention?

A **robot** is a computer-controlled device that can physically manipulate its surroundings. There are a wide variety of sizes and shapes of robots, each designed with a particular use in mind. Often these uses are functions that would be tedious or even dangerous for a human to perform. The most common industrial robots sold today are mechanical devices with five or six directions of motion, so that they can rotate into proper position to perform their tasks (Figure 4).

Recently, **vision robots,** with the help of a TV-camera eye, have been taught to see in living color—that is, to recognize multicolored objects solely from their colors. This is a departure from the traditional approach, whereby robots recognize objects by their shapes (Figure 5), and from vision machines that "see" only a dominant color. For example, a robot in an experiment at the University of Rochester was able to pick out a box of Kellogg's Sugar Frosted Flakes from 70 other boxes. Among the anticipated benefits of such visual recognition skills is supermarket checkout. You cannot easily bar code a squash, but a robot might be trained to recognize it by its size, shape, and color.

RoboBug

They call it "situational awareness": the ability to detect the enemy. The worst part about being in a land war is that you know some folks are out to get you, but you do not know where they are. So reach into your pocket and pull out a cigar-like tube; open it to release a 3-inch robotic "bug" equipped with infrared detectors, acoustic sensors, and video cameras. You have sent forth a creepy-crawly spy, whose range is 500 yards. The actual bug is made of ceramic-coated metal and looks something like a daddy long-legs made from a tiny Erector set.

InfoBit

Human and robot performance diverge on versatility. Although there are robots that can weld or swim as well as humans, there are no robots that have anything like the range of behavior of a human being. The same human can walk and talk and weld and swim, but each factory robot is confined to a single specialty.

(a)

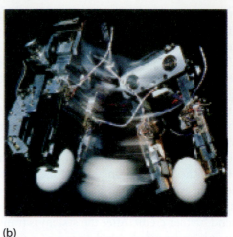

(b)

Figure 4 Industrial robots. (a) These standard robots are used in the auto industry to weld new cars. (b) This robot is not making breakfast. Hitachi uses the delicate egg, however, to demonstrate that its visual-tactile robot can handle fragile objects. The robot's sensors detect size, shape, and required pressure, attaining sensitivity almost equal to that of a human hand.

Field Robots

Think of some of the places you would rather not be: inside a nuclear power plant, next to a suspected bomb, at the bottom of the sea, on the floor of a volcano, or in the middle of a chemical spill. But robots readily go to all those places. Furthermore, they go there to do some dangerous and dirty jobs. These days, **field robots**—robots "in the field"—inspect and repair nuclear power plants, dispose of bombs, inspect oil rigs used for undersea exploration, explore steaming volcanos, clean up chemical accidents, and even explore a battlefield in advance of soldiers. Field robots are also used to check underground storage tanks and pipelines for leaks and to clean up hazardous waste dumps. An undersea robot ventured into the icy waters off Finland and scanned the sunken ferry *Estonia*, sending back pictures of its weakened bow, thought to be a cause of the disaster. Newer undersea robots are being designed to swim like fish (Figure 6a). Going in another direction, space researchers look forward to the day when "astrobots" can be stationed in orbit, ready to repair faulty satellites. Field robots may be equipped with wheels, tracks, legs, fins, or even wings (Figure 6b). A future goal, scientists hope to use robots to construct a space station and base on the moon.

Field robots have largely been overshadowed by factory robots, mainly because until recently they have lacked the independence of their manufac-

Figure 5 The seeing robot. Robots "see" by casting light beams on objects and matching their shapes to those of already "known" objects. In this machine-vision sequence, (a) the object is seen by the robot, (b) the object is matched to known shapes, (c) inappropriate shapes are eliminated, and (d) the object is recognized.

(a)

(b)

(c)

(d)

GETTING PRACTICAL

ROBOTS IN OUR LIVES

If you think robots are not practical in your own life, think again. Like computers before them, robots will soon be everywhere. Here are some examples.

- **Fill it up.** If filling your car's gas tank is not a favorite chore, you will be pleased to know that robots are taking over. Drivers pull up to a specially equipped station, swipe a plastic "tank card," and enter an identification number. The unit identifies the make and model of the auto, then guides the robotic arm to the car's fuel filler door. Once it is open, the robot then places the right grade and amount of gas in the tank and even replaces the cap.
- **My doctor the robot.** If you have orthopedic surgery, you may find that a key player alongside the surgeon is a robot. For example, to make room for a hip implant, a robotic arm drills a long hole in a thigh bone. Robotic precision improves the implant, reduces pain after surgery, and speeds healing.
- **Lending a hand.** Robots may soon be of significant use to the disabled. Researchers have already developed a robot for quadriplegics. The machine can respond to dozens of voice commands by

answering the door, getting the mail, and even serving soup.
- **Road maintenance.** In California, road signs may soon say, "Robots at Work." Robots use lasers to spot cracks in the pavement and dispense the right amount of patch material. Soon robots will also be painting the road stripes.
- **Man's best friend.** The ultimate toy, a pet robot, can walk, lie down, and play games. Shown here, the Sony labs critter known as D21 is a prototype of things to come. The puppy weighs 2.8 pounds and packs a 64-bit microprocessor, 8 megabytes of memory, and a supersensitive camera eye. It knows commands too: Stick out your hand and it will sit.
- **One cool clerk.** The very latest in modern technology and artificial intelligence has been used to create the Super RoboShop, the world's most convenient convenience store. Human store clerks have been replaced by the cheery little Robo, a computer-controlled bucket that

does your shopping for you. Can't find batteries? Robo can, sparing the weary shopper from wandering the aisles or interacting with another human being. RoboShop is basically a gigantic vending machine delivering an eclectic mix of products—everything from cookies to comic books to cologne. Customers enter code numbers for desired products in an ATM-like keypad, pay the machine, and Robo whizzes into action, picking each item from the display cases without smashing so much as a single egg. This

shop may not be in your life just yet: The first dozen RoboShops were in Japan and they are just now being developed in New York City.
- **Going bump in the night.** Chip, the chunky errand boy on the night shift at Baltimore's Franklin Square Hospital, fetches medicine, late meals, medical records, and supplies. A robot, Chip finds his way using sensitive whiskers and touch pads. Nurses love him because he saves them from having to run all over the hospital.

Figure 6 Field robots. (a) Nicknamed Robotuna, this undersea robot will, scientists hope, be able to map the ocean floor, track schools of real fish, or detect pollution—and then swim home with the data. (b) Can a robot really fly? Yes. Flying robots have both military and civilian uses. This Sentinel robot can soar up to 10,000 feet to spy on an enemy or to inspect high-voltage wires or to spot forest fires. (c) The robot called Spider checks gas tanks for cracks and sends computer images back to the ground, saving engineers from making a dangerous climb.

(a)

(b)

(c)

Critical Thinking

So far, robots cannot speak, understand, or reason as well as most humans. What other examples can you think of where robots also fall far short of human standards of performance? (There are many possible suggestions here, but students may have some difficulty coming up with the most obvious—there are no two-legged walking robots, and there are no robots capable of covering the variety of urban terrain and conditions that even average humans are easily capable of traversing.)

Critical Thinking

What characteristics of the human visual system can you think of that might be desirable for vision robots? (Some possibilities include stereo vision [using two cameras to provide depth perception just as two eyes do], the ability to operate under a wide range of illumination conditions, the ability to veer quickly from one target to another, color vision, and even protection from damage—eyelids.)

turing counterparts, needing to be remotely controlled by human operators. Now, however, enough computer power can be packed into a field robot to enable it to make most decisions independently. Field robots need all the power they can get. Unlike factory robots, which are bolted to the ground and blindly do the same tasks over and over again, field robots must often contend with a highly unstructured environment, such as changing terrain and changing weather.

Virtual Reality

The concept of **virtual reality,** sometimes called just **VR,** is to engage a user in a computer-created environment so that the user physically interacts with that environment. In fact, the user becomes so absorbed with the virtual reality interaction that the process is called **immersion.** Virtual reality alters perceptions partly by appealing to several senses at once—sight, hearing, and touch—and by presenting images that respond immediately to one's movements.

The visual part is made possible by sophisticated computers and optics that deliver to a user's eyes a three-dimensional scene in living color. The source of the scene is a database used by a powerful computer to display

(a)

(b)   (c)

Figure 7 Virtual reality. (a) Users can "tour" a building by physically reacting—a turn of the head shows a different scene. (b) The data glove in the foreground has fiber-optic sensors to interact with a computer-generated world. (c) Virtual reality technology can be used to let people who are in wheelchairs design their own apartments.

graphic images. The virtual reality system can sense a user's head and body movements through cables linked to the headset and glove worn by the user. That is, sensors on the user's body send signals to the computer, which then adjusts the scene viewed by the user. Thus the user's body movements can cause interaction with the virtual (artificial) world the user sees, and the computer-generated world responds to those actions (Figure 7).

Travel Anywhere, but Stay Where You Are

At the University of North Carolina, computer scientists have developed a virtual reality program that lets a user walk through an art gallery. A user puts on a head-mounted display, which focuses the eyes on a screen and shuts out the rest of the world. If the user swivels his or her head to the right, pictures on the right wall come into view; similarly, the user can view any part of the gallery just by making head movements. This action/reaction presents realistic continuing changes to the user. Although actually standing in one place, the user feels as if he or she is moving and wants to stop short as a pedestal appears in the path ahead. It is as if the user is actually walking around inside the gallery.

In another example, scientists have taken data about Mars, sent back by space probes, and converted it to a virtual reality program. Information about hills, rocks, and ridges of the planet are used to create a Mars landscape that is projected on the user's head screen.

The Promise of Virtual Reality

An embryonic technology such as virtual reality is filled with hype and promises. It is the practical commercial applications for real-world users that

FOCUS ON *Ethics*

Virtual Reality for Good or Evil

Virtual reality has been lauded as an inexpensive and relatively painless way to lessen a person's sensitivity to heights and other apprehensions. However, behavior modification can cut two ways, for good or for evil. What are the ethical implications for the use of VR on the general populace? Could VR be used to condition a person in antisocial ways? Another problem is that VR can cause vertigo, nausea, disorientation, and even motion sickness in susceptible individuals. In view of those possibilities, is it ethical to use human subjects for VR experiments?

2000 and Beyond

FROM THE VIRTUAL TO THE REAL

Afraid of flying? We can help you with that, and you won't have to get near an airplane. Afraid of heights? We can give you the same fearful sensation without leaving the ground—and make you feel good about it. Need some expensive hands-on training? Now it can be simulated for half the price.

Soon enough we will all be participating in virtual activities as they permeate society and economic markets. By donning a headset and using sensor controls, you can behave as if you were somewhere you are not. Trainers who help fearful flyers can let them simulate the identical experi-

ence, which is so real that sweaty palms are included. People who fear heights can "walk" a plank over a canyon, even lean daringly over the edge. Conventional treatment for pho-

bias involves repeated exposure to experiences that cause anxiety. Virtual therapy saves time and money and has been shown to have a high success rate.

Training by virtual reality is being embraced by various segments of the community. Two important early users were doctors and pilots. But VR is moving to more generic audiences. The Oregon Research Institute, for example, is using virtual reality to help children learn to operate a motorized wheelchair (see photo). Not only does the training make them more self-sufficient, it gives them a sense of accomplishment. While you personally may not yet be using virtual reality, it is emerging from the lab to various segments of society. Whether it someday joins the mainstream is yet to be seen.

shows where this technology might lead. Here are some applications under development:

- Wearing head mounts, consumers can browse for products in a "virtual showroom." From a remote location, a consumer will be able to maneuver and view products along aisles in a warehouse.
- Similarly, from a convenient office perch a security guard can patrol corridors and offices in remote locations.
- Using virtual reality headsets and gloves, doctors and medical students will be able to experiment with new procedures on simulated patients rather than real ones.

Any new technology has its drawbacks. Some users experience "simulator sickness," even though they know the experience is not real. The developers of virtual reality are faced with daunting costs. Many hurdles remain in the areas of software, hardware, and even human behavior before virtual reality can reach its full potential.

▲

The immediate prospects for expert systems, robots, and virtual reality systems are growth and more growth. You can anticipate both increased sophistication and more diverse applications.

CHAPTER REVIEW

Summary and Key Terms

- **Artificial intelligence (AI)** is a field of study that explores how computers can be used for tasks that require the human characteristics of intelligence, imagination, and intuition. AI has also been described as the study of how to make computers do things that—at the present time—people can do better.

- Artificial intelligence is considered an umbrella term to encompass several subsets of interests, including problem solving, natural languages, expert systems, and robotics.

- In the early days of AI, scientists thought that it would be useful just to stuff facts into the computer; however, facts are useless without the ability to interpret and learn from them.

- An early attempt to translate human languages by providing a computer with vocabulary and rules of grammar was a failure because the computer could not distinguish the context of statements. This failure impeded the progress of artificial intelligence.

- The study of artificial intelligence is predicated on the computer's ability to learn and to improve performance on the basis of past errors.

- A **knowledge base** is a set of facts and rules about those facts. An **inference engine** accesses, selects, and interprets a set of rules. The inference engine applies rules to the facts to make up new facts.

- People rarely solve problems using the step-by-step logic most computers use. The brain beats the computer at solving problems, because it has millions of neurons working simultaneously.

- **Data mining** is the process of extracting previously unknown information from existing data.

- **Natural languages** are associated with artificial intelligence because humans can make the best use of artificial intelligence if they can communicate with the computer in human language. Furthermore, understanding natural language is a skill thought to require intelligence. A key function of the AI study of natural languages is to develop a computer system that can resolve ambiguities.

- An **expert system** is a software package used with an extensive set of organized data that presents the computer as an expert on a specific topic. The expert system works by figuring out what the question means and then matching it against the facts and rules that it "knows."

- For years, expert systems were the exclusive property of the medical and scientific communities, but in the early 1980s they began to make their way into commercial environments.

- Some organizations choose to build their own expert systems to perform well-focused tasks that can easily be crystallized into rules, but few organizations are capable of building an expert system from scratch.

- Some users buy an **expert system shell,** a software package that consists of the basic structure used to find answers to questions. It is up to the buyer to fill in the actual knowledge on the chosen subject.

- The person working to extract information from the human expert is sometimes called a **knowledge engineer.**

- A **robot** is a computer-controlled device that can physically manipulate its surroundings. Most robots are in factories.

- **Vision robots** traditionally recognize objects by their shapes or else "see" a dominant color. But some robots can recognize multicolored objects solely from their colors.

- **Field robots** inspect and repair nuclear power plants, dispose of bombs, inspect oil rigs for undersea exploration, put out oil well fires, clean up chemical accidents, and much more.
- **Virtual reality,** sometimes called just **VR,** engages a user in a computer-created environment, so that the user physically interacts with the computer-produced three-dimensional scene. Since the user is so absorbed with the interaction, the process is called **immersion.**

Discussion Questions

1. Describe the differences in the way humans and machines learn.

2. Is it possible to create an expert system for doing term papers? Why or why not?

3. What kinds of jobs are threatened by robots? Consider some jobs you may wish to have, now or in the future. Are the workers who perform them likely to be replaced by robots?

Student Study Guide

Multiple Choice

1. The kind of robot that can recognize objects by their shape is called a(n)
   a. factory robot   c. field robot
   b. expert robot   d. vision robot

2. The VR process is referred to as
   a. inference   c. immersion
   b. a shell   d. data mining

3. The worker extracting knowledge from a human expert is called a(n)
   a. data miner   c. field robot
   b. inference engine   d. knowledge engineer

4. Most robots can be found in
   a. factories   c. VR
   b. the field   d. an underwater environment

5. The umbrella term that includes problem solving, expert systems, and robotics is
   a. virtual reality   c. artificial intelligence
   b. data mining   d. inference engine

6. The software that holds the structure to ask questions of an expert system is called an
   a. expert system engine   c. expert system language
   b. expert system shell   d. expert system robot

7. The process of extracting previously unknown information from existing data is called
   a. data reality   c. data inferring
   b. data mining   d. data immersing

8. A computer-controlled device that can manipulate its surroundings is called a(n)
   a. knowledge base   c. expert system
   b. shell   d. robot

9. A set of facts and rules about those facts is called a(n)
   a. knowledge base   c. inference engine
   b. data mine   d. expert shell

10. The kind of robot that can take on dangerous jobs in locations unfit for humans is called a(n)
    a. factory robot   c. field robot
    b. expert robot   d. vision robot

True/False

T F   1. Artificial intelligence has always enjoyed wide respect from scientists and the government.

T F   2. Artificial intelligence is an umbrella term that covers many subjects.

T F   3. A knowledge base is a set of facts and rules about those facts.

T F   4. Early artificial intelligence scientists were called knowledge engineers.

T F   5. Early attempts to translate human language failed.

T F   6. An expert system is software.

T F   7. An expert system shell is used by the end-users of the expert system.

T F   8. Vision robots have sight capability that is significantly less than human capability.

T F   9. Field robots can do many tasks that are undesirable for humans.

T F   10. A knowledge engineer is a customer who uses an expert system.

T F   11. Using virtual reality, a user physically walks along hallways and from room to room.

T F   12. Most organizations that want expert systems do not attempt to build them from scratch.

T F   13. Using computers to mimic natural language is a relatively easy task for computer experts.

T F 14. Immersion refers to the environment of undersea robots.

T F 15. Computers generally solve problems in a step-by-step fashion.

T F 16. People always solve problems in a step-by-step fashion.

T F 17. An underlying assumption of artificial intelligence is that the computer can learn.

T F 18. Data mining means extracting previously unknown information from data files.

T F 19. An inference engine is the same as a knowledge base.

T F 20. Understanding natural language is a skill thought to require intelligence.

T F 21. At one time AI scientists were the subject of ridicule.

T F 22. In general, a given word in a natural language has a single meaning.

T F 23. Part of the need for data mining functions is related to a high volume of data.

T F 24. Most computer chess programs can still be beaten by average human chess players.

T F 25. Most robots today are used in scientific experiments.

T F 26. Artificial intelligence is a subset of the field of expert systems.

T F 27. Some robots can swim, some robots can walk, and some robots can fly.

T F 28. Part of the difficulty of making a computer understand natural language is language ambiguities.

T F 29. The field of artificial intelligence has enjoyed broad support for several decades.

T F 30. Data mining involves both underground cables and underground storage.

Fill-In

1. The generic term for using computers for jobs requiring human characteristics is

   _____.

2. The term for software that can be used to build an expert system is _____.

3. The software that interprets facts and rules is known as _____.

4. The kind of robot that can perform inspections and other dangerous tasks is the

   _____.

5. The person who extracts information from a human expert is called a(n)

   _____.

6. When a person is totally involved in a VR experience, it is called _____.

7. A device that can physically manipulate its surroundings is called _____.

8. A set of facts and a set of rules about those facts is called a(n) _____.

9. The language used by humans is called

   _____.

10. The kind of robot that can distinguish objects by their shape or color is known as a(n)

   _____.

Answers

True/False

1. F	6. T	11. F	16. F	21. T	26. F
2. T	7. F	12. T	17. T	22. F	27. T
3. T	8. T	13. F	18. T	23. T	28. T
4. F	9. T	14. F	19. F	24. F	29. F
5. T	10. F	15. T	20. T	25. F	30. F

Fill-In

1. artificial intelligence
2. expert system shell
3. inference engine
4. field robot
5. knowledge engineer
6. immersion
7. robot
8. knowledge base
9. natural language
10. vision robot

Multiple Choice

1. d	6. b
2. c	7. b
3. d	8. d
4. a	9. a
5. c	10. c

AMERICANA

There is not a lot to say about this last topic, a topic of mixed words and rich images. A search engine will pull up many thousands of sites for the word *Americana*. Some are patriotic sites with sentiments such as "Our country was founded on powerful principles."

The vast majority of sites, however, are for hobbyists who want to show and trade memorabilia and collectibles or, as one put it, "neat old stuff." In addition, you can find sites for businesses of every kind that have tacked the word Americana in front of their names: Americana Bank, Americana Software, *Americana* Media Consulting, and Americana Motel.

We simply want to share some of our discoveries on the Internet, displaying some images we have come across that show "neat old stuff." No exercises either. Take a break.

PLANET INTERNET

Dear Timmy,
I'll always be here when you need me. A nice card from you would make any day special.

ps: Write more often. You know how your mother worries.

A **YEAR ROUND** Tribute to Mom.

Omega Oil For Sun Burn For Weak Backs

Omega Oil For Athletes Trial Bottle 10¢

Omega Oil For Stiff Joints For Sore Muscles

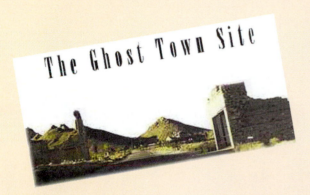

The Ghost Town Site

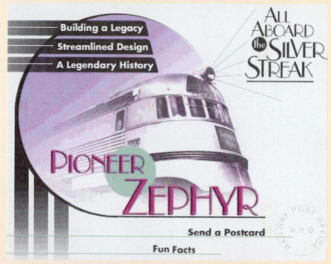

HISTORY AND INDUSTRY

The Continuing Story of the Computer Age

MITS ALTAIR 8800 COMPUTER

LEARNING OBJECTIVES

- Understand the story of how computer technology unfolded, with particular emphasis on the "generations"
- Understand how people and events affected the development of computers
- Become familiar with the story of personal computer development

Although the story of computers has deep roots, the most fascinating part—the history of personal computers—is quite recent. The beginning of this history turns on the personality of Ed Roberts the way a watch turns on a jewel. It began when his foundering company took a surprising turn.

Like other entrepreneurs before him, Ed Roberts had taken a big risk. He had already been burned once, and now he feared being burned again. The first time, in the early 1970s, he had borrowed heavily to produce microprocessor-based calculators, only to have the chip producers decide to build their own product and sell it for half the price of Ed's calculator.

Ed's new product was based on a microprocessor, too—the Intel 8800—but it was a computer. A little computer. The "big boys" at the established computer firms considered computers to be industrial products; who would want a small computer? Ed was

not sure, but he found the idea so compelling that he decided to make the computer anyway. Besides, he was so far in debt from the calculator fiasco that it did not seem to matter which project propelled him into bankruptcy. Ed's small computer and his company, MITS, were given a sharp boost by Les Solomon, who promised to feature the new machine on the cover of *Popular Electronics.* In Albuquerque, New Mexico, Ed worked frantically to meet the publication deadline, and he even tried to make the machine pretty, so it would look attractive on the cover (Figure 1).

Making a good-looking small computer was not easy. This machine, named the Altair (after a heavenly *Star Trek* destination), looked like a flat box. In fact, it met the definition of a computer in only a minimal way: It had a central processing unit (on the chip), 256 characters (a paragraph!) of memory, and switches and lights on a front panel for input/output. No screen, no keyboard, no storage.

But the Altair was done on time for the January 1975 issue of *Popular Electronics,* and Roberts made plans to fly to New York to

demonstrate the machine for Solomon. He sent the computer on ahead by railway express. Ed got to New York, but the computer did not—the very first personal computer was lost! There was no time to build a new computer before the publishing deadline, so Roberts cooked up a phony version for the cover picture: an empty box with switches and lights on the front panel. He also placed an inch-high ad in the back of the magazine: "Get your own Altair kit for $397."

Ed was hoping for perhaps 200 orders. But the machine—that is, the box—fired imaginations across the country. Two thousand customers sent checks for $397 to an unknown Albuquerque, New Mexico, company. Overnight, the MITS Altair personal computer kit was a runaway success.

Ed Roberts was an important player in the history of personal computers. Unfortunately, he never made it in the big time; most observers agree that his business insight did not match his technical skills. But other entrepreneurs did make it. In this appendix we will glance briefly at the early years of computers and then examine more recent history.

Babbage and the Countess

Born in England in 1791, Charles Babbage was an inventor and mathematician. When solving certain equations, he found the hand-done mathematical tables he used filled with errors. He decided that a machine could be built that would solve the equations better by calculating the differences between them. He set about making a demonstration model of what he called a **difference engine** (Figure 2). The model was so well received that in about 1830 he enthusiastically began to build a full-scale working version, using a grant from the British government.

However, Babbage found that the smallest imperfections were enough to throw the machine out of whack. Babbage was viewed by his own colleagues as a man who was trying to manufacture a machine that was utterly ridiculous. Finally, after spending its money to no avail, the government withdrew financial support.

Despite this setback, Babbage was not discouraged. He conceived of another machine, christened the **analytical engine,** which he hoped would perform many kinds of calculations. Although it was never built in his time, a model was eventually put together by his son. It was not until 1991 that a working version of the analytical engine was built and put on public display in London. It embodied five key features of modern computers: an input device, a storage place to hold the number waiting to be processed, a processor, a control unit to direct the task to be performed and the sequence of calculations, and an output device.

If Babbage was the father of the computer, then Ada, the Countess of Lovelace, was the first computer programmer (Figure 3). The daughter of English poet Lord Byron and of a mother who was a gifted mathematician, Ada helped develop the instructions for doing computations on the analytical engine. Lady Lovelace's contributions cannot be overvalued. She was able to see that Babbage's theoretical approach was workable, and her interest gave

Figure 1　The Altair. The term *personal computer* had not been coined yet, so Ed Roberts's small computer was called a "minicomputer" when it was featured on the cover of *Popular Electronics.*

Figure 2　Charles Babbage's difference engine. Babbage's second difference engine was not completed in his lifetime. The one shown here was built in 1991 by the London Science Museum, according to Babbage's original design, in honor of Babbage's 200th birthday.

Figure 3 **Ada, the Countess of Lovelace.** Augusta Ada Byron, as she was known before she became a countess, was Charles Babbage's colleague in his work on the analytical engine and has been called the world's first computer programmer.

him encouragement. In addition, she published a series of notes that eventually led others to accomplish what Babbage himself had been unable to do.

Herman Hollerith: The Census Has Never Been the Same

Because the hand-done tabulation of the 1880 United States census had taken seven and a half years, a competition was held to find some way to speed the counting process of the 1890 census. Herman Hollerith's tabulating machine won the contest. As a result of the adoption of his system, an unofficial count of the 1890 population (62,622,250) was announced only six weeks after the census was completed.

The principal difference between Hollerith's and Babbage's machines was that Hollerith's machine used electrical rather than mechanical power (Figure 4). Hollerith realized that his machine had considerable commercial potential. In 1896 he founded the successful Tabulating Machine Company, which, in 1924, merged with two other companies to form the International Business Machines Corporation—IBM.

Watson of IBM

For more than 30 years, from 1924 to 1956, Thomas J. Watson Sr. ruled IBM with an iron grip. Cantankerous and autocratic, supersalesman Watson

Figure 4 **Herman Hollerith's tabulating machine.** This electrical tabulator and sorter was used to tabulate the 1890 census.

made IBM a dominant force in the business machines market, first as a supplier of calculators, then as a developer of computers.

IBM's entry into computers was sparked by a young Harvard professor of mathematics, Howard Aiken. In 1936, after reading Lady Lovelace's notes, Aiken began to think that a modern equivalent of the analytical engine could be constructed. Because IBM was already such a power in the business machines market, with ample money and resources, Aiken worked out a careful proposal and approached Thomas Watson. In one of those make-or-break decisions for which he was famous, Watson gave him $1 million. As a result, the Harvard Mark I was born.

The Start of the Modern Era

Nothing like the **Mark I** had ever been built before. It was 8 feet high and 55 feet long, made of streamlined steel and glass, and it emitted a sound during processing that one person said was "like listening to a roomful of old ladies knitting away with steel needles." Unveiled in 1944, the Mark I was never very efficient. But the enormous publicity it generated strengthened IBM's commitment to computer development. Meanwhile, technology had been proceeding elsewhere on separate tracks.

In the early 1940s, American military officials approached Dr. John Mauchly at the University of Pennsylvania and asked him to build a machine that would rapidly calculate trajectories for artillery and missiles. Mauchly and his student J. Presper Eckert relied on the work of Dr. John V. Atanasoff, a professor of physics at Iowa State University. During the late 1930s Atanasoff had spent time trying to build an electronic calculating device to help his students solve mathematical problems. He and an assistant, Clifford Berry, had succeeded in building the first digital computer that worked electronically; they called it the **ABC,** for **Atanasoff-Berry computer** (Figure 5).

After Mauchly met with Atanasoff and Berry in 1941, he used the ABC as the basis for the next step in computer development. From this association ultimately came a lawsuit based on attempts to get patents for a commercial version of the machine Mauchly built. The suit was finally decided in 1974, when a federal court determined that Atanasoff had been the true originator of the ideas required to make an electronic digital computer actually work. (Some computer historians dispute this court decision.) Mauchly and Eckert were able to use the principles of the ABC to create the **ENIAC,** for **Electronic Numerical Integrator and Calculator.** The main significance of the ENIAC is that, as the first general-purpose computer, it was the forerunner of the UNIVAC I, the first computer sold on a commercial basis.

The Computer Age Begins

The remarkable thing about the computer age is that so much has happened in so short a time. We have leapfrogged through four generations of technology in about 40 years—a span of time whose events are within the memory of many people today. The first three computer "generations" are pinned

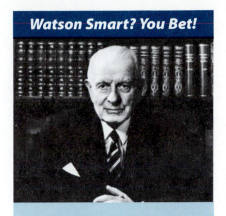

Watson Smart? You Bet!

Just as computers were getting off the ground, Thomas J. Watson Sr. saw the best and brightest called to arms in World War II. But he did not just bid his employees a sad adieu. He paid them. Each and every one received one quarter of his or her annual salary in twelve monthly installments. The checks continued to arrive throughout the duration of the war. Every month those former employees thought about IBM and the generosity of its founder.

The result? A very high percentage of those employees returned to IBM after the war. Watson got his brain trust back, virtually intact. The rest is history.

Figure 5 The ABC. John Atanasoff and his assistant, Clifford Berry, developed the first digital electronic computer.

to three technological developments: the vacuum tube, the transistor, and the integrated circuit. Each has drastically changed the nature of computers. We define the timing of each generation according to the beginning of commercial delivery of the hardware technology. Defining subsequent generations has become more complicated because the entire industry has become more complicated.

The First Generation, 1951–1958: The Vacuum Tube

The beginning of the commercial computer age can be dated to June 14, 1951. This was the day the first **UNIVAC—Universal Automatic Computer—** was delivered to a client, the U.S. Bureau of the Census, for use in tabulating the previous year's census. The date also marked the first time that a computer had been built for a business application rather than for military, scientific, or engineering use. The UNIVAC was really the ENIAC in disguise and was, in fact, built by Mauchly and Eckert, who in 1947 had formed their own corporation.

In the first generation, **vacuum tubes**—electronic tubes about the size of lightbulbs—were used as the internal computer components (Figure 6). However, because thousands of such tubes were required, they generated a great deal of heat, causing many problems in temperature regulation and climate control. In addition, although all the tubes had to be working simultaneously, they were subject to frequent burnout, and the people operating the computer often did not know whether the problem was in the programming or in the machine.

Another drawback was that the language used in programming was machine language, which uses numbers. (Present-day higher-level languages are more like English.) Using numbers alone made programming the computer difficult and time-consuming. The UNIVAC used **magnetic cores** to provide memory. These consisted of small, doughnut-shaped rings about the size of pinheads, which were strung like beads on intersecting thin wires (Figure 7). To supplement primary storage, first-generation computers stored data on punched cards. In 1957 magnetic tape was introduced as a faster, more compact method of storing data.

Figure 6 Vacuum tubes. Vacuum tubes were used in the first generation of computers.

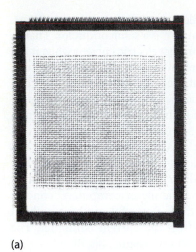

(a)

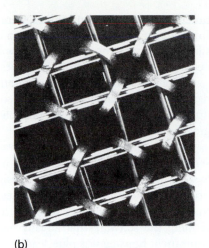

(b)

Figure 7 Magnetic cores. (a) A 6- by 11-inch magnetic core memory. (b) Close-up of magnetic core memory. A few hundredths of an inch in diameter, each magnetic core was mounted on wires. When electricity passed through a wire on which a core was strung, the core could be magnetized as either on or off.

The Second Generation, 1959–1964: The Transistor

Three Bell Lab scientists—J. Bardeen, H. W. Brattain, and W. Shockley—developed the **transistor,** a small device that transfers electronic signals across a resistor. (The name *transistor* began as a trademark concocted from *trans*fer plus res*istor*.) The scientists later received the Nobel Prize for their invention. The transistor revolutionized electronics in general and computers in particular. Transistors were much smaller than vacuum tubes, and they had numerous other advantages: They needed no warm-up time, consumed less energy, and were faster and more reliable.

During this generation another important development was the move from machine language to **assembly languages,** also called **symbolic languages.** Assembly languages use abbreviations for instructions (for example, L for LOAD) rather than numbers. This made programming less cumbersome.

After the development of symbolic languages came **high-level languages,** such as **FORTRAN** (1954) and **COBOL** (1959). Also, in 1962 the first removable disk pack was marketed. Disk storage supplemented magnetic tape systems and enabled users to have fast access to desired data.

Throughout this period computers were being used principally by business, university, and government organizations. They had not filtered down to the general public. The real part of the revolution was about to begin.

The Third Generation, 1965–1970: The Integrated Circuit

One of the most abundant elements in the earth's crust is silicon, a non-metallic substance found in common beach sand as well as in practically all rocks and clay. The importance of this element to Santa Clara County, which is about 30 miles south of San Francisco, is responsible for the county's nickname: Silicon Valley. In 1965 Silicon Valley became the principal site for the manufacture of the so-called silicon chip: the integrated circuit.

An **integrated circuit** (**IC**) is a complete electronic circuit on a small chip of silicon. In 1965 integrated circuits began to replace transistors in computers. The resulting machines were called third-generation computers. Integrated circuits are made of silicon because it is a **semiconductor.** That is, silicon is a crystalline substance that will conduct electric current when it has been "doped" with chemical impurities implanted in its lattice-like structure.

The chips were hailed as a generational breakthrough because they had desirable characteristics: reliability, compactness, and low cost. Mass-production techniques have made possible the manufacture of inexpensive integrated circuits.

The beginning of the third generation was trumpeted by the IBM 360 series (named for a full circle of service—360 degrees) in 1964. The System/360 family of computers, designed for both business and scientific use, came in several models and sizes. The "family of computers" concept made it possible for users to move to a more powerful machine without redoing the software that already worked on the current computer. The equipment housing was blue, leading to IBM's nickname, Big Blue.

The 360 series was launched with an all-out, massive marketing effort to make computers business tools—to get them into medium-size and smaller business and government operations where they had not been used before. Perhaps the most far-reaching contribution of the 360 series was IBM's decision to **unbundle** the software, that is, to sell the software separately from the hardware. This approach led to the creation of today's software industry.

Software became more sophisticated during this third generation. Several programs could run in the same time frame, sharing computer resources. This approach improved the efficiency of computer systems. Software systems were developed to support interactive processing, which used a terminal to put the user in direct contact with the computer. This kind of access caused the customer service industry to flourish, especially in areas such as reservations and credit checks.

The Fourth Generation, 1971–Present: The Microprocessor

Through the 1970s computers gained dramatically in speed, reliability, and storage capacity, but entry into the fourth generation was evolutionary rather than revolutionary. The fourth generation was, in fact, an extension of third-generation technology. That is, in the early part of the third generation, specialized chips were developed for computer memory and logic. Thus all the ingredients were in place for the next technological development—the general-purpose processor-on-a-chip, otherwise known as the **microprocessor,** which became commercially available in 1971.

Nowhere is the pervasiveness of computer power more apparent than in the explosive growth in the use of the microprocessor. In addition to the common applications of the microprocessor in digital watches, pocket calculators, and personal computers, you can expect to find one in virtually every machine in the home or business—cars, copy machines, television sets, bread-making machines, and so on. Computers today are 100 times smaller than those of the first generation, and a single chip is far more powerful than ENIAC.

The Fifth Generation: Onward

The term *fifth generation* was coined by the Japanese to describe the powerful, "intelligent" computers they wanted to build by the mid-1990s. Later the term evolved to encompass elements in several research fields related to computer intelligence: artificial intelligence, expert systems, and natural language.

But the true focus of this ongoing fifth generation is connectivity, the massive industry effort to permit users to connect their computers to other computers. The concept of the information superhighway has captured the imaginations of both computer professionals and everyday computer users.

The Story of Personal Computers

Personal computers are the machines you can "get closest to," whether you are an amateur or a professional. There is nothing quite like having your very own personal computer. Its history is very personal too, full of stories of success and failure and of individuals with whom we can readily identify.

Apple Leads the Way

As we noted in the beginning of this appendix, the very first personal computer was the MITS Altair, produced in 1975. But it was a gee-whiz machine, loaded with switches and dials but with no keyboard or screen. It took two teenagers, Steve Jobs and Steve Wozniak, to capture the imagination of the public with the first Apple computer. They built it in that time-honored place of inventors, a garage, using the $1300 proceeds from the sale of an old Volkswagen. Designed for home use, the Apple was the first to offer an easy-to-use keyboard and screen. Founded in 1977, Apple Computer was immediately and wildly successful. (Figure 8 shows the cover page of the user's manual for the first commercial Apple computer.)

The first Apple computer, the Apple I, was not a commercial success. It was the Apple II that anchored the early years of the company. In fact, it was the combination of the Apple II and the spreadsheet software called VisiCalc that caught the attention of the business community and propelled personal computers into the workplace.

The IBM PC Standard

Announcing its first personal computer in the summer of 1981, IBM proceeded to capture the top market share in just 18 months. Even more important, its machine became the industry standard (Figure 9). The IBM machine included innovations such as an 80-character screen line, a full upper- and lowercase keyboard, and the possibility of adding memory. IBM also provided internal expansion slots, so that peripheral equipment manufacturers could build accessories for the IBM PC. In addition, IBM provided hardware schematics and software listings to companies who wanted to build products in conjunction with the new PC. Many of the new products accelerated demand for the IBM machine. Even more important, many new companies sprang up just to support the IBM PC.

IBM made its computer from nonproprietary parts, opening the door for other manufacturers to do the same. Thus other personal computer manufacturers emulated the IBM standard, producing IBM **clones,** copycat computers that can run software designed for IBM computers. Almost all the major personal computer manufacturers today—Compaq, Dell, Gateway,

APPLE-1
OPERATION
MANUAL

APPLE COMPUTER COMPANY
770 Welch Road
Palo Alto, Calif. 94304

Figure 8 Apple manual. Shown here is a collector's item: the very first manual for operation of an Apple computer. Unfortunately, the early manuals were a hodgepodge of circuit diagrams, software listings, and handwritten notes. They were hard to read and understand, enough to frighten away all but the most hardy souls.

Figure 9 The IBM PC. Launched in 1981, this early IBM PC rose to the top of the best-seller list in just 18 months.

The Entrepreneurs

Ever thought you'd like to run your own show? Make your own product? Be in business for yourself? Entrepreneurs are a special breed. They are achievement oriented, like to take responsibility for decisions, and dislike routine work. They also have high levels of energy and a great deal of imagination. But perhaps the key is that they are willing to take risks.

Steve Jobs
Of the two Steves who formed Apple Computer, Steve Jobs was the true entrepreneur. Although they both were interested in electronics, Steve Wozniak was the technical genius, and he would have been happy to have been left alone to tinker. But Steve Jobs

would not let him alone for a minute; he was always pushing and crusading. In fact, Wozniak had hooked up with an evangelist, and they made quite a pair.

When Apple was getting off the ground, Jobs wanted Wozniak to quit his job so that he could work full-time on the new venture. Wozniak refused. His partner begged and cried. Wozniak gave in. While Wozniak built Apple computers, Jobs was out hustling, finding the best marketing person, the best venture capitalist, and the best company president. This entrepreneurial spirit paid off in a spectacular way as Apple rose to the top of the list of personal computer companies.

Bill Gates
When Bill Gates was a teenager, he swore off computers for a year and, in his words, "tried to act normal." His parents, who wanted him to be a lawyer, must have been relieved when Bill gave up on the computer foolishness and

went off to Harvard in 1974. But Bill started spending weekends with his friend Paul Allen, dreaming about personal computers, which did not exist yet. When the MITS Altair, the first personal computer for sale, splashed on the market in January 1975, both Bill and Paul moved to Albuquerque to be near the action at MITS. But they showed a desire even then to chart their own course. Although they wrote software for MITS, they kept the rights to their work and formed their own company. It was called Microsoft.

When MITS failed, Gates and Allen moved their software company to their native Bellevue, Washington. They had 32 people in their employ in 1980 when IBM came to call. Gates recognized the big league when he saw it and put on a suit for the occasion. He was offered a plum: the chance to develop the operating system (a crucial set of software) for IBM's soon-to-be personal computer. Although he knew he was betting the whole company, Gates never hesitated to take the risk. He purchased an existing operating system, which

he and his crew reworked to produce MS-DOS—Microsoft Disk Operating System. It was this product that sent Microsoft on its meteoric rise.

Michael Dell
The rise of the Dell Computer Corporation, founded by Michael Dell, is astonishing by any standard. It would be hard to say who is more pleased--customers, stockholders, or Mr. Dell himself. Customers, large and small, have learned that Dell personal computers are excellent and that company service is even better. Stockholders have enjoyed owning the fastest rising stock of the 1990s. And Michael Dell? In addition to untold billions, he has the satisfaction of inventing a business model that is now copied worldwide.

The business began not in a fabled garage, but in a place just about as noteworthy for a good story line: Michael Dell's dorm room at the University of Texas. It was 1983 and he was 19 years old. He began with the premise of delivering high-performance computer systems directly to the end user. By not using resellers, Dell reduces both the cost of the computer and the time of delivery. Along the way, Dell adopted the Internet as a key sales tool. Dell generates millions in revenue every day from its web site.

Now, in his early thirties, Michael Dell oversees one of the most profitable and innovative companies in the world.

and many more—are IBM clones. In fact, clone computers now dominate the personal computer market, leaving IBM with a market share that is small when compared with its original success.

The Microsoft/Intel Standard

In the history of the computer industry, the spotlight has been on the fast-changing hardware. However, personal computer users now focus more on the tremendous variety of software. The dominant force in personal computer software is the Microsoft Corporation.

Microsoft supplied the operating system—the underlying software—for the original IBM personal computer. This software, called MS-DOS, was used by IBM and by the IBM clones, permitting tiny Microsoft to grow quickly. Microsoft eventually presented more sophisticated operating systems, notably Windows. The Windows operating system is used on computers powered by a microprocessor from the Intel Corporation; this potent combination, nicknamed *Wintel*, has become the dominant force in personal computer sales.

Nevertheless, the Wintel standard is ever open to challenge. Efforts to offer computers that simply bypass Windows have not made significant inroads. It is noteworthy, however, that handheld models such as the Palm, which use neither Microsoft nor Intel products, are being used, to some degree, in lieu of personal computers. Furthermore, Linux, developed by Linus Torvalds at the University of Helsinki in Finland, offers personal computer users a graphical user interface operating system. Although copyrights are held by various creators of Linux's components, its distribution stipulations require that any copy be free. Despite its lack of a commercial marketing mechanism, Linux is making some inroads.

The Internet Revolution

The word *revolution* is never far away when the discussion is about computers. But nothing in computer history has captured the attention of computer users as the Internet has. Even the acceptance of the personal computer pales in comparison. *Revolution* is truly an appropriate word.

There are two critical points to be understood regarding the history of the Internet. The first is that the Internet was started as ARPANet, a network of equal computers that could survive a nuclear attack. Second, the Internet was made attractive to the average user by Dr. Tim Berners-Lee, who came up with the notion of links, and Marc Andreesen, who produced the first browser.

Unlike other parts of computer history, the Internet is well documented online. It makes sense to go to the source, rather than read an abbreviated version here. If you want to know more, submit words such as *Internet, history,* and *ARPANet* to a search engine, and several appropriate sites will be offered.

▲

History is still being made in the computer industry, of course, and it is being made incredibly rapidly. A book cannot possibly pretend to describe all the very latest developments. Nevertheless, as we indicated earlier, the four areas of input, processing, output, and storage describe the basic components of a computer system, whatever its date.

APPENDIX REVIEW

Summary and Key Terms

- Charles Babbage is called the father of the computer because of his invention of two computation machines. His **difference engine,** which could solve equations, led to another calculating machine, the **analytical engine,** which embodied the key parts of a computer system. Countess Ada Lovelace, who helped develop instructions for carrying out computations on Babbage's device, is often called the first programmer.

- The first computer to use electrical power instead of mechanical power was Herman Hollerith's tabulating machine, which was used in the 1890 census in the United States. Hollerith founded a company that became the forerunner of International Business Machines Corporation (IBM).

- Thomas J. Watson Sr. built IBM into a dominant force in the business machines market. He also gave Harvard professor Howard Aiken research funds with which to build an electromechanical computer, the **Mark I,** unveiled in 1944.

- John V. Atanasoff, with assistant Clifford Berry, devised the first digital computer to work by electronic means, the **Atanasoff-Berry Computer (ABC).**

- The **ENIAC (Electronic Numerical Integrator and Calculator),** developed by John Mauchly and J. Presper Eckert at the University of Pennsylvania in 1946, was the world's first general-purpose electronic computer.

- The first computer generation dates to June 14, 1951, with the delivery of the **UNIVAC (Universal Automatic Computer)** to the U.S. Bureau of the Census. First-generation computers required thousands of **vacuum tubes,** electronic tubes about the size of lightbulbs. The main form of memory was **magnetic core.**

- Second-generation computers used transistors, which were small, needed no warm-up, consumed less energy, and were faster and more reliable. During the second generation, **assembly languages,** or **symbolic languages,** were developed. Later, **high-level languages,** such as **FORTRAN** and **COBOL,** were also developed.

- The third generation featured the **integrated circuit (IC)**—a complete electronic circuit on a small chip of silicon. Silicon is a **semiconductor,** a substance that will conduct electric current when it has been "doped" with chemical impurities.

- With the third generation, IBM announced the System/360 family of computers, which made it possible for users to move up to a more powerful machine without redoing the software that already worked on the current computer. IBM also **unbundled** the software, that is, sold it separately from the hardware.

- The feature of the fourth generation—the microprocessor, a general-purpose processor-on-a-chip—grew out of the specialized memory and logic chips of the third generation.

- The term *fifth generation,* coined by the Japanese, evolved to encompass developments in artificial intelligence, expert systems, and natural languages. But the true focus of the fifth generation is connectivity, permitting users to connect their computers to other computers.

- The first personal computer, the MITS Altair, was produced in 1975. However, the first successful computer to include an easy-to-use keyboard and screen was offered by Apple Computer, founded by Steve Jobs and Steve Wozniak in 1977.

- IBM entered the personal computer market in 1981 and captured the top market share in just 18 months. Other manufacturers began to produce IBM **clones,** copycat computers that could run software designed for IBM computers.

- The leading software company worldwide is the Microsoft Corporation, which supplied the operating system for the original IBM personal computer and then went on to develop a variety of successful applications software.

GLOSSARY

A

Access arm   A mechanical device that can access all the tracks of one cylinder in a disk storage unit.

Access time   The time needed to access data directly on disk, consisting of seek time, head switching, and rotational delay.

Accumulator   A register that collects the results of computations.

Acoustic coupler   A modem that connects to a telephone receiver rather than directly to a telephone line.

Acquisition by purchase   Buying an entire system for use by the organization, as opposed to designing a new system.

Active badge   A badge that, embedded with a computer chip, signals the wearer's location by sending out infrared signals, which are read by computers distributed throughout a building.

Active cell   The cell currently available for use in a spreadsheet. Also called the *current cell*.

Address   A number used to designate a location in memory.

Address register   A register used to help locate where instructions and data are stored in memory.

Affiliate   A web site whose owner has contracted with the owner of a web site that agrees to carry its banner ad.

Alphanumeric data   Letters, digits, and special characters such as punctuation marks.

ALU   See *Arithmetic/logic unit*.

America Online (AOL)   A major online service that offers a variety of services.

Amplitude   The height of the carrier wave in analog transmission. Amplitude indicates the strength of the signal.

Amplitude modulation   A change of the amplitude of the carrier wave in analog data transmission to represent either the 0 bit or the 1 bit.

Analog transmission   The transmission of data as a continuous electrical signal in the form of a wave.

Analytical engine   A historically significant machine designed by Charles Babbage that embodied the key characteristics of modern computers.

Anchor tag   In HTML, the command used to make a link. The key attribute of the anchor tag is HREF, which indicates a link destination. The anchor tag also includes the name of the word or words—the hypertext—that will be clicked to initiate the move to the new site.

ANSI   American National Standards Institute.

Antivirus   A computer program that stops the spread of a virus. Also called a *vaccine*.

AOL   See *America Online*.

Applet   A small program that can provide animation such as dancing icons and scrolling banners on a web site.

Applications software   Programs designed to perform specific tasks and functions, such as word processing.

Arithmetic/logic unit (ALU)   Part of the central processing unit, the electronic circuitry of the ALU executes all arithmetic and logical operations.

Arithmetic operations   Mathematical calculations that the ALU performs on data.

ARPANet   A network, established in 1969 by the Department of Defense, that eventually became the Internet.

Artificial intelligence   The field of study that explores computer involvement in tasks requiring intelligence, imagination, and intuition.

ASCII (American Standard Code for Information Interchange)   A coding scheme using 7-bit characters to represent data characters. A variation of the code, called ASCII-8, uses 8 bits per character.

Assembler program   A translator program used to convert assembly language programs to machine language.

Assembly language   A second-generation language that uses abbreviations for instructions, as opposed to only numbers. Also called *symbolic language*.

Atanasoff-Berry Computer (ABC)   The first electronic digital computer, designed by John V. Atanasoff and Clifford Berry, in the late 1930s.

Attribute   In object-oriented programming, a fact related to an object.

Asynchronous transmission   Data transmission in which data is sent in groups of bits, with each group of bits preceded by a start signal and ended with a stop signal. Also called *start/stop transmission*.

ATM   See *Automated teller machine*.

Audio-response unit   See *Voice synthesizer*.

Audit trail   A method of tracing data from the output back to the source documents.

Automated teller machine (ATM)   An input/output device connected to a computer used by bank customers for financial transactions.

Automatic recalculation   In a spreadsheet, when one value or calculation is changed, all values dependent on the changed item are automatically recalculated to reflect the change.

Automatic reformatting   In word processing, automatic adjustment of text to accommodate changes such as margin width.

Auxiliary storage   Another name for secondary storage, which is storage for data and programs. Auxiliary storage is most often on disk.

Axis   A reference line of a graph. The horizontal axis is the x-axis. The vertical axis is the y-axis.

B

Backbone   The major communication links that tie Internet servers across wide geographical areas.

Background   (1) In large computers, the memory area for running programs with low priorities. Contrast with *Foreground*. (2) On a web site, the screen appearance behind the text and images.

Backup system   A method of storing data in more than one place to protect it from damage or loss.

Bandwidth   The number of frequencies that can fit on one communications line or link at the same time, or the capacity of the link.

Banner ad   On a web site, a clickable ad, often in the shape of a rectangle, that can take a user to the site of the advertiser.

Bar code   A standardized pattern of vertical marks that represents the Universal Product Code (UPC) that identifies a product.

Bar code reader   A stationary photoelectric scanner that inputs bar codes by means of reflected light.

Bar graph   A graph made up of filled-in columns or rows that represent the change of data over time.

BASIC (Beginner's All-purpose Symbolic Instruction Code)   A high-level programming language that is easy to learn and use.

Batch processing   A data processing technique in which transactions are collected into groups, or batches, for processing.

Binary   Regarding number systems, the binary number system uses exactly two symbols, the digits 0 and 1.

Binary system   A system in which data is represented by combinations of 0s and 1s, which correspond to the two states off and on.

Biometrics   The science of measuring individual body characteristics; used in some security systems.

Bit   A binary digit.

Body tags   In HTML, a pair of tags that enclose the content of the page.

Bomb   An application that sabotages a computer by triggering damage—usually at a later date. Also called a *logic bomb*.

Boolean logic   Regarding search engines on the Internet, a mathematical system that can be used to narrow the search through the use of operators such as AND, OR, and NOT.

Bpi   See *Bytes per inch*.

Broadcasting   A method of file transmission that sends one copy of a file from one computer to every computer on the network.

Bridge   A device that recognizes and transmits messages to be sent to other similar networks.

Browser   Software used to access the Internet.

Bus or bus line   An electronic pathway for data travel among the parts of a computer. Also called a *data bus*.

Bus network   A network that has a single line to which each device is attached.

Button   Clickable icons that represent menu choices or options.

Byte   Strings of bits (usually 8) used to represent one data character—a letter, digit, or special character.

Bytes per inch (bpi)   An expression of the amount (density) of data stored on magnetic tape.

C

C   A sophisticated programming language invented by Bell Labs in 1974.

C++   An object-oriented programming language; a version of C.

Cable modem   A fast communications link that uses coaxial television cables already in place without interrupting normal cable TV reception.

Cache   A relatively small amount of very fast memory that stores data and instructions that are used frequently, resulting in improved processing speeds.

CAD/CAM   See *Computer-aided design/computer-aided manufacturing*.

Candidates   In systems analysis and design, alternative plans offered in the preliminary design phase of a project.

Carrier sense multiple access with collision detection (CSMA/CD)   The line control method used by Ethernet. Each node has access to the communications line and can transmit if it hears no communication on the line. If two stations transmit simultaneously, they will wait and retry their transmissions.

Carrier wave   An analog signal used in the transmission of electric signals.

Cathode ray tube (CRT)   The most common type of computer screen.

CD-R   A technology that permits writing on optical disks.

CD-ROM   See *Compact disk read-only memory*.

Cell   The intersection of a row and a column in a spreadsheet. Entries in a spreadsheet are stored in individual cells.

Cell address   In a spreadsheet, the column and row coordinates of a cell. Also called the cell reference.

Cell contents   The label, value, formula, or function contained in a spreadsheet cell.

Cell reference   In a spreadsheet, the column and row coordinates of a cell. Also called the *cell address*.

Central processing unit (CPU) Electronic circuitry that executes stored program instructions. It consists of two parts: the control unit and the arithmetic/logic unit. The CPU processes raw data into meaningful, useful information.

Centralized Description of a computer system in which hardware, software, storage, and computer access is in one location. Contrast with *Decentralized*.

CERN The name of the site of the particle physics lab where Dr. Tim Berners-Lee worked when he invented the World Wide Web; sometimes called the birthplace of the Web.

Change agent The role of the systems analyst in overcoming resistance to change within an organization.

Character A letter, number, or special character such as $.

Characters per inch (cpi) An expression of the amount (density) of data stored on magnetic tape.

Chief information officer (CIO) Manager of an MIS department.

Circuit One or more conductors through which electricity flows.

CISC See *Complex instruction set computer*.

Class In object-oriented programming, an object class contains the characteristics that are unique to that class.

Click stream The set of a series of mouse clicks that link from site to site.

Click through Leaving the current web site for an advertised site.

Client (1) An individual or organization contracting for systems analysis. (2) In a client/server network, a program on the personal computer that allows that node to communicate with the server.

Client/server A network setup that involves a server computer, which controls the network, and clients, other computers that access the network and its services. In particular, the server does some processing, sending the client only the portion of the file it needs or possibly just the processed results. Contrast with *File server*.

Clip art Illustrations already produced by professional artists for public use. Computerized clip art is stored on disk and can be used to enhance any kind of graph or document.

Clock A component of the CPU that produces pulses at a fixed rate to synchronize all computer operations.

Clone A personal computer that can run software designed for IBM personal computers.

CMOS See *Complementary metal oxide semiconductor*.

Coaxial cable Bundles of insulated wires within a shielded enclosure. Coaxial cable can be laid underground or undersea.

COBOL (COmmon Business-Oriented Language) An English-like programming language used primarily for business applications.

Cold site An environmentally suitable empty shell in which a company can install its own computer system.

Collaborative software See *Groupware*.

Collision The problem that occurs when two records have the same disk address.

Command A name that invokes the correct program or program segment.

Commercial software Software that is packaged and sold in stores. Also called *packaged software*.

Compact disk read-only memory (CD-ROM) Optical data storage technology using disk formats identical to audio compact disks.

Compare operation An operation in which the computer compares two data items and performs alternative operations based on the results of the comparison.

Compiler A translator that converts the symbolic statements of a high-level language into computer-executable machine language.

Complementary metal oxide semiconductor (CMOS) A semiconductor device that does not require a large amount of power to operate. The CMOS is often found in devices that require low power consumption, such as portable computers.

Complex instruction set computer (CISC) A CPU design that contains a large number of instructions of varying kinds, some of which are rarely used. Contrast with *Reduced instruction set computer*.

Computer A machine that accepts data (input) and processes it into useful information (output). A computer system requires four main aspects of data handling—input, processing, output, and storage.

Computer Fraud and Abuse Act A law passed by Congress in 1984 to fight computer crime.

Computer Information Systems (CIS) The department responsible for managing a company's computer resources. Also called *Management Information Systems (MIS)*, *Computing Services (CS)*, or *Information Services*.

Computer literacy The awareness and knowledge of, and the capacity to interact with, computers.

Computer Matching and Privacy Protection Act Legislation that prevents the government from comparing certain records in an attempt to find a match.

Computer operator A person who monitors and runs the computer equipment in a large system.

Computer programmer A person who designs, writes, tests, and implements programs.

Computer-aided design/computer-aided manufacturing (CAD/CAM) The use of computers to create two- and three-dimensional pictures of products to be manufactured.

Computing Services The department responsible for managing a company's computer resources. Also called *Management Information Systems (MIS)*, *Computer Information Systems (CIS)*, or *Information Services*.

Concurrently With reference to the execution of computer instructions, in the same time frame but not simultaneously. See also *Multiprogramming*.

Conditional replace A word processing function that asks the user whether to replace text each time the program finds a particular item.

Consortium   A joint venture to support a complete computer facility to be used in an emergency.

Context sensitive   In reference to an ad on a web site, one that is related to the subject matter on the screen.

Continuous word system   A speech recognition system that can understand sustained speech so that users can speak normally.

Control unit   The circuitry that directs and coordinates the entire computer system in executing stored program instructions. Part of the central processing unit.

Cookie   An entry in a file stored on the user's hard drive that reflects activity on the Internet.

Coordinating   In systems analysis, orchestrating the process of analyzing and planning a new system by pulling together the various individuals, schedules, and tasks that contribute to the analysis.

Copyrighted software   Software that costs money and must not be copied without permission from the manufacturer.

CPU   See *Central processing unit.*

CRT   See *Cathode ray tube.*

CSMA/CD   See *Carrier sense multiple access with collision detection.*

Current cell   The cell currently available for use in a spreadsheet. Also called the *active cell.*

Cursor   An indicator on the screen; it shows where the next user-computer interaction will be. Also called a *pointer.*

Cursor movement keys   Keys on the computer keyboard that allow the user to move the cursor on the screen.

Custom software   Software that is tailored to a specific user's needs.

Cut and paste   In word processing and some other applications, moving a block of text by deleting it in one place (cut) and adding it in another (paste).

Cylinder   A set of tracks on a magnetic disk, one from each platter, vertically aligned. These tracks can be accessed by one positioning of the access arm.

Cylinder method   A method of organizing data on a magnetic disk. This method organizes data vertically, which minimizes seek time.

D

DASD   See *Direct-access storage device.*

DAT   See *Digital audio tape.*

Data   Raw input to be processed by a computer.

Data communications   The process of exchanging data over communications facilities.

Data communications systems   Computer systems that transmit data over communications lines, such as public telephone lines or private network cables.

Data compression   Making a large data file smaller by temporarily removing nonessential but space-hogging items such as tab marks and double-spacing.

Data Encryption Standard (DES)   The standardized public key by which senders and receivers can scramble and unscramble messages sent over data communications equipment.

Data entry operator   A person who keys data for computer processing.

Data flow diagram (DFD)   A diagram that shows the flow of data through an organization.

Data item   Data in a relational database table.

Data mining   The process of extracting previously unknown information from existing data.

Data mirroring   In RAID storage, a technique of duplicating data on a separate disk drive.

Data point   Each dot or symbol on a line graph. Each data point represents a value.

Data striping   In RAID storage, a technique of spreading data across several disks in the array.

Data transfer   The transfer of data between memory and the place on the disk track—from memory to the track if writing, from the track to memory if reading.

Data transfer rate   The speed with which data can be transferred to or from a disk and a computer.

Database   An organized collection of related files stored together with minimum redundancy. Specific data items can be retrieved for various applications.

Database management system (DBMS)   A set of programs that creates, manages, protects, and provides access to the database.

DBMS   See *Database management system.*

Debugging   The process of detecting, locating, and correcting logic errors in a program.

Decentralized   Description of a computer system in which the computer and its storage devices are in one place but devices that access the computer are in other locations. Contrast with *Centralized.*

Decision support system (DSS)   A computer system that supports managers in nonroutine decision-making tasks. A DSS involves a model, a mathematical representation of a real-life situation.

Decision table   A standard table of the logical decisions that must be made regarding potential conditions in a given system. Also called a *decision logic table.*

Default settings   The settings automatically used by a program unless the user specifies otherwise, thus overriding them.

Delete key   The key used to delete the text character at the cursor location or a text block that has been selected or marked.

Demodulation   The reconstruction of the original digital message after analog transmission.

Density   The amount of data stored on magnetic tape; expressed in number of characters per inch (cpi) or bytes per inch (bpi).

Dependent variable   Output of a computerized model, particularly a decision support system. Called dependent because it depends on the inputs.

DES See *Data Encryption Standard.*

Desk-checking A programming phase in which a programmer mentally checks the logic of a program to ensure that it is error-free and workable.

Detail design A systems design subphase in which the system is planned in detail, including the details of output, input, files and databases, processing, and controls and backup.

DFD See *Data flow diagram.*

Diagnostics Error messages provided by the compiler as it translates a program. Diagnostics inform the user of programming language syntax errors.

Difference engine A historically significant machine designed by Charles Babbage to solve polynomial equations by calculating the successive differences between them. See also his other machine, *Analytical engine.*

Digital audio tape (DAT) A high-capacity tape that records data using a method called helical scan recording, which places the data in diagonal bands that run across the tape rather than down its length.

Digital subscriber line (DSL) A service that uses advances electronics to send data over conventional copper telephone wires.

Digital transmission The transmission of data as distinct on or off pulses.

Digital versatile disk A form of optical disk storage that has a double-layered surface and can be written on both sides, providing significant capacity. Also called *DVD-ROM.*

Direct access Immediate access to a record in secondary storage, usually on disk.

Direct conversion A system conversion in which the user simply stops using the old system and starts using the new one.

Direct file organization An arrangement of records so that each is individually accessible.

Direct file processing Processing that allows the user to access a record directly by using a record key.

Direct-access storage device (DASD) A storage device, usually disk, in which a record can be accessed directly.

Disaster recovery plan Guidelines for restoring computer processing operations if they are halted by major damage or destruction.

Discrete word system A speech recognition system limited to understanding isolated words.

Disk drive A machine that allows data to be read from a disk or written on a disk.

Disk pack A stack of magnetic disks assembled together.

Diskette A single disk, made of flexible Mylar, on which data is recorded as magnetic spots. A diskette is usually 31/2 inches in diameter, with a hard plastic jacket.

Displayed value The calculated result of a formula or function in a spreadsheet cell.

Distributed data processing A computer system in which processing is decentralized, with the computers and storage devices and access devices in dispersed locations.

Documentation The instruction manual for packaged software.

Domain The name of the Internet service provider, as it appears in the Uniform Resource Locator.

Dot pitch The amount of space between dots on a screen.

Download In a networking environment, to receive data files from another computer, probably a larger computer or a host computer. Contrast with *Upload.*

DRAM See *Dynamic random-access memory.*

DSL See *Digital subscriber line.*

DSS See *Decision support system.*

DVD See *Digital versatile disk.*

Dynamic random-access memory (DRAM) Memory chips that are periodically regenerated, allowing the chips to retain the stored data. Contrast with *Static random-assess memory.*

E

EDI See *Electronic data interchange.*

EFT See *Electronic fund transfer.*

Electronic data interchange (EDI) A set of standards by which companies can electronically exchange common business forms such as invoices and purchase orders.

Electronic fund transfer (EFT) Paying for goods and services by transferring funds electronically.

Electronic mail (e-mail) Sending messages from one terminal or computer to another.

Electronic software distribution Downloading software from the originator's site to a user's site, presumably for a fee.

Electronic spreadsheet A computerized worksheet used to organize data into rows and columns for analysis.

E-mail See *Electronic mail.*

Encapsulation (1) In object-oriented programming, the containment of both data and its related instructions in the object. (2) A way to transfer data between two similar networks over an intermediate network by enclosing one type of data packet protocol into the packet of another. Also called *tunneling.*

Encryption The process of encoding data to be transmitted via communications links, so that its contents are protected from unauthorized people.

ENIAC (Electronic Numerical Integrator and Computer) The first general-purpose electronic computer, built by Dr. John Mauchly and J. Presper Eckert, Jr., and was first operational in 1946.

Equal-to condition (=) A logical operation in which the computer compares two numbers to determine equality.

Erase head The head in a magnetic tape unit that erases any data previously recorded on the tape before recording new data.

Ergonomics The study of human factors related to computers.

ESS See *Executive support system.*

Ethernet A popular type of local area network that uses a bus topology.

E-time   The execution portion of the machine cycle; E-time includes the execute and store operations.

Executive support system (ESS)   A decision support system for senior-level executives who make decisions that affect an entire company.

Expansion slots   The slots inside a computer that allow a user to insert additional circuit boards.

Expert shell   Software having the basic structure to find answers to questions that are part of an expert system; the questions themselves can be added by the user.

Expert system   Software that presents the computer as an expert on some topic.

External cache   Cache (very fast memory for frequently used data and instructions) on chips separate from the microprocessor.

Extranet   A network of two or more intranets.

F

Facsimile technology (fax)   The use of computer technology to send digitized graphics, charts, and text from one facsimile machine to another.

Fair Credit Reporting Act   Legislation that allows individuals access to their own credit records and gives them the right to challenge them.

Fax   See *Facsimile technology.*

Fax modem   A modem that allows the user to transmit and receive faxes without interrupting other applications programs, as well as performing the usual modem functions.

Feasibility study   The first phase of systems analysis, in which planners determine if and how a project should proceed. Also called a *system survey* or a *preliminary investigation.*

Federal Privacy Act   Legislation stipulating that government agencies cannot keep secret personnel files and that individuals can have access to all government files, as well as to those of private firms contracting with the government, that contain information about them.

Fiber optics   Technology that uses glass fibers that can transmit light as a communications link to send data.

Field   A set of related characters.

Field name   In a database, the unique name describing the data in a field.

Field robot   A robot that is used on location for such tasks as inspecting nuclear plants, disposing of bombs, cleaning up chemical spills, and other chores that are undesirable for human intervention.

Field type   In a database, a category describing a field and determined by the kind of data the field will accept. Common field types are character, numeric, date, and logical.

Field width   In a database or spreadsheet, the maximum number of characters that can be contained in a field.

File   (1) A repository of data. (2) A collection of related records. (3) In word processing, a document created on a computer.

File server   A network relationship in which an entire file is sent to a node, which then does its own processing. Also, the network computer exclusively dedicated to making files available on a network. Contrast with *Client/server.*

File transfer protocol (FTP)   Regarding the Internet, a set of rules for transferring files from one computer to another.

File transfer software   In a network, software used to transfer files from one computer to another. See also *Download* and *Upload.*

Firewall   A dedicated computer whose sole purpose is to talk to the outside world and decide who gains entry to a company's private network or intranet.

Flaming   Sending insulting e-mail messages, often by large numbers of people in response to spamming.

Flash memory   Nonvolatile memory chips.

Flatbed scanner   A desktop scanner that scans a sheet of paper, thus using optical recognition to convert text or drawings into computer-recognizable form.

Flowchart   The pictorial representation of an orderly step-by-step solution to a problem.

Font   A complete set of characters in a particular size, typeface, weight, and style.

Font library   A variety of type fonts stored on disk. Also called *soft fonts.*

Footer   In word processing, the ability to place the same line, with possible variations such as page number, on the bottom of each page.

Footnote   In word processing, the ability to make a reference in a text document to a note at the bottom of the page.

Foreground   In large computers, an area in memory for programs that have a high priority. Contrast with *Background.*

Format   (1) The process of preparing a disk to accept data. (2) The specifications that determine how a document or worksheet appears on the screen or printer.

Formula   In a spreadsheet, an instruction placed in a cell to calculate a value.

FORTRAN (FORmula TRANslator)   The first high-level programming language, introduced in 1954 by IBM; it is scientifically oriented.

Fourth-generation language   A very high-level language. Also called a *4GL.*

Frames   The capability of some browsers to display pages of a site in separate sections, each of which may operate independently.

Freedom of Information Act   Legislation that allows citizens access to personal data gathered by federal agencies.

Freeware   Software for which there is no fee.

Frequency   The number of times an analog signal repeats during a specific time interval.

Frequency modulation   The alteration of the carrier wave frequency to represent 0s and 1s.

Front-end processor   A communications control unit designed to relieve the central computer of some communications tasks.

FTP   See *File transfer protocol.*

Full-duplex transmission   Data transmission in both directions at once.

Full justification   In word processing, making both the left and right margins even.

Function   A built-in spreadsheet formula.

Function keys   Special keys programmed to execute commonly used commands; the commands vary according to the software being used.

G

Gantt chart   A bar chart commonly used to depict schedule deadlines and milestones, especially in systems analysis and design.

Gateway   A collection of hardware and software resources to connect two dissimilar networks, allowing computers in one network to communicate with those in the other.

GB   See *Gigabyte.*

General-purpose register   A register used for several functions, such as arithmetic and addressing purposes.

Gigabyte (GB)   One billion bytes.

Graphical user interface (GUI)   An image-based computer interface in which the user sends directions to the operating system by selecting icons from a menu or manipulating icons on the screen by using a pointing device such as a mouse.

Graphics   Pictures or graphs.

Graphics adapter board   A circuit board that enables a computer to display pictures or graphs as well as text. Also called a *graphics card.*

Graphics card   See *Graphics adapter board.*

Greater-than condition (>)   A comparison operation that determines whether one value is greater than another.

Groupware   Software that lets a group of people develop or track a project together, usually including electronic mail, networking, and database technology. Also called *collaborative software.*

GUI   See *Graphical user interface.*

H

Hacker   (1) An enthusiastic, largely self-taught computer user. (2) Currently, a person who gains access to computer systems illegally, usually from a personal computer.

Half-duplex transmission   Data transmission in either direction, but only one way at a time.

Halftone   In desktop publishing, a reproduction of a black-and-white photograph; it is made up of tiny dots.

Handheld scanner   A small scanner that can be passed over a sheet of paper, thus using optical recognition to convert text or drawings into computer-recognizable form.

Hard copy   Printed paper output.

Hard disk   A metal platter coated with magnetic oxide that can be magnetized to represent data. Hard disks are usually in a pack and are generally in a sealed module.

Hardware   The computer and its associated equipment.

Head crash   The result of a read/write head touching a disk surface and causing all data to be destroyed.

Header   In word processing, the ability to place the same line, with possible variations such as page number, on the top of each page.

Helical recording   Storing data on tape by placing it in tracks that run diagonally across the tape.

Hierarchy chart   See *Structure chart.*

High-level language   An English-like programming language that is easier to use than an older symbolic language.

Home page   The first page of a web site.

Host computer   The central computer in a network, to which other computers, and perhaps terminals, are attached.

Hot list   Regarding the Internet, a list of names and URLs of favorite sites.

Hot site   For use in an emergency, a fully equipped computer center with hardware, communications facilities, environmental controls, and security.

HTTP   See *HyperText Transfer Protocol.*

Hyperregion   On the World Wide Web, an icon or image that can be clicked to cause a link to another web site; furthermore, the cursor image changes when it rests on the hyperregion.

Hypertext   On the World Wide Web, text that can be clicked to cause a link to another web site; hypertext is usually distinguished by a different color and perhaps underlining; furthermore, the cursor image changes when it rests on the hypertext.

HyperText Transfer Protocol (HTTP)   A set of rules that provide the means of communicating on the World Wide Web by using links. Note the http at the beginning of each web address.

I

IC   See *Integrated circuit.*

Ice   A web page that page does not fill a larger screen but is anchored to the right side of the screen. See *jello, liquid.*

Icon   A small picture on a computer screen; it represents a computer activity.

Imaging   Using a scanner to convert a drawing, photo, or document to an electronic version that can be stored and reproduced when needed. Once scanned, text documents may be processed by optical recognition software so that the text can be manipulated.

Immersion   Related to virtual reality. When a user is absorbed by virtual reality interaction, the process is said to be immersion.

Impact printer   A printer that forms characters by physically striking the paper.

Implementation   The phase of a systems analysis and design project that includes training, equipment conversion, file conversion, system conversion, auditing, evaluation, and maintenance.

Independent variable   Input to a computerized model, particularly a decision support system. Called independent because it can change.

Indexed file organization   The combination of sequential and direct file organization.

Indexed file processing   A method of file organization that represents a compromise between sequential and direct methods. Indexed processing stores records in the file in sequential order, but the file also contains an index of keys; the address associated with the key is then used to locate the record on the disk.

Indexed processing   See *Indexed file processing.*

Inference engine   Related to the field of artificial intelligence, particularly how computers learn; a process that accesses, selects, and interprets a set of rules.

Information   Input data that has been processed by the computer; data that is organized, meaningful, and useful.

Information center   A company unit that offers employees computer and software training, help in getting data from other computer systems, and technical assistance.

Information Services   The department responsible for managing a company's computer resources. Also called *Management Information Systems (MIS), Computer Information Systems (CIS),* or *Computing Services.*

Information utility   A commercial consumer-oriented communications system, such as America Online or the Microsoft Network, that offers a variety of services, usually including access to the Internet.

Inheritance   In object-oriented programming, the property meaning that an object in a subclass automatically possesses all the characteristics of the class to which it belongs.

Ink-jet printer   A nonimpact printer that forms output text or images by spraying ink from jet nozzles onto the paper.

Input   Raw data that is put into the computer system for processing.

Input device   A device that puts data in computer-understandable form and sends it to the processing unit.

Input requirements   In systems design, the plan for input medium and content and forms design.

Instance   In object-oriented programming, a specific occurrence of an object.

Instruction set   The commands that a CPU understands and is capable of executing. Each type of CPU has a fixed group of these instructions, and each set usually differs from that understood by other CPUs.

Integrated circuit (IC)   A complete electronic circuit on a small chip of silicon.

Integrated   Services Digital Network (ISDN)   A type of digital network that links computers and other devices in a single, very fast system.

Interlaced   A screen whose lines are scanned alternatively, first the odd-numbered lines, and then the even-numbered lines, allowing for a lower refresh rate without producing flicker. See *Non-interlaced.*

Internal cache   Cache (very fast memory for frequently used data and instructions) built into the design of the microprocessor. Contrast with *External cache.*

Internal font   A font built into the read-only memory (a ROM chip) of a printer.

Internal modem   A modem on a circuit board. An internal modem can be installed in a computer by the user.

Internal storage   The electronic circuitry that temporarily holds data and program instructions needed by the CPU.

Internet   A public communications network once used primarily by businesses, governments, and academic institutions but now also used by individuals via various private access methods.

Internet service provider (ISP)   An entity that offers, for a fee, a server computer and the software needed to access the Internet.

Internet Tax Freedom Act   A federal law that imposes a three-year moratorium (beginning in October 1998) on taxes imposed on the Internet, and calls for a committee to study the matter.

Intranet   A private Internet-like network internal to a certain company.

Interrupt   In multiprogramming, a condition that temporarily suspends the execution of an individual program.

IP switches   Internet protocol switches used to direct communications traffic among connected networks that have adopted the Internet protocol.

ISDN   See *Integrated Services Digital Network.*

ISP   See *Internet service provider.*

I-time   The instruction portion of the machine cycle; I-time includes the fetch and decode operations.

J

Java   A network-friendly programming language that allows software to run on many different platforms.

Jello   A web page does not fill a larger screen but is centered. See *ice, liquid.*

Joystick   A graphics input device that allows fingertip control of figures on a CRT screen.

Justification   In word processing, aligning text along the left or right margins, or both.

K

K or KB   See *Kilobyte.*

Kerning   In word processing or desktop publishing, adjusting the space between characters to create a more attractive or readable appearance.

Key   A unique identifier for a record.

Key field   In a database, a field that has been designated as a key can be used as the basis for a query of the database.

Keyboard   A common computer input device similar to the keyboard of a typewriter.

Kilobyte (K or KB)   1024 bytes.

Knowledge base Related to the field of artificial intelligence, particularly how computers learn; a set of facts and rules about those facts.

Knowledge engineer Related to building an expert system, the person working to extract information from the human expert.

L

Label In a spreadsheet, data consisting of a string of text characters.

LAN See *Local area network.*

LAN manager A person designated to manage and run a computer network, particularly a local area network (LAN).

Laptop computer A small portable computer, usually somewhat larger than a notebook computer.

Laser printer A nonimpact printer that uses a light beam to transfer images to paper.

LCD See *Liquid crystal display.*

Leading In word processing or desktop publishing, the vertical spacing between lines of type.

Less-than condition A logical operation in which the computer compares values to determine whether one is less than another.

Librarian A person who catalogs processed computer disks and tapes and keeps them secure.

Light pen A graphics input device that allows the user to interact directly with the computer screen.

Link (1) A physical data communications medium. (2) On the World Wide Web, clickable text or image that can cause a change to a different web site.

Link/load phase A phase that takes the machine language object module and adds necessary prewritten programs to produce output called the load module; the load module is executable.

Liquid A web page that fills the entire screen, no matter what the screen size. See *ice, jello.*

Liquid crystal display (LCD) The flat display screen found on some laptop computers.

Live banner A type of web site banner ad that lets a user get more information about a product without leaving the current site.

Load module An executable version of a program.

Local area network (LAN) A network designed to share data and resources among several computers, usually personal computers in a limited geographical area, such as an office or a building. Contrast with *Wide area network.*

Logic chip A central processing unit on a chip, generally known as a microprocessor but called a logic chip when used for some special purpose, such as controlling some under-the-hood action in a car.

Logic error A flaw in the logic of a program.

Logic flowchart A flowchart that represents the flow of logic in a program.

Logical field In a database, a field used to keep track of true and false conditions.

Logical operations Comparing operations. The ALU is able to compare numbers, letters, or special characters and take alternative courses of action depending on the result of the comparison.

Lurking Reading messages in newsgroups without writing any.

M

Machine cycle The combination of I-time and E-time, the steps used by the central processing unit to execute instructions.

Machine language The lowest level of language; it represents data and instructions as 1s and 0s.

Magnetic core A small, flat doughnut-shaped piece of metal used as an early memory device.

Magnetic disk An oxide-coated disk on which data is recorded as magnetic spots.

Magnetic tape A magnetic medium with an iron-oxide coating that can be magnetized. Data is stored on the tape as extremely small magnetized spots.

Magnetic tape unit A data storage unit used to record data on and retrieve data from magnetic tape.

Magnetic-ink character recognition (MICR) A method of machine-reading characters made of magnetized particles. A common application is checks.

Magneto-optical (MO) A hybrid disk that has the high-volume capacity of an optical disk but can be written over like a magnetic disk. It uses both a laser beam and a magnet to properly align magnetically sensitive metallic crystals.

Mail merge Adding names and addresses, probably from a database, to a prepared document, such as a letter prepared using word processing.

Main memory The electronic circuitry that temporarily holds data and program instructions needed by the CPU.

Main storage The electronic circuitry that temporarily holds data and program instructions needed by the CPU.

Mainframe A large computer that has access to billions of characters of data and is capable of processing large amounts of data very quickly. Notably, mainframes are used by such data-heavy customers as banks, airlines, and large manufacturers.

MAN See *Metropolitan area network.*

Management Information Systems (MIS) A department that manages computer resources for an organization. Also called *Computing Services* or *Information Services.*

Mark In word processing, one marks a certain section of text, called a block, by using some sort of highlighting, usually reverse video; the marked text is then copied, moved, or deleted.

Mark I An early computer built in 1944 by Harvard professor Howard Aiken.

Master file   A semipermanent set of records.

MB   See *Megabyte.*

Megabyte (MB)   One million bytes. The unit often used to measure memory or storage capacity.

Megaflop   One million floating-point operations per second. One measure of a computer's speed.

Megahertz (MHz)   One million cycles per second. Used to express microprocessor speeds.

Memory   The electronic circuitry that temporarily holds data and program instructions needed by the CPU.

Memory management   The process of allocating memory to programs and keeping the programs in memory separate from one another.

Memory protection   In a multiprogramming system, the process of keeping a program from straying into other programs in memory.

Message   In object-oriented programming, a command telling what—not how—something is to be done, which activates the object.

Method   In object-oriented programming, instructions that tell the data what to do. Also called an *operation.*

Metropolitan area network (MAN)   A network than spans a city.

MHz   See *Megahertz.*

MICR   See *Magnetic-ink character recognition.*

MICR inscriber   A device that adds magnetic characters to a document, in particular, the amount of a check.

Microcomputer   A relatively inexpensive type of computer, usually used by an individual in a home or office setting. Also called a *personal computer.*

Microprocessor   A general-purpose central processing unit on a chip.

Microsecond   One-millionth of a second.

Micro-to-mainframe link   A connection between microcomputers and mainframe computers.

Microwave transmission   Line-of-sight transmission of data signals through the atmosphere from relay station to relay station.

Millisecond   One-thousandth of a second.

MIPS   Millions of instructions per second. A measure of how fast a central processing unit can process information.

MIS   See *Management Information Systems.*

MIS manager   A person, familiar with both computer technology and the organization's business, who runs the MIS department.

MITS Altair   Generally considered the first personal computer, offered as a kit to computer hobbyists in 1975.

MMX   See *Multimedia extension chip.*

Model   (1) A type of database, each type representing a particular way of organizing data. The three database models are hierarchical, network, and relational. (2) In a DSS, an image of something that actually exists or a mathematical representation of a real-life system.

Modem   Short for modulate/demodulate. A device that converts a digital signal to an analog signal or vice versa. Used to transfer data between computers over analog communications lines.

Modulation   Using a modem, the process of converting a signal from digital to analog.

Monitor   Hardware that features the computer's screen, includes housing for the screen's electronic components, and probably sits on a stand that tilts and swivels.

Monochrome   A computer screen that displays information in only one color, usually green, on a black background.

Monolithic   Refers to the inseparable nature of memory chip circuitry.

Mouse   A handheld computer input device whose rolling movement on a flat surface causes corresponding movement of the cursor on the screen. Also, a mouse button can be clicked to make selections from choices on the screen.

Motherboard   Inside the personal computer housing, a board that holds the main chips and circuitry of the computer hardware, including the central processing unit chip.

Motion Picture Experts Group (MPEG)   A set of widely accepted video standards.

MPEG   See *Motion Picture Experts Group.*

Multicasting   A method of file transmission that sends one copy of the file from one computer to the computer of each designated recipient.

Multimedia   Software that typically presents information with text, illustrations, photos, narration, music, animation, and film clips—possible because the high-volume capacity of optical disks can accommodate photographs, film clips, and music. To use multimedia software, you must have the proper hardware: a CD-ROM drive, a sound card, and speakers. Multimedia also is offered on several Internet sites.

Multimedia extension chip (MMX)   A microprocessor that boosts a computer's ability to produce graphics, video, and sound by including many of the needed functions on the chip itself.

Multiprocessing   Using more than one central processing unit, a computer can run multiple programs simultaneously, each using its own processor.

Multiprogramming   A feature of large computer operating systems under which different programs from different users compete for the use of the central processing unit; these programs are said to run concurrently.

N

Nanosecond   One-billionth of a second.

Natural language   A programming language that resembles human language.

Navigation bar   A set of links on a web page.

NC   See *Network computer.*

Netiquette   Appropriate behavior in network communications.

Network   A computer system that uses communications equipment to connect two or more computers and their resources.

Network computer   A computer used in conjunction with a television set to access the Internet. Also called a *net computer* or *net box* or *Web TV.*

Network interface card (NIC)   A circuit board that can be inserted into a slot inside a personal computer to allow it to send and receive messages on a local area network (LAN).

Network manager   A person designated to manage and run a computer network.

Newsgroup   An informal network of computers that allows the posting and reading of messages in groups that focus on specific topics. More formally called Usenet.

NIC   See *Network interface card.*

Node   A device, usually a personal computer, that is connected to a network.

Noise   Electrical interference that causes distortion when a signal is being transmitted.

Nonimpact printer   A printer that prints without striking the paper.

Non-interlaced (NI)   A description of screens that scan all lines in order, a procedure that is best for animated graphics. See *Interlaced.*

Notebook computer   A small portable computer.

O

Object   In object-oriented programming, a self-contained unit that contains both data and related facts and functions—the instructions to act on that data.

Object module   A machine language version of a program; it is produced by a compiler or assembler.

Object-oriented programming (OOP)   A programming approach that uses objects, self-contained units that contain both data and related facts and functions—the instructions to act on that data.

OCR   See *Optical character recognition.*

OCR-A   The standard typeface for characters to be input by optical character recognition.

Office automation   The use of technology to help achieve goals in an office. Often associated with data communications.

OMR   See *Optical mark recognition.*

Online   In a data communications environment, a direct connection from a terminal to a computer or from one computer to another.

Online service   A commercial consumer-oriented communications system, such as America Online or the Microsoft Network, that offers a variety of services, usually including access to the Internet. Also called an *information utility.*

OOP   See *Object-oriented programming.*

Operating environment   Software designed as a shell, an extra layer, for an operating system, so that the user does not have to memorize or look up commands.

Operating system   A set of programs that lies between applications software and the computer hardware, through which a computer manages its own resources.

Operation   In object-oriented programming, instructions that tell the data what to do. Also called a *method.*

Optical character recognition (OCR)   A computer input method that uses a light source to read special characters and convert them to electrical signals to be sent to the computer.

Optical disk   Storage technology that uses a laser beam to store large amounts of data at relatively low cost.

Optical mark recognition (OMR)   A computer input method that uses a light source to recognize marks on paper and convert them to electrical signals to be sent to the computer.

Optical recognition system   A category of computer input method that uses a light source to read optical marks, optical characters, handwritten characters, and bar codes and convert them to electrical signals to be sent to the computer.

Organization chart   A hierarchical diagram depicting lines of authority within an organization, usually mentioning people by name and title.

Output   Raw data that has been processed by the computer into usable information.

Output device   A device, such as a printer, that makes processed information available for use.

Output requirements   In systems design, the plan for output medium and content, types of reports needed, and forms design.

Outsourcing   Assigning the design and management of a new or revised system to an outside firm, as opposed to developing such a system in-house.

P

Packaged software   Software that is packaged and sold in stores. Also called *commercial software.*

Packet   A portion of a message to be sent to another computer via data communications. Each packet is individually addressed, and the packets are reassembled into the original message once they reach their destination.

Page composition   Adding type to a layout. In desktop publishing, the software may be called a page composition program.

Page layout   In publishing, the process of arranging text and graphics on a page.

Page table   The index-like table with which the operating system keeps track of page locations.

Page template   A predesigned page that can contain page settings, formatting, and page elements.

Pages   Equal-size blocks into which a program is divided to be placed into corresponding noncontiguous memory spaces called page frames. See also *Page frame.*

Pagination   In word processing, options for placing the page number in various locations on the document page.

Paging   The process of dividing a program into equal-size pages, keeping program pages on disk, and calling them into memory as needed.

Pan   To move the cursor across a spreadsheet or a database to force into view fields that do not fit on the initial screen.

Parallel conversion   A method of systems conversion in which the old and new systems are operated simultaneously until the users are satisfied that the new system performs to their standards; then the old system is dropped.

Parallel processing   Using many processors, each with its own memory unit, that work at the same time to process data much more quickly than with the traditional single processor. Contrast with *Serial processing.*

Participant observation   A form of observation in which the systems analyst temporarily joins the activities of the group.

Partition   A separate memory area that can hold a program, used as part of a memory management technique that simply divides memory into separate areas. Also called a *region.*

Pascal   A structured, high-level programming language named for Blaise Pascal, a seventeenth-century French mathematician.

PC card   A credit-card-sized card that slides into a slot in the computer, most often a modem, in which a cable runs from the PC card to the phone jack in the wall. Originally known as PCMCIA cards, named for the Personal Computer Memory Card International Association.

PDA   See *Personal digital assistant.*

Peer-to-peer network   A network setup in which there is no controlling server computer; all computers on the network share programs and resources.

Pen-based computer   A small portable computer that accepts handwritten input on a screen with a penlike stylus. Also called *personal digital assistant.*

Peripheral equipment   All of the input, output, and secondary storage devices attached to a computer.

Personal computer   A relatively inexpensive type of computer, usually used by an individual in a home or office setting. Also called a *microcomputer.*

Personal digital assistant (PDA)   A small portable computer that is most often used to track appointments and other business information and that can accept handwritten input on a screen. Also called a *pen-based computer.*

Phase   (1) In data transmission, the relative position in time of one complete cycle of a carrier wave. (2) In systems analysis and design, a portion of the systems development life cycle (SDLC).

Phased conversion   A systems conversion method in which the new system is phased in gradually.

Picosecond   One-trillionth of a second.

Pie chart   A pie-shaped graph used to compare values that represent parts of a whole.

Pilot conversion   A systems conversion method in which a designated group of users try the system first.

Pipelining   A processing arrangement whereby one instruction's actions—fetch, decode, execute, store—need not be complete before another instruction begins.

Pixel   A picture element on a computer display screen; a pixel is merely one dot in the display.

Platform   The hardware and software combination that comprises the basic functionality of a particular computer.

Plot area   The area in which a graph is drawn, that is, the area above the x-axis and to the right of the y-axis.

Plug-in   Software that can be added to a browser to enhance its functionality.

PNG   See *Portable Network Graphic.*

Point   A typographic measurement equaling approximately 1/72 inch.

Pointer   An indicator on a screen; it shows where the next user-computer interaction will be. Also called a *cursor.*

Point-of-sale (POS) terminal   A terminal used as a cash register in a retail setting. It may be programmable or connected to a central computer.

Polymorphism   In object-oriented programming, polymorphism means that when an individual object receives a message it knows how, using its own methods, to process the message in the appropriate way for that particular object.

Pop-up menu   A menu of choices that appears, popping upward, when an initial menu choice is made.

Portable Network Graphic (PNG)   A file format commonly used on Internet sites; PNG is non-proprietary and is replacing the GIF format.

Portal   A web site that is used as a gateway or guide to the Internet.

POS terminal   See *Point-of-sale (POS) terminal.*

Preliminary design   The subphase of systems design in which the new system concept is developed.

Preliminary investigation   The first phase of the systems analysis and design life cycle, in which planners determine if and how a project should proceed. Also called a *feasibility study* or a *system survey.*

Primary memory   The electronic circuitry that temporarily holds data and program instructions needed by the CPU.

Primary storage   The electronic circuitry that temporarily holds data and program instructions needed by the CPU.

Printer   A device for generating computer-produced output on paper.

Process   (1) The computer action required to convert input to output. (2) An element in a data flow diagram that represents actions taken on data: comparing, checking, stamping, authorizing, filing, and so forth.

Processor   The central processing unit (CPU) of a computer, a microprocessor.

Program   A set of step-by-step instructions that directs a computer to perform specific tasks and produce certain results. More generically called software.

Programmable read-only memory (PROM)   Chips that can be programmed with specialized tools called ROM burners.

Programmer/analyst   A person who performs systems analysis functions in addition to programming.

Programming language   A set of rules that can be used to tell a computer what operations to do. There are many different programming languages.

Project management software   Software that allocates people and resources, monitors schedules, and produces status reports.

PROM   See *Programmable read-only memory.*

Protocol   A set of rules for the exchange of data between a terminal and a computer or between two computers.

Prototype   A limited working system or subset of a system that is developed to test design concepts.

Pseudocode   An English-like way of representing the solution to a problem.

Public domain software   Software that is uncopyrighted, and thus may be altered.

Pull-down menu   A menu of choices that appears, as a window shade is pulled down, when an initial menu choice is made.

Push technology   Software that automatically sends — pushes—information from the Internet to a user's personal computer. Also called *webcasting.*

Q

Query languages   A variation on fourth-generation languages that can be used to retrieve data from databases.

R

RAID   See *Redundant array of inexpensive disks.*

RAM   See *Random-access memory.*

Random-access memory (RAM)   Memory that provides temporary storage for data and program instructions.

Range   A group of one or more cells, arranged in a rectangle, that a spreadsheet program treats as a unit.

Raster-scan technology   A video display technology. The back of the screen display has a phosphorous coating, which will glow whenever it is hit by a beam of electrons.

Read-only memory (ROM)   Memory containing data and programs that can be read but not altered. Data remains in ROM after the power is turned off.

Read/write head   An electromagnet that reads the magnetized areas on magnetic media and converts them into the electrical pulses that are sent to the processor.

Real storage   That part of memory that temporarily holds part of a program pulled from virtual storage.

Real-time processing   Processing in which the results are available in time to affect the activity at hand.

Record   (1) A set of related fields. (2) In a database relation, one row.

Reduced instruction set computer (RISC)   A computer that offers only frequently used instructions. Since fewer instructions

are offered, this is a factor in improving the computer's speed. Contrast with *Complex instruction set computer.*

Redundant array of inexpensive disks (RAID)   Secondary storage that uses several connected hard disks that act as a unit. Using multiple disks allows manufacturers to improve data security, access time, and data transfer rates.

Refresh   To maintain an image on a CRT screen by reforming the screen image at frequent intervals to avoid flicker. The frequency is called the scan rate; 60 times per second is usually adequate to retain a clear image.

Register   A temporary storage area for instructions or data.

Region   A separate memory area that can hold a program, used as part of a memory management technique that simply divides memory into separate areas. Also called a *partition.*

Relation   A table in a relational database model.

Relational database   A database in which the data is organized in a table format consisting of columns and rows.

Relational model   A database model that organizes data logically in tables.

Relational operator   An operator (such as , or =) that allows a user to make comparisons and selections.

Removable hard disk cartridge   A supplemental hard disk, that, once filled, can be replaced with a fresh one.

Resolution   The clarity of a video display screen or printer output.

Resource allocation   The process of assigning resources to certain programs.

Response time   The time between a typed computer request and the response of the computer.

Retrovirus   A virus that is powerful enough to defeat or even delete antivirus software.

Reverse video   The feature that highlights on-screen text by switching the usual text and background colors.

Ring network   A "circle" of point-to-point connections between computers at local sites. A ring network does not contain a central host computer.

RISC   See *Reduced instruction set computer.*

Robot   A computer-controlled device that can physically manipulate its surroundings.

ROM   See *Read-only memory.*

ROM burner   A specialized device used to program progammable read-only memory (PROM) chips.

Rotational delay   For disk units, the time it takes for a record on a track to revolve under the read/write head.

Router   A special computer that directs communications traffic when several networks are connected together.

S

Sampling   In systems analysis, collecting a subset of data relevant to the system under study.

Sans serif   A typeface that is clean, with no serif marks.

Satellite transmission   Data transmission from earth station to earth station via communications satellites.

Scan rate   The number of times a CRT screen is refreshed in a given time period. A scan rate of 60 times per second is usually adequate to retain a clear screen image.

Scanner   A device that uses a light source to read text and images directly into the computer. Scanners can be of several varieties, notably handheld, sheetfeed, and desktop.

Screen   A television-like output device that can display information.

Scrolling   A feature that allows the user to move to and view any part of a document on the screen.

SDLC   See *Systems development life cycle.*

Sealed module   A disk drive containing the disks, access arms, and read/write heads sealed together.

Search engine   Regarding the Internet, software that lets a user specify search terms that can be used to find web sites that include those terms.

Secondary storage   Additional storage, often on disk, for data and programs. Secondary storage is separate from the CPU and memory. Also called *auxiliary storage.*

Sector method   A method of organizing data on a disk in which each track is divided into sectors that hold a specific number of characters. Data on the track is accessed by referring to the surface number, track number, and sector number where the data is stored.

Security   A system of safeguards designed to protect a computer system and data from deliberate or accidental damage or access by unauthorized persons.

Seek time   The time required for an access arm to move into position over a particular track on a disk.

Select   In word processing, to mark a certain section of text, called a block, by some sort of highlighting, usually reverse video. The text is usually selected in advance of some other command upon the text, such as Move.

Semiconductor   A crystalline substance that conducts electricity when it is "doped" with chemical impurities.

Semiconductor storage   Data storage on a silicon chip.

Sequential file organization   The arrangement of records in ascending or descending order by a certain field called the key.

Sequential file processing   Processing in which records are usually in order according to a key field.

Serial processing   Processing in which a single processor can handle just one instruction at a time. Contrast with *Parallel processing.*

Serif   Small marks added to the letters of a typeface; the marks are intended to increase readability of the typeface. Contrast with *Sans serif.*

Server   (1) In a client/server network arrangement, the computer that controls and manages the network and its services; the server usually has hard disks that hold files needed by users on the network. (2) A computer used to access the Internet; it has special software that uses the Internet protocol.

Shareware   Software that is given away free, although the maker hopes that satisfied users will voluntarily pay for it.

Sheetfeed scanner   A scanner that uses a motorized roller to feed a sheet of paper across the scanning head, thus using optical recognition to convert text or drawings into computer-recognizable form.

SIMM   See *Single in-line memory module.*

Simplex transmission   Transmission of data in one direction only.

Simulation   The use of a computer model, particularly a decision support system, to reach decisions about real-life situations.

Single in-line memory module (SIMM)   A board containing memory chips that can be plugged into a computer expansion slot.

Sink   In a data flow diagram, a destination for data going outside the system.

Site license   A license permitting a customer to make multiple copies of a piece of software.

Smalltalk   An object-oriented language that supports a particularly visual system.

Smart terminal   A terminal that has some processing ability.

Social engineering   A tongue-in-cheek term for con artist actions, specifically hackers persuading people to give away their passwords over the phone.

Soft copy   Computer-produced output displayed on a screen.

Soft font   A font that can be downloaded from the font library on disk with a personal computer to a printer.

Software   Instructions that tell a computer what to do. Also called *programs.*

Software piracy   The unauthorized copying of computer software.

SOHO   Abbreviation for small office, home office, a designated group for which software is designed.

Source   In a data flow diagram, an origin outside the system.

Source data automation   The use of special equipment to collect input data as it is generated and send it directly to the computer.

Source document   An instrument, usually paper, containing data to be prepared as input to a computer.

Source module   A program as originally coded, before being translated into machine language.

Source program listing   The printed version of a program as the programmer wrote it, usually produced as a byproduct of compilation.

Spamming   Mass advertising on the Internet, usually done with software especially designed to send solicitations to users via e-mail.

Speech recognition   Converting input data given as the spoken word to a form the computer can understand.

Speech recognition device   A device that accepts the spoken word through a microphone and converts it into digital code that can be understood by a computer.

Speech synthesis   The process of enabling machines to talk to people.

Spooling   A process in which files to be printed are placed temporarily on disk.

SRAM   See *Static random-access memory*.

Star network   A network consisting of one or more computers connected to a central host computer.

Start/stop transmission   Asynchronous data transmission.

Static random-access memory (SRAM)   A type of RAM that requires a continuous current to hold data. SRAM is usually faster but larger and more expensive than dynamic RAM. Contrast with *Dynamic random-access memory (DRAM)*.

Storage register   A register that temporarily holds data taken from or about to be sent to memory.

Streaming   The downloading of live audio, video, and animation content.

Structured interview   In systems analysis, an interview in which only planned questions are used.

Structured programming   A set of programming techniques that includes a limited number of control structures and certain programming standards.

Style   In word processing, the way a typeface is printed—for example, in italic.

Suite   A bundle of basic software designed to work together.

Supercomputer   The largest and most powerful category of computers.

Supervisor program   An operating system program that controls the entire operating system and calls in other operating system programs from disk storage as needed.

Supply reel   A reel that has tape with data on it or on which data will be recorded.

Surge protector   A device that prevents electrical problems from affecting data files.

SVGA (Super VGA)   A superior screen standard with 800x600, 1024x768, 1280x1024, or 1600x1200 pixels. All SVGA standards support a palette of 16 million colors, but the number of colors that can be displayed simultaneously is limited by the amount of video memory installed in a system.

Symbolic address   The meaningful name for a memory location. Instead of just a number, for example, a symbolic address should be something meaningful, such as NAME or SALARY.

Symbolic language   A second-generation language that uses abbreviations for instructions. Also called *assembly language*.

Synchronous transmission   Data transmission in which characters are transmitted together in a continuous stream.

Synonym   The name for a record's disk address, produced by a hashing scheme, that is the same as a pre-existing address for a different record.

Syntax   The rules of a programming language.

Syntax errors   Errors in the use of a programming language.

Synthesis by analysis   Speech synthesis in which a device analyzes the input of an actual human voice, stores and processes the spoken sounds, and reproduces them as needed.

Synthesis by rule   Speech synthesis in which a device applies linguistic rules to create an artificial spoken language.

System   An organized set of related components established to perform a certain task.

System journal   A file whose records represent real-time transactions.

System requirements   A detailed list of the things a particular system must be able to do, based on the results of the systems analysis.

System survey   The first phase of systems analysis, in which planners determine if and how a project should proceed. Also called a *feasibility study* or a *preliminary investigation*.

System testing   A testing process in which the development team uses test data to determine whether programs work together satisfactorily.

Systems analysis   A phase of the systems development life cycle, involving studying an existing system to determine how it works and with an eye to improving the system.

Systems analyst   A person who plans and designs computer systems.

Systems design   A phase of the systems development life cycle, involving developing a plan for a new or revised system based on the results of the systems analysis phase.

Systems development   A phase of the systems development life cycle, whose activities include programming and testing.

Systems development life cycle (SDLC)   The multiphase process required for creating or revising a computer system.

Systems flowchart   A drawing that depicts the flow of data through some part of a computer system.

Systems software   All programs related to coordinating computer operations, including the operating system, programming language translators, and service programs.

T

Tag   In HTML, a command that performs a specific function.

Take-up reel   A reel that always stays with the magnetic tape unit.

Tape drive   The drive on which reels of magnetic tape are mounted when their data is ready to be read to or written on by the computer system.

Target frame   In a web page with frames, the frame that holds the page currently referenced in the table of contents frame.

TCP/IP   See *Transmission Control Protocol/Internet Protocol*.

Telecommuting   Using telecommunications and computers at home as a substitute for working at an office outside the home.

Teleconferencing   A system of holding conferences by linking geographically dispersed people together through computer terminals or personal computers.

Template   (1) In desktop publishing, a predetermined page design that lets a user fill in text and art. (2) In a spreadsheet program, a worksheet that has already been designed for the solution of a specific type of problem, so that a user need only fill in the data. (3) In FrontPage, a predesigned page format.

Teraflop   One trillion floating-point operations per second. One measure of a computer's speed, especially as related to parallel processors.

Terminal   A device that consists of an input device (usually a keyboard), an output device (usually a screen), and a communications link to the computer.

Terminal emulation software   Data communications software that makes a personal computer act like a terminal, so that it can communicate with a larger computer.

Text block   A continuous section of text in a document that has been marked or selected.

Text editor   Software that is somewhat like a word processing program, used by programmers to create a program file.

Theme   A unified set of design elements and color schemes that can be apply to a web page to give it a consistent and attractive appearance.

Thesaurus program   With a word processing program, this program provides a list of synonyms and antonyms for a selected word in a document.

Time slice   In time-sharing, a period of time—a fraction of a second—during which the computer works on a user's tasks.

Time-sharing   A special case of multiprogramming in which several people use one computer at the same time.

Title   The caption on a graph that summarizes the information in the graph.

Token passing   The protocol for controlling access to a Token Ring network. A special signal, or token, circulates from node to node, allowing the node that "captures" the token to transmit data.

Token Ring network   A network protocol that uses token passing to send data over the shared network cable. A computer that wants to send a message must capture the token before sending.

Top-level domain   Regarding the Internet, in a Uniform Resource Locator (URL), the last part of the domain name, representing the type of entity, such as organization or education or country.

Topology   The physical layout of a local area network.

Touch screen   A computer screen that accepts input data by letting the user point at the screen to select a choice. The finger touching the screen interrupts the light beams on the monitor's edge, pinpointing the selected screen location.

Track   On a magnetic disk, one of many data-holding concentric circles.

Trackball   A ball used as an input device; it can be hand-manipulated to cause a corresponding movement of the cursor on the screen. Trackballs are often built in on portable computers.

Transaction file   A file that contains all changes to be made to the master file: additions, deletions, and revisions.

Transaction processing   The technique of processing transactions one at a time, in the order in which they occur.

Transistor   A small device that transfers electrical signals across a resistor.

Translator   Software, typically a compiler, that converts a program into the machine language the computer can understand.

Transmission Control Protocol/Internet Protocol (TCP/IP)   A standardized protocol permitting different computers to communicate via the Internet.

Transparent   Computer activities of which a user is unaware even as they are taking place.

Transponder   A device in a communications satellite that receives a transmission from earth, amplifies the signal, changes the frequency, and retransmits the data to a receiving earth station. The transponder makes sure that the stronger outgoing signals do not interfere with the weaker incoming signals.

Trojan horse   An application that covertly places destructive instructions in the middle of a legitimate program but appears to do something useful.

Tunneling   A way to transfer data between two similar networks over an intermediate network by enclosing one type of data packet protocol into the packet of another. Also called *encapsulation*.

Twisted pairs   Wires twisted together in an insulated cable. Twisted pairs are frequently used to transmit data over short distances. Also called *wire pairs*.

Type size   The size, in points, of a typeface.

U

Unbundle   To sell software separately from the hardware on which it will run.

Unicasting   A method of file transmission that sends a copy of a file from one computer to the computer of each designated recipient.

Uniform Resource Locator (URL)   The unique address of a web page or other file on the Internet.

Unit testing   Testing an individual program by using test data.

UNIVAC I (Universal Automatic Computer I)   The first computer built for business purposes.

Universal Product Code (UPC)   A code number unique to a product. The UPC code is the bar code on the product's label.

Unstructured interview   In systems analysis, an interview in which questions are planned in advance, but the questionnaire can deviate from the plan.

UPC   See *Universal Product Code*.

Update   To keep files current by changing data as appropriate.

Updating in place   The ability to read, change, and return a record to its same place on the disk.

Upload   In a networking environment, to send a file from one computer to another, usually to a larger computer or a host computer. Contrast with *Download*.

URL   See *Uniform Resource Locator*.

Usenet   An informal network of computers that allows the posting and reading of messages in newsgroups that focus on specific topics. Also called *newsgroups*.

User-friendly   A term to refer to software that is easy for a novice to use.

User involvement   The involvement of users in the systems development life cycle.

V

Vaccine   A computer program that stops the spread of a virus. Also called an *antivirus*.

Vacuum tube   An electronic tube used as a basic component in the first generation of computers.

Value   In a spreadsheet, data entered into a cell.

Variable   (1) On a graph, the items that the data points describe. (2) In a program, a name assigned to a memory location, whose contents can vary.

Vector   An arrow—a line with directional notation—used in a data flow diagram.

Vertical market   A market consisting of a group of similar customers, such as dentists, who are likely to need similar software.

Very high-level language   A fourth-generation language.

Video graphics   Computer-produced animated pictures.

Video Privacy Protection Act   Legislation that prohibits video vendors from revealing what videos their customers rent.

Videoconferencing   Computer conferencing combined with cameras and wall-size screens.

Virus   A set of illicit instructions that passes itself on to other programs with which it comes into contact.

Virtual memory   See *Virtual storage*.

Virtual private network (VPN)   Technology that uses the public Internet backbone as a channel for private data communication.

Virtual reality (VR)   A system in which a user is immersed in a computer-created environment, so that the user physically interacts with the computer-produced three-dimensional scene.

Virtual storage   A technique of memory management in which part of the application program is stored on disk and is brought into memory only as needed. The secondary storage holding the rest of the program is considered virtual storage.

Virus   A set of illicit instructions that passes itself on to other programs with which it comes into contact.

Vision robot   A robot that can recognize an object by its shape or color.

Voice input   Using the spoken word as a means of entering data into a computer.

Voice output device   See *Voice synthesizer*.

Voice synthesizer   A device that converts data in main storage to vocalized sounds understandable to humans. Also called an *audio-response unit* and *voice output device*.

Volatile   Subject to loss when electricity is interrupted or turned off. Data in semiconductor storage is volatile.

Volume testing   The testing of a program or a system by using real data in large amounts.

VPN See *Virtual private network*.

VR   See *Virtual reality*.

W

Walkthrough   A process in which a group of programmers—your peers—review your program and offer suggestions in a collegial way.

WAN   See *Wide area network*.

Wand reader   An input device that scans the special letters and numbers on price tags in retail stores and sends that input data to the computer. Often connected to a point-of-sale terminal in a retail store.

Web   See *World Wide Web*. Also, using FrontPage software, a set of web pages.

Web site   An individual location on the World Wide Web.

Web TV   See *Network computer*.

Webcasting   Software that automatically sends—pushes—information from the Internet to a user's personal computer. Also called *push technology*.

Weight   In word processing or desktop publishing, the variation in the visual heaviness of a typeface; for example, words look much heavier when in boldface type.

"What-if" analysis   The process of changing one or more spreadsheet values and observing the resulting calculated effect.

Wide area network (WAN)   A network of geographically distant computers and terminals. Contrast with *Local area network*.

Wire pairs   Wires twisted together in an insulated cable. Wire pairs are frequently used to transmit data over short distances. Also called *twisted pairs*.

Wireless   Transmitting data over networks using infrared or radio wave transmissions instead of cables.

Word   The number of bits that constitute a common unit of data, as defined by the computer system.

Word processing   Computer-based creating, editing, formatting, storing, retrieving, and printing of a text document.

Word wrap   A word processing feature that automatically starts a word at the left margin of the next line if there is not enough room for it on the line.

Worksheet   Another name for an electronic spreadsheet, a computerized version of a manual spreadsheet.

Workstation   A computer that combines the compactness of a desktop computer with power that almost equals that of a mainframe.

World Wide Web (the Web)   An Internet subset of sites with text, images, and sounds; most web sites provide links to related topics.

WORM   See *Write-once, read-many media*.

Worm   A program that spreads and replicates over a network.

Write-once, read-many media (WORM)   Media that can be written on only once; then they become read-only media.

WYSIWYG   An acronym meaning what you See is what you get; in FrontPage WYSIWYG refers to the fact that you See the page as it will look as you create it.

X

XGA (extended graphics array)   A high-resolution graphics standard that provides high resolutions, supports more simultaneous colors than SVGA, and can be non-interlaced. Contrast with *SVGA*.

Z

Zone recording   Involves dividing a disk into zones to take advantage of the storage available on all tracks, by assigning more sectors to tracks in outer zones than to those in inner zones.

CREDITS

Fronticepiece:©Don Bishop.

Cummins/FPG; 06.17:©Patti McConville/The Image Bank; 06.18:©Joe Cornish/TSI.

Chapter Seven
Chapter Opener:©Christian Michaels/FPG; ©Louis Psihoyos/Matrix; 07.03:Courtesy of Netscape Communications; 07GP:©Wendy Grossman.

Chapter Eight
Chapter Opener:©Telegrah Colour Library/ FPG; 08.01: Courtesy of BabyCenter.com, Courtesy of UPS, Courtesy of Lilly, Courtesy of Vitesse, Courtesy of Merrill Lynch, Courtesy of General Electric Corporation; 08.02:Courtesy of The Nature Conservancy, Courtesy of Fox Corporation; 08.03:Courtesy of Exploria, Courtesy of J.Crew, Courtesy of The Nature Company, Courtesy of Office Max; 08.04:Courtesy of Lands End; 08MN:Courtesy of Peapod; 08.05:Courtesy of Chrysler Corporation; 2000 and Beyond:©Wendy Grossman; 08GP:Courtesy of The Mountain Zone, Courtesy of Chef's, Courtesy of Ethel M. Chocolates; 08MN:Courtesy of Procter and Gamble; 08MRC:Courtesy of Ebay.

Chapter Nine
Chapter Opener:©Charley Franklin/FPG; 09GP:©Nick Koudis/1999 Photodisc; 09.17, 09.21, 09.22, 09.23:©Corbis.

Chapter Ten
Chapter Opener:©William Schick/The Stock Market; 10MN:©The New York Times; 10.04:Courtesy of American BioMetric; 10.05:Courtesy of Technology Recognition Systems; 10MN:©Terry Hefferman/Apple Computer, Inc.; ©James Porto/FPG.

Chapter Eleven
Chapter Opener:©Chip Simons/FPG; 2000 and Beyond:©Corbis; 11MRC:©Herbert Simms; 11.19:©Adam Zakin/Benjamin-Cummings.

Chapter Twelve
Chapter Opener:©Arthur Tilley/FPG; 12MRC:Courtesy of CyberMedia.

Chapter Thirteen
Chapter Opener:©John Brooks/Tony Stone Images; 13MRC:Courtesy of Microsoft.

Chapter Fourteen
Chapter Opener:©Ron Chapple/FPG; 2000 and Beyond:©Tom Draper Design/Seattle; 14GP:©Michael Simpson/FPG; 14MRC:©Rick Tomlinson.

Chapter Fifteen
Chapter Opener:©Zephyr Images; 15GP:©Telegraph Colour Library/FPG.

Chapter Sixteen
Chapter Opener:©Kaluzny/Thatcher/ Tony Stone Images; 2000 and Beyond:Courtesy of Hewlett Packard; 16.03:©Peter Wiant.

Chapter Seventeen
Chapter Opener:©Glenn McLaughlin/The Stock Market; 17MRC:©Paul and Lindamarie Ambrose/FPG; 17.02:©Ed Kashi/PhotoTake; 17.04a:©Andy Sacks/TSI; 17.04b:Courtesy of Japan Airlines; 17.05:Courtesy of Thinking Machines Corporation; 17.06a:Courtesy of Dave Barrett/MIT; 17.06b:Courtesy of Control Data Corporation; 17.06c:©Fujiphotos/The Image Works; 17.07a:©P.Howell/Gamma-Liaison; 17.07b:Courtesy of VPL Research; 17.07c:Courtesy of David Sutton; 2000 and Beyond:©Peter Chapman.

Making Microchips Gallery
Opener: ©Manfred Kage/Peter Arnold, Inc.; 2: ©Geoff Tompkinson/SPL/Photo Researchers; 3: Courtesy of Precision Visuals International/SPL/Photo Researchers; 4: ©Robert Holmgren; 5: AT&T Archives; 6: Courtesy of IBM; 7: ©Ted Horowitz/The Stock Market; 8:

Courtesy of TRW Inc.; 9: Courtesy of Micron Technology, Inc.; 10: ©Mel Lindstrom/TSI; 11: ©Andrew Syred/SPL/Photo Researchers; 12: AT&T Archives; 13, 14, 15: Courtesy of Hewlett-Packard Company; 16: ©Astrid & Hanns-Frieder Michler/SPL/Photo Researchers; 17: Courtesy of Advanced Micro Devices Inc.; 18: ©Mark Segal/TSI; 19: ©Telegraph Colour Library/FPG; 20: ©Rosenfeld Images Ltd./SPL/Photo Researchers; 21: ©Phil Matt/PhotoTake NYC.

Computer Graphics Gallery
Opener:Courtesy of Corel. Art by Dave Martland; 6:Courtesy of Corel. Art by Bill Frymire; 7:Courtesy of Corel. Art by Antonio De Leo; 8:Courtesy of Corel. Art by Karin Kuhlmann; 9:©Joseph Maas; 10:Courtesy of Corel. Art by Huan Le Tran; 11:©Marcus Benko; 12:©Jeremy Birn; ©13:David Brickley; 14:©Kyle Nau; 15:©Kris Lazoore; 16:©Alberto Giorgi; 17:©Kevin Odhner; 18:©Steve Gowers; 19, 23:©Nathan O'Brien; 20:©Gautam Lad; 21:©Ian Armstrong; 22:©Adrian Baumann.

Computers at Work Gallery
Opener:©George Shelley/The Stock Market; 5:©Andy Sacks/Tony Stone Images; 6:©The Stock Market; 7:©Joe Baraban/The Stock Market; 8:©Roger Tully/Tony Stone Images; 9:©Mark Harmel/FPG; 10:©Stock Works/The Stock Market; 11:©The Stock Market; 12:©Zephyr Images; 13:©Joe Feingersh/The Stock Market; 14:©Andy Sacks/Tony Stone Images; 15:©Sally Werner Grotta/The Stock Market; 16:©Robert E. Daemmrich/Tony Stone Images; 17:©Robert Frerck/Tony Stone Images; 18:©Michael Keller/The Stock Market; 19:©Ronnie Kaufman/The Stock Market; 23: Courtesy of Corel. Art by Matthias Gleirscher.

INDEX